Case Studies in Crisis Communication

Case Studies in Crisis Communication: International Perspectives on Hits and Misses was organized to fill the gap for a much-needed textbook in case studies in crisis communication from international perspectives. The events of September 11, 2001, other major world crises, and the ongoing macro-economic challenges of financial institutions, justify the need for this book. While existing textbooks on the subject focus on U.S. corporate cases, they may not appeal equally to students and practitioners in other countries, hence the need to analyze cases from the United States and from other world regions.

Amiso M. George is an associate professor of journalism at Texas Christian University, Fort Worth, Texas, USA where she teaches crisis communication and public relations campaigning. A former director of the strategic communication graduate program at TCU, she developed and taught the first course in crisis communication in 2003 at the Reynolds School of Journalism, University of Nevada, Reno, where she was also director of the public relations program.

Cornelius B. Pratt is a contributing editor of *Public Relations Quarterly* and a professor at Temple University School of Communications and Theater, USA. Before joining the Temple faculty in 2006, he served for nearly six years in the U.S. Department of Agriculture, in Washington, DC, and for eleven years on the faculty at Michigan State University, the last eight years as full professor.

Case Studies in Crisis Communication

International Perspectives on
Hits and Misses

Edited by

Amiso M. George
Texas Christian University,
Fort Worth, Texas

Cornelius B. Pratt
Temple University, Philadelphia;
and Temple University Japan

Routledge
Taylor & Francis Group

NEW YORK AND LONDON

First published 2012
by Routledge
711 Third Avenue, New York, NY 10017

Simultaneously published in the UK
by Routledge
2 Park Square, Milton Park, Abingdon, Oxon OX14 4RN

Routledge is an imprint of the Taylor & Francis Group,
an informa business

Library of Congress Cataloging in Publication Data
George, Amiso M.
  Case studies in crisis communication: international perspectives
  on hits and misses / Amiso M. George, Cornelius B. Pratt.—1st ed.
  p. cm.
  Includes index.
  1. Crisis management—Case studies. 2. Public relations—
  Management—Case studies. 3. Social media. 4. Communication,
  International—Case studies. I. Pratt, Cornelius B. II. Title.
  HD49.G46 2011
  658.4'056—dc23
  2011034597

ISBN: 978–0–415–88989–6 (hbk)
ISBN: 978–0–415–88990–2 (pbk)
ISBN: 978–0–203–19066–1 (ebk)

Typeset in Sabon
by Florence Production Ltd, Stoodleigh, Devon

To our hard-driving, crisis communication students
whose insightful questions inspired this work

Contents

Illustrations

Figures

Tables

Contributors

Wole Adamolekun (Ph.D., University of Abuja, Nigeria) has more than 30 years' experience in corporate communication in the downstream oil sector, microcredit administration, youth and social development, and strategic communication. Until recently, he was acting executive secretary at and chief executive officer of the Petroleum Products Pricing Regulatory Agency in Nigeria. Currently, he is general manager of corporate services in that agency, where he provides oversight for formulating, communicating, and executing organizational policy. He is also secretary general of the African Public Relations Association, whose headquarters are in Abuja, Nigeria. He is the author of *Public Relations Possibilities: Selected Seminar and Conference Papers* (Spectrum Books, 2005); and a co-author of *Interactive Public Relations* (Spectrum Books, 2007). E-mail: lolese123@yahoo.com

Joseph Ajami (Ph.D., Ohio University) is chairperson of the Department of Mass Communication and associate professor at Notre Dame University, Lebanon. He finished his B.A. in Journalism at the Lebanese University in 1978 and in the process he earned a scholarship to pursue both his M.S. and Ph.D. in Journalism at Ohio University. He taught for seven years at three American universities before returning to Lebanon in 1994. Ajami's research interests include international communication, public relations, advertising creativity, media and society, and media ethics. He has published several articles in refereed journals in the areas of public relations, advertising and political communication. E-mail: jajami@ndu.edu.lb; joeajami@hotmail.com

Emmanuel C. Alozie (Ph.D., University of Southern Mississippi) is a professor of journalism and mass communication at Governors State University. Alozie is an author, freelance journalist, and social commentator. A former assistant editor of *Democratic Communiqué*, Alozie's publications include *Marketing in Developing Countries: Nigerian Advertising in a Global and Technological Economy* (Routledge, 2009); *Cultural Reflections and the Role of Advertising in the Socio-Economic and National Development of Nigeria* (Edwin Mellen, 2005); and *Toward the Common Good:*

Perspectives in International Public Relations (Allyn and Bacon, 2004), which has been selected as one of the 100 most influential and indispensable books in international public relations by *Communication Director, Magazine for Corporate Communications and Public Relations*. E-mail: alozieemmanuel@hotmail.com

Olugbenga C. Ayeni (Ph.D., University of Southern Mississippi) is associate professor of communication at Eastern Connecticut State University. He is the author of *A Comparative Study of the Political Communication Styles of Bill Clinton and Tony Blair* (Edwin Mellen, 2005). His primary research area is public relations. E-mail: ayenio@easternct.edu

Isaac A. Blankson (Ph.D., Ohio University) is associate professor in and chair of the Department of Speech Communication, Southern Illinois University Edwardsville, and special assistant to the dean, College of Arts and Sciences, on international and diversity initiatives. He teaches public relations and intercultural communication. Blankson also holds an M.A. from the University of Oslo, Norway; and a B.A. from the University of Ghana. Dr. Blankson's recent publications include *Negotiating Democracy: Media Transformations in Emerging Democracies* (2008); "Public Relations Practices in sub-Saharan Africa," in *Global Public Relations: Spanning Borders, Spanning Cultures* by Freitag and Stokes (2009); and "Stranger in our Midst: An Adventure of an International Faculty," in *Adventures in the Academy: Professors in the land of Lincoln and Beyond* by LaFond, Berger and Romero (2010). E-mail: iblanks@siue.edu

Robert Brown (Ph.D., University of Rochester) is professor of communication at Salem State College in Massachusetts. A former speechwriter for corporate CEOs, his speech on the management of crises is published in the June 2010 issue of *Vital Speeches of the Day*. Brown's byline has appeared 13 times on the op ed page of the *Boston Globe*, and he has written for *Los Angeles Times, Toronto Globe & Mail* and *Honolulu Advertiser*. He taught a graduate lecture class on crisis management at Universidad Externado, Bogota, Colombia, for two summers. He is a frequent contributor to, and editorial board member of the *Public Relations Review* and a member of the editorial board of *Public Relations Inquiry*, a forthcoming journal from Sage Publications. E-mail: rbrown@salemstate.edu

Weidan Cao is a doctoral student in the Mass Media and Communication Program at Temple University, United States. Her current research interests include crisis communication, health communication, social networks, psychological processing of media, intercultural communication, and comic art. With regard to crisis communication, she is particularly interested in the influence of cultural factors on ethical perceptions and on crisis communication practices, as well as in the effective use of social media in disaster communication. E-mail: weidan@temple.edu; cecilia.cao@gmail.com

Ronald Lee Carr (M.F.A., University of California, Los Angeles) is an associate professor in and director of the Department of Communication at Temple University Japan. He is also the executive producer of Global Lives, Asia, and of Urban Villages, a Temple University-funded research project that brings awareness and solutions to serious issues plaguing Asian urban communities. Professor Carr produces stories on disaster relief in Manila, Philippines, and on the struggles of informal settlers in that country. His research and creative projects have taken him to far-flung places such as Beirut, Sapporo, and Varnasse. He resides in Tokyo with his family. E-mail: carr@tuj.ac.jp

W. Timothy Coombs (Ph.D., Purdue University) is a professor in the Nicholson School of Communication at the University of Central Florida. He is the 2002 recipient of Jackson, Jackson and Wagner Behavioral Science Prize from the Public Relations Society of American for his crisis research. His research includes 37 journal articles, 27 book chapters, 110 conference paper presentations, and the award-winning book *Ongoing Crisis Communication*. He co-authored the award-winning books *It's Not Just Public Relations* and *PR Strategy and Application*, with Sherry Holladay; and *Today's Public Relations*, with Robert Heath. He is also co-editor of *The Handbook of Crisis Communication*. E-mail: Timothy.Coombs@ucf.edu

Christopher Galloway (Ph.D., Monash University, Australia) is senior lecturer and discipline leader in advertising and public relations, at the Faculty of Higher Education, Swinburne University of Technology, Melbourne, Australia. He specializes in research and writing to do with risk, risk communication, and public relations and has many publications in those areas. He is a co-author with Kwamena Kwansah-Aidoo of *Public Relations Issues and Crisis Management: Asia, Australia and New Zealand*. He is a frequent consultant in risk communication in Australia, New Zealand, Asia and the Middle East. E-mail: CGalloway@groupwise.swin.edu.au

Amiso M. George (Ph.D., Ohio University; accredited in public relations by the Public Relations Society of America [PRSA]; fellow PRSA) is associate professor of strategic communication and former director of the graduate program at Schieffer School of Journalism, Texas Christian University, Fort Worth. She developed and taught the first course in crisis communication and was director of the public relations program at the Reynolds School of Journalism, University of Nevada in Reno. Earlier, she taught at University of Texas San Antonio and worked as a radio and television journalist and freelance broadcaster at Nigerian Television Authority and Voice of America (Africa Service) and at C-SPAN-TV as a consultant, before embarking on an academic career. George has published book chapters and journal articles on crisis communication and public relations. She consults in crisis communication for nonprofits and small to mid size companies. E-mail: a.george2@tcu.edu

Jaime S. Gómez (Ph.D., University of Utah) is professor of communication at Eastern Connecticut State University. He teaches digital media production, media aesthetics, mass media, and organizational communication and technology courses. He is co-author of a media production book and also wrote and published another one, in Spanish, on technology and education in Colombia. He has also served as a consultant on media and education issues for several Colombian national institutions and was a grant recipient for the Colombian National Television Commission. He worked for several years as director and producer of Telecaribe, the Colombian Caribbean Region Television Network, where he produced many community-oriented media campaigns. E-mail: gomezj@easternct.edu

Alfonso González-Herrero (Ph.D., Complutense University of Madrid, Spain) is manager of external communications at IBM Spain, Portugal, Greece and Israel. He is also an associate professor at the Rey Juan Carlos University of Madrid. González began his career as a consultant at the New York office of Hill and Knowlton. Later, he joined the public affairs practice of Burson-Marsteller's Madrid office, where he became manager. He holds an M.A. in public relations management from Michigan State University, and a B.A. in advertising and public relations from Complutense University of Madrid. He also serves as regional coordinator in Spain of the European Association of Communication Directors. E-mail: agonzalezherrero@yahoo.com

Bitrus P. Gwamna (Ph.D., Ohio University) is professor of communication at Iowa Wesleyan College, Mount Pleasant, Iowa. He is a former broadcaster at Radio Nigeria, Kaduna, and editor and communication consultant to nonprofit organizations, including the Iowa chapter of the National Federation of the Blind. His research interests are in intercultural communication. E-mail: bgwamna@iwc.edu

Ali M. Kanso (Ph.D., Ohio University) is professor in the Department of Communication at the University of Texas at San Antonio. He is an international public relations and integrated marketing communication expert. His professional background includes work as a reporter, community relations director, advertising copywriter, and media consultant. Kanso's teaching, research, and consulting areas focus on cross-cultural communication, strategic planning in public relations, issues management, and international advertising. He has been named as one of the top 14 contributors to international advertising research in credited journals. Kanso received his B.A. from the Lebanese University. E-mail: ali.kanso@utsa.edu

Dean Kruckeberg (Ph.D., University of Iowa; accredited in public relations by the Public Relations Society of America [PRSA]; fellow, PRSA) is the executive director of the Center for Global Public Relations and professor in the Department of Communication Studies at the University of North Carolina at Charlotte. Kruckeberg is the co-author of *Public Relations and Community: A Reconstructed Theory*, and is the author and co-author of book chapters, articles and papers on international public relations and international public relations ethics. He is co-author of *This Is PR: The Realities of Public Relations*. Since 1997, Professor Kruckeberg has been co-chair of the National Commission on Public Relations Education. E-mail: Dean.Kruckeberg@uncc.edu

Kwamena Kwansah-Aidoo (Ph.D., Queensland University of Technology, Australia) is an associate professor of public relations, head of Communications Academic Group and associate dean, International, at the Faculty of Higher Education, Swinburne University of Technology in Melbourne, Australia. His research interests include the areas of crisis and cross-cultural communication. He is the author of many articles, book chapters and two books, including *Public Relations Issues and Crisis Management: Asia, Australia and New Zealand* which he co-authored with Christopher Galloway. From 2001–2007, he developed, nurtured and directed the public relations program at Monash University in Australia. Kwansah-Aidoo sits on the editorial board of *Environmental Communication: A Journal of Nature and Culture*, an international journal published by Routledge. E-mail: kkwansah@swin.edu.au

Jacqueline Lambiase (Ph.D., University of Texas at Arlington) is associate professor of strategic communication at the Schieffer School of Journalism at Texas Christian University, Fort Worth. Her published research uses qualitative methods to scrutinize gendered media images, public relations ethics, rhetorical branding strategies, and social media. Most recently with two co-authors, she analyzed a San Francisco Zoo crisis using two non-Western ethical philosophies in the *Western Journal of Communication* (2010). E-mail: j.lambiase@tcu.edu

Soledad Leal (M.A., Universidad Autónoma de Mexico) is an associate professor and coordinator of the organizational communication track in the department of communication and journalism at the Universidad Autónoma del Caribe in Barranquilla, Colombia. She also works as a consultant for political and organizational communications campaigns and has been a newspaper reporter and broadcast journalist for more than 16 years. E-mail: soleal@hotmail.com

Thierry Libaert (Ph.D., University of Louvain, Belgium) is professor of organizational communication at the Catholic University of Louvain (Belgium) where he chairs the laboratory of research in communication

(LASCO). Previously he has worked for the state industry department, for a public relations agency and subsequently as public relations manager for one of France's leading companies. He is also scientific director of the International Crisis Watch and adviser to the European Economic and Social Committee. He has published 20 books, including *La communication de crise* (Dunod Editions, 3rd edition, 2010). E-mail: Thierry. Libaert@uclouvain.be

Min Liu (Ph.D., North Dakota State University) is an assistant professor in the Department of Speech Communication at Southern Illinois University Edwardsville. Min Liu has presented and published crisis communication research that examined various international public health crises, including the SARS outbreak, the Melamine milk contamination incident in China, and HIV/AIDS as a public health issue in China. E-mail: mliu@siue.edu

Sorin Nastasia (Ph.D., University of North Dakota) is an assistant professor in the Department of Speech Communication at Southern Illinois University Edwardsville. He teaches public relations case studies, public relations campaigns, and related courses. Nastasia has presented and published research in U.S. and international settings on the role of U.S. public relations models in shaping French and Romanian public relations practices, new technologies in Western and Eastern Europe, Eastern European identities in transition and in diaspora, and youth issues in election campaigns. E-mail: snastas@siue.edu

Doug A. Newsom (Ph.D., University of Texas, Austin; accredited in public relations by the Public Relations Society of America [PRSA]; fellow PRSA) is the author of one textbook, *Bridging Gaps in Global Communication*, 2008, and co-author of three others: *Media Writing* (with the late James Wollert); *This Is PR* (with Judy VanSlyke Turk and Dean Kruckeberg) and *Public Relations Writing* (with the late Bob Carrell) and now Jim Haynes. She is co-editor of a book of women's colloquium papers, *Silent Voices* (also with Bob Carrell). She is professor emerita at Texas Christian University in Fort Worth and a public relations practitioner. Newsom and Haynes give webinars and presentations on crisis planning/management and public relations writing. E-mail: d.newsom@tcu.edu

Alexander G. Nikolaev (Ph.D., Florida State University) is an associate professor of communication in the Department of Culture and Communication at Drexel University, Philadelphia. His areas of expertise include public relations, crisis communication, political communication, and international communication, negotiations and news coverage. He has published articles in those areas in trade and scholarly journals, as well as several book chapters in the United States and elsewhere. He is the author of *International Negotiations: Theory, Practice, and the Connection with Domestic Politics*. He also edited *Ethical Issues in International*

Communication and co-edited (with E. Hakanen) *Leading to the 2003 Iraq War: The Global Media Debate*. E-mail: agn24@drexel.edu

Kunle Ogedengbe holds a master's degree in communication studies from Lagos State University and another master's in finance from the University of Calabar, Nigeria. As country representative (Nigeria) for *The Banker*, Financial Times Group, United Kingdom, he is an observer of Nigeria's financial crisis. Between 2002 and 2009, he worked in the Nigerian financial industry, and served as a research assistant on *Insight Nigeria*, a paper presented at the University of Hertfordshire, United Kingdom, in 2009. He lectures on crisis communication and marketing communication in tertiary institutions in Nigeria. He is the author of several books and research articles, including *Media of Public Relations* (PR Plus Consulting, Lagos, 2004). E-mail: ogedengbekunle@yahoo.com

Cornelius B. Pratt (Ph.D., University of Minnesota at Twin Cities; accredited in public relations by the Public Relations Society of America [PRSA]) is a professor in the Department of Strategic Communication at Temple University, United States. He also teaches at Temple University Japan. Professor Pratt is an honorary visiting professor of mass communication at Bingham University, New Karu, Nasarawa State, Nigeria. He serves on the editorial review boards of six journals, including *The South East Asian Journal of Management*, *Public Relations Review*, and the *Journal of Public Relations Research*. His research interests include international communication, ethics, public relations, and communication for national and regional development, particularly in emerging economies. E-mail: cbpratt@temple.edu; cbpratt@msu.edu

Andreas Schwarz (Ph.D., Ilmenau University of Technology, Germany) is assistant professor at the Department of Media Studies at Ilmenau University of Technology, Germany, where he received his Ph.D. in crisis communication in 2009. Since 2006 he has been managing director of the International Research Group on Crisis Communication (www.crisis-communication.de). He is the founding chair of the Temporary Working Group on Crisis Communication at the European Communication Research and Education Associaton. His research has been published in journals such as *Public Relations Review* and *International Journal of Strategic Communication*. Besides crisis communication, his research interests include public relations (nonprofit public relations, international public relations), journalism, and cross-cultural communication. He teaches in the areas of public relations, journalism, communication theory, and crisis management. E-mail: andreas.schwarz@tu-ilmenau.de

Abdul Karim Sinno (Ph.D., University of Wisconsin at Madison) provides quality teaching, research, and public service in the academic and business environments, using business and academic expertise to enhance understanding of the important social, technological, managerial, and public policy role of communication. His doctorate is in mass communication (with focus on advertising and persuasion). Dr. Sinno is the author of two books, a motivational speaker, and workshops leader. He is professor of communication and chairman of the Communication Department at Clarke University, Dubuque, Iowa. E-mail: abdul.sinno@Clarke.edu

J. Chris Skinner (M.A., University of Cambridge; and M.A., University of Zululand, South Africa) is a fellow and former chairman of the Accreditation Board of the Public Relations Institute of Southern Africa (PRISA). He is co-author of the *Handbook of Public Relations* which is the widely used text in Southern Africa as well as a number of other books and articles on public relations and related disciplines. Currently he is a visiting lecturer and researcher in the Department of Information Systems and Technology in the Faculty of Management Studies at the University of KwaZulu Natal. E-mail: chris.skinner@telkomsa.net

Ashli Quesinberry Stokes (Ph.D., University of Georgia) is an assistant professor in the Department of Communication Studies at the University of North Carolina—Charlotte. Dr. Stokes pursues a variety of research topics in public relations, specializing in rhetorical approaches to analyzing public relations controversies. She has published in the *Journal of Public Relations Research*, *Journal of Communication Management*, *Public Relations Review*, *the Southern Communication Journal*, *Studies in Communication Sciences*, and the *Encyclopedia of Public Relations*. She is co-author of a textbook about international public relations with colleague Dr. Alan Freitag, published by Routledge in 2009, and has also published a number of book chapters. E-mail: aqstokes@uncc.edu

Chiara Valentini (Ph.D., University of Jyväskylä, Finland) is an associate professor in the Department of Business Communication, Business and Social Sciences, Aarhus University, Denmark, where she teaches undergraduate and graduate courses in public relations and in public and political communication. She has worked in and consulted with several organizations and public institutions, including the Italian Representation of the European Commission in Rome and the European Movement International Secretariat in Brussels. She is the author and co-author of several books and papers on public relations and relationship management, crisis communication, public and political communication, public affairs and public diplomacy, and on the European Union. E-mail: chv@asb.dk

Monika Vij (Ph.D., University of Delhi) is an assistant professor in the Department of Geography, Miranda House, University of Delhi, where she teaches graduate and undergraduate courses. Her multidisciplinary research interests focus on communication of socio-spatial concerns of developing nations. In her work on participatory research appraisal, she evaluated the development communication activities, information dissemination, social mobilization, and behavior change of women in marginalized communities in Madhya Pradesh, one of India's least developed states. Currently, Dr. Vij is a postdoctoral fellow at the Indian Council of Social Sciences Research New Delhi, where she is working on the use of communication to reduce street crime in Delhi. E-mail: monikavij@hotmail.com

Foreword

It is high time a book that examines the topic of crisis management from a global or multi-country perspective was written, so this volume should become a mandatory resident on the bookshelf of every public relations executive or student.

Not only are the many case studies rich in detail and full of lessons but they are also topical so will be fresh in the memory of most readers. They have also, for the most part, occurred in the era in which social media on the Internet have played a major role in shaping communication during a crisis and have, on occasion, been the launch pad for the crisis.

The book is especially valuable for the way in which it marries scholarly theory to the practice of crisis communication. It rightly argues that a stronger and better developed theory for crisis management should help communicators and managers adopt a more systematic approach when confronted with a crisis and decisions must be made quickly. It represents an important step on the way to the development of analytics and action templates for dealing with a variety of crises that will be of real practical value.

A review of the crises covered in this volume also shines the spotlight on certain important factors that can cause poor handling of a major crisis affecting any global organization. Two in particular stand out.

The first is the culture of the organization itself as well as its "home" country when the crisis itself might be centered primarily in another country. My own experience of a number of such situations suggests that there is invariably a clash of views on the crisis strategy and action plan between management at headquarters and the local management in the market concerned. The result is either too long a delay in the all-important initial response or too wrong or insensitive responses. Either can lead to more difficult and much longer phases of damage control and reputation recovery.

The second is the continued poor record of issues identification and management on the part of many organizations. I have always held the view that only on exceptional occasions can crises be a surprise. And among the cases in this book almost all could—and should—have been anticipated and the issue(s) should have been managed so that a crisis was averted. For example, Toyota was aware over a period of years that there had been reports of unintended acceleration in its vehicles but chose not to confront and resolve the problem and inform stakeholders. Toyota paid the price in the loss of its carefully nurtured stellar reputation and revenues while some car owners were injured and several paid the ultimate price with their lives.

If, as I hope, this important work motivates transnational organizations to reorganize their management structures so as to harmonize different cultures and to pay as close attention to issues identification and management as they do to prepare for the crisis as if it were inevitable, it will have provided a vital service.

Michael Morley
Deputy Chairman, Edelman
Adjunct Professor, New York University School of
Continuing Professional Studies

Preface

Organizational and governmental communications are becoming increasingly important in a world of expanding technological dependence, of growing sociopolitical challenges, and of daunting environmental uncertainties. Technology is also enabling the restructuring of our communication patterns at the social level, as well as at the organizational and governmental levels, more so with the burgeoning use—and misuse—of social- or alternative- media platforms. Facebook, for example, has more than 800 million subscribers worldwide—and that number is expected to increase to more than one billion by 2020. The scope of activities in the blogosphere is becoming more complex and extensive by the day, raising mammoth questions about privacy; about the criteria for identifying the accuracy of information; about the real intent of a blogger; and about the fleeting, blurring boundaries among news, views, and opinions. A challenge of communication practitioners is to harness and manage this communication development in ways beneficial to their organizations or governments—that is, to enable the world community to navigate effectively a terrain that is vulnerable, to a large extent, to the dictates of nature.

Japan's triple disaster of March 11, 2011, for example, is a fervent reminder of the limits of the human mind; of the susceptibility of our well-being to Mother Nature; of the importance of prompt, swift public communication in a crisis of unexpected proportions; and of the reassuring efforts of the Japanese government and its communication staff, particularly those at Nippon Hōsō Kyōkai, Japan's only public radio and television corporation, to place the crisis quickly and publicly in a broader national context. The point here is that human-induced crises also require appropriate communication responses as a critical step to ameliorating the consequences of a crisis on an organization's activities, public standing, and reputation, and on the well-being of its disparate stakeholders.

Those concerns make this book a must-read. It shares organizational practices in crisis communication. And its goal is to help students, scholars, and communication practitioners glean directions as much from best practices as from questionable practices—all from disparate cultural and functional backgrounds on a global scale. This book will also help students, scholars and practitioners enhance their worldviews of communication for crisis management, in light of the increasing reality that organizational actions are either increasingly global or have major global implications. We hope that it will expand the reaches of the knowledge on and the practice of communication for crisis management to those that address the effects of the confluence of globalization and technology on business paradigms and on practitioner competencies.

We believe that this book fills a gap for a much-needed discussion of situations in crisis communication from international perspectives. The events of September 11, 2001, and other major world crises, including Toyota's runaway crisis, a magnitude-9.0 earthquake and tsunami in Japan, anti-government protests in the Middle East and North Africa, the Chilean miners rescue, corporate fraud, and oil rig explosions, justify the need for this book. While many books on crisis communication tend to focus on U.S. corporate cases, they may not appeal equally to students and practitioners in other parts of the world, hence the need to analyze cases from the United States and from other countries.

The variety and the international focus of cases in this book make it more appealing to a wider audience. And the reader will note the depth of the cases and the palpable attempt by the book's editors and contributors to avoid using a shop-worn, cookie-cutter approach to case analyses. The cases, therefore, examine sociocultural issues associated with responding to a variety of crises. Additionally, a unique feature of this book is a section titled "Views from an expert," which appears at the end of each case. The expert in question is not connected to the crisis; thus, she or he can share disinterested opinions and views on the specifics of a crisis that an organization confronts. "Views from an expert" is, therefore, written in a consistent, down-to-earth manner.

This book is organized into three parts. Part I provides the background and theoretical framework within which each case is analyzed. It emphasizes the importance of theory to effective crisis communication. As social psychologist Kurt Lewin wrote in the mid-twentieth century, "There is nothing so practical as a good theory." Similarly, German philosopher Immanuel Kant (1724–1804) wrote that a critical test of any theory is its capacity to guide action in fruitful ways. And in 2008, U.S. ethics scholar Clifford G. Christians averred: "Theories ought not to be treated in static, scholastic terms . . . [They] should be redefined as meaningful portraits and not statistically precise formulations derived from artificially fixed conditions." Thus, this section also includes sociocultural views of crisis communication. And it defines crisis in all its forms and presents types of crises, highlighting concepts such as crisis management, reputation management, issues management, image restoration, disaster communication, and risk communication. It also discusses the elements of an effective crisis communication. This discussion will enable readers to understand how and why some crises are effectively managed and why others are not.

Part II discusses the three phases or stages of effective crisis planning and communication. They include what organizations do to prepare to communicate before a crisis occurs, the nature of communication during the crisis, and communication post-crisis. It also includes tips and sample forms that may be adapted for use during a crisis.

Part III discusses the individual cases drawn from Africa, Asia, Australia, Europe, Middle East and the Americas. From Africa, we have cases that range from the social media role in anti-government protests in Egypt, election violence and the effect on tourism in Kenya, a financial crisis in Nigeria to an oil refinery explosion in South Africa. The Asian cases include tainted infant formula in China; reactions in China to the Olympic Torch protests in France; corporate fraud in India; Japan's triple disaster (earthquake, tsunami, nuclear reactor malfunctioning) and Toyota's auto-acceleration crisis; and political uncertainties and protests in Thailand. Australia offers a fascinating case of the 2009 catastrophic bushfires. Europe provides us with "Climategate" from England, which casts doubt on global warming. The case from France gives insights into the crisis management of the exceptional fraud at Société Générale Bank. Germany's Love Parade tragedy underscores the power of images in influencing public opinion. Russia's case study illustrates government communication during the 2008 war in South Ossetia. A scandal at Eurovision, Europe's largest TV show, serves as a coda to cases from Europe.

Similarly, the Middle East provides interesting cases, from Iran's Twitter revolution to Lebanon's attempt to revive its tourism sector in the wake of the Israeli–Lebanese war of 2006.

In North America, the analysis of BP's crisis management in the aftermath of the oil rig explosion in the Gulf of Mexico offers important lessons in crisis communication. And from Mexico comes a campaign to rebrand the Mexican resort town of Rosarito Beach. One of the two cases from South America focuses on the triumph of the Chilean government's response to a mining accident; the other is on the massive floods in Colombia's Atlántico State. A chapter on social media highlights the intersection of social media and crisis communication, particularly in our growing dependence on all things virtual.

The chapters are written by scholars or professionals with expertise or research interests in those parts of the world on which their chapters are focused. And the cases cover a broad spectrum: multinational corporations, nonprofit organizations, and governments. Several discussion questions are presented in each chapter.

We hope that this book provides you with useful insights into crisis communication from international perspectives and stimulates global discussions in the classroom, in the boardroom, or by the water fountain. We welcome your comments and suggestions.

Acknowledgments

Ideas for book manuscripts generally do not flourish in a vacuum. A convergence of factors provided the impetus for developing this book. Our students, to whom this book is aptly dedicated, played a significant role in getting us thinking seriously about models of educational and training tools in crisis communication. We thank our students for sharing with us the strengths and limitations of traditional instructional offerings in crisis communication. Those strengths are inarguably compelling.

Except that crisis communication, as a specialty of public relations, did not have an eclectic collection of international cases that would provide the depth and the breadth of analyses that would engage students inside and outside the classroom.

Except that "standards for graduate education in public relations [needed to] reflect its body of knowledge and practice expectations," as recommended by the Commission on Public Relations Education, a body of practitioners and educators in communication and related fields.

Except that crisis-communication practitioners, even as they apply meaningful theoretical models to their strategic considerations for formulating and implementing crisis-response strategies, could not avail themselves of a wide range of situations—in governments, in nonprofit organizations, in corporate settings—that have heuristic implications for their everyday responsibilities, particularly for those on crises.

And except that managers in non-communication positions did not have a single source from which they could glean snippets of information that could position them at the ready to contribute invaluably to preventing, analyzing and resolving crises.

A serendipitous meeting between Amiso George, co-editor, and John Szilagyi, commissioning editor at Routledge Publishing, at a business conference in Dallas in February 2010 moved preliminary ideas for this book to the next phase. We thank Mr. Szilagyi for consistently supporting our work and for graciously offering key suggestions for broadening its appeal, which was further enhanced by the brilliance and enthusiasm of our cadre of global contributors.

We also thank Sara Werden, editorial assistant in business and management at Routledge, in New York City, for her patience and professionalism in guiding us through the arduous process of book publishing. Our thanks also go to Alfred Symons and his team. Mr. Symons is the production editor in Routledge's United Kingdom office. James Sowden and Jane Fieldsend of Florence Production, in the UK, both edited our work with precision; Jane our copyeditor, ensured uniformity and clarity in language. We thank them for their bold encouragement and unalloyed support in bringing this book to fruition.

We appreciate the comments of the anonymous reviewers of our proposal. Their suggestions helped us to refine the direction of this book.

We are profoundly grateful to Pedro Alejandro Wunderlich, a recent graduate of the Schieffer School of Journalism at Texas Christian University, where he enrolled in classes from the first editor and was active in the school's chapter of the Public Relations Student Society of America and Advertising Club. During a weekend, Mr. Wunderlich, then a senior at TCU, created four sample designs of the cover for this book. He was characteristically gratuitous: he neither received extra course credit nor any form of remuneration for his creative products.

We must acknowledge the invaluable insights we received on some of our field's pedagogical needs that our colleagues at Texas Christian and Temple universities shared with us. Similarly, our colleagues at the Greater Fort Worth Public Relations Society of America (PRSA), particularly Carolyn Bobo, Accredited in Public Relations (APR), Fellow, PRSA; and Dan Keeney, APR, of DKPR of Dallas and Houston, provided compelling illustrations for some of our arguments. We thank them all.

Part I

Theoretical Approaches to and Sociocultural Perspectives in Crisis Communication

Cornelius B. Pratt

This chapter summarizes various definitions of crisis—definitions that indicate the multiplicity of perspectives in the growing specialty of crisis communication. It outlines types of crises and describes key communication theories (e.g., the theory of image restoration discourse and the situational crisis communication theory) and related theoretical formulations that undergird crisis management (e.g., the blog-mediated crisis communication model) that practitioners will continue to find useful in crisis response. Finally, it addresses the interplay between societies' dominant cultural practices and their influence on crisis communication. It illustrates that interplay primarily from the Asian perspective, noting that the high-context attributes and Confucian principles dominant in Asian and sub-Saharan African cultures result in nuanced, indirect crisis communication, whereas communicators in dominant United States' culture and those of the United Kingdom, France, and Germany, with their low-context attributes, are wont to be direct and sometimes confrontational in their communication.

Introduction

The nearly two dozen cases in this book, all of which are based on events or incidents that occurred after 2006, have stoked the interest of communication practitioners, teachers, and students worldwide in how best to communicate *in* or *about* a crisis. Each case is presented in accordance with the best practices in the field; that is, a background or analysis of each case is provided, then the initial response of major stakeholders is presented and quickly coupled with the goals, objectives, strategies, and tactics used by the key stakeholders. Because each case focuses on a crisis, we begin our analysis by describing that concept and identifying some of the key theories that serve as "field guides" for communication practitioners as they develop or implement plans for responding to crises.

4 Cornelius B. Pratt

This chapter iterates the importance of theories, which many communication practitioners use, sometimes unwittingly, in a crisis. The lessons learned from each crisis are outlined as take-away gems. The next chapter takes readers to some of the nuts and bolts of crisis communication—setting the stage for providing prompt, effective responses to crises.

This chapter has five sections. The first outlines the importance of theory to crisis communication. The second and third summarize sample definitions, characteristics, and types of crises. The fourth identifies key theories that undergird the use of crisis communication strategies. And the fifth presents the interplay between a sociocultural environment and crisis communication.

Theory and Crisis

Why are theories important to our understanding of how we can communicate effectively *in* or *about* a crisis? Consider: You are about to launch a major communications campaign, this time on a nebulous, shifting terrain. You now have persuasive data on your publics: their psychographics (e.g., attitudes, use of social media, and quality and patterns of social relationships); and their demographics (e.g., ethnicity, education, and income). And you know you still need to amass, perhaps in short order, additional information on the campaign to ensure that its implementation is not tantamount to a fool's errand. So you analyze a welter of data to decipher relevant information. Enter theory.

Our knowledge of relevant communication theories ensures that all possible contingencies have been considered well before a rollout. That essential knowledge of theory, Toth (1986) noted, "can provide a framework for coping with reality" (p. 30). From the standpoint of "normal science," as Kuhn (1996), a philosopher of science, wrote, theory is used in "puzzle-solving" (pp. 35–42); that is, to answer questions and to solve specific scientific problems. Similarly, from the standpoint of the social sciences, a general theoretical perspective "allows scientists to go about solving the puzzles they continually generate" (Eckberg and Hill, 1979, p. 929). That perspective can enable us to do some stocktaking even as various facets of our campaign are being implemented—sometimes simultaneously. How? Because theories are indeed a lighthouse in the dark, a Global Positioning System, of sorts, such as a Garmin or a TomTom; they tell us precisely how we can most effectively implement our programs and how we can identify, segment, and connect strategically with, say, our publics—without possibly veering off course. Theories are indeed our field guide. In essence, they are also searchlights that ensure that we have a step-by-step approach to understanding, anticipating, and addressing sticky campaign or communication situations. Observations (or phenomena) on our campaign are described (what is happening here?) and accounted for and explained (what are these campaign-related phenomena and activities? How do they occur? And why and when do they occur?). We want a clear idea of what to expect as our campaign takes on a life of its own—

that is, to be better able to predict processes and constraints on outcomes; to hedge our bets, if necessary; to have some order in and control of each phase of the campaign; to identify how actions undertaken in one phase and the outcomes they engender relate in an organized way to other actions in and outcomes from other phases. Thus, the practitioner has reliable descriptions and systematic explanations of possible campaign processes and outcomes. Those explanations contribute to a better understanding of how one part of the campaign or program relates to (or interacts, intersects, or unifies with) other parts. They offer compelling interpretations of the significance of each turn and each outcome. Armed with theories, practitioners are not, as it were, operating in the dark, in a vacuum. In fact, the practitioner's actions can contribute in meaningful ways to theory building in public relations, as Botan (1989) noted:

> When a public relations practitioner offers an explanation for why a public relations effort succeeded or failed, he or she is taking the first step in propounding a theory. The generally accepted explanations and ways of doing things that have evolved over the years in public relations are therefore rudimentary theories.
>
> (Botan, 1989, p. 102)

Since about the mid-1990s, the scholarly literature on crisis communication has identified several theories that communication practitioners find useful in formulating and identifying apppropriate crisis-response strategies, in predicting constraints on crisis interventions, and in implementing and evaluating crisis-communication programs. Unbeknown to some such practitioners, however, their actions were already well grounded in theories, even as crisis-communication researchers (e.g., Coombs, 1999, 2007a; Sisco et al., 2010) bemoan the fragmentation of theoretical constructs in our specialty and the paucity of investigations of their implications for or direct relevance to crisis communication.

Two crisis-communication theories—both of which will be addressed in some detail in a subsequent section of this chapter—are the theory of image restoration discourse, which focuses on what corporations can say when faced with a crisis (Benoit, 1995, 1997; Harlow et al., 2011); and the situational crisis communication theory (SCCT) (Coombs, 2007a, b, c; Coombs, 2009; Coombs and Holladay, 2010), which states that some public relations crises are best resolved if organizations adopt specific crisis-response strategies in their attempt to restore their reputations. Coombs (1995) and Coombs and Holladay (1996) illustrate, for example, how attribution theory is used to classify crises, resulting in categories that, in turn, help practitioners determine the response strategies that they should adopt.

Technology company Foxconn's rash of 15 suicides—from that of a 19-year-old male employee on January 23, 2010, through that of the most recent in February 2011—falls into Coombs's (2007a) preventable crisis cluster in which the company's community raises the question: Why so much pain at this Shenzhen plant? That question is framed within the context of SCCT. And organizational responses are appropriately identified. Little wonder that more organizations are benefiting from effective crisis communication and crisis management, even from their unwitting applications of theoretical perspectives to communicating and managing their crises. But, first, what is a crisis?

Crisis: Definitions and Characteristics

Let us examine briefly the situation in which the world's largest contract manufacturer of electronics found itself early in 2010. Foxconn Technology Group, whose parent company is Taipei-based Hon Hai Precision Industry Co. Ltd, has more than 920,000 employees in China and 420,000 in a sprawling factory complex in Shenzhen, China's coastal city in Guangdong province. That complex also has dormitories in which the company's migrant work force lives in cramped quarters, separate from families. The company's clients include Apple, Cisco, Dell, Hewlett-Packard, IBM, Nokia, and Sony. During the first six months of 2010, beginning on January 23, 16 Foxconn employees at the Shenzhen factory attempted suicide, 12 others killed themselves, and an additional 20 were stopped from committing suicide. That was a major crisis, compounded by three factors. First, austere, bare-bones employee living quarters, which, some argued, exacerbated an intimidating corporate environment. Second, perhaps because of the preceding factor, employees' mental health was in question. Third, the company's hard-charging, take-no-prisoners, suffer-no-fools-gladly culture projected an organizational environment not at once conducive to employee well-being and productivity. News reports dubbed the culture militaristic and the management non-human-based, resulting in burnout among employees ("Foxconn case," 2010). But because Foxconn produces electronic parts for high-end technology companies, it requires excellence in productivity and zero tolerance for fallibility. The crisis that emanated from that corporate culture illustrates Hermann's (1963) working definition of an organizational crisis as that which "(1) threatens high-priority values of the organization, (2) presents a restricted amount of time in which a response can be made, and (3) is unexpected or unanticipated by the organization" (p. 64).

Developing effective definitions of crisis has been a dynamic effort for decades, with early definitions being event- or incident-oriented and some current definitions taking a process-oriented approach, even as both approaches overlap and are complementary (Jaques, 2009). Snyder et al. (2006) state that the vague definitions of organizational crisis result in the lack of a unifying conceptualization of the concept. Even so, the numerous definitions of crisis have a common theme: unexpected events that engender unwholesome outcomes. Some such definitions and descriptions:

- Barton (2008) defines a crisis as *"any event that can seriously harm the people, reputation, or financial condition of an organization"* (p. 3).
- Coombs and Holladay (2010) identify the following key descriptors of a crisis: *"unpredictable, expectations, serious impact/negative outcomes,* and *perception"* (p. 238). They also state, "The term *crisis* should be reserved for serious events or threats."
- Fearn-Banks (2011) says that it is a "major occurrence with a potentially negative outcome affecting the organization, company, or industry, as well as its publics, products, services, or good name. A crisis interrupts normal business transactions and can sometimes threaten the existence of the organization" (p. 2).
- Fink (2002) states that a crisis "is *not* necessarily bad news—merely reality" (p. 1), an observation reflected in his definition of crisis as "an unstable time or state of affairs in which a decisive change is impending— either one with the distinct possibility of a highly undesirable outcome or one with the distinct possibility of a highly desirable and extremely positive outcome. It is usually a 50–50-proposition, but you can improve the odds" (p. 15).
- Fishman (1999) outlines five characteristics of crises: events are unpredictable; threats are evident on an individual or organization; causes of the crisis are discernible; events are time-sensitive; and occurrences are a dynamic, multidimensional set of relationships.
- Gilpin and Murphy (2010) define crises specifically from a two-pronged perspective: perception and effects. They write: "Thus how an event is perceived and how it affects the people linked to an organization, both individually and as a group, will determine whether or not it is classified as a crisis and how it is subsequently handled" (p. 14). They note that crises can also be defined from a number of perspectives that include psychological attributes (how do managers feel about their involvement in a crisis?); cause (is it natural, technological, confrontational, malevolent, skewed management values, deceptive, or untoward management conduct?); and business impacts (what public perception or business shift does it engender?)
- Heath and Millar (2004) adopt a two-dimensional, rhetorical definition of crisis: technical or managerial (for example, accidents, human errors, or threats to the environment); and communication response (for example, how an organization prepares for, accommodates to, and recovers from disruptive outcomes).
- Maitlis and Sonenshein (2010) say that crises are "often situations characterized by ambiguity, confusion, and feelings of disorientation" (p. 552).
- Ogilvy Public Relations Worldwide identifies eight characteristics that underlie all corporate crises: events that occur suddenly and are driven by media exposure; information that is short on relevant facts of crisis; flow

of events that hampers management's understanding of crisis and its persuasive response; loss of control over perception of crisis and its impact on company; scrutiny from corporate insiders and outsiders, including the media, government regulatory agencies, and activist groups; onset of corporate siege mentality that encourages company officials to hide behind legal aspects of crisis, making the company more vulnerable to the crisis; panic that paralyzes corporate decision making; and issue that tends to be resolved in the public arena to the satisfaction of outsiders, including the media, government regulatory agencies, and activist groups, and to the detriment of the company itself (Tortorella, 2004).

- Pearson and Clair (1998) define it strictly within an organizational context as "a low-probability, high-impact situation that is perceived by critical stakeholders to threaten the viability of the organization and that is subjectively experienced by these individuals as personally and socially threatening" (p. 66).

- Roux-Dufort (2007, 2009) takes a processual approach to crisis, viewing it as both an event and a process of the gradual organizational accumulation of weaknesses, imperfections, and vulnerabilities at different levels of the organization. Those pre-existing conditions produce a triggering event that leads to a crisis. Crisis is, thus, conceptualized as an organization's proneness to institutional and environmental prerequisites, which lead to "the transition from a situation of normality to one of imbalance and then to a disruption" (Roux-Dufort, 2009, p. 5); and reflect the managerial ignorance that precedes the eruption of an event. Earlier, Turner (1976), in writing about "the accumulation of unnoticed events that are at odds with beliefs shared on the dangers and means of avoiding them" (p. 381), spelled out some of the fundamentals of the processual theory of crisis. Research by Shrivastava et al. (1988) built upon that perspective, which views crises as combinations of several loosely coupled and interdependent events, each one preparing the ground for the other to occur in a chain reaction.

- Snyder et al. (2006) define "organizational crisis as an extraordinary condition that is disruptive and damaging to the existing operating state of an organization. An organization crisis, if ignored or mismanaged, will threaten competitiveness and sustainability of the affected entity" (p. 372).

- Ulmer et al. (2011) view crises as "dangerous moments or turning points in an organization's life cycle" (p. 3). Their working definition of organizational crisis: "a specific, *unexpected*, and *nonroutine* event or series of events that create high levels of uncertainty and simultaneously present an organization with both *opportunities* for and *threats* to its *high-priority goals*" (p. 7).

- Zaremba (2010) identifies three "recurring characteristics" of the definitions of crises as involving atypical events that might be predictable but not expected when they occur, as damaging to an organization or individual, and as necessitating communications with various audiences to minimize the fallout from the crises. He says it is "an anomalous event that may negatively affect an organization and requires efficient organizational communication to reduce the damage related to the event" (p. 21).

It is clear from the preceding list that, at the very least, a crisis is a situation or event that can be organizationally unnerving, disruptive, or interruptive, even as the Chinese-language symbol for crisis, *wei ji*, means *both* a crisis and an opportunity (Ulmer et al., 2011). And, as Augustine (2000) observes, "Almost every crisis contains within itself the seeds of success as well as the roots of failure" (p. 4), making the harnessing of that success and the understanding of that failure pivotal to effective crisis management. But a crisis, depending on type, can be more manageable than others, a subject to which we now turn.

Types of Crises

As the literature on crisis and crisis communication shows, there have been a number of descriptions and characterizations of what is or constitutes a crisis. That scholarly dynamic is indicated in the categories or typologies of crises. The diversity of scholarly disciplines involved in research in crisis communication may explain "'the tower of Babel' effect" (Shrivastava, 1993, p. 33) on, and the difficulties in reaching a common understanding of, the definitions of terms and concepts in the specialty (Jaques, 2009).

Coombs (2007a, 2008) and Coombs and Holladay (2002, 2010) draw upon attribution theory to develop three types or clusters of crises: (a) victimized, that is, by natural disasters, rumors, and workplace violence; (b) accidental, such as challenges and technical-error accidents; and (c) preventable, such as human-error accidents and organizational misconduct. Earlier, Coombs (1995) developed a two-by-two crisis-type matrix, grounded in attribution theory and based on intentionality and locus of control: (a) accidents (unintentional and internal), (b) transgressions (intentional and internal), (c) faux pas (unintentional and external), and (d) terrorism (intentional and external).

Lerbinger (1997) identifies seven types of crises subsumed under three causes: (a) nature and technology, both crises of the physical world, as illustrated in the still-mysterious explosion that killed 11 workers on a British Petroleum drilling rig off the Louisiana coast on April 20, 2010; (b) confrontation and malevolence, both crises of the human and social environment, as illustrated in protest movements in Iran over the 2009 presidential election that declared President Mahmoud Ahmadinejad victorious over challenger Mir Hossein Mousavi, and in Thailand over its Red Shirt–Yellow Shirt confrontation; and (c) concern with corporate profits at the expense of other stakeholder interest, deception, and misconduct, all crises of management failure, as illustrated in the global financial crisis that began in the summer of 2007 and precipitated by subprime mortgages in the United States.

Linke (1989) takes a significantly different approach to developing a typology of crises, grounding his in the amount of time an organization has to respond to a crisis: (a) exploding; (b) pressing, that is, immediate; (c) building; and (d) continuing.

Similarly, Mitroff (2004), Mitroff and Anagnos (2001), and Mitroff and Pearson (1993) developed a six-item typology of crises based on causes: (a) economic attacks, (b) information attacks, (c) organizational malfunction, (d) catastrophic malfunction, (e) "psycho" attack, and (f) occupational health crises.

Skinner et al. (2007) have a three-pronged typology of crises: (a) immediate, which happens suddenly and unexpectedly; (b) emerging, which brews over time; and (c) sustained, which persists for months or years.

Ulmer et al., (2011) categorized crises according to intent: (a) intentional crises, such as terrorism, sabotage, workplace violence, poor employee relationships, and unethical management, tend to be human-provoked; and (b) unintentional crises, such as natural disasters, disease outbreaks, unforeseeable technical interactions, and product failure, tend to be outside the realm of intentional human provocation.

Finally, Zaremba (2010) provides a summary of categories of crises culled from works of several writers: natural disaster, management/employee misconduct, product tampering, megadamage, rumor, technical breakdown/accident, technical breakdown/not entirely accidental, challenge, human error, and workplace violence.

The triggering events for crises are numerous and diverse, making each crisis situation an instructive experience for organizations as they attempt to align the crisis type with the appropriate theory-informed response. Crisis-communication managers have at their disposal a number of theories that can provide the guiding light to what such response *should* be.

Crisis-communication Theories

Avery et al. (2010) reported that a majority of the research studies on crisis management and communication in public relations over an 18-year period was guided by two primary theories: Benoit's (1995, 1997) theory of image restoration or repair, and Coombs's (2007a) situational crisis communication theory. Both those theories, as well as others that undergird crisis communication, have been well documented (e.g., Brinson and Benoit, 1999; Brown and White, 2011; Coombs, 2007a; Coombs and Holladay, 2002; Coombs and Schmidt, 2000; Hearit, 1999; Jin and Liu, 2010; Marsh, 2006, 2010; Meng, 2010; Zaremba, 2010); therefore, their key features and their illustrations will be summarized here in short order.

Theory of Image Repair Discourse

An inevitability of the corporate environment is an image crisis; therefore, this theory is grounded in two key assumptions: (a) that communication is goal-directed activity, and (b) that an important goal of communication is to maintain a favorable reputation. According to this theory, a starting point in resolving a crisis is to understand its causal factors as well as the nature of the threat. Benoit's (1995, 1997) image restoration theory holds that, because image and reputation are essential to organizations and individuals, any (offensive) act that undermines an organization's standing with its stakeholders could be addressed through an image restoration discourse to develop and understand images that respond to such an image crisis. The theory extends Ware and Linkugel's (1973) theory of *apologia*, which identifies four factors in self-defense: denial (this company had nothing to do with the alleged act); bolstering (this company is a significant employer in this community; differentiation (this company is expanding its services rapidly to better serve you, our customers who are our top priority); and transcendence (this company's rapid growth in its services and its growing pains can translate into more community involvement and support).

Benoit's (1995, 1997) expansive theory focuses on message options—that is, the content of crisis communication or the messages that an organization uses to change stakeholders' perceptions when confronted with a crisis. According to Benoit, five general self-defense strategies underpin the messages: (a) denying charges, accusations or allegations; (b) evading responsibility for an offensive act; (c) reducing the severity of the offensiveness of a wrongful act; (d) taking corrective actions; and (e) admitting or confessing wrongdoing and begging for forgiveness (mortification).

Relating this theory to Foxconn's experience leads us to the following conclusions:

- The company neither denied accusations and allegations of its high-pressure work environment nor the severity of the issue. And Foxconn did not shift the blame for the crisis to someone else.
- The company did not evade its responsibility; it accepted it. The events on its plant were not a consequence of defeasibility (that is, lack of information or of the ability to respond to them). In fact, Foxconn's immediate response included welcoming Apple's then-chief operating officer Tim Cook to a fact-finding mission on the Shenzhen plant in June 2010; hiring counselors for its 24-hour care center; and attaching large nets to factory buildings, hoping that that device would serve as a deterrent to further suicide attempts.
- The company did not diminish the offensiveness of the incidents, either by minimization by saying that they were infrequent or an aberration or, by attacking its accusers, or by proposing up front that it would compensate victims' families.

- The company took immediate corrective action, promptly seeking employee contributions to resolving the embarrassing weakness of its corporate culture and seeking the services of mental-health counselors to help create an environment more conducive to employee well-being. And its U.S. public relations firm disseminated timely information on corrective measures being undertaken.
- The company did not seek mortification; it did not apologize for the realities of the cookie-cutter environment in which its operations are conducted, even as it ensured that the situations in the workplace that led to a spate of suicides were being improved.

On balance, Foxconn's eclectic response strategies helped create a public perception of a responsive company whose quick action was in the overall interest of its employees.

Situational Crisis Communication Theory

Coombs's (2007a, 2008, 2009) situational crisis communication theory (SCCT), grounded in attribution theory (Claeys et al., 2010; Coombs, 2007a; Coombs and Holladay, 2005, 2010), posits an audience-centered approach to crisis communication, focusing on how stakeholders respond to a crisis and on the best response strategies organizations can adopt to restore their reputations. Different crises generate different predictable levels of responsibility for the crises. The more the cause of a crisis is perceived as beyond an organization's or an individual's control, the lower the attribution of responsibility for a crisis to that organization or individual; higher perceptions of controllability lead to higher attributions of responsibility for a crisis. As Jeong (2009) and Zaremba (2010) state, stakeholders' attributions of responsibility in crisis communication are affected by relationship history (that is, a negative relationship leads to additional damage to corporate reputation), external versus internal control (that is, whether a crisis is caused or controlled by people internal to or external to the organization); and personal control (that is, whether someone close to the crisis could have controlled it).

SCCT segments crises into three types of clusters—victim (low attributions of crisis responsibility), accidental (moderate attributions of crisis responsibility), and preventable (high attributions of crisis responsibility)—each of which requires specific organizational responses grouped into three postures: deny, which indicates low concern for crisis victims; diminish, which seeks to reduce organization's vulnerability to the crisis; and deal, which indicates high concern for victims and high acceptance of responsibility. As Coombs (2008) notes, the deny posture includes attacking the person or group that claims that an organization has engaged in a wrongful act; the diminish posture is used by the crisis manager eager to minimize organizational responsibility or the perceived damage it may have caused; and the deal posture includes ingratiation (crisis managers remind stakeholders about the positive traits of organization), concern, compensation, and apology.

SCCT also matches crisis managers' response recommendations to crises, by situations: for rumors, use denial strategies; for product tampering, use instructing information; for accidents and human error, deal strategies; to victims of crisis, demonstrate concern (Coombs, 2008).

The resolution of Foxconn's suicide crisis was a throwback to Coombs's (2007a, 2008) SCCT: the company assumed neither the deny nor the diminish posture; rather, it adopted pointedly the deal posture, demonstrating utmost, urgent concern for victims and their families. The causes of the crisis (hallmarks of attributions of responsibility for a corporate culture) evoke anger toward the event (for example, through employee protests) that in turn leads to motivation for action (for example, Foxconn's retaining WPP Burson Marsteller to investigate and implement corrective measures). The degree to which Foxconn did all of those things was at some level consistent with some of the key elements of SCCT; it demonstrated the latter's application to a situation that had major implications for corporate communications.

The remainder of this section highlights four related theoretical formulations that are used by crisis managers to undergird crisis communication—and, in one instance, to help them track blog-mediated organizational rumors and resolve such "victim crises" (Coombs and Holladay, 2010, pp. 248–249) in the blogosphere, which is exploding with activities large and small.

Blog-mediated Crisis Communication Model

Granted, models and theories have overlapping features; however, the former do not necessarily have explanatory and predictive characteristics, two hallmarks of *all* theories. But the descriptive and interactive features of models are so palpable that the blog-mediated crisis communication (BMCC) model, for example, helps crisis managers identify influential external blogs and bloggers and to engage them. It places priority on using blog-mediated public relations' strategies and tactics to reach key publics associated with a crisis and to foster relationships with them in light of organizations' limited resources to address crises and to connect with those publics through the crisis-information flows generated by influential external blogs or user- or public-generated content (Jin and Liu, 2010). While understanding influential blogs (that is, blog content) is important, it is equally important that crisis-communication managers identify the dissemination process of that content, for example, whether it is through e-word-of-mouth communication.

Additionally, Jin and Liu (2010) proposed two types of blogger involvements: (a) issue involvement, which occurs when bloggers' direct or indirect experiences with an issue motivate them to talk with others about an organization to relieve the excitement or disappointment caused by the issue; and (b) self-involvement, which occurs when bloggers seek self-affirmation by talking with others about a service, or product, thus building their credentials as leaders or authorities on the subject.

Stakeholder Theory

To the degree that a crisis is usually noteworthy largely because of its effects or consequences on an organization's diverse stakeholders, stakeholder theory is a bedrock of public relations and the fulcrum of crisis communication. And because such stakeholders have disparate concerns about, interests in, and demands on the organization, it is important that stakeholder theory be brought to bear in segmenting publics for specific forms of communication. Crisis-response strategies are invariably sensitive to the importance of stakeholders in the organization's environment. As Ulmer (2001) observes, "The benefits of investing in stakeholder relationships precrisis has profound implications for crisis-stricken organizations" (p. 593).

Freeman's (1984) seminal work on stakeholder theory concluded that because environmental "shifts" were occurring among internal stakeholders (customers, employees, and suppliers) and external stakeholders (regulatory agencies, competitors, and special-interest groups), effective organizations need to "take into account all of those groups and individuals that can affect, or are affected by, the accomplishment of the business enterprise" (p. 25). Therefore, such a list of stakeholders—what Freeman (2010) calls "the stakeholder map of an organization" (p. 67)—can enable communication practitioners to place stakeholders at the center of strategic thinking, to assign ranks to the stakeholders, and to develop a relational view of organizational communication. Crisis managers can then communicate effectively *in* or *about* a crisis. Grunig and Repper (1992) wrote: "Communication at the stakeholder stage—ideally before conflict [read: crisis] has occurred—is especially important because it helps to develop the stable, long-term relationships that an organization needs to build support from stakeholders and to manage conflict when it occurs" (pp. 126–127). Along that vein, Freeman (2010) argued that integrating stakeholder concerns into business operations makes corporate social responsibility as a distinct, separate activity moot. The point here is that adopting or disregarding stakeholder theory by crisis managers can facilitate recovery from a crisis in a turbulent organizational environment or exacerbate that crisis.

Situational Theory of Publics

Related to stakeholder theory is a theory that helps us assess the communication behaviors of different publics. The situational theory of publics tells us what stakeholders—or publics—will do if they recognize a problem (or a risk or crisis), if they perceive themselves as being involved with the problem, or if they think they are constrained in resolving the problem. Will a stakeholder who recognizes a risk merely process or actively seek information on it? How likely will risk messages—that is, those on communicating the seriousness of the safety, environmental, or health risks associated with consuming or using a product, on engaging in an activity, or on buying into an idea—encourage stakeholders to seek more information about threats? And what additional measures will risk communicators take in response to stakeholder risk concerns and needs?

Crisis and risk communications are so tightly woven into each other in practice and are both so undergirded by the situational theory of publics that one can serve as a substitute for the other. The definition of risk communication clarifies that interface: ". . . a dialogue between organizations creating risks and the constituents that must bear the risk . . . [O]rganizations explain what the risk is . . . while risk bearers try to voice their concerns and fears about the risk" (Coombs and Holladay, 2010, p. 219). The theory purports that certain factors—problem recognition, level of involvement, and constraint recognition—influence whether individuals will merely process information about a problem or whether individuals will actively seek out more information about a problem. Thus this theory is the degree to which a perceived risk can evolve into a problem and quickly morphs into a crisis (problem recognition), and calls for an assessment of an organization's strategic responses to that problem (constraint recognition), and necessitates assessing organizational involvement with that problem (level of involvement), followed by stakeholders' processing or seeking information on the problem or risk.

Rhetorical Stasis Theory

This theory falls squarely in the genre of rhetorical theories of self-defense whose strategies Ware and Linkugel (1973) articulated as (a) denying, that is, stating categorically that the alleged wrong act did not occur; (b) bolstering, that is, reinforcing favorable traits to encourage stakeholders' positive feelings toward an alleged wrongdoer; (c) differentiating, that is, redefining the facts of a larger context; and (d) transcending, that is, persuading stakeholders to look at a crisis from a broader perspective of the organization's overall strengths.

Stasis theory helps crisis managers identify core issues in a crisis and provides a hierarchical structure for selecting response strategies to it, and for identifying specific actions within those strategies (Marsh, 2006), particularly in the theory's application to corporate *apologia*, which Hearit (1994) defines as "a defense that seeks to present a compelling counter description of organizational actions" (p. 115). (Stasis means an issue.) Marsh presents four forms of stasis: (a) stasis of fact, by which an organization acknowledges or denies its responsibility for a crisis or shifts blame to another target (did BP damage the Gulf of Mexico?); (b) stasis of definition, by which an organization places a crisis in a large, absolving context (did BP's pollution of the Gulf of

Mexico constitute a socially irresponsible act?); (c) stasis of quality, by which an organization minimizes its responsibility for a crisis (did the circumstances of this environmental crisis mitigate BP's guilt?); and (d) stasis of jurisdiction, by which we question the appropriateness of, say, the court of public opinion as the proper venue for judging crisis-related actions.

Sociocultural Contexts of Crisis Communication

Erez and Earley (1993) argue that organizational culture, aside from debates on its existence or meaning, is a product of societal culture: ". . . culture acts as a moderator in the relationship between managerial techniques and employee behavior" (p. 4). Similarly, cultures have moderating effects on organizational behavior—that is, on the attainment of organizational group goals, on intragroup communication, on group performance, and on economic incentives (or rewards) for group goal attainment, which, in turn, enhance the level of motivation (Erez and Somech, 1996).

Therefore, in the same breath, cultural differences account for communication differences. There is a growing body of research that concludes that cultural factors influence theory building and perspectives in and the practice of public relations (Botan, 1992; Grunig et al., 1995; Kent and Taylor, 1999; Kim and Kim, 2010; Rhee, 2002; Sriramesh, 2007; Sriramesh and Kim, 1999; Vasquez and Taylor, 2000), and crisis response strategies (An et al., 2010; Taylor, 2000). Communicators in dominant sub-Saharan African cultures, like those in Asia, because of their high-context attributes, are likely to engage in nuanced, indirect communications whereas those in dominant United States' culture and in the United Kingdom, France, Germany, and Switzerland, with their low-context attributes, are wont to be open and direct in their crisis communication. Several studies (e.g., Kang and Mastin, 2008; Kim and Kim, 2010; Vasquez and Taylor, 2000) have, for example, investigated the effects of most of Hofstede's (2001, 2011) and Hofstede et al.'s (2010) six dimensions of national cultures (power distance, uncertainty avoidance, individualism–collectivism, masculinity–femininity, long- to short-term orientation, and indulgence–restraint) on communication values and practices. Power distance is the acknowledgement and acceptance of unequal power distribution or status differences in a community, organization, or social setting. Examples of high power-distance countries include Malaysia, Guatemala, Panama, and the Philippines. Low power-distance countries include Austria, Israel, and Denmark.

Uncertainty avoidance focuses on how cultures respond to ambiguity, change, and uncertainties. Cultures high in uncertainty avoidance seek consensus, whereas people in low uncertainty-avoidance cultures tend to be more willing to take risks. Countries high on this index include Greece, Poland, and Belgium. Some low uncertainty-avoidance countries are Singapore and those in the West.

The individualism–collectivism dimension measures the extent to which a society encourages independent thought and action versus one that encourages interdependence and conformity. High-individualism countries include Australia, Belgium, the Netherlands, and the United States, while Indonesia, Venezuela, and Guatemala are high collectivistic countries.

The masculinity–femininity dimension refers to whether a society values masculine traits (e.g., competition and ambition) more than it does feminine traits (e.g., service to others and quality-of-life issues). Countries with high scores on the masculine index include Japan, Austria, Venezuela, Italy, and Switzerland. Those that score lowest on that index include Sweden, Norway, and the Netherlands.

Long- to short-term orientation, earlier labeled Confucian work dynamism, focuses on perseverance, sense of shame, and thrift, enabling us to pose questions such as: (a) Do I want instant or delayed gratification? (b) Are we planning for the next year or for the next five years?

Indulgence versus restraint, the newest of the six dimensions, describes indulgent cultures as primarily concerned with encouraging individuals to express opinions freely, to feel healthier and happier, and to engage in a leisure ethic, whereas restraint cultures are primarily concerned with curbing such human drives. High-indulgent nations include Venezuela, Mexico, Puerto Rico, and El Salvador; high-restraint nations include Ukraine, Latvia, Egypt, and Pakistan.

All of those dimensions influence individual communication and, in turn, organizational communication (Gudykunst, 1997), and, by extension, provide the framework for crisis communication. High power-distance countries such as South Korea, Singapore, Malaysia, Japan, and Taiwan use newscasting to convey authoritative and official narratives, whereas low power-distance countries such as Spain, the Netherlands, Denmark and Sweden use casual narratives that project more personal relationships (Kang and Mastin, 2008). Because organizations interact with culturally diverse stakeholders, they can avoid crises by acknowledging globalization, respecting the multiethnic nature of their work force, and avoiding ethnocentrism (Kent and Taylor, 1999; Zaremba, 2010). Cast against the preceding background, then, what is the interplay between cultures and crisis communication? To answer that question, the remainder of this chapter focuses on illustrations from Asia and Africa.

Illustrating Cultural Influences on Crisis Communication in Asia

It must be stated unequivocally that Chinese public relations is influenced by Western theories, concepts, and practices (Liu et al., 2009; Zhang et al., 2009) and also by the country's cultural, political, and economic environments. In September 2006, the U.S. Food and Drug Administration (FDA) recalled pet foods imported from China because of reports of renal failure in some pets.

Similar recalls occurred in Europe and South Africa. The crisis came to a head in March 2007 when a Canadian-based pet food manufacturer alerted the FDA about pets' physical well-being after they had consumed pet foods made in China. The Chinese government's initial image-repair strategy was to deny responsibility for it and to shift blame to others: that the pet foods from China did not cause the deaths in pets (Peijuan et al., 2009). Such a denial strategy, as well as a distancing strategy, is effective only in cases in which there is clear, unequivocal evidence that an organization is not at fault. If, however, a company were responsible, either in part or in whole, for an incident, then denial or distancing will exacerbate the situation.

The Chinese government then engaged in bolstering, asserting that China had strict supervision of exported foods. In the same breath, the government attacked the accuser, namely, the U.S. news media. In the face of a mountain of evidence, China finally took corrective action, revoking the business licenses of two companies implicated in the export of the tainted food.

What is the cultural explanation for the initial denial of exporting toxic pet foods and the significant turnaround in responses by the same government? Within the context of the Confucian tradition, face-saving and "soft landing" are preferred to direct, brazen confrontation. And the government's attack on the media is premised on the principle of inequality in the power relationships between a government and news organizations. According to Hofstede and Bond (1987), Confucian philosophy has four principles:

1. "*The stability of society is based on unequal relationships between people* . . .
2. "*The family is the prototype of all social organizations* . . .
3. "*Virtuous behavior toward others consists of treating others as one would like to be treated oneself* . . .
4. "*Virtue with regard to one's tasks in life consists of trying to acquire skills and education, working hard, not spending more than necessary, being patient, and persevering*" (p. 8, emphasis in original).

By extension, neo-Confucian or new Confucianism not only asserts the value of the preceding centuries-old principles as geographically bound, but also seeks to advance them as a universal model for and as a contributor to a mutual understanding in a world community (Tsai, 2008).

In contrast to the preventable crisis of toxic pet foods, the Sichuan earthquake crisis in 2008 provided the Chinese government with opportunities to attract much-needed positive publicity, to improve its global image, and to translate a natural disaster into an opportunity (Chen, 2009). The government's responses (a) emphasized open, timely communication with the nation; (b) adopted two-way asymmetrical communication, by which it set and framed the agenda on the crisis; (c) defined the crisis in ways that indicated that the government was in control of the crisis; (d) sought to strengthen stakeholder relations; (e) used the new media only moderately; (f) took action to build and cultivate relationships; and (g) sought to be compassionate and empathic toward victims.

In a factor-analytic study of Taiwan's top 500 companies' crisis-communicative strategies—the actual responses organizations use to address crises—five factors emerged, four of which were consistent with those in Western organizational cultures (Huang et al., 2005). A new, Taiwan-specific factor, diversion, indicates the Chinese emphasis on interpersonal relationships (or *quanxi*), making diversion a means of avoiding direct confrontation in the Asian context. Information strategy did not emerge as a distinct factor, suggesting that, whereas Western companies use communication for information exchange, Chinese communication is geared toward maintaining and cultivating relationships, more commonly known as *quanxi*.

Cultural influences were also brought to the fore in the aftermath of charges by both consumers and the Osaka City Hall that Snow Brand Milk Products Co., Ltd., of Japan, sold poisonous milk products in 2000. But the inflexibility of the company's culture, fueled in large measure by societal practices of high power distance, high levels of uncertainty avoidance, harmonious interpersonal relationships, and group solidarity, prevented open communication about the issue and stifled warnings from employees about a possible problem with the product (Wrigley et al., 2006). It is this interplay between cultural values and the immediate demands of crises that prompts us to consider it as a major factor in assessing the effectiveness of crisis communication and of crisis management within cultural and organizational contexts.

Confucian Work Dynamism

There is some association between primarily Confucian cultural values and economic growth in Asian economies, including those in Mainland China, Hong Kong and Taiwan (Ahlstrom et al., 2010). Thus, given the Confucian virtue of ideal human relations, characterized by the principles of "humanity" or "*ren*" and of familistic (not Western individual) patterns of decision making (Fan, 2002, 2010), concerns have been expressed about the relevance to Eastern values of the results of Hofstede's (1980) seminal survey of work-related values: the possibility that they could be culture-bound and that they reflected the imposition of "mental programming" (Yeh, 1988, p. 150) on Chinese and Japanese values (The Chinese Culture Connection, 1987; Yeh, 1988). A 22-country survey undertaken by the Chinese Culture Connection (1987) reported that an additional dimension—Confucian work dynamism—did not correlate with any of Hofstede et al.'s (2010) dimensions developed from a survey of the workplace in 50 countries and three regions, suggesting that, from the Asian perspective, it was a separate dimension in its own right. Consequently, Hofstede and Bond (1987) reported that nations that score high in Confucian work dynamism emphasized long-term characteristics such as being persistent and thrifty, and observing order. It has also been reported that such Confucian attributes are evident as harmonious, tolerant Chinese management style, loyalty to top management, and reciprocal loyalty to productive employees and valued suppliers (Ahlstrom et al., 2010).

Similarly, Confucianism, on the one hand, has positive influences on public relations in some Asian countries (e.g., Rhee, 2002); on the other, it influences media relations negatively (Kim and Kim, 2010). The Chinese Confucian traditions tend to hinder effective crisis management and communication. Those traditions emphasize face and harmony and expect the Chinese to save face and avoid shame and conflicts (Chen, 1996; Moon and Franke, 2000). De Mente (1998) noted that Confucianism influenced South Korean business culture: "The first priority is to avoid any kind of direct confrontation . . . In business situations this may include not telling the truth about something, withholding bad news and not bringing up mistakes that have been made" (p. 55). Thus, in crises, an organization or a government that adheres to Confucian traditions tends to withhold information on a crisis from the public and attempts to resolve the crisis privately to save its own face or reputation. One example is that of Sanlu Group, which was criticized by the public for covering up a contamination issue, an action that precipitated its collapse (see Cao's chapter, "China's Sanlu's Infant Formula Proves Fatal," in this book). Another is Chinese government's covering up the outbreak of SARS in 2003. But as China evolves into an even more formidable, influential player on the global scene and engages the rest of the world more politically, it is likely that its mindset on liberalism, humanistic tendencies, and benevolent communism will also evolve to a point in which its government and people could better understand the enduring issues in Confucian traditions. Chen (2009) concluded that the Chinese government's communication in the aftermath of the Sichuan earthquake in 2008 was 100 times more effective than that of SARS in 2003, because the government "placed unprecedented emphasis on open, timely and direct communication with the publics" (p. 191).

In sum, Asia's eclectic, yet selective, use of Western and Eastern practices in crisis communication affords it the best of both worlds, formulating strategic responses to crises largely determined by the typology and cause of a crisis.

Illustrations from Sub-Saharan Africa

Crisis communication in sub-Saharan Africa, a region that shares some of the high-context cultural traits and Confucian principles dominant in Asia, is as global as it is local in both structure and delivery. Global, in that crisis managers avail themselves of all the strategic options inherent in the theories presented in this chapter, yet local, in that they are susceptible to the constraints and limitations of a communication environment influenced by cultural values. Denying, dragging one's foot, and distancing oneself from a crisis, even when those actions could be detrimental to the reputation of an organization, are reflective of the tendency of sub-Saharan Africans not to "wash their dirty linen in public." On the other hand, making amends and taking corrective action are consistent with the African cultural value of *Ubuntu*, which translates into "Because we are one community, I am because we are." Therefore, crisis communication in sub-Saharan Africa strives for the proper balance between being forthright about a situation and sharing selective sensitive organizational information on it. At one extreme, Olaniran and Williams (2008) found that Shell Petroleum Development Company's responses to its oil spills in Nigeria's Delta region contradicted "guidelines for a relationally oriented crisis response" (p. 58). The strategies used were scapegoating, that is, blaming communities for the sabotage that led to the oil spills; and denying and evading responsibility, that is, denying responsibility for environmental pollution and degradation.

At the other extreme are Nigerian governments' communication efforts to rein in the country's ethno-religious crises, which the governments acknowledged could deepen ethnic divides in the country. Within the contexts of Benoit's (1995) and Coombs's (2007a) crisis-response strategies, the governments employed corrective actions and a deal posture. As part of their communication responses to the crisis, the governments set up commissions of inquiry, which called for memoranda, organized public hearings, and visited crises areas. Nigeria's Institute of Governance and Social Research, the Nigerian Institute of International Affairs, and the Nigerian Red Cross organized several fora, peace conferences, roundtables, and workshops on how best the country can address the ethnic crisis.

Discussion and Conclusion

This chapter presents the growing scholarship in crisis communication that offers crises managers theory- and evidence-based strategic options for building and protecting the reputations of their organizations or clients. The broad, interdisciplinary character of those options indicates the opportunities, broad interest and appeal that the specialty attracts. But the advances in crisis-communication research are not without limitations, one of which, as Shrivastava (1993) put it, is fragmentation that results from building new vocabularies and frameworks that do not cohere: ". . . the lack of efforts to build systematic connections with past research gives the field an ad hoc character. It is a barrier to developing cumulative understanding of crises" (p. 33). Those difficulties are also reflected in the dearth of the application of theories to crisis-communication activities. Coombs (2008) emphasizes the need to link theory more directly to practice: "Crisis communication theory should be able to tell crisis managers what to expect in a crisis and how best to respond communicatively to the crisis" (p. 263). This chapter provides theoretical guidance in that regard, noting the eminence of both Benoit's theory of image repair discourse (1995, 1997) and Coombs's (2007a, 2008) SCCT.

But the application of the crisis-response strategies indicated in the theories presented in this chapter is also contingent upon sociocultural dimensions advanced in part by Hofstede (1980, 2001, 2011). This chapter uses Asia's cultural landscape as a platform for discussing the extent to which those dimensions influence corporate values and practices. At some level, the globalizing realities of the workplace make unnecessary a rigid separation of Western and Eastern cultures. So, on the ground, crisis communication in, say, Asia integrates Western and domestic communication values; the latter in some ways are also responsive to globalizing influences. The point here is that Benoit's (1995, 1997) image-restoration strategies or Coombs's (2007a) crisis-response strategies by postures are both enriching and expanding the body of knowledge and the tools with which crisis managers fight to safeguard or enhance reputations. While both those theories are applied to crisis communication in sub-Saharan Africa, that region shows extremes in the use of management's response strategies, which depend largely on crisis type and on specific stakeholders affected by it.

The next chapter presents guidelines for developing strategic organizational plans for managing crises effectively. Key elements of such plans include crisis-management teams and crisis-operations centers. Planning for crises can be instructive to organizations whose crisis preparedness requires improvement and to those such as German nonprofit organizations that tend to be substantially lacking in crisis preparedness, with fewer than one-third using crisis plans, crisis management teams, or crisis scenarios (Schwarz and Pforr, 2011). The point here is to establish a company-wide framework that ensures that organizations can prevent some crises up front or cannot be blindsided by the occurrence, complexity, and consequences of crises, and are at the ready to respond to them.

References

Ahlstrom, D., Chen, S., and Yeh, K. S. (2010). Managing in ethnic Chinese communities: Culture, institutions, and context. *Asia Pacific Journal of Management*, 27, 341–354.

An, S.-K., Park, D.-J., Cho, S., and Berger, B. (2010). A cross-cultural study of effective organizational crisis response strategy in the United States and South Korea. *International Journal of Strategic Communication*, 4, 225–243.

Augustine, N. R. (2000). Managing the crisis you tried to prevent. In *Harvard Business Review of Crisis Management* (pp. 1–32). Cambridge, MA: Harvard Business School Press.

Avery, E. J., Lariscy, R. W., Kim, S., and Hocke, T. (2010). A quantitative review of crisis communication research in public relations from 1991 to 2009. *Public Relation Review*, 36, 190–192.

Barton, L. (2008). *Crisis leadership now: A real-world guide to preparing for threats, disaster, sabotage, and scandal.* New York: McGraw-Hill.

Benoit, W. L. (1995). *Accounts, excuses, and apologies: A theory of image restoration strategies.* Albany, NY: State University of New York Press.

Benoit, W. L. (1997). Image repair discourse and crisis communication. *Public Relations Review, 23,* 177–186.

Botan, C. H. (1989). Theory development in public relations. In C. H. Botan and V. Hazleton Jr. (Eds.), *Public relations theory* (pp. 99–110). Hillsdale, NJ: Lawrence Erlbaum Associates.

Botan, C. H. (1992). International public relations: Critique and reformulation. *Public Relations Review, 18,* 149–159.

Brinson, S. L., and Benoit, W. L. (1999). The tarnished star: Restoring Texaco's damaged public image. *Management Communication Quarterly, 4,* 483–510.

Brown, K. A., and White, C. L. (2011). Organization-public relationships and crisis response strategies: Impact on attribution of responsibility. *Journal of Public Relations Research, 23,* 75–92.

Chen, N. (1996). Public relations in China: The introduction and development of an occupational field. In H. Culbertson and N. Chen (Eds.), *International public relations: A comparative analysis* (pp. 121–154). Mahwah, NJ: Lawrence Erlbaum.

Chen, N. (2009). Institutionalizing public relations: A case study of Chinese government crisis communication on the 2008 Sichuan earthquake. *Public Relations Review, 35,* 187–198.

The Chinese Culture Connection. (1987). Chinese values and the search for culture-free dimensions of culture. *Journal of Cross-Cultural Psychology, 18,* 143–164.

Claeys, A-S., Cauberghe, V., and Vyncke, P. (2010). Restoring reputations in times of crisis: An experimental study of the situational crisis communication theory and the moderating effects of locus of control. *Public Relations Review, 36,* 256–262.

Coombs, W. T. (1995). Choosing the right words: The development of guidelines for the selection of the "appropriate" crisis-response strategies. *Management Communication Quarterly, 8,* 447–476.

Coombs, W. T. (1999). Information and compassion in crisis responses: A test of their effects. *Journal of Public Relations Research, 11,* 125–142.

Coombs, W. T. (2007a). Attribution theory as a guide for post-crisis communication research. *Public Relations Review, 33,* 135–139.

Coombs, W. T. (2007b). *Ongoing crisis communication: Planning, managing, and responding* (2nd ed.). Thousand Oaks, CA: Sage.

Coombs, W. T. (2007c). Protecting organization reputations during a crisis: The development and application of situational crisis communication theory. *Corporate Reputation Review, 10,* 163–176.

Coombs, W. T. (2008). The development of the situational crisis communication theory. In T. L. Hansen-Horn and B. D. Neff (Eds.), *Public relations: From theory to practice* (pp. 262–277). Boston, MA: Allyn and Bacon.

Coombs, W. T. (2009). Conceptualizing crisis communication. In R. L. Heath, and H. D. O'Hair (Eds.), *Handbook of risk and crisis communication* (pp. 99–118). New York: Taylor and Francis.

Coombs, W. T., and Holladay, S. J. (1996). Communication and attribution in a crisis: An experimental study of crisis communication. *Journal of Public Relations Research, 8,* 279–295.

Coombs, W. T., and Holladay, S. J. (2002). Helping crisis managers protect reputational assets: Initial tests of the situational crisis communication theory. *Management Communication Quarterly, 16,* 165–186.

Coombs, W. T., and Holladay, S. J. (2005). Exploratory study of stakeholder emotions: Affect and crisis. In N. M. Ashkanasy, W. J. Zerbe, and C. E. J. Hartel (Eds.), *Research on emotion in organizations: Volume 1: The effect of affect in organizational settings* (pp. 271–288). New York: Elsevier.

Coombs, W. T., and Holladay, S. J. (2010). *PR strategy and application: Managing influence*. Malden, MA: Wiley-Blackwell.

Coombs, W. T., and Schmidt, L. (2000). An empirical analysis of image restoration: Texaco's racism crisis. *Journal of Public Relations Research, 12*, 163–178.

De Mente, B. L. (1998). *NTC's cultural dictionary of Korea's business and cultural code words*. Lincolnwood, IL: NTC Publishing Group.

Eckberg, D. L., and Hill, L. Jr. (1979). The paradigm concept and sociology: A critical review. *American Sociological Review, 44*, 925–937.

Erez, M., and Earley, P. C. (1993). *Culture, self-identity, and work*. New York: Oxford University Press.

Erez, M., and Somech, A. (1996). Is group productivity loss the rule or the exception? Effects of culture and group-based motivation. *Academy of Management Journal, 39*, 1513–1537.

Fan, R. (2002). Reconsidering surrogate decision making: Aristotelianism and Confucianism on ideal human relations. *Philosophy East and West, 52*, 346–372.

Fan, R. (2010). *Reconstructionist Confucianism: Rethinking morality after the West*. New York: Springer.

Fearn-Banks, K. (2011). *Crisis communications: A casebook approach* (4th ed.). New York: Routledge.

Fink, S. (2002). *Crisis management: Planning for the inevitable*. Lincoln, NE: iUniverse.

Fishman, D. A. (1999). Valujet Flight 592: Crisis communication theory blended and extended. *Communication Quarterly, 47*, 345–375.

Foxconn case shows job burnout. (2010, July 8). *People's Daily*. Retrieved from www.zjsjt.gov.cn/art/2010/7/8/art_872_106711.html

Freeman, R. E. (1984). *Strategic management: A stakeholder approach*. Boston, MA: Pitman.

Freeman, R. E. (2010). *Strategic management: A stakeholder approach*. New York: Cambridge University Press.

Gilpin, D. R., and Murphy, P. J. (2008). *Crisis management in a complex world*. New York: Oxford University Press.

Grunig, J. E., and Repper, F. C. (1992). Strategic management, publics, and issues. In J. E. Grunig (Ed.), *Excellence in public relations and communication management* (pp. 117–157). Hillsdale, NJ: Lawrence Erlbaum Associates.

Grunig, J. E., Grunig, L. A., Sriramesh, K., Huang, Y-H., and Lyra, A. (1995). Models of public relations in an international setting. *Journal of Public Relations Research 7*, 163–186.

Gudykunst, W. B. (1997). Cultural variabilities in communication: An Introduction. *Communication Research, 24*, 327–348.

Harlow, W. F., Brantley, B. C., and Harlow, R. M. (2011). BP initial image repair strategies after the Deepwater Horizon spill. *Public Relations Review, 37*, 80–83.

Hearit, K. M. (1994). Apologies and public relations crises at Chrysler, Toshiba, and Volvo. *Public Relations Review, 20*, 113–125.

Hearit, K. M. (1999). Newsgroups, activist publics, and corporate *apologia*: The case of Intel and its Pentium chip. *Public Relations Review, 25,* 291–308.

Heath, R. L., and Millar, D. P. (2004). A rhetorical approach to crisis communication: Management, communication processes, and strategic responses. In D. P. Millar and R. L. Heath (Eds.), *Responding to crisis: A rhetorical approach to crisis communication* (pp. 1–17). Mahwah, NJ: Lawrence Erlbaum Associates.

Hermann, C. F. (1963). Some consequences of crisis which limit the viability of organizations. *Administrative Science Quarterly, 8,* 61–82.

Hofstede, G. (1980). *Culture's consequences: International differences in work-related values.* Beverly Hills, CA: Sage.

Hofstede, G. (2001). *Culture's consequences: Comparing values, behaviors, institutions and organizations across nations* (2nd ed.). Thousand Oaks, CA: Sage.

Hofstede, G. (2011). Culture's continuing consequences. Paper presented at the Asia Service Business Research Institute, Waseda University, Tokyo, June.

Hofstede, G., and Bond, M. H. (1987). The Confucius connection: From cultural roots to economic growth. *Organizational Dynamics, 16*(4), 5–21.

Hofstede, G., Hofstede, G. J., and Minkov, M. (2010). *Cultures and organizations: Software of the mind* (3rd ed.). New York: McGraw-Hill.

Huang, Y-H., Lin, Y-H., and Su, S-H. (2005). Crisis communicative strategies in Taiwan: Category, continuum, and cultural implication. *Public Relations Review, 31,* 229–238.

Jaques, T. (2009). Issue and crisis management: Quicksand in the definitional landscape. *Public Relations Review, 35,* 280–286.

Jeong, S-H. (2009). Public's responses to an oil spill accident: A test of the attribution theory and situational crisis communication theory. *Public Relations Review, 35,* 307–309.

Jin, Y., and Liu, B. F. (2010). The blog-mediated crisis communication model: Recommendations for responding to influential external blogs. *Journal of Public Relations Research, 22,* 429–455.

Kang, D. S., and Mastin, T. (2008). How cultural difference affects international tourism public relations websites: A comparative analysis using Hofstede's cultural dimensions. *Public Relations Review, 34,* 54–56.

Kent, M. L., and Taylor, M. (1999). When public relations becomes government relations. *Public Relations Quarterly, 44*(3), 18–22.

Kim, Y., and Kim, S-Y. (2010). The influence of cultural values on perceptions of corporate social responsibility: Application of Hofstede's dimensions to Korean public relations practitioners. *Journal of Business Ethics, 91,* 485–500.

Kuhn, T. S. (1996). *The structure of scientific revolutions* (3rd ed.). Chicago, IL: The University of Chicago Press.

Lerbinger, O. (1997). *The crisis manager: Facing risk and responsibility.* Mahwah, NJ: Lawrence Erlbaum Associates.

Linke, C. G. (1989). Crisis: Dealing with the unexpected. In B. Cantor and C. Burger (Eds.), *Experts in action: Inside public relations* (pp. 166–178). New York: Longman.

Liu, X., Chang, Z., Zhao, P. (2009). Is it simply a matter of managerial competence? Interpreting Chinese executives' perceptions of crisis management. *Public Relations Review, 35,* 232–239.

Maitlis, S., and Sonenshein, S. (2010). Sensemaking in crisis and change: Inspiration and insights from Weick (1988). *Journal of Management Studies, 47*, 551–580.

Marsh, C. (2006). The syllogism of *apologia*: Rhetorical stasis theory and crisis communication. *Public Relations Review, 32*, 41–46.

Marsh, C. (2010). The *National Review* "fires" Christopher Buckley: Image restoration and the rhetoric of severance and restraint. *Public Relations Review, 36*, 376–382.

Meng, J. (2010). SK-II China and its skin cream scandal: An extended analysis of the image restoration strategies in a non-Western setting. *Public Relations Review, 36*, 66–69.

Mitroff, I. I. (2004). *Crisis leadership: Planning for the unthinkable*. Hoboken, NJ: Wiley.

Mitroff, I. I., and Anagnos, G. (2001). *Managing crises before they happen*. New York: AMACOM.

Mitroff, I. I., and Pearson, C. M. (1993). *Crisis management: Diagnostic guide for improving your organization's crisis-preparedness*. San Francisco, CA: Jossey-Bass.

Moon, Y. S., and Franke, G. R. (2000). Cultural influences on agency practitioners' ethical perceptions: A comparison of Korea and the U.S. *Journal of Advertising, 29*, 51–65.

Olaniran, B. A., and Williams, D. E. (2008). Applying anticipatory and relational perspectives to the Nigerian Delta region oil crisis. *Public Relations Review, 34*, 57–59.

Pearson, C. M., and Clair, J. A. (1998). Reframing crisis management. *Academy of Management Review, 23*, 59–76.

Peijuan, C., Ting, L. P., and Pang, A. (2009). Managing a nation's image during crisis: A study of the Chinese government's image repair efforts in the "Made in China" controversy. *Public Relations Review, 35*, 213–218.

Rhee, Y. (2002). Global public relations: A cross-cultural study of the excellence theory in South Korea. *Journal of Public Relations Research, 14*, 159–184.

Roux-Dufort, C. (2007). A passion for imperfections: Revisiting crisis management. In C. M. Pearson, C. Roux-Dufort, and J. A. Clair (Eds.), *International handbook of organizational crisis management* (pp. 221–252). Thousand Oaks, CA: Sage.

Roux-Dufort, C. (2009). The devil lies in details! How crises build up within organizations. *Journal of Contingencies and Crisis Management, 17*, 4–11.

Schwarz, A., and Pforr, F. (2011). The crisis communication preparedness of nonprofit organizations: The case of German interest groups. *Public Relations Review, 37*, 68–70.

Shrivastava, P. (1993). Crisis theory/practice: Towards a sustainable future. *Industrial & Environmental Crisis Quarterly, 7*, 23–42.

Shrivastava, P., Mitroff, I. I., Miller, D., and Miglani, A. (1988). Understanding industrial crises. *Journal of Management Studies, 25*, 285–303.

Sisco, H. F., Collins, E. L., and Zoch, L. M. (2010). Through the looking glass: A decade of Red Cross crisis response and situational crisis communication theory. *Public Relations Review, 36*, 21–27.

Skinner, C., Von Essen, L., Mersham, G., and Motau, S. (2007). *Handbook of public relations* (8th ed.). Cape Town, South Africa: Oxford University Press Southern Africa.

Snyder, P., Hall, M., Robertson, J., Jasinski, T., and Miller J. S. (2006). Ethical rationality: A strategic approach to organizational crisis. *Journal of Business Ethics*, *63*, 371–383.

Sriramesh, K. (2007). The relationship between culture and public relations. In E. L. Toth (Ed.), *The future of excellence in public relations and communication management: Challenges for the next generation* (pp. 507–526). Mahwah, NJ: Lawrence Erlbaum Associates.

Sriramesh, K., and Kim, Y. (1999). Public relations in three Asian cultures: An analysis. *Journal of Public Relations Research*, *11*, 271–292.

Taylor, M. (2000). Cultural variance as a challenge to global public relations: A case study of the Coca-Cola scare in Europe. *Public Relations Review*, *26*, 277–293.

Tortorella, A. (2004). What is a corporate crisis? An Ogilvy PR definition. Retrieved from www.ogilvypr.com/files/corporate-crisis.pdf

Toth, E. L. (1986). Broadening research in public affairs. *Public Relations Review*, *12*(2), 27–36.

Tsai, Y. (2008). Selfhood and fiduciary community: A Smithian reading of Tu Weiming's Confucian humanism. *Dao: A Journal of Comparative Philosophy*, *7*, 349–365.

Turner, B. (1976). The organizational and interorganizational development of disasters. *Administrative Science Quarterly*, *21*, 378–397.

Ulmer, R. R. (2001). Effective crisis management through established stakeholder relationships: Malden Mills as a case study. *Management Communication Quarterly*, *14*, 590–615.

Ulmer, R. R., Sellnow, T. L., and Seeger, M. W. (2011). *Effective crisis communication: Moving from crisis to opportunity* (2nd ed.). Thousand Oaks, CA: Sage.

Vasquez, G. M., and Taylor, M. (2000). What cultural values influence American public relations practitioners? *Public Relations Review*, *25*, 433–449.

Ware, B. L., and Linkugel, W. A. (1973). They spoke in defense of themselves: On the generic criticism of *apologia*. *Quarterly Journal of Speech*, *59*, 273–283.

Wrigley, B. J., Ota, S., and Kikuchi, A. (2006). Lightning strikes twice: Lessons learned from two food poisoning incidents in Japan. *Public Relations Review*, *32*, 349–357.

Yeh, R. (1988). On Hofstede's treatment of Chinese and Japanese values. *Asia Pacific Journal of Management*, *6*, 149–160.

Zaremba, A. J. (2010). *Crisis communication: Theory and practice*. Armonk, NY: M. E. Sharpe.

Zhang, A., Shen, H., and Jiang, H. (2009). Culture and Chinese public relations: A multi-method "inside out" approach. *Public Relations Review*, *35*, 226–231.

Part II

The Phases of Crisis Communication

Amiso M. George

Risk Management and Crisis Communication

As human beings we take risks daily; whether it is driving to work, taking a plane ride somewhere, swimming in a pool, or investing our money in the stock market. We accept the risks that come with those activities or decisions, even though we know that the probability of getting in harm's way may be low. We consider two issues when we assess a risk: the likelihood of harm that may be caused to us, and the cost of that harm. As humans, we also face personal and professional crises, and sometimes we are prepared to handle them; other times we are not. Organizations are similar in the sense that they, too, face risks and crises. How do they prepare?

This chapter discusses the phases of crisis management: prevention—preparing before a crisis occurs; managing—communicating during the crisis; and recovery—communicating postcrisis. However, it is imperative to introduce the concept of risk management as it impacts crisis management.

With the constant threat of all kinds of crises ranging from natural disasters, technological, workplace violence, industrial accidents, and others, every organization, no matter how large or small, needs both a risk assessment and crisis communication plans. Often, companies focus on one or the other; however, both plans are necessary for the successful management of an organization, because ineffective risk management and communication may result in a crisis. Ideally, they work in tandem.

Risk is variously defined as potential injury, liability, damage, threat, or loss caused by external or internal susceptibilities of a vulnerable organization, that may be defused through preventive measures. Risk is also defined as a measure of the probability and severity of adverse effects (Lowrance 1976), the likelihood of loss or injury and the extent of likelihood of such a loss (Kaplan and Garrick, 1981), and "the potential for an adverse outcome assessed as a function of threats, vulnerabilities, and consequences associated with an incident, event, or occurrence" (FEMA, 2010, p. 27).

Risk management is the deliberate "process of identifying, analyzing, assessing, and communicating risk and accepting, avoiding, transferring or controlling it to an acceptable level considering associated costs and benefits of any actions taken" (FEMA, 2010, p. 30).

Risk management begins with an assessment—a process whereby organizations assess areas of vulnerability and determine how they would use their resources to respond to or minimize those vulnerabilities. They also ascertain the consequences of not addressing or responding to the issues they identified. Effective risk assessment must be part of an organization's strategic plan and culture and must have the support of management and staff. A typical risk assessment process involves the following:

- identification of the hazards or risks;
- ascertaining potential victims and how they may be harmed;
- evaluating the risks and choosing preventive methods that have the maximum benefit/cost for reducing the risks;
- documenting findings and implementing them, and reviewing assessment for modification (HSE, 2010).

Risk potential is dependent on (1) location of organization, (2) type of organization, and (3) demographics of organization.

Risk communication, which has its origins in environmental health, but has since been adopted by other organizations, is defined severally as an interactive exchange of information and opinion among individuals, groups, and institutions, with the goal of assessing, minimizing, and regulating risks. Ropeik (2008) defines it as "actions, words, and other interactions that incorporate and respect the perceptions of the information recipients, intended to help people make more informed decisions about threats to their health and safety" (p. 59). In essence, it is the sharing of information with the public or institutions about the probability and consequences of harmful events. Risk communication enables the public to respond to crisis and reduces the possibility of misinformation.

Effective risk communication involves trust between the organization or people communicating the risk and the audience receiving the information. Miscommunication may potentially result in a crisis situation.

Crisis Communication

The previous chapter aptly captured the many definitions of crisis. At the core of these definitions is the agreement that crisis is a significant threat that can jeopardize an organization's image, reputation, and financial stability, and may result in injuries and death. Crisis is dynamic, often unexpected, and necessitates immediate and effective response to minimize harm. Crisis may be caused by natural disasters, technological breakdown, confrontation, malevolence, organizational misdeeds, workplace violence and rumors (Lerbinger, 1997).

Crisis management is an organizational process that enables an organization to prepare for and respond to crisis situations in order to minimize its effect on stakeholders. Crisis management often entails the execution of planned actions to contain the crisis, restore confidence in the organization and maintain business continuity. Crisis communication, an integral part of crisis management, is the process of active communication with stakeholders to minimize any damage to the organization's image or reputation.

Dan Keeney, president of Texas-based DPK Public Relations and a crisis communication expert, states that in spite of organizations' proactive efforts to identify and assess their vulnerabilities, and prepare for crisis, sometimes, the assessment process results in unexpected outcomes that may compel the organization to bridge the disconnect between its assumptions about its stakeholders or issues and reality (D. Keeney, personal communication, April 6, 2011). It is these kinds of assessments within organizations that reveal potential vulnerabilities that, if not managed, may lead to a crisis. Given that companies are becoming more aware of the need for risk and crisis management, the two entities are rightfully considered integral parts of effective organizations' policies.

Crisis communication has taken on a new dimension since 9/11 and the many subsequent crises that have affected organizations and governments worldwide. Social media, an important arsenal in crisis communication, have become a vital part of some organization's crisis management policy; yet, in a survey of companies with a social media crisis plan commissioned by German company Gartner Communications, and reported in *PR Week*, only 20.7 percent of companies polled worldwide admit that they have a social media crisis plan. Nonetheless, 84.8 percent of companies said that while they do not have a social media crisis plan, they have traditional crisis plans (Maul, 2010). This result further reinforces the worldwide importance of crisis communication.

Bad news travels faster than good news. In today's social media era, bad news circulates minutes after it happens. Organizations no longer have the luxury of waiting for a few hours or days before responding to a crisis. Speed and accuracy are of the essence. Effective preparedness is assumed. The first step to effective crisis management is to ascertain potential risks and issues in the organization. Before an organization encounters any crisis, it is imperative that it develops a proactive public relations program. Part of the program includes building strong and positive relationships with all of its stakeholders, whether it is through responsibility toward the community and environment in which it operates, or through its clients, regulatory agencies, and ensuring an excellent relationship with the media. It is also important that the organization develops fully multimedia platforms through which it can communicate with its key external and internal stakeholders. If stakeholders perceive an organization positively, a crisis situation may not spell its downfall, especially if the crisis is managed effectively and efficiently. To ensure that the organization survives a crisis, it must develop a detailed crisis communication plan or procedure.

Crisis communication occurs in three phases: *prevention*—preparing before a crisis occurs; *managing*—communicating during the crisis; and *recovery*—communicating postcrisis.

Phase 1: Prevention—Planning/Preparing before Crisis Occurs

In the first stage of crisis communication management, an organization's main goal is to anticipate, prepare for potential crises, and attempt to prevent them before they occur. The key function of the prevention stage is to research and prepare an issue or risk management plan and a response to the plan.

Mitroff and Pearson (1993) state that crisis preparation is the difference between secure and insecure organizations. They further stated that "crisis-prepared organizations constantly scrutinize their operations and management structures whereas crisis-prone organizations tend to miss or ignore signals indicating potential weakness in operations and structure" (p. 22). They also propose that to prepare for a potential crisis, every organization should conduct a SWOT (strength, weakness, opportunity, and threat) assessment. This strategy enables an organization to identify areas where it is prepared and where it is vulnerable so it could plan accordingly.

Part of the planning stage is the establishment of a Crisis Communication Team (CCT) that would help to execute the crisis plan. Ideally, this team will consist of managers from all key departments and the organization's legal counsel.

A crisis plan must have a goal, objectives and tactics. It must be packaged on multiple platforms for easy accessibility to the crisis team. That means that it should be in hard copy, on the company's website, and downloadable on hand-held electronic devices.

Goal

A crisis communication plan is a document that delineates the policies and guidelines for coordinating effective communication among members of the crisis team in an organization, between the organization and the media and between the organization and other stakeholders.

The crisis communication plan should be written in conjunction with a crisis plan. It should address a variety of crises that the organization may face and provide guidelines on how to rapidly manage the crisis and communicate the organization's response before, during, and after the crisis.

The crisis communication plan should also be executed by the designated crisis team and in conjunction with the organization's crisis plan. A good plan has three characteristics: (a) it is detailed, but must be adaptable to changes in the crisis; (b) it triggers a response to how the crisis team is notified and how the team in turn notifies the organization's stakeholders and others; (c) it has the buy-in of the organization's management if it is to be effective. It is important to remember that the plan is a resource and not a panacea to crisis management.

Objective

The objectives of a typical crisis communication plan are as follows:

- to analyze the crisis situation and ascertain what, and if any, action should be taken;
- to assemble a CCT that will propose appropriate and unified response to the crisis;
- to execute the proposals recommended in the plan: communicate with stakeholders, stem negative effects of crisis, restore stakeholders' confidence, and maintain business continuity; and
- to review the effectiveness of the plan after the crisis.

Tactics

In a generic crisis communication plan, the tactics are the specific actions taken when a crisis strikes.

- The first act is to gather facts or incident reports.
- If the first respondent believes that the crisis warrants action, depending on the organization, the person will notify the appropriate authority that would make the decision to convene the CCT. In some organizations, the first responder may be the crisis communication manager or leader.
- The CCT then executes the crisis communication plan.

Outcome

The aftermath of the crisis depends on a number of issues, including how effectively the crisis communication plan was executed, lessons learned, and the process of healing.

Writing the Crisis Communication Plan

1. Establish a Crisis Communication Team

A Crisis Communication Team (CCT) is a group of key individuals in and outside an organization, specially created to identify a crisis, develop a plan on how to manage the crisis, and execute the crisis communication plan.

- A crisis communication team of key decision makers such as president or CEO, vice presidents, and managers of key departments such as information technology, human resources and facilities, public relations or communication managers, social media experts, legal counsel subject matter experts, chief security and risk managers, administrative assistants, and others who may be appointed on an ad-hoc basis. An effective team also seeks help from crisis experts from other organizations who may bring in fresh insights or views.

- The crisis team must designate a chief spokesperson, who would:
  - be the chief liaison with the media and must be well versed in working with all forms of media;
  - be knowledgeable about the organization and the crisis;
  - be able to convey the organization's message in a calm, confident and deliberate manner. In the event of a major crisis, the CEO will be the spokesperson; an assistant spokesperson substitutes in the event the spokesperson is not available; and
  - be able to coordinate with subject matter experts who can answer technical questions about the crisis.

- A crisis team must have a manager and assistant manager to ensure effective and efficient coordination and execution of the plan by team members. The crisis manager is also responsible for:
  - coordinating communication to key stakeholders via emergency notification system put in place before the crisis. This notification could take the form of phone and e-mail blasts and SMS text messages;
  - ensuring that team members perform their roles effectively; and
  - creating sub-teams within the crisis team to handle specific tasks. For instance, public relations or communication members of the team should be assigned as the crisis/media team—responsible for preparing materials for the media kit that can be posted online or distributed to the media. Such information would include current organizational fact sheets, product or organization's backgrounders, speeches, biographies of key personnel, press releases, and media alerts.

- Team members roles should be clearly defined or described to ensure that all parties understand their roles, train for their roles, and are able to perform their designated functions at optimum level during the crisis.
- Media coverage monitor—works closely with the media team to monitor and document all media coverage, including social media, to correct errors and to use information in postcrisis assessment.
- Safety team—supervised by the safety officer—to ensure that all functions are conducted in a safe and efficient manner.

- Scenario coordinator—works with team to develop scenarios that would help the organization ferret out potential gaps in its crisis plan.
- Community groups and brand ambassadors—provide support and promote the organization in a positive way to key audiences.
- Phone bank workers—specially trained to work in crisis situations where key stakeholders want a human voice to answer their questions.
- Administrative assistant—assigned to document all correspondence.

The Crisis Communication Plan includes the following:

- CCT member roles and contact information: The crisis team members' roles should be listed with their names and all contact information about the individuals. The designation and contact information should be used to create a master list, which is made available to all team members on multiple communication platforms.
- Contact information for emergency services such as police, fire, and hospitals must be in the plan. Also include information about other non-emergency community services that may be needed.
- Contact information for multimedia platforms, including social media communicators such as influential bloggers and tweeters that could be used to communicate to audiences during a crisis.
- Organization's media kit: Include fact sheet, media release, media advisory, brief biographies (with high resolution pictures) of key executives of the organization, backgrounders, and key messages and frequently asked questions (FAQs). The media kit should also be available on the company's website, with links to social media efforts, including blogs, Twitter feeds, and YouTube. The media kit becomes part of the crisis kit once a crisis is underway.
- Include sample incident reporting forms (for potentially useful information) and phone logs to document phone calls from the media and other inquiries.
- Educate employees about crisis, so they can direct all media inquiries to the crisis team.

2. Identify an Emergency Operations Center or Command Center
Often in a crisis, the organization may have to move its emergency operations away from the location of the crisis to another place. This Emergency Operations Center or EOC is a physical location that functions as a central command or headquarters where the crisis could be monitored by the team. It is also where all decisions about the crisis, such as media briefings and crisis updates are made.

The EOC should be centrally located to accommodate the influx of media personnel, volunteers, and crisis team members. Equally important is the inclusion of a virtual EOC that allows crisis team members to communicate from remote locations through wireless networks and hand-held electronic devices. A virtual EOC not only connects crisis team members electronically, it makes room for flexibility in the event of changes to the crisis.

The EOC must be equipped with, among others, the following:

- kitchenette
- food and beverage
- laptop computers with Internet connection, iPads
- copier, scanner
- pens, pencils, markers
- notepads, phone lines
- clipboards
- staples, paperclips
- rubber bands
- cell phones, walkie-talkies
- generator, flash lights, lighters
- maps, Global Positioning System (GPS)
- phone directories
- media kits
- first aid kit
- chairs and tables
- chalkboard, chalks
- lectern with company logo
- radio, television sets
- fully functional "Crisis Kit."

The Crisis Kit includes the following items:

- notepads
- company letterheads
- preprinted "incident report forms"
- initial media statement forms
- pens, pencils, markers
- masking tapes
- first aid kit
- list of emergency personnel, including contact information
- list of community resource personnel, including contact information
- list of local, regional and national media personnel and contact information
- crisis communication team list including contact information
- organization's building plans, including maps of floor plans, security alarm

- locations, images of interior and exterior of the building
- local, city and state maps.

The crisis kit, like any emergency kit, should be readily accessible to members of the team at the onset of a crisis.

3. Maintain current contact information
In addition to maintaining current contact information of all CCT members and organization's top management in both hard and downloadable electronic copies, the plan should also include all contact information for the following:

- external crisis professionals
- local media
- public emergency services at local state and national levels
- local police, hospital and fire departments
- local non-emergency community services.

If possible, the contact list should also be designed in a wallet-sized and electronic format, accessible via hand-held devices and distributed to the crisis communication team. The contact list should be updated regularly to ensure that it remains current.

4. Identify crisis scenarios
Working with the crisis team, think through and identify a variety of crisis scenarios that an organization may encounter. These scenarios may vary depending on the type of organization. Nonetheless, consider including in the scenario at least one type of crisis from each of the categories of crisis: natural disaster, technological, workplace violence, fire, fraud, and many others.

Write out the crisis and be as detailed as possible. Use subject matter experts to make sure the crisis is as authentic as possible.

5. Develop/evaluate response to your crisis scenarios
The response or simulation of the crisis scenario is one way to ensure that in an actual crisis, the crisis team will respond efficiently and effectively. To ensure success, the response should fully address the crisis scenario identified in step 4. That means:

- individuals assigned would gather information about the crisis, identify what happened, who was involved, where it happened, when it happened, how it happened, and why it happened (if the person has information about the reason for the crisis). This incident report would be reported to the appropriate personnel;

- the Crisis Communication Team will be activated and members assigned to their various functions;
- the team will establish a fully operational EOC, as well as a virtual EOC;
- the team will anticipate the media's tough questions and prepare the spokesperson for them;
- the team will prepare a variety of media statements, talking points and FAQs for the spokesperson;
- the team will activate the crisis page (dark site) on the organization's website;
- the team will identify and activate all communication channels to the organization's stakeholders on multiple media platforms;
- the team will use third party endorsers and brand ambassadors to tell the organization's story to different stakeholders;
- the team will reconvene to evaluate its response to the simulated crisis;
- the team will identify lessons learned from the simulation and what could have been done differently.

With this simulation, the team is ready to tackle a real crisis.

Phase 2: Managing—Communicating During the Crisis

Once a crisis occurs, it is important to ascertain what happened, assess the impact of the crisis, and move quickly to contain the crisis, minimize its impact, and bring it to a successful conclusion. Some organizations fail to understand the importance of a quick response to a crisis and suffer the consequences. Toyota's recalls provide an apt example of reputational damage as a result of delayed response to a crisis.

Millar and Heath (2004) note that communicating during a crisis can include fairly and correctly assigned blame. It could also entail apology depending on the crisis and the organization's goals. However, in communicating these messages, the organization must consider how the issue could be handled without shocking its audiences unnecessarily (p. 7). Some crisis experts state that an apology is effective if it is considered sincere, offers a solution and comes from the organization's CEO. The Toyota crisis also serves as an example of the use of this approach.

Organizations decide on who becomes the chief spokesperson based on the severity of the crisis. In the Toyota case, CEO Akio Toyoda, had to appear as the face of the company, because the crisis was the severest the company had faced in its recent history. Jet Blue's CEO, David Neeleman, took the same approach during the company's crisis involving stranded passengers on New York City airport tarmac in 2007.

Another issue that organizations face during a crisis is prioritizing of communication. Who should be notified first? Given that social media channels have made information available instantly to all, some crisis experts favor notification of employees before other stakeholders. However, Lukaszewski (1997) proposed an order of response to stakeholders during a crisis—he suggested that the order of response should be first: "Those most directly affected (victims, intended and unintended), second: employees, third: those indirectly affected—neighbors, friends, families, relatives, customers, suppliers, government, regulators, and third parties) and fourth: the news media and other channels of external communication" (p. 8).

Many experts agree that effective communication during a routine crisis generally follows these steps:

1. Gather the facts: accurate information is crucial to enable the crisis team to respond properly. Call the emergency services, if necessary.
2. Ensure that employees are safe.
3. Notify the CEO of the organization or the crisis team manager.
4. Convene the CCT: members will decide how to proceed in response to the crisis, depending on the level of the crisis. Crises levels can range from minimally intense which may attract little attention to highly intense which attract wide media and social media coverage. For instance, a highly intense crisis is one where the media appear on the premises seeking answers and the victims or their supporters express outrage, and also take to social media to criticize the organization. In that case, the CEO may have to make the initial statement and express empathy for the victims.
5. Prepare an initial statement and background information about the crisis. Such information should consists of the four Ws and H: Who, What, Where, When and How? The "Why" may be determined by the appropriate personnel if that information is not immediately known. Do not volunteer information unless it is confirmed to be accurate (see appendix for sample statement). If possible, develop a statement on how the organization will respond to resolve the crisis.
6. Identify key stakeholders: Determine how and in what order the stakeholders will be notified of the crisis.
7. Notify key stakeholders using the appropriate channel of communication.
8. Communicate first with internal audiences: Employees must be in the loop. They must be told the facts of the crisis via all communication channels (e-mail blasts, SMS text messages, and phone blasts). Employees should be directed to forward all inquiries about the crisis to the CCT leader.
9. Communicate with direct stakeholders: These may be shareholders, clients, or partners. Use all communication channels that you have used before the crisis to communicate with stakeholders.

10. Activate your EOC and virtual EOC for team members in remote areas.

11. Communicate with external audiences: Arrange a press conference or issue a media statement depending on the nature and gravity of the crisis. If a press conference is scheduled, provide necessary items, such as company logo, lectern and images.

12. Activate the "dark site" on the company's website. The "dark site" is a website that is prepared prior to a crisis, but not visible to anyone. The site is made accessible once a crisis erupts. Post initial statement on this now-activated crisis site and provide updates about the crisis on that site. Information on the "dark site" should include: Fact sheets about the crisis, company profile, top management biographies, maps, photos, of organization's infrastructure, section for newsroom and message updates, and useful Web links.

13. Use social media: blogs, vblogs, Facebook, Twitter, YouTube, and Flickr to post texts and images and updates on the crisis.

14. Designate a trained spokesperson for the crisis. In the event of a catastrophic crisis, the CEO should be the spokesperson. The crisis team should keep the spokesperson informed of new developments in the crisis and a subject expert should also be available to provide specific information on the crisis.

15. Develop key messages: Use message mapping or scripted messages during the first critical hours of the crisis. Keep messages clear, concise (about three key points) and consistent (see appendix for sample).

16. Post messages on organization's website, Facebook, blog, and YouTube and tweets by the designated individual.

17. Maintain a log of all media inquiries and calls and return their calls, e-mails or, text messages. This record enables the team to assess media coverage of the crisis and also to correct inaccuracies (see appendix for sample log form).

18. Use third party endorsers or brand ambassadors to bolster your crisis communication tactics and to dispel rumors.

19. Ensure business continuity by keeping organization as operational as possible.

20. Remain calm.

Tips for communicating with the media during crisis (what the designated spokesperson and organization should do):

• Have a clear and consistent message. In essence, tell the truth.
• Apologize if organization is at fault. Show empathy with the affected stakeholders.
• Be able to convey key messages of the organization in an effective and efficient manner. The key messages should be limited to three. The messages should be repeated at every media opportunity.

- Be able to respond to "difficult" or "hostile" questions from the media. This confidence is achieved through previous media training provided to the spokesperson.
- Be able to work with subject matter experts on the crisis to ensure accurate response to the media.
- Be able to avoid saying "no comment." That leads to media speculation and definition of the crisis situation instead of the organization doing so.
- Be able to avoid making unrelated off-the-cuff or off-the-record comments to reporters. Assume that every comment would be recorded.
- Be able to recognize questions designed to mislead. Such questions include:

  - accusatory questions
  - false questions containing inaccurate details
  - labeling questions
  - leading/loaded questions
  - multiple-part questions
  - presumptuous questions
  - speculative questions.

- Spokesperson statement should be uploaded and posted on the organization's website, Facebook, blog, vblog, and other social media channels to reiterate the organization's position on the crisis.
- Organization should take advantage of Twitter to post updates on crisis situation. Updates should follow social media format—140 characters for Twitter.
- Communication with media must be timely and consistent.
- Monitoring of media coverage must be ongoing.

Phase 3: Recovery—Communicating Postcrisis

The postcrisis or postmortem stage begins immediately after the crisis has been brought to a conclusion. This stage may last only a few months or years, depending on the type and severity of the crisis.

For Coombs (2007), postcrisis communication is what the organization says and does after a crisis. Reynolds and Seeger (2005) argue that "post-crisis is also a period when the media and the public become more critical and questioning regarding the cause of the crisis, the appropriateness of responses, and who would take the blame and responsibility" (p. 50).

Millar and Heath (2004) define postcrisis response as communication that "demonstrates how, why and when the organization has put things right as well as what it plans to do to prevent the recurrence of a similar crisis" (p. 8). Seeger et al. (2003) take the definition one step further by stating that organizations undergo three effective postcrisis communication stages: salvaging legitimacy, learning, and healing.

Salvaging legitimacy: Organizations should restate a larger social purpose or value and highlight their benefits to stakeholders (p. 142). Organizations should use issues management to reclaim their social legitimacy and "image restoration, which entails denial, evading responsibility, reducing offensiveness of the event, corrective action, and mortification" (p. 143) to salvage their tarnished image.

Learning: This stage includes what the authors call retrospective sensemaking, structural reconsideration, and vicarious learning. They state that retrospective sensemaking occurs when the organization recognizes issues that it ignored and assumptions that it did not question, which may have led to the crisis. Structural reconsideration occurs when an organization implements changes in "leadership, mission, and general practices" to regain its legitimacy (p. 147). Vicarious learning occurs when organizations learn from best practices of other firms.

Healing: This process involves explanation, forgetting, remembering, and renewal. Explanation answers the question of what happened and how the crisis came about. Forgetting is the ability to replace negative feelings about the crisis with positive ones (p. 149). Remembering is an organization's effort to recollect aspects of the crisis that illustrate unity and resilience (p. 150) and renewal focuses on the future by determining how to overcome previous weaknesses and take advantage of new opportunities (p. 150).

Organizations generally use this stage to:

1. declare the crisis officially over through the same media platforms used to communicate during the crisis;
2. evaluate their performance before, during, and after the crisis and lessons learned;
3. review specific response(s) to all stakeholders;
4. evaluate media coverage of crisis and respond to media critics;
5. update media, emergency personnel and community resources lists;
6. update website and social media;
7. reinforce their value to their stakeholders and their community;
8. reaffirm their commitment to their stakeholders and attract new stakeholders by reinforcing business continuity;
9. identify and publicly recognize heroes and heroines whose efforts made a difference during the crisis (the recognition format is determined by the organization); and
10. debrief crisis team, review and make appropriate revisions to crisis plans and prepare for the next crisis.

Acknowledgments

Many thanks to the public relations professionals who provided useful insights and answers from their experiences with crisis communication. Special thanks to colleagues in the Greater Fort Worth PRSA, especially Carolyn G. Bobo, APR, Fellow PRSA and Dan Keeney, APR, DKPR, Dallas and Houston, Texas, USA.

Appendix

Crisis Communication Team Directory

This directory should be updated and made available to all crisis team members in both electronic form and print. A wallet-sized version of the directory could be produced for team members.

Last name	First name	Title	Office	Home	Cell	E-mail

Subject Matter/Content Experts

Area of expertise	Name/Title	Organization	Contact information
Legal			
Human resources			
Corporate reputation			
Environmental			
Crisis and risk communication			
Security			

Important Community Resources

Local Emergency

Contact	*Name*	*Phone numbers/E-mail addresses*
Local police	List names of key personnel	
Local fire department	List names of key personnel	
Local hospitals	List key departments, including ER	
Ambulance/Emergency Medical Service (EMS)	List name of nearest ambulance service	
Local Red Cross	List name of key personnel	
Local shelter/ community kitchen	List name of key personnel	

Local Media Directory

Contact	*Name*	*Phone numbers/E-mail addresses*
Local television stations	Names of news director/news editor/ beat reporter	
Local radio stations	Names of news director/news editor/ beat reporter	
Community cable stations	Names of news director/news editor/ beat reporter	
Local newspapers	Names of news editor/beat reporter	
Local webmedia	Name of contents editor/bloggers	

Sample Media Log

Last name	First name	Phone numbers/ E-mail addresses	Date	Question(s) asked	Media organization	Responder's name	Additional follow-up needs	Notes

Sample Messaging Steps

Sample Initial Media Statement on Crisis

"(Identification of speaker): A (what happened) at (where it happened) involving *(who was involved)* occurred today at *(location and time).* The incident is under investigation and we will provide you with additional information as soon as we get them."

Key Messages

- *Message to staff*
  - On (date), (incident) occurred (tell what happened) at (where it happened) involving (who was involved).
  - The incident is under investigation and more information will be provided as we receive them.
  - (Show empathy) ABC Company is committed to the safety of its employees.
  - Please direct all media inquiries to the (Crisis team leader) or public relations department.

- *Message to customers*
  - On (date), (incident) occurred (tell what happened) at (where it happened) involving (who was involved).
  - The incident is under investigation and more information will be provided as we receive them.
  - (Show empathy) ABC Company is committed to the safety of its customers.
  - Please call this number (123–456–7890) if you have questions.
  - Also visit our website and Facebook page for updates.
  - Follow us on Twitter @ABC Company.

- *Message to media*
  - On (date), (incident) occurred (tell what happened) at (where it happened) involving (who was involved).
  - We will notify you as we get additional information about the situation.
  - ABC Company is committed to the safety of its employees and customers.
  - We will have updates on our website www.abccompany.com/newsroom.
  - You can also find us on blogpost at ABCcoyblogpost.com, Facebook at ABC Company, and on Twitter @ABC Company.

Sample Media Release

COMPANY LOGO
FOR IMMEDIATE RELEASE/RELEASE DATE

Contact (Name/Title)
Phone number/E-mail/Skype
Facebook/LinkedIn/Blog

Media Release Headline

- [Location] [date]: The [name of organization] has evacuated customers from the ABC remote location in [name of place] as a result of a gas leak in [specify area of gas leak].
- Briefly describe when leak occurred, how it was detected, and action taken by the company.
- Indicate time of day company notified local authorities and what other arrangements have been made.
- Quote company source as to what action the company has taken or is taking to minimize the effect of the gas leak or to plug the leak [cite company official's name and title].
- Direct media to website and social media links for additional information.
- Indicate if there would be a press conference or a public comment about the crisis at a later time and place.

Sample Social Media Release Format

Contact information	Organization: Phone #/Skype E-mail/Facebook Website	Spokesperson: Phone #/Skype E-mail/Facebook/LinkedIn IM/Website/Blog/Twitter
Include release date	MEDIA RELEASE HEADLINE: (subhead)	
	KEY FACTS or MESSAGE Use bullets or number	Tag your release with key words and phrases to make for easier Internet search.
	LINK to RSS FEED (to ensure regular update on web content)	Link to previous releases in organization's "newsroom."
Link to relevant PHOTO/GRAPHIC	Link to PODCAST	Link to relevant VIDEO/YOUTUBE
Link to all organization's social Media: Website, Facebook, LinkedIn, Blogs, Twitter, Flickr	Link to approved KEY QUOTES by company executives, experts on the crisis.	Link to relevant sites for third party endorsement of crisis efforts or brand ambassadors comments
Insert LOGO for social media links identified earlier: RSS, YouTube, Facebook, Twitter, LinkedIn	Boilerplate Information	Insert LOGO for social media links Identified earlier: RSS, YouTube, Facebook, Twitter, LinkedIn

References

Coombs, T. W. (2007). Attribution theory as a guide for post-crisis communication research. *Public Relations Review*, *33*(2), 135–139.

FEMA. (2010). Risk steering committee. DHS Risk lexicon. 2010 Edition. (September). Homeland Security. Retrieved from www.fema.gov/pdf/gov/grant/fy11_hsgp.lexicon_pdf

HSE (2011). Five steps to risk assessment. Health and Safety Executive. Retrieved from www.hse.gov.uk

Kaplan, S., and Garrick, B. J. (1981). On the quantitative definition of risk. *Risk Analysis*, *1*(1), March, 11–27.

Lerbinger, O. (1997). *The crisis manager: Facing risk and responsibility*. Mahwah, NJ: Erlbaum.

Lowrance, W. W. (1976). *Of acceptable risk: Science and determination of safety*. Los Altos, CA: W. Kaufmann.

Lukaszewski, J. E. (1997). Establishing individual and corporate crisis communication standards: The principles and protocols. *Public Relations Quarterly*, *42* (3), 7–14.

Maul, K. (2010). Companies lack social media crisis plans. Retrieved from www.prweekus.com/pages/companies-lack-social-media-crisis-plans/article/177167

Millar, D. P. and Heath, R. L. (2004). *Responding to crisis: A rhetorical approach to crisis communication*. Mahwah, NJ: LEA.

Mitroff, I. I. and Pearson, C. M. (1993). *Crisis management: A diagnostic guide for improving your organization's crisis-preparedness*. San Francisco, CA: Jossey-Bass Publishers.

Reynolds, B., and Seeger, M. W. (2005). Crisis and emergency risk communication as an interactive model. *Journal of Health Communication*, *10*(1), 43–55.

Ropeik, D. (2008). Risk communication: More than facts and feelings. *IAEZ Bulletin 50*(1), September. Retrieved from www.iaea.org/Publications/Magazines/Bulletin/Bull501/Risk_Communication.html)

Seeger, M., Sellnow, T. L., and Ulmer, R. (2003). *Communication and organizational crisis*. Westport, CT: Praeger.

Part III
Case Studies

Section 1
Africa

Egypt

Social Media Stoke a Political Revolution in Egypt

Olugbenga C. Ayeni

The quiet plan to assemble like-minded people to protest against a government that grew apart from its citizens soon became a global event that led to a revolution. This would not have been possible without the enormous reach of the Internet and the social networking sites in particular. In a manner that has virtually reversed the structure of the agenda-setting role of the traditional media, social networking has citizens not just fully controlling the content and production but also, by extension, largely influencing the media's agenda as well. Even though the precipitating video blog calling for public protests in Egypt triggered the revolution, blog posts on the political situation started a few years earlier. Because of the outcome of the protests, the Egyptian crisis thus became a success story for all bloggers and social networking advocates who now see the empowering role of these mass mobilization channels as having huge transformative powers to shape political and social landscapes across the globe. That President Hosni Mubarak's 30-year rule was brought to an end was a significant outcome of a plot that was hatched on the Internet and executed on the streets of Egypt.

Introduction

> This "network of networks" would not only "promote the functioning of democracy by greatly enhancing the participation of citizens in decision making," but its distributed intelligence would help "spread participatory democracy" leading to a new Athenian Age of democracy forged in the fora the GII will create.
>
> (Al Gore, former U.S. vice president, 1994, p. 14)

The use of the new media platforms made possible by advanced communication technology has led to the growth of citizen journalism and civic engagement, a trend that was made popular by citizen journalists and reporters, bloggers, and social networkers. Citizen journalism has been defined by Rosen (2008) as what happens, "when the people formerly known as the audience employ the press tools they have in their possession to inform one another" (p. 34). Bowman and Willis (2003) also described it as "the act of a citizen, or a group of citizens, playing an active role in the process of collecting, reporting, analyzing and disseminating news and information" (p. 9). In looking at the future of citizen journalism and its consequences, Gillmor (2006) noted that the new models of citizen journalism will ultimately erase "the lines between producers and consumers [and] the communications network itself will become a medium for everyone's voice" (p. 45).

Social media in the last decade assumed new mass popularity and provided limitless platforms for the growth of citizen journalism and mass participation in social and political discourse. With the emergence of online publishing, networking techniques, and user-generated content, social media ignited hopes of the potential to fuel the process of democratization in otherwise autocratic countries. With the new social media came new ways of inclusion and direct citizen participation. The unfettered nature of social media and their attributes of openness, author-produced, interactive, timely, and uncensored content were soon going to pose challenges to repressive and autocratic governments worldwide. Hitherto, politically passive young populations found a new arena in which ideas can be more freely discussed, causes passionately championed, and the rise of activism through mobilization effectively achieved.

When protests erupted on the streets of Iran in 2009, following disputed election results, the use of Twitter was no longer in doubt. The turnout of people in support of the demonstrations spearheaded by the opposition group, the Green Movement, and the swiftness with which images and videos of the riots were covered in traditional mass media outlets were unprecedented. Those occurrences marked *the* Twitter revolution of sorts. Moldova's demonstrations followed the same pattern as that of Iran in their quick spread as a result of social media. Reverberations of the demonstrations resulted in unrests in other European countries.

From about the second half of 2010 to about the first half of 2011, there was a wave of citizen activism and mass mobilization that took the entire world by surprise. Far-flung countries, particularly in Africa and the Middle East, erupted into a contagious wave of civil unrest whose nuclei were traced to citizen journalism and social networking sites through the use of the Internet and camera phones. From Tunisia to Bahrain, Egypt to Yemen, and Saudi Arabia to Libya, despotic governments were forced to listen to the voices of their citizens who had been oppressed for decades. Rheingold (2002) acknowledged the role of social media in helping people "gain new forms of social power and new ways to organize their interactions and exchanges just in time and just in place" (p. xii).

Restricted through media blackouts, censorships, and prohibitive laws, despotic, tyrannical leaders held their citizens on a tight leash and controlled dissidence to the barest minimum. However, with the emergence of the new media and social networking sites, camera phones and other similar communication gadgets, newly initiated and technologically savvy citizens became empowered through unfettered access to the world with direct access to the traditional media outlets through which their mass mobilization messages found vent.

However, not all citizen-led movements were able to assume revolutionary status that resulted in landmark regime change or an end to all corrupt governments across the globe. In fact, as was seen in many of the cases involving mass movements fueled by social networking sites, regime changes did not occur in many of the affected countries, as was the case in Iran where government cracked down violently to shut off opposition. A lingering crisis ensued in Libya after mass protests that had erupted there were met with stiff resistance by forces loyal to the president. The protesters had demanded the resignation of longtime despot, Muammar Gaddafi, who had held on to power for nearly 40 years. The Libyan revolution succeeded with the toppling of the government, capture and assassination of Colonel Gaddafi. In parts of the world where civil rights records are suspect, leaders have resorted to monitoring access to the Internet, to disabling international cell-phone access, or to confiscating "offensive" gadgets, and to imposing jail time for those caught in the act of using their device to communicate embarrassing messages about the government to the outside world.

In a report by *Global Voices Advocacy*, the Chinese government cut off Internet and SMS access, following the riots that erupted in Urumqi in July 2009. In Xinjiang, Internet access was shut down for several months allowing only authorized government agencies very controlled and limited access. Many countries have put in place devices through which online interaction and communication can be monitored and filtered. The Ethiopian government banned the use of the Internet for two years in 2005, when a contested election was about to ignite into citizen movement against the government (Lam, 2010).

Background of the Crisis

Egypt's revolution of January 2011 started in an unusual manner through the silent mobilization efforts that were fueled by interactive video blogs and social networking sites. The movement was intended to comprise peaceful protests, civil disobedience, demonstrations, and marches to press home citizens' demands for political and economic changes in Egypt. The Egyptians had lived for 30 years under the tyrannical leadership of 83-year-old Hosni Mubarak, who, according to media reports, engaged in citizen intimidation through police brutality and violent clampdown on opposition. The high rate of unemployment, runaway inflation, extreme mass poverty, absence of rule of law, and endemic corruption made life a living hell for ordinary citizens.

It was just a matter of time for something to happen to make change possible, but no one knew how until around the beginning of January 2011.

The answer came from nearby Tunisia where massive protests had led to the removal of another despot, Zine El Abidine Ben Ali, after the brave act of self-immolation by Mohamed Bouazizi triggered massive riots and protests. Bouazizi was humiliated following the seizure of his unlicensed vegetable cart owing to nonpayment of official tax as required by the government. The fine of 10 dinar (about $7) imposed was equivalent to a day's wage in Tunisia, but Bouazizi was going to pay to ensure that he continued to be gainfully employed (*New York Times*, January 21, 2011). It was the humiliating ordeal that he suffered in the hands of the arresting police woman that triggered his decision to set himself ablaze on December 17, 2010, in front of the police headquarters. The policewoman had spat on his face and insulted his father. In the Islamic world, that was the worst form of humiliation, and Mohamed Bouazizi had had enough. He died a few days later in a hospital (Kareem, 2011).

When a 26-year-old Egyptian woman, Asma Mahfouz, posted a video blog calling on all Egyptians to join a protest on January 25, 2011, many people were fueled by the act of self-sacrifice by the Tunisian Bouazizi, and the unrelenting suffering in the hands of Mubarak's corrupt government (*The Canadian Charger*, 2011). Mahfouz's video blog and social media posts went viral, and soon gathered impressive following with April Youth Movement and the main opposition group in Egypt, the Muslim Brotherhood, pledging their support to the protests. Cairo's protests began with street demonstrations that called for the resignation of President Hosni Mubarak. President Mubarak, who was a military chief himself, ascended to power in 1981, following the assassination of the peace-loving Anwar El-Sadat. Having served as vice president to President Sadat before his gruesome assassination, upon taking over power, President Mubarak ran a tight-fisted government for 30 years without any clear succession structure or a vice president. Muffled rumors of President Mubarak's son, Gamal Mubarak, taking over the reins of power from his father were all in the air, fueling suspicion in Egypt that the people's suffering would never end.

In a gale of protests reported to have been sparked by the inflammable nature of social media, Cairo was soon on fire. Protesters in their thousands took to the streets of Cairo, spilling over to surrounding cities of Alexandria, Mansura, Tanta, Sinai Peninsula, Ismaila, and Beni Suef, and extending as far away as Zag Zig. In a brazen manner protesters showed grit and bravery, and did not hide their frustration and disdain for the regime of Mubarak, which hitherto had led the people with apparent disdain and insensitivity.

The first day, dubbed "The Day of Revolt," witnessed civilian police clashes, and reported cases of injuries. The protests continued despite the curfew as world attention had now shifted from Tunisia to Cairo (*The Guardian*, 2011). Within 24 hours of the protest, hundreds of thousands had joined in the actual protests while millions used social network sites to follow the progress and galvanize support. On February 26, Mubarak's government responded by shutting down Internet access to limit communication among protesters and shut out the entire world from monitoring or following the unravelling scenario in Egypt.

It was not until Friday, January 28, that the real fury of the protesters began to manifest. Dubbed "Friday of Anger," protesters mobilized after the Friday Muslim prayers and took to the streets where there were more reports of skirmishes, looting, and freeing of prison inmates. Mubarak's attempts to claw his way back into power through thugs fighting on his behalf led to more bloodshed.

Four days after the start of the protests, Mubarak made his first televised address during which he promised new government reforms. As the protests increased, the military was called in to secure the cities, and vigilante groups guarded neighbourhoods to avoid looting by thugs. Mubarak sacked his government and appointed a trusted ally and head of the Egyptian General Intelligence Directorate, Omar Suleiman, as vice president. It was seen in government as a big deal since Mubarak had a tight lid on authority before the crisis.

More concessions were made by Mubarak during his second speech on February 1. He promised not to run for another term in office, but wanted to remain in office as president to midwife the elections in September, to guarantee stability of the nation. The protesters did not buy that. Despite two major speeches made by President Mubarak to appeal to the citizens to abandon their cause, the incensed protesters were unyielding. Mubarak's government was challenged by the multilevel task of facing the barrage of criticisms coming from all direction about the mishandling of the crisis. There was aloofness and self-importance in the delayed speech delivered by Mubarak four days after the riots broke on the streets of Cairo, showing crass disregard for public sensitivity.

Mubarak's self-laudatory rhetoric raised the protesters' anger to the peak. The tone of his message fell far short of the people's expectations, while ineffective tactics of apologia were exploited. A good example is the opening sentence of his speech which ironically was prophetic. Mubarak said:

> I talk to you during critical times that are testing Egypt and its people which could sweep them into the unknown . . . Those protests were trans-formed from a noble and civilized phenomenon of practicing freedom of expression to unfortunate clashes, mobilized and controlled by political forces that wanted to escalate and worsen the situation.

Leaders of government or corporate leaders finding themselves in such crisis typically employ tactics as they seek to, "distance themselves from their illegit-imate behaviours and then create identifications with the public values they are reputed to have violated" (Hearit, 1995, p. 4).

Situation Analysis

Evidently the political and economic situation in Egypt gave ample credence to the agitations of the protesters. President Mubarak had overspent his goodwill and reputational equity that he may have had when he assumed leadership in Egypt 30 years ago. His harsh policies and unresponsive attitude to the needs of the people quickly eroded any likelihood for him to salvage his presidency following the breakout of these rashes of protests. Prevailing emergency laws had made pluralist democracy impossible until 2005; before then, only Mubarak could stand for presidential election on a yes or no vote. Elections were more of a selection process since most of them were rigged and falsified. Mubarak claimed to have won five consecutive presidential elections with a questionable sweeping majority in all of them. When an opposing candidate, Ayman Nour, planned to run against Mubarak he was imprisoned before the 2005 elections (Sharp, 2009).

Free speech, one of the key ingredients in any democratic society, is not free in Egypt. Government had sweeping powers to censor anything that was considered a threat to "public safety and national security." A fine of 20,000 pounds ($3,650) and up to five years in prison could be imposed on any reporter or blogger found to criticize the government. The Moltaqa Forum for Development and Human Rights Dialogue reported that between January and March 2009, 57 journalists from 13 newspapers faced legal penalties for their governmental critiques. To keep the citizens on a leash, the Egyptian government owns stock in the three largest daily newspapers while licensing and distribution of all papers in Egypt were in the strong hands of the government (U.S. Department of State Bureau of Democracy, Human Rights and Labor, 2010).

The social networking websites, blogspots, and the Internet as a whole thus came to the rescue of all Egyptians, and indeed all the admirers of people's will and citizen power in every corner of the earth. That explains the fact that external stakeholders were equally as important as the internal ones. Each stakeholder had unique agendas to pursue and interests to protect.

The Stakeholders

The array and diversity of the stakeholders in this crisis were as diverse as the social problems plaguing Egypt and the rest of the Arab world. These stakeholders comprised:

- the Egyptian government;
- the U.S. government and its allies whose interests are being threatened;
- the nearly 80 million Egyptian citizens seeking political and social changes;
- the Arab countries who are watching for what comes next to them;
- the international community.

The stakeholders in the Egyptian crisis include the suffering masses of Egypt, who had the highest stakes in the crisis, government leaders and officials, the police, and the military, the Arab world, Israel, and of course, the United States. For each of the stakeholders, the outcomes were significantly different.

The Protesting Egyptians

The Egyptian people put their lives on the line to confront the 30-year tyrannical and oppressive government of President Mubarak, a former military leader who ruled with draconian powers under a semi dictatorship, despite the semblance of democratic structures in place. Obviously, the government, which had claimed to hold on to power on behalf of the people suddenly lost face and was being challenged by the same people it claimed to protect.

They had a list of demands that they wanted Mubarak to deliver; chief among them were the suspension of the emergency laws to be replaced by the rule of law, provision of employment, and better life for the people. The global economic downturn had slowed down any economic reforms that were earlier put in place by Mubarak. Employment among the youth was said to be as high as 10 percent, while in 2010, close to half of the population, 40 percent of Egypt's 80 million people, lived on income equivalent of roughly US$2 per day, with a large part of the population relying on subsidized goods. The protests were therefore the only means left through which the voices of the people could be heard, and because they had a lot at stake, they were willing to stake their lives to press on their demands.

The United States Government

The reaction from the U.S. government through President Obama was quick, even though tentative in tone. Many had hoped that the U.S. government would offer more prompt but wholesome support to the protesters and condemn Hosni Mubarak sooner for the high-handed manner he handled the protests. It did appear that from the position of the United States, using that approach would be considered meddling in the internal affairs of another country.

The position of the U.S. government was tentative for a reason. U.S. government officials felt that in the unpredictable political climate in Egypt at the time, when no clear leader had emerged, making a statement overtly supporting the protests would have been dangerous for Egypt, the Arab world, and the interests of the United States, especially Israel. Obama's speech was delivered soon after Mubarak's, and he reiterated that Egypt was a strong ally and should listen to the voice of its people.

In his speech about the situation in Egypt, President Obama said:

> going forward, this moment of volatility has to be turned into a moment of promise. The United States has a close partnership with Egypt and we've cooperated on many issues, including working together to advance a more

peaceful region. But we've also been clear that there must be reform—political, social, and economic reforms that meet the aspirations of the Egyptian people.

(White House, 2011)

Treading a path of caution, Obama never let the chance to express support for human and people's rights pass by when he said that:

Violence will not address the grievances of the Egyptian people. And suppressing ideas never succeeds in making them go away. What's needed right now are concrete steps that advance the rights of the Egyptian people: a meaningful dialogue between the government and its citizens, and a path of political change that leads to a future of greater freedom and greater opportunity and justice for the Egyptian people.

(*New York Times*, February 10, 2011)

The Arab Countries

There were varied reactions from Arab countries as there were from the rest of the international community. It was particularly difficult to tag these protests as imported from Western countries, even if Mubarak had in his post-protest messages hinted at the "us versus them" gambit. Whereas Tunisia and, surprisingly, Iran supported the protests strongly, Saudi Arabia condemned the protests. Israel, which had hitherto enjoyed a favorable relationship with Egypt, was cautious in embracing the protests, particularly since the identities of those spearheading the movement were not so clear.

There was an ominous warning that what was happening in Egypt could have a bandwagon effect in those Arab countries. This put many of the Arab leaders in an uncomfortable position as they were not sure if their actions or inactions would trigger similar protests in their home lands. Saudi Arabia began quickly to announce palliative measures to its citizens when there were rumors of an impending demonstration in the Saudi Kingdom, just as others made wide-ranging offers of social reforms.

The International Community

The Egyptian crisis and the doggedness of its leaders was a quick reminder to all people who were under despotic leaders that people's power surpassed military power. The Western countries were unanimous in their support. United States was the main cheerleader, while France, Germany, and Britain supported the protests and called for a peaceful resolution and the restoration of democratic institutions that guarantee all human freedoms.

The effective use of new media outlets, and the wall-to-wall coverage by most news and cable networks in the United States made the Egyptian crisis the hot-button issue at the center of international media attention all through the entire period. Tahrir Square became the epicenter as well as the Ground Zero for the struggle.

Egyptian Government's Initial Response

President Mubarak responded by:

- shutting down the Internet and restricting access to mobile telephone networks so as to contain and crush the protests without external influence;
- deploying police to the streets to unleash violence on the protesters;
- delivering terse televised message to the people;
- firing the cabinet and appointing a vice president for the first time in 30 years;
- offering piecemeal reforms to whittle down the protests;
- deploying thugs riding camels into the midst of the protesters to discredit the noble cause of the protests; and
- imposing curfews to limit movement and frustrate the protesters.

It could be said that the initial response of the government of Mubarak evidently confirmed that he had lost touch with the people, and did not have much to offer in terms of the needs of the teeming population.

Goals and Objectives

Goal 1: To limit the scope of the protests and contain them in the fiercest manner possible.

Objective: To use the police and other government machinery to contain the spread of the protests.

Strategy: To deploy police on the streets to confront the protesters.

Tactics:

- brutalized and arrested many of the protesters to serve as deterrent to others to abandon the cause; and
- imposed curfews to control movement.

Goal 2: To cripple the protesters' communication networks.

Objective: To contain the situation and shield it from the international media with hopes that it would end the problem, and bring protests to an end.

Strategy: Kept news of the protests from filtering out of Egypt.

Tactics: Ordered the telecommunications company to block access to the Internet and paralyzed international communications channels.

Goal 3: To introduce some reforms and palliatives for the citizens.

Objective: To present the impression of a responsive government in a bid to end the protests.

Strategy: Offered to meet some of the demands of the protesters to appease them.

Tactics:

* pledged to form a new government;
* pledged not to run for office again; and
* appointed a vice president.

Goal 4: To infiltrate the ranks of the protests and raise counter-protest in support of the government.

Objective: To hijack the protesters so that the cause of the activists and advocates will lose legitimacy.

Strategy: Disintegrated society provided opening for a counter-protest to impede further progress for the protesters.

Tactics:

* withdrew the police from the streets soon after the first few clashes that led to looting; and
* sponsored camel riding thugs to attack protesters.

The Rest of the World

Whereas the United States was in the forefront in supporting demonstrations, many critics of the Obama administration said the delayed reaction in Egypt was costly. However, in the rest of the Arab world, countries such as Tunisia and Iran supported the protesters while neighboring Israel was cautiously supporting change. Egyptian protesters' agendas were a cause célèbre, making the revolution the number one news event worldwide. Reporters thronged to Cairo to get the scoop of the decade. The revolution in Tunisia and then in Egypt served as a wake-up call to all other Arab leaders that the fire next time may well be ignited in their backyard. Many of the countries hurriedly announced palliatives for the citizens with promises of reforms to stem the tide of any planned protests.

Goal: To provide as much support to the causes of the protesters as possible.

Objective: To support the freedoms of all oppressed people as enshrined in the United Nations charter guaranteeing all freedoms.

Strategy: Exerted pressure on their own governments to speak out against the government of Mubarak.

Tactics:

- held rallies across the world to rally support for the Egyptians; and
- supported the protesters' actions through public condemnation of acts of cowardice by the Mubarak government.

The Egyptian People

Goal 1: To ensure that the government of Mubarak was removed immediately.

Goal 2: To ascertain that pluralist democracy returned to Egypt permanently.

Objective: To bestow on the people an inclusive democratic government of which they can be proud.

Strategy: Kept a sustained attitude and focus on the goal of the protests

Tactics:

- united in their demands for Mubarak's resignation;
- ignored calls for curfew;
- risked their lives in the face of intimidation;
- used traditional and new media to showcase their agenda; and
- coordinated their movement effectively even if there were no clear leaders.

The Government of the United States

Goal 1: To offer support for the protesters without being intrusive.

Goal 2: To ensure that there was minimum bloodshed.

Goal 3: To ensure that the will of the Egyptian people prevailed.

Objective: To ensure that the intended goal of the protesters is accomplished.

Tactics:

- discouraged the Egyptian government from using force to address the protesters' demands;
- offered support for freedom and democracy; and
- provided legitimacy to the struggle through diplomatic consultations and statements.

Outcomes Assessment

Summary of Government Action (and Reaction)

After four days of persistent street protests that spanned nearly the entire country, President Mubarak, rather than deliver the speech of his life to assuage those yearning for his removal, chose to respond through a terse televised message that the executive cabinet of his government was sacked. He defiantly clung to power as president, and did not address the core request of the people that he step down from office. While the rest of the world was shocked that the leader took so long to respond to the clamor for change that had enveloped his entire country, the protesting population was incensed by that move. This was a clear evidence of arrogance of power and proof that the disdain that the world's despotic leaders have for the common man on the streets was without limit. Hosni Mubarak seemed to have lost touch with the people he swore to lead and serve.

The beleaguered government of Mubarak knew that the trouble was hatched through the Internet and the social networking sites of Facebook and Twitter, and also through cell phone technology. Initial panicky response was to shut down the citizens' access to these communication tools. Despite that initial wrong move by the government, news of the protests still trickled out of Cairo to the rest of the world. The police were brought in to crush the riots during which people were violently attacked and lives were lost. The world reacted in disgust and America waded in and called for all violence to stop.

Mubarak immediately sacked his cabinet and appointed for the first time in 30 years his trusted ally, and intelligence chief, Omar Suleiman, as vice president—a move that many thought was just akin to treating the symptoms rather than the cause of the problem. The reaction of the protesting population was evidently unrelenting as more people poured into the streets and demanded the exit of Mubarak.

Many of the demands of the protesters were met by the government of Hosni Mubarak but it seemed that the Egyptian people's major wish was to see Mubarak step down as president. However before Mubarak reluctantly stepped down, other demands by the protesters were met, such as the cancellation of the emergency law and the dismantling of the State Security Intelligence, an agency used to repress the citizens' rights, which was a welcome change. One could say then that the crisis in Egypt was more a communication problem as it was a social responsibility crisis.

The Egyptian government under Hosni Mubarak failed to seize the moment by avoiding the crisis in Egypt even though he had a teachable moment with what happened next door in Tunisia. Lessons were not learned from the Tunisian crisis that led to the removal of a longstanding despot. Initial response of the Egyptian government was wrong as it was late. It is often said that crises have the tendency of bringing irreparable consequences when they occur, but when crisis situations are met with wrong and late reactions from those affected, they often lead to huge failure and monumental damages. Mubarak was evidently caught unprepared and he applied the wrong solutions when he responded.

Public communication during the crisis was ineffective, lackluster and insufficient to make any significant impact on the crisis. Key issues that informed the protests were visibly not part of the government response when it became necessary. Mubarak never allayed the fears of the stakeholders. Neither was there a coordinated public information channel that had direct link with the protesters.

Lessons Learned

• The will of the people cannot be suppressed.

Despite many reforms that were earned though bloodshed by the protesters, it was the prize of ending the 30-year-old tyranny and corruption of the Mubarak government that made all the headlines. Mubarak, to the ordinary citizens, had become the symbol of repression and no matter how many reforms were offered to the protesters, it was Mubarak's exit that meant so much to the people.

• The failure of the Mubarak government to identify the pre-crisis stage of the problem.

Every crisis begins with a prodromal stage, the point where signs of an impending crisis are evident. The stage where organizations search for signs of an impending crisis is known as signal detection (Coombs, 2007). In the case of Egypt, the leaders had the example in nearby Tunisia to alert them to the possibility of a crisis at home.

It was surprising that Egypt did not see the signs, or the signs were deliberately ignored in an act typifying arrogance of power. The *Washington Post* sounded the ominous warning before the Egyptian Revolution but no one listened: "The Jasmine Revolution should serve as a stark warning to Arab leaders—beginning with Egypt's 83-year-old Hosni Mubarak—that their refusal to allow more economic and political opportunity is dangerous and untenable" (*Washington Post*, January 15, 2011).

- When effectively deployed, prompt crisis communication response is helpful in dousing the raging fire of rage of public protests.

The crisis communication plan deployed during the Egyptian Revolution was weak, slow, faulty, inappropriate, and ineffective, thereby making the concessions offered by the government of Mubarak of little or no significance. For corrective action to be appreciated, it must come promptly earlier in the crisis before citizens' become emboldened and unappreciative of those corrective actions.

- Effective use of apology can lead to quick restoration of strained relationships.
- Crisis communications plan is a useful tool to guide in times of crises.
- Peaceful protests can lead to unprecedented changes, a fact that was attested to by President Obama following the resignation of Mubarak. He said:

> There are very few moments in our lives where we have the privilege to witness history taking place. This is one of those moments. This is one of those times . . . This is the power of human dignity, and it could never be denied. Egyptians have inspired us, and they've done so by putting the lie to the idea that justice is best gained through violence.
> (White House, 2011)

Discussion Questions

1. Could a well-coordinated crisis communication plan have affected the outcomes of the Cairo crisis in any different way? If so, how?
2. Which step taken by the Egyptian authorities do you find most offensive and why?
3. The government of Hosni Mubarak introduced some landmark changes following the protests. Do you believe those changes if presented better could have reversed the situation? Why or why not?
4. How crucial was the role of social media in the success of the Egyptian crisis?

References

BBC News. (2011). Egypt: Mubarak sacks cabinet and defends security role. January 29, 2011. Retrieved from www.bbc.co.uk

Bowman, S., and Willis, C. (2003). *WeMedia: How audiences are shaping the future of news and information.* Washington, DC: American Press Institute.

The Canadian Charger. (2011). Asmaa Mahfouz, a woman behind Egypt's pro-democracy revolution, February 5. Retrieved from www.canadiancharger.com

Coombs, W. T. (2007). *Ongoing crisis communication: Planning, managing and responding.* London, UK: Sage Publications Inc.

Gillmor, D. (2006). *We the media: Grassroots journalism by the people, for the people.* Sebastopol, CA: O'Reilly.

Gore, A. (1994). Remarks prepared for delivery at International Telecommunications Union, Buenos Aires, Argentina, March 21. Retrieved from www.web.simmons.edu/~chen/nit/NIT'94/94-Appendices-367.html

The Guardian (2011) Protests in Egypt—As it happened. Live blog, January 26. Retrieved from www.guardian.co.uk

Hearit, K. M. (1995). Mistakes were made: Organizations, apologia, and crises of social legitimacy. *Communication Studies, 46,* 1–17.

Kareem, F. (2011). Slap to a man's pride set off tumult in Tunisia. *New York Times,* January 21. Retrieved from www.nytimes.com

Lam, O. (2010). When the network was out in Xinjiang. Global Voices Advocacy, October 13. Retrieved www.globalvoicesonline.org

Phelps, T. (2011). Revolution might not be a cure for Egypt's extreme poverty. *Los Angeles Times World,* February 20. Retrieved from http://articles.latimes.com

Rheingold, H. (2002). *Smart mobs: The next social revolution.* Cambridge, MA: Perseus Publishing.

Rosen, J. (2008). A most useful definition of citizen journalism *PressThink: Ghost of democracy in the media machine,* July 14. [Web log comment]. Retrieved from http://journalism.nyu.edu/pubzone/weblogs/pressthink/2008/07/14/a_most_useful_d.html

Sharp, J. (2009). Egypt: Background and U.S. relations. Congressional Research Service. Retrieved from www.fas.org/sgp/crs/mideast/RL33003.pdf

U.S. Department of State Bureau of Democracy, Human Rights and Labor. (2010). *2009 Human Rights Report: Egypt,* March.

The Washington Post (2011). Editorial: Tunisia's revolution should be a wake-up call to Mideast autocrats, January 15. Retrieved from www.washingtonpost.com

White House (2011). Remarks made by the president on Egypt, February 11. Retrieved from www.whitehouse.gov/the-press-office/2011/02/11/remarks-president-egypt

VIEWS FROM AN EXPERT

EDMOND CHIBEAU

Edmond Chibeau (Ph.D., Northwestern) is concerned with how communication is performed across new media and how decisions are made about what is appropriate content for emerging technologies. He teaches writing for performance and history of media at Eastern Connecticut State University.

Crisis management and the new media have gone hand in hand throughout history. Egypt has been in the forefront of new technology and revolutionary communication since the carving of the Rosetta Stone, and the attempt by Thothmose III to erase all references to Hatsheput, the first female Pharaoh.

Whoever controls the media controls the people. But if the people take control of the means of communication then the government is in danger. To keep control of the government those in power must stay on top of an ever-changing media environment.

We can imagine two contending schools of crisis communication: one that believes in clear carefully formulated on-message top-down broadcast of authoritative proclamations; and another that believes in widely distributed and eclectically sourced multipoint dissemination of up-to-the-minute data. One is slow, the other is fast. One is precise, the other is messy.

Bureaucracies are not nimble. Revolutionary movements very often are. In January 2011 there was a classic match between the big, slow, centralized, entrenched, and powerful Egyptian Government communication apparatus on the one side, and the small, nimble, decentralized, fluid, and unorganized ad hoc communication system of the revolution on the other side. Both camps were facing a crisis and both needed to communicate quickly with two constituencies; their loyal base on the one hand, and the uncommitted and uninformed majority on the other.

The standard government move in this game is to reduce opportunities for communication and diffusion of innovative ideas (revolutionary ideas). The standard move for the insurgent forces is to find ways to communicate quickly and widely to their constituencies.

In the British colonies of North America leading up to the American Revolution of the 1770s, the leaders of the protest movement against the king of England formed Committees of Correspondence using the Post Road system to share information.

In the 1950s in Cuba, Fidel Castro and the guerrilleros in the Sierra Madre Mountains communicated by word of mouth. When one campesino would pass another walking in the mountains he would mention where he had seen government troops and the direction they were going. This was called the "Radio Bamba." The interlocking network of mountain pathways in Cuba in the 1950s became the Internet and Twitter of Egypt in 2011.

Just as a networked economy becomes more valuable the more people use it, a networked public sphere becomes more voluble the more people are connected to it. The fighters for a more democratic Egypt used democratic social media to stand against a plutocracy that was trying to turn a virtually non-rivalrous and non-exclusionary public good (the Internet social media) into a scarce resource. Public media are the abode of democracy in the first decades of the twenty-first century. They became a site of contention in the info-war between the Mubarak monolith and cloud-distributed popular revolt that is spreading across the Islamic world.

The question that can only be answered by time is whether these new multipoint personal media can remain technologies of freedom or whether they will be co-opted to become technologies of oppression.

Kenya

Wooing Tourists Back after a Civil Strife: The Kenyan Example

Bitrus P. Gwamna

In 2008, Kenya erupted in violence as voters protested against the award of election victory to incumbent president, Mwai Kibaki. Travel warnings by European and U.S. governments led to cancellation of bookings to Kenyan tourist sites, causing a slump in revenue by that country's greatest revenue earner. This chapter discusses strategies and tactics by Kenya's tourism industry to win back visitors. It argues for a robust crisis management team, which would plan and execute communication strategies to safeguard the tourism industry in times of civil strife.

Introduction

Tourism is the export that generates the most revenue to the Kenyan economy. Thousands of visitors troop to the country to seek gratification from its most unique features: wildlife and beaches. The export-revenue earning potential of the tourism industry in Kenya is threatened each time there is a terrorism attack, or a threat, as in the 1998 bombing of the U.S. consulate in Mombasa, or the post-election violence of 2008. The chapter examines, discusses, and analyzes communication strategies and tactics resorted to by the Kenyan Tourist Board and relevant stakeholders to repopulate the Kenyan beaches and forests with fee-paying visitors after the political turmoil that ensued following the December elections of 2007.

Background to the Crisis

Shortly after Christmas in 2007, Kenyans went to polling booths to vote for president and members of parliament. Many were looking for change, and it would appear from election results from various stations that they would have their wish. However, on New Year's Eve, many Kenyans were displeased at what they thought was the last-minute switching of election results, which gave the incumbent, President Mwai Kibaki victory over his opponent Raila Odinga. Otieno-Onyando (2008), writing in *The Nation Group* newspaper, reported that Mr. Odinga led with 4.3 million votes to Kibaki's 3.7 million, a few hours before the final announcement. The *Royal Media Services*, according to Otieno-Onyando, showed a similar margin. Mr. Odinga's lead was expected to fall marginally as results from some Kibaki strongholds not yet tallied trickled in. Then, the unexpected happened; the last batch of results announced at the KICC tallying center indicated huge inconsistencies from the ones announced at constituencies. As the European Union observer mission indicated in its report, Otieno-Onyando's article explains, the EU's representative in Molo in the former White Highlands witnessed the recording of 50,000 votes for Kibaki, contrary to the result announced in Nairobi, which gave him nearly 75,000 votes (Otieno-Onyando, 2008).

Many constituency results were reported rigged in Kibaki's favor by simply crossing his numbers from the field and inserting higher figures. According to Otieno-Onyando, the Orange Democratic Movement (ODM) alleged that at least 750,000 votes were stolen this way; that the 230,000 margin announced for Mr. Kibaki camouflaged a 500,000 vote victory for Mr. Odinga. The announcement was followed by a hurried swearing-in ceremony for Kibaki at State House, Nairobi. Spontaneous demonstrations erupted throughout the country, with youths barricading roads in Mombasa, Nairobi, Kisumu, Eldoret, and other towns (Otieno-Onyando, 2008). They chanted pro-ODM slogans, expressing outrage at the perceived injustice. They swore not to relent until their candidate, who they believed won the election, took over at State House (Otieno-Onyando, 2008). At constituency level, where doctoring results is much harder, voters rejected an astounding 20 of Kibaki's cabinet ministers. Kibaki's own party won only 43 seats in the new parliament, less than half of ODM's 99 in a 210-member house (Otieno-Onyando, 2008).

The ensuing political violence, as reported on a BBC website, claimed the lives of over 600 people, and a quarter-million people were driven from their homes. The Kikuyu dominate economic life in Kenya, but many of their businesses were burned, and farmers driven from their property (Greste, 2008); opposition leaders launched boycotts of companies owned by top allies of Kibaki, who they believed stole the election.

As television images of rioting Kenyans were broadcast worldwide, American and European tourists began canceling vacations in Kenya. In the coastal region, hotels and resorts that operated at 85 percent capacity at that time of year were only 20 percent full. Munene Kilongi, in his article, stated that although there was no reported violence on tourists, the U.S. Embassy nonetheless issued a travel alert that noted the volatility of the situation in Kenya, and cautioned care by U.S. tourists. Kilongi further explained that the embassy had a travel warning for Kenya for more than four years, owing largely to a 2002 attack by Al Qaeda suspects on a hotel outside Mombasa that was popular with Israeli tourists.

The French Ministry of Foreign Affairs also announced a travel advisory discouraging tourists from traveling to Kenya until the situation was stabilized (Interface Tourism 2008). Following further advice from the French Association of Tour Operators, travel to Kenya was frozen. The ethnic conflict and the travel advisories by the U.S. and European countries took a toll on the Kenyan economy, particularly the tourism sector. According to the Kenyan Tourist Board (KTB), the tourism industry revenue dropped 32 percent in the first six months of 2008, against the same period the previous year, as reported by Reuters. KTB said that the tourist inflow in Kenya dropped 36 percent to slightly over half a million visitors in the first half of 2008 from over 800,000 visitors in the same period in 2007. With the fall in tourist arrivals, the industry revenue also plummeted from an estimated $507.14 million recorded in 2007 to $344.04 million at the end of June 2008. Also, the average hotel room booking dropped between 35 and 40 percent during the same period. The Interface Tourism website stated that by the end of January 2008, experts feared that 20,000 jobs might have been lost in the coastal region where an estimated four in five residents depend on tourism for their livelihood, and an additional 120,000 jobs might have been lost by March that year (Kilongi, 2008).

It was not just Kenya that suffered as a result of the violence; no fewer than five neighboring states channel their exports and imports through the Kenyan port of Mombasa on the Indian Ocean. In a statement by the United Nations credited to the BBC, the World Bank said a quarter of the gross domestic product of Uganda and Rwanda and a third of Burundi's found it difficult to pass through Kenya, including essential commodities. South Sudan, the eastern Democratic Republic of Congo and northern Tanzania, which also lean heavily on Kenya both for trans-shipments and imports of essentials such as maize, became concerned about the effects of the violence on their economic activities (Greste, 2008).

Intervention by leading international organizations and figures including the former U.N. Secretary-General, Kofi Annan, led to the establishment of a government of unity with Mwai Kibaki as president and Raila Odinga as prime minister. Presidential and parliamentary elections were scheduled for the following year in which Mwai Kibaki would not seek re-election.

Situation Analysis

The stakeholders in this crisis abound among the tourism industry and the Kenyan people:

1. Tourists: Tourists pour millions of dollars into the Kenyan economy by spending on food, hotels, and packaged tours and in some cases, contribute to charity works in the country.

2. Tourism industry: These include tour operators, the hotel and motel industry, restaurant operators, and all the allied services connected to the tourism industry and tourists.
3. The Kenyan people: A large percentage make their living from services they provide to the tourism industry, as employees or as business owners who cater to tourists.

Tourism Industry and Kenya Tourist Board Reaction

Once a semblance of peace was restored, the tourists began to return not in droves but in trickles. Relevant stakeholders in the industry had to embark on a mission to save their businesses from extinction. The Kenyan government, through the Kenyan Tourist Board, worked with the tourism industry to galvanize efforts in executing a crisis communication plan to restore confidence in Kenya. Interface Tourism, one of the top tourism operators, which has represented the Kenya Tourist Board in France since 2004, developed a plan to encourage international tourists, especially English and French tourists, to return to Kenya.

Interface Tourism

Goal: To restore confidence in Kenya as a safe vacation destination.

Objective: To lobby French and international institutions against discouraging their members from traveling to Kenya.

Strategy: Constitute a crisis management team made up of major French tourism trade and press associations and headed by a chief executive.

Tactics:

- lobbied the French Embassy in Kenya, and the French Ministry of Foreign Affairs to lift the global negative travel advisory on Kenya;
- successfully sought an official open letter by Elisabeth Barbier, the French ambassador to Kenya, to reassure the French public that Kenya was stable and safe;
- met with the French media, trade representatives, and French officials to convince them that Kenya was safe;
- lobbied the French Association of Tour Operators, the French Association of Travel Agents, and airlines to resume flights to Kenya; and
- invited and briefed 250 international journalists and 150 travel agents and gave them 15 different itineraries to the country and encouraged them to go and see for themselves that Kenya is safe for tourists (Interface Tourism, 2008).

*Kenyan Tourist Board Collaboration with Others to Ensure a
Unified Campaign to Repair Kenya's Tarnished Image and Bring
Tourists Back to Kenya*

The Kenyan Tourist Board, in tandem with major tour operators, used public relations and marketing tactics to bring tourists back to Kenya.

Goal: To restore confidence in Kenya as a safe vacation destination.

Objective: To call to action partnerships with tour operators to restore Kenyan tourism within a short time.

Strategy: With the cooperation of Virgin Atlantic and some major tour operators, began a promotion campaign on the London Underground to woo back British tourists.

Tactics:

- published e-newsletters dedicated to events in Kenya;
- developed tour promotions and communication campaigns on different websites including travel selling websites (see for example www.tourism. go.ke; and www.katakenya.org);
- created a mini-website, placed advertisement in up-market lifestyle magazines;
- invited Nouvelles Frontières to operate a direct flight to Kenya for winter 2008/2009 with charter airline Air Méditérannée (Interface online); and
- in conjunction with Britain and Virgin Atlantic airlines, sponsored 35 UK journalists and operators to demonstrate Kenya's preparedness for the return of tourists, following the political violence in January 2008.

The case for Kenya's readiness for tourists was re-echoed by Richard Branson of Virgin Atlantic who, at the opening ceremony of a primary school, urged the international press to inform everyone that Kenya was safe (www. travelweekly.com). However, he warned Kenyan authorities that any revival of the political violence would dissuade Virgin Atlantic from flying into and out of the country.

While acknowledging that Kenya's tourism would have a slow recovery in spite of these campaigns, the country's tourism minister Najib Balala, in 2008, informed a magazine editor that the priority of the industry was to entice tourists familiar with Kenya to return. "Emerging markets such as China, Eastern Europe, Russia, Canada, Australia and India are good, but in a recovery strategy you don't invest in new markets," he said (Perrett, 2008). Balala also added that tourists were helping to eradicate poverty. According to him, the revenues from tourism will be put into building schools, giving free education and healthcare, and building roads.

Outcomes

Relative peace has meant more tourists to Kenya. The increase in the number of tourists from Europe and North America is in large part owing to the efforts by stakeholders to lobby foreign governments, and implementation of initiatives to assure visitors of safety throughout the country, particularly tourist sites. For example, the strategies embarked by Interface Tourism on behalf of the Kenya Tourist Board led to a change in the travel advisory by the French Ministry of Foreign Affairs five months after it was issued. The Interface Tourism website reports that there was an official open letter by Elisabeth Barbier, the French ambassador to Kenya, reassuring the French public that Kenya was stable and safe. The Association of Tour Operators recommended sales to Kenya on March 3, 2008, while the national carrier reopened its direct route to Kenya on June 11, 2008. There was also positive coverage generated by Interface Tourism in the French media immediately after the press trip to various destinations in Kenya (www.interfacetourism.com).

The campaign by a partnership of tour operators led to a boost of last minute sales to Kenya for the summer of 2008. Between December 2008 and March 2009, charter flights from France brought over 3,000 passengers to Kenya. Nouvelles Frontières is said to have realized nearly five million euros in sales. According to Dori Saltzman, in an online travel market report on Kenya's tourism, barely 600,000 tourists visited the country in 2009. The U.S. State Department continues to update an existing travel warning that is still enforced. Globus, along with other operators, are entering or returning to the Kenyan tourist market (Saltzman, 2011).

Saltzman also quotes the Kenyan Ministry of Tourism as confirming that there was a slow return of tourists to Kenya. According to the ministry, between January and August 2010, tourists numbered slightly over 700,000 (Saltzman, 2011). Although rekindled interest in Kenya's tourist sites can be partially explained by the absence of nonviolence in Kenya's political activity leading up to 2012 elections, it must be argued that the public relations activities embarked on by stakeholders in Kenya's tourism industry would account for the slow upsurge of visitors to Kenya.

Lessons Learned

Civil strife is not an uncommon phenomenon in Kenya. Indeed, since independence in 1963, the various ethnic groups that make up the country have had reason to bicker among themselves resulting in some disruption to the country's economic activity, particularly the tourism trade. For example, following the multiparty elections of 1992, the Kalenjins and the Kikuyus became embroiled in civil strife leading to the deaths of 1,500 Kenyans (Murphy, 2003). Additionally, multiparty elections since 1992 have been marred by civil strife, with the 2007 elections being the most violent. Murphy (2003) notes that these disturbances impact the gross domestic product of the country. According to him, during election years (1991–92 and 1997–98) there was a fall in the GDP, which might be attributed to ethnic violence. "The GDP fell from 1.4% to 0.8% from 1991–92, and it fell again from 3.0% to –0.8% from 1997–1998. Kenya witnessed another decline in GDP from 1999 to 2000 when the GDP fell from 1.4% to –0.4%" (Murphy, 2003).

The terrorism attacks in 1998 and 2002, coupled with threats of repeat attacks, negatively impacted the tourism trade as foreign nations cautioned their citizens against traveling to the country. It is therefore incredulous to note these incidents did not prompt the establishment of a communication crisis team prior to the aftermath of the 2008 civil unrest. Even then, the crisis management teams set up by the Kenya Tourist Board and Interface Tourism of France set their sights on preparing and implementing communication programs to cope with the aftermath of the 2008 violence. Consequently, strategies and tactics employed by both teams were short-term and could only succeed in achieving limited results. In view of the significance of tourism to Kenya's gross domestic product, the Kenya Tourist Board will need a more robust communication crisis plan to protect the industry from the negative consequences of civil strife. Kuto and Groves (2004) subscribe to the view that the Kenya Tourism Board should develop a:

> guide for managing the aftermath of terrorism. This guideline will save time by providing a roadmap to follow in a time of confusion resulting from a terrorism attack and will facilitate the recovery of tourism from the negative occurrences, thus rebuilding Kenya's image. Second, a crisis management task force needs to be set up. This task force should consist of committees or departments that should be headed by dedicated locals. Whenever possible, the heads of each department should be professionals, with expertise in the respective disciplines.

The strategies executed by the Kenya Tourism Board and other stakeholders have been aimed at European and North American tourists. With competition by other African countries for these same customers, stakeholders in the tourism industry in Kenya must begin to devise and execute tactics for exposing citizens of the emerging markets of Brazil, India, and China. There is also the need to sensitize Kenyan citizens, especially the upwardly mobile, to the pleasures derived from the patronage of their nation's tourist sites. It must be understood however, that communication strategies will produce no results unless there is a concerted effort by the political class to avoid incendiary statements that could inflame ethnic tensions and threaten the security of pleasure seekers, foreign and domestic.

Discussion Questions

1. Are there any advantages to the Kenya Tourism Board of retaining an international crisis communication team?
2. Provide a rationale for a home-grown crisis management team.
3. How would you advise the Kenya Tourism Board to stay ahead of its competitors?
4. How can social media strengthen the programming efforts of the Kenya Tourism board's crisis management team?

References

Greste, P. (2008). Kenyan crisis hammers tourism sector. *BBC News*, January 9. Retrieved from http://news.bbc.co.uk/2/hi/business/7179577.stm

Interface Tourism. (2008). Kenya 2008 political crisis—How to manage crisis communication & implement a relevant post-crisis recovery strategy. Retrieved from www.interface.com/clients/case-studies/kenya-2008-political-crisis-how-to/htm

Kilongi, M. (2008). Political crisis devastates Kenya's tourism. *McClatchey News*, January 18. Retrieved from www.mcclatchydc.com/2008/01/18/v-print/25005/political-crisis-devastates-kenya.html

Kuto, B. and Groves, J.L. (2004). The effects of terrorism: evaluating Kenya's tourism crisis. *ERTR*, 2(4), 88–97. Retrieved from http://ertr.tamu.edu.88

Murphy, C. (2003). How ethnicity emanates in present-day Kenya. *Africa Today*. Retrieved from www.du.edu/korbel/sfa/violenceinkenya.doc

Otieno-Onyando, J. (2008). Redefining the public interest: The scandal of Kenyan media. *Nandi gaa Kaburwo Blogspot*, January 30. Retrieved from http://nandi-kaburwo.blogspot.com/2008/01/redefining-public-interest-scandal-of.html

Perrett, M. (2008) Analysis: Kenya is back on the tourism map after political unrest. *Travel Weekly*, May 22. Retrieved from www.travelweekly.co.uk/articles/2008/05/22/27668/analysis-kenya-is-back-on-the-tourism-map-after-political.html

Saltzman, D. (2011).Learning from history: the impact of civil unrest on Kenya's tourism. *Travel Market Report*, February 3. Retrieved from www.travel marketreport.com

VIEWS FROM AN EXPERT

MUSA D. ILU

Musa D. Ilu, Ph.D. is an associate professor of sociology at University of Central Missouri, Warrensburg. Dr. Ilu received his doctorate from University of Missouri-Columbia in 2001. A keen observer and researcher on Kenyan politics and the role of tourism in Kenyan society, he also studies sociology of organizations and urban sociology.

The violence that occurred in Kenya following the presidential elections of 2007, caused a huge disruption to the tourism industry of Kenya. Aside from lives lost to the mayhem, thousands of tourists from Europe and North America canceled bookings to Kenya's tourist sites owing to insecurity, leading to a loss of revenue, and great unemployment. The negative impact of the post-election violence on this most vital economic resource of Kenya was not unexpected. Since the commencement of multi-party politics in 1991, Kenya has experienced civil strife during elections, causing a dislocation in the tourism industry.

Unfortunately, stakeholders are always caught unprepared to handle the aftermath of the resultant unrest. Following the first civil disturbance, which threatened the tourism trade, the Kenya Tourist Board and other stakeholders should have constituted a crisis committee to develop a communication plan for guaranteeing the continued interest in this industry by customers. This communication crisis outfit would have put in place strategies for informing, educating, and persuading the Kenyan populace to be mindful of the harm to the tourism industry when it resorts to violence as a means for seeking redress after a negative electioneering outcome. Communication tools at the disposal of the committee could have been advanced to blunt the negative images on worldwide media, which depicted Kenya as an unsafe environment for new and returning visitors. Again, interested stakeholders could, prior to any electioneering activity, alert political party functionaries of the need to dissuade supporters from engaging in acts capable of scaring visitors to the country, as any civil strife could have a catastrophic consequence on employment.

During political campaigns, it would behove politicians of all stripes to engage each other with civil tongues, with the media—both local and international—giving prominence to these interactions in coverage of electioneering activities. Testimonials by returning visitors to Kenya, especially immediately after any upheaval, would reflect well on the tourism industry. More importantly, stakeholders must take responsibility for encouraging Kenyan citizens to take pride in the flora and fauna of their beloved nation, for, as they are depicted enjoying tourist scenes during and after a civil strife, foreign visitors would feel encouraged to react positively to programs wooing them back to Kenya. Kenyans will also find it in their interest to refrain from political violence when they are made to feel that their social and economic livelihoods are at risk by recourse to unconstitutional methods for seeking redress for political grievances.

Overall, this case highlights the importance of planning for a crisis before it occurs.

Nigeria

Crisis in Nigeria's Banking and Financial Industry: Government Actions Reassure Skittish, Jittery Publics

Wole Adamolekun, Kunle Ogedengbe, and Cornelius B. Pratt

Values-driven communication practices are crucial in times of economic downturns—more so whenever such situations affect an industry whose credibility waned from 2008 to 2010 because inappropriate banking practices undermined public trust and confidence in that industry. This case study examines various communication strategies and tactics used by both the Central Bank of Nigeria and the country's banking and financial industry to reassure skittish, jittery publics—investors and everyday customers—that the nation's banking sector is still worthy of its credibility even after it violated several banking regulations and was affected by a faltering global financial system. The Central Bank of Nigeria quickly went into an offensive, injecting billions of naira into a fragile banking industry and consolidating the industry by reducing the number of banks from 80 to 24 over several months before the crisis. Communication practitioners in the industry launched a series of public-information campaigns to restore the stability of the industry and to reassure the nation that a crisis-ridden industry is still viable. Finally, to inform future actions that can engender customer confidence in the industry and guide practitioners' further investigations into how best to strengthen and expand their values-driven practice on behalf of an industry in an emerging economy, this case presents propositions as codas to corporate strategies for a more effective crisis communication.

Introduction

> The Central Bank's actions were aimed at restoring confidence [in the financial industry]. There was a high level of confidence before but this was shaken because of the doubts as to the true financial position of many banks.
>
> (Bismarck Rewane, CEO of Nigeria's Financial Derivatives Limited, in Obayiuwana, 2009, p. 31)

> Many [Nigerians] do not trust banks, creating a real barrier to the development of a savings culture. On a larger level, corruption also impedes direct foreign investment and economic development.
>
> (Wheary, 2009, p. 80)

In late February 2007, the world awoke to perhaps the first initial indications of a financial industry that was just beginning to unravel, providing stark, lucid reminders about risks associated with offering sizable home mortgages with low down-payments to borrowers with weak credit ratings—that is, subprime loans. The U.S. housing market was beginning to weaken. In the United States, several initial events precipitated a mortgage-market turmoil that eventually engulfed the global financial market in the second half of 2008, resulting in a full-blown global financial crisis through 2009.

- Item: The U.S. Federal Home Loan Mortgage Corporation (Freddie Mac) announced on February 27, 2007, that it would no longer buy the riskiest subprime mortgages (loans made to borrowers with weak credit ratings) and mortgage-related securities, making it the first sign that the U.S. economy was headed for a meltdown.
- Item: New Century Financial Corporation, a major subprime mortgage lender, filed for Chapter 11 bankruptcy protection on April 2, 2007.
- Item: Standard and Poor's and Moody's Investor Services on June 1, 2007, downgraded more than 100 bonds backed by second-lien subprime mortgages.
- Item: Bear Sterns liquidated, on July 31, 2007, two hedge funds that invested in mortgage-backed securities.
- Item: American Home Mortgage Investment Corporation, on August 6, became the second financial firm to file for Chapter 11 bankruptcy protection.
- Item: Lehman Brothers Holdings Incorporation filed for Chapter 11 bankruptcy protection on September 15, 2008.

Those events resulted in a burgeoning industry in its own right—one that generated interest in the causes of and recommendations for immediate and short-term actions for reforming financial systems in Western economies and in Africa (e.g., Arieff et al., 2009; "Fiscal implications," 2009; Grauwe, 2010; Kolb, 2010; Murinde, 2009; Onadele, 2009; Sanda, 2009; Stiglitz, 2010a, b; Williams, 2010). And it has also resulted in essays on how "studies in communication contribute to its understanding" (Chakravartty and Downing, 2010, p. 693). To complement those recommendations and the thrust of those essays on the crisis, this chapter also proposes corporate strategies backed by propositions for effective management of communication in response to the crisis.

A cause of the financial meltdown was growth in inequality within and between countries, resulting in a significant increase from the 30:1 ratio of income in the richest 20 percent to 103:1 in the poorest 20 percent (Seguino, 2010; United Nations Development Programme, 2005). The outcomes have been a decline in inflation-adjusted incomes, leading to a decline in consumption, an increase in relocation of firms and finance across borders, and growth in outsourcing production (Seguino, 2010). These have further slowed wage growth, undermined the unions' bargaining power, and reduced job growth.

Bexley et al. (2010), for example, attribute the crisis to a "domino effect" of several significant events such as the call on July 11, 2007, by Standard and Poor's for a credit watch classification on 612 subprime-backed mortgages and Countrywide Financial Corporation, one of the nation's largest mortgage lenders putting the Securities and Exchange Commission on notice of its "difficult financial condition." Bank of America purchased Countrywide on January 11, 2008, for $4 billion in stock.

The U.S. government's Financial Crisis Inquiry Commission placed the blame on the failure of the Federal Reserve Bank to develop mortgage-lending standards, loans that fueled the housing bubble, increases in banks' purchase of mortgage-backed securities, mismanagement of financial risk-taking by financiers, and breaches in accountability and of ethics at all levels (Financial Crisis Inquiry Commission, 2011).

Importance of Case

Analyzing communication strategies and tactics for managing communication programs can be crucial to improving the conduct of Nigeria's banks in a crisis (e.g., Pratt et al., 2011). But more than that, integrating that analysis with propositions on future investigations into corporate responses to crises is important for three reasons. *First*, to the degree that the recent global recession—an effect of unconscionable, unethical, and questionably risky practices in the world's major financial markets—affects banking and financial institutions in ways that include growing consumer dissatisfaction and a crisis of confidence, coupled with a diminution of trust, it is imperative that the banking industry respond to the crisis outside of governments' mandate that the industry implement a monetary policy or lend more and charge lower rates, and of banks' expectations of fiscal stimuli and bailouts. *Second*, to the degree that threats to the financial industry's reputation is fueled by a crisis of confidence and diminished trust, the stakes are higher for Nigeria's crisis communication practitioners who must now work even harder to earn the understanding and trust of their key stakeholders—both commercial entities and individual investors—as a condition for maintaining, sustaining, and expanding their market share. *Third*, in light of the preceding observations, it is important that this chapter outlines strategies and tactics that corporate affairs managers of financial institutions, particularly in emerging economies, have taken in Nigeria and elsewhere to improve the reputation of their industry. It accomplishes that purpose by presenting several propositions on communication management, thereby enabling communication practitioners in Nigeria's banking and financial industry to better enhance their key constituents' perceptions of four organizational factors: reliability, responsibility, credibility, and trustworthiness. Fombrun (1996) notes that those four factors are critical to building strong, favorable corporate reputation; to maintaining and gaining customer support; and to boosting profits in the long run.

Background of the Crisis

The International Monetary Fund predicts that the global economy will grow from 3.9 percent in 2010 to 4.3 percent in 2011 (International Monetary Fund, 2010). The World Trade Organization reported a decline of 23 percent in world merchandise trade in 2009—the largest decline in more than 50 years (World Trade Organization, 2010). The world's gross domestic product declined by 2.4 percent in 2009; in that same year, Nigeria's exports declined by 36 percent, imports by 22 percent.

The World Economic Forum held in Dalian, China, in early September 2009 reassured the global community that some headway was being made in jumpstarting limping economies and financial institutions in a good many countries, foremost among which were those in China and Japan. But at its January 2011 forum in Davos, Switzerland, while it expressed some optimism about the world economy, it was particularly concerned about geopolitical issues: the political impact of rising food prices; upheavals in the Arab world; and the January 24, 2011, Moscow's Domodedovo Airport bombing that killed 35 people and injured nearly 200.

But recessions have their upsides: they could provide opportunities for reflexivity and stock taking at both the individual and organizational levels. Reflexivity occurs when "social practices are constantly examined and reexamined in the light of incoming information about those very practices, thus constitutively altering their character" (Giddens, 1990, p. 38). Difficult economic circumstances could be a boon to crisis communication managers, a constraint on their professional responsibilities, or a threat to the very survival of their organizations. Differences in outcomes indicate differences in approaches to availing oneself or one's organizations of the challenges that emerge in an economic downturn. The Chinese, described as the "Patron Saints of Africa" (Wrong, 2009, p. B6), have offered an instructive, telling expression for crisis, "interpreted as *dangerous opportunity*" (Ulmer et al., 2011, p. 3), or *wei ji*, which means both a crisis and an opportunity; thus, the recent worldwide fiscal crisis, in the Chinese dialectical view, also presented opportunities for brand positioning and product development. Crisis communicators are expected to parlay the evolving challenges of an economic downturn into a wellspring of integrated activities and programs conducive to building and strengthening organizational reputations. The point here is that when typical marketing problems (e.g., investor relations, product distribution, and pricing) occur in turbulent environments engendered by an economic downturn and unethical business practices, they tend to spur nonmarketing problems (e.g., mistrust, dissatisfaction, incredulity, confrontation, and hostility toward an organization), calling communication practitioners to find comprehensive solutions to both marketing and nonmarketing problems; hence, the growing acknowledgment of the organizational value of ethical management, particularly in a market whose reputation has been besmirched.

Worldwide, particularly since the 1980s, major financial crises have hobbled national economies initially and regional and global economies subsequently. From the late 1980s through the 1990s, Japan's economy experienced high unemployment, an increase in public debt, a banking system saddled with high-risk loans, political instability, and failures in foreign policy, all of which resulted in what had been dubbed a "lost decade" to the people and government of Japan (Dobson, 2005; Hughes, 2004; Inoguchi, 2002; Yoshikawa, 2001). The failure of the world's then-second-largest economy reverberated regionally. In 1997, for example, the East Asian financial crisis started shortly after the Thai government devalued and floated its national currency, the baht, resulting in massive losses in the country's import sector, in weak economies in much of Asia, and in the International Monetary Fund's infusing $40 billion to stabilize the economies of Indonesia, South Korea, and Thailand. In 1998, Russia floated the ruble, leading to an inflationary spiral that peaked at 84 percent. The Swedish banking crash of the late 1990s, during which more than 70 percent of Sweden's largest banks were insolvent, was preceded by high unemployment, massive bankruptcies, and a contraction of liquidity in the banking system. That economic landscape reoccurred in 2008, when major Swedish banks lost heavily in real estate in the Baltic States. To stabilize losses from subprime mortgages and avert further losses from a debt-fueled growth in real estate, the government developed a rescue plan that injected billions of kronor into the ailing economies of its Baltic neighbors: the new democracies of Estonia, Latvia, and Lithuania.

In South America, falling exports and rising inflation and unemployment have led to grim economic predictions for the region, except in Brazil, one of the few bright spots there. Between 1999 and 2002, investors lost so much confidence in banks in Argentina that they withdrew massive amounts from their accounts and transferred huge sums to foreign banks; such capital flight led to street riots, unprecedented inflation, and unemployment.

In the United States, financial institutions, even when backed by government guarantees, continue to offer risky loans under byzantine financial structures and to trade in questionable derivatives that offer short-term profits, from which some top bankers get their sizable bonuses. U.S. financial institutions call such bonuses "I.B.G.," which means "I'll be gone after I earn my bonus," leaving the U.S. government with massive debts. The outcomes have been the highest unemployment rate since 1983 and the worst economic slowdown since the Great Depression.

Finally, in 2004, Central Bank of Nigeria (CBN) required the nation's 84 banks to recapitalize, stating that licenses would only be approved for banks that had a minimum capital base of $165 million. Mergers resulted in 24 banks meeting that threshold. In the country's stock market, however, its volatility resulted in a 70 percent loss in its value in 2008–2009. One discernible change in Nigeria's business climate is its higher-than-average strength of investor protection index of 5.7, on a 0–10 scale, with higher values indicating greater protection (World Bank, 2011). That index is a composite of three indices: (a) disclosure index, that is, disclosure of proposed transactions to the public and shareholders (5); (b) director liability index, that is, the ability of investors to hold a board of directors liable for damages (7); and (c) shareholder suits index, that is, the availability of documents that can be used during trial and the access of litigants to witnesses (5). Such scores indicate Nigeria's increasingly hospitable business environment, on which the financial industry would do well to capitalize.

Situation Analysis

Nigeria's banking and financial crisis is at some level an aberration, fueled ironically by a buoyant, growing economy and perpetuated in part by a failure of ethical conduct and by a disregard among bankers and financial counselors for compliance with strict federal regulations. Granted, the ongoing crisis of confidence has been exacerbated by significant knock-on effects of the recent global recession on the nation's economy. Onadele (2009) and Sanda (2009) identify several areas in which the global financial crisis took a toll on Nigeria: decline in government revenue, growth in deficits in balance of payments, weakness of currency exchange rates, reduction in foreign exchange reserves, increase in unemployment, and loss of confidence in the stock market and in economic reforms. Those outcomes could, however, have been managed proactively by the banking and financial industry if ethics had been fully integrated into both the workplace and corporate communications, more so as today's communication practitioners understand that achieving corporate strategic goals not only calls for communicating effectively, but also for doing so integratively, ethically, and symmetrically.

For Nigeria's banking and financial industry, then, the loss of investor confidence is a critical challenge. For the leadership of the banking industry, it was another stain on its tenuous reputation for propriety. Tinubu (2009) summarized the key issues: "Rather than adhere to best practices in lending and prudence in risk management, they seem to have fully embraced insider lending, share price manipulation and other fraudulent techniques for personal gain" (p. 3). The banking and financial landscape had all the markers of an industry at risk for collapse: mortgage speculation, housing bubble, Ponzi schemes. Even so, as recently as January 2007, the then-governor of CBN, Chukwuma Soludo, said that the banking and financial sector was the soundest it had ever been, that the nation's newly capitalized 24 commercial megabanks were "strong and reliable," that the Nigerian banking industry was the fastest growing in Africa, and that stakeholder confidence in the economy was growing. But in a February 2009 roundtable sponsored by the Nigerian Economic Society, Michael Obadan, a professor of economics at the University of Benin, Edo State, Nigeria, expressed a contrary view:

> A contingency plan for a possible bailout of banks needs to be in place so as to contain the macroeconomic implications of possible distress in the banking system. This would take the form of injection of funds into sick banks through acquisition of shares which would be bought back when they recover.
>
> (Michael Obadan, in Onwuamaeze, 2009, p. 21)

At the crux of the crisis in Nigeria, then, are three major issues: (a) customer dissatisfaction, (b) crisis of confidence, and (c) a diminution of trust and of relationship commitment.

Hon and Grunig (1999) defined *satisfaction* as "[t]he extent to which each party feels favorably disposed toward the other because positive expectations about the relationship are reinforced. A satisfying relationship is one in which the benefits outweigh the costs" (p. 3). Customer dissatisfaction, therefore, typically occurs when the risks to the customer are high and the benefits are minuscule.

Trust, however, has had a variety of definitions: it is a commodity maintained and nurtured by relationships, accountability, credibility, and by the organizational systems in which transactions occur (Brown, 2008; Dasgupta, 1988); a communicative act (Luhmann, 1979); and a product of confidence (Giddens, 1990).

Hon and Grunig, iterating Giddens, defined it as "[o]ne party's level of confidence in and willingness to open oneself to the other party" (1999, p. 3). They identified three dimensions of trust: integrity, dependability, and competence, all of which communication practitioners consider vital to their exchanges with stakeholders. From the standpoint of relationship marketing, Morgan and Hunt (1994) similarly conceptualize trust "as existing when one party has confidence in an exchange partner's reliability and integrity" (p. 23). Rotter (1967), iterating both "dependability" and "reliability," defined trust as "a generalized expectancy that the oral or written statements of other people can be relied upon" (p. 653).

But Luhmann (1979, 1988) makes a distinction between confidence and trust, noting that the former shows an absence of doubt whereas the latter is inherently linked to the awareness of risk, to uncertainty and anxiety (as in a global recession), to emotions, and to the absence of appropriate knowledge. Social theorists argue that interpersonal trust enables a people to manage the complexities and anxieties that are part of modern society (Giddens, 1990;

Luhmann, 1988). The higher the investor's awareness of risk, the lower the confidence in the financial institution—and vice versa. A commonality between these two social phenomena is the nature of the action or inaction by a financial staffer. Absent communication that fosters institutional proximity to the client, the banker remains abstruse to the client, undercutting any possibility for exchange and understanding on both sides, and heightening the possibility among clients that the financial institution does not support their best interests.

Such anxieties have been exacerbated by corporate practices that engendered an economic downturn in the first place and that further eroded the fragile confidence that customers had in financial institutions.

Within the crisis communication context, trust is undermined when one party loses confidence in an exchange partner's integrity, dependability, and competence. Thus, when organizations engage in, or perpetuate, practices that undermine the very essence of customer–institutional bonds, crisis communications are placed on a Sisyphean task.

Hon and Grunig (1999) define *commitment* as "[t]he extent to which each party believes and feels that the relationship is worth spending energy to maintain and promote" (p. 3). Its dimensions are continuance commitment and affective commitment.

Customer satisfaction is a strong, positive predictor of trust and trust is a strong predictor of commitment (Ki and Hon, 2007). Interestingly, when trust was controlled for in a path model, there was a significant but weak direct effect of satisfaction on commitment, indicating that organizations should go well beyond customer satisfaction if they want to have a constant stream of repeat customers and to expand their operations, a finding supported by earlier research (Hon and Grunig, 1999; Huang, 2001; Jo, 2006). All three constructs, as global measures of organization–public relationships (Jo, 2006), can be instrumental in addressing the everyday corporate anxieties that stem from a global recession.

Such corporate anxieties are also palpable in Nigeria, Africa's second-largest economy. The country has paltry foreign exchange reserves of between $32 billion and $36 billion (as of Septmber 2011), a negligible foreign debt, a trade surplus, and a foreign direct investment that quadrupled between 2000 and 2006. Its telecommunications industry is poised to overtake the continent's largest—that of South Africa. In recent months, its credibility and legitimacy among its stakeholders have been questioned. In essence, then, Nigeria's banking and financial crisis is an outcome of the country's economic success, business growth, and political sophistication. And its corporate affairs managers have benefited professionally from their memberships of organizations such as the Association of Corporate Affairs Managers of Banks, the Nigerian Institute of Public Relations, African Public Relations Association, and the International Public Relations Association, and are, thus, able to articulate effectively "the import of communication as the *only* [emphasis added] way for banks to keep their heads above water" (Dangogo, 2008, p. 213). At the industry's core, however, are concerns about a crisis of confidence and concerns over its future, both enabled by abstruse, opaque, perhaps illegal, conditions under which some major loans were offered or irregular transactions undertaken.

This case study on Nigeria's banking and financial industry in particular and on Africa's financial institutions in general is grounded in three realities—part historical, part immediate. First, historically, Nigeria's banking industry has been a driving force in political developments, business growth, and economic sustenance. Well before Nigeria's looming independence from British colonial administration in 1960, its two colonial banks—the British Colonial Bank established in 1916 and acquired in 1925 by Barclays Bank Ltd. and renamed Barclays Bank (Dominion, Colonial and Overseas) and the Bank of British West Africa Ltd.—responded strategically to changing political and economic realities on the ground (Bostock, 1991). The Barclays Overseas Development Corporation was incorporated on January10, 1946, as a wholly-owned finance and development subsidiary of Barclays (DCO); it professed interest in Nigeria's indigenous economy, particularly in agricultural banking. The Bank of British West Africa provided direct medium- and long-term loans, of which colonial and native administrations availed themselves.

At the dawn of Nigeria's independence, both banks refocused their competitive practices to the dismay of upstart indigenous banks (e.g., the National Bank of Nigeria Ltd., Agbonmagbe Bank, and the African Inter-continental Bank Ltd.). Those practices gave them a hooded, predatory look and feel among Nigerian patriots, nationalists, and elites whose denunciation of the exploitation of Africa to support the nondomestic interests of the colonial administration stoked the nationalists' suspicion and ire. Consequently, the colonial banks were pressured into endearing themselves to Nigerian investors not only by increasing small-business lending to them, but by offering them loans at unusually favorable terms; by implementing and publicizing national development programs; and by engaging in corporate philanthropy through society-focused campaigns that are still the hallmarks of today's Nigeria's fully indigenous banking industry. Barclays (DCO), for example, immediately emphasized "commercial education, encouragement of savings and financial assistance to small businesses in retail and manufacturing. Hence Barclays expected the emerging middle class to be a pool for potential staff as well as customers" (Decker, 2006, p. 11). The point here is that Nigeria's banking industry's *sui generis* history of helping ensure the birth and the development of a fledgling nation, of establishing major stakes in the country's economic and social well-being, and of building non-usurious financial institutions prima facie underscores the importance of this topic.

The second reality is explosive global growth in Africa's banks, which are opening offices and establishing partnerships in Asia (Norbrook, 2009). And the continent's emerging markets offer significant business and investment opportunities that have fueled the growth of a lucrative, sophisticated financial sector and a revolution of sorts in the banking sector (Babarinde, 2009; Campbell, 2009). In 2009, the region attracted nearly $1 billion in net fund inflows ("Africa attracts," 2009). From 2004 to 2007, Nigeria had the highest proportion (34.8 percent) of foreign direct investment inflows (a major source of external finance) on the continent; that of South Africa, the continent's largest economy and second-largest recipient of fund inflows, was less than one-half Nigeria's (Arieff et al., 2009). Nigeria is becoming increasingly cosmopolitan, and its banks are the fastest-growing in Africa and are among the fastest-growing in the world. In 2010, the country had the second-highest number (three) of the top 20 banks in Africa and most (18) of Africa's 200 largest banks ("The top 200," 2011). Its growing population, political transformation, and economic reforms are attracting massive foreign investment and an economic revival. The latter is being buoyed in part by the country's "Vision 20: 2020," by which it is striving to become one of the 20 largest economies in the world by 2020.

Third, the country's banking industry, beginning in July 2004, was overhauled massively through consolidating 80 commercial banks into 24 stronger megabanks, a move "necessitated by the pervasive weaknesses and uncertainty of the banking system and the need to re-engineer and fast-track a system that will engender confidence and power a new economy" (Soludo, 2007, p. 1). CBN had provided nearly $2 billion to bail out eight ailing banks and was taking several widespread measures to sustain and enhance the health of the country's financial system.

Government's and Industry's Initial Responses

Government

Nigeria's government's actions were undertaken initially to protect and enhance the credibility of a faltering, teetering financial industry. Those actions included the following: established principles for corporate governance; set up a CBN/Banks Sinking Fund, a $1.3 billion commercial Agricultural Credit Scheme, and a CBN backing for foreign credits; regulated "margin" lending, scope of banking activities and ancillary matters, and currency outsourcing and cash management; adopted universal banking and included the Chinese yuan as a foreign currency of exchange and trade in Nigeria; and launched a "Know Your Customer Campaign."

CBN Governor Sanusi (2010) identified eight factors that had contributed to a fragile banking industry:

- large and sudden capital inflows that cause macro-economic instability;
- major failures in corporate governance;
- serious lack of investor and consumer protection;
- inadequate disclosure and transparency about banks' financial position;
- critical gaps in the regulatory framework and regulation;
- uneven supervision and enforcement;

- unstructured governance and management processes at CBN;
- significant weaknesses in Nigeria's business environment.

Several incidents underscore the extent of the challenge. A CBN audit that began early in 2009 identified 10 banks that had offered large loans without having adequate collateral, which were then invested in a volatile stock market. On August 14, 2009, Sanusi fired five chief executive officers of those banks: Afribank, FinBank, Intercontinental Bank, Oceanic Bank, and Union Bank. Several months later he fired the CEOs of three additional banks: Bank PHB, Equatorial Trust Bank, and Spring Bank. Two other banks—Unity Bank and Wema Bank—were advised to improve their management. Additionally, the CBN streamlined banks' governance, for example, by separating managing director from the chief executive officer position and limiting tenure in each to 10 years.

To further reassure skittish investors and a jittery general public about the vitality of the financial industry, the CBN daringly infused $3.9 billion into nine banks as liquidity support and long-term loans. And to ensure the return and maintenance of the international community's confidence in Nigeria's banks, the country's federal government required that banks adopt, by the end of 2010, the International Financial Reporting Standards, which require quarterly and annual reports consistent with the best international practices.

Erastus Akingbola, CEO of Intercontinental Bank and one of five bank CEOs fired in mid-August 2009 by Sanusi for mismanagement, symbolizes the banking climate that is a concern to CBN and to the Economic and Financial Crimes Commission (EFCC), which filed criminal charges against him for money laundering. He fled to the United Kingdom to avoid prosecution. Beginning January 2010, the EFCC began confiscating his assets and properties in Dubai, Ghana, Nigeria, and the United Kingdom. On August 4, 2010, he returned voluntarily to Nigeria to face criminal charges.

Cecilia Ibru, a former managing director and chief executive officer of Oceanic Bank and also one of the five fired top bank executives, was prosecuted by the EFCC for multibillion-dollar banking irregularities in August 2009. She pleaded guilty to three of 25 charges against her, was sentenced to a six-month jail term on October 8, 2010, and was ordered to forfeit $1.2 billion in cash and assets to the government.

In August 2009 and again in October 2009, the EFCC arrested Peter U. Ololo, a stockbroker and founder of Falcon Securities Ltd., and charged him with conspiring with two bank officials at Afribank and Union Bank to manipulate the value of their banks' stocks; the two bank officials were also charged with making improper loans to Ololo. It was alleged that Ololo's brokerage firm used funds provided by banks eager to have the price of their stocks inflated to buy large quantities of stocks, creating the impression that those stocks were desirable. When the value of the stocks was artificially high, Ololo would then announce a public offering at a discount price. That scheme paid huge dividends to Falcon Securities and to the conniving banks.

On July 19, 2010, the government signed into law an Asset Management Corporation of Nigeria to "stimulate the recovery of the financial system by acquiring nonperforming loans [toxic assets] from the banks and assisting them in improving their capital and liquidity" (Ohai, 2010, p. 4).

And on August 5, 2010, Nigeria Securities and Exchange Commission (SEC) fired Ndi Okereke-Onyiuke, director-general and CEO of the Nigerian Stock Exchange (NSE), for "its inadequate oversight of affairs under its purview, ongoing litigation, allegations of financial mismanagement, governance challenges, and the inordinate delays in the implementation of the succession plan for The Exchange" ("Headliners," 2010, p. 16) The SEC also suspended the NSE president, Aliko Dangote, "pending the outcome of the ongoing litigation" against his appointment.

Industry

The initial response of the industry was tantamount to playing a wait-and-see game, particularly because the audit report was issued piecemeal—and at two different times. The industry collaborated with the government by complying fully with its directives. Even though CBN's actions were challenged in the courts, those legal actions were perceived as vehicles toward resolving the disparate interests of the key players. This was because no stakeholder questioned the integrity of the CBN in auditing the banks and its subsequent actions. The industry in one way or the other supported the CBN action.

Communication Goals, Objectives, Strategies, and Tactics

With new management in place, letting the stakeholders know the true position of things in the affected banks became a major issue. The CBN urged the banks to appoint public relations consultants to help manage the crisis, emphasizing media relations.

Central Bank of Nigeria

Goal 1: To ensure the health of Nigeria's banking and financial industry.

Objective: To enforce regulations on banking and financial practices.

Strategy: Alerted the banking and financial community of the CBN's resolve to ensure the financial health of the industry.

Tactics:

- held meetings with executives of major Nigerian banks;
- sent auditors to review periodically banks' declared assets;

- indicted executives whose banks did not have a healthy liquidity;
- threatened to shut down near-insolvent banks; and
- increased the capital base of banks from $13.3 million to $166.67 million.

Goal 2: To ensure communications between industry and the general public.

Objective: To bring key constituents in the banking industry frequently updated on CBN's activities and programs.

Strategy: Used in-house professionals to accomplish communication activities

Tactics:

- used CBN's website as the preferred medium to update information on the crisis; and
- held meetings with executives of the banking and financial industry.

The Banking and Financial Industry

Goal 1: To restore stakeholders confidence in the nation's banking and financial institutions.

Objective: To enhance the banking and financial institutions' status and to expand their market share.

Strategy: Engaged in structured communications with all stakeholders: regulators, shareholders, staff, customers, and international credit organizations.

Tactics:

- announced banks' recovery plans in the media, for example, as the managing director and chief executive officer of Oceanic International Bank did on several occasions;
- used social media internally as conversational fora to enable their employees to better understand organizational roles, to encourage group cohesiveness and improved work processes, to develop strong professional ties with their customers, and to respond to customer complaints; and
- used social media externally to promote several aspects of the industry's operations and products. Guaranty Trust Bank (GTBank), a trendsetter in the use of social media among Africa's financial institutions—the bank is on YouTube, Twitter, Flickr and Facebook—has a program titled "15 minutes with Tayo Aderinokun," a former managing director at the bank. In that webcast, he enunciates his bank's strong culture of professionalism

and its passion for integrity, connects with customers, and responds to questions posted on his bank's website. GTBank also uses an e-magazine, NDANI, for that same purpose. Zenith Bank has "Just for Fun," by which its employees communicate with customers on just about every banking subject.

Goal 2: To increase revenue sources.

Objective: To diversify the income base from interest income and management fees.

Strategy: Retained services of a media-relations consultancy and employed those of Eddy Ademosu, one of the country's top communication experts in the banking industry.

Tactics:

- launched campaigns, such as "Today is a new day to start something new" (Oceanic Bank);
- held press briefings, during which efforts in managing the financial crisis were relayed to stakeholders;
- used social media to encourage retail banking, to generate customer deposits, and to improve revenue generation;
- popularized catch phrases, such as those of Union Bank: "To be the best of the best to bank on" and "To be the foremost financial institution with the most satisfied customers";
- used slogans, for example, "Big, Strong, Reliable Bank" (Union Bank); and
- updated various stakeholders on the ideals and events in the bank.

Outcomes Assessment

Today, all of Nigeria's 24 commercial megabanks are operating at full throttle, largely because of the timely intervention of CBN, which announced in January 2011 in a paid advertisement that none of the banks in the country would be liquidated. That advertisement was signed by Muhammed M. Abdullahi, director of CBN's corporate communication. Anecdotal evidence suggests that public perceptions of the industry are now generally positive. Even so, some of the banks in which public relations was given short shrift are still grappling with significant losses to their reputations.

Lessons Learned

The first two authors of this case study are active members of Nigeria's and of the international communication practitioner communities, and the first serves as secretary general of the African Public Relations Association, a continent-wide organization of educators and practitioners. The lessons listed below (in short order) are a culmination of the first two authors' many years of public relations practice, as well as those that emanated from discussions of the Association of Corporate Affairs Managers of Banks, to which the third author presented an earlier version of this case study on September 24–27, 2009.

- Communication is even more critical in crises, and that the downgrading of communications departments of some of Nigeria's major banks, except Union Bank and Spring Bank, was a factor in the onset of the industry's credibility crisis. Today, Intercontinental Bank has an assistant general manager of communications who manages the bank's image-restoration activities; the previous occupant of that post had been fired during the crisis.
- For public relations to be effective, it must operate as a top-management function. In organizations in which it is peripheral or incidental, its impact is minuscule. Banking and financial institutions, for example, Union Bank and Spring Bank, in which the function operated at the core of management, weathered the crisis much more easily than those in which the function operated as peripheral to the organizational mission.
- The banks that retained outside consultants limited their contracted activities to media relations, undermining all possibilities for engaging in the strategic use of public relations. Little wonder, then, that such tactical approach to a key issue of image enhancement and restoration left the banks reeling from massive damage to their credibility and financial health.
- Nigeria's banking and financial crisis was exacerbated by the absence of formal crisis communication plans. The downside of the absence of such proactive measures was evident in the banks' failure to contain the crisis early on.
- The banks' failure to use the strategic first voice in crisis communication robbed them of the advantages of that voice; therefore, the credibility and persuasiveness of that voice were lost to all unknowing cadre of communication practitioners in the banking and financial industry.

Proposed Strategies and Propositions

The communication strategies of Nigeria's banking and financial industry have been largely discrete rather than coordinated, perhaps a reflection of the semantic ambiguity over the true meaning of integrated communications, particularly when used during a crisis. This case proposes the blending, unifying, aligning, and coordinating various communication and promotional activities and campaigns in an integrated communications program. Three caveats on the strategies: (a) that practitioners in that sector variably use some of these strategies, which, collectively, offer mammoth opportunities for an integrated approach to a more effective management of crisis communications; (b) that they are presented here largely as touchstones of optimal crisis communications; and (c) that they can be accomplished using extant resources either in their original state or in slightly modified ways to avoid incurring significant additional expenses or as add-ons to existing activities, all of which can be reasonably justified in the midst of current corporate economic challenges.

While all of those problems are related in some measure to the structural operations of Nigeria's banking and financial industry and to the characteristics of its environment, the directions taken in this case are strictly normative-behavioral—that is, identifying strategies that underpin the conduct of those operations. Against the background of the preceding observations, we present six strategies for effective crisis communication, each of which is backed by a proposition as coda.

Strategy 1: Build Trust in Every Facet of the Stakeholder Experience

More than a dozen years ago, Pine and Gilmore (1999) declared that goods and services were no longer enough; that customer satisfaction as we knew it was becoming blasé; that the service economy was peaking; and that a new, emerging economy, which they labeled "the experience economy," which engaged individuals in a personal, memorable way, was coming of age. They wrote: "While commodities are fungible, goods tangible, and services intangible, experiences are memorable . . . and inherently personal" (pp. 11–12). Experiential communications can ensure that customers have a seamless total experience that is unique to each customer; that is both mediated and direct; and that serves simultaneously as a strategic expression of the customer's self-identity, social group, culture or subculture, and emotion or affect.

Consider, for example, some slogans of Nigeria's banks: "Expanding your world" (Skye Bank); "Touching your life in more ways than one" (Diamond Bank); and "In your best interest" (Zenith Bank). All seek to appeal to the customer's personal, unique experience as a reason for becoming associated with a particular financial institution, in contradistinction to "Big, Strong, Reliable" (Union Bank) and "Inspired. Motivated. Involved" (Stanbic IBTC Bank), each of which focuses on a bank's attributes. Experiential marketing has the potential to make consumer-focused slogans a lived experience—and it could ameliorate the effects of a crisis on an organization.

Two consumer trends make personalization of communications even more critical. The first is the growing impact of the attention economy in which the low cost of transmitting advertising and the burgeoning number of marketing channels available to consumers create a scarcity of consumer attention. Thus, consumer attention in an attention economy is an increasingly rare commodity (Davenport and Beck, 2001). The second is the growing attraction of the "demand-pull" information model, by which customers are actively seeking out, from social networks such as Facebook, Twitter, MySpace, blogs and podcasts, information that emotionally appeals to their unique sense of self, their needs and wants, quite apart from the offerings on "supply-push" traditional media. Globally, social media wield significant influences on both interpersonal and organizational communications. On the interpersonal front, they are used to create and share information (Zhong et al., 2011). Organizationally, they are used by employees to better understand organizational roles, to encourage group cohesiveness and improved work processes, and to develop strong professional and personal ties (Baehr and Alex-Brown, 2010; Baehr and Schaller, 2010). Outside of organizations, employees have been known to use those media to promote their company on by posting photographs of company events, products, and promotional items and by moderating discussion fora (Freeman and Chapman, 2010). It is understandable, then, that Nigeria's banking industry seems enamored with those media.

It has been argued, however, that the dominance of entertainment and tourism on YouTube videos from Africa undermines their informative and educational value to viewers (Wall, 2009); however, there is also the possibility for the increasing use of that medium to present business news and to create and project the desired persona of the banking and financial industry. Brody (2001) underscores that point: "Ability to shape audience experience grows ever more important in public relations as the impact of traditional media deteriorates" (p. 20). Personalizing the banking experience is consistent with four banking and financial industry models proffered by Sanusi (2010) and which could be implemented over 10 years: (a) international; (b) national; (c) regional; and (d) mono-line and specialized banks (e.g., interest-charges-free Islamic banking). All will have varying capitalization base.

What do stakeholders in, say, focus groups, tell us about how we could more innovatively personalize our bank? Some recommendations: that the banking and financial industry consider minimally renovating and appointing its premises as a social setting—that is, as also site for social gatherings or as a neighborhood gathering place; for intellectual discussions of financial issues; for lectures, seminars and workshops; for walk-in professional consultations on small-business management and on investment plans; and for ancillary financial services such as vetting or verifying the authenticity of certain documents. Banks should offer a *total* experience. They could also adopt new message-distribution strategies by participating in social networks in which their own customers already participate and engage them frequently on bank-related issues. The perception of a bank as an ogre—a cold, staid, remote place—is inconsistent with the experience economy. Banks should be welcoming and inviting and engaging in extensive, consistent stakeholder studies to identify needs, wants, attitudes and values, and implement plans to make experiential communications a reality. For the (individual) business customer, for example, a lobby could be equipped with computer work-stations, free high-speed wi-fi, and other low-cost office essentials. Such facilities can humanize even a financial behemoth and convey a message of a bank that is truly "As unique as you" (Ecobank Nigeria). The preceding analysis leads us to the first proposition.

P1: Customers' personal or individual experiences with their banks predict their level of involvement with, their loyalty to, and their confidence in their banks and in their products—three variables that can explain the extent of a public fallout from a bank's crisis.

Strategy 2: Emphasize Ethics in the Workplace and in all Communications

The Nigerian business environment, not least that of the banking and financial industry, has historically been challenged by unethical practices (Erondu et al., 2004; Onah, 1991). Akinsola Akinfemiwa, a former group managing director and chief executive of Skye Bank, told a conference of top Nigerian government officials that "The case for business to uphold ethical standards is not only a matter of doing the right thing; it also makes business sense in the long run" (Akinfemiwa, 2001, p. 4). Bunke (1988), in stating the importance of ethics, said that a

> business system will endure only so long as it is solidly rooted in a meaningful idealism; that, in the end, the pursuit of money—or as taught in finance, maximizing profits—is legitimate as long as it is a form of scorekeeping on activities designed to "do good."
>
> (Bunke, 1988, p. 7)

The ethical climate of banks in Nigeria taxes crisis communication. How does a bank's corporate affairs department communicate its defense of alleged wrongdoing by a handful of employees? Under what circumstances should it disclose all that it knows in an attempt to keep stakeholders as informed about allegations of unethical, let alone illegal, practices as they are encouraged to be loyal to their financial institution? Shouldn't a bank's media relations operation field occasional on-site media visits? Answers to those questions suggest the second proposition.

P2: To the degree that a bank's crisis communication programs serve as its conscience, crisis communication in the bank's markets should be demonstrably guided by delineated standards, principles, and codes of ethical corporate behavior.

Strategy 3: Expose Crisis Communication Practitioners to Applied Ethics

Several national and continent-wide programs provide opportunities for improving organizational ethics in Africa. On February 19, 2009, for example, a nonprofit organization, Leadership, Effectiveness, Accountability and Professionalism (LEAP), convened, in Lagos, officials from both business and government to discuss "Business Ethics—A Prerequisite for Successful and Sustainable Business in Nigeria." Similarly, in August 3–5, 2009, the Business Ethics Network of Africa, which has memberships in 25 African countries, held a conference to facilitate discussions of business ethics between academics and practitioners and to disseminate information on the continent's best ethical practices.

The Lagos Business School, as well as scores of higher-education institutions in Nigeria and elsewhere on the continent, offers intensive courses in ethics (Gichure, 2006; Milanzi, 1997). Such courses generally use role-play, simulations, and case studies to strengthen participants' commitment to improving business ethics in Africa.

Even though crisis communication practitioners have benefited immensely from such exchanges, questions have arisen regarding their scope and content. Gichure (2006) argues that the cultural orientation of the community must be integrated into such instruction. For example, virtue ethics focuses on an individual's disposition (e.g., character and integrity) rather than on the group; even so, the individual is not alone, an attribute consistent with the African proverb, "a person becomes virtuous through the virtue of others." The virtuous crisis communicator would not merely create opportunities for a commitment between a manager and a client, but between the latter and the bank, thereby improving wholesale organizational performance.

An empirical study of commercial bank employees in Nigeria confirmed the applicability of ethical theories to the Nigerian banking environment (Erondu et al., 2004). Therefore, it is recommended that training modules integrate a country's cultural landscape, as argued by Gichure (2006), into classical ethical theories such as the following:

- Teleological theories (e.g., utilitarianism)—an act is moral if it results in more good than harm.
- Deontological theories hold that the morality of an act is based on its conformity to moral principles or rules, not on its consequences. Kant (1964), perhaps the best-known deontologist, developed the categorical imperative as the ultimate test of morality, stating that a moral rule, maxim, or principle must be universal and unchanging and that people never should be used merely as means, but must have the ability to choose for themselves.

- Virtue ethics grounds ethics in character, not rules; it focuses on the disposition of people to act morally (professional competence, honesty, courage, and compassion). And this theory of virtue ethics interfaces with Nigeria's communitarian notion of ethics (Limbs and Fort, 2000), which balances individual values with community-shared values and practices.
- Universal ethical egoism (or the self-interest criterion), in which the individual's (or the bank's) best interest dominates the ethical decision-making process.
- Situation ethics or ethical relativism, while not a classical ethical theory in its own right, has had a large following since Boas (1887) argued that "civilization is not something absolute, but that it is relative, and that our ideas and conceptions are true only so far as our civilization goes" (p. 589). Christians et al. (1993) write: "Ethical relativism is the belief that because moral judgments vary across cultures and historical periods, all moral systems are equally good, even if they are antithetical" (p. 59). Such has been a longstanding issue that threatens business ethics. A challenge to classical ethical theory is the endearing appeal of moral relativism couched within the frameworks of cultural diversity and of cultural relativism. Banking practices in Nigeria, for example, the exchange of significant gifts in transactions, could be culturally justified. But can such cultural relativism be decoupled from moral relativism—or should it?

Such an attempt to enhance the ethical conduct of crisis communication practitioners has the potential to transform perceived institutional liability and leadership, their demonstrated commitment to ethics in planning, decision making, program implementation and communication, and their integration of ethics into everyday corporate activities. And such attempts go well beyond codes of ethics, which "seem pale and toothless" (Bunke, 1988, p. 7), and about which professionals from investment banks are ambivalent (Norberg, 2009). The organizational importance of and concern for ethics suggest the third proposition.

P3: Corporate governance, based on disclosure, transparency, and board liability, is effective crisis communication management that draws upon and adheres to the tenets of classical ethical theories.

Strategy 4: Elevate Strategic Action to Communicative Action

Strategies grounded in research and guided by core organizational values are the lynchpins of the goals and objectives of crisis communication. But such strategies are inherently hamstrung in their reach in building the reputations of our financial institutions. Crisis communicators are, therefore, encouraged to adopt a communicative response to managing organizational diminution of trust.

Enter Jürgen Habermas, a critical theorist and rationalist. Habermas (1984, 1987) distinguishes between strategic action and communicative action, asserting that the former is success-oriented, the latter grounded in an orientation toward reaching an understanding. Because communicative action has the hallmarks of communication symmetry—openly inviting stakeholders to accept, challenge, refute, deliberate, discuss, negotiate, or reject the bases of ideal speech acts and symmetry conditions—it has a much stronger potential than strategic action to maximize opportunities for using crisis communication to respond to industry challenges. All of those possible outcomes emphasize full community participation as the desideratum of making significant inroads into a subject that, for some banks in Nigeria, has been an overwhelmingly enduring blot on their public perception. As Erondu et al. (2004) disconcertingly note, "Nigerian business is considered by many to be one of the most corrupt environments in the world. [I]t appears that Nigerian bank employees share the same ethical and moral compass as people in other business environments" (p. 356).

Habermas distinguishes between genuine and false consensus through an emphasis on what he describes as an ideal speech situation, a symmetry condition in which there is unconstrained dialogue to which all speakers have access, and in which they have the prevailing force of better judgment. It is devoid of domination or sheer influence and bereft of all coercive distortion. Holtzhausen (2000) argues that it is difficult for communication managers to buy into real symmetry because consensus associates with the demise of thinking, represents an unjust outcome that does not satisfy any party, and engenders challenges from the postmodern concepts of dissensus and dissymmetry. "Seeking consensus," Holtzhausen argues, implies seeking an unjust settlement in which the most powerful, usually organizations, get their way ... In addition, consensus sacrifices the recognition of differences for superficial treatment" (pp. 106–107).

But Habermas's ideal speech, defined in relation to a number of symmetry conditions, does not subscribe to the Holtzhausen (2000) position in that ideal speech conditions require that (a) there must be a symmetrical distribution of opportunities to contribute to discussions—that is, all can speak; (b) there must be opportunities for participants to raise any and all subjects they wish to see addressed, that is, nothing is "off the table"; and (c) there must be an inviting environment to discuss every topic fully and to the satisfaction of those who raised the topic (Habermas, 1990). Actors seek, through speech acts, an orientation toward understanding, consensus and agreement rather than toward fulfilling their own specific agendas or personal goals. Such a theoretical perspective emphasizes planning for crisis through widespread community participation, dialogue, consensus, cooperation, and negotiation, not necessarily through strategic action. Habermas identifies as a speech act that which is being engaged by both senders and receivers of linguistic acts (read: message content) geared toward understandings that are rationally negotiated by all parties. But there are limits to such negotiations. While, say, parties to a speech act can understand the conditions under which a message recipient (a bank's current or prospective customer) can understand, accept and endorse the speech act and be persuaded by its validity claims, neither the recipient nor the sender can know the conditions of the acceptability of the speech act relative to the actual attitudes and beliefs of the individual other, thereby, fostering openness and the absence of coercion in exchanges.

To summarize, communicative action should be *the* activity of choice among communication practitioners of the banking and financial industry for good reason: its exchanges are free from the distorting influences of high power distance, which is typical in the Nigerian culture; unequal, asymmetrical relationships; closed, myopic thinking; fixed, unchallenged assumptions; and a subtle, manipulative orientation. It, therefore, overcomes barriers to efforts toward reaching a true consensus, a possible outcome that leads to the fourth proposition.

P4: Organization–client communication grounded in symmetry as communicative action will engender more favorable perceptions among stakeholders and limit the fallout from a bank's crisis than will strategic action.

Strategy 5: Emphasize Cause Marketing Communication as a Promotional Device for the Corporate Brand

An illustration of brand uniqueness is provided by Glitnir Bank, one of the top three commercial banks in Iceland. In 2006, its media-relations program coordinated a massive campaign in response to that country's declining international profile and reputation, particularly in financial markets. Glitnir had benefited immensely from a robust economy fueled in large part by a booming real-estate market and market expansions in Norway, Denmark, Luxembourg, and in the United Kingdom. In 2005, the year before Iceland's economic crisis occurred, Glitnir posted a 60 percent increase in profits. But Iceland's economy declined suddenly early in 2006 on the heels of financial reports that downgraded the country's sovereign debt and the ensuing negative media reports about a looming macroeconomic crisis. The bank, which interpreted the crisis as an opportunity, charged its communications staff with raising the awareness of current and prospective investor publics about Iceland's overall strong economy and with reassuring them about its stronger economic prospects. A commercial bank was in the forefront of coordinating a nation's efforts in educating skittish stakeholders about a media-fueled situation.

Consumers do not stop using bank services because of a limping economy; they stop patronizing banks because of their perceived higher or additional investment or transaction risks, their abysmally low satisfaction from their interactions, and their maligned trust in organizations. One innovative, proactive area in which branding, as a marketing tool, can be particularly helpful to Nigeria's commercial and investment banks is in the country's anticorruption efforts. While this might appear counterintuitive in the current ethical climate, governments alone cannot fight corruption—even in the banking and financial industry. Consequently, the World Bank, the United Nations Global Program Against Corruption, the World Economic Forum Partnering Against Corruption Initiative are working to bring fairness and integrity to businesses worldwide. The World Bank (2006) sees a "crucial role [for] . . . the business community in demanding better governance, especially where government leadership is lacking" (p. vi). It engages the private sector as vital partners in promoting the demand for good governance and anticorruption and in championing environmental and social causes. To the degree that Nigeria's banks operate in environments in which they are vulnerable to corrupt practices, their integrity inherently raises questions. And to the degree that a corporation has "a main role to play in promoting transparency and curbing corruption" (Calderón et al., 2009, p. 321), and is considered a partner against corruption, it stands to reason that Nigeria's maligned banking industry can still link its brand image to a nagging, gnawing social phenomenon; increase its visibility within the context of a major cause; and enhance its stature nationally and globally. When one's brand is so connected with a cause the payoff can be robust. As Warner (2009) observes, "What many fail to realize . . . is that there's a great opportunity to flourish, build and/or reinvent a brand during difficult economic times" (p. 2).

Nigeria's Skye Bank, for example, has identified several causes that include providing health care for all Nigerians, promoting obedience for the law, and assisting the federal government to accomplish "Vision 20: 2020," by which Nigeria strives to become one of the 20 largest economies in the world by 2020. GTBank champions the social and professional importance of earning trust by asserting matter-of-factly that "[t]rust is earned, never given," and by exhorting Nigerians to "[b]e trustworthy. Earn the trust of people around you." Crisis communicators could capitalize on similar opportunities on various governments' and social institutions' agendas—for example, improving public health or enhancing higher education—and causes—for example, defusing ethnic and religious tensions—as veritable initiatives in revamping their reputations as they build *the* preferred brand image. Such attempts could result in the banking industry's engaging in "communicative governance" as its branding program. The brand is indicative of the essence of the product.

P5: The preferred—and desired—product brand is a function of the nature of the communicative governance of a financial institution and serves as a bulwark against a public fallout from an institution's crisis.

Strategy 6: Determine Communication Outcomes and Apply Results to Subsequent Programs

Measuring the outcomes of communication efforts is crucial to ascertaining and ensuring that communication objectives (attitudinal—how people feel about a crisis, behavioral—how people act in a crisis, and knowledge or awareness—what people know about a crisis) are accomplished; that necessary program changes are justified; that communications are being optimized; and that management support is enlisted for acquiring resources even for those communication efforts (e.g., engaging in publicity to communicate the right messages or fostering effective media relations) that are viewed as cost, not profit, centers. In essence, outcomes assessments are an indication of how well we use scarce resources during a macroeconomic crisis to, say, maintain brand loyalty.

Even though a variety of assessment methods are used in different communication circumstances, evaluation research is conducted to enable an organization to conclude confidently that its interventions contributed to its desired outcomes. This also could mean using a pretest-posttest design with control groups or a control construct design (Fischer, 1995); or longitudinal surveys (e.g., trend, panel or cohort-trend); or interrupted time-series design (or in-group comparisons). The control construct design has four key strengths: (a) ease of design and use, (b) inexpensiveness, (c) appropriateness in measuring campaign effectiveness in meeting specific attitudinal and behavioral objectives, and (d) acceptance by management.

If a campaign objective were to have a positive media portrayal of one's financial institution, then a systematic content analysis of news and opinion articles could empirically document the success of the institution's media relations and outreach efforts, initially as a measure of process evaluation and then as outcomes evaluation among message recipients. But it must be noted that the audiences for traditional media are shrinking while those for social media are increasing exponentially; therefore, content analysis of those technology-enabled social networks that hold animated discourses are critical to assessing organizational reputation. Measuring effects cuts two ways: as a tool of outcomes assessment and as a tool for repositioning a corporate effort under way.

P6: Marshaling evidence on the attitudinal and behavioral outcomes of corporate efforts offers crisis communication practitioners three opportunities that are (a) prescriptive (what should we engage in?); (b) instructive (how should we now engage in that which we want to engage in?); and (c) indicative (what are the outcomes of such an engagement?)

Future Landscape

CBN has publicly acknowledged the various shortcomings of Nigeria's banking sector. And it has been bold about calling the attention of bankers and financial counselors to the possibility of heady days ahead. But more than those, policy changes and actions that CBN has taken so far point to a banking landscape that will be less mismanaged and significantly more ethical than that of the past. The twin forces of CBN and EFCC make wanton disregard of ethical proprieties more an occurrence of the past than a possibility of the future. And to ensure the return and maintenance of the international community's confidence in Nigeria's banks, Nigeria's federal government required that banks adopt, by the end of 2010, the International Financial Reporting Standards, which require quarterly and annual reports consistent with the best international practices. While such an accounting process augurs well for improving investor and customer confidence in a maligned financial system, it must be noted that Banco Santander of Spain weathered the financial crisis not because of strict government regulations but because of its strong reputational risk-management programs (Xifra and Ordeix, 2009).

The recent global recession, the deepest downturn since World War II, presented communication practitioners, particularly corporate affairs managers of banks, with opportunities for growth—in their organizations' market share, preferred brand image, business reputations, corporate profitability, and in their crisis-communication evaluation techniques. For crisis communicators to maximize their potential for effective, persuasive communications on behalf of the banking and financial industry requires that they engage in values-driven practices that are well grounded in integrity, honesty, symmetry, reflexivity, and openness. But, absent instrumental leadership that initiates structure and specifies rules, standards, norms and expectations for employee conduct (Grojean et al., 2004; Mulki et al., 2009), and an ethical transformational leadership that seeks to promote greater organizational performance through employee motivation and professional well-being, all of the six strategies presented in this chapter will not lead to expected outcomes.

Thus, it is important that crisis communication programs be developed and implemented in an organizational climate conducive to meeting the growing challenges of ensuring optimal communications for establishing *the* preferred brand image, for sustaining organizational interests, for expanding markets, and for meeting customers' inherently personal, unique needs. Anything less will be inimical to resolving the industry's crisis and to attaining its long-term goals.

Discussion Questions

1. Assume that the Association of Corporate Affairs Managers of Banks, headquartered in Lagos, Nigeria, has requested that you consult with it on how its membership can maximize its use of social media as a business tool. What additional tactics will you propose, particularly to help the industry that it represents enhance its reputation?

2. If you were to advocate the application of classical ethical theories to everyday practices of corporate communicators in Nigeria's banking and financial industry, what key elements of those theories will you emphasize—and why?
3. Propose at least three additional strategies as complements to those presented in this chapter. Justify each.
4. The six propositions presented in this chapter are essentially touchstones for investigating the communication management landscape in Nigeria. Make a case for extending their geographical relevance.
5. Jürgen Habermas uses the modifier "strategic," as in strategic action, in contradistinction to how communication practitioners generally use "strategic," as in strategic communication. In practical terms, is there really a contradiction in terms here? Why or why not?
6. Use the illustrations in this chapter to distinguish between ethics per se and applied ethics.
7. This chapter identifies actions that Nigeria's regulatory agencies have taken so far in response to professional misconduct in the country's banking and financial sector. Argue that those actions are, indeed, on solid ground.

References

Africa attracts $1 billion in fund flows this year. (2009). *Africa Good News*, August 3. Retrieved from www.africagoodnews.com/economy/africa-attracts-1-billion-in-fund-flows-this-year.html

Akinfemiwa, M. A. (2001). Ethics of bribe in the banking sector. Paper presented at the First Conference of Permanent Secretaries, Abuja, Nigeria, August.

Arieff, A., Weiss, M. A., and Jones, V. C. (2009). The global economic crisis: Impact on sub-Saharan Africa and global policy responses. Congressional Research. Service Report for Congress Prepared for Members and Committees, Report No. 7–5700, August 25. Washington, DC: Congressional Research Service.

Babarinde, O. A. (2009). Africa is open for business: A continent on the move. *Thunderbird International Business Review, 51*, 319–328.

Baehr, C., and Alex-Brown, K. (2010). Assessing the value of corporate blogs: A social capital perspective. *IEEE Transactions on Professional Communication, 53*, 358–369.

Baehr, C., and Schaller, B. (2010). *Writing for the Internet: A guide to real communication in virtual space.* Santa Barbara, CA: Greenwood Press.

Bexley, J. B., James, J. F., and Haberman, J. (2010). The financial crisis and its issues. *Research in Business and Economics, 3*, 1–7.

Boas, F. (1887). Museums of ethnology and their classification. *Science, 9*, 587–589.

Bostock, F. (1991). The British overseas banks and development finance in Africa after 1945. *Business History, 33*(3), 157–176.

Brody, E. W. (2001). Who is measuring outcomes? The "attention" economy. *Public Relations Quarterly*, 46(3), 18–21.

Brown, P. R. (2008). Trusting the new NHS: Instrumental versus communicative action. *Sociology of Health & Illness*, 30, 349–363.

Bunke, H. C. (1988). Should we teach business ethics? *Business Horizons*, 31(4), 2–8.

Calderón, R., Alvarez-Arce, J. L., Mayoral, S. (2009). Corporation as a crucial ally against corruption. *Journal of Business Ethics*, 87, 319–332.

Campbell, C. (2009). Private equity in Africa: Lessons learned. *Thunderbird International Business Review*, 51, 403–405.

Chakravartty, P., and Downing, J. D. H. (2010). Media, technology and the global financial crisis. *International Journal of Communication*, 4, 693–695.

Christians, C. G., Ferré, J. P., and Fackler, P. M. (1993). *Good news: Social ethics and the press*. New York: Oxford University Press.

Dangogo, K. (2008). *Strategic public relations management: Beyond the banking hall*. Kaduna, Nigeria: Timex Communications.

Dasgupta, P. (1988). Trust as a commodity. In D. Gambetta (Ed.), *Trust: Making and breaking cooperative relations* (pp. 49–72). Oxford, UK: Basil Blackwell.

Davenport, T. H., and Beck, J. C. (2001). *The attention economy: Understanding the new currency of business*. Boston, MA: Harvard Business School Press.

Decker, S. D. (2006). *How to gain local goodwill and influence politicians: British companies and economic nationalism in Nigeria and Ghana, 1945 to 1977*. Paper presented at the International Economic History Conference, Helsinki, Finland, August 21.

Dobson, H. (2005). Review article: Rethinking Japan's "lost decade." *Global Society: Journal of Interdisciplinary International Relations*, 19, 211–223.

Erondu, E. A., Sharland, A., and Okpara, J. O. (2004). Corporate ethics in Nigeria: A test of the concept of an ethical climate. *Journal of Business Ethics*, 51, 349–357.

Financial Crisis Inquiry Commission (2011). *The financial crisis inquiry report: Final report of the National Commission on the causes of the financial and economic crisis in the United States*, January. Washington, DC: Government Printing Office.

Fiscal implications of the global economic and financial crisis (2009). Occasional paper No. 269. Fiscal Affairs Department. Washington, DC: International Monetary Fund.

Fischer, R. (1995). Control construct design in evaluating campaigns. *Public Relations Review*, 21, 45–58.

Fombrun, C. J. (1996). *Reputation: Realizing value from the corporate image*. Boston, MA: Harvard Business School Press.

Freeman, B., and Chapman, S. (2010). British American Tobacco on Facebook: Undermining Article 13 of the Global World Health Organization Framework Convention on Tobacco Control. *Tobacco Control*, 19, e1-e9. doi: 10.1136/tc.2009.032847.

Gichure, C. W. (2006). Teaching business ethics in Africa: What ethical orientation? The case of East and Central Africa. *Journal of Business Ethics*, 63, 39–52.

Giddens, A. (1990). *The consequences of modernity*. Palo Alto, CA: Stanford University Press.

Grauwe, P. D. (2010). The banking crisis: Causes, consequences and remedies. In L. S. Talani (Ed.), *The global crash: Towards a new global financial regime?* (pp. 10–31). Basingstoke, UK: Palgrave Macmillan.

Grojean, M. W., Resick, C. J., Dickson, M. W., and Smith, D. B. (2004). Leaders, values, and organizational climate: Examining leadership strategies for establishing an organizational climate regarding ethics. *Journal of Business Ethics, 55,* 223–241.

Habermas, J. (1984). *The theory of communicative action: Reason and the rationalization of society, Vol. 1* (T. McCarthy, Trans.). Boston, MA: Beacon Press (Original work published 1981).

Habermas, J. (1987). *The theory of communicative action: Lifeworld and system: A critique of functionalist reason, Vol. 2* (T. McCarthy, Trans.). Boston, MA: Beacon Press (Original work published 1981).

Habermas, J. (1990). *Moral consciousness and communicative action.* Cambridge, MA: MIT Press.

Headliners of 2010: Business (2010). *The Nigerian Voice,* 29 December. Retrieved from www.thenigerianvoice.com/nvnews/42219/1/headliners-of-2010-business.html

Holtzhausen, D. R. (2000). Postmodern values in public relations. *Journal of Public Relations Research, 12,* 93–114.

Hon, L. C., and Grunig, J. E. (1999). *Guidelines for measuring relationships in public relations.* Gainesville, FL: Institute for Public Relations.

Huang, Y-H. (2001). OPRA: A cross-cultural, multiple-item scale for measuring organization-public relationships. *Journal of Public Relations Research, 13,* 61–90.

Hughes, C. W. (2004). *Japan's security agenda: Military, economic and environmental dimensions.* Boulder, CO: Lynne Rienner.

Inoguchi. T. (Ed.). (2002). *Japan's Asian policy: Revival and response.* Basingstoke, UK: Palgrave Macmillan.

International Monetary Fund (2010). *World economic outlook update: A policy-driven multispeed recovery.* Washington, DC: International Monetary Fund.

Jo, S. (2006). Measurement of organization–public relationships: Validation of measurement using a manufacturer–retailer relationship. *Journal of Public Relations Research, 18,* 225–248.

Kant, I. (1964). *Groundwork of the metaphysics of morals* (H. J. Paton, Trans.). New York: Harper & Row (Original work published 1785).

Ki, E-J., and Hon, L. C. (2007). Reliability and validity of organization–public relationship measurement and linkages among relationship indicators in a membership organization. *Journalism & Mass Communication Quarterly, 84,* 419–438.

Kolb, R. W. (Ed.). (2010). *Lessons from the financial crisis: Causes, consequences, and our economic future.* Hoboken, NJ: John Wiley & Sons.

Limbs, E. C., and Fort, T. L. (2000). Nigerian business practices and their interface with virtue ethics. *Journal of Business Ethics, 26,* 169–179.

Luhmann, N. (1979). *Trust and power.* Chichester, UK: John Wiley & Sons.

Luhmann, N. (1988). Familiarity, confidence, trust: Problems and alternatives. In D. Gambetta (Ed.), *Trust: Making and breaking cooperative relations* (pp. 94–108). Oxford, UK: Basil Blackwell.

Milanzi, M. C. (1997). Business ethics in eastern and southern Africa. *Journal of Business Ethics, 16,* 1549–1553.

Morgan, R. M., and Hunt, S. D. (1994). The commitment–trust theory of relationship marketing. *Journal of Marketing*, *58*, 20–38.

Mulki, J. P., Jaramillo, J. F., and Locander, W. B. (2009). Critical role of leadership on ethical climate and salesperson behaviors. *Journal of Business Ethics*, *86*, 125–141.

Murinde, V. (2009). *Global financial crisis: Implications for Africa's financial system.* Paper presented at the European Development Report Conference, Accra, Ghana, May 21–23.

Norberg, P. (2009). "I don't care that people don't like what I do"—business codes viewed as invisible or visible restrictions. *Journal of Business Ethics*, *86*, 211–225.

Norbrook, N. (2009). Finance: Africa's banking leaders go global. *The Africa Report*, *19*, October–November, 84–86, 88.

Obayiuwana, O. (2009). Nigerian banks still in the firing line. *New African*, November, pp. 30–31.

Ohai, C. (2010). Jonathan to constitute Asset Management Corporation board. *Nigerian Best Forum*, August 28. Retrieved from www.nigerianbestforum.com/generaltopics/?p=63180

Onadele, B. (2009). *Global financial crisis: Implications for Nigerian banks.* Paper presented at a roundtable organized by the Nigerian Economic Society, Nigerian Institute of International Affairs, Victoria Island, Lagos, February.

Onah, J. O. (1991). Marketing ethics and social responsibilities of marketing. In E. Kaynak (Ed.), *Sociopolitical aspects of international marketing* (pp. 295–313). New York: The Haworth Press.

Onwuamaeze, D. (2009). The road to the turmoil in the banks. *Newswatch*, *50*(14), October, 21–23.

Pine, B. J., and Gilmore, J. H. (1999). *The experience economy: Work is theatre and every business a stage.* Boston, MA: Harvard Business School Press.

Pratt, C. B., Ademosu, E. A., Adamolekun, W., Alabi, L., and Carr, R. L. (2011). Managing a crisis of confidence in Nigeria's banking and financial industry. *Public Relations Review*, *37*, 71–73.

Rotter, J. B. (1967). A new scale for the measurement of interpersonal trust. *Journal of Personality*, *35*, 651–665.

Sanda, A. U. (2009). *Effects of global financial crisis on the Nigerian economy.* Paper presented at a roundtable organized by the Nigerian Economic Society, Nigerian Institute of International Affairs, Victoria Island, Lagos, February.

Sanusi, S. L. (2010). *The Nigerian banking industry: What went wrong and the way forward.* A lecture at the annual convocation ceremony at Bayero University, Kano, February 26.

Seguino, S. (2010). The global economic crisis, its gender and ethnic implications, and policy responses. *Gender & Development*, *18*, 179–199.

Soludo, C. C. (2007). The safety and soundness of the Nigerian banking system. Press briefing in Abuja, Nigeria, June 12.

Stiglitz, J. E. (2010a). The financial crisis of 2007–8 and its macroeconomic consequences. In S. Griffith-Jones, J. A. Ocampo, and J. E. Stiglitz (Eds.), *Time for a visible hand: Lessons from the 2008 world financial crisis* (pp. 19–49). New York: Oxford University Press.

Stiglitz, J. E. (2010b). Responding to the crisis. In S. Griffith-Jones, J. A. Ocampo, and J. E. Stiglitz (Eds.), *Time for a visible hand: Lessons from the 2008 world financial crisis* (pp. 76–98). New York: Oxford University Press.

The top 200 banks in Africa 2010. (2011). *The Africa Report*, January 26. Retrieved from www.cp-africa.com/2011/01/26/top-200-banks-africa-2010/

Tinubu, B. (2009). The Nigerian financial sector: Escape from crisis or new trouble? *The Nation*, October 1, p. 3.

Ulmer, R. R., Sellnow, T. L., and Seeger, M. W. (2011). *Effective crisis communication: Moving from crisis to opportunity* (2nd ed.). Thousand Oaks, CA: Sage.

United Nations Development Programme. (2005). *Human development report 2005*. New York: UNDP.

Wall, M. (2009). Africa on YouTube: Musicians, tourists, missionaries and aid workers.*The International Communication Gazette*, 71, 393–407.

Warner, C. (2009). Build a power brand during an economic downturn. *Boston Herald*, September 1. Retrieved from www.bostonherald.com/business/womens/general/view.bg?articleid=1194413&srvc=womens&position=14

Wheary, J. (2009). One step forward, two steps back. *World Policy Journal*, 26(4), 80–81.

Williams, M. T. (2010). *Uncontrolled risk: The lessons of Lehman Brothers and how systemic risk can still bring down the world financial system*. New York: McGraw-Hill.

World Bank (2006). *Strengthening bank group work in governance and anti-corruption*, July 20. Washington, DC: World Bank.

World Bank (2011). *Doing business 2011, Nigeria: Making a difference for entrepreneurs*. Washington, DC: World Bank.

World Trade Organization (2010). *International trade statistics 2010*. Geneva, Switzerland: World Trade Organization.

Wrong, M. (2009). Patron saints of Africa, *The Washington Post*, August 16, p. B6.

Xifra, J., and Ordeix, E. (2009). Managing reputational risk in an economic downturn: The case of Banco Santander. *Public Relations Review*, 35, 363–360.

Yoshikawa, H. (2001). *Japan's lost decade*. Tokyo: Trust/International House of Japan.

Zhong, B., Hardin, M., and Sun, T. (2011). Less effortful thinking leads to more social networking? The associations between the use of social network sites and personality traits. *Computers in Human Behavior*, 27, 1265–1271.

VIEWS FROM AN EXPERT

PETER WALKER

Peter Walker is a fellow and former president of the Chartered Institute of Public Relations, United Kingdom, and a chartered public relations practitioner. He is also a fellow of the Communication Advertising and Marketing Education Foundation in the United Kingdom. In 2010, he was named fellow of the Nigerian Institute of Public Relations. Walker was instrumental in establishing the Centre for Corporate Responsibility in the United Kingdom in 1975 and served as its director from 1995 to 1999. Walker lectures and writes extensively on public relations and communication management nationally and internationally. He has taught at several higher-educational institutions, including the University of Southern California; the University of Miami; University of Florida, Gainesville; Brunel University; and Brookes University, Oxford.

It would be unfair and unrealistic to hold the crisis communication performance of the Nigerian banking sector up to scrutiny in isolation. A prolonged period of global economic growth fueled by a lax national financial regulatory regime in most developed countries, with the exception of Australia and Canada, coupled with an increasing complexity of financial products marketed to eager investors and political economic populism had created a decade that dulled risk management sensibilities. Public relations directed at issues or crisis communication for banks throughout the world was consumer marketing-focused, designed to stimulate borrowing with property as promoted as the asset whose inflation would secure increased personal and corporate borrowing.

In Nigeria, the second Obasanjo presidential term (2003–2007) heralded a rapid and even brutal approach to deregulation, consolidation, and competitive capitalization of the banking and financial services sector. No one looking back can fail to admire the ways in which the banking sector responded. A series of mergers and rounds of investment created a strong, vibrant, competitive, and profitable banking sector whose dozen major players soon established themselves as a force in banking in Nigeria, Africa, and internationally, in London and New York City in particular.

Any close scrutiny of their public relations departments would recognize them as being marketing-driven, but also taking on the concepts of diversity— support for women; philanthropy and the arts; culture and sports support, and corporate social responsibility. There were also signs of excesses, criticisms of customer relations, complaints from small businesses on the lack of financial support, and questions on high operational costs. An examination of the public evidence suggests that public relations played little part in dealing with these issues or the incidents that drove them. It is impossible to know whether any public relations professionals argued or debated at board level on these issues and the professional management of the incidents.

Several issues the public face and the behavior of many in the banking sector had not gone unnoticed by the Central Bank of Nigeria. At least two attempts were made by the immediate past governor of the bank, Professor Chukwuma Soludo, to establish some form of generic public relations based on publicity-driven programs to promote the banking sector and its contribution to the Nigerian economy.

The advent of Umaru Yar'Adua, Nigeria's new president, with his strong interest in private-sector development, his commitment to an enterprise economy, and his appointment in 2009 of a risk-management-based Central Bank Governor Mallam Sanusi Lamido Sanusi, was a game-changer. With the support of the president, Sanusi moved quickly and decisively to audit and make public the deficiencies or the criminal and fraudulent behavior of senior management, even populist chief executives. It is no coincidence, then, that Sanusi believes his role is to speak the truth to the bigwigs in the financial industry. Speaking the truth is a mantra for every public relations professional, especially for those involved in crisis communication.

Crisis communication managers in the Nigerian banking sector, as outlined in this case analysis, have performed no worse and possibly better in some instances than their counterparts in the rest of the world. In the next phase of structuring the banking sector into tiers comprised of international, national, regional, and specialized banks defined by regulation and capital adequacy standards, crisis communication anchored on professional public relations management and banking management have a considerable role to play. Based on the evidence of their performance during the Nigerian financial crisis, there are crucial lessons the world can learn about crisis communication as applied to Nigeria's financial crisis.

South Africa

Hotspot: South Durban Basin, South Africa—The Engen Oil Refinery Explosion

J. Chris Skinner

The South Durban basin, KwaZulu Natal, South Africa, forms the backdrop for a special study of the chemical industry and in particular the major role played in the region by two of the country's major oil refineries, Engen and SAPREF. After outlining the scope of these developments and their impact on the environment, the Engen case study is used to illustrate the crisis management scenario to protect the interest of those communities living close to Engen.

Introduction

If one were to select one region in the world that illustrates the classical interaction of politics, economics, and social engineering it would possibly be the South Durban basin of KwaZulu Natal, South Africa. Blighted by 50 years of apartheid, which left communities segregated and in close proximity with chemical manufacturing plants and other industries that employed them, it is a region that today is one of the environmental hotspots on the planet. Much has been done to alleviate the situation in the post-apartheid era since 1994, but the legacy of poor health, safety, and security still remains despite all the efforts of the authorities to make a difference. This is why the study of emergency and crisis communication in this region has real meaning and where lessons can be learned that have both national and international implications. It is thus an area that has great scope for research in a variety of fields including health, welfare, education, economics, and environmental planning.

While the study focuses on one case, the Engen Refinery fire, the international model that follows is at the heart of all emergency planning and provides the framework for a strategic communication analysis for all the organizations that operate within the South Durban basin. The model is adopted from APELL for Mining (2001) (Figure 1.1).

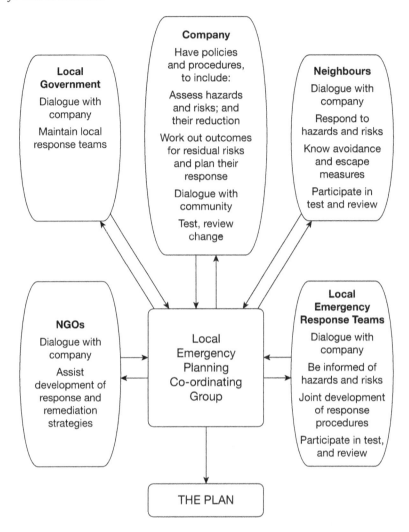

Figure 1.1 The APELL planning model.

Background of the Case: Engen Oil Refinery Fire

Petroleum refineries and the petro-chemical industry which piggyback onto these are the key industries in South Durban, South Africa. Linked to this is the development by Transnet in 2009 of a multi-fuel pipeline linking the port of Durban to Gauteng.

The port of Durban is South Africa's busiest port and the largest in Africa. It is visited annually by 4,000 commercial vessels, supports 400 port-related industries and handles two-thirds of South Africa's container cargo trade. With the container terminal already drawing more than 300 trucks daily, the transport of goods to and from the port has become a critical issue. Current port activities in addition to affiliated businesses, such as trucking and container storage have created serious environmental impacts in surrounding communities, especially Clairwood and the Bluff. Residents have to battle serious pollution as a result of the comingling of residential and industrial zones.

The relocation of the Durban International Airport in May 2010 and proposals on how to use the vacant property would exacerbate the current congested situation with all its attendant pollution problems.

Situated approximately 20 kilometers from Durban and adjoining the South Durban basin is also one of the largest concentrations of chemical manufacturing companies in South Africa. The Umbogintwini Industrial Complex (UIC) currently has 13 major operating companies, 12 of which manufacture a variety of chemical products, animal feeds, and textiles (UIC, 2009) (Figure 1.2).

Adjacent to this industrial complex are also two new shopping complexes, Arbour Crossing with an area of 43,000 square meters of retail space and over 50 stores, which was opened in 2008, and the Galleria Mall with over 81,603 square meters of retail space and over 200 stores, which was opened in 2009 (Figure 1.3). Together they handle some 5,000 shoppers at peak times. There is no doubt that the proximity of both shopping complexes to the chemical site has added a further dimension to the safety, security, and access

Figure 1.2 Front cover of the latest Umbogintwini Industrial Complex, Safety, Health and Environmental Report for 2009.

Figure 1.3 Aerial view looking south of the Arbour Crossing and Galleria shopping complex, which was completed in 2009. It is adjacent to the UIC, which houses thirteen chemical companies.

of emergency services to the area and the need therefore, for an integrated disaster management strategy for the region if and when the need should arise.

It is within this context that this chapter analyzes one case, the Engen Refinery fire, to illustrate the need for integrated crisis management and communication strategy for the region.

In recent years there have been a series of major disasters in the South Durban basin. Among the most notable ones are the Engen Oil Refinery explosions. Engen, according to its website, was originally founded as the Standard Vacuum Oil in 1881 and was backed by J. D. Rockefeller Standard Oil Trust. In 1910, the name Mobil was added to Vacuum Oil. It subsequently changed to Mobil Oil. The company thereafter reinvented itself as Engen Refinery. The company focuses on "the refining and marketing of petroleum and petroleum-based products, and the provision of retail convenience services, through an extensive network of service stations across 17 countries in Sub-Saharan Africa" (www.engen.co.za). The Engen refinery in Durban is the oldest in the area with a production capacity of 135,000 barrels a day (www.engen.co.za). What is of most concern to critics is that the refinery is located in the densely populated urban residential areas of Merebank, Asterville and Wentworth and the Bluff. This close proximity, for over 50 years, has increased health, safety, and air pollution concerns for the residents of the residential communities (www.sheqafrica.com/engen-refinery-fire).

Timeline of the Refinery Fires

On September 18, 2007, a series of massive explosions shook Durban Harbor, the Bluff residential area and the Durban Central Business District. What followed was a series of huge fires in the Island View liquid storage tank zone which contained more than 1,000 liquid fuel tanks.

On November 20, 2007, a storage tank with more than seven million liters of petrol caught fire and burned for 58 hours at the Engen refinery, as a result of lightning. Although Engen had its own firefighting crews specifically trained to deal with fuel tank fires, the company called in the eThekwini Metro Fire Department as well as city disaster crews.

Just a year later on November 13, 2008, another explosion rocked the refinery causing over R200 million of damage (Figure 1.4).

In all of these cases, the explosions caused fear and panic and in particular a concern that the Engen refinery was prone to accidents and that the local authority, eThekwini Municipality lacked an effective emergency evacuation plan should the need arise to handle an emergency on this scale.

Situation Analysis

The various stakeholders that have a direct bearing on the study and who provide the framework for the analysis for the case study include the following:

International Council of Chemical Associations (ICCA)
The ICCA is the worldwide voice of the chemical industry, a sector with 2007 turnover of more than $3 trillion. ICCA members come from countries that account for more than 70 percent of global chemical manufacturing operations. The ICCA's mission is therefore to increase membership and its representation on a global front and thereby improve the image of the industry worldwide. Additionally, the Council promotes the practice of sound and productive chemicals management, international climate negotiations, advocacy and communications, and Responsible Care, the chemical industry's unique global initiative that drives continuous improvement in health, safety, and environmental (HSE) performance, together with open and transparent communication with stakeholders.

Through the participation of over 50 national chemical manufacturing associations, and through them, thousands of chemical sites around the world, Responsible Care forms an essential part of ICCA's contribution to the United Nation's Strategic Approach to International Chemicals Management (SAICM).

The chemical industry in South Africa
Chemical and Allied Industries' Association of South Africa (CAIA) represents 206 companies of which 67 manufacturers account for over 90 percent of chemical production in South Africa. It is of strategic importance to the

Figure 1.4 The front page story of November 21, 2008, in the local newspaper, the *Southlands Sun*, reporting on the Engen fire.

economy, contributing 5 percent to the country's GDP and approximately 25 percent of its manufacturing sales; no other industry group is more concerned with the regulation of its current practices and procedures, its safety and security, and in particular its communication exchanges with key stakeholders to minimize risk if an accident does occur, than the chemical industry represented in South Africa by the CAIA.

CAIA's primary goals are to promote responsible care and to monitor its implementation, earn public trust for the chemical industry, improve the effectiveness of its advocacy initiatives with government and NGOs, support education initiatives in science, engineering, and technology; and to create maximum value for its members (CAIA, 2008, 2009).

The communities nearest to the refinery
Although the South Durban basin is considered as one of the economic hubs of South Africa, it also continues to be the "environmental hotspot" in South Africa. This "environmental hotspot" has a unique spatial plan that has several heavy industries integrated with highly populated residential areas. While these industries are considered as having positive economic impact, they contribute to several negative impacts in the area including air and water pollution, poor health conditions in the neighboring communities, exposing the residents to high risks in events of industrial accidents and malfunctions.

As a result of these negative impacts, the fight for "environmental justice" continues to be the cornerstone of the communities in the South Durban Basin. (SDCEA, 2008, 2009). The many activities that contribute negatively to the environment in the South Durban basin have been identified as:

- two oil refineries with a total processing capacity of approximately 250 million barrels of crude oil a day;
- a paper mill with a processing capacity of 550,000 tons per annum;
- several bulk storage tank facilities that also store hazardous and toxic chemicals in bulk;
- approximately 300 other industries including the manufacture of chemicals, food, and pharmaceutical products and the motor and allied industries; and
- a high volume of heavy vehicle traffic owing to the poor rail infrastructure in the basin and loss of green belts, buffer zones, and other sensitive areas to housing estates and commercial centers.

Initial Response of Engen Refinery to the Explosion

The November 2007 explosion in which approximately 7.5 million liters of petrol caught fire and burned at the Engen refinery because of a reported lightning strike did not result in any death or injury. However, it not only caused massive damage to the refinery to the tune of R120 million, it created mass hysteria in the nearby communities as a previous explosion had occurred at a nearby petrochemical company in September of the same year.

The response was two-pronged—Engen and the city of Durban. The city had to be a part of this crisis response because of the large residential communities surrounding the refinery. Engen's initial response was to send in its specially trained fire fighters who specialize in fuel tank fires. The company also brought in the eThekwini Metro Fire Department as well as the city' of Durban's disaster management crews.

According to news reports summarized in SheqAfrica.com, Africa's leading online occupational safety, health, environment, and quality (Sheq) magazine, the communities near Engen Refinery were not evacuated. William Oosthuizen, Engen's general manager was quoted as saying: "At this stage it does not look like evacuation of residents is necessary. The best thing is to stay indoors and keep the windows closed." Rather, he stated that the disaster management crews were instructed to drive through the residential areas and warn people, through loudspeakers, to stay home (*SheqAfrica* Online Magazine, 2007).

The city of Durban's emergency crew worked in tandem with Engen's disaster team to respond to the crisis. While Durban's city manager, Dr. Mike Sutcliffe, acknowledged the existence of a crisis management plan, his response to media inquiries did not assuage the fears of the community. Sutcliffe said: "The city does have a disaster management plan, but each disaster has a different level of operation . . . We can't always use the same procedure, so it is not something that can be placed on paper and handed out to residents" (Naidu and SAPA, 2007).

Community Reaction to Engen and Durban City Response

Reaction to the city's and Engen's response to the disaster was swift. Residents of the communities accused Engen of gross negligence and of not having a crisis management plan that it should have activated. They also accused the city of Durban of attempting to minimize the damage and the environmental and health effects of the chemical fire on the community. In interviews with various news organizations, some residents said that when they contacted Engen's environment office, they were rebuffed. So, rather than heed Engen's warning to stay indoors, most residents fled their homes. The city was also not forthcoming with information. A resident of one of the communities noted in a news report, that neither he nor his neighbors had been given a crisis management plan by either the city or Engen. "I've sat on different community forums and the issue of a disaster management or evacuation plan has been brought up numerous times, but the municipality hasn't assisted us with any information" (Naidu and SAPA, 2007).

The negative community reaction from one of Engen's important stake-holders meant that the company had to activate its plan to deal with the disaster.

Goals: The goal was to reassure the general public and in particular the local residents that the Engen Refinery was safe and well managed and that indeed the city did have an emergency evacuation plan that could be executed at short notice if the need arose.

Objectives: With these twin goals in mind both parties, the company and the city, embarked on their objectives, which were:

- to provide information (facts) on what had happened in the various accidents and what steps were being taken to improve safety and security at the plant;
- to deploy emergency services to the disaster scene as speedily and efficiently as possible when called upon to do so.

Strategies: Although it appeared that Engen and the city of Durban did not have an effective crisis management plan, Engen used:

- conventional media to disseminate information on the possible causes of the accident;
- nonconventional media (mobile public address system) to reach at least one of its target audience or stakeholders; and
- the city, working with Engen, also used both conventional and non-conventional media to communicate to the residents of the communities surrounding the refinery.

Tactics:

- Engen sent press releases to local and regional newspapers and radio stations about the chemical fire accident that occurred on November 20, 2007. The release gave information on the nature of the accident and its possible causes. Throughout the period, the company continued to disseminate media releases and to avail the refinery manager for special interviews. This constant communication was designed to update the public on what progress was being made in the plant investigation into causes of the accident and what subsequent action it was taking to return to normal operations.
- The response to this and a subsequent chemical accident at the same refinery on November 13, 2008, generated a lot of discussion in radio talk shows and letters to the newspapers. The responses also included an open letter to the manager of the eThekwini Municipality, Dr. Mike Sutcliffe, released by the chairman of the South Durban Community Environmental Alliance (SDCEA) Mr. Desmond D'Sa entitled "IVS incident fails to produce emergency plan" in which he criticized the lack of an Emergency Response Plan for the area (see Figure 1.6).
- Additionally, with foreign funding, SDCEA produced a special community brochure to advise its members on what practical steps they should take in case of emergency (SCDEA, 2008). It is reproduced in Figure 1.5 and a full copy is available from SDCEA itself.

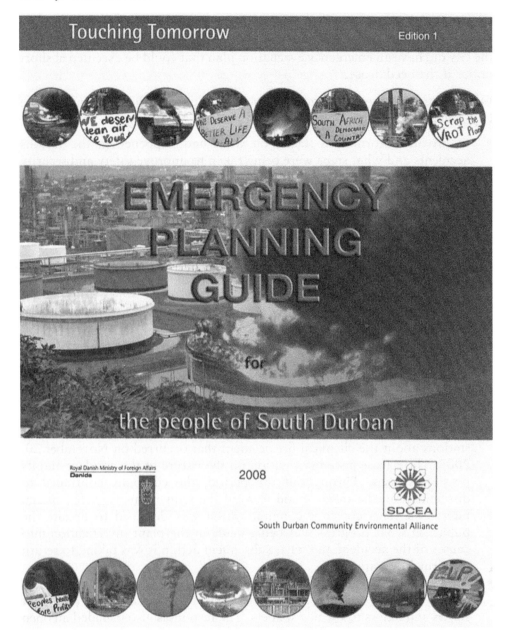

Figure 1.5 The Emergency Planning Guide produced by SDCEA to help the community cope with emergencies such as the Engen fire. It was written and compiled by the community itself and was sponsored independently.

Sun *News*

Fire heightens fears

Residents decry lack of emergency plan

ONE of the major setbacks which will affect Engen Refinery's ability to start up its operation following Thursday morning's crippling blaze, is the ordering of new materials.

This includes API standard refinery pumps, which will be imported.

"It could take up to three months to receive them," said William Oosthuizen, refinery general manager.

The refinery will lose close on R6-m for every day that it is not operating.

"This one is big, this can run into a several hundred million rand loss for Engen," said William. In terms of the country's fuel stock, he believes "you will see a dip, but it will recover very quickly."

RULED

William strongly ruled out age and lack of maintenance as the cause of the fire. He described the refinery, which has operated on the site since 1954, as "young facilities by international standards." Engen spends in the region of "R200 million per year on plant maintenance and over the past decade spent an average of nearly R60 million per year on projects to improve our environmental footprint." He also thinks it's "unlikely a skill issue."

However, it is only a year since one of Engen's storage tanks holding seven million litres of petrol burnt for 58 hours.

He described the refinery's four fires in the last two years as a "worrying trend for us".

SDCEA chairman, Desmond D'Sa protests outside Engen Refinery.

"We couldn't sleep last night, my chest was tight. The fire was out of control, blazing very high. This is happening too often. The refinery scaring us. We heard the hooters and we wanted to run. They are aware that its going to leak. Who is going to compensate us?" shouted an angry local, Joan Ryan.

On Thursday morning, hours after the blaze, the South Durban Community Environmental Alliance (SDCEA) along with the Wentworth community protested outside Engen. "Phanzi Engen, phansi" was loudly heard through the hailer.

Desmond D'Sa, chairman of SDCEA said: "There's still no disaster management or emergency plan for the people. We can only ask why there's been no effort from local government to tighten standards and restrictions and fine industries.

The absolute paranoia of the people as they gathered in groups on the roads into the morning makes me shudder to think how these matric pupils will perform in their exams with no sleep and added stress.

The refinery doesn't understand just how it affects ordinary people," he said.

CARRY OUT

Engen confirmed the refinery's environmental team will carry out regular air sampling during and after the fire. These samples will be sent to specialised laboratories in Italy for analysis.

According to William, the results are due in a fortnight, after which they will be presented to the South Durban Basin community.

Figure 1.6 Further editorial coverage about the fire, voicing the concerns of the community.

- A number of community meetings were also convened during this period to discuss the way forward and regular contact was maintained between the community and the Engen Community Liaison forum.

The media coverage of the specific accident of November 13, 2008, is also reproduced as Figure 1.6 to show the extent of the community's concern for its safety.

Outcomes

All parties monitored the media coverage. Following the initial communication between Engen and the community, the city of Durban, and among the three parties, it is important to note that liaison and personal contacts among the various players in the scenario described above have improved and that they are now working more closely together. However, thousands of people continue to reside right next to the refinery and SDCEA continues to monitor daily the air pollution and the general health and welfare of its residents. These figures are discussed with the company monthly and any exceedances of emissions are raised immediately with both the company and the municipality. The nature of the operations, however, could result in unforeseen accidents. "Expect the unexpected" is therefore still the watchword and accidents similar to those experienced in 2007 and 2008 could happen again. On October 10, 2011, another explosion ocurred at the refinery.

Lessons to be Learned

It would be heartening to report that, as a result of this emergency that cost Engen in the vicinity of $50 million in lost production, greater understanding between the municipality, industry, and the surrounding communities that are directly affected by the disaster(s) would occur. It is true that the formation of Community Liaison Forums by the key operators in the basin have improved communication but the risks are still there and the pollution continues to be a real threat to the health of people living so close to their work. All parties are working on a win–win situation but the very nature of the operations puts people at risk despite all the precautions taken. Whether it happens today or in 2012 and beyond there is an even greater need to inform the public of danger and what immediate action needs to be taken jointly by the various parties. This is why the discussion on the role of social media in assisting parties in crisis communication, which appears at the end of the chapter, has such relevance.

Dealing with the Media During Emergencies

Of all the topics for discussion in this area of specialization, dealing with the media during emergencies is probably the most important and vital for success.

The subject is dealt with extensively in two books; the *Handbook of Public Relations* (Skinner et al., 2010) and *Disaster Management: A Guide to issues management and crisis communication* (Skinner and Mersham, 2002), both published by Oxford University Press. In conducting this research, a number of personal interviews have been conducted with journalists to get their standpoint and some of their requirements are set out below.

Media Perspective

- We have respect for what you do but it is not our job to be nice. We have to ask the awkward questions.
- During emergencies we do not want to get in the way. We are mindful of the task at hand but we do want first-hand information.
- It may be useful for companies to know who we are and the audiences we write for, so do your homework and find out who the journalists are on your local papers and community radio stations as well the regional press.
- As journalists we want to be helpful but you must assist us. Do not therefore send us urgent news in the middle of the night when clearly we have logged off!
- However, let us know immediately about a crisis. We can help mitigate the impact of an emergency. By all means have your emergency meeting with authorities and emergency services but please keep us informed. Send us an alert and please tell us something is happening. An initial brief can be followed up by more details or a press conference.
- We understand that most press statements have to be signed off by management. To us that information is sanitized: it helps to give the information as you have it. However, to put it bluntly, do not spin. Give us the truth right from the start as it is far less damaging.
- Sometimes the "boss" or the senior in charge does not want to be interviewed. We understand this, but we are not prepared to accept this because there are things we want to hear from the horse's mouth.
- If we sense that information is being withheld from us we will go behind your back. Always remember that after every disaster or emergency there will a good investigative journalist doing a meticulous follow-up. If there is a good story to be found, we will find it and publish it!
- So after the emergency is over, share with us your findings and advise what people can do to help in the event of another emergency. By doing so it will help to recapture what your relationship with the media was during the actual emergency. This could have the real benefit of strengthening relationships with key journalists and thus avoid future misunderstandings.
- These candid views can be used as the basis of discussion in evaluating company media strategies.

Company Perspective

- Just as the journalist's view of a crisis may be important, it is also important to marry the company's perspective as well. In the heat of the moment it is crucial that speed in replying to a query is all-important—journalists have deadlines.
- Keep cool. If a reporter gets snappy, chances are it's because he or she is under considerably more pressure at that moment than you are. Try to cooperate to the greatest extent possible.
- If you don't know the answer, attempt to get it for the reporter.
- Never ask to see or vet a reporter's story. Time is usually a key factor.
- There is seldom a reason why you should not be quoted by name. As a member of management and one charged with public relations, you are speaking for the company.
- Never flatly refuse to supply information. Always give a good reason why it is not available (for example, you want to be sure facts are correct, next of kin must be notified, official investigation is not yet complete).
- Always know to whom you are talking. Get his or her name and phone number and e-mail address in case you need to contact that person later.
- Never give an answer that you feel might not stand up. It can embarrass you later.
- Never falsify, color, or slant your answers. Reporters are trained to see a curved ball coming a mile away, and have fielded many of them before.
- Be especially alert for photographers. You have no control over photographs taken off company property, but you have every right to control those taken within the plant. Remember, photos can be as harmful as words.
- Be sure there is no time lag between the time you get information that can be put out and the time it is actually given to news people.
- Have safety, labor, and employee records available for your reference if possible.
- Be quick to point out long safety records and any acts of heroism by employees.
- If damage must be estimated for the press immediately, confine your statement to a general description of what was destroyed. Avoid putting a figure to the damage and the cost to the company.
- If possible always accentuate the positive. If your public relations is good, so are your chances of an even break!
- Provide regular and informative updates on your website with quotes from management and leading people that you are happy to be copied and pasted. Add photos and or graphics if you can.
- These two contrasting perspectives can be used as the basis for discussion on media relations in a crisis and a spokesperson from both sides would add to the authenticity and relevance of the debate.

Role of NGOs and Community Liaison Forums

Another interesting aspect of this debate is a discussion on the role of NGOs and community liaison forums (CLFs) in expanding the communication network. There are a number of NGOs and CLFs operating throughout the South Durban basin. Many of the larger companies have formed their own CLFs and use them as part of their corporate social responsibility platform. They invite representation from the communities in which they physically operate and from whom they often draw their labor support.

One of the most active in the field is the SAPREF CLF whose mission is to "seek out the right partnerships with local organizations and to develop the capacity of these organizations to gain access to the resources that government, companies and also SAPREF have available to support community development." Contact with a selection of these organizations has revealed that most of them are under-resourced and under strength and battle for survival particularly in the current economic climate.

What then are your findings from the areas in which you reside concerning the effectiveness and efficiency of CLFs?

The Role of Social Media in Crisis Management

In a final discussion area, it would be interesting to assess the role of social media in disseminating news about a disaster and to contrast it with the use of traditional media. Nowhere is this better illustrated than in the South Durban basin where communities live almost at the factory gates of the Engen refinery, one of the largest oil refineries in Southern Africa. The disaster that occurred at the plant in November 2008 has already been discussed. But five years on how could social media have played an ever-increasing role in informing the public on what to do as the drama unfolded?

Conclusion

This chapter has been wide ranging in its scope and diversity in the context of emergency and disaster management planning. With the watchword "Expect the unexpected," it has highlighted the importance of communication in dealing with disaster management. The BP oil rig disaster in the Gulf of Mexico in 2010 illustrates only too clearly what can happen to an operation if things go wrong—in BP's case to the tune of $20 billion. What will be remembered is how the company handled the news and the unfolding tragedy. In retrospect it is a record that the company will not be proud of. We therefore need to learn from these mistakes. Only a combination of practice, good communication, and trust will see a disaster through to its successful conclusion.

References

APELL for Mining (2001). Guidance for the mining industry in raising awareness and preparedness for emergencies at local level. (Technical Report 41 of 2001): SCP Publications.

Chemical and Allied Industries' Association (2008, 2009) *Responsible care performance reports for 2008 and 2009*. Johannesburg: CAIA.

Naidu, R., and SAPA (2007). Durban's refinery damage hits r120 m. *iOL News*, November 21. Retrieved from www.iol.co.za/news/south-africa/durban-refinery-damage-hits-r120m

SDCEA (2008). Emergency Planning Guide for the people of South Durban. Retrieved from www.sdcea.co.za

SDCEA (2009). Climate Change for the people of South Durban. Retrieved from www.sdcea.co.za

SheqAfrica Online Magazine (2007). Lightning blamed for Durban's Engen refinery blaze, November 20. Retrieved from www.sheqafrica.com/engen-refinery-fire/

Skinner, J. C., and Mersham, G. M. (2002). *Disaster management: A guide to issues management and crisis communication*. Cape Town: Oxford University Press.

Skinner, J. C., von Essen, L. M., Mersham, G. M., and Motau S. (2010). *Handbook of public relations* (9th ed.). Cape Town: Oxford University Press.

VIEWS FROM AN EXPERT

KAREN LOTTER

Karen Lotter is a journalist and writer based in Durban, South Africa. She runs a company (www.ethekwiniweb.co.za/) specializing in creating websites and blogs, writing creative and interesting content and optimizing sites for search engines. She has written profiles, political speeches, features, advertising copy, obituaries, press releases, and columns in magazines, company newsletters, and newspapers, and written and produced corporate scripts. She has been a Feature Writer at Suite 101.com (www.suite101.com/profile.cfm/ethekwini girl), a Canadian-based contents website for over three years. She is also a Web writing tutor at SA Writers' College (www.sawriterscollege.co.za).

The SDCEA have produced and distributed an excellent Emergency Planning Guide. Community members' phone numbers could be put onto a database and they could be educated with regular text messages with regard to emergency procedures. If/when an emergency occurred, people could be kept updated. Key elements of this could be summarized and sent out by text message (SMS) by Engen or a joint company/community task force set up for such an occasion to practically cover everyone in the community. Regular updates could be provided as to the progress in containing the fire.

Just as the organization's website needs to be more interactive with regards to the media, it also needs to be interactive with regards to the community. Social media, such as Facebook, Twitter, Mixit, and other relevant sites can be used to build relationships, and engage in conversations with the community—not only to communicate with them when there is a disaster!

Those on Facebook could be provided with current information and could see the emergency plans being put in place via Facebook pages. Through pages they can also comment or post enquiries. Although the pages must be monitored, it would be a good idea to set up a comments policy—no abuse, hate speech, etc., which will justify deleting some comments. Companies must learn to toughen up a bit and NOT delete comments that are negative just for the sake of doing so. The pages also allow people to vent their feelings. Reply as best you can. But if comments overstep your comments policy, delete them.

Those on Twitter could provide updated information too and could direct the authorities to those in the community that need immediate attention. Twitter is a great medium because of its immediacy and also because most people can tweet from their mobile phones. We have seen across the world how Twitter has been the "first responder" in many disasters. It is the responsibility of the companies to build up their Twitter followers and ensure that it includes a large amount of other people directly affected by their industry, as well as journalists.

Keep them informed and updated at all times. Give them good information about products and services and when there is an emergency, be clear.

Learn how to create searchable Twitter posts; learn about hashtags. The all clear could be provided to all those involved in the emergency through radio, cell phones, and computers—via websites and social media.

What has happened in the past is that the company Engen and the SDCEA have worked independently and that little coordination of effort has occurred. The local radio station, East Coast Radio, has been the principal source of external communications. East Coast Radio has a very popular website and this is the case with most regional radio stations.

Depending on the emergency, one could ask the radio station to run a feed from the company/industry's Twitter on their website so that more people could be drawn in. The radio would broadcast the news of the fire/explosion. However, beamed as it is to the whole of KwaZulu Natal, it has tended to attract unwanted visitors to the accident scene and has hindered rather than helped in the emergency operation.

Section 2

Asia

China

China's Sanlu's Infant Formula Proves Fatal

Weidan Cao

Sanlu Group Co., one of China's former dairy giants, was at the center of a poisonous infant formula crisis that shocked the nation and the world in 2008. That crisis resulted in the company's collapse early in 2009. This case focuses on Sanlu's unethical conduct: neglecting humanism, preventing free flow of information, and shifting its responsibility for the crisis. This case offers three major lessons: the necessity of improving the organization's ethics, the importance of increasing the organization' crisis prevention and preparation awareness, and the necessity of acting effectively during a crisis response.

Introduction

> Those in the Chinese food industry, especially dairies, consider Sept 11 itself to be the "day of terror," when baby formula tainted with melamine from dairy giant Sanlu Group was exposed and snowballed to involve 22 domestic dairies, leading to at least six infant deaths and 294,000 others sickened by the products.
>
> (Zhu, January 6, 2009, para. 4)

"Outbreaks of food-borne illness, caused by eating food presumed to be safe, produced one of the most common forms of organizational crises" (Ulmer et al., 2007, p. 83). During the past decade, every continent reported serious outbreaks of foodborne disease ("WHO global strategy," 2002). Such diseases can seriously affect consumers, especially young children ("WHO global strategy," 2002), and have the potential to ruin the organizations responsible (Ulmer et al., 2007). Take baby foods, as an example. Infant foods in Belgium, the United States, China, France, the United Kingdom, Brazil, the Gambia, Gabon, Argentina, the Netherlands, South Korea, and Cyprus were once found contaminated with *Enterobacter sakazakii* during the period from 2000 to 2007("Product recall list," n.d.). In France, for example, Mead Johnson's infant formula, Pregestimil, was reported contaminated with *Enterobacter sakazakii* in late 2004 ("Pregestimil infant formula," 2005; "Product recall list," n.d.). In Argentina, Mead Johnson's infant formula Enfamil AR was also found contaminated with *Enterobacter sakazakii* in July, 2005 ("Product recall list," n.d.). In 2006, metal particles were discovered in baby foods in the United States, South Korea, China, and Australia ("Product recall list," n.d.). Many companies (e.g., Mead Johnson, Nestle, Wyeth) that had baby food problems recalled their products.

The collapse of the Sanlu Group Co., Ltd., previously one of the biggest dairy companies in China, once boasting high-quality products and record sales in the nation, drew international attention in 2008. Its infant formula had been contaminated by melamine, a chemical that can be used in plastics and other industries but can by no means be added to food such as raw milk. However, to boost the apparent amount of protein and to fool food-quality inspectors, melamine was added to watered-down raw milk supplies by some milk dealers to pursue profits at the expense of other people's health. The tainted milk was then sold to Sanlu and other dairy companies. The Sanlu Group was criticized for selling substandard products and trying to cover up the tainted milk issue. Six babies died and more than 300,000 had kidney stones and renal failure from consuming the tainted infant formula.

After the outbreak, a panic over dairy products made in China had spread nationwide and to other countries (Zhu, 2008). The World Health Organization was immediately notified. The U.S. Food and Drug Administration issued a warning on infant formula made in China and Chinese dairy products were banned internationally.

Background of the Crisis

Sanlu's Precipitous Collapse

Based in Shijiazhuang, Hebei province, the Sanlu Group, established in 1996 from several corporate acquisitions, was originally Happiness Milk Producers Cooperative, founded in 1956, and later grew into Shijiazhuang Dairy Company. Its founding chairwoman and general manager, Wenhua Tian, served from 1996 to 2008. Before the scandal, the group led the nation's dairy industry for many years and its products were popular nationwide. In 2006, Sanlu evolved into a joint-venture company, with 43 percent of its shares owned by Fonterra Cooperative Group Ltd., a New Zealand dairy company. Also in 2006, Sanlu celebrated its fiftieth anniversary and became a formidable and reputable dairy company (Feng and Nie, 2006). Two years later, it fell into disrepute: it was at the center of a food crisis that brought it to its knees.

Infant Formula Crisis

Beginning December 2007, consumers began to complain to Sanlu ("Sanlu's three meetings," 2009), questioning the quality of its infant formula and alleging that there were red sediments in their babies' urine.

The first report of a baby with kidney stones occurred in Nanjing, China, at the beginning of March 2008. In May, more customers complained to Sanlu, claiming their children's urine samples showed abnormalities after they had consumed Sanlu's infant formula. Meanwhile, there was a significant increase in the number of infants diagnosed with kidney stones nationwide. Parents argued that their affected infants had consumed Sanlu's milk for a long time.

However, it was not until September 11, 2008, that the public knew that Sanlu's infant formula had been contaminated by melamine. By September 13, according to Chinese health officials, about 1,200 babies were sickened and at least 432 cases of infant's kidney stones due to the consumption of the milk powder were reported ("China starts emergency response," 2008; "China's tainted milk," 2008).

On September 12, China's General Administration of Quality Supervision, Inspection and Quarantine (GAQSIQ) started to inspect infant formula nationwide. The Ministry of Health collected the cases of the disease and issued recommended treatment. Meanwhile, Sanlu's infant products were ordered to be removed from shelves and destroyed in the nation. On September 13, Hebei provincial government ordered the Sanlu Group to halt the production and sale of its product.

On September 15, it was confirmed that two deaths in two counties in Gansu province were related to the poisonous milk powder. On September 16, the GAQSIQ reported the inspection result, identifying 22 companies whose infant formula was tainted with melamine. In the next few days, Sanlu's chairwoman, Wenhua Tian, was removed from office and detained by the police. Four Sanlu managers were arrested. Government officials responsible for the oversight of the dairy industry were removed from office for dereliction of duties. On September 23, to ease consumers' concerns and to restore trust, many Chinese dairy companies and distribution businesses issued a proclamation of food quality commitment. Later, a Chinese court accepted the bankruptcy petition of the group. In 2009, a local Chinese court declared Sanlu insolvent and approved its takeover by Beijing Sanyuan Food Company.

Two milk dealers, Yujun Zhang and Jinping Geng, were arrested. The former was convicted of producing 776 tons of "protein powder" (a mixture containing melamine) and selling more than 600 tons of it to middlemen (Zhu, November 25, 2009) from September 2007 to August 2008. The latter was found guilty of adding 434kg of the "protein powder" to about 900 tons of raw milk (Zhu, November 25, 2009). Jinping Geng and other criminals then sold the adulterated milk to the Sanlu Group and other dairy companies from October 2007 to August 2008 (Zhu et al., 2009). Both dealers were sentenced to death.

Sanlu's chairwoman and general manager, Wenhua Tian, was sentenced to life imprisonment for producing and selling fake or substandard products. Other Sanlu executives received five- to 15-year sentences. Figure 2.1 provides an overview of the milk crisis.

Figure 2.1 An overview of the milk crisis.

Source: Courtesy *China Daily*.

Situation Analysis

In this scandal, consumers, particularly babies and their families, were most seriously affected. The dairy farmers, Sanlu's shareholders, its distributors, and its employees were also greatly affected. The other dairy companies and even the entire industry suffered great loss. The government agencies as well as the media were also involved.

The consumers. As one of the most serious food-safety breaches in China, Sanlu's consumers, especially the consumers with brand loyalty, were the main victims of the crisis. They included six babies killed and more than 300,000 babies hospitalized owing to the consumption of the poisonous infant formula over a long period of time.

The victims also included the heartbroken parents who lost their beloved new-borns and who are haunted by the bitter memories, as well as the anxious parents who are more concerned about the long-term health conditions of their hospitalized children than the compensation from Sanlu or the execution of the criminals. Hundreds of scandal-shocked parents converged on Sanlu demanding refunds and asking what milk powder was safe for their infants ("Toxic milk," 2008). A lot of babies affected by melamine-laced milk were from extremely poor rural areas and their parents sacrificed all their savings only to buy such toxic baby food.

Other consumers would also worry about their health conditions even though no symptoms of urinary tract ailments were detected at that time. Consumers lost confidence in Sanlu and even in the entire dairy industry. During the critical period, what the shocked parents needed most was the money and knowledge to take care of their babies hospitalized while all the consumers needed most was a safe source of milk powder.

The dairy farmers. These were also seriously affected by the scandal (Liu, 2008; Zhu and Cui, 2008). At the bottom of the nation's dairy industry, they provided raw milk to middlemen who also connected to the dairy companies. After the incident, farmers were losing money since no one wanted to drink milk anymore. The farmers could not make ends meet and needed immediate financial support because the milk price was plummeting while the feeding cost was increasing after the crisis ("Dairy farmers," 2009).

> In the entire production–marketing chain from farming to consumption, farmers always bear the brunt whenever a disaster, whether natural or artificial, occurs during the procedure. They are the most vulnerable to risks but the least powerful when it comes to profit-sharing.
>
> (Liu, 2008, para. 8)

Given the farmers' vulnerable and powerless status, Sanlu did not try to improve their status and economic situation before the crisis nor help them during the crisis. Instead, Sanlu attacked the dairy farmers by declaring that they tainted the milk and should be responsible for the crisis.

Sanlu's shareholders, distributors, and employees. Fonterra, Sanlu's largest shareholder, was aware of the contamination six weeks before the scandal was exposed and contacted the Chinese local officials, but failed to persuade them to issue a public recall of the milk powder (Van Den Gergh, 2008). Sanlu's scandal seriously damaged Fonterra's corporate image and reputation, and caused Fonterra's financial loss.

Sanlu's distributors were facing severe financial difficulties after the scandal became public. No supermarkets or other outlets wanted their products, so they had no income to help themselves out. Sanlu failed to provide the cash compensations to them in a timely manner. The distributors also suffered a loss of credibility during the crisis.

Thousands of Sanlu's employees faced the problem of supporting themselves and even their families after Sanlu had been ordered to halt production and business after the crisis. After the breakdown of the group, it would be hard for some of those employees who had spent many decades in that group to find another job to support themselves.

Other dairy companies and the entire dairy industry. Since the outbreak of Sanlu Group's scandal, many other dairy companies' products were also inspected and 22 companies' products were confirmed to be tainted by melamine. Thus, other dairy companies (such as Mengniu, Yili, and Guangming) were also facing huge financial losses. The scandal has severely damaged the entire dairy industry in the nation (Zhu, November 25, 2009) and has resulted in bans of dairy ingredients made in China internationally (Chao, 2009). The entire market was in depression ("Dairy farmers," 2009).

The government. The central government warned the public on September 11, 2008, that Sanlu's infant milk powder was highly suspected to be contaminated by melamine. It was not until the involvement of the central government that Sanlu issued a public recall. The government started "the first-class national food safety emergency response" ("China starts emergency response," 2008, para. 1) to deal with the contamination issue. Meanwhile, as the investigation of the scandal went further, the government officials found inadequate in leadership during the crisis were removed from office and "1244 government employees were investigated on corruption accusations" ("60 arrested," 2009).

The media. Several newspapers reported the cases of kidney stones and related the cause of the disease to the products of "some brand," without directly mentioning "Sanlu" in their reports. It was not until September 11, 2008, that a conscientious journalist named Guangzhou Jian wrote an article titled "Sanlu's milk powder, a possible cause of the kidney disease afflicting 14 infants in Gansu province." It was published before the central government's warning. The article was immediately reproduced and cited by many most frequently visited websites in China.

Sanlu's Initial Response

According to journalist Guangzhou Jian's recount ("An interview," n.d.), after the release of his report, Sanlu privately required him through phone calls to withdraw the article, arguing it was not the quality of Sanlu's products that were to blame and that the drinking water could be the cause of the kidney diseases ("An interview," n.d.).

Sanlu officially responded to Jian's report in a phone interview at 10 a.m. on September 11, 2008. The details of the interview were posted on some major Chinese websites. Sanlu's response:

> Our company is highly concerned about the issue. We have already sent staff to Gansu province for further investigation. Sanlu is a famous brand in our dairy industry. The milk powder is produced according to the national food quality standards. Thus the products are qualified. Currently no evidence shows that it is the consumption of Sanlu's milk powder that caused the diseases. If this is really the case, we believe that the food quality inspection department will give us an answer.
>
> ("Sanlu Group's response," 2008, para. 3)

Sanlu's officials also argued that there were many possible causes of the infants' kidney stones, that comprehensive knowledge was needed to raise babies, and that people should not just focus on a single aspect ("Sanlu Group's response," 2008).

At 1 p.m. that day, Haoyi Zhou, Chairman of Sanlu's cooperative company, firmly asserted again to the reporters:

> Although some consumers argued that our baby formula was the cause of the children's development of kidney stones a month ago, the results of the products inspection indicated they are all qualified products, which were stringently produced and inspected according to the national standards. We are highly conscientious to our customers.
>
> (Xu, 2009, p. 24)

Later that day, Sanlu's Yanfeng Cui, in charge of the Communications Department, told reporters:

> As a well-known national company with more than 60 years of history, Sanlu has become an icon of our national milk powder. We have a high sense of social responsibility. Our infant milk powder is produced exclusively for babies. The processes of production and inspection all meet the requirements of the national standards. However, these days, we have heard all kinds of negative feedback about our products. Since we don't know the reason currently, I feel puzzled. The entire industry and the experts also feel confused. So, we hope that our customers can inspect the products themselves. At the same time, I hope that the national authority will provide a persuasive report soon, since we are here to solve the problem, not to evade it. However, I am certain that all our products are qualified.
>
> ("Sanlu's declaration," 2008, para. 4)

However, at about 9:00 p.m. that day, the Ministry of Health announced the test result that Sanlu's products contained melamine, a chemical that will cause kidney stones in humans' unitary tract systems. Half an hour later, Sanlu Group finally admitted the issue and officially declared it would recall the products produced before August 6, 2008. Sanlu admitted that its self-test indicated some of its infant formula produced before August 6 were contaminated by melamine and there were about 700 tons of tainted products in the market. Sanlu's Production Department also warned people to stop consuming Sanlu's infant formula.

Goals, Objectives, Strategies, and Tactics

Sanlu's goals during the critical situation can be reflected in Sanlu's three important high-level managers' meetings from May to August 2008 regarding its product's quality and the kidney stones cases. The meetings indicated that the leaders realized the problem but were concerned more about the company instead of public health in that critical situation ("Sanlu's three meetings," 2009). From those three meetings, Sanlu's goals and objectives were deciphered. The reader is cautioned against assuming that the standard distinction between goals and objectives used in the West also applies to crisis communication programs in the East. Sanlu seemed oblivious to the warning signs of a looming corporate crisis and was hardly prepared for it from a communications standpoint (Wen, 2008; Xu, 2009); therefore, each of its objectives did not have a time element. Its crisis planning and program implementation were largely reactive. Sanlu's strategies and tactics reflected its crisis communication goals and objectives.

1. Goals, objectives, strategies, and tactics before the exposure of the scandal by the central government

Goal 1: To identify the cause of the kidney stones (when realizing an acute increase of infants' kidney stones cases in hospitals).

Objective 1: To determine whether Sanlu's infant milk powder is related to the kidney stones.

Strategy: Carried out self-investigation to determine whether its products were related to the cases of kidney stones.

Tactics:

- sent its samples to labs in Beijing, Shanghai, and Tianjin to test its quality;
- supervised the source of the fresh milk; and
- inspected the ingredients and the amount of ingredients of its products.

Objective 2: To identify why the amount of non-protein nitrogen in Sanlu's baby formula is so high after confirming that its products were related to the kidney stones in young children.

Strategy: Investigated the reason the amount of non-protein nitrogen in its products was so high.

Tactics: Sent samples of its products to Hebei Entry–Exit Inspection and Quarantine Bureau Technical Center secretly for inspection.

Goal 2: To cover up the issue (after confirming the contamination issue) to protect the company's image.

Objective 1: To keep the contamination issue out of public scrutiny.

Strategy: Kept the contamination issue a secret, after confirming through inspection that the infant formula was tainted with melamine.

Tactics:

- required everyone in high-level management to keep the contamination issue confidential;
- allowed no notes to be taken during the meeting on the issue;
- chose not to report it to the government before August ("China's Sanlu apologizes," 2008); and
- chose not to inform the public about the contamination issue ("China's Sanlu apologizes," 2008).

Objective 2: To settle customers' complaints.

Strategy: Compensated complaining consumers privately.

Tactics:

- compensated the customers who complained with Sanlu's other products; and
- compensated the customers who complained with money to pay for their infants' medical inspection fees.

Objective 3: To increase positive media coverage and to reduce negative media coverage.

Strategy 1: Suppressed the media's negative reports and disseminated through the media the false messages touting the high quality of its products (Bandurski, 2008).

Tactics:

- appointed one of Sanlu's vice general managers to tackle the media;
- required the consumers to remove their complaints from the BBS;
- required privately the reporter who first named Sanlu in his story to withdraw his report; and
- disseminated false messages by acting as reporters contributing articles eulogizing Sanlu through major print media and websites in China (Bandurski, 2008).

Strategy 2: Denied that its products were the cause of the cases of kidney stones through media before the central government's public warning of its product contamination.

Tactics:

- stated in a phone interview that its products were qualified and argued that there were many possible causes of the infants' kidney stones;
- claimed to the reporters that Sanlu's products were qualified and were produced and inspected in accordance with the national standards, and that Sanlu was highly conscientious toward its consumers; and
- told reporters that Sanlu was a company of rich history and a company with a high sense of social responsibility and that they were sure that their products were qualified.

Goal 3: To solve the contamination issue quietly (after confirming the issue).

Objective: To remove the products tainted with melamine from the market.

Strategy 1: Relied on the government to solve the contamination issue.

Tactics:

- submitted two written reports on the contamination issue to the Shijiazhuang local government on August 2 and on August 29 (Cui, 2009; Zhu and Cui, 2009); and
- decided to follow the local officials' directions and didn't inform the public. (Officials opted for a trade recall (Kwok, September 18, 2008; "Sanlu's three meetings," 2009) because they worried about negative publicity (Fan, 2008), especially during the period when China was hosting the 2008 Olympic Games.)

Strategy 2: Implemented a trade recall instead of a public recall (Kwok, September 17, 2008).

Tactics: Notified privately all the distributors of the contamination issue and recalled those products quietly in August (Chao, 2009).

Strategy 3: Replaced the products with a higher amount of melamine on the market with the products with less melamine.

Tactics:

- planned to produce melamine-free milk powder to replace the products with melamine in the market, but finally gave it up once under pressure; and
- used the products with 20 mg/kg melamine in stock to replace the products with a higher amount of melamine in the market (Zhu et al., 2009).

2. Goals, objectives, strategies, and tactics after the exposure of the scandal by the central government.

Goal: To protect the company from being devastated by the crisis.

Objective: To restore the company's image.

Strategy 1: Issued a public recall and warned the public after the central government's warning of Sanlu's contamination.

Tactics:

- declared officially to recall the products produced before August 6, 2008, half an hour after the central government's public warning on September 11;
- admitted the contamination issue; and
- warned people to stop consuming Sanlu's infant formula.

Strategy 2: Regarded itself as a victim and blamed the other parties.

Tactics:

- declared on September 12 that it was the dairy farmers who had illegally mixed melamine into the raw milk and the farmers should be responsible for victim compensation;
- stated on September 12 that the reason why they did not test the amount of melamine was that there were currently no national standards for reference ("A comprehensive report," 2008; Xu, 2009); and
- declared that the group was also the victim.

Strategy 3: Apologized to the public through the media.

Tactics:

- On September 15, Sanlu's Vice President Zhenling Zhang apologized to the sickened infants and young children as well as their families in a news conference. Zhenling Zhang read the following letter of apology:

  > The serious safety breach of the Sanlu's infant formula milk powder has caused severe harm to the affected babies and their families. We really feel distressed about this issue. Sanlu Group extends its most sincere apology to you. At 9 a.m. on September 15, our group got the news from news conference held by the Public Security Department of Hebei province that 19 suspects who may have been involved in tainting the milk were detained and 2 were arrested. We thank the Public Security Department for their hard work. We solemnly declare that we will recall all the products produced prior to August 6. If consumers have doubts and concerns about those produced after that date, we will also make a recall. Also, we will try to help cure the sickened babies at all costs.
  >
  > (Li and Wu, 2008, para. 2)

- On September 18, Sanlu's newly appointed chairman also apologized to the public.

Strategy 4: Compensated the victims after the crisis.

Tactics: Secured a loan of 902 billion yuan (142 billion dollars) on December 19, 2008, to pay for the medical fees for the sickened infants and children ("60 arrested," 2009).

Most of Sanlu's goals and objectives were completely against the company's mission statement and philosophy. The name of the group (i.e., Sanlu) means three deer, a symbol of benevolence, longevity, peace, and prosperity in Chinese culture (Li and Ma, 2009). One of the company's business goals is an endless effort to create nutritious products for the customers' health (Liu, 2003). Its core values include: humanistic orientation, honesty, harmony, innovation, as well as responsibility, with a humanistic orientation and honesty as the basic and ultimate value (Feng and Nie, 2006). Its chairwoman, Wenhua Tian, once said in an interview: During these 50 years, what the group valued most were the people (including the customers, the employees, and the dairy farmers), honesty and sincerity, as well as the quality of their products and service (Feng and Nie, 2006). She also said that the group should be credible to its customers, dairy farmers, distributors, and even the entire society (Feng and Nie, 2006). However, its strategies and tactics employed before and after the exposure of the scandal reflected its true goals and objectives, and thus were against the previously stated business goals and corporate values.

Outcomes Assessment

Responsibility and accountability, access to information, as well as humanism and care are all ethical issues (Ulmer et al., 2007). Sanlu's unethical conduct (i.e., neglecting humanism, preventing the free flow of information, and shifting responsibility) during the scandal are the major reasons for its collapse. "Humanism is a philosophical standpoint and value system that emphasizes the uniqueness and inherent worth of human beings" (Ulmer et al., 2007, pp. 172–173). However, Sanlu's crisis communication goals (e.g., covering up the milk powder issue to protect the group when facing the crisis) and strategies (e.g., using less tainted products in stock in exchange for severely tainted products in the market, disseminating the false reports, hiding the truth from the consumers) revealed that they neglected humanism. What they truly valued was the organization's reputation, financial situation, and sustainability. They did not take the consumers' health or even their lives into account, obviously in contradiction with a humanist orientation.

The group's strategy of preventing the free flow of information (e.g., suppressing the media's negative reports and hiding the truth of the product contamination from the public) led to the development of the crisis and created a devastating effect. If the public had been informed directly after the group's confirming the contamination, consumers could have taken measures earlier and fewer people would have been victimized.

Sanlu is responsible for the crisis. It failed to respond promptly and appropriately, did not stop producing and selling the tainted products, and did not administer a public recall after confirming the contamination ("Sanlu's three meetings," 2009). Sanlu tried by every means possible to cover up the issue ("Sanlu's three meetings," 2009; Xu, 2009; Zhu et al., 2009). An official investigation demonstrated Sanlu's lying about the contamination ("Crisis management helps," 2008); thus, many families were still using Sanlu's milk formula to feed the infants developing kidney stones and receiving treatment in hospitals (Chao, 2009). Moreover, it assigned responsibility to the dairy farmers and the government agencies and declared that it was also the victim. Due to those unethical attitudes and behaviors, Sanlu lost its reputation, credit, and the consumers' confidence (Wen, 2008).

A lack of crisis communication knowledge also contributed to Sanlu's collapse. First, the group was not aware of crisis prevention. The initial warning sign appeared at the end of 2007, when Sanlu received the first customer's complaints. But owing to its lack of crisis management knowledge and lack of crisis prevention awareness, it failed to take the warning signs seriously. It suppressed the warning signs by privately compensating the consumers who complained, with the hope of protecting the reputation of the company and reducing customer complaints. No actions were taken to evaluate the warning signs to prevent the potential harm. It began to take the warning signs seriously in May when more and more infants were diagnosed with kidney stones, about half a year after the first warning sign appeared. Second, the group's actions in response to the crisis were not only unethical and inadequate, but also slow. Official public recall, public warning, public apology, and victim compensation came too late. Third, its relationships with different stakeholders are questionable. It relied too much on the local government for decisions and communicated too little with the customers, its vital stakeholders. Not only does government need information, but so do consumers, as they are the primary stakeholders, and need to know how such a crisis affects their lives, and what they can do to protect themselves in the crisis (Coombs, 2007). "In fact, an organization should fully disclose any and all information about a crisis if there are risks of further harm or even death resulting from the crisis" (Coombs, 2007, p.133). However, the group did not tell the customers what to do to protect themselves nor inform and help the victims by providing necessary information, resources, guidance, and support. As to its relationship with the dairy farmers, the group failed to establish a cooperative and equal relationship with the dairy farmers by ignoring the fact that the dairy farmers are politically powerless and economically disadvantaged. Moreover, when the scandal was exposed and no one wanted milk, the group shifted the responsibility to the dairy farmers who were already disadvantaged, triggering national resentment. Also, Sanlu's relationship with the media was not only inappropriate but also unethical. All those factors damaged the relationships between Sanlu and its primary stakeholders (i.e., the consumers and the dairy farmers) and led to Sanlu's collapse.

Lessons that can be Learned

Admittedly, the industry's present structure (middlemen connecting dairy farmers and dairy companies) needs to be improved because dairy companies have no way to monitor the quality of fresh milk (Zhu and Cui, 2008; Zhu, January 6, 2009). Also, the nation's food safety supervision loopholes need to be mended and food safety standards and regulations need to be improved (Li, 2009; Zhu, January 6, 2009). However, those steps will only partially solve the problem. Sanlu deserved punishment because, when facing a potential crisis and later hit by the crisis, it did not engage in proper crisis management that can protect health and lives, lower potential damage to a company's reputation, and save an organization's future. Many lessons can be learned from Sanlu's case of crisis management and crisis communication.

The most important lesson is the necessity of improving organizations' business and social ethics. Sacrificing ethics for profits, a path leading to disaster, should by no means be adopted by any organizations or individuals. When facing a crisis, it is even critical for an organization to demonstrate sound social ethics and the priority should be given to physically, mentally, and economically vulnerable victims created by a crisis (Ulmer et al., 2007). A humanistic and caring orientation toward the victims, potential victims, and all other human beings should guide the organization's crisis communication goals, strategies, and tactics. Unethical deeds such as lying and deceiving should be replaced by ethical ones such as honest, forthright communication to prevent the crisis or limit the negative effects of the crisis on victims, other stakeholders, and the company itself. Understanding corporate social responsibilities and a willingness to accept responsibilities after an outbreak of a crisis are ethical, while attempting to avoid responsibilities is unethical (Ulmer et al., 2007). After the crisis, the organization should actively engage in helping the victims by providing physical, emotional, and economic support.

Another important lesson learned is that China's organizations should increase the awareness of crisis prevention and preparation. Crisis prevention and preparation are important parts of crisis communication (Coombs, 2007; Regester and Larkin, 2005). But Sanlu Group did not realize the importance of crisis scanning, warning signs, and the necessity of an effective crisis-sensing mechanism (Wen, 2008), nor did it know the functions of risk management and reputation management. Because a crisis can influence the organization, the organization's stakeholders, and the environment (Coombs, 1999, 2007; Fearn-Banks, 2011; Heath and Millar, 2004; Zaremba, 2010) by preventing an organization from achieving its vital objectives (Heath and Millar, 2004; Ulmer et al., 2007), by threatening or damaging its reputation (Fearn-Banks, 2011; Lerbinger, 1997), by creating potential or actual financial loss (Lerbinger, 1997), by violating stakeholders' expectation toward the organization (Coombs, 2007), by affecting the stakeholders' interests (Heath and Millar, 2004), by leading the stakeholders in attributing cause and responsibility (Coombs and Holladay, 1996), as well as by harming the relationship between the organization and its stakeholders (Heath and Millar, 2004), an organization should proactively prevent a crisis rather than passively respond to a crisis when it hits.

The third important lesson is that an organization should act effectively in the crisis response period in a timely manner. It should respond quickly and actively with appropriate ethics as guidance, not waiting and relying on the government or other stakeholders. "Chinese companies were notoriously bad at communicating"(Van Den Gergh, 2008). When facing a crisis, the organization should seize the time to communicate with all kinds of stakeholders through appropriate channels and take appropriate actions to reduce the negative effects of the crisis.

Discussion Questions

1. Comment on the appropriateness of Sanlu's crisis communication goals.
2. What strategies might have changed the outcomes?
3. What is your take on Sanlu's initial response?

References

60 arrested over melamine-tainted Sanlu milk powder. (2009, January 11). Retrieved from www.chinaview.cn

A comprehensive report on Sanlu's milk powder: Getting closer to truth. (2008, September 17). Retrieved from www.zhgpl.com/doc/1007/4/8/1/100748166.html?coluid=0&kindid=0&docid=100748166

An interview with Jian Guangzhou: Why I mentioned Sanlu's brand name in my report. (n.d.). Retrieved from http://news.qq.com/zt/2008/dialog/jgz.htm

Bandurski, D. (2008). Sanlu's public relations pawns: A relay of lies in China's media, September 28. Retrieved from http://cmp.hku.hk/2008/09/28/1259/

Chao, L. (2009). World news: Ex-executive pleads guilty in China's tainted-milk case. *Wall Street Journal* (Eastern ed.), January 2. Available from EBSCO Academic Search Premier database (Accession No. 36146824).

China starts emergency response over tainted milk powder incident. (2008, September 13). Retrieved from www.chinaview.cn

China's Sanlu apologizes for milk powder contamination. (2008, September 15). Retrieved from www.chinaview.cn

China's tainted milk scandal grows; company apologizes as government braces for more stricken infants. (2008). *Grand Rapids Press* (Michigan), September 17. Available from LexisNexis Academic database.

Coombs, W. T. (1999). *Ongoing crisis communication: Planning, managing, and responding*. Thousand Oaks, CA: Sage.

Coombs, W. T. (2007). *Ongoing crisis communication: Planning, managing, and responding* (2nd ed.). Los Angeles, CA: Sage.

Coombs, W. T., and Holladay, S. J. (1996). Communication and attribution in a crisis: An experimental study of crisis communication. *Journal of Public Relations Research*, 8, 279–295.

Crisis management helps China's dairy industry recover. (2008, September 25). Retrieved from www.chinaview.cn

Cui, X. (2009). Dairy firm's former chairwoman denies cover-up. *China Daily*, January 1. Retrieved from www.chinadaily.com.cn

Dairy farmers to get $36.6 million subsidies. (2009). *China Daily*, April 24. Retrieved from www.chinadaily.com.cn

Fan, M. (2008). China's tainted-milk crisis grows despite official claims; A dozen countries banning, recalling nation's dairy products. *The Washington Post*, September 28. Available from LexisNexis Academic database.

Feng, Y., and Nie, Y. (2006). Those who have got deer will gain the world: An interview with Sanlu's Chairwoman Wenhua Tian. *China Dairy*, 11, 4–7.

Fearn-Banks, K. (2011). *Crisis communications: A casebook approach*. Mahwah, NJ: Lawrence Erlbaum Associates.

Heath, R. L., and Millar, D. P. (2004). A rhetorical approach to crisis communication: Management, communication processes, and strategic responses. In D. P. Millar and R. L. Heath (Eds.), *Responding to crisis: A rhetorical approach to crisis communication* (pp. 1–17). Mahwah, NJ: Lawrence Erlbaum Associates.

Kwok, K. (2008). Officials "knew of tainted milk for a month"; Local government accused of failing to pass on information to provincial leaders. *South China Morning Post*, September 17. Retrieved from www.lexisnexis.com.libproxy.temple.edu/hottopics/lnacademic/?verb=sr&csi=8422&sr=lni(4TG4–9S50-TX36–903F)

Kwok, K. (2008). Trade recall chosen over public alert. *South China Morning Post*, September 18. Retrieved from www.lexisnexis.com.libproxy.temple.edu/hottopics/lnacademic/?verb=sr&csi=8422&sr=lni(4TGB-90V0-TX36–919J)

Lerbinger, O. (1997). *The crisis manager: Facing risk and responsibility*. Mahwah, NY: Lawrence Erlbaum Associates.

Li, S., and Ma, Y. (2009). The origin and changes of China's deer culture. *Journal of Northeast Agricultural University*, 7(5), 75–78.

Li, W., and Wu, Y. (2008). Sanlu apologized to the customers as well as sickened babies and their families. *Hebei Daily*, September 16. Available from CNKI database (doi: CNKI:PCN:13–0001.0.2008–09–16.0027).

Li, X. (2009). Conviction in Sanlu case just a start. *China Daily*, January 22. Retrieved from www.chinadaily.com.cn

Liu, S. (2008). Protecting interest of farmers. *China Daily*, October 15. Retrieved from www.chinadaily.com.cn

Liu, X. (2003). *A study on developing strategy of Hebei Sanlu Group Co.* (Master's thesis). Available from CNKI database (doi: CNKI:CDMD:2.2004.126572).

Pregestimil infant formula recall. (2005, January 20). Retrieved from www.fsai.ie/details.aspx?id=5868

Product recall list (from 2000 to 2007). (n.d.). Retrieved from www.ibfan.org/art/85–23.pdf

Regester, M. and Larkin, J. (2005). *Risk issues and crisis management: A casebook of best practice* (3rd ed.). Philadelphia, PA: Kogan Page.

Sanlu Group's response to the milk powder issue: Products were in accordance with the national standards. (2008, September 11). Retrieved from http://news.sina.com.cn/c/2008–09–11/105416273760.shtml

Sanlu's declaration: We don't have the 18 yuan milk powder and the lowest retail price is 25 yuan. (2008, September 11). Retrieved from http://news.163.com/08/0911/19/4LJ6KDH70001124J.html

Sanlu's three meetings. (2009, January 8). Retrieved from http://finance.cctv.com/20090108/103353.shtml

Toxic milk fears grow. (2008, September 20). Available from LexisNexis Academic database.

Ulmer, R. R., Sellnow, T. L., and Seeger, M. W. (2007). *Effective crisis communication: Moving from crisis to opportunities*. Thousand Oaks, CA: Sage.

Van Den Gergh, R. (2008). Fonterra's melamine response "too late." *The Dominion Post*, November 10. Available from LexisNexis Academic database.

Wen, M. (2008). Three major mistakes committed by Sanlu's crisis communication. *Foreign Business*, 10, 36–37.

WHO global strategy for food safety: Safer food for better health. (2002). Retrieved from www.who.int/foodsafety/publications/general/en/strategy_en.pdf

Xu, Q. (2009). *An investigation on Sanlu's crisis management* (Doctoral dissertation). Available from CNKI database (doi: CNKI:CDMD:2.2009.204056).

Zaremba, A. J. (2010). *Crisis communication: Theory and practice*. London, UK: M. E. Sharpe.

Zhu, F., Yang, S., and Zhang, H. (2009). Sanlu Group's cover-up uncovered. *China Animal Husbandry Bulletin* 2, 32–33.

Zhu, Z. (2008). Govt shows milky way to troubled dairy firms. *China Daily*, November 20. Retrieved from www.chinadaily.com.cn

Zhu, Z. (2009). Feeding a formula for disaster. *China Daily*, January 6. Retrieved from www.chinadaily.com.cn

Zhu, Z. (2009). 2 executed over milk powder scandal. *China Daily*, November 25. Retrieved from www.chinadaily.com.cn

Zhu, Z., and Cui, X. (2008). Tough, uncertain days ahead. *China Daily*, October 15. Retrieved from www.chinadaily.com.cn

Zhu, Z., and Cui, X. (2009). Sanlu ex-boss aware of tainted milk. *China Daily*, January 1. Retrieved from www.chinadaily.com.cn

VIEWS FROM AN EXPERT

XIANHONG CHEN

Xianhong Chen is director of the Department of Advertising and assistant dean of School of Journalism and Communication at Huazhong University of Science and Technology, China. She is also the vice director of the China Public Relations Association and a member of China International Public Relations Association. Her research interests include comparison research on public relations theory, government public relations, new media public relations, crisis management, as well as advertising and brand communication.

As we all know, Sanlu's public relations practices were both expected and criticized by the public during the poisonous milk crisis. On the one hand, the inappropriate deeds of the unethical public relations firm (e.g., one PR firm tried to give 3 million yuan, i.e., 0.47 million dollars, to the online media and asked them to ban Sanlu's negative coverage online) were greatly criticized. On the other hand, the public and the organization greatly expected that public relations could act like saviors and save the organization from the crisis. How can we analyze Sanlu's poisonous milk scandal in the context of effective crisis communication?

Public relations is not a panacea. If an organization like Sanlu acts unethically by neglecting the public interest to pursue profits, the organization's department of public relations is to be blamed. If it is outside public relations firms (e.g., the firm suggesting using 3 million yuan to ban the online negative reports) that led to Sanlu's unethical deeds, the public relations firms are to be blamed because of their abuse of public relations knowledge and skills.

First, not only the strategies, but more importantly, the ethics should be the essence of public relations. The ethical issues are also philosophical issues, related not only to the conduct of public relations practitioners, but also to the worldviews and methodologies as well as the core and the construction of the discipline of public relations. Social responsibility should be the basis of public relations. Effective public relations is based on actual actions and policies. If organizations do not take the public interest into account, its actions of public relations will not be supported by the public. Thus, the actions of public relations should take both the public's interest and the organization's interest into account.

Second, the essence of crisis communication is not only an issue of methodologies, but also an issue of philosophical perspective. That is, actively being socially responsible should be regarded as the worldview and methodology for crisis communication. Generally speaking, an organization's social responsibility should include economic responsibility, legal responsibility, ethical responsibility, and philanthropic responsibility. That is to say, when an organization is making profits and being responsible for the shareholders, it should also be responsible for its employees, consumers, the environment, and its community. Those responsibilities include: obeying laws and regulations, ensuring employees' health and safety, protecting workers' rights, following business ethics, protecting the environment, supporting philanthropy, making donations to charity, and protecting vulnerable social groups. Studies indicate that when public relations practices are responsible and ethical, public relations is productive for the organization and even the world by enhancing mutual understanding among different groups and by settling conflicts. However, when the practices are irresponsible and unethical, public relations are all about manipulation and deception.

To carry out effective crisis communication, an organization should incorporate social responsibility into organizational culture, in order to prevent irresponsible thoughts and conduct. Moreover, when a crisis comes, an organization should actively take on social responsibility by recalling the products in a timely manner, by comforting and compensating the victims, by making an apology, and by other methods. Thus, Sanlu's shutdown was inevitable. It did not have modern public relations programs. Its strategies and tactics were against the theories and methodologies of crisis communication. Therefore, Sanlu demonstrated a bad example of public relations.

Maybe someone will ask whether there could have been a way to save Sanlu. The answer there is most likely positive. For example, at the beginning of the poisonous milk issue, if Sanlu had taken full responsibility (such as recalling all of their products and compensating the consumers) to protect the consumers and the brand name, it would not have gone bankrupt. Facing a crisis, an organization should first protect consumers, then the brand. If consumers are protected, then the brand name will be protected, and the organization will survive the crisis.

China and France

Olympic Torch Protests in France, Reactions in China: Carrefour Learns about International Crises

W. Timothy Coombs

When French pro-Tibet protesters attacked the 2008 Olympic Torch on its trip through France, it initiated a series of events that created an international crisis for the French retailer Carrefour. Chinese citizens, in a show of national pride, protested against Carrefour stores in China. The protesters were striking back against France by attacking Carrefour. Communicative actions by Carrefour and the Chinese government helped to ease the crisis. This case examines the events that precipitated the crisis, how the three main actors (Chinese protesters, Carrefour management, and the Chinese government) responded to the crisis, and the effectiveness of those responses. The analysis extends our understanding of international crises and the effective use of crisis response strategies along with demonstrating the analytic value of the rhetorical arena model of crisis communication.

Introduction

A torch relay is held immediately before each Olympics. The torch is lit in Greece and runs a route through various countries on its way to the next Olympic venue. The torch is a symbol of the Olympics and is shared with other countries through the torch relay. The idea is to spread the Olympic message of peace and friendship as well as to build interest in the games themselves. On March 24, 2008, the torch was lit for the summer Olympics to be held in Beijing, China. The 129-day trip was called the Journey of Harmony. Unfortunately, the 2008 Olympic Torch relay was far from the ideal of peace and friendship or harmony. In many locations the Olympic Torch relay was met with protests. Most protesters were pro-Tibet and were upset by China's treatment of Tibet, while other protesters were using the Olympics as a chance to feature China's poor human rights record. Protests occurred in the U.S., Australia, Japan, the U.K., South Korea, and France. However, the most vocal and violent of the protests transpired in France. In fact the Olympic Torch was extinguished in France and, at times, the torch had to be kept in the support van as more security was added and the torch relay route shortened in France. It should be noted the support van carries the true flame and relay torches are simply lit from that flame. If a torch is extinguished for any reason, including a malfunction of the torch, the Olympic flame still burns.

Hosting the Olympic Games is a significant public diplomacy effort for an emerging country. Being an Olympic host is one way for a country to announce its entry onto the world stage. For instance, Mexico City in 1968 and Seoul in 1988 were examples of the Olympics marking the global arrival of its hosts. So, in 2008, the Beijing Summer Games were to announce the arrival of China as a major international actor. However, when the games were awarded to Beijing, the protests began. The focal point was human rights including China's control of Tibet and possible connections to the brutal situation in Darfur. Human Rights Watch was one of the leaders of the protests claiming China's human rights record should have precluded it from hosting the games. Many protesters targeted the top-level Summer Olympics sponsors including Atos Origin, Coca-Cola, General Electric, Manulife, Johnson and Johnson, Kodak, Lenovo, McDonald's, Omega (Swatch Group), Panasonic, Samsung and Visa ("Rights group", 2008). In March of 2008, there were violent clashes been protesters and Chinese forces in Tibet. The violence in Tibet sparked negative media coverage for China as their human rights policies were questioned.

Beijing was considered by many to be a controversial pick to host the Olympics. However, China's emergence as a major global force needed to be recognized and hosting the Olympics is an accepted form of global recognition. The Chinese government and its people were rightfully excited about hosting the Olympics and took great pride in their hosting duties. It was not surprising that the torch attack in France created a negative reaction in China. The torch attack was an attack on the Olympic host, China. One of the attacks involved Jin Jing, a disabled Chinese fencer. Her refusal to allow a protester to take the torch from her made her a hero in China. An anti-French sentiment had already been building in China because French President Nicolas Sarkozy had said he might not attend the Summer Olympics because of the Chinese crackdown on dissenters in Tibet ("China protests", 2008).

In response to the French attacks, many Chinese citizens decided to retaliate by protesting against France. Unfortunately for the retail giant Carrefour, they are a symbol of France and have a strong presence in China. Chinese citizens went online to organize boycotts of Carrefour and to stage protests at Carrefour stores in China. Other French symbols were targeted as well but Carrefour was the most visible (Lawrence, 2008).

Carrefour suddenly found itself in the middle of a crisis simply because it was French, not because of anything the corporation had done. Moreover, Carrefour was encountering the challenging realm of an international crisis. As corporations become more transnational, the likelihood of an international crisis increases. Transnational corporations produce goods or market service in more than one country. There will be a home country where operations are based and multiple host countries where assets are located. An international crisis might involve a host or a global crisis. A host crisis is a crisis limited to one or a few host countries. The transnational corporation faces challenges associated with managing a crisis in an unfamiliar locale—the host countries. A global crisis involves the home country and one or more host countries. Again, the transnational corporation faces concerns with addressing a crisis in an unfamiliar host country as well as dealing with the situation in the home country (Coombs, 2008). At times, the crisis management demands of the host and home crisis can conflict, thereby increasing the complexity of the crisis management effort (Frandsen and Johansen, 2010). Figures 2.2 and 2.3 present visual depictions of the host and global crises.

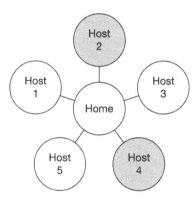

Figure 2.2 Varieties of international crises—host crisis.

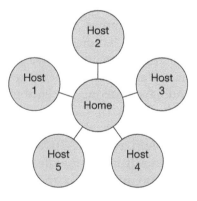

Figure 2.3 Global crisis.

Carrefour was in a global crisis. There were problems in the host country of China and concerns in the home country of France. The Olympic Torch boycotts clearly were news in France, so the home country was involved in the crisis. In a global world, whatever actions Carrefour took in China would be known back home to stakeholders in France. Hence, Carrefour management would need to consider home country stakeholders when reacting to the crisis.

Background of the Crisis

To understand the 2008 Beijing Olympics, we need to go back to September 24, 1993. It was on that date that Sydney, Australia was awarded the 2000 Summer Olympics. Why is this important? Beijing, China was considered the frontrunner for the 2000 Summer Olympics making the Sydney announcement a surprise. The suspected reason for the defeat was China's human rights record and continued repression of dissidents (Riding, 1993). Greece was the favorite for 2004 Summer Olympics because of a felt need to return to Athens, the birthplace of the Olympics. Athens failed to win the 1996 Olympics but did secure the 2004 Summer Olympics.

For Beijing, 2008 was next chance to really secure the Summer Olympics. On July 13, 2001, the announcement was made that Beijing would host the 2008 Summer Olympics. Beijing won by a wide margin in the voting. Concerns were still raised about human rights but the Chinese had argued their human rights record was improving and many other countries argued that hosting the Olympics will deepen China's commitment to improving human rights. Many human rights groups disagreed and began their protests the day the Olympics were awarded to Beijing. Another important point is that by 2001 China was a global superpower. Their important place within the realm of global events could not be denied. The global prominence of China is one reason given for the overwhelming Olympic voters' support for the 2008 Beijing bid (Longman, 2001). The Chinese government pledged it would work to improve human rights, freedom of the press, and environmental concerns. There were issues of air quality in Beijing and the danger it might pose to the athletes, and how freely foreign journalists would be allowed to operate while covering the Olympics.

When the French protesters attacked the Olympic Torch on April 7, 2008, it was not a sudden event but part of a long concern over China, the Olympics, and human rights. For Carrefour, the Olympic Torch attack in France suddenly made it a major player in this long-simmering crisis. The Chinese people were very proud of hosting the Summer Olympics. Hosting an Olympics is recognition of a country's position in the world. Again, the French attacks on the Olympic Torch were viewed as an attack on China. Many Chinese people used the Internet to defend China's honor by attacking France. How do average people attack a country? The answer is by using the marketplace and attacking the products of that country through protests and boycotts. Enter

Carrefour, a French retail giant with a strong presence in China. Carrefour was to feel the wrath of customers upset with France and looking to defend the honor of their homeland.

Carrefour is described as a retailer and has hypermarkets (a supermarket that is combined with a department store), supermarkets, hard discount, and convenience stores. Carrefour is the second-largest retail chain in the world and the largest in Europe. Walmart is the world's largest retail chain. At the time of the protests and boycotts, Carrefour had 122 stores in China ("China protests", 2008)

The Chinese protests and boycotts of Carrefour were created by Internet and cell phone messages. A number of websites appeared in China, calling for Carrefour boycotts. By April 14, 2008, there were over 170,000 "boycott Carrefour" web pages online ("Paris torch relay", 2008). E-mails were sent urging people not to buy from Carrefour. One message asked people to not shop the big May 1 sale Carrefour was planning. Another requested that people not shop at Carrefour for 17 days, the length of time the Summer Olympics would be held in Beijing ("Chinese netizens", 2008). Part of the Internet chatter included a rumor encapsulated in this sample message, "No one should shop at Carrefour, because the biggest shareholder of Carrefour donated huge money to the Dalai Lama, a lot of French people support the independence of Tibet, and even the French president has announced boycott of the Beijing Olympics" ("Chinese netizens", 2008, para. 3). The rumor held that shareholders of Carrefour were funding the Dalai Lama and support for pro-Tibetan efforts in the West. The information was not factual; hence, it is being labeled as a rumor. However, the rumor helped to increase negative views of Carrefour and a willingness to take action against the corporation.

The actions went beyond boycotts to physical protests at Carrefour stores. A number of Carrefour stores across China were the site for protesters to voice their complaints against Carrefour, France, and the West in general. The protests would often attract hundreds and perhaps even over a thousand protesters in locations such as Beijing, Shanghai, Changsha, Fuzhou, Chongqing, and Shenyang (McDonald, 2008; "More protests", 2008). Carrefour canceled its planned advertising for the major May 1 holiday sale and operated in crisis mode. Carrefour managers were trying to understand the situation and how best to address the crisis.

Situation Analysis

A key to understanding this global crisis is to examine the major actors involved in the crisis situation. The major actors represent the different voices that appear during the "Olympic Torch Crisis." The crisis actors comprise what Frandsen and Johansen (2010) call the rhetorical arena. The rhetorical arena is unique in that it utilizes a multivocal approach to crisis communication. A multivocal approach examines how the different crisis communication voices arise and intermix during a crisis. For the Olympic Torch Crisis case, it is instructive to identify the major crisis communicators and their stake in the crisis.

The Carrefour Group

Carrefour has had operations in China since 1995. That initial effort was a joint venture. By 2000, Carrefour had become the largest retailer in China. Carrefour carefully cultivated its China market strategy. Wisely, Carrefour treated China as a number of smaller markets rather than one large market. Moreover, Carrefour stocks many items manufactured in China creating the sense of being local. Carrefour is dedicated to growth in the China market opening its 169th hypermarket in November of 2010 ("China Carrefour inaugurated", 2010). In 2007, a sale of cooking oil during a time of rising cooking oil prices created a stampede that killed three customers in Chongqing ("Three die", 2007). Later, two Carrefour executives were sentenced to jail time for safety lapses leading to the deaths (Buckley, 2010). China is a critical market for Carrefour and the market cultivation process has not been without its problems.

The stake for Carrefour in the Olympic Torch Crisis was market share in China and revenues in general. A boycott could create a temporary loss of revenue for Carrefour. For instance, the May 1 holiday sales were estimated to be 20 percent below the previous year (Carrefour, 2008). Of course a boycott's impact on sales are typically temporary. However, if resentment remained over the Olympic Torch Crisis, Carrefour could risk a permanent drop in its Chinese market share. Carrefour had a strong economic stake in the crisis. The crisis threatened to derail Carrefour's expansion and profitability in the China market.

The Chinese Government

The Summer Olympics were to be a global moment of recognition and validation of China as a superpower—it was to be a celebration. China would get to show the world what it had become and demonstrate its ability to deliver a spectacular Olympic Games. The various groups trying to make human rights abuses a part of the 2008 Summer Olympic news coverage detracted from China's goals. Hosting an Olympics is supposed to generate positive media coverage for the host. In turn, that positive media coverage would help to build a positive reputation for the Olympic host in the minds of people all around the world. That is why hosting the Olympic Games is considered to be a valuable element of public diplomacy. In addition, staging major, international sporting events (mega-events) is one means of generating favorable, international media coverage of the host country (Manheim, 1994).

The Chinese government's stake is reputation enhancement via positive media attention. Any interjections of human rights discussions into the

Olympic media coverage would erode the reputation-building effects of hosting the 2008 Summer Olympics. The Carrefour boycott was a reaction to the protests in France. The protests in France were a function of human rights complaints toward China. It follows that the media coverage of the reaction to the torch relay attacks served to perpetuate the discussion of human rights. The crisis threatened to lessen the positive impact hosting the Summer Olympics would have on China's global reputation.

The Chinese Protesters

The Chinese citizens protesting Carrefour were expressing their displeasure over perceived insults to their country. Those boycotting and protesting were showing pride in and support for their country. The attack on France, through Carrefour, was a means of venting frustration and responding to a character attack. The stake for the Carrefour protesters is national pride. That is a nebulous stake but is what binds the protesters to this crisis—the motivation for their actions. The Carrefour protesters in China were not trying to destroy Carrefour by never shopping there again. Instead, they were trying to make a point about standing up for their own country and used tools available to them for making that point.

Summary of Problems and Opportunities

The Olympic Torch Crisis was clearly a problem for Carrefour. They were facing financial and marketing share loss. There was a need for Carrefour management to craft an effective response that could diffuse the crisis. The Chinese government was facing a minor problem. Overall media coverage of the 2008 Summer Olympics was still positive but the Olympic Torch Crisis was keeping the human rights issue alive in the media. The Chinese protesters saw the Olympic Torch Crisis as an opportunity. It was an opportunity for them to show their national pride and to retaliate against a country that had insulted them.

Responses to the Crisis

The analysis covers the three main entities involved in the Olympic Torch Crisis. Those entities are Carrefour, the Chinese government, and the Chinese protesters. The responses of Carrefour and the Chinese government reflect crisis communication efforts designed to manage the crisis while the Chinese protesters used communication to initiate the crisis.

Carrefour Response

Even though there are three primary actors in the crisis, Carrefour is the primary crisis manager. Carrefour is at the center of the crisis and the party most affected by the protests. The crisis was essentially a rumor with some elements of a challenge crisis. Carrefour did not support pro-Tibet groups and did not oppose the Beijing Olympics. The corporation was simply a victim of guilt by association. Carrefour was French and some French people had insulted China with the torch attacks. The challenge was that Carrefour was part of the French effort to support pro-Tibet groups and to attack the Beijing Olympics. Perceptions do matter in a crisis. If your stakeholders perceive the organization is in crisis, there is a crisis (Coombs, 2007). Chinese protesters perceived a problem with Carrefour so Carrefour was in a crisis.

The initial response from Carrefour was virtually no response. Carrefour management seemed stunned by the breadth and depth of the boycotts and protests because initially there was no statement. As the crisis intensified, Carrefour began to construct its crisis response. Carrefour's strategy was built around denial and ingratiation. The denial crisis response strategy seeks to demonstrate there is no connection between the crisis and the organization and/or no crisis occurred. The ingratiation crisis response strategy seeks to praise stakeholders (Benoit, 1995; Coombs, 2007). Carrefour was seeking to dissociate itself from the Olympic Torch protests, reaffirm its commitment to China and the Beijing Olympics, and correct misinformation about its supposed support for pro-Tibet groups.

The initial Carrefour crisis response was offered at a press conference by Gean Luc Lhuillier, Carrefour China's vice president, "We and all our employees feel regretful about what happened in Paris and support the Beijing Olympics 100 percent" (Carrefour, 2008). Similar sentiments were expressed by Carrefour Chairman Jose Luis Duran:

> Obviously, recent sabotage incidents in Paris during the Olympic Torch relay hurt the feelings of the Chinese people, made them angry and triggered their protests. I hope that the preparations for the Olympics will be implemented with a harmonious atmosphere. The success of the Beijing Olympics will benefit all the people.
>
> ("Carrefour supports", 2008)

Carrefour began its crisis response with adjusting information, a recommended base response for crisis management. Adjusting information helps people to cope psychologically with a crisis (Sturges, 1994). One element of adjusting information is to express sympathy or concern for those affected by the crisis (Coombs, 2007). Carrefour expressed concern for those Chinese who were offended by the Olympic Torch attack in France. Carrefour validated the Chinese emotions rather than complaining about or attacking them. In addition, Carrefour engaged in ingratiation by praising the Beijing Olympics, thus praising China as well. By praising the Olympics and condemning the torch attacks, Carrefour differentiated itself from those in France who opposed China and the Beijing Olympics. The expression of concern and ingratiation set the stage for the more difficult task of denial.

Denial is a difficult crisis response strategy to use effectively because stakeholders must accept the organization is not responsible for an event or that no event occurred. Denial is the appropriate strategy when faced with a rumor. Neither Carrefour nor its major shareholder had provided financial support for pro-Tibet groups. Still, that rumor was circulated on the Internet and mobile phone messages used to garner support for the anti-Carrefour actions. Chairman Duran denied any Carrefour store had given money to pro-Tibet groups, "these allegations are groundless. Carrefour and its branches have given no direct or indirect support to any political or religious group. Whether in China or anywhere else, Carrefour has never done these and will never do these" ("Carrefour supports", 2008). Vice president Lhuillier directly denied the Internet messages claiming Carrefour was linked to support for pro-Tibet groups, "Carrefour is innocent, but we understand the feeling of the Chinese people ... Carrefour never ever did and will not do anything concerned with politics and religion" ("Carrefour China", 2008).

Rumors need to be refuted but are powerful because they are believable on some level. Carrefour employed a skilled approach to debunking the rumor. First, Carrefour acknowledged why people might believe the information. Second, Carrefour explained why the rumor was untrue. Finally, Carrefour stated the "truth" about the situation. The crisis response recognized that statements about Carrefour supporting pro-Tibet groups were made and believed. They then worked to explain that Carrefour had never provided support (the incorrect information) and noted their policy of not getting involved with politics and religion (the correct information).

Chinese Government Response

The Chinese government was in a conflicted position. The State media in China was refuting critics of the Beijing Summer Olympics. Hence, the protests were a reflection of the Chinese government's own anger over many international statements about human rights and the Beijing Summer Olympics ("China protests", 2008). The national pride displayed in the protests were an echo of the Chinese government's position. However, the protests were a distraction as well, taking media attention away from the positive aspects of the Beijing Summer Olympics. The initial Chinese government response was muted with little said about the protests. But as the protests lingered, the Chinese government began to assert its need to project a positive view of the Beijing Olympics in the international media. That meant removing the Carrefour protests as a source for media coverage.

The Chinese government switched from a passive to an active response by discouraging anti-French protests, highlighted by Carrefour, through words and actions. The Chinese government asked its people to be more positive in their displays of patriotism. Government editorials and statements requested that citizens display patriotism "rationally" (Lawrence, 2008). Rational displays of patriotism included seeing that the Games were a success and that "the best way to love your country is to do your job well" ("China protests", 2008). The actions were more direct in ending the Carrefour boycotts and protests. The government began deleting calls for boycotts from websites (McDonald, 2008). Though low key, the Chinese government was making it known they no longer approved of the Carrefour boycotts and protests.

Chinese Protesters

The Chinese protesters were a trigger event for the Olympic Torch Crisis. Their boycotts and actions were creating the crisis that Carrefour management and Chinese government officials were managing. The responses from the Chinese protesters can be divided into two categories: (1) the Carrefour rumor and (2) national pride. The Carrefour rumor was the misinformation about Carrefour supporting pro-Tibetan organizations. Here is a sample Carrefour rumor message:

> No one should shop at Carrefour, because the biggest shareholder of Carrefour donated huge money to the Dalai Lama, a lot of French people support the independence of Tibet, and even the French president has announced boycott of the Beijing Olympics.
>
> (Guest, 2008)

The rumor was increasing the anger felt toward Carrefour. In turn, anger in a crisis is a powerful motivator to action such as boycotts and protests (Coombs and Holladay, 2007). The Carrefour rumor was an important energizing element in the Olympic Torch Crisis. The rumor was a response to the French protests, not the Olympic Torch Crisis itself. Still, the Carrefour rumor was an important communicative element in the Olympic Torch Crisis.

The second set of messages revolved around national pride. Again, the attack on the Olympic Torch was viewed as an attack upon China's reputation. Angry Chinese citizens wanted a means of showing their national pride and actions against Carrefour provided just such an outlet. Here is a sample national pride message: "We want to let all foreigners know that China is very angry today. We have to let Chinese people in China know that we are united" (McDonald, 2008). This message was delivered by a protester that was being placed in a police van. As such, the message does serve as a reaction to the crisis situation. The boycotts and the protests were about national pride, not hatred of France or Carrefour. The boycotts and protests were a way for the average Chinese citizen to express his or her support for China by striking back against those that would insult their country. The Chinese protester national pride response reflects the underlying dynamic that was fueling the Carrefour backlash in China.

Communication Goals, Objectives, Strategies, and Tactics

The communication analysis will follow the three main actors for the Olympic Torch Crisis: (1) Carrefour management, (2) the Chinese government, and (3) the Chinese protesters. These three actors are the primary voices that appear in the rhetorical arena for the crisis

1. Carrefour Management

Goal: To reduce anger over French pro-Tibetan Olympic Torch protests and end actions against Carrefour in China.

Objective 1: To correct misinformation about Carrefour's support for pro-Tibetan groups.

Strategy: An opinion/knowledge dissociation is used to debunk the pro-Tibetan rumor. The strategy involved acknowledging the rumor, noting why it was wrong, providing the correct information, and noting support for China's policies. Denial is a key element in this approach. Carrefour needed to establish they never provided support for pro-Tibetan groups.

Tactics: Interviews with the news media, especially the Chinese media, and public statements of support for China.

Objective 2: To show Carrefour's support for the Beijing Summer Olympics.

Strategy (a): Provide bolstering by praising China's hosting of the 2008 Summer Olympics.

Strategy (b): Expression of regret for the Olympic Torch attacks in France.

Strategy (c): Dissociation using individuals and groups. Carrefour argued that only some French people were pro-Tibetan and that Carrefour was part of the group in France that supported China.

Tactics: Interviews with the news media, especially the Chinese media, and public statements of support for China.

2. Chinese Government

Goal: To end negative international media coverage of the Olympics that focused on the anti-France protests.

Objective: To convince Chinese citizens to express patriotism in a way other than through protests and boycotts.

Strategy: Use of transcendence to place patriotic response in a new context—redefine what constitutes patriotism for Chinese citizens.

Tactics:

- erase references to Carrefour protests and boycotts from websites; and
- statements from the government to change expressions of patriotism.

3. *Chinese Protesters*

Goal: To express anger over insults to China.

Objective: To punish a highly visible French target through direct actions.

Strategy: Provocation as the Chinese protesters were responding to the Olympic Torch attacks by French protesters.

Tactics:

- protest Carrefour in person;
- post comments and calls for action against Carrefour online; and
- send phone messages calling for action against Carrefour.

Outcomes Assessment

The Beijing Olympic Games are now a part of Olympic history. Carrefour continues its push to expand in the Chinese market. So how do we evaluate the crisis communication efforts of the three primary actors in the Olympic Torch Crisis? Interestingly, an argument can be made that all three actors achieved their objectives and had a measure of success in the crisis. The outcome objectives will be considered in reverse order from their presentation in the previous section. The reason for this change is that the Chinese protesters were non-traditional crisis managers. They are crisis managers in that their actions precipitated and were the focal point of the crisis.

1. *Chinese Protesters*

It would be accurate to describe the Chinese protesters as issues managers. They were trying to raise awareness of what they considered to be international insults to China. However, one person's issue can be another person's crisis (Coombs, 2007). So the Chinese protesters were a type of crisis managers because their actions were feeding the crisis. Their provocation strategies were very effective at attracting international media coverage and generating Internet discussions of how China had been insulted by Olympic Torch attacks. The

Chinese protesters had made their point by drawing attention to their concern for over two weeks. Boycotts are rarely intended to drive a company out of business and such was the case here. Chinese protesters were not trying to remove Carrefour from China; they were trying to make a point about how they perceived the actions by French protesters. The Chinese protesters were using provocation because that strategy is a response to the actions of others (Benoit, 1995). The Chinese protesters were able to express their anger, show patriotism, and present their interpretation of the Olympic Torch attacks to the world.

2. Chinese Government

The Chinese government wanted to end the anti-French actions in order to focus media coverage on the positive aspects of the Beijing Olympic Games. Once the Chinese government took action, the highly visible boycotts and protests of Carrefour ended and media coverage turned to other issues related to the Olympics. Whether the Chinese protesters accepted the effort to transform what should be considered patriotic actions is hard to determine and, to a degree, irrelevant to the outcome. The key is whether or not the actions stopped, thereby depriving the news media of a reason to continue to cover anti-French sentiment. The Chinese government was able to end the Carrefour protests and boycotts, thereby achieving their objective. To a degree the Chinese government agreed with the Chinese protesters but could not allow the Olympic Torch Crisis to linger in the global media environment.

3. Carrefour Management

Carrefour management was pursuing the interrelated objectives of debunking the rumor that Carrefour supported pro-Tibetan groups and showing their support for the Beijing Olympics. It can be argued that these two objectives were part of larger effort to end the protests and boycotts. If the Chinese protesters believed Carrefour did not support pro-Tibetan groups and did support China; that should be grounds for ending actions against Carrefour. Of course Carrefour was just a substitute for France so we must look more closely at the two objectives. The rumor was creating anger toward Carrefour that was related to the anti-French sentiment. Carrefour management needed to debunk the rumor and prove its loyalty to China or risk long-term damage to its reputation, and potentially its sales, in China.

Unfortunately there is no direct evidence about Carrefour's success at debunking and bolstering. We do know the messages were delivered to the Chinese citizenry but do not have an assessment of their reaction to the messages. The strategy and tactics were appropriate for the crisis using situational crisis communication theory (Coombs, 2007). The messages were sent through channels that would reach the target and fit with theory so we can make the assumption they were successful. The only objective evidence for success is that Carrefour continued to expand in China and increase its market share. Had there been residual hatred toward Carrefour, such success would have been unlikely. By acknowledging the Chinese citizens had a right to be angry—expressing concern—the Carrefour response was not a refutation of the protests themselves. Hence, Carrefour did not create an "us against them" feeling in the crisis.

Lessons Learned

A critical feature of the Carrefour–Olympic Torch Crisis is its international nature. A variety of trends suggest that international crises will be on the rise. First, globalization continues to increase with trade, foreign direct investment, and international travel and tourism. Second, corporations are increasingly becoming transnational, even many nongovernment organizations are now transnational. One illustration of increased transnationalism is supply chains becoming geographically dispersed. As supply chains disperse, the number of host countries increases for a corporation. Finally the Internet makes messages global rather than local. Crises are not just managed locally.

International crises create more complex crisis arenas for crisis managers. Frandsen and Johansen (2010) developed the rhetorical arena model of crisis communication to help account for just such complexity. They argue for a multi-vocal approach to crisis communication that looks beyond having one, dominant crisis communicator to including all the relevant actors communicating about the crisis. The rhetorical arena has a macro level that includes all crisis voices that are heard before, during, and after a crisis. There is a micro level as well, consisting of four parameters (context, media, genre, and text) and three elements (crisis communication, sender, and receiver) (Frandsen and Johansen, 2010; Johansen and Frandsen, 2007). The macro level of the rhetorical arena helps to illuminate the Olympic Torch Crisis because of the three main communicators. The micro elements of crisis communication and text are relevant to the examination of the selection and application of rhetorical strategies (crisis response strategies).

Coupled-Crisis

Organizations must be aware that another's crisis can cause them collateral damage by spawning a second crisis that will involve them. On the surface, the French protesters attacking the Olympic torch is not a crisis for Carrefour because they are not involved in this initial rhetorical arena. However, the Chinese protesters enter the rhetorical arena and their communicative efforts draw Carrefour into the rhetorical arena with them. A second crisis is created by the reactions of the Chinese protesters. The crises are coupled because one precipitates the other. Crisis managers should monitor crises that have the potential to be coupled and draw them into the rhetorical arena. One illustration is a crisis within an organization's industry. The crisis could easily spread to others in the industry. Globally, organization must anticipate how anger against a particular country can create a coupled crisis. An organization that is associated with a "disliked" country (its home country) can create a coupled crisis in a host country. Consider how Arla Foods suffered costly boycotts in the Middle East over the Muhammed cartoons published in a Danish newspaper. Arla Foods (a Danish–Swedish company) is closely associated with Denmark (a home country) and suffered boycotts in a variety of host countries throughout the Middle East (Frandsen and Johansen, 2010).

Rhetorical Arena Insights

Within the rhetorical arena for the Olympic Torch Crisis, the Chinese government and Carrefour had similar goals. Both wanted the anti-French protests to end though each had a different stake in the goal. Carrefour and the Chinese government worked well in tandem. The Chinese government helped to dissuade citizens from protesting while Carrefour helped to diffuse the anger by providing reasons why Chinese citizens should once again like Carrefour. The Chinese government acknowledged shared efforts by noting Carrefour had taken positive actions by stating their support for the Beijing Olympics and their opposition to Tibet independence ("China welcomes", 2008).

Initially, the goal of the Chinese protesters drove the Olympic Torch Crisis. The anger of the Chinese protesters motivated the anti-French protests. The Chinese protesters had made their point through weeks of protests so any further extension of the anti-French protests was not entirely necessary. Goal conflict, real or perceived, is a driving force in challenge crises. By looking at the rhetorical arena as a whole, we can see how the goals of the three crisis communicators were eventually consistent. The Chinese government asked the Chinese protesters to take a new direction with their patriotism while Carrefour noted the validity of the Chinese protesters concerns but argued Carrefour itself was an inappropriate target. On some level, there was a type of goal congruency. Crisis managers should consider the various goals of those involved in the rhetorical arena to determine where there is goal compatibility, where there is goal conflict, and whether the goal conflict will be long or short term.

Crisis Communication Theory Application

The analysis of the crisis response strategies employed in this case applied a variety of crisis communication theory. The successful outcomes for the three crisis communicators illustrate the potential value of these crisis response strategies. The Chinese protesters effectively employed provocation to attract the attention of Carrefour, the international media, and their own government.

Provocation can be used to express anger and to attract attention to an issue. The Chinese government coupled Internet editing with transcendence to redirect Chinese patriotism to other expressive outlets. Within the Chinese context, power and transcendence can be used to alter behaviors. Carrefour appropriately attempted to debunk the rumor through an opinion/knowledge dissociation while bolstering its position in China through expression of support for the Beijing Summer Olympics (Hearit, 2006). Dissociation and bolstering appear to be an effective means to debunk a rumor and reduce the anger generated by the rumor and fit well with recommendations from SCCT. These conclusions about crisis communication strategies are tentative and require additional research.

Discussion Questions

1. What risks were Carrefour management taking by supporting the Beijing Summer Olympics and opposing Tibet independence groups?
2. How is it that the crisis communication efforts of the Chinese Protesters and Carrefour management were both conflicting and complementary?
3. Why were the actions of the Chinese protesters so readily covered by the international news media? Why is that important to the case?
4. Do you think the communicative efforts of Carrefour management helped to reduce the life cycle of the crisis—end it more quickly? Why or why not?
5. What other actors could be added to the Olympic Torch Crisis rhetorical arena? What might each of the new actors contribute to the analysis of the case?

References

Benoit, W. L. (1995). *Accounts, excuses, and apologies: A theory of image restoration.* Albany, NY: State University of New York Press.

Buckley, C (2010). China Carrefour managers jailed for deadly stampede. Retrieved from www.reuters.com/article/idUSL555655120081106

Carrefour chairman: Carrefour supports Beijing Olympics. (2008, April 23). Retrieved from http://news.xinhuanet.com/english/2008–04/23/content_8034795.htm

Carrefour China reiterates support for Beijing Olympics. (2008, April 29). Retrieved from www.china.org.cn/olympics/news/2008–04/29/content_15031311.htm

Carrefour supports Beijing Olympics. (2008, April 23). Retrieved from www.china daily.com.cn/olympics/2008–04/23/content_6638543.htm

Carrefour China inaugurated eight new Carrefour stores. (2010, November 16). Retrieved from www.carrefour.com/cdc/group/current-news/china—-opening-of-eight-new-carrefour-stores.html

China protests French retailer Carrefour. (2008). Retrieved from www.msnbc.msn.com/id/24218173/

China welcomes Carrefour's stance. (2008, April 23). Retrieved from www.chinadaily.com.cn/olympics/2008–04/23/content_6637911.htm

Chinese netizens calling in a boycott of Carrefour in wake of troubled Olympic torch. (2008, April 16). Retrieved from http://josieliu.blogspot.com/2008/04/chinese-netizens-calling-on-boycott-of.html

Coombs, W. T. (2007). *Ongoing crisis communication: Planning, managing, and responding* (2nd ed.). Los Angeles, CA: Sage.

Coombs, W. T. (2008). The future of crisis communication from an international perspective. In T. Nolting and A. Tieben (Eds.), *Krisenmanagement in der Mediengesellschaft (Arbeitstitel)Potenziale und Perspektiven in der Krisenkommunikation* (pp. 275–287). Wiesbaden, Germany: VS-Verlag.

Coombs, W. T., and Holladay, S. J. (2007). The negative communication dynamic: Exploring the impact of stakeholder affect on behavioral intentions. *Journal of Communication Management, 11*, 300–312.

Frandsen, F., and Johansen, W. (2010). Apologizing in a globalizing world: crisis communication and apologetic ethics. *Corporate Communications: An International Journal, 15*(4), 350–364.

Guest blogger: Chinese netizens call for boycott of Carrefour. (2008). Retrieved from http://chinadigitaltimes.net/2008/04/chinese-netizens-calling-on-boycott-of-carrefour-in-the-wake-of-troubled-olympic-torch-rely-josie-liu/

Hearit, K. M. (2006). *Crisis management by apology: Corporate response to allegations of wrongdoing.* Mahwah, NJ: Lawrence Erlbaum Associates.

Johansen, W. and Frandsen, F. (2007). *Krisekommunikation: Når virksomhedens image ogomdømme er truet.* Frederiksberg: Forlaget Samfundslitteratur.

Lawrence, D. (2008). Carrefour boycott has China reining in supporters, April 28. Retrieved from www.bloomberg.com/apps/news?pid=newsarchive&sid=aw1fs XdRYEvU&refer=asia

Longman, J. (2001). Olympics: Beijing wind bid for 2008 Olympic games, July 14. Retrieved from www.nytimes.com/2001/07/14/sports/olympics-beijing-wins-bid-for-2008-olympic-games.html

Manheim, J. B. (1994). *Strategic public diplomacy and American foreign policy: The evolution of influence.* New York: Oxford University Press.

McDonald, J. (2008). Protests target Carrefour stores in China, May 1. Retrieved from www.usatoday.com/news/world/2008–05–01–3419792923_x.htm

More protests erupt at China Carrefour stores, 9 detained. (2008). Retrieved from http://goldsea.com/805/01carrefour.html

Paris torch relay disruption prompts Carrefour boycott call in China. (2008, April 18). Retrieved from www.chinastakes.com/2008/4/paris-torch-relay-disruption-prompts-carrefour-boycott-call-in-china.html

Riding, A. (1993). Olympics: 2000 Olympics to Sydney in surprise setback for China, September 24. Retrieved from www.nytimes.com/1993/09/24/sports/olympics-2000-olympics-go-to-sydney-in-surprise-setback-for-china.html

Rights group decries Olympic sponsors. (2008, August, 9). Retrieved from www.upi.com/Top_News/2008/08/19/Rights-group-decries-Olympic-sponsors/UPI-993512 19195808/

Sturges, D. L. (1994). Communicating through crisis: A strategy for organizational survival. *Management Communication Quarterly, 7*(3), 297–316.

Three die in China sale stampede. (2007). Retrieved from http://news.bbc.co.uk/2/hi/asia-pacific/7088718.stm

VIEWS FROM AN EXPERT

ISAAC A. BLANKSON

Isaac A. Blankson is associate professor and chair of the Department of Speech Communication, Southern Illinois University Edwardsville, and Special Assistant to the Dean, College of Arts and Sciences, on international and diversity initiatives. He teaches public relations and intercultural communication. His professional experience includes serving as a consultant on crisis management to international organizations.

Professor Coombs's chapter presents a successful example of international crisis management that involves international actors. He acknowledges the complexity and multidimensional nature of international crisis communication, especially when played out in the global arena. In this case, the three actors were the Chinese protesters, the Chinese government, and Carrefour, a global corporation. The author presents effectively the historical background of the crisis, as well as how each of the actors dealt with it. But, more important, the case hints at important areas in international public relations, specifically in crisis communication.

Upfront, the author draws attention to the complexities of the global marketplace in which international corporations and practitioners function. The chapter tells us that a win–win situation in the global sphere can be achieved when all stakeholders perceive a sense of harmony in their relationships and in the public rhetoric arena. It reminds us of the extent to which public loyalty and national pride can create activism around an issue and its potential to harm an otherwise innocent entity, Carrefour. Also, well discussed is the importance of the guilty-by-association principle in international crises management. The chapter demonstrates that the public's perceived association of a global business with its parent country has the potential to threaten the corporation's operation and relationships regardless of whether the association is warranted, true or not, and can force the business to act. One of the lessons presented is that, in the eyes of the perspective of a host nation, international corporations represent their parent countries abroad. Global corporations should not take this perceived association for granted.

Finally, the chapter presents a provoking insight into a case where a country (China) with a tainted international image seized on an opportunity to effectively repair this image in the global community by using the Olympics, a symbol of international peace and unity, as a public relations tool.

Even though the chapter manages to bring these issues together, there are a few critical unanswered questions that need further inquiry. The key question centers on which actor's or actors' public relations efforts were key to ending the crises. Was it the Chinese government's messages to its people urging them to display patriotism more rationally, coupled with its control of the protesters' communication capabilities that ended the boycotts and protests? Or, was it Carrefour's public relations strategies that centered on ingratiation and refutation strategies that worked? Also, was it the Chinese people's loyalty to their government, their national pride, and to the symbolism of the Olympics games to their nation that made them stop their protests and boycotts? It would be worthwhile for future research to examine these questions, particularly within the context of the cultural landscape. Of particular curiosity would be an investigation into the role that the Chinese government's control of protesters' use of social media and electronic channels (shutting down websites, blocking cell phones, slowing Internet traffic) played in the management of the crises. Recent events in the Middle East and North Africa call on media and public relations scholars to re-examine this issue thoroughly. This is because in two countries (Egypt and Tunisia) the people's free access to social media tools and electronic communication channels was credited for their ability to organize and overthrow the Mubarak and Ben Ali governments early in 2011. In other countries (e.g., Libya, Bahrain, Syria, and Yemen) similar attempts did not result in such an outcome in part because those governments denied the public access to social media and other communication tools.

In summary, the chapter leaves us with an appreciation of the uncertainty, complexity, and multidimensional nature of the global rhetorical arena in which international corporations operate, and the public relations challenges they face. It also teaches us that in a globalizing world, what ultimately matter are the harmonious relationships the public relations practitioner develops and maintains with each of the many stakeholders or publics with which she or he interacts.

India

Corporate Fraud in India: Satyam in the Spotlight

Monika Vij

The US$1 billion corporate-accounting fraud at Satyam Computer Services Ltd, in India, came to light in January 2009. The financial world was stunned when Chairman Ramalinga Raju resigned and announced publicly that he had falsified his company's balance sheet. The scandal was quickly dubbed India's Enron. Besides financial implications, much more was at stake. Satyam was an example of India's growing success in its transition into a global economy. The objective was to protect India's image as the information technology hub of the world along with saving the company. In less than half a year, the company's assets were boosted miraculously by as much 20 percent. This was possibly the only instance in the corporate world where, after such a big fraud, a company was brought back on the rails without any financial support or bailout from the government.

Introduction

> The truth is as old as the hills.
>
> (Mahatma Gandhi, 1936, p. 49)

We all remember the collapse of energy giant Enron in 2001 in the United States. That fraud was labeled the mother of all accounting frauds and the biggest audit failure ever, only to be surpassed by WorldCom's bankruptcy seven months later. We are also aware of the accounting irregularities exposed in HealthSouth corporation in the United States; the Tylenol package-tampering scare of 1982 and 1986; the horror of Union Carbide's chemical accident in Bhopal, India, in 1984; the incidents leading to the collapse of major U.S. financial institutions such as Lehman Brothers in 2008 and AIG in 2004; the falsified accounting documents of Parmalat in 2003 in Italy; and the Anglo-Irish Bank hidden loans controversy (also known as the circular transactions controversy) in Ireland, 2008. And, of course, the global macroeconomic crisis that was attributed to the subprime meltdown in the United States; the U.S. auto industry; the collapse of Fannie Mae and Freddie Mac . . . the list goes on. There has been a tremendous increase in the number of corporate frauds during the last two decades, leading to losses in billions—mainly the incomes and savings of common people—and untold suffering to millions (Rajagopalan and Zhang, 2009).

Since January 7, 2009, when the US$1 billion corporate-accounting fraud at Satyam computer services became public, the scandal has been called India's Enron. There are many similarities: Inflated assets, a disgraced but politically powerful chairman, a suspected auditor under a cloud, even an attempted suicide. But there is a big difference. The outcome of the Satyam Saga did not go the Enron way.

Background of the Crisis

India has long been known to be one of the most highly regulated economies in the world. Realizing the need for change in a globalizing economy, the government of India implemented various strategies by which it could open up the economy and liberalize trade. The relaxed restrictions of course proved helpful to business in India, eventually leading to the information technology (IT) outsourcing industry's rapid growth. The major outsourcing companies in India are Wipro, Infosys Technologies, Tata Consultancy Services (TCS) and Satyam (now Mahindra Satyam). The Western firms were anxious to outsource and take advantage of high-skill, low-wage workers. This trend created a new breed of businessmen for the twenty-first century and generated many fortunes literally overnight. The IT boom in India was fueled by young, middle-class, educated, budding Indian entrepreneurs. The story of Satyam is one such fortune created and demolished by the same person (Ahmad et al., 2009).

Satyam Computer Services Limited as Leading Global Business and Information

The technology services company, headquartered in Hyderabad India, had core competencies in consulting, system integration, and outsourcing. Ironically, "Satyam" means "truth" in the ancient Indian language, Sanskrit. As of 2008, Satyam serviced 690 clients, including 185 Fortune 500 companies, in 20 industries and more than 66 countries.

Satyam employed more than 53,000 associates in engineering and product development, supply chain management, client relationship management, business process quality, business intelligence, enterprise integration and infrastructure management, among other key capabilities. Its revenue exceeded US$2 billion and Satyam became the first company to launch a secondary listing on Euronext Amsterdam under the New York Stock Exchange (NYSE),

Figure 2.4
B. Ramalinga Raju, former Chairman of
Satyam Computer Services Limited.

Source: Courtesy: *The Hindu Archives*. Reprinted
by permission.

Euronext being the new "fast path" process for cross listings in New York
and Europe.

Interestingly, however, before 2008, Satyam's beginning was quick and
promising. The company was incorporated as a private limited company on
June 24, 1987, for providing software development and consultancy services
to large corporations. The company was promoted by a highly talented
entrepreneur, B. Ramalinga Raju (Figure 2.4), and his brother, Rama Raju,
with fewer than 20 employees. On August 26, 1991, Satyam was recognized
as a public limited company after its initial public offering: It was listed on
the Bombay Stock Exchange (BSE). Also in 1991, Satyam obtained its first
Fortune 500 customer in a software project with John Deere and Company.
By 1999 Satyam had established its presence in 30 countries. In the following
year the associate count within Satyam reached a new level at 10,000. In 2001,
Satyam was listed on the NYSE under the ticker symbol "SAY," and five years
after listing on the NYSE, Satyam reported revenues that exceeded US$1
billion. The business community recognized Satyam as a global leader in
information technology outsourcing (Figure 2.5).

Satyam was an example of India's growing success. Satyam won numerous
awards for innovation, governance, and corporate accountability. In 2007,
Ernst & Young awarded Raju with the entrepreneur of the year award.
Satyam was acknowledged as being among the top three best employers in
India by Hewitt and Mercer in independent surveys in 2007. The American
Society of Training and Development (ASTD) named it as the best globally,
for its learning practices—the first company outside the United States to be
awarded this honor. On April 14, 2008, Satyam won awards from MZ
consultants for being a leader in India in Best Investors Relations in websites

Figure 2.5 The quick and promising growth of Satyam Computer Services Limited.

in the Asia Pacific and Africa regions. UK Trade and Investment (UKTI) India business awarded Satyam for corporate social responsibility. Teleos, in association with Know Network, declared Satyam as the "Most Admired Knowledge Enterprise" (MAKE). In September 2008, the World Council for Corporate Governance awarded Satyam with the "Global Peacock Award" for Global Excellence in Corporate accountability. Unfortunately, less than five months after winning the Global Peacock Award, Satyam became the centerpiece of a massive accounting fraud.

The Fraud

The stock markets around the world collapsed during 2008. The enormous losses caused investors to withdraw large amounts of cash from their investments. These cash withdrawals in turn triggered the discovery of several cases of financial fraud in America, as perpetrators could no longer hide the results. The discovery of high profile financial scandals increased scrutiny on governance practices and companies' financial statements. The Indian Stock Exchange, the Sensex, also fell from a high of more than 21,000 to below 8,000 between January 2008 and October 2008. Satyam continued to report positive results during 2008 and claimed success in navigating the economic crisis. In October, Satyam reported net income of US$ 132.3 million, an increase of 28 percent from the same quarter the previous year. Satyam asserted that despite the challenging environment, it continued to find opportunities for growth.

The first blow to the company's reputation came during October 2008, when the World Bank barred Satyam Computer Services from doing business with it for eight years on charges of data theft. The World Bank debarment—the harshest sanction made by the bank, was meted out for "improper benefits to bank staff" and "lack of documentation on invoices." In addition, one stock analyst drew attention to large cash balances in non-interest-bearing bank accounts of Satyam during an October conference call, reporting earnings. The analyst expressed reservations about the accuracy of the numbers. Investors ignored the analyst comments and the Satyam stock prices rose with the reports of positive earnings and revenue growth (Winkler, 2010).

On December 16, 2008, the real stroke to the image of Satyam as a well-managed company came when Satyam's Board of Directors unanimously announced that it would acquire a 100 percent stake in Maytas properties Limited and 51 percent in Maytas Infrastructure—both of which were companies that developed properties in smaller cities in India. Both these companies were completely unrelated to the information technology field. The Raju family was the controlling shareholder in both these companies.

The decision was made without seeking the approval of minority share-holders who controlled over 90 percent of voting shares in Satyam. At that time, Ramalinga Raju anticipated that the market would "be delighted" by the two transactions as it would provide Satyam with greater diversification (Nocera, 2009). However, investors were outraged and retaliated by dumping the stocks, which lost over 30 percent of their value in a single day of trading on the BSE. Satyam immediately aborted the transaction. However, the damage had already been done as investors had lost their faith in the management of the company. On December 22, 2008, the World Bank confirmed the eight year ban on Satyam from providing services to the World Bank (Figure 2.6).

After the incident, chaos ensued. Analysts immediately soured on the company and put "SELL" recommendations on its stocks. Satyam's shares dropped and, adding to the crisis, four of the five independent directors resigned. The Securities and Exchange Board of India (SEBI), the primary market regulator of the Indian capital market, decided to investigate the

Figure 2.6 Unrelated companies with similar names and shared finances.

corporate governance issues concerning the Satyam–Maytas Deal. Satyam's stock continued its freefall, eventually shedding 69 percent of its value from its 52 week high. Since the company was declared "unethical" by the World Bank, everyone doubted its credibility. In a bid to placate investors' anger, Satyam hired DSP Merill Lynch to explore strategic opportunities to enhance shareholder value. However, a week after being hired, the Merill Lynch team found material accounting irregularities and resigned from the assignment. ("DSP Merill Lynch terminates engagement with Satyam," 2009) (Figure 2.7).

On January 7, 2009, Ramalinga Raju mailed a letter to the board members of Satyam, the SEBI, as well as various stock exchanges at which Satyam traded, in which he detailed the massive fraud perpetrated by him (Text of Ramalinga Raju's statement, 2009).

Ramalinga Raju claimed that he overstated assets on Satyam's balance sheet by US$1.47 billion. Nearly US$1.04 billion in bank loans and cash that the company claimed to own was nonexistent. Satyam also underreported liabilities on its balance sheet. The holes in the balance sheet were owing to inflated profits recognized in the past several years. Satyam overstated income nearly every quarter in order to meet analysts' expectations over the course of several years. For example, results announced on October 2009 overstated quarterly revenues by 75 percent and profits by 97 percent (D'Monte, 2008). He wrote:

> What began as a small gap between actual and reported performance soon swelled in size and each failed attempt to cover up the scam resulted in a larger gap ... It was like riding a tiger not knowing how to get down without being eaten ... The stress of hiding the fraud grew too much for

Figure 2.7 The shocking collapse of Satyam Computer Services.

me to bear. I am now prepared to subject myself to the laws of the land and face consequences thereof.

(Text of Ramalinga Raju's statement, January 8, 2009)

Responsible Parties

Ramalinga Raju was the primary individual responsible for the fraud. Indian authorities accused Raju and subsidiary players such as the chief financial officer (CFO), a managing director, and the company's global head of internal audit with responsibility for the fraud and filed charges against them. Additionally, Satyam auditors and the Board of Directors were responsible for the fraud. Finally, the analysts believe that the ownership structure of Indian Business contributed to the Satyam scandal.

Ramalinga Raju initially asserted that he acted alone in perpetrating the fraud. However, Indian authorities also charged Ramalinga Raju's brother Rama Raju, as well as the company's chief financial officer, the company's global head of internal audit and one of the managing directors. In association with the company's global head of internal audit, Ramalinga Raju used a number of different techniques to perpetrate the fraud. Using a personal computer, he created 6,000 fake salary accounts, falsified the bank statements over years and appropriated the money after the company deposited it (Figure 2.8).

The company's global head of internal audit created fake customer identities and generated fake invoice against their names to inflate revenue. He also forged board resolutions and illegally obtained loans for the company. Ramalinga Raju initially asserted that he did not divert any money to his personal accounts and that the company was not as profitable as it had reported. However, during later interrogations, Ramalinga Raju revealed that he had diverted a large amount of cash to other firms that he owned and that he had been doing this since 2004.

Several commentators criticized Pricewaterhouse Coopers (PWC), the auditors for Satyam since 2000, for failing to detect the fraud (Blakely, 2009). PWC signed Satyam's financial statements and was responsible for the numbers

Figure 2.8 The financial irregularities.

under Indian law. According to the accounting professionals, one particular item was concerning the US$1.04 billion that Satyam claimed to have on its balance sheets in non-interest-bearing deposits. This large amount of cash should have been on a red flag for the auditors, because reasonably, it should have been either invested into an interest bearing account or the excess cash returned to the shareholders. The fraud went on for a number of years and involved manipulations of balance sheets and income statements without the auditors discovering the fraud. It is also interesting that PWC audited the company for over nine years and did not uncover the fraud, whereas Merill Lynch discovered the fraud as part of its due diligence in merely ten days (Figure 2.9). Missing the red flags implies that either the auditors were inept or in collusion with the company in committing the fraud. The auditors did not independently verify with the banks in which Satyam claimed to have deposits (Timmons and Kahn, 2009). PWC initially asserted that it performed the company's entire audit in accordance with applicable auditing standards, but the two PWC partners who had signed the Satyam's audit since 2000 were arrested and charged with cheating, forgery, criminal breach of trust, and criminal conspiracy.

Figure 2.9 PWC audited the company for over nine years and did not uncover the fraud whereas Merill Lynch discovered the fraud as part of its due diligence in merely ten days.

Satyam's board of directors consisted of nine members. Five members of the board were independent as required by the Indian listing standard. The board comprised several prominent figures in the business world, a fact that likely contributed to the lack of scrutiny that Satyam received. The board came under fire on three accounts: First, when it approved Satyam's purchase of real estate companies in which Ramalinga Raju owned a large stake. It gave the impression that the board was not actively monitoring Satyam. Second, the board should have caught some of the red flags that the auditors, PWC, missed. Third, the board of directors should have been concerned with the knowledge that Raju decreased his holdings of Satyam significantly over the three years from 15.67 percent in 2005–2006 to 2.3 percent in 2009. The Central Bureau of Investigation (CBI) said in a report that the members of the board of directors had acted as "rubber stamps," unwilling to oppose the fraud. Not a single note of dissent was recorded in the minutes of the board meetings (Guha, 2009).

Analysts believed that the ownership structure of Indian Businesses also contributed to Satyam's Scandal. Family Business groups dominate the ownership of Indian corporations. The problem with such businesses is that the independent directors often succumb to serving the interests of the family group instead of the interests of the corporation as a whole, thus harming the minority shareholders ("Scandal at Satyam," 2009).

Situation Analysis

The Indian stock market fell dramatically upon the disclosure of the Satyam scandal. All the stake holders—the investors, shareholders, clients and employees—felt cheated. There was a crisis of confidence. India's image as IT capital of the world was at stake. Politicians feared that the loss of trust in the market would take years to regain (Timmons and Wassener, 2009).

That situation resulted in several difficulties, including the more than 53,000 positions that had to be saved, salaries that had to be paid, an international brand that had to be saved, and reassurances that had to be provided to customers (see Figure 2.10) ("Satyam was rescued," 2010).

The size and scope of the fraud raised questions about regulatory oversight in India. The observers raised questions about accounting standards and whether similar problems might be buried elsewhere (Ramachadran, 2009). Questions such as: "If a company's Chairman itself says they built fictitious assets whom do you believe here?" were raised. The fraud had put a question mark on the entire corporate governance system in India (Jayasekara and Kumara, 2009). The news of the scandal, quickly compared with the collapse of Enron, tremendously affected the Indian stock market. The BSE Index fell more than 5 percent and the shares in Satyam fell more than 70 percent (Kripalani, 2009).

The financial crisis and tightened lending standards made it extremely difficult for Satyam to find liquidity. The company was quickly running out

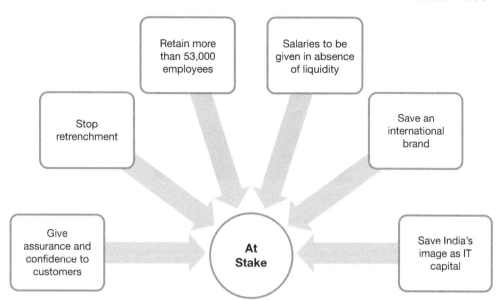

Figure 2.10 The immediate concerns after the Satyam fraud revelation.

of cash. The corporate sector looked to the government to bail Satyam out, as they were the only ones who could raise the capital required in a short period of time.

Initial Response

Immediately after Ramalinga Raju's revelation of the fraud, the Indian government reacted at a very swift pace and in a decisive manner (Figure 2.11). The existing board was dissolved and new board members were appointed to work toward a solution that would prevent the total collapse of the firm. The authorities quickly instituted an investigation into the irregularities, falsification, and the apparent fraud, and persuaded criminal actions against Satyam executives and auditors. At the same time, they initiated steps to ensure that the employees, customers, and shareholders did not suffer. Indian officials acted quickly to save Satyam from the same fate that met Enron and WorldCom when they experienced large accounting frauds. As we are aware, both Enron and WorldCom had filed for bankruptcy, creating a large upheaval in the capital market, as well as an increase in unemployment. The Indian government immediately started the investigation while at the same time limiting its direct participation with Satyam because it did not want to appear as though it was responsible for the fraud and now attempting to cover it up ("Scandal at Satyam," 2009).

PWC claimed its innocence. In a statement that was released, PWC said that there is "not an iota of material to link them with the accusations leveled against them." However, the two PWC partners were both arrested and

Figure 2.11 The quick and decisive government response.

charged with cheating, forgery, criminal breach of trust, and criminal conspiracy under the Indian Penal Code (IPC). The SEBI and the Registrar of Companies (RoC) launched a probe into Pricewaterhouse. The new board at Satyam dropped PWC and appointed Deloitte and KPMG as its auditors.

Goals, Objectives, Strategies, Tactics

This was the biggest accounting fraud of the Indian corporate sector ever. There were many goals to be accomplished—both long and short term. The most important long-term goal was to protect India's image in IT sector services worldwide to avoid severe implications for India's economy. The immediate short-term goal was to ensure that the company continued with its operations, safeguarded the interests of its employees, and that the company did not lose its customers. In the given situation, the only option apparent was to find a new home for Satyam. In order to meet these goals, various strategies and tactics were adopted by the government of India and the interim management at Satyam and succeeded in restoring the company—"the glory of Satyam." The newly appointed board worked very closely with the customers, employees, financial institutions, and other stakeholders and prepared a roadmap for the future.

The crisis-communication goals, objectives, strategies, and tactics, which covered all short-term and long-term goals, are presented below.

Goal 1: To protect India's image in IT sector services and give assurance to customers to ensure they remain loyal to the company.

Objective: To ensure continuity of operations and ascertain that the employees, customers, and shareholders do not suffer and lose their confidence in the company.

Strategy (a): Took steps to prevent the total collapse of the firm and brought stability and confidence back to the company.

Strategy (b): Took steps toward strengthening corporate governance requirements for publicly traded corporations listed in the country.

Tactics:

- India's Prime Minister asked his office to give this matter top priority.
- The government superseded and replaced the existing board of Satyam by a government-nominated board comprising eminent and globally renowned individuals from diverse disciplines.
- An interim CEO was appointed to steer the company through this challenging phase.
- SEBI revised corporate governance requirements as well as financial reporting requirements for strengthening the regulatory environment in the securities market.
- The Indian Ministry of Corporate Affairs drafted a new corporate code and devised more stringent disclosure obligations for Indian publicly listed companies.

Goal 2: To navigate the company through the fraud fallout and assuage concerns of various stakeholders in a highly fluid and challenging situation.

Objective: To create a task force to keep the business running and reach out to the customers to meet its business commitments, assure employees, and also ascertain the company's liquidity position.

Strategy: Took steps to prevent the total collapse of the firm and bring stability and confidence back to the company.

Tactics:

- The interim CEO held a press conference at Hyderabad and announced its future navigation plan.
- Satyam's top management team ("Leadership Council") declared its decision not to resign despite the revelation.
- It expressed confidence that the company will be able to overcome this latest development and continue to provide excellent service to clients, while delivering value to shareholders in the medium to long term.
- The leadership council committed to uphold the highest levels of corporate transparency with the relevant regulatory authorities to conduct detailed investigations into this matter.

- It also promised to keep stakeholders informed of the developments on a regular basis.
- Formed a SWAT team consisting of senior leaders with a minimum of 10 years' experience in the company and more than 20 years in the industry.
- SWAT team represented all customer facing units, key horizontal competency units, and critical support units.
- The Leadership Council conducted "U SPEAK" (meet the leadership seniors) in each city in India where Satyam offices were located, and organized numerous "webinars" to address associates in various countries to retain confidence in the company.
- January 2009 salaries were paid to all the employees.

Goal 3: To find a new home for Satyam (Figure 2.12).

Objective: To sell the company within 100 days and take whatever steps needed to achieve that without profitability, balance sheet numbers, and all pending legal cases on an "as is where is" basis.

Strategy: Devised a plan of sale of Satyam.

Tactics:

- The board met with the bankers, lawyers, accountants, and government officials to devise a suitable strategy.
- The board hired Goldman Sachs and Avendus Capital as investment bankers to the IT firm and charged them with the task of selling the company.
- The board also appointed Boston Consulting Group (BCG) as management advisers to the board itself and Satyam's management.

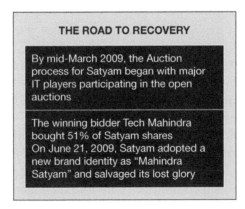

Figure 2.12 Satyam gets a new home.

- The SEBI appointed a retired Supreme Court Justice to oversee the process and instill confidence in the transaction.
- In order to ensure greater transparency, the government-appointed Satyam board decided to have an open auction by bidders to select a new owner.

The interim chief executive of the beleaguered Satyam Computer Services wrote an unedited, impassioned open letter to all the employees of the company, asking them to stand together in the turbulent times. He wrote:

> Over the past twenty-one years, with your passion and commitment we have built significant customer assets, formidable service offerings, excellent delivery processes and scalable support systems . . . Let us fight this battle together . . . What we have been trained for, we will now put to work. Let us continue to handle our respective areas with total autonomy, freedom and control. On behalf of our new leadership team, I apologize to you for the uncertainty and inconvenience that this incident has caused to you and your families. I am confident that we will emerge stronger, together . . . We shall soon be a successful case study of how organizations have turned over a new leaf.
>
> (Unedited open letter from Satyam interim CEO, 2009)

By mid-March, several major players in the IT field had gained enough confidence in Satyam operations to participate in the auction process. The SEBI appointed a retired Supreme Court Justice, Justice Bharucha, to oversee the process and instill confidence in the transaction. Several companies bid on Satyam. The winning bidder, Tech Mahindra, bought 51 percent of Satyam for US$1.13 per share—less than a third of its stock market value before the fraud was admitted—and salvaged its operations. Tech Mahindra and SEBI were fully aware of the extent of the fraud (Ribeiro, 2009).

On June 21, 2009, Satyam adopted a new brand identity as "Mahindra Satyam." In a company statement it declared that "the strategic move paves the way for the emergence of a robust brand which draws from the core value of the Mahindra Group and the inherent strength of the Satyam brand." The managing director of the rebranded Satyam believed that "customer centricity, high standard of corporate governance, impeachable ethics form the corner stone of Mahindra group"; this was well amalgamated with Satyam's fabled expertise and its identity which signified "commitment, purpose and proficiency of the organization and its people." The new board also outlined its new program to re-energize its brand and reignite its growth while retaining key talent and review cost structure and liabilities (Figure 2.13).

Thus, the acquisition provided Satyam with a corporate identity and resources to survive as a company and continue competing in the offshore IT services market. The stocks again stabilized and Satyam was once again on its way towards a bright future.

Figure 2.13 What a tragic fall. B. Ramalinga Raju, founder of Satyam Computer
Services and an icon of India's software success, is now a prisoner in
Hyderabad's Chanchalguda jail.

Source: Courtesy of *The Hindu Archives*. Reprinted by permission.

Outcomes Assessment

The outcome of the Satyam saga did not go the Enron way. Enron imploded:
it was put into liquidation, its assets were sold piecemeal, its employees were
kicked to the curb and the result was more or less a disaster. In the case of
Satyam, the immediate and effective response of the government within the
strategic framework, the quality commitment and swift action of the new
constituent board members who put in unprecedented levels of effort, and the
dedication and untiring work of the Satyam team shepherded the company
out of the crisis. Analysts argued, if this had happened to a consumer finance
company or a small or even big manufacturing company, the government
would not have come out and superseded the board. The normal procedures
for bankruptcy and liquidation would have taken place. After all, Enron, like
Satyam, had its business and assets—namely power plants and the marketing,
commercial, and administrative infrastructure—intact, power, which was
Enron's product and an essential utility, and had an assured market. Despite
all these positives, Enron was simply allowed to collapse, causing pain all
around (Vasudev, 2010).

As additional details of the fraud emerged it became evident that the fraud was perpetuated by a select group of individuals and did not reflect a failure of Satyam's business and operating model or the erosion of the core capabilities and competency sets. The Indian government portrayed the Satyam scandal as an aberration and salvaged the confidence in its capital market and IT sector (Jain, 2009). However, the scandal pointed at the need for strengthening the regulatory environment in the securities market.

In response to the scandal, the SEBI revised corporate governance requirements as well as financial reporting requirements for all publicly traded corporations listed in the country. The SEBI adopted International Financial Accounting Reporting Standards (IFARS) and increased personal liability of board members. It made mandatory that publicly listed companies carry director and officer liability insurance in order to protect shareholders from damages (Behan, 2009). Two weeks after Satyam's collapse, the SEBI also made it mandatory for controlling shareholders to disclose any share pledges. Pledging stocks is the process whereby a person offers his or her stock to a bank or other institution as collateral for a loan. The problem with controlling shareholder pledging stocks is that once the stock drops below a certain level, the drop will trigger a margin call. After receiving the margin call, the person who pledged the stocks must provide additional collateral. If the person cannot provide additional collateral, the lender will liquidate the stock, causing a significant decline in the company's stock price. This hurts the minority shareholders who are unaware that the controlling shareholder had pledged his or her stock. In the case of Satyam, in times of financial crisis, they borrowed money against their own holding. This borrowed money had been used to start other businesses like Maytas real estate and infrastructure, run by Ramalinga Raju's sons. During the global financial crisis, stock prices collapsed, banks wanted more shares and at that time they did not have shares; they had pledged all their holding. Some banks sold the pledged shares and that is the time they decided to acquire Maytas Infrastructure Limited and Maytas Properties Limited.

The Satyam scandal highlighted the importance of securities laws and corporate governance in emerging markets. In addition to the new SEBI regularity requirements, the Indian Ministry of Corporate Affairs drafted a new corporate code for Indian publicly listed companies (Banerjee, 2009). The new code imposed more stringent disclosure obligations. The SEBI asked companies to disclose their balance sheet positions twice a year. Pre-Satyam, the regulations only required disclosure of balance sheet positions once a year. This reporting would provide investors with more information on the stability of a company's financial position and provide Indian citizens with the confidence to invest in the financial markets (Chakrabarti et al., 2008).

Thus, in the process of achieving the goal of Satyam salvage, a new global model for government–corporate–stakeholder partnerships was created for managing the aftermath of such scams.

Lessons Learned

The Satyam debacle has definitely provided the corporate world many lessons. The biggest issue it raises is about the social responsibility of business. As Jin and Drozdenko (2009) suggest, a corporate's pursuit of profit cannot ignore society or its obligation to it. The first lesson to be learned is that a company's independence to make profits ends at that point where it starts affecting other members of the society. There is a need for various social control mechanisms to keep corporations in check and maintain full transparency. But when these systems are not robust enough and corporates are not self-regulating, they raise issues of ethics and the interests of stakeholders. Basu (2009) suggests, now that India, with all its recent economic reforms, is breaking away from the shackles of the License Raj (the red tape required for business between 1947 and 1990), it has to be prepared to grapple with the more novel crimes associated with market capitalism—the crimes that come from giving more license to the Rajus.

The second lesson is about stakeholder value, especially that of the shareholders. Investors, in fact, were the biggest victims; they had no opportunity to independently verify financial statements. They had to take the auditors' word, and they were rational in having confidence in a publicly traded company with audited financial results. While their plight was understandable, the lesson that needs to be learned is about their role. The very shape and idea of the stakeholder has changed. No longer do shareholders come in as providers of capital who remain invested for reasonably long periods. Now, they are investors aiming to make quick money. The interest is short term and only for quick profits. In an effort to retain shareholder interest, very often managements become slaves to the stock market. The practice of quarterly reporting worsens matters as corporates feel obliged to show growth in every quarter. This is difficult to achieve from core activities, so managements sometimes turn to financial re-engineering. Taking the case of Satyam, the accounts of Satyam were declared every quarter after the three leading companies, TCS (Tata Consultancy Services), Infosys, and Wipro. Satyam was always the last of the top four to announce quarterly results. The growth rates and numbers were all manipulated, thus misusing the wealth that was not theirs. This kind of financial re-engineering led to the collapse of Enron, WorldCom, Arthur Andersen, Parmalat, and several other companies.

The third lesson to be learned is that there should also be concern whenever a promoter/owner has a very low holding in a company and its value keeps declining (Angur, 2009). In Satyam's case, Ramalinga Raju's family holding in the company was very low and his sons were not even on the board of the company. As Belan (2009) suggests, the ownership structure of Indian businesses also contributed to the Satyam scandal. Family business groups dominate the ownership of Indian corporations. As of 2006, family ownership structure, and to a lesser extent state-owned structures, comprised 60 percent of the 500 largest companies. Such business structures present unique challenges for effective corporate governance. One problem with such consolidated control is that it is more difficult for board members to be independent (Figure 2.14).

The independent directors in family businesses often succumb to serve the interests of the family group instead of the interests of the corporation as a whole—thus harming the minority shareholders (Gongmeng et al., 2006). Among several, one such tactic involves the the "tunneling" of corporate gains to other entities within the group in which they own a larger share. In the Satyam case, during later interrogations, Ramalinga Raju revealed that he had diverted a large amount of cash to other firms that he owned and that he had been doing this since 2004 (Belan, 2009).

The fourth and a very important lesson is about communication. In a precarious environment clear and consistent communication is critical. During a crisis, stakeholders instinctively grasp for any shred of information to hang on to and often misinterpret this information. They can end up feeling abandoned, confused, or distrustful. Companies must also be sure to focus on employees, who too often are the last to receive information. The employees are the first point of contact for many stakeholders (Sims, 2009). They should be able to project an air of confidence and stability to angst-ridden consumers and investors. On the other hand, lack of information may lead to employee anxiety, unrest, or mistrust and can soon permeate beyond the company walls to be picked up by the public. Public fear compounded by persistent media coverage can further chip away trust. In the Satyam case, consistent and continuous messaging was done at all levels. The Indian government stepped in and provided the required handholding. The communication from the government side was swift and precise. This gave tremendous confidence to all stakeholders. There was a general assurance that "there is no chance the government will allow the company to go down. It is important for employees, for Indian corporates and for the government."

The decision of top management at Satyam to stay put provided the necessary reassurance. The government's move to fire the existing board followed by new appointments were welcomed by Satyam in a clear statement saying that "it had complete confidence in them and pledged to work closely

---

"All that is necessary for evil to triumph is for good men to do nothing"

Edmund Burke

Figure 2.14

and in full cooperation with the new board." Indian corporate culture has also long been grounded by an unspoken bond between workers and management that is based on loyalty. Many employees declared that they are staying out of loyalty to the company (Figure 2.15).

On January 15, 2009, several hundred Satyam employees gathered outside Chanchalguda prison in Hyderabad, where Ramalinga Raju was being held, to express support for their former boss. This way the company was able to preserve its goodwill with the external stakeholders—as they were open and honest about their own role and responsibility in this wake of uncertainty.

The fifth lesson is on the role of the media. They help in information processing by selecting the most relevant information, by cross-checking the veracity of news. This approach gives them the watchdog role. The media failed to play its role. Oftentimes, journalists simply do not know what is happening even with the companies they track. The media also has a tendency to quickly liaise with seemingly successful businesspersons. The media initially hails them and promptly throws them to the wolves once the truth emerges. It must be more responsible in its reporting of corporates and act as informal regulators and watchdogs of the corporate governance process.

Figure 2.15 Employees and well-wishers place flowers and placards as a mark of support at the gate of Chanchalguda jail, in Hyderabad.

Source: courtesy of *The Hindu Archives*. Reprinted by permission.

The biggest lesson is that business should be managed honestly—that is, with utmost integrity. The regulatory bodies, the outside agencies, the internal auditors, and the external auditors should be more vigilant, and even the employees of the company must come out and complain to the regulators when they suspect something.

Discussion Questions

1. As an auditor of a fraudulent company how would you deal with the issues of the chairman's accounting?
2. What challenges does PWC face in India? What communication platform should PWC use to convey to the stakeholders that their reputation can still be trusted?
3. From the perspective of crisis communication expert, what is the most important lesson learned from this crisis? What could have been done better?

References

Ahmad, T., Malawat, T., Kochar, Y., and Roy, A. (2009). Satyam scam in the contemporary corporate world: A case study in Indian perspective. *IUP Journal*. Retrieved from http://papers.ssrn.com/sol3/papers.cfm?abstract_id=1460022

Angur, M. (2009). Are we ignoring the early warning signs in our corporate governance system? Corporate governance system—revisited, *Journal of Indian Business Research*, 1(1), 66–70.

Banerjee, R. (2009). Listed firms to get new conduct code. *Financial Chronicle*, October 25. Retrieved from www.mydigitalfc.com/news/listed-firms-get-new-conduct-code-949

Basu, K. (2009). India's lessons from Satyam. *BBC NEWS/ SOUTH ASIA*, January 26. Retrieved from http://news.bbc.co.uk/2/hi/south_asia/7850818.stm

Behan, B. (2009). Governance lessons from India's Satyam. *Business Week*, January 16. Retrieved from www.businessweek.com/managing/content/jan2009/ca2009 0116_465633.htm

Blakely, R. (2009). Investors raise questions over PWC Satyam audit. *Times Online*, January 8. Retrieved from

Chakrabarti, R., Megginson, W., and Yadav, P. K. (2008). Corporate governance in India. *Journal of Applied Corporate Finance*, 20(1), 59–72.

D'Monte, L. (2008). Satyam: just what went wrong? *Rediff India Abroad*, December 19. Retrieved October 4, 2011 from www.rediff.com/money/2008/dec/19satyam-just-what-went-wrong.htm

DSP Merill Lynch terminates engagement with Satyam. (2009) *Outlook India.com*, January 7. Retrieved from www.outlookindia.com/article.aspx?239403

Gandhi, M. K. (1936). *Harijan*. Ahmedabad, India, p. 49, March 28.

Gongmeng, C., Firth, M., Gao, D.N., and Rui, O. M. (2006). Ownership structure, corporate governance, and fraud: Evidence from China. *Journal of Corporate Finance*, 3, 424–448.

Guha, R. (2009). Wider fraud is seen at India's Satyam. *Wall Street Journal*, November 26. Retrieved from http://online.wsj.com/article/SB10001424052748703499404574559263208602726.html

ICIA finds ex Satyam CFO, Pricewaterhouse auditors guilty. (2009) *Outlook India.com*, September 29. Retrieved from http://business.rediff.com/report/2009/sep/29/satyam-ex-cfo-pw-auditors-guilty-says-icai.htm

Jain, V. (2009). Satyam fraud is not a system failure. *Outlook India.com*, January 26. Retrieved from http://news.outlookindia.com/item.aspx?652667

Jayasekara, D., and Kumara, K. (2009). India: gigantic corporate fraud at Satyam computers deals body-blow to Indian elite's global ambitions. *World Socialist Web Site*, January 27. Retrieved from www.wsws.org/articles/2009/jan2009/indi-j27.shtml

Jin, K., and Drozdenko, R. (2009). Relationships among perceived organizational core values, corporate social responsibility, ethics, and organizational performance outcomes: An empirical study of information technology professionals. *Journal of Business Ethics*, 3, 341–359.

Kripalani, M. (2009). India's Madoff Satyam scandal rocks outsourcing industry. *Business Week*, January 7. Retrieved from www.businessweek.com/globalbiz/content/jan2009/gb2009017_807784.htm

Lessons from Satyam revolt. (2008). *Livemint.com*, December 19. Retrieved from www.livemint.com/2008/12/18222135/Lessons-from-Satyam-revolt.html

Nocera, J. (2009). In India, crisis pairs with fraud. *The New York Times*, January 9. Retrieved from www.nytimes.com/2009/01/10/business/10nocera.html?_r=1

Paying the price: Satyam's auditors face plenty of questions. (2009). *India Knowledge @ Wharton*, January 22. Retrieved from http://knowledge.wharton.upenn.edu/india/article.cfm?articleid=4346

PricewaterhouseCoopers (2009). Moving forward: global acceptance of IFRS. *Bangkok Post*, November 10. Retrieved from www.bangkokpost.com/business/economics/27159/moving-forward-global-acceptance-of-ifrs

Rajagopalan, N., and Zhang, Y. (2009). Recurring failures in corporate governance: A global disease? *Business Horizons*, 52(6), 545–552.

Ramachadran, S. (2009). Raju brings down Satyam, shakes India. *Asia Times Online Ltd*, January 9. Retrieved from www.atimes.com/atimes/South_Asia/KA09Df01.html

Range, J. (2009). Additional $100 Million said to be missing from Satyam. *Wall Street Journal (Eastern Edition)*. Retrieved from http://online.wsj.com/article/SB124109291445272905.html?mod=googlenews_wsj

Ribeiro, J. (2009). Indian government approves Satyam takeover. *IDG News Service*, April 16. Retrieved from www.itworld.com/business/66503/indian-government-approves-satyam-takeover

Satyam explores possible merger. (2009). *The Economic Times*, January 5, Retrieved from www.livemint.com/2009/01/05120636/Satyam-explores-possible-merge.html

Satyam was rescued to preserve India's image. (2010). *Livemint.com*, January 6. Retrieved from www.livemint.com/2010/01/06212549/Deepak-Parekh—Satyam-was-res.html

Scandal at Satyam: Truth, lies, and corporate governance. (2009). *Little India*, February 12. Retrieved from http://knowledge.wharton.upenn.edu/india/article.cfm?articleid=4344

Sims, R. (2009). Toward a better understanding of organizational efforts to rebuild reputation following an ethical scandal. *Journal of Business Ethics*, 90(4), 453–472.

Text of Mr. Ramalinga Raju's statement. (2009). *Business Line*, January 8. Retrieved from www.thehindu.com/todays-paper/article370641.ece

Timmons, H. and Wassener, B. (2009). Satyam chief admits huge fraud. *New York Times Online*, January 7. Retrieved from www.nytimes.com/2009/01/08/business/worldbusiness/08satyam.html

Timmons, H. and Kahn, J. (2009). Auditor in cross hairs over fraud at Satyam. *The New York Times*, January 9, Retrieved from www.nytimes.com/2009/01/09/business/worldbusiness/09iht-09outsource.19206831.html?scp=220&sq=fraud&st=Search

Unedited open letter from Satyam interim CEO Ram Mynampati. (2009). *The Times of India*, January 7. Retrieved from http://economictimes.indiatimes.com/unedited-open-letter-from-satyam-interim-ceo-ram-mynampati/articleshow/3947512.cms

Vasudev, P. M. (2010). Satyam and Enron: A tale of two companies and two countries. *Deccan Herald*. Retrieved from www.deccanherald.com/content/96271/satyam-amp-enron-tale-two.html

Winkler, D. (2010). UICIFD Briefing Paper No. 8: India's Satyam Accounting Scandal. Retrieved from www.uiowa.edu/ifdebook/briefings/docs/satyam.shtml

VIEWS FROM AN EXPERT

K. M. SHRIVASTAVA

Professor K. M. Shrivastava is on the faculty of the Indian Institute of Mass Communication, New Delhi. His specialties are media ethics, journalism, and public relations. His research has also been published in Political Communication in Action *(Hampton Press, USA, 1996);* Human Rights Reporting in Asia *(AMIC, Singapore, 2000);* Media Ethics in Asia *(AMIC, Singapore, 2002);* Global Media Journal, *the* Blackwell International Encyclopedia of Communication *and* News Agencies in the Turbulent Era of the Internet *(Catalan News Agency, 2010). He can be reached at kmsiimc@rediffmail.com*

From the crisis communication perspective the Satyam case is unique. On January 7, 2009 when his position became impossible to defend, Chairman and Founder B. Ramalinga Raju sent in a letter tendering resignation and detailing financial irregularities. The top management of the company acted swiftly. The letter, dated January 7, 2009, was circulated to all existing members of the board, several senior leaders, and copied to the Chairman of Securities and Exchange Board of India (SEBI) and the stock exchanges where Satyam was listed.

"We are obviously shocked by the contents of the letter. The senior leaders of Satyam stand united in their commitment to customers, associates, suppliers and all shareholders. We have gathered together at Hyderabad to strategize the way forward in light of this startling revelation," said Ram Mynampati, Interim CEO (pending ratification by the Board) and Member of the Board, who was mandated by the Board to steer the company through this crisis.

A press release dated January 7, 2009, announced:

> Satyam confirmed that its immediate priorities are to protect the interests of its shareholders, protect the careers and security of its approximately 53,000 associates, and meet all its commitments to its customers and suppliers.
>
> "We recognize that our associates have committed a significant part of their careers to build Satyam. We will pursue all avenues to secure their future in the company," added Mynampati.
>
> Satyam believes that its underlying business model, customer assets and growth prospects remain sound, even in the current challenging financial environment. Satyam leadership expressed confidence that the company will be able to overcome this latest development and continue to provide excellent service to clients, while delivering value to shareholders in the medium to long term.
>
> Satyam is committed to uphold the highest levels of corporate transparency and will cooperate with the relevant regulatory authorities to conduct detailed investigations into this matter. Satyam will keep stakeholders informed of the developments on a regular basis.
>
> The company will conduct a press conference at its headquarters within the next 24 hours.

This was perhaps one of the best examples of corporate communication in serious crisis where the Chairman accepted the financial irregularities and resigned. The remaining leadership got together quickly and assured all stakeholders and the government agencies for highest levels of corporate transparency. The post-crisis period did not create a leadership vacuum and the company was able to overcome the crisis and continued to provide excellent services to clients, while delivering value to shareholders in the medium to long term.

This was so effective that on February 21, 2009 the company could announce "new purchase orders and work extensions totaling over US$250 million, since January 7, 2009." The newly appointed Chief Executive Officer, A. S. Murty, went to Singapore and assured the world on February 3, 2009, that

Satyam's foundation in Singapore and the Rest of the World region is still quite strong. Our customer base remains intact and all of our clients have chosen to stand by us during these challenging times. And, since the beginning of 2009, we have seen a record level of new contracts in the region, which shows the confidence our customers and the industry continue to have in us.

Law is taking its own course as far as Mr. B. Ramalinga Raju is concerned. Thanks to unity of top management and to proper corporate communication during the crisis, Satyam survived and finally became a healthy part of the more than US$7 billion-worth Mahindra Group and became Mahindra Satyam. The Satyam crisis, however, underscores the need for robust risk management in global outsourcing.

Japan (Disaster)

A Triple Disaster in One Fell Swoop: Rethinking Crisis Communication in Japan after March 11

Isaac A. Blankson, Sorin Nastasia, and Min Liu

In March 2011, within days, the northeastern region of Japan experienced an earthquake, a tsunami, several nuclear reactor meltdowns, loss of thousands of lives, the destruction of buildings and towns, and challenges in fulfilling basic human needs such as safe drinking water. The mega-crisis has had local, national, and international resonance, manifesting in natural disasters, industry failures, humanitarian disasters, and a legitimacy crisis faced by the government and a troubled nuclear industry. This case study makes an argument for a crisis communication analytical framework that recognizes the complexity and variety of the multiple crises. Focusing on local communities, the central government, and Tokyo Electric Power Company (TEPCO), the analysis examines the various crisis communication exigencies and challenges that the different players faced, details their crisis communication goals and strategies, and presents a critical assessment of the intended and unintended outcomes of how the crises were handled. Theoretical implications and practical lessons to be learned are explored.

Introduction

> As I awake each day I am humbled by the courage of the Japanese people enduring an unprecedented adversity . . . I read that so many people are still sheltered, no, quarantined for more than a week now in their homes . . . I hear the quiet calls from here, 11,000 kilometers away, asking for help, food and water as they sit patiently in this devastation. I have so many questions . . . And I remember, as it is all over the world, when they cannot control atomic power they will try to control the information.
>
> (Paul Gunter for Kyodo News, March 22, 2011)

Extra-Strength Tylenol capsule poisonings in 1982. Bhopal pesticide plant leaks in 1984. Challenger space shuttle breakup in 1986. Exxon Valdez oil spill in 1989. Mad cow disease outbreak in 1996. Columbine high school shootings in 1999. World Trade Center attacks, 9/11 2001. SARS outbreak in 2002. Columbia space shuttle breakup in 2003. New Orleans hurricane-related flooding in 2005. Virginia Tech University shootings in 2006. Deepwater Horizon oil spill in 2010. Each of these disasters provoked what communication experts—both professionals and scholars—call a *crisis*.

The field of crisis communication continues to expand, which is unfortunately in part owing to the increasing frequency of crises around the globe. Coombs (1999) observed:

> Pick any day of the week and you will find stories about train derailments, plane crashes, funds used inappropriately at a nonprofit organization, explosions in a manufacturing facility, workers shot or injured on the job, or *E. coli*-tainted beef, turkey, chicken, or even bean sprouts.
>
> (Coombs, 1999/2007, p. 1)

Crises come in different shapes and forms, and, as a result, communication specialists have attempted to categorize what leads to a crisis, what defines a crisis, and how to respond to a crisis (Mileti and Sorensen, 1990; Fearn-Banks, 1996/2009; Coombs, 1999/2007; Lucaszewski, 2001; Mitroff and Anagnos, 2001; Mitroff, 2003, 2005; Heath and Millar, 2004; Millar and Heath, 2005 Ruff and Aziz, 2003; Seeger et al., 2003; Ulmer et al., 2007/2011).

Such discussions have been instrumental in both establishing the area of studies of crisis communication and helping groups and organizations cope with adversities or catastrophes they face. In the case of the 2011 Japan crises, within days, the region experienced an earthquake, a tsunami, several nuclear reactor meltdowns, the death of thousands of people, the destruction of hundreds of thousands of buildings, and challenges in fulfilling basic human needs such as safe drinking water. The issues have had local, national, and international resonance. As such, relying on any singular model of crisis communication or emergency response would be insufficient in facilitating an understanding of the complexity and variety of circumstances. Similarly, as several critical scholars (Toth, 2008; Dunn, 2010) have argued, a comprehensive account of a crisis cannot be achieved without acknowledging and cross-examining the multiplicity of presences and voices connected to a crisis, especially those of people and communities affected by the crisis.

Several crisis typologies exist that are relevant to the current study. For example, Coombs (1999/2007) asserted that crises occur as a result of natural disasters (such as floods), megadamage (such as oil spills), human malevolence (such as product tampering), human breakdowns (such as errors), organizational misdeeds (such as harming stakeholders), challenges (such as protests), workplace violence (such as verbal/physical clashes), rumors (such as gossip), and technological breakdowns (such as computer failures). Similarly, Seeger et al. (2003) affirmed that a typology of crises should include depicted natural disasters, airline crashes, terrorist attacks, human resource crises, industrial crises, product/service crises, public perception crises, organizational environment crises, and economic crises.

It is important to recognize in the case of the 2011 Japan crises, multiple crises of different kinds were unfolding simultaneously. The mega-crisis encompasses natural and human-made disasters, as well as human and systemic failures. It incorporates two natural disasters (earthquake and tsunami), numerous physical disasters (wiping out of residential and industrial facilities), major industry failures (problems with multiple reactors at two nuclear plants) and subsequent production issues (problems with nuclear power in Japan and internationally), alleged human malevolence and evidenced human breakdown (regarding handling of nuclear power capacities), alleged organizational misdeeds and evidenced reputation challenges (regarding how the national government handled the aid for the region and how corporate and governmental bodies handled activities at and information about nuclear reactors), societal challenges and reputation challenges (increases in anxiety and decreases in trust), and an array of technological and economic breakdowns. Given that the crisis events are ongoing at the time of the book's publication, the list is likely to grow longer.

How key stakeholders define the nature of a crisis often determines how crisis responses will be evaluated. Different kinds of crises are considered to manifest different forms of threat, lead to different information needs, and create different communication exigencies (Pauchant and Mitroff, 1992; Reynolds and Seeger, 2005). As in the case of Tokyo Electric Power Company (TEPCO), industrial crises are triggered by natural disasters. However, the public generally assumes that natural disasters are beyond the control and responsibility of corporate organizations, and "preparation and management of these events usually falls to government agencies" (Seeger et al., 2003, p. 55). Crisis communication during a natural disaster, mostly in the form of emergency public information, has focused primarily on protecting "health, safety, and the environment" (Mileti and Sorensen, 1990, p. 4), and on restoring public confidence in an organization's (or government's) ability to manage the situation. Therefore, it is believed to be in the best interest of industry organizations to have crises classified as natural disasters rather than as industry failure crises caused by human factors (Dezenhall and Weber, 2007), and as documented in this chapter this was the approach taken by TEPCO leaders. The current analysis recognizes that local communities, national governments and for-profit organizations (such as TEPCO) are interdependent actors in responding to the 2011 crises with different crisis communication exigencies, leading to different goals and objectives, demanding different communication strategies and tactics.

A brief review of the current crisis communication scholarship uncovers various scholarly approaches with different assumptions of how to best understand a crisis and what makes some crisis communication more successful than others. For example, an approach offered by Seeger et al. (2003) recommends that communication experts understand the precrisis, crisis, and postcrisis stage, and communication challenges and opportunities in each stage. Coombs (2006) developed "a prescriptive system of matching crisis responses to crisis situation" (p. 171), itemizing mitigation strategies according to types of publics approached.

The complexity of the mega-crises in Japan 2011 calls for an integrative approach to understanding and evaluating crisis communication. There are too many incidents, too many stakeholders, and too many facets to rely solely on any single definition or paradigm of crisis communication. Instead of attempting to formulate a set of principles to be pursued and rules to be followed, this case study allows for multiple stories to be told and multiple voices to be heard. This case study places several types of discourses (of the local communities in northeastern Japan, the national government of Japan, the international corporation TEPCO, and to some extent the international media), and the goals, objectives, strategies, and tactics associated with these discourses, into cross-dialogues.

Background of the Crisis

Japan's Tohoku Region

Japan has a history of severe natural disasters (Karan and Gilbreath, 2005, p. 34). Its coastline, especially the Sanriku coast in the Tohoku region situated in northeastern Japan, has always been in danger of powerful earthquakes and large tidal waves. Two major tectonic plates, the Pacific Plate and the North American Plate, come together off the Sanriku coast, periodically causing earthquakes. Moreover, the Sanriku coast has a shoreline with many bays positioned in a zig-zag pattern, and this increases the size of tidal waves striking the area. An earthquake and tsunami hit the Sanriku coast in 1896, killing over 20,000 people. Another sequence of such disasters struck Japan in 1923, killing approximately 100,000 people. Other earthquakes and tsunamis have occurred in this region of Japan in more recent times.

The Tohoku region has suffered from depopulation, migration of its youth to urban areas, and aging of its residents because of potential natural disasters and its rural character. Traphagan and Knight (2003) wrote about "the negative long-term effects of depopulation on Tohoku agricultural communities" in the following terms:

> The scarcity of young people, the disproportionate number of senior citizens, unequal access to educational opportunities, the lack of good jobs,

and the deficiency of funds to provide needed health and social services are but a few of the symptoms.

(Traphagan and Knight, 2003, p. 89)

These authors affirmed that the negative effects are increased by "current demographic trends nationally such as declining fertility and the unprecedented rapid aging of the general population" that led to problems regarding welfare policies and long-term care (p. 90).

Japan's National Government

In Japan, there is a close connection between politicians and business executives (Vogel, 2006). Japan's internal affairs have historically been controlled by powerful bureaucrats. Prominent corporations operate with an extensive influence on personal lives, and their executives are often posed as model citizens. Numerous powerful bureaucrats retire to better-paid jobs in the very industries they once regulated, a practice known as *amakudari* (Colignon and Usui, 2003). But over the past decade, the bureaucrats' authority has been reduced, and corporations are losing power. Yet, no strong political class has emerged instead. Four prime ministers have come and gone in less than four years. The current government was formed by the Japan Democratic Party, elected after 50 years of domination by the Liberal Democratic Party.

Japan's national government regulators and utility companies have particularly close relations, as they have worked hand in hand to promote nuclear energy in order to reduce Japan's reliance on imported fuels. University of Southern California professor Najmedin Meshkati, a long-time critic of the nuclear industry's deceptive behaviors, blamed the Japanese government for being "complicit with the nuclear industry" to such an extent that once regulatory officials gave a whistleblower's name to a utility plant (PBS, March 17, 2011). A diplomatic cable obtained by Wikileaks reveals that in 2008 a member of Japan's legislative body, Taro Kono, opposed criticism by U.S. diplomats who were stating that Japanese officials had been "covering up nuclear accidents and obscuring the true costs and problems associated with the nuclear industry" ("U.S. embassy," 2008, para. 6).

Japan's Nuclear Industry

Japan is the only nation in the world that has endured an atomic bomb attack (Saito, 2010). On August 6 and August 9, 1945, in the final stages of World War II, the United States army conducted two atomic bombings against the cities of Hiroshima and Nagasaki. This history, together with the constant danger of natural disasters, has created some opposition to nuclear power. Although nuclear energy has been a national priority of the Japanese government since the 1970s when the nation was heavily dependent on imported fuel, and although the country is today the world's third largest nuclear power user with 54 nuclear reactors working and 12 being considered (Kageyama, March 17, 2011), environmentalists and left-leaning media outlets have expressed lack of trust in nuclear power production businesses and their regulators.

TEPCO, the largest power utility in Japan and Asia, owns 17 nuclear reactors and supplies about one-third of Japan's electrical needs, covering Tokyo and other densely populated areas (PBS, March 17, 2011). TEPCO has had its share of safety issues (Smith et al., 2011). In 2002, the company was accused of false reporting in routine inspections of nuclear facilities over many years (Gregory, March 16, 2011); the company admitted to 200 occasions in which information had been falsified between 1977 and 2002. The company's top executives resigned after the scandal. Two employees who had complained that the company falsified inspection records were fired. TEPCO's Kashiwazaki Kariwa plant had to shut down all its seven reactors following the 6.8 magnitude Shuetsu offshore earthquake in 2007, which inflicted major losses on the company. When TEPCO finally gained approval for restarting a reactor at this plant in May 2009, the progress was believed to be crucial to the company's fulfilling its promise to shareholders of returning a profit in 2009–2010 for the first time in three years (IHS Global Insight, 2009).

Since the 1970s, safety inspectors at the U.S. Atomic Energy Commission (AEC) have warned that General Electric (GE) reactors such as those used at TEPCO plants are vulnerable to explosions and radiation release if a meltdown occurs after a natural disaster. Yet, no actions were taken by the Japanese government to modify nuclear plant standards (Asahi.com, 2011, March 25, 26). Additionally, the Japanese nuclear industry has had a dismal record of safety violations leading to disasters, including a 1997 fire and explosion at a Tokaimura plant exposing 37 workers to radiation, a 1999 violation of safety standards at the same plant killing two workers and exposing hundreds to radiation, a 1999 accident in a Tsuruga plant where radiation levels 11,500 times the safety limit leaked from a pipe, and malfunctions at the Kashiwazaki Kariwa plant after the 2007 earthquake, including radioactive water spills and fires (Kageyama, 2011, March 17).

Japan's Cultural Background

Japanese culture is rooted in a highly collectivist emphasis on conformity, in-group solidarity, and high power-distance, and thus frowns upon dissent (Donahue, 1998). This cultural disapproval for dissent can help explain both government hesitance to push for more rigorous safety checks at nuclear power plants and community groups' hesitance to raise their voices against governmental and business entities dealing with nuclear energy. While approaching an industry believed to be of vital importance to the country's long-term development, regulatory officials may have chosen to overlook lapses for fear that more sanctions would be viewed as disturbing the harmony and interests of the community and society in general. For the same reasons, community activists and media groups may have toned down their protests.

It is also relevant for this case study to discuss the meaning of apology in the Japanese culture. Researchers studying Japanese and U.S. students found that Japanese consider acknowledging fault as an appropriate apology, whereas Americans view a statement that explains or justifies behavior as an appropriate apology. Also, many Japanese believe that it is better to apologize even when the other party is at fault. As such, some scholars have argued that apology needs to be understood as a culturally contextualized act (Sugimoto, 1998), and that an apology in the Japanese cultural context is an "indication of an individual's wish to maintain or restore a positive relationship with another person" (Wagatsuma and Rosett, 1986, p. 472). These authors also argue that in Japan apologizing is not necessarily an admission of fault; for example, the cultural assumption is that when a car accident occurs, the two parties should immediately apologize to each other and thus restore positive relationships, regardless of whose fault it is.

Situation Analysis

The crises in Japan unfolded in a rapid succession. Thus, the authors consider it appropriate to provide a chronological account of the crises as they occurred from Friday, March 11, when devastating natural disasters hit Japan until March 30, when this analysis was completed.

Friday, March 11, 2011

- 2:46 p.m.: An 8.8 Tohoku–Taiheiyou–Oki earthquake occurred. Japan Meteorological Agency issued tsunami warnings. Minutes later a deadly tsunami swept through the northeastern communities leaving thousands dead, several thousand missing, and extensive damage to infrastructure, houses, etc. (Figure 2.16).
- TEPCO nuclear power stations at Fukushima Daiichi Nuclear Power Station were severely damaged. Units 1 to 3 of the reactors were shut down. Units 4 to 6 experienced power outage. TEPCO released an immediate apology for the anxiety and inconvenience caused to its 4.05 million household customers.
- Prime Minister Naoto Kan held a press conference to assure the nation of the safety of nuclear power plants. He also called on the public to remain calm.

Figure 2.16 Earthquake and tsunami devastation in one of Japan's communities.
Source: Courtesy of Kyodo International News Inc. Reprinted by permission.

March 12

- Explosive sound and white smoke was confirmed near Unit 1 reactor.
- 6:00 a.m.: The national government instructed an evacuation for local residents within 3 km radius of Fukushima Daiichi Nuclear Power Station.
- 7:00 a.m.: The national government extended the evacuation zone from 3 km to within 10 km radius of Fukushima Daiichi Nuclear Power Station and Fukushima Daini Nuclear Power Station. Voluntary evacuation was instructed for local residents between 20 km and 30 km radius of the plant.
- 8:20 p.m.: TEPCO started to inject water (and later seawater, and then boric acid, which absorbs neutrons) into the reactor after experiencing abnormal heating.

March 14

- 11:01a.m.: Explosion followed by white smoke occurred near Unit 3 after experiencing abnormal increase in pressure of reactor containment vessel. Four workers sustained injuries.
- 1:25 p.m.: TEPCO notified local and national government officials of failure of reactor cooling function in Unit 2 as required by Clause 1, Article 15 of Act on Special Measures Concerning Nuclear Emergency Preparedness.
- TEPCO started implementation of rolling blackout (planned blackout alternates from one area to another) to avoid unexpected blackout. Company assured affected customers that it was working to restore power supply. Unaffected customers were asked to reduce electricity usage. TEPCO advised the public not to touch cut-off electric wires and to switch off electric appliances when leaving homes.

March 15

- 6:00 a.m.: An explosion damaged the roof of Unit 4 reactor building, causing decreasing pressure inside the compression chamber (Figure 2.17). TEPCO began to inject seawater to cool reactor. Employees not in charge of injection work were evacuated to safer locations.

March 16

- 5:45 a.m.: A fire at the northwestern corner of the Unit 4 Nuclear Reactor Building was detected and reported to the fire department and the local government.
- TEPCO considered using the Self-Defense Forces to spray water by helicopters. The idea was canceled.

Figure 2.17 Partially damaged building housing the No. 4 reactor of the Fukushima
        Daiichi nuclear power station in Fukushima Prefecture.
Source: Courtesy of Kyodo International News Inc. Reprinted by permission.

March 17–25

• TEPCO collaborated with several agencies to spray water or inject
  seawater to cool the reactors. Agencies include the Self-Defense Forces,
  the United States Armed Forces, police units, Tokyo Fire Department's
  Hyper Rescue and Osaka City Fire. TEPCO reported using 13 fire engines
  from regional fire departments and Tokyo Fire Department.

March 21–28

• Radioactive materials such as iodine and cesium were found in seawater,
  air samples, and puddles near Fukushima Daiichi Nuclear Power Station.
• TEPCO released a statement to assure public safety and promise
  continuous monitoring of the environment.

March 24

• TEPCO reported progress.
• Three emergency workers were exposed to high radiation and sent to
  Fukushima Medical University hospital and later to National Institute of
  Radiological Sciences. All three workers were later discharged.

March 26–28

- Lights in the main control rooms of all units were restored.
- Blackouts were resolved.
- TEPCO continued to monitor activity and radiation levels.

March 29–30

- Extremely high levels of plutonium, iodine, and cesium were detected in water puddles in and around the plant.
- TEPCO continued to monitor and work to reduce radiation levels.

Problem and Opportunity (PO) Statements

Crises can be seen in terms of the challenges they present as well as the opportunities they offer (Coombs, 1999/2007; Ulmer et al., 2007/2011). For the crises discussed here the problems are multifaceted and stem from an unprecedented series of natural, human, and technological disasters; yet the opportunities are also numerous and complex, and they range from enhanced community engagement to more sustainable regional reconstruction to increased governmental body accountability to more open conversations about nuclear power. A Reuters article on March 24, 2011 announces:

> As the world's third construction market, Japan has the resources, skills, and social cohesiveness required to rebuild quickly, but the disaster may also spur it to think harder about how—and where—to rebuild devastated towns and villages, experts say.
>
> ("After the disaster," 2011, para. 12)

Others have called for a new type of Japanese politics and the revival of Japanese pride.

Three primary actors are identified in Japan's crises: the local communities in Tohoku (represented by local government officials and individual citizens), the national government of Japan (represented by the Prime Minister and heads of Ministries), and the international corporation TEPCO. There have been additional actors in these crises, such as foreign governments, the international media, and international aid agencies, but these have not played major roles in managing the crises and will not be considered separately in the economy of this chapter. The remainder of this chapter is discussed in line with the three primary actors.

- *PO Statement of the local communities in Tohoku*: The northeastern coast communities are threatened by natural and nuclear concerns and must demonstrate resilience needed for recovery.

- *PO Statement of the national government of Japan*: Japan's government, as protector of citizens and regulator of nuclear industry, is capable of managing the crises.
- *PO Statement of the international corporation TEPCO*: TEPCO has the ability to solve its nuclear plant failures and to rebuild public/stakeholder confidence in its operations.

Initial Responses to the Crises

In the immediate aftermath of the March 11 disasters in Japan, people from around the world were shocked by images of massive destruction of human life and property, yet also amazed by the evidence of extraordinary fortitude of the Japanese people and communities. A BBC account on March 20, 2011 specifies:

> There was an almost total blackout, but there was hardly any crime reported. There were shortages of essential supplies, but people in the city would queue calmly for up to two hours at a time rather than taking from the empty shops . . . they were cooperating.

Yet the account also mentions the following statement by Professor Jeff Kingston from Temple University in Tokyo: "In Japan people smile with their face and cry inside."

Immediately after the earthquake and tsunami struck, the Japan government set up an emergency management headquarters headed by Prime Minister Naoto Kan, who ordered all ministers to do their utmost to save and help disaster victims and survivors. The government mobilized the military's Self-Defense Forces (SDF), police units, and firefighters to work with prefectural governments in providing relief assistance. The SDF was charged with control of shipment of aid to ensure speedy delivery of needed resources and the evacuation of victims in hard-to-reach areas.

Report of damaged reactors at TEPCO's nuclear power plants soon diverted the Japanese government's attention away from the relief efforts. Prime Minister Kan and Chief Cabinet Secretary Yukio Edano held several press conferences to assure the Japanese people of their safety and that the government was working with TEPCO to address the problems.

The government's initial response to the nuclear crisis was to leave TEPCO in charge of the emergency operations at the Fukushima plant. However, as stipulated by Japan's Law on Special Measures Concerning Nuclear Emergency Preparedness, the government declared a state of emergency on March 11 after TEPCO notified officials of the nuclear reactor failures. Six days later, the government dispatched the Self-Defense Forces to assist TEPCO. According to a ministry of defense spokesman, the SDF had to wait for TEPCO to request help.

Immediately following the earthquake on March 11, TEPCO released its first press statement at 2:46 pm, which acknowledged that the Fukushima Daiichi nuclear power units 1 to 4 had automatically shut down because of the earthquake. The company notified relevant entities of the incident (the Minister of Economy, Trade, and Industry, the Governor of Fukushima Prefecture, the Mayor of Okuma Town, and the mayor of Futaba Town) as required by Article 10, Clause 1 of the Act on Special Measures Concerning Nuclear Emergency Preparedness. The Act obligates TEPCO to notify the nation, prefectures, cities and towns in order for them to take necessary actions and in a timely manner. It also assured the public that the company was taking steps to determine the exact cause of the shutdown of their emergency generators and also working toward restoration. On March 25, TEPCO reported progress. However, between March 26 and March 31, when this analysis was completed, extremely high levels of plutonium, iodine, and cesium were detected in water puddles in and around the plant. TEPCO continued to monitor and work to reduce radiation levels.

Communication Goals, Objectives, Strategies, and Tactics

The crisis-communication goals, objectives, strategies, and tactics will be presented from a three-pronged perspective: of the local communities, of the national government, and of the international corporation. We must note that, because these players have different configurations, their communication planning sets differ in their concerns of degrees of consistency. We must also note that, because the crises are still ongoing, the goals, objectives, strategies, and tactics of these players might keep changing.

1. The Local Communities in Tohoku

Goal 1: To create public awareness of the effects of the disaster on their livelihood and society.

Objective: To frequently and urgently communicate with domestic and international entities about their situation.

Strategy (a): Communicated critical needs of the community to the national government and humanitarian agencies.

Strategy (b): Cooperated with local, national, and international entities in the recovery efforts (Figure 2.18).

Tactics:

- kept all communication channels open with the national government and aid agencies;

Figure 2.18 Government response to devastation in Japan's communities. A junior high school serving as an evacuation center in Rikuzentakata, Iwate Prefecture.

Source: Courtesy of Kyodo International News Inc. Reprinted by permission.

- listened for and complied with local and national government directives;
- looked for and contributed to relief efforts organized by aid agencies;
- posted data about survivors and the deceased on walls and in virtual environments;
- organized search and rescue teams to locate survivors and the deceased;
- gave scores of interviews to the domestic and international media; and
- citizens shared their experiences in local, national and international media.

Goal 2: To increase public knowledge of local concerns about the safety of utility plants in the region.

Objective 1: To provide extensive locally/self-generated data about the nuclear problems.

Objective 2: To cultivate significant public interest in self-generated data about radiation levels.

Strategy (a): Monitored, collected, and disseminated locally/self-generated information about the situation at the nuclear power plants.

Strategy (b): Kept local, national, and international community apprised of developments.

Tactics:

- gathered data about nuclear reactor issues from national and international, governmental and nongovernmental bodies;
- citizens purchased and used personal radiation detector devices to generate own data;
- used local and international media to release self-gathered data about nuclear reactor issues; and
- used new media (blogs, Twitter, Facebook, websites) to disseminate radiation level data.

Goal 3: To communicate a sense of hope and vision for the future.

Objective 1: To organize massive community efforts to clean up and rebuild.

Objective 2: To increase significantly local community participation in determining the future of the communities.

Strategy (a): Initiated civic dialogues to engage discussions about the region and its future.

Strategy (b): Developed collaborations with concerned entities to begin the process of rebuilding.

Tactics:

- local government officials held scores of media interviews and appearances to organize and announce cleanup plans;
- citizens used new/social media outlets such as blogs and websites (JapanStatus.org) to communicate their participation and experiences in cleanup efforts;
- local government officials used the local media to communicate their vision for the future for the region; and
- used community forums to discuss future plans for the communities and region.

2. The National Government of Japan

Goal 1: To maintain constant information flow between the national government and the communities affected by the crises.

Objective 1: To cultivate significant and immediate assurance of government support and assistance to local governments and communities.

Objective 2: To significantly reduce concerns of national and international stakeholders about support to communities affected by the disasters.

Strategy (a): Kept periodic information updates to local representatives and various stakeholders.

Strategy (b): Called for political groups and governmental bodies to work together to address community needs and to solve the crises.

Tactics:

- used official channels and the media to communicate information about and from the area affected by the crises;
- kept communication channels open among themselves, with local authorities, and with rescue workers;
- officials traveled to affected communities to demonstrate concern and pledge support;
- officials used various media channels to communicate their assessment of the situation in the affected area; and
- appointed members of opposition parties to key positions to coordinate and help manage the disaster.

Goal 2: To alleviate safety concerns after the earthquake and tsunami and during the nuclear emergencies.

Objective 1: To manage information flow on the crises.

Objective 2: To cultivate and maintain significant public trust and confidence in the government's ability to manage the situation.

Objective 3: To reinforce an image of a competent regulator of the nuclear industry.

Strategy (a): Issued necessary orders and guidelines to protect the public and property.

Strategy (b): Provided periodic information about efforts being made to solve the nuclear power plant emergencies.

Tactics:

- used official channels and the media to convey information about the nuclear power plants;
- kept communication channels open with power plant officials and communities;
- provided prescriptive guidelines to the public and community officials on actions to take in response to the crises;
- used on-site visits and worked extensively with plant officials; and
- communicated measures taken to protect people from risks of radiation (including measures about water, vegetables, milk, seafood).

Goal 3: To increase a sense of public hope for government assistance/support and in the future.

Objective 1: To organize significant and immediate nationally-administered clean-up efforts.

Objective 2: To provide frequent and timely information about support services available to communities and people.

Strategy (a): Assured public and communities of continued government support for the region.

Strategy (b): Provided significant guidelines and alerts to the communities and public about improving circumstances following the crises.

Tactics:

- used official channels and the media to inform the communities and public about government efforts and plans for the region;
- collaborated with local government representatives to relocate surviving victims and to provide them with essential services;
- established an application process for housing units for people who lost their homes as a result of the earthquake and tsunami and those relocated owing to high radiation levels; and
- used variety of channels (official and media) to communicate official assessment reports pertaining to the region.

3. The International Corporation TEPCO

Goal 1: To notify relevant governmental and community bodies about the nuclear problems and efforts to solve the problems.

Objective 1: To provide immediate and accurate information about the state of the nuclear power emergencies as they unfold.

Objective 2: To provide immediate and accurate information about possible public safety concerns relating to the explosions and radiation levels.

Strategy: Kept national government, local governments, and public informed of efforts to solve the problems facing their nuclear plant.

Tactics:

- used the media to announce incidents to key stakeholders as they unfolded; and
- held press conferences to disseminate efforts being made to the public.

Goal 2: To convey a larger sense of legitimacy and control over the unfolding incident.

Objective 1: To frequently communicate apologies as a way of soliciting sympathy and patience from the Japanese people.

Objective 2: To create a sustained image (locally and internationally) of a company in control of the situation.

Strategy (a): Reminded the public that the problems facing the nuclear plant resulted from natural disasters and not from human or organizational error.

Strategy (b): Provided frequent and timely updates of company's efforts to address the problems.

Tactics:

- used various press conferences to refute allegations of company not doing enough to solve the problems but only protecting its bottom line;
- issued hourly reports through press releases to update stakeholders of the crises as they unfolded;
- issued hourly progress reports through press releases;
- issued televised public apologies; and
- used company website to update local and international community of the status of the crises and efforts being made to address them.

Goal 3: To maintain goodwill and confidence in the harmonious coexistence of nuclear power plants and local communities.

Objective 1: To maintain a sustained positive image of TEPCO as a good neighbor of the community.

Objective 2: To frequently demonstrate heroic actions of company employees.

Strategy (a): Presented and emphasized the positive contributions the plant has made to the local communities.

Strategy (b): Demonstrated the hard work and dedication of the company's workers.

Tactics:

- used opportunities in the media to talk about the company's past and future contributions to the communities;
- provided national and local media with images of the plant and heroic actions of emergency workers;
- used press conferences to emphasize the company is working to solve the crises; and
- issued press releases on company website and to media to address some of the allegations of criticisms against the company.

Outcomes Assessment

1. The Local Communities in Tohoku

The orderliness and resilience of the Japanese citizens after the earthquake, tsunami, nuclear meltdowns, and radiation dangers, is currently admired around Japan and in the whole world. Local officials' and local residents' statements of courage and determination have been cited by a variety of media outlets (see BBC News, 2011; Beech, 2011; "Nuclear workers," 2001; Voigt, 2011). An NPR report from March 23, 2011, cites the mayor of a small town in the Tohoku region stating that "We live our lives here . . . We are all together here. When you think about that, it's impossible for us to leave here" (Beaubien, 2011).

Community residents from northeastern Japan were also viewed with admiration by many for their determination to find their missing loved ones following the disasters. A CNN report from March 22, 2011, includes the following story:

> Toyoko Numayama walks from town to town, clutching a photograph of her husband and praying someone recognizes him. "Of course, I have to hope," she says . . . Survivors sift through evacuation centers and hospital logs as the government's tally of the missing grows daily.

There has been little good news from the communities in northeastern Japan about finding loved ones, but many local residents are still expressing hope when interviewed by the media representatives. Some have also expressed dissent, which is uncommon in the Japanese culture. Dissent has primarily been voiced by local citizens and some officials regarding the national government's decision to bury the dead (often without coffins and in mass graves, owing to lack of resources and fear of diseases) rather than cremate them as Japanese traditions require. As an article from *The Wall Street Journal* from March 22, 2011, depicts, "Some families are reported to have hauled away relatives to organize cremation on their own. In at least one town, officials are resisting burying its dead, though it lacks alternatives." The article cites Futoshi Toba, mayor of Rikuzentakata, a fishing village in the Iwate prefecture, saying: "The prospect of pulling the deceased from under the rubble—only to bury them again in soil, without even a coffin—is just not something I am prepared to do." Rikuzentakata has 700 dead and a crematorium that can burn seven people a day, so the mayor of the village is asking neighboring towns for help and the national government for understanding (Wakabayashi, 2011).

Community residents are also looking for those who have been separated owing to the nuclear crisis. Numerous accounts from *The Japan Times* (see Hongo, 2011; "Iwate evacuees," 2011; "Tsunami survivors," 2011; "The young volunteers," 2011) and international media outlets state that in some families the younger people and the children have left seeking safety from high radiation, while older people, those ill, and many without many resources have been left behind. In an ABC report on March 24, 2011, a woman declared that in her family there were seven people and only five places in the car, so she told her husband to go with the children and she remained in her town. The sympathy of national and international communities has also been directed towards those who now live in public places in their local areas and their traumatic experiences of sleeping on cold floors of sports arenas or transportation buildings, as well as about help they are receiving from people who are bringing food, taking strangers into their own homes, or who have volunteered to do fundraising. Many in the media and communities are seeing signs that Japan's younger generation is acquiring a taste for civic engagement (Kubota, 2011).

Japanese people from the suffering northeast are also engaged in monitoring the situation and reporting about it. A BBC report from March 21, 2011, shows that, since governmental and corporate reports about radiation levels have not been reliable, people have organized in such ways as to report radiation levels themselves. The article calls this "crowd-sourcing": people have bought radiation detection equipment, are reading radiation levels, and are posting their data on websites such as JapanStatus.org. Many are not just protesting against measures taken by the national government or TEPCO that they find unfair or not in tune with their traditions, but are also taking their own measures to prevent governmental and corporate abuses.

Local government and representatives have also collaborated intensely to start clean-up efforts and to envision a sustainable society of the future in the region affected by the disasters.

2. The National Government of Japan

In the aftermath of the multiple disasters, the national government attempted to maintain information flow to and from the region affected by the crises, to alleviate safety concerns in and about the region, and to maintain public hope in the future. Several measures were taken for accomplishing these goals, including various forms of enhanced communication and increased collaboration.

After March 11, 2011, Chief Cabinet Secretary Yukio Edano became the face of the government, delivering countless updates to the media and the Japanese people via live press conferences and interviews. Although before the crises opposition parties were asking for the resignation of Japan's Prime Minister owing to economic problems, shortly after the crises all the opposition parties, including the Liberal Democratic Party which is the main adversary of the Kan government, began to cooperate with the government.

In spite of efforts to provide intense communication and to showcase collaboration between various political groups, the government has been criticized by the media and to some extent is losing the trust of the populations (Hodge et al., 2011; Kaufmann and Penciakova, 2011). Media outlets in Japan and internationally have indicated that more than 200,000 people remain in temporary shelters, where there are still acute shortages of food, water, electricity, heating, and other essential amenities. Media sources blame this on the inadequacy of the government's emergency response to the earthquake and tsunami (Fukue, 2011; ABC News, 2011). There have been voices also accusing the government of not providing sufficient and reliable information about the region's future, including clean-up, housing, infrastructure, and job creation plans.

The nuclear issues tested the strength of Japan's government in handling this magnitude of a crisis, and arguably the government did not demonstrate the leadership necessary to take charge of the situation. Rather, its responses were dominated by lack of transparency, reluctance to release information, and preoccupation with protecting TEPCO. It also did not demonstrate the ability to improvise and to act resolutely in the unprecedented and fast evolving crises.

Prime Minister Kan and Chief Cabinet Secretary Edano appeared to be overwhelmed by the challenges of the nuclear accident (Dominowski, 2011). After the nuclear plant breach was known on March 11, Prime Minister Kan held a press conference reassuring the public of the safety of nuclear power plants. He called on the public to remain calm. The next day, the government announced plans to evacuate hundreds of thousands of people residing within 20 kilometers of the plant as a cautionary step to protect locals from exposure to radiation. Chief Cabinet Secretary Edano was also reported as seeming unable to make sense of the fast-evolving crises. On March 16, he reportedly caused confusion when he announced at a press conference that staff members of the plant were being temporarily moved to a safe place because of an increase in radiation levels from smoke from Reactor No. 3 at Fukushima Daiichi. Some of the foreign media interpreted his statement as meaning that TEPCO staff members were leaving the plant. Critics have also charged that the government has not been forthcoming with disclosing information. Most communications from the government officials were described as vague, confusing, and untimely.

Recently, radioactive materials have been detected in seawater, vegetables grown in the area, and in Tokyo's water supply. This has forced the government to act more resolutely, although sometimes with confusing statements. After discovering dangerous levels of radioactive iodine in the tap water in Tokyo on March 23, the government warned parents to prevent their infants from drinking tap water. This triggered confusion over the safety of the drinking water and a rush to purchase bottled water. Chief Cabinet Secretary Edano had to use a press conference on March 24 to reassure the public of the safety of tap water except for infants. To demonstrate the safety of the water an official publicly drank water from the tap. The government also pledged to deliver bottled water to homes with one-year-old infants or younger.

Since March 24, the government has taken measures to alleviate concerns over dangerous levels of radioactive contamination found in milk and 11 kinds of vegetables in Fukushima and neighboring prefectures. It placed restrictions on agricultural products in Japan. It ordered affected prefectures to halt all shipments of vegetables, and suspended raw milk shipments from Fukushima and Ibaraki. To answer international concerns, it also insisted that no fish are being caught near the reactors, and that Japan is diligently testing seafood and has found no dangerous levels of radiation.

3. The International Corporation TEPCO

The earthquake and tsunami set off a succession of nuclear emergencies for TEPCO that required emergency responses. However, the company's communication has not been sustained or trustworthy, being marked by reluctance to release information, confusing statements, and public apologies that came across as formal rather than honest (Weisul, 2011).

Public safety issues were not clearly delineated by TEPCO. On March 12, after having initially denied problems at its power plants, TEPCO announced that its facilities have been seriously damaged, and power shortages may occur. TEPCO officials explained that "A big sound and white smoke were recorded near Reactor No. 1." The matter "was under investigation" (TEPCO, 2011). In a press release at 7:00 a.m., TEPCO stated: "Evacuation has been instructed by the national government to the local residents within 10 km radius of

Fukushima Daiichi Nuclear Power Station and Fukushima Daini Nuclear Power Station." An hour later it retracted this information, stating that:

> The national government has instructed evacuation for those local residents within 3 km radius of the periphery and indoor standby for those local residents between 3 km and 10 km radius of the periphery. We are very sorry to have informed wrongly about evacuation area ...
>
> (TEPCO, March 12, 2011)

Reactor cooling efforts were also not made clear by TEPCO. On March 12, the company announced that it was putting top priority on cooling down the reactor core. At first, TEPCO emergency workers and military fire trucks sprayed water onto the reactor using temporary fire pumps to prevent the fuel from overheating and releasing radiation. It later switched to injecting seawater and boric acid, which absorbs neutrons into the reactor core. Media reports speculated that TEPCO management was too slow to accept the necessity of drastic measures. Crucial efforts to cool down the nuclear reactors were delayed because TEPCO did not want to lose the reactors as productive assets. Using seawater would make it difficult to reuse the reactors in the future, and thus affect the bottom line. Critics claimed that Prime Minister Kan ordered TEPCO on Sunday to use seawater. But the company's spokesperson Hiro Hasegawa claimed the company was taking the safety of the plant and the appropriate timing into consideration.

TEPCO's communication of what it called "planned power outages," first announced on March 13, was also unclear. In the aftermath of the earthquake and destruction of TEPCO's facilities, its power generation capacity fell to 31 million kilowatts causing a shortage of 10 million kilowatts for its customers. Under the plan, the areas and hours of blackouts were to be decided in advance to ensure public awareness. TEPCO divided its service areas into five groups and stated that it would suspend power supply to each group for three hours a day. However, on March 14, the company retracted this plan stating that the company would not implement the power cut in the first of the five groups as demand had been found less than expected. An hour later, TEPCO retracted this announcement, affirming that it will start the outages as planned. According to company officials, electricity demand was deemed smaller than expected because railway companies (major customers of TEPCO) had cut train service in preparation for the outages. The company has meanwhile implemented some planned power outages and is planning to continue until the end of April.

TEPCO's leadership has also not been very strong. It was not until March 13, two days after the nuclear emergency and hours after the explosion in Reactor No. 1, that the President of TEPCO Masataka Shimizu gave his first press conference. Shimizu informed the public that the scope of nuclear radiation was under review, but that he did not think it would have immediate consequences for human health. Shimizu was not seen for two weeks after his press conference. According to TEPCO, the president was suffering from dizziness and high blood pressure and had been hospitalized. The company's chairman, Tsunehisa Katsumata, took over operations. Since March 11, several top leaders of TEPCO, who affirmed that the dangers of meltdowns and radiation were small, have retracted their affirmations; they have apologized publicly, but they have not matched these public apologies with action (Figure 2.19). News accounts alleged that a Japanese reporter had told a TEPCO official at a press conference that he wanted to hear concrete plans and not that the official felt sorry for the situation.

However, since the beginning of the crises TEPCO officials have highlighted the ways in which the corporation benefits Japanese communities and offers work to people in communities. These officials have also focused on the ways in which workers of TEPCO do their duty diligently and choose to remain at the nuclear reactors even under danger. However, critics have pointed out that nuclear plant issues have hurt agriculture in northeastern Japan, and that plant workers do not have any other choice but to remain under danger since jobs in the region are scarce.

Figure 2.19 TEPCO Vice President Sakae Muto (second from right) and other executives bow to apologize during a press conference over errors in analyzing the concentration of radioactive substances in water found in the nuclear power plant.

Source: Courtesy of Kyodo International News Inc. Reprinted by permission.

Lessons Learned

In a world that is more interconnected than ever before, we can no longer consider crises, big or small, as isolated, local events that can be contained. As the Japan 2011 crises unfolded, with real time coverage of the events all over the world, billions of people saw repeated images of devastated communities and dislocated people. Additionally, footage of buildings being swept away were posted on Youtube, requests for prayers for the 50 Fukushima workers were posted on Twitter by a family member, and all of these helped keep the rest of the world informed, engaged as part of the crisis, and collaborating to shape global awareness of this crisis. As one researcher eloquently stated, "real time media coverage, social network technologies, impact and change our perception of the world as ever smaller, more inter-connected, and certainly more dangerous, unsafe, and crisis prone" (James, 2008, p. 10).

Crisis responses have to be considered in terms of the needs of local communities and citizens immediately affected by the crisis, but also of the diverse needs of those who feel connected to or part of the crisis events even though they may live thousands of miles away. These stakeholders' needs for accurate and timely information, for safety and hope reassurance, for messages of self-efficacy and civic engagement, for example, should be addressed by crisis responses. Additionally, issues about local and international attempts to envision and put to practice communities of the future that would be more sustainable, more interconnected, and thus more capable of responding to disasters should also be addressed.

The Japanese government's handling of the 2011 crises arguably presents the biggest test regarding its public trust since World War II. How it handles the nuclear crisis poses a particularly significant threat to the government's legitimacy. On the one hand, it is a top priority of the government to facilitate a productive nuclear industry, which is seen as key to Japan's long-term growth and sustainability as a nation. On the other hand, the government's willing-ness and ability to regulate the industry is called to question every time an incident occurs. Given the difficulty in justifying the existence of an unstable and volatile industry, the government needs to realign its relationship with the nuclear industry and to reinforce an image of competence and rigor in its regulatory capacity in the eyes of specific local communities and the general public.

Crises with global ramifications such as the one Japan is facing should take into account larger crisis management plans that engage key international stakeholders. The cooperation of the international community, particularly the United States and the International Atomic Energy Agency (IAEA) should have been sought. But TEPCO and the Japanese government seem determined to solve the crises with little international involvement. After waiting for an invitation from Japan for days, the IAEA decided to dispatch an expert commission to Japan even though its expertise had not been solicited for by Japan.

Mega-crises call for reasonable transparency. The lack of transparency and the reluctance in releasing information to local communities and the international community has created distrust and frustration. Countries such as the United States took matters into their own hands and issued statements that contradicted those of the Japanese government. For example, after the reactor explosions, the U.S. government instructed its civilians to evacuate up to 80 kilometers from the nuclear plant. This contradicted the Japanese government's evacuation area of 20 kilometers around the plant. European countries, Australia, South Korea, and others followed the United States' lead in setting wider evacuation areas for their nationals and evacuating their citizens to safer places. The chairman of the U.S. Nuclear Regulatory Commission Gregory Jaczko made this statement that also contradicted the official Japanese position: "We believe that radiation levels are extremely high, which could possibly impact the ability to take corrective measures." His statement was quickly rebutted by officials of TEPCO and Japan's nuclear regulatory agency. The involvement of international agencies could have reduced the distrust in information coming from Japan and could have prevented the overreactions of foreign governments.

Discussion Questions

1. The multiple crises in Japan were still unfolding as the case study was written and sent to print. Based on how the events evolved after March, 2011, how would you amend the authors' analysis presented in this chapter? What new "lessons learned" would you draw from the later developments of this crisis?
2. How can local and regional communities be configured as full partners into the communication processes taking place during complex crisis situations?
3. How can local community residents and representatives better coordinate their needs and resources with those of national governments, corporations, and the international community during a complex crisis?
4. Compare and contrast the role of apology in crisis management in Japan and the United States or another Western country.
5. How can national governments better function as intermediaries between citizens and communities of their country and of the world and for-profit organizations and corporations?
6. The Japanese government and TEPCO did not engage the international community in a major way. Do you agree with their approach? What could the international involvements have brought to this case had they been consulted extensively? What implications could it have on the TEPCO's and the Japanese government's image?

References

6 days on, government still looking for aid supply plan. (2011, March 18). Retrieved from www.yomiuri.co.jp/dy/national/T110317004454.htm

ABC News (2011). Atomic refugees, March 24. Retrieved from http://news.yahoo.com/video/world-15749633/24652118

After the disaster: Japan's age-old problem. (2011). Reuters, March 24. Retrieved from http://www.reuters.com/article/2011/03/24/us-japan-quake-rebuild-idUSTRE 72N4KA20110324

Asahi.com (2011). Nuclear expert: Hubris led to disaster, March 25. Retrieved from www.asahi.com/english/TKY201103250201.html

Asahi.com (2011). TEPCO ignored latest research on tsunamis, March 26. Retrieved from www.asahi.com/english/TKY201103250387.html

BBC Mobile (2011). Crowd-sourcing aids Japan crisis, March 21. Retrieved from www.bbc.co.uk/news/technology-12803643

BBC News (2011). Japan quake: Disaster tests country's famed "stoicism", March 20. Retrieved from www.bbc.co.uk/news/mobile/world-asia-pacific-12798799

BBC News (2011). Works resumes at stricken Japan nuclear plant, March 24. Retrieved from www.bbc.co.uk/news/world-asia-pacific-12844346

Beaubien, J. (2011). In Fukushima city shelter, evacuees imagine future. *NPR*, March 23. Retrieved from www.npr.org/2011/03/23/134792191/in-fukushima-city-shelter-evacuees-imagine-future

Beech, H. (2011). How Japan will reawaken. *Time*, March 28, 44–47.

CNN News (2011). In northeastern Japan, hope dwindles as death toll mounts, March 22. Retrieved from www.edition.cnn.com/2011/WORLD/asiapcf/03/21/japan.disaster/index.html?iref=topnews

Colignon, R. A. and Usui, C. (2003). Amakudari: The hidden fabric of Japan's economy. Ithaca, NY: Cornell University Press.

Coombs, W. T. (2006). Crisis management: A communicative approach. In C. H. Botan and V. Hazelton (Eds.), *Public relations theory II* (pp. 171–197). Mahwah, NJ: Lawrence Erlbaum Associates.

Coombs, W. T. (1999/2007). *Ongoing crisis communication: Planning, managing, and responding*. Los Angeles: Sage.

Dezenhall, E., and Weber, J. (2007). *Damage control: Why everything you know about crisis management is wrong*. New York: Portfolio Hardcover.

Dominowski, M. W. (2011). Earthquake and tsunami, nuclear crisis overwhelmed government, Japanese official says. *AP*, March 22. Retrieved from www.silive.com/news/index.ssf/2011/03/earthquake_and_tsunami_nuclear.html

Donahue, R. T. (1998). *Japanese culture and communication: Critical cultural analysis*. Lanham, MD: University of Press America.

Dunn, C. K. (2010). Power and place: A case study approach to rethinking crisis communication. Unpublished doctoral dissertation, East Carolina University, Greenville, NC.

Fearn-Banks, K. (1996/2009). *Crisis communications: A casebook approach*. New York: Routledge.

Fukue, N. (2011). Evacuees served hot meals: Budokan first shelter in capital to offer square fare to displaced. *The Japan Times Online*, March 24. Retrieved from http://search.japantimes.co.jp/cgi-bin/nn20110324a4.html

Gregory, M. (2011). Is Tokyo Electric Power becoming Japan's BP? *BBC News*, March 16. Retrieved from www.bbc.co.uk/news/mobile/business-12764458

Gunter, P. (2011). Information controlled when atomic power out of control. *Kyodo News*, March 22. Retrieved from http://english.kyodonews.jp/news/2011/03/80140.html

Heath, R. L., and Millar, D. P. (Eds.). (2004). *Responding to crisis: A rhetorical approach to crisis management*. Mahwah, NJ: Lawrence Erlbaum Associates.

Hodge, N., Weisman, J. and Morse, A. (2011). Japan reassures, others flee, March 18. Retrieved from http://ebird.osd.mil/ebird2/ebfiles/e20110318809253.html, p. 1.

Hongo, J. (2011). Signs of disaster were there to see: Seismology experts warned for years nuclear plant can't withstand true worst-case scenario. *The Japan Times Online*, March 26. Retrieved from http://search.japantimes.co.jp/cgi-bin/nn2011 0326x3.html

IHS Global Insight. (2009). Tepco gains approval for Kashiwazaki Kariwa NPP restart in Japan. Retrieved March 20, 2011 from www.ihs.com/products/global-insight/industry-economic-report.aspx?ID=106595557&pu=1&rd=globalinsight_com#

Iwate evacuees apply for housing. (2011). *The Japan Times Online*, March 26. Retrieved from http://search.japantimes.co.jp/cgi-bin/nn20110326x2.html

James, R. K. (2008). *Crisis intervention strategies* (6th ed.). Belmont, CA: Brooks-Cole/Thompson.

Kageyama, Y. (2011). Bungling, cover-ups define Japanese nuclear power, March 17. Retrieved from http://hosted2.ap.org/APDEFAULT/cae69a7523db45408eeb2b3a 98c0c9c5/Article_2011–03–17-AS-Japan-Earthquake-Nuclear-Scandals/id-dda657 ff723241ac83018e21567b5d74

Karan, P. P., and Gilbreath, D. (2005). *Japan in the 21st century: Environment, economy, and society*. Lexington, KY: The University Press of Kentucky.

Kaufmann, D. and Penciakova, V. (2011). Japan's triple disaster: Governance and the earthquake, tsunami and nuclear crises, March 16. Retrieved from www.brookings.edu/opinions/2011/0316_japan_disaster_kaufmann.aspx

Kubota, Y. (2011, March 24). After the disaster: Japan's age-old problem. Retrieved from www.reuters.com/article/2011/03/24/us-japan-quake-rebuild-idUSTRE72 N4KA20110324

Lukaszewski, J. E. (2001). Crisis communication management: Protecting and enhancing corporate reputation and identity. In P. J. Kitchen and D. E. Schultz (Eds.), *Corporate communications in the 21st century* (pp. 199–245). New York: Palgrave.

Mileti, D. S., and Sorensen, J. H. (1990). Communication and emergency public warning. ORLN-6609. Washington, DC.

Millar, D. P., and Heath, R. L. (Eds.). (2005). *Responding to crisis: A rhetorical approach to crisis communication*. Mahwah, NJ: Lawrence Erlbaum Associates.

Mitroff, I. I. (2003). *Crisis leadership: Planning for the unthinkable*. New York: John Wiley & Sons.

Mitroff, I. I. (2005). *Why some companies emerge stronger and better from a crisis: Seven essential lessons for surviving disaster*. New York: AMACOM.

Mitroff, I. I., and Anagnos, G. (2001). *Managing crises before they happen: What every executive and manager needs to know about crisis management*. New York: Amacom.

Nuclear workers can quit; few do. (2011). *The Japan Times Online*, March 27. Retrieved from http://search.japantimes.co.jp/cgi-bin/nn20110327a4.html

Pauchant, T. C., and Mitroff, I. I. (1992). *Transforming the crisis-prone organization: Preventing individual, organizational, and environmental tragedies.* San Francisco, CA: Jossey-Bass.

PBS. (2011). Get to know Tepco: Japan's biggest power company, March 17. Retrieved from www.pbs.org/newshour/rundown/2011/03/get-to-know-tepco-japans-biggest-power-company.html

Reynolds, B. and Seeger, M. W. (2005). Crisis and emergency risk communication as an integrative model. *Journal of Health Communication Research*, *10*, 43–57.

Ruff, P., and Aziz, K. (2003). *Managing communication in a crisis.* Aldershot, UK: Gower Publishing Company.

Saito, H. (2010). *A history of Japan.* New York: Routledge.

Seeger, M.W., Sellnow, T. L., and Ulmer, R.R. (2003). *Communication and organizational crisis.* Westport, CT: Praeger Press.

Smith, R., Casselman, B., and Obe M. (2011, March 22). Japan plant had troubled history. Retrieved from http://online.wsj.com/article/SB10001424052748704433 90457621298046388179 2.html

Sugimoto, N. (1998). Norms of apology depicted in U.S. American and Japanese literature on manners and etiquette. *International Journal of Intercultural Relations*, *22*, 251–276.

TEPCO (2011). Corporate ethics and compliance. Retrieved from www.tepco.co.jp/en/corpinfo/overview/restor-e.html

TEPCO (2011, March 12). Press release. Retrieved from www.tepco.co.jp/en/press/corp-com/release/11031104-e.html

TEPCO's poor publicity led to metropolitan mess. (2011, March 16). Retrieved from www.yomiuri.co.jp/dy/editorial/T110315004137.htm

The young volunteers. (2011). *The Japan Times Online*, March 27. Retrieved from http://search.japantimes.co.jp/cgi-bin/ed20110327a2.html

Toth, E. L. (2008). Crisis communication: The public first/organization last paradox. Paper presented to the International Forum on Public Relation and Advertising, Crisis Management and Integrated Strategic Communication Conference.

Traphagan, J. W., and Knight, J. (2003). *Demographic change and the family in Japan's aging society.* Albany, NY: State University of New York's Press.

Tsunami survivors face monstrous cleanup task. (2011). *The Japan Times Online*, March 26. Retrieved from http://search.japantimes.co.jp/cgi-bin/nn20110326a5.html

Ulmer, R. R., Sellnow, T. L., and Seeger, M.W. (2007/2011). *Effective crisis communication: Moving from crisis to opportunity.* Thousand Oaks, CA: Sage.

U.S. embassy cables: MP criticizes Japanese nuclear strategy. (2008). Wikileaks, October 27. Retrieved from http://www.guardian.co.uk/world/us-embassy-cables-documents/175295

Vogel, S.K. (2006). *Japan remodeled: How government and industry are reforming Japanese capitalism.* Ithaca, NY: Cornell University Press.

Voigt, K. (2011). Are the Japanese different? *CNN*, March 25. Retrieved from http://articles.cnn.com/2011–03–25/world/Japan.quake.culture_1_japanese-modern-history-japanese-people-japan-watchers?_s=PM:WORLD

Wagatsuma, H., and Rosett, A. (1986). The implications of apology: Law and culture in Japan and the United States. *Law and Society Review, 20,* 461–498.

Wakabayashi, D. (2011). After flood, deaths overpower ritual. Prospect of mass graves raises tensions in country where cremation is the rule. *The Wall Street Journal,* March 22, A10.

Weisul, K. (2011). So sorry! The art of the corporate (non)-apology, March 16. Retrieved from www.bnet.com/blog/business-research/so-sorry-the-art-of-the-corporate-non-apology/1079

The Yomiuri Shimbun (2011). Multiple crises call for clear command structure, March 21. Retrieved from www.asianewsnet.net/home/news.php?id=18015

VIEWS FROM AN EXPERT

SHARI R. VEIL

Shari R. Veil, MBA, Ph.D. is the director of risk sciences and assistant professor of communication at the University of Kentucky College of Communications and Information Studies. She coordinates research and funding opportunities and establishes education and training programs specific to risk and crisis communication. Previously, she was the director of the Center for Risk and Crisis Management and assistant professor of strategic communication at the University of Oklahoma. She is currently a co-principal investigator on two projects funded by the Department of Homeland Security's National Center for Food Protection and Defense to analyze traditional media and social media coverage of food safety crises. Her work has been published in several reputable communication and risk management journals. Her research interests include organizational learning in high-risk environments, community preparedness, and communication strategies for crisis management.

When a crisis occurs, the failures that led to the crisis are quickly defined and tallied in an attempt to find both cause and fault. A reoccurring failure referenced following the 9/11 terrorist attacks and Hurricane Katrina in the U.S. and the devastating series of events that occurred in Japan in March 2011 has been described as a "failure of imagination." Despite the countless reports and precipitating events that warned of the impending crises, the extent of damage caused overwhelmed even the most imaginative risk analysts. How do you prepare for damage you cannot even imagine is possible? In Japan in particular, the events clearly demonstrated how natural hazards could interact with technological advances to cause a catastrophic disaster. And even though Japan had prepared for the salient risks of earthquakes and tsunamis along the northeast coast, the additional threat of nuclear exposure from damaged power plants compounded response capabilities. Sociologist Charles Perrow's now classic 1984 book *Normal Accidents: Living with high-risk technologies* thoroughly explains how seemingly unrelated events can interact to create catastrophic outcomes. Thus, we know these low-probability, high-impact events can occur. However, our capacity for realizing the immensity of the potential interactional effects is limited.

The authors mention that at the time of press they still did not know the full scope of the 2011 Japan crisis' adverse affects. However, since mass graves and rubble entombed unknown victims and the long-term effects of radiation exposure are still being studied, the full extent can only be estimated. The case study presented here outlines the response strategies of three key stakeholder groups during the initial crisis into goals and objectives so we can understand how members of the international audience perceived the strategies enacted just one month after the events occurred. Perspectives will change with time. Key stakeholders will change, depending on the perspective. Considering the number of retracted statements in the last month, facts will even likely change. However, to have excluded an event that will greatly affect a prominent nation and the world economy during this period of history would have immediately made this book irrelevant. Truly, this case study provides one of the first historical accounts ever written on the 2011 Japan crisis and could be used as a starting point for the hundreds of studies that will follow, each dissecting and analyzing different aspects of the multiple hazards and disasters encompassed in the crisis.

The authors admirably chose to take a wide-angle view of the crisis. The information vacuum created so soon after a crisis does not limit the number of research questions that can be asked; however, limiting a case analysis so early in a crisis can hinder our consideration of contributing factors to the crisis and the future directions for risk and crisis research. Like risk analysts, researchers too can suffer from a "failure of imagination." The authors' first discussion question acknowledges the limitations of providing this analysis while the crisis is developing. However, the inclusion of this case as this book is going to press demonstrates the impact the 2011 Japan crisis has already had and will continue to have for years to come.

Japan (Toyota)

Delays, Denials, Recalls, and Apologies: Fixing the Dent in Toyota's Image

Amiso M. George

A fatal California crash in August 2009 involving a family of four riding in a Lexus ES350 forced the Toyota crisis onto media headlines. The California crash brought to light a rash of other Toyota car crashes whose reportage had been minimized. It also highlighted the role that Toyota corporate culture and Japanese culture played in how the crisis was managed. Most important, the case provides important lessons in corporate crisis communication.

Introduction

Since September 2009, global automaker Toyota has had two major crises: (a) the 2009 international recall of Toyota vehicles, mostly in the United States, and the dozens of lawsuits—seven of them by insurance companies—that accompanied the recalls; and (b) the effects of the earthquake, tsunami, and nuclear-reactor damage that occurred in Japan at midday on Friday, March 11, 2011, shaking the world's third-largest economy at its core, and forcing the company to temporarily shut down its plants in Japan; although operations in the United States were not affected. Thus, within months, the auto giant implemented communication plans in response to the fallout from crises that emanated from both natural and human-induced causes. This chapter focuses on the recall crisis.

Background of the Recall Crisis

In August 2009, an off-duty California Highway Patrol officer, Mark Saylor, was driving with three of his family members in a 2009 Lexus ES350. The car unexpectedly accelerated, reportedly at more than 100 miles per hour, hit another car, tumbled down the side of the highway and burst into flames. One of the occupants of the car, Saylor's brother in-law, managed to call

911 to report the unusual acceleration before the crash that killed all four occupants.

According to a report in *The San Diego Union-Tribune*, a previous renter of the same Lexus had complained to the dealer about the sudden acceleration caused by interference of the gas pedal with the driver's side floor mat, but no action was apparently taken by the dealership or Toyota. In the meantime, the crash continued to raise questions (Baker and Gustafson, 2009).

Shortly after reports of the crash, Toyota launched an investigation to ascertain the cause. Preliminary results from Toyota revealed that the brakes did not cause the crash; rather, the Lexus that the late Saylor was driving had a faulty, or wrongly installed, floor mat that obstructed the gas pedal. Toyota's press statement did not address the Saylor case in particular, but responded to the controversy surrounding its safety recall ("Our point of view," 2009).

In September 2009, Toyota announced an initial recall of 3.8 million Toyota automobiles, including the Lexus model, to deal with the floor mat problem. The company directed Toyota and Lexus dealers to install adaptable floor mats in a way that did not interfere with the functions of the brake (Welch, 2009). According to news reports, months later, the number of recalled vehicles was increased to 4.2 million, the largest recall in U.S. history (Taylor, 2010).

At the same time, Toyota denied that the problem was related to electronics. In a news release announcing the recall, Bob Daly, Toyota Motor Sales (USA) senior vice president, noted that the U.S. National Highway Traffic Safety Administration's (NHTSA) investigation into the unintended acceleration involving Toyota and Lexus vehicles revealed nothing more than "an unsecured or incompatible driver's floor mat" ("Toyota begins interim notification," 2009).

A few months after the initial recall, in December 2009, the day after Christmas, four friends driving in a Toyota Avalon sedan died after their car spun out of control and flipped into a six-foot-deep pond in Southlake, Texas. Eyewitnesses said that the driver drove through an intersection, crashed through a fence and landed in a pond (Diaz and Traham, 2009). Although local police and paramedics were able to get the passengers out of the pond, all later died at a local hospital. Police reports say the car was traveling at only 45 miles an hour before the crash. The same reports indicate that the floor mats were put in the car's trunk, just as Toyota had advised owners to do (Diaz and Trahan, 2009).

Unfortunately, it was not just the floor mats that were a problem for Toyota; the September recall opened a Pandora's box dating back to 2000. Investigative news reports indicated that Toyota had previous problems with unintended acceleration of its vehicles, but did not make the information public. There were also problems with gas pedals that did not return to the neutral position after being pressed down (see *Timeline*, Bloxham, 2011).

Most important, the problems that led *Consumer Reports* to delist Toyota Camry as one of its top choice cars in 2007 began in 2000 when, according to reports, Toyota began a program called "Construction of Cost Competitiveness for the 21st Century." The goal of the program was to trim costs by about 30 percent across the board for purchases of all of its car parts.

> The bold plan to squeeze its own network of traditional suppliers, known as a keiretsu, was designed to make sure the Toyota group would retain its competitive edge against a spate of global auto alliances such as DaimlerChrysler (DCX), which promised gigantic synergies from their bigger size.
>
> (Dawson and Anhalt, 2005)

This quest for a competitive edge, increased market share, rapid growth and profits, contributed to a slack in quality of Toyota products. As a March 11, 2010, article in *Business Week* aptly put it:

> As grave as the current troubles are, they are symptomatic of a larger problem at Toyota: It got carried away chasing high-speed growth, market share, and productivity gains year in and year out. All that slowly dulled the commitment to quality embedded in Toyota's corporate culture.
>
> (Ohnsman et al., 2010)

Toyota went from delay to respond, to denial of the depth of the problems raised by customers and other critics, to subsequent apologies by Toyota CEO, Akio Toyoda, first at a press conference in Japan and subsequently in the United States. In a testimony before Congress, Toyoda took "full responsibility" for the safety defects in Toyota cars that led to fatalities. "I myself, as well as Toyota, am not perfect . . . I, more than anyone, wish for our customers' cars to be safe," he said. While the apology served to temper some of the criticism of the company, it was not a panacea to Toyota's credibility problem (Altman, 2010).

A Litany of Complaints

The September 2009 recall was not the first for Toyota. Complaints from individuals and insurance companies to NHTSA dating as far back as 2004, had focused on such issues as electronic throttle malfunction and unexpected acceleration. Investigations by NHTSA in response to the complaints turned up no clear evidence of those complaints, even though Toyota's former CEO, Katsuaki Watanabe, expressed regret for "quality glitches" in the company's automobiles (Cato, 2010). Toyota delayed the rolling out of some new models by six months (Kim and Bailey, 2010). Subsequently, unpublicized recalls had taken place in 2007 following a March 2007 investigation by NHTSA of a fatality from a suspected "pedal entrapment" in a Camry (Kim and Bailey, 2010). Toyota was forced to recall 55,000 all-weather floor mats for the 2007 and 2008 model Camry and Lexus ES350.

The auto company's woes were not limited to the United States. In January 2009, Toyota was compelled to recall about 1.3 million vehicles worldwide because of problems associated with seat belts and exhaust. About a year later, in February 2010, another round of recalls was announced. This time 437,000 cars were affected. This included the popular Prius, a car embraced by energy efficiency advocates worldwide. Toyota attributed the recall to "brake problems" ("Toyota Prius recall extended worldwide," 2010).

Within a few months, in July 2010, Toyota again had to recall 270,000 cars, including its luxury brands, owing to engine defects that could stop the car while in motion. The Associated Press reports indicated that more than 90,000 Lexus and Toyota Crown cars were recalled in Japan alone, 138,000 in the United States, and the rest in Europe, the Middle East, China, Canada, and other countries (Kageyama, 2010).

In total, Toyota had recalled 5.3 million cars by January 2010 and paid $32.4 million in civil penalties to NHTSA and families of individuals who sued the company (Drives, 2011).

Table 2.1 Key dates in Toyota crisis and recalls

2007 Recalls	
January 2007	Complaints from five owners of Lexus ES350 about unintended acceleration prompt Toyota to begin an investigation to ascertain connection between floor mats and accelerator pedals.
March 29, 2007	NHTSA launches an investigation based on the complaints of the five Lexus owners.
July 26, 2007	A fatal crash of a 2007 Toyota Camry in California prompts an investigation.
September 13, 2007	An NHTSA investigation concludes that the crash resulted from the "entrapment of an accelerator pedal by an all-weather floor mat." NHTSA informs Toyota to order a recall.
September 26, 2007	Toyota announces a recall of 55,000 floor mats designed as an "optional equipment on its Toyota Camry and Lexus ES models."
2009 Recalls	
January 2009	Toyota announces a recall of 1.3 million vehicles worldwide because of "problems associated with seat belt and exhaust."
August 2009	Toyota recalls about 690,000 automobiles made in China, the largest recall in China. The reason was "faulty window switches."
April 27, 2009	Toyota engineers in Europe report sticky pedal problems to Toyota engineers in the United States.

August 2009	California Highway patrolman Mark Saylor and his family perish in an accident while Saylor was driving a 2009 Lexus ES350. Accident is attributed to sticky gas pedal and faulty floor mat.
September 29, 2009	Toyota announces the recall of 3.8 million cars, the biggest in the automaker's history. The company issues a "customer safety advisory" in which it acknowledges that floor mats can be entangled with the gas pedal. The company advises owners to remove their floor mats and put them in the trunk. It also urges dealers to use zip ties to secure the floor mats in their vehicles to avoid interference with the gas pedal.
November 2, 2009	Toyota announces that it would voluntarily recall floor mats, and claims that the NHTSA's findings found no mechanical problems with Toyota. NHTSA refutes Toyota's statement.
November 25, 2009	Toyota announces that it would shorten by three quarters of an inch all gas pedals on affected cars to avoid the sticky acceleration problems.
December 26, 2009	An accident in Southlake, Texas, involving a Toyota Avalon, kills all four occupants of the car.

2010 Recalls

January 2010	Toyota recalls an additional 2.3 million vehicles in the U.S. to repair faulty accelerator pedals.
January 26, 2010	Toyota postpones sales and production of eight models in the United States and North America.
January 28, 2010	Toyota announces recalls in Europe and China. Congress begins inquiry into accelerator problems.
January 29, 2010	Toyota admits European recalls could reach 1.8 million cars and eight models, including Yaris and Auris.
February 3, 2010	Toyota owners in the United Kingdom and the United States are warned to stop driving their Toyota cars pending investigation.
February 9, 2010	Toyota confirms it will recall 8,500 third-generation Prius cars in the United Kingdom.
February 24, 2010	Toyota CEO, Akio Toyoda, testifies in Congress, apologizes for the accelerator problem and promises to do all he can to regain public trust in Toyota.

2011 Recalls and Redemption

January 26, 2011	Toyota announces recall of 19,000 Avensis and Lexus IS 250 models because of the risk of fuel leaks.
February 8, 2011	NHTSA report finds "no electronic flaws to explain sudden, unintentional acceleration." The report is the result of a 10-month investigation of Toyota cars.

Source: Bloxham (2011); Owles and McDermon (2010).

How did Toyota go from being the most profitable and highly rated automobile company in the world to one whose reputation was now in doubt as a result of the recalls and other mistakes along the way?

To understand the crisis, it is important to review the Toyota story in Japan.

Brief History of Toyota

According to the Toyota Global Website, the company's history began in 1924 when Sakichi Toyoda invented the Toyoda Model G Automatic Loom used in the silk and cotton industry in Japan. The sale of the automatic loom to a British company in 1929 provided the initial funding to start the company. Looking for a way to expand as orders for automatic looms slowed because of the Great Depression, Toyoda allowed his son, Kiichiro Toyoda, in 1937, to spin off an automobile department within the Toyoda Automatic Loom Works. This company eventually became a fully functioning automobile company named Toyota Motor Corporation, a subsidiary of Toyota Industries, but not before it produced its first passenger car, the Toyota AA (History of Toyota, n.d.).

According to Toyota historians, the name change came about as a result of a logo design competition, among other reasons. The chosen design replaced the "d" in Toyoda with a "t," conforming to the style of the Japanese katakana alphabet. The word "Toyota" is written in only eight brushstrokes, while Toyoda is written in ten; eight is considered a lucky number. Additionally, the company wanted to dissociate itself from the name Toyoda, which means "fertile rice paddies," a farming reference. Furthermore, other historians have noted that the name change was also designed to separate the car company from the loom outfit in order to completely break from the past. The new name "Toyota" was trademarked and formally became known as Toyota Motor Company in 1937. The company, whose headquarters are in Toyota City, Japan, and known for its innovative design and technical

Table 2.2 Key dates in Toyota Motors history

1924	Sakichi Toyoda invents Toyoda Model G Automatic Loom.
1937	Toyota Motor Co., Ltd. is established.
1950	Company faces a financial crisis; Toyota Motor Sales Co., Ltd. is established.
1955	The Toyopet Crown, Toyopet Master, and Crown Deluxe are launched.
1957	The first prototypes of the Crown are exported to the United States; Toyota Motor Sales U.S.A., Inc. is established.
1982	Toyota Motor Co., Ltd. and Toyota Motor Sales Co., Ltd. are merged into Toyota Motor Corporation.
1984	Joint venture with General Motors (New United Motor Manufacturing, Inc.) begins production in the USA.
1988	Toyota Motor Manufacturing, USA, Inc. (present TMMK) begins production.
1989	The Lexus brand is launched in the USA.
2005	The Lexus brand is introduced in Japan.
2008	Worldwide Prius sales top 1-million mark.
2010	Worldwide Prius sales top 2-million mark.

Source: www.toyota-global.com/company/history_of_toyota

excellence, went on to export its first passenger car, the Toyopet Crown, to the United States in 1957 and established Toyota Sales USA, Inc. In 1972, Toyota opened its first manufacturing plant in the United States. In 1986, it began producing vehicles and introduced its luxury brand, Lexus, three years later. It sold its first hybrid car in 2000 and in 2007 rolled out its built-in-America Tundra, thereby completing an impressive first 50-year run in the United States (History of Toyota, n.d.).

Today, Toyota Motors Corporation is a part of the Toyota Group, which, according to the 2010 ranking of the world's largest corporations, is the world's fifth-largest company (Fortune Global 500, 2010). Toyota Motors also holds the distinction of being the largest manufacturer of automobiles by sales and production. In 2010, Toyota sold about 8.42 million cars (Kageyama, 2011).

The Nexus Between Toyota Corporate Culture and the Japanese Culture

Toyota's Corporate Culture

Toyota has been criticized for its handling of the crisis; however, to understand how the intersection of Toyota's corporate culture and Japanese culture influenced the company 's response to the crisis, it is imperative to first define culture.

While many definitions of culture abound, it can generally be defined as the accepted behaviors, beliefs, values, symbols, and institutions of a group of people that are transmitted through communication and imitation from one generation to the next. Anthropologist Edward T. Hall defines culture as the deep, common, unstated experiences that members of a given culture share, communicate without knowing, and which form the backdrop against which all other events are judged (Hall, 1966). "Culture is the collective programming of the mind which distinguishes the members of one group or category of people from another" (Hofstede, 1984, p. 51). For Gudykunst and Kim (1992), culture is the systems of knowledge shared by a relatively large group of people. In their own case, Rogers and Steinfatt (1999) see culture as the total way of life of a people, composed of their learned and shared behavior patterns, values, norms, and material objects.

Edward Hall helps us to see the nexus between culture and communication through his theory of high- and low-context culture (Hall, 1976). Low-context cultures have explicit rules and messages that are clearly communicated in writing; hence knowledge is transferable. Members are individualistic, prefer facts, logic, directness, are task-oriented and have less sense of loyalty to others. Low-context cultures are found in Western Europe and North America.

On the other end of the spectrum are the high-context cultures that have many contextual elements that enable members to understand the unwritten or implied rules and messages; maintenance of social order, hierarchy, importance of the group and the environment and social context within which communication occurs, hence words are often not very important. As a result, knowledge is also situational. Such societies are more traditional, collectivist, or interdependent. High-context cultures can be found in Africa, Middle East, parts of South America, and Asia.

Toyota, Japan, and High-Context Culture

Toyota's corporate culture is a microcosm of Japanese culture and as a top-notch Japanese and international company, Toyota's way of conducting business is reflective of the high-context culture described earlier. At the same time, it embodies some elements of low-context culture.

One of the elements of a high-context culture in the Toyota crisis is *deference and loyalty to hierarchy* and team. Employees defer to their bosses or superiors and maintain team or group harmony at all times. That means that the boss is never criticized even when the individual makes the wrong decisions for the company or project. Loyalty to the group or team and to the boss is more important. This failure to criticize reaches deep into the culture of *"saving face."* In essence, the boss may not be corrected or criticized so as to "save the face" of the boss and maintain group cohesion. Face can be lost, earned, or saved (Kingston, 2010).

Homogeneity in decision making is another negative corporate culture that impacted crisis communication at Toyota. When groupthink overrides individual decision making, plausible strategies and tactics, while contrary to the accepted group decision to problem solving, are suppressed.

Nonverbal communication is a key element of high-context cultures. Since there are unwritten or implied rules, members of the group are wont not to break them; hence, gestures, actions, and body language often communicate volumes.

Toyota, Japan, and Low-Context Culture

While Toyota and Japan are clearly recognized as fitting in the high-context culture category, Toyota also maintains qualities of low-context cultures. Among these qualities is the documentation and accessibility of knowledge, transfer of knowledge and rules. The Toyota Production System (TPS) aptly illustrates this point.

The TPS is the guidelines and business process that enable Toyota to "provide the customer with the highest quality vehicles, at lowest possible cost, in a timely manner with the shortest possible lead times" (Toyota Production System, n.d., sec. 1).

According to the Toyota website, TPS was established based on two concepts: The first is called *jidoka* (which can be loosely translated as "automation with a human touch") which means that when a problem occurs, the equipment stops immediately, preventing defective products from being produced; the second is the concept of "Just-in-Time" (or lean manufacturing), in which each process produces only what is needed by the next process in a continuous flow (Toyota Production System, n.d., sec. 3).

Sakichi Toyoda, Toyoda industries founder, is credited with the introduction of the jidoka concept in his automatic loom business. He designed the loom machine to stop functioning whenever a thread was cut. The same concept was adapted successfully in Toyota production whereby such quality assurance allowed employees to focus on other issues in the production process. His son, Kiichiro Toyoda, introduced the Just-in-Time (JIT) concept or lean manufacturing. This concept was designed to eliminate unnecessary supplies. The TPA system ensures that the Toyota Production System was efficient and effective, a concept that many organizations around the world had adopted (Toyota Production System, n.d., para. 1).

How then does the culture, which reflects characteristics of high-context culture and some elements of low-context culture, affect Toyota's response to the U.S. crisis? How does culture underpin the making of a crisis in the U.S. market?

Situation Analysis

Toyota Stakeholders

The stakeholders affected by the Toyota crisis are varied and many. However, the ones most directly affected include Toyota owners or customers worldwide, Toyota employees, dealers, the Japanese government, government regulatory agencies (especially in the United States), the U.S. government, financial media, and automobile analysts.

- *Toyota owners and customers*: Toyota owners cover all demographics and psychographics. Many news reports show that Toyota owners buy the vehicle because they trust the reliability and utility of the brand. The media coverage of the multiple recalls has tarnished the image of the brand.
- *Toyota employees:* Employees can sabotage a company if they are ignored or feel insecure about their job. They must be kept abreast of developments about the crisis via internal communication
- *Toyota dealers:* As the first line of attack, they must be kept updated about changes, recalls, and any information that a customer would like to know about the vehicles.
- *Toyota shareholders:* They are concerned about the effect of the crisis on their shares. Toyota must assure them that the company will weather the storm intact.

- *Automobile industry analysts/Automobile media/Influential auto industry and technology bloggers*: These professionals can investigate and write damaging or enhancing stories about the design and technology that drives Toyota Motors.
- *Financial analysts/Financial media*: They can investigate and write damaging or complimentary reports of the ups and downs of Toyota stocks or shares in the financial market.
- *Mainstream media*: They, as well as the specialized media, can create damaging or enhancing headlines about the crisis.
- *Japanese government*: Toyota has a symbiotic relationship with the Japanese government. It is Japan's largest company and receives many incentives from the government; so what affects Toyota affects the Japanese government.
- *Government (U.S.) Regulatory Agencies* (such as NHTSA): They have an interest in the crisis and thus can investigate, regulate and or force recalls of automobiles.

Theory of Image Restoration

Image is a concept based on perception. It is how a person, group, or organization is perceived by others based on the actions and rhetoric of the person, group, or organization. Image is also "the corporation as seen through the eyes of its constituencies" (Argenti, 2003, p. 44).

   Image restoration theory, rooted in rhetoric and social science, and widely used in public relations, especially crisis communication, presumes that upholding a good reputation is a key goal of communication. Thus, when an organization's reputation is maligned every effort is made to restore the image (Benoit, 1997). Benoit and Pang (2008) describe these persuasive efforts or strategies as *denial, evading responsibility, reduce offensiveness, corrective action, and mortification*. Benoit and Pang state that the first strategy of response to a tarnished image would be a denial. This response employs such tactics as a simple denial of whatever the accused was accused of, or, shifting blame to someone else. Another strategy is evasion of responsibility, whereby the accused can claim that their actions were provoked; they could also claim defeasibility because of lack of information or ability. Other tactics include claiming the action was an accident or that they had good intentions. The aggrieved could also use reduction of offensiveness as a strategy, whereby such tactics as bolstering (stressing good traits of the aggrieved), minimization (minimizing the enormity of the act), differentiating (presenting the act as less serious than previous or similar ones), transcending (that there are more important considerations), attack (whereby the accused party attacks the attacker of an offense. The aim is to reduce the credibility of the accuser) and compensate (to reimburse the victims). Another strategy of the accused is corrective action. The action is taken to solve or prevent the reoccurrence of the alleged offense. Finally, there is mortification: a defensive strategy in which the accused admits responsibility for the offense, apologizes and accepts demand for restitution and punishment.

Benoit and Drew (1997) conclude that of all the image repair strategies, mortification (apologies, concessions) and corrective action were found to be more effective and appropriate. However, it is important to note that while mortification and corrective action may be the most effective strategies, cultural differences must be considered in analyzing communication response to a tarnished image.

The Toyota recall crisis and the negative press that accompanied it have lasted since 2009. Toyota has used some of the image restoration tactics in its attempt to restore its tarnished reputation. All international media, including virtual media sites and crisis communication experts have comprehensively covered Toyota's response to the recall crisis.

Toyota's Initial Response

Toyota, known worldwide for reliability, quality, and innovation, dropped the ball in its initial handling of the recall crisis. While the company did not follow the classic apologia route, it exhibited elements of the strategies described earlier.

Toyota's obvious non-reaction was ignoring initial reports that described the problems associated with some of its brands. For instance in the Santee, California, crash in which four family members were killed, Toyota argued that the crash could not be blamed on the automaker's sticky floor mats. After a very costly delay of two weeks in which Toyota's inaction was roundly pilloried in international media, Toyota CEO Akio Toyoda, in a press conference in Japan and subsequently in a testimony in Congress, offered an apology where he acknowledged that "four precious lives had been lost." He expressed remorse for giving Toyota customers "cause for grave concern" and, according to a translated text, said that "truly we think of our customers as a priority and we guarantee their safety."

Referring to the near collapse of the company's once strong reputation for safety and quality, Toyoda said, "I would like for the people to trust us." The company reinforced Toyoda's apology with the release of a Progress Report, where it noted that it is "listening more closely to our customers, responding more quickly to their concerns and those of our regulators, and taking concrete actions to ensure we are among the industry's leaders in safety" (Toyota Progress Report, May 2010, para. 1)

It is important to note that the inability of Toyota's management to recognize the depth of the crisis, an absence of crisis communication plan or policy, and the juxtaposition of Toyota's corporate culture and Japanese culture may have contributed to the initial lack of aggressive response from Toyota. Jeff Kingston's excellent *Wall Street Journal* article "A crisis made in

Japan," also notes that "Toyota's botched response to its escalating problems has deep roots in Japan's legal system and corporate tradition" (Kingston, 2010). The tradition, according to Kingston and others, is one in which the legal system makes little distinction between Japanese corporate needs and those of the country.

The initial silence (no response from Toyota for over a week) illustrates Kingston's description of the Japanese proverb: "if it stinks, put a lid on it." In essence, Toyota's approach to crisis was to wish it away instead of open communication. Toyota also used denial (where Toyota stated in a press release that its findings did not support the assertion about the sticky floor mats and unintended acceleration, and local Toyota dealers, affirming the assertion, did not make any repairs to the cars). Toyota's assertion was condemned by NHTSA as "inaccurate and misleading" (Linebaugh et al., 2010).

Toyota blamed the customers when it claimed that drivers must have mistakenly hit the gas pedal instead of the brake. The company blamed the improperly installed floor mats as well. Toyota also used reduction of offensiveness, whereby the company tried to minimize the impact of the recalls by asserting that no serious accidents could be attributed to the sticking gas pedals or floor mats (Ramsey and Mitchell, 2010). None of these image repair strategies and tactics did much to endear Toyota to angry customers.

Toyota recognized these gaffes when Jim Wiseman, a communication official at Toyota Motors North America, admitted in a *New York Times* article: "We acknowledge that we could have communicated better as a company . . . However, we have taken significant steps to address these issues" (Kanter et al., 2010).

Toyota also tried to compensate for its late start in crisis communication by releasing a series of media statements reinforcing its plans to minimize the impact of the recalls and assuage angry customers (Figure 2.20).

In the face of the mounting criticism from Toyota customers worldwide and U.S. federal agency NHTSA, Toyota embarked on a campaign to repair its tarnished image. The auto giant used all forms of media, including social media, to communicate its actions and regain the trust of its audience. The company used corrective action (fixing the sticky gas pedals and floor mat problems, compensation (a settlement agreement of $32.4 million with NHTSA that addressed among others, the sticky pedal and improperly installed floor mats issues and their victims, but without admitting guilt) and mortification (apologies of Akio Toyoda) ("Toyota issues statement regarding NHTSA settlement," 2010, www.toyota.com/newsroom).

Communication Goals, Objectives, Strategies, and Tactics

At a meeting at company headquarters in Toyota City, Japan, CEO Akio Toyoda, was quoted by *Japan Times* as saying:

Figure 2.20 Toyota Progress Report (May 20, 2010).
Reprinted by permission.

We need to assert a renewed commitment to "customer first" in reviewing all our work processes from a customer perspective . . . In addressing recent quality problems, I really came to understand that products are our lifeline. If we can regain customer trust in our quality, we can increase production volumes and regain profits . . . Then, everything can work positively.

(Nakata, 2010)

Toyota's crisis communication plan is derived from Akio Toyoda's editorial in major U.S. newspapers, his address to Toyota executives at the company's headquarters in Japan, press statements, Toyota commercials from the company's website (www.toyota.com), and media publications both in Japan and the United States.

Goal 1: To restore public trust in Toyota.

Objective: To make special efforts to repair recalled vehicles within a few months.

Strategy: Used multiple media and third party endorsers to communicate Toyota's plan to restore public trust in its products.

Tactics:

- took out print advertisement in 20 U.S. newspapers justifying its decision to temporarily stop production of cars with possible acceleration problem. The ad read: "A temporary pause . . . to put you first." Then it went on further to explain why it took that action;
- repaired nearly 3.5 million recalled vehicles by May 2010;
- ran TV commercials during the 2010 Winter Olympics and at other times. Among these was the Toyota Commitment Commercial. It stated: "In recent days, our company hasn't been living up to the standards that you've come to expect from us or that we expect from ourselves . . . We stopped production so we could focus on our customers first." The announcer further stressed how Toyota would "restore your faith in our company";
- used social media: Facebook, Twitter, and YouTube to communicate commitment to customers and vows to restore public trust;
- used third party endorser: Commercial where a female Toyota owner described and demonstrated the "Stopping procedure for sticking accelerator pedal";
- developed a very active Facebook page with 622,590 "friends" as of December 2011; and
- created "autobiographies" on Facebook, where Toyota owners write their own unique stories—from the sublime to the outlandish.

Goal 2: To improve customer satisfaction.

Objective 1: To use teams of experts throughout the U.S. to aggressively increase the speed of response to customer complaints, sometimes within 24 hours.

Objective 2: To increase the number of overseas executives from 13 to 15 for a rapid response to complaints based on regional needs.

Strategy (a): Gave North American leaders a greater voice in safety decision making, including a direct path to Toyota's global president.

Strategy (b): Gave more autonomy to regional managers to respond to customer concerns.

Strategy (c): Trained global staff in quality issues.

Strategy (d): Used media to communicate Toyota's contrition, safety, service and appreciation.

Tactics:

- completed 2,000+ vehicle inspections for unintended acceleration complaints with none linked to the company's electronic throttle control system (as of May 2010);
- responded within hours after a magazine voiced concern about the Lexus GX in April 2010 and announced the Lexus LS steering recall after just 12 complaints;
- responded promptly to customer complaints about Prius and Lexus HS250h anti-lock brake systems;
- set up "CF" (customer first) training centers by July 2010 in Japan, North America, Europe, Southeast Asia, and China to cultivate quality professionals in each region;
- used television commercials, print ads, Facebook, YouTube, and Twitter to communicate the importance of customer safety and service. One TV ad read: "At Toyota, your safety will be a top priority in any and all of our decisions . . .";
- made a two-minute ad featuring Jim Lentz, President and CEO of Toyota Motor Sales USA, in which he "sincerely apologize[d] for the recall. I know that we let you down . . ."; "I apologize for the situation. I hope you will give us a chance to earn back your trust . . . Thank you for your patience and understanding"; and
- made another ad that thanked customers for their support: "Your Toyota dealers appreciate the support a lot of folks have given them recently . . . and these deals . . . among them, zero percent financing for 60 months on Camry and Corolla models . . . are their way of saying thanks."

Goal 3: To highlight quality controls.

Objective 1: To increase the number of technology offices in North America to seven from one, and set up seven new offices in Europe, six in China and more in other regions.

Objective 2: To equip all new cars and trucks with more advanced safety technologies, including brake override across entire product range by the end of 2010 and improve event data recorders.

Objective 3: To open Toyota technology to unprecedented levels of independent review, including a study by NASA.

Strategy: Enlisted four third-party experts to review improvement measures adopted by the "special committee for global quality" and release publicly results of the review and Toyota's response to the findings.

Tactics:

• suspended production of eight models in five plants in North America pending repairs of gas pedal problem;
• used social media (Facebook, YouTube, and Twitter) to communicate its efforts at quality control;
• recruited third-party experts from each region, including a North American team chaired by Rodney Slater, former U.S. Transportation Secretary to assess quality-improvement measures on a regional basis; and
• named six chief quality officers (CQO) to oversee "recall and other safety decision making on a global basis."

Goal 4: To increase outreach to government agencies.

Objective: To open lines of communication with government safety and regulatory agencies such as NHTSA.

Strategy: Communicated proactively and frequently to ensure vigilance in responding to safety or other regulatory issues.

Tactics: Toyota has proactively issued recalls and alerts voluntarily.

Outcome Assessment

A Matter of Culture Clash

The combination of Japanese and Toyota corporate culture affected the outcome of this crisis. It is obvious from the analysis that Toyota did not act on time to stem the fallout from the crisis. Toyota's initial response of denial, blaming the accusers, minimizing the enormity of the crisis and subsequent apology, stems from a corporate culture where the top hierarchy is shielded from criticism, communication is linear—from top to bottom, employees have group-think mentality, and thus would not point out errors, according to many experts, including Professor Jeff Kingston, head of Asian Studies at Temple University Japan. Additionally, open communication and crisis communication are not well developed in Japan (Kingston, 2010). If Toyota had a crisis plan, no one seemed to have activated it.

The insularity of Toyota's top echelon may have contributed as well. Toyota's board of directors lacked diversity of opinion. Toyota's first and only non-Japanese board member, Jim Press, president of its North American operations, was appointed in April 2007, but he resigned five months later to join Chrysler. At that time, Press joined a board that consisted of 29 Toyota executives who were all Japanese and all male.

The esteemed position of Toyota in the hierarchy of Japanese culture, the fact that Japan is not a litigious society, the difficulty for outside criticism of the company to gain traction in the media, and the Japanese media's deference for that same reason, all add to the perfect storm that resulted in Toyota's public relations nightmare.

On the other hand, in the United States, Toyota's delay and initial denial, minimizing the crisis and shifting of responsibility were construed as guilt, as evidenced in the rash of media reports. Most criticized Toyota as "arrogant," "out of touch with the needs of its customers," and hit at Toyota's core by questioning its vehicle technology. When Akio Toyoda finally apologized, first at a press conference in Japan shortly after taking the helm, and later during his testimony in Congress, pundits and industry experts called Akio Toyoda's apology too little, too late. They noted that Toyota was forced to apologize since the United States is a crucial trade partner. The Japanese media criticized the apologetic bow itself, a 60-degree bow, which was not considered as contrite as a 90-degree bow, given the gravity of the crisis.

In describing the importance attached to the bow in Japanese culture, Brian Palmer of Slate.com categorized the Japanese bow as:

> *eshaku*, a simple 15-degree bend or nod of the head; *keirei*, a 30-degree tilt to show respect; *saikeirei*, a full 45- to 90-degree bow intended to show the deepest veneration or humility; and *dogeza* a fetal prostration expressing utter subjection or contrition.

Palmer described Toyoda's bow as an unsatisfactory *keirei*, whereas critics believed he should have performed a *saikeirei* (Palmer, 2010).

In spite of these criticisms, Liker and Ogden (2011, p. 200) forcefully argue that

> It's not about PR strategies or charismatic leadership, or vision, or any specific action by any individual. It's not about policies or procedures or risk mitigation processes. It's about the actions that have been programmed into the individuals and teams that make up a company before the crisis starts.

Secret or Open and Better Communication?

While Toyota is a global entity, it is very much a Japanese organization where decision making on all major aspects of the company is centralized in Japan, communication is limited or guarded, and top officials at the home office rarely give interviews in crisis situations. Hence, when U.S. executives and communication staff pressed Toyota to respond quickly to reports of the sticky pedals and unintended acceleration, given the negative media, top officials in Japan who called the shots, chose instead to focus on dealing with the problem. The Japanese officials did not consider the intensity of the storm that was about to drench Toyota. Liker and Ogden (2011) aptly describe this "gap in perception between Toyota Japan and the United States" (p. 105) as one in which Toyota saw its action of recalling the problematic cars as evidence of "putting customers first." The description of this gap not only reveals a breakdown in communication between Toyota's headquarters and its U.S. office, but also reveals how Toyota's crisis management approach differs sharply from what normally obtains in the United States—one in which open and early communication of the problem and proffered solutions are offered.

A New Way of Thinking: What Toyota Has Done

Toyota is not just a Japanese company, it is an international organization that purports to respect and adapt its vision to fit the region of operation. To that end, Toyota has taken a few commendable steps listed in the company's crisis plan. In addition, the company has made efforts to "streamline and diversify management." Toyota began this process by removing the bureaucracy of decision making and making top executives accessible to employees.

The company also decentralized certain management decisions, giving regional managers autonomy to make the right decisions for the region. Pending board approval, Toyota noted it would slash board members from 27 down to 11, a dramatic downsizing that CEO Akio Toyoda believes will make for a more nimble board.

In another move, Toyoda appointed Canadian executive, Ray Tanguay, to the newly created position of senior managing officer, making Tanguay the only non-Japanese on the board. This, in Toyoda's view, marks a shift from the "old" way of thinking at Toyota (Greimel, 2011).

A Better Crisis Management Approach

In direct reaction to the crisis, Toyota should have adhered to effective crisis management and communication strategies:

- Take proactive action.
- Practice your vision.
- Diversify crisis team and ensure that management buys into the crisis plan.

- Establish a fully functioning virtual Emergency Operations Center (EOC), in addition to a bricks and mortar EOC, where business can be done effectively with hand-held devices.
- Develop an adaptable crisis plan that is simulated a few times a year by a crisis team, and part of that simulation must be media training of spokespersons for the company.
- Develop a good relationship with the media before a crisis.
- Develop a functioning "dark site" on the company website where information can quickly be uploaded/downloaded in times of crises cannot be overstated. But when that is not possible, prepare to react quickly by doing the following:

  - Have crisis teams and use them!
  - Have a nimble crisis plan and use it!
  - Tell the truth, and tell it quickly. If not, the media will get hold of the information and define you as they did with Toyota.
  - Avoid denial, shifting blame, or minimizing the crises. Show and express concern and apologize if necessary. Stakeholders are more likely to be sympathetic.
  - Correct or rectify faults as soon as possible and communicate that action to your stakeholders.
  - Take a global and cultural view of your crisis communication. What works in Japan may not work in North America or Europe.
  - Take full advantage of social media and tell your story on multiple media platforms. Toyota failed to do so quickly, giving anti-Toyota groups the opportunity to set up blogs, vblogs, websites, Facebook, and Twitter solely to criticize the company.
  - Continuously update information on these media platforms and link all of them with the right key words or phrases.
  - Use third party endorsers (brand ambassadors) early in the game to help tell your stories in all media. When Toyota finally discovered social media, it did not take full advantage of them right away by using Toyota brand ambassadors to tell their Toyota story.
  - Use a spokesperson who can show empathy. Body language as well as what is said are equally important. Bring in the CEO in a very serious crisis, but train him or her to effectively present the company's case.
  - Avoid saying "no comment" because a non-response may imply guilt.
  - After the crisis, continue communication of actions taken with your stakeholders through the same multiple media platform used during the crisis.
  - Use the opportunity to heal and repair the pain and inconvenience caused to your stakeholders during the crisis.

Having said all these, once Toyota realized that this was not a crisis that it could ignore, the company acted by taking the right short-term and long-term steps—not just to repair its tarnished image, win back its customers, and in the process gain news ones, but to become a new and improved Toyota. Akio Toyoda's apology, while it did not include a "deep bow," was acceptable. He sounded contrite and humble.

While this image repair would not be a sprint, Toyota is already on its way to refocusing on the quality, reliability, and style and regaining the confidence that millions of Toyota users had in it.

Post-script—Good News for Toyota

In February 2011, the government announced the result of the joint National Highway Traffic Safety Administration and the National Aeronautics and Space Administration study of allegations of electronic throttle control system defects in Toyota cars. The 18-month investigation, also known as the NHTSA/NASA Report, exonerated Toyota of the electronic defects. According to the report, "NASA did not find an electronic cause of large throttle openings that can result in UA incidents. NHTSA did not find a vehicle-based cause of those incidents in addition to those causes already addressed by Toyota recalls" (NHTSA-NASA Study, 2010). A preliminary report in 2009 reached the same conclusion.

In March 2011, Toyota received additional good news when J.D. Power and Associates announced the results from its 2011 Vehicle Dependability Study (VDS), covering 2008 model year vehicles that Lexus and Toyota owners rated both as best for quality and dependability (Toyota.com/newsroom).

In early April 2011, the company won a crucial case on the unintended acceleration case claims in U.S. District Court in New York (Figure 2.21). The case, according to Toyota and outside experts, demolished the oft-argued theories that led to multiple lawsuits on acceleration claims against the company. Previous lawsuits against Toyota in November 2010 were also dismissed because plaintiffs failed to identify electronic defects acceleration.

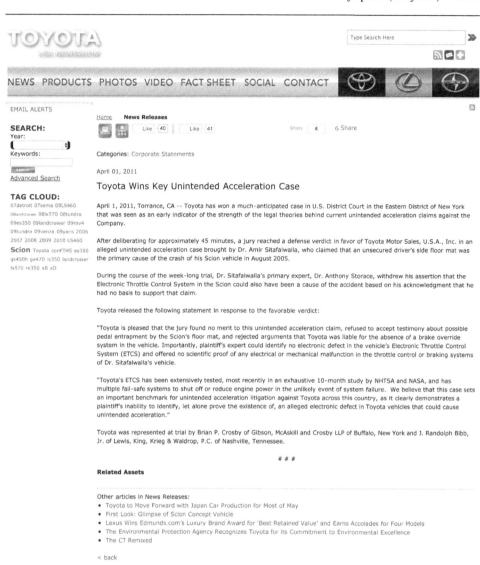

Figure 2.21 Toyota wins key unintended acceleration case (April 1, 2011).
Reprinted by permission.

Discussion Questions

1. Identify and discuss the major mistakes Toyota made when the crisis erupted. What would you have done differently?
2. Identify the objectives of Toyota in light of the crisis. Are the objectives specific, time bound, and measureable? If not, how would you have phrased them?
3. Identify examples of tactics that Toyota used in its attempt to repair its image. Hint: Those tactics are available on the Internet and at Toyota's website.
4. Assume that you were part of Toyota's crisis team based in the United States, what advice would you give to the team at the headquarters in Japan on how to prepare CEO Akio Toyoda for his testimony to Congress?
5. Overall, how effective was Toyota's crisis management and communication? Give specific examples to support your answer. Could you design a better crisis plan for Toyota?

References

Altman, A. (2010). Congress puts Toyota (and Toyoda) in the hot seat. *Time*, February 24. Retrieved from www.time.com/time/nation/article/0,8599,1967654,00.html

Argenti, P. (2003). *Corporate communication* (3rd ed.). Boston, MA: McGraw Hill Irwin.

Baker, D., and Gustafson, C. (2009). Fatal crash continues to raise questions. *San Diego Union Tribune*, August 31. Retrieved from www.signonsandiego.com/news/2009/aug/31/bn31chp-lexus-crash/

Benoit, W. L. (1997). Image repair discourse and crisis communication. *Public Relations Review*, 23(2), 177–186.

Benoit W., and Drew, S. (1997). Appropriateness and effectiveness of image repair strategies. *Communication Reports*, 10(2), 153–163.

Benoit, W. L., and Pang, A. (2008). Crisis communication and image repair discourse. In T.L. Hansen-Horn and B. D. Neff (Eds.), *Public relations: From theory to practice* (pp. 244–261). Boston, MA: Pearson.

Bloxham, A. (2011) Timeline: Toyota recalls. *The Telegraph*, January 26. Retrieved from www.telegraph.co.uk/motoring/news/8283023/Timeline-Toyota-recalls.html

Cato, J. (2010). Recall madness a crisis for Toyota. *Globe & Mail*, January 27. Retrieved from www.theglobeandmail.com/globe-drive/driving-it-home/recall-madness-a-crisis-for-toyota/article1446308/

Dawson, C., and Anhalt, K. N. (2005). A "China price" for Toyota. *Business Week*, February 21. Retrieved from www.businessweek.com/magazine/content/05_08/b3921062.htm

Diaz, M., and Trahan, J. (2009). Four dead after car plunges into Southlake pond. *WFAA-TV/Dallas Morning News*, December 26. Retrieved from www.wfaa.com/news/local/accident-80138632.html

Drives, P. (2010). Toyota to pay $32.4 million fine for recalls. *CNN Money*, December 21. Retrieved from www.money.cnn.com/2010/12/20/autos/toyota_fine/index.htm

Fortune Global 500. (2010) Our annual ranking of the world's largest corporations. *CNN Money.* Retrieved from www.money.cnn.com/magazines/fortune/global500/2010/snapshots

Greimel, H. (2011). Toyota, aiming to double profit, promotes Canada chief as top non-Japanese exec. North America gains more autonomy. *Auto News*, March 9. Retrieved from www.autonews.com/apps/pbcs.dll/article?AID=/20110309/OEM/303099982

Gudykunst, W., and Kim, Y. Y. (1992). *Communicating with strangers: An approach to intercultural communication* (2nd ed.). New York: McGraw-Hill.

Hall, E. T. (1966). *The hidden dimension.* New York: Anchor Press/Double Day.

Hall. E. (1976). *Beyond culture* (pp. 85–128). New York: Doubleday.

History of Toyota, (n.d.) *Toyota.com.* Retrieved from www.toyotaglobal.com/company/history_of_toyota

Hofstede, G. (1984). National cultures and corporate cultures. In L. A. Samovar and R. E. Porter (Eds.), *Communication between cultures.* Belmont, CA: Wadsworth.

Kageyama, Y. (2010). Toyota worldwide recall includes luxury models. *Associated Press*, July 6. Retrieved from www.staradvertiser.com/business/20100706_Toyotas_worldwide_recall_includes_luxury_models.html

Kageyama, Y. (2011). Toyota sold 8.4m vehicles in 2010 to hold top spot. *Associated Press*, January 24. Retrieved from http://abcnews.go.com/Business/wireStory?id=12745584

Kanter, J., Maynard, M., and Tabuchi, H. (2010). Toyota has pattern of slow response on safety Issues. *The New York Times*, February 6. Retrieved from www.nytimes.com/2010/02/07/business/global/07toyota.html?pagewanted=all

Kim, S., and Bailey, D. (2010). Timeline: Toyota's rise and run-up to its recall crisis. *Reuters*, February 9. Retrieved from www.reuters.com/article/2010/02/23/us-toyota-timeline-idUSTRE61M0IT20100223

Kingston, J. (2010). A crisis made in Japan. *The Wall Street Journal*, February 5. Retrieved from http://online.wsj.com/article/SB100014240527487045332045750473706332344141.html?mod=rss_Today's_Most_Popular#printMode

Liker, J., and Ogden, T. N. (2011). *Toyota under fire: Lessons for turning crisis into opportunity.* New York: McGraw-Hill.

Linebaugh, K., Searcey, D., and Shirouzu, N. (2010). Secretive culture led Toyota astray. *The Wall Street Journal*, February 8. Retrieved from http://online.wsj.com/article/SB10001424052748704820904575055733096312238.html#printMode

Nakata, H. (2010). Toyota takes steps to improve image: New panel of experts to call shots on recalls. *Japan Times*, March 31. Retrieved from www.japantimes.co.jp/cgi-bin/nb20100331a1.html

Ohnsman, A., Green, J., and Inoue, K. (2010). The humbling of Toyota. *Business Week*, March 11. Retrieved from www.businessweek.com/magazine/content/10_12/b4171032583967_page_2.htm.

Our point of view: Unintended acceleration: Toyota addresses the issues. (2009). *Toyota.com*, November 6. Retrieved from http://pressroom.toyota.com/article_display.cfm?article

Owles, E., and McDermon, D. (2010). A Toyota timeline. *The New York Times*, February 10. Retrieved from www.nytimes.com/interactive/2010/02/10/business/20100210_Toyota_timeline2.html

Palmer, B. (2010). How many ways can you bow in Japan? *Slate.Com*, February 8. Retrieved from www.slate.com/default.aspx?id=3944&qt=categories+of+japanese+bowing

Ramsey, M., and Mitchell, J. (2010). U.S. study points to driver error in many Toyota crashes. *The Wall Street Journal*, August 11. Retrieved from http://online.wsj.com/article/SB10001424052748704164904575421603167046966.html?mod=googlenews_wsj

Rogers, E. M., and Steinfatt, T.M. (1999). *Intercultural communication.* Prospect Heights, IL: Waveland Press.

Taylor III, A. (2010). How Toyota lost its way—Full version. *CNN Money*, July 10. Retrieved from http://money.cnn.com/2010/07/12/news/international/toyota_recall_crisis_full_version.fortune/index.htm

Toyoda, A. (2010). Toyota's plan to repair its public image. *Washington Post*, February 9. Retrieved from www.washingtonpost.com/wpdyn/content/article/2010/02/08/AR2010020803078_pf.hml

Toyota announces two voluntary recalls and amends potential floor mat interference recall announced in 2009. (2011). *Toyota.com*, February 24. Retrieved from www.pressroom.toyota.com/pr/tms/toyota/toyota-consumer-safety-advisory-102572.aspx?srchid=K610_p228906387#link1

Toyota begins interim notification to owners regarding future voluntary safety recall related to floor mats. (2009) *Toyota.com*, November 2. Retrieved from www.pressroom.toyota.com/pr/tms/toyota/toyota-begins-interim-notification-112088.asp

Toyota issues statement regarding NHTSA settlement. (2010). *Toyota.com*, December 20. Retrieved from www.toyota.com/newsroom)

Toyota outlines new vision after recall fiasco. (2011). *MSN.com*, March 9. Retrieved from http://att-news.mobile.msn.com/enus/article_biz.aspx?aid=41985003&afid=1&pg1=2501

Toyota Prius recall extended worldwide. (2010). *CBS News*, February 9. Retrieved from www.cbsnews.com/stories/2010/02/09/business/main6188378.shtml

Toyota Production System. (n.d.). *Toyota.com*. Retrieved from www.toyota.com.au/about/toyota-production-system

Toyota Production System. (n.d.). *Toyotaglobal.com*. Retrieved from www.toyotaglobal.com/company/vision_philosophy/toyota_production_system

Toyota Progress Report (2010). *Toyota.com*, May. Retrieved from www.pressroom.toyota.com/pr/tms/toyota-progress-report-159009.aspx)

Toyota remains world's largest automaker for third year straight. (2011). *Automotive.com*, January 25. Retrieved from www.blogs.automotive.com/6739692/miscellaneous/toyota-remains-worlds-largest-automaker-for-third-year-straight/index.html.

Toyota stakeholders. (n.d.) Toyota stakeholders' dialogues. *Toyotaglobal.com*. Retrieved from www.toyotaglobal.com/sustainability/stakeholders/toyota_stakeholder_dialogues/

Toyota sued by insurance companies over alleged acceleration-related crashes. (2011). *Los Angeles Times Blogs*, January 3. Retrieved from http://latimesblogs.latimes.com/money_co/2011/01/toyota-sued-by-seven-insurance-companies-sudden-acceleration.html

Toyota wins key unintended acceleration case. (2011, April 1). Retrieved from www.pressroom.toyota.com/releases/toyota-wins-key-unintended-acceleration-case.htm

Welch, D. (2009). Toyota recalls 3.8 million vehicles. *BusinessWeek*, September 29. Retrieved from www.businessweek.com/autos/autobeat/archives/2009/09/toyota_recalls.html

VIEWS FROM AN EXPERT

CAROLYN BOBO

Carolyn Bobo, APR, Fellow PRSA has worked in higher education, health care and professional services public relations in Texas, New Mexico, and South Carolina. She is a graduate of the University of Texas at Austin and Syracuse University Newhouse School of Public Communication. Carolyn has been an adjunct instructor at TCU's Schieffer School of Journalism and at South Carolina's Furman University. She has been the professional adviser for the award-winning PRSSA Bateman Team at TCU.
She has published articles in Public Relations Quarterly, PR Tactics and Journal of Employee Communications Management. *She was a contributor to the book,* Crisis Communications in Health Care: A Delicate Balance, *and to the instructor's guide for editions of* This is PR *textbook.*

Toyota Crisis Observations

Toyota's failure to follow standard crisis event response was surprising, even shocking. The company is a global manufacturing giant, and the expectations of customers, media, and regulators is that its ability to respond to an alarming safety-related incident would be equal to its marketplace clout.

However, Toyota stumbled through almost two years of controversy when it failed to follow basic crisis response rules: respond quickly, tell the truth, apologize if necessary, and announce a plan of action. Although vehicles were recalled early on, Toyota's public statements did not rise to the level of the major crisis that developed. The subsequent official apology, criticized as inadequate, was an indication of festering public distrust, surprising for a Japanese icon.

Organizational culture predicts organizational communications style, and some of Toyota's difficulties were culturally based, public relations errors rooted in the system of organizational beliefs and operational behaviors found in Japanese companies, and in its formal, authoritarian management. Unfortunately, that style also dictates a method of public relations likely to create a trust gap between customers, regulators, and media.

Toyota also believed that the problem was not a technological issue and viewed the acceleration incidents as driver errors. Toyota essentially said that consumers were wrong, ignoring the fact that many purchased a Toyota because of the company's reputation for superior technology and manufacturing. Consumers want to enjoy technology without hazards, and when an incident occurs, publics expect the organization to remove the risk, not blame the customer. Rather than alienating customers, perhaps the company could have used them (through social media) to build understanding and support for Toyota's initial and planned actions. When customers are not satisfied by company action, they expect regulatory bodies to solve the problem—in this case, the National Highway Transportation and Safety Administration.

Also of significance is the apparent need for a senior level adviser as part of the executive team or the board. Such a presence—as outside counsel or as a member of the dominant coalition, the formal or informal leaders who make critical decisions—could have recommended strategic communications activities that would have mitigated the erosion of customer and regulator trust, and assisted with media relations.

A senior public relations counselor also could have managed cultural translation. The cultural translator/senior public relations practitioner's role is to recognize issues, use research and other resources to predict public responses and to identify and manage execution of tactical communication response. This senior position is responsible for boundary spanning, for scanning the market environment in search of threats to the company's reputation, and by extension, to sales and profits.

It's easy to note that a company should have a powerful, executive-level public relations individual or function, and an executive management group that listens to, supports and responds to such counsel. In fact, it is not so common or so easy for that practitioner to be extant or to function without compromise. The assertive senior level public relations executive may risk loss of organizational clout, ridicule, and in the case of Toyota, loss of face. Of course, he or she also may risk loss of employment. However, part of excellent crisis communications planning and response—and the reputation management and marketplace success that accompanies it—is the recognition that senior-level practitioners should be involved early, often and permanently.

Thailand

"Bringing the Government Down": Managing Thailand's Political Crisis

Cornelius B. Pratt and Ronald Lee Carr

Protest movements, like other forms of social movements, generally encourage citizens, organizations, and governments to reflect on public issues; to take stock of their programs, strategic actions, and activities; and to respond to them accordingly. Massive, sometimes violent, protests by two major vibrant groups—the Red Shirts and the Yellow Shirts —struck Thailand in April and May 2010. The Red Shirts described the current government of Prime Minister Abhisit Vejjajiva, a military-supported politician of the Democrat Party, as illegitimate and as a front for aristocrats, called for his resignation and demanded that he grant amnesty to their revered politician in exile, former Prime Minister Thaksin Shinawatra, of the Thai Rak Thai party. The Yellow Shirts supported the prime minister and King Bhumibol Adulyadej. In skirmishes between both protest groups, 91 people were killed, and nearly 2,000 injured. Beginning April 7, 2010, Abhisit declared a state of emergency in Bangkok and in five other provinces; that decree was extended eventually to 18 additional provinces. On May 3, 2010, Abhisit announced a five-pronged program of national reconciliation. To the degree that Abhisit's government is healing the wounds of the crisis, this case study re-emphasizes the importance of continuing government communications as major contributions to national policy, as well as the verity of protest movements as a tool in participatory democracy and deliberation, as a channel for citizen input, as a medium for national reflection, and as a necessary action for democratic reforms.

Introduction

The now ubiquitous street politics may sometimes be uncivil, but there has been a mobilization in other areas as well. Voting, community radio, political publications, and all kinds of discussion and activism have expanded. The downside is that there has also been a rise in political cynicism, particularly among the middle class.

(Hewison, 2010, p. 131)

> The quality of Thai democracy has suffered incisive erosion, with the result that Thailand today might be termed a tutelary democracy—a form of defective or unstable democracy.
>
> (Chambers, 2010, p. 837)

Protest events. Social movements. Political activism. Union movements. Protest rallies and marches. Demonstrations and uprisings. We see them in major cities, in small towns, in rural areas, on plant sites, on college campuses worldwide. And we see them with increasing frequency, particularly since February 15, 2003, when "the largest protest event in human history" (Walgrave and Rucht, 2010, p. xiii) occurred in hundreds of cities across the globe on a single day against an imminent U.S.-led war on Iraq. They are activist groups riled over the perceived misgivings of more powerful entities: governments, corporations, international organizations. They are social movements aimed at mobilizing a consensus (that is, persuading people about a good cause) or mobilizing an action (that is, bringing people to the streets) (Klandermans, 1984, 1997). And they are the New York City Occupy Wall Street demonstrations that spread to other U.S. cities and to other countries. Protests, social movement participation, collective action participation, and political activism are becoming ever more formidable as channels for expressing discontent with government or corporate policies or programs, and for facilitating collective public participation in an issue that could otherwise be ignored by the targets of the groups' concerns. And, of course, for getting an electorate all worked up. Early in 2011, such movements, armed with Facebook and Twitter, sought immediate political reforms, brought down the government of Tunisian President Zine El Abidine Ben Ali, and exacerbated political tensions over Hosni Mubarak's authoritarian government in Egypt, threatening similar governments in the Arab world.

In April and May 2010, thousands of antigovernment protesters demonstrated in several cities in Thailand, calling on the government to annul the 2007 Constitution and to restore democracy to the Southeast Asian nation of 68 million people ruled by a coalition government they perceived as illegitimate, particularly because the pro-Thaksin Pheu Thai Party was the largest in parliament, and as a front for aristocrats and the military elite. The protesters also demanded amnesty for one of their own—former Prime Minister Thaksin Shinawatra.

The protests illustrated the relevance of three research findings: (a) that personal ties with friends, peers, and family members play a significant role in recruiting and mobilizing people to participate in political activism; (b) that organizations and associations mobilize people to participate in political activism; and (c) that single-issue protest events rely on social infrastructure—that is, organizational and personal ties—to encourage protesters to participate in those events (Fisher, 2010).

Why do people participate in protests? Valocchi (2010) observes that engaging in "activism is not a monocausal or determinant process. Nor is it an 'all or nothing phenomenon' as if a switch is flipped and people suddenly become activists" (pp. 109–110). He states that the pathway to participation and commitment is a dynamic model that reveals "multiple influences and interactions across influences" (p. 123) that combine three elements: (a) biography such as family socialization and favorable dispositions toward social movement participation; (b) social networks such as the settings that inspire participants to take action; and (c) critical events and external shocks to a system that can motivate people to engage in collective action, irrespective of their attitudinal dispositions.

Such protests are used to (a) control their image and manipulate how others view the organization; (b) rebuff management's demands for concessions; (c) cultivate and present an image of success and uniqueness, particularly when the field is crowded, thus gaining access to a wider audience for recruitment purposes and increasing the odds for positive attention; and (d) increase solidarity among their members (Martin, 2010).

Protest movements are organized as high-profile critics of government or business practices; of meetings and conferences of international governmental organizations such as the World Trade Organization, the World Economic Forum, and the World Bank; and of societies and multinational corporations to which are directed internationally coordinated campaigns that frame transnational public debates (Beyeler and Kriesi, 2005; Crossley, 2002a, b, 2003; Smith, 2001). Movements "pursue change or stability of a system and in the system" (Oommen, 2010, p. 19); they use websites to structure negative communications that persuade the public to avoid companies that have wronged them (Ward and Ostrom, 2006).

Mobilization is the engine that drives a protest movement, which occurs as a "demand" or as the will of a segment of a population to show its discontent (e.g., Does the movement address issues of concern to people?) and as a "supply" or the offer from the protesters (e.g., Does the movement stage activities that appeal to people?) (Klandermans, 2004; Stekelenburg and Klandermans, 2009; Walgrave and Klandermans, 2010). Structural conditions and societal changes can also enable the emergence of such movements (Fuchs, 2006).

In what forms do protest events occur? Dalton (1996) writes that they range from conventional petitioning to more conflictual activities that have four thresholds:

- transition from conventional to unconventional politics such as signing a petition and participating in lawful demonstrations. Porta and Diani (2006, p. 176) describe this as the "logic of bearing witness";
- shift to direct action such as boycotts. Porta and Diani (2006, p. 171) describe this as the "logic of numbers";
- strikes that are unofficial and take over or occupy a building in a nonviolent manner. Porta and Diani, again, describe this as the "logic of numbers"; and

- injury inflicted on other people or damage to property in violent confrontations. Porta and Diani (2006, p. 173) describe this as the "logic of damage".

From an organizational standpoint, effective political protests have been likened more to improvisational jazz than to classical symphony (Rosen et al., 2010). The former, according to Rosen et al., tends to be decentralized and open, providing room for interpretation and flexibility of group direction; the latter, as formally established "mobilizing structures" (McAdam et al., 1996), is centralized and hierarchical, with individuals being less able to contribute to decision making or to communicate freely with others because of an intricate network of communication channels. Both forms promote key messages and tactics of social movement organizations in a variety of institutional settings and engender mobilization potential (Minkoff and McCarthy, 2005).

We all read, hear about or see major protest movements across the globe.

- Item: Occupy Wall Street protesters camped and demonstrated in and around Zuccotti Park, in Lower Manhattan, New York City, beginning September 17, 2011, directing their furor at high unemployment, economic inequality, and excessive corporate greed. Similar movements emerged in several other U.S. cities and in other countries, including Canada, England, Germany, Iran, and Italy, and the Hong Kong Special Administrative Region.
- Item: Thousands of university students demonstrated in central London and in several other British cities, beginning November 10, 2010, against a new Conservative-led coalition government's austerity proposal that could triple university tuition.
- Item: Increases in tuition proposed for California's two public-university systems resulted in student protests in 2009 and 2010. On November 10, 2010, for example, students at the California State University System protested against a 15.5 percent tuition hike over two years.
- Item: Millions of French citizens, under the aegis of labor and trade unions, protested in October 2010 against the center-right government's pension-reform measures: raising the age for receiving full state pension from 65 to 67 and that for legal retirement from 60 to 62. There were no fatalities from the conflicts with government's security forces, but 30 percent of international flights and 50 percent of domestic flights were canceled; social services, for example, garbage collection, were disrupted; gasoline deliveries to nearly 13,000 gas stations were reduced significantly, resulting in long lines at the pumps. Nicolas Sarkozy's government insisted on making the reforms, and the French Parliament approved them on October 27. During 20 days in October and November 2005 in *banlieues* (or suburbs) of Paris and in a few other cities in France, minority French

youths, mostly of North African heritage, in loosely coordinated riots vandalized government property, set buildings and 10,000 cars on fire, and attacked government's security personnel, all to express their disdain over their perception of racial injustice. Then-Minister of the Interior Nicolas Sarkozy had described the rioters as "trash," fueling additional resentment from them.

- Item: Protests organized by opposition groups were held on October 20, 2010, in several Indonesian cities on the first anniversary of President Susilo Bambang Yudhoyono's second term because of widespread frustration with inaction of the popularly elected president in reforming the economy and fighting widespread corruption.

- Item: Protests supported by an opposition candidate to Iran's incumbent president began June 13, 2009, and escalated in various Iranian cities and in other world regions, following the announcement of the results of 2009 presidential election that declared President Mahmoud Ahmadinejad victorious over his challenger, Mir Hossein Mousavi. Fatalities, arrests, and injuries were each estimated in the hundreds.

The preceding overview tells us, among other things, that protests are symbols, instructive discourses, and contentious actions by which individuals engage political systems in which they seek changes. That singular purpose is the framework for our analysis of Thailand's evolving management of its political crisis.

Background of the Crisis

Thailand, a constitutional monarchy, had had a series of destabilizing military coups, unpredictable changes in government, rivalries among units of its armed forces and government agencies, and deep social and economic divisions between the rural poor and the urban elite. Its political crises had made its governments vulnerable to military incursions: the military seized power 18 times in the past 79 years. So far-reaching was its "crisis-centered politics" that McCargo (2000) concluded more than a decade ago that "Crisis and reform are not antithetical in Thailand: rather, they enjoy a symbiotic relationship, each thriving on the other" (p. 136).

The remote cause of the 2010 protests was a watershed event in 1932, when a military coup abolished the absolute monarchy, making it titular, placing Thailand on a path toward establishing a representative, parliamentary government that ensured that Thais had universal voting rights. Thais parlayed such newfound civic responsibility into other areas of civil life, particularly into organizing protest movements.

Thailand's 1997 "People's Constitution" (Phongpaichit and Baker, 2004, p. 2) spelled out major reforms of the electoral and political processes, including discouraging the odious practices of buying votes, manipulating business–politician relationships for personal gains, and making promises to and having tradeoffs with political parties. Thus, it established seemingly independent, powerful constitutional bodies to rein in such activities. Three such institutions were the Election Commission, which investigated the validity of election results; the National Counter-Corruption Commission (NCCC), which investigated election fraud and ministers' declaration of assets; and the Constitutional Court, which adjudicated constitutional issues.

The fulcrum of the 2010 protests that left 91 dead and nearly 2,000 injured was Thaksin, founder of the Thai Rak Thai (TRT; Thais Love Thais) political party in July 1998. TRT's campaign themes for the January 6, 2001, general election focused on three issues: low-cost health care for the poor, government funds for each village for community development, and debt relief for farmers unable to repay government bank loans, all of which critics labeled "populist." TRT won the election in a landslide, landing Thaksin in the premiership in February 2001, for a four-year term. Those elections resulted in an unprecedented parliamentary majority, thus reshaping, as McCargo and Pathmanand (2005) concluded, Thailand's political landscape. Thaksin's vision for the country and his party's programs were an immediate catalyst for protests from opposition groups.

TRT had won the election on a platform of moving Thailand toward making economic and social reforms, of engaging in a reformist agenda, and of implementing policies that would enhance the well-being of the poor. But the new Thaksin government had been bedeviled from its start, in the aftermath of a finding by the NCCC in December 2000 that the then-billionaire candidate was guilty of concealing assets worth more than $200 million when he was deputy prime minister in the 1997 Chavalit Yongchaiyudh administration. The case was referred to the new Constitutional Court, which, if it had upheld the ruling of the NCCC, would have had the option of imposing a five-year ban on Thaksin's participation in politics.

Thaksin, whose disdain for the corruption commission and for the Constitutional Court was public knowledge, took his case to the court of public opinion and mobilized his supporters to impress upon the court that their prime minister was "a savior sent to redeem Thailand from its troubles— an argument that reflected popular belief in the capacity of strong, charismatic leadership" (McCargo and Pathmanand, 2005, p. 15).

In an 8–7 vote, the Constitutional Court on August 3, 2001, reversed the findings of the NCCC. Two days later, Thaksin said, "It's strange that the leader who was voted by 11 million people had to bow to . . . two organizations composed of only appointed commissioners and judges, whom people do not have a chance to choose" (in Peleggi, 2007, p. 141). Widespread notions of judicial interference and questions about the court's independence fueled concerns about a possible derailment of the TRT's reformist, "think new, act new" agendas. A suspicious cloud hung over the prime minister's government until the next parliamentary election in February 2005. TRT won decisively, with 57 percent of the vote in the national election, making Thaksin the first prime minister of Thailand to serve two consecutive terms (2001–2006); the second was half-term. The integrity of that election victory, nonetheless, was questioned and opposition to and pressures on his government increased. And to Thaksin's critics, his authoritarian tendency as an alternative to liberal democracy was indicated in his reducing government to the first-person singular in his key messages: "I give to all of you"; "I belong to you"; "I am the mechanism which can translate the will of the people into state action" (Phongpaichit and Baker, 2008, pp. 68–69).

Thaksin resigned in April 2005 as head of his government. TRT, however, used brinksmanship to reinstate him, but the monarchy and some powerful segments of the military were still incredulous and disenchanted about his leadership. On January 23, 2006, the Shinawatra family sold, tax-free, its stake in the Shin Corporation to Singapore government's Temasek Holdings. Even though there were no irregularities in the transaction, Thaksin was criticized for selling a national icon to another government. In March 2006, the People's Alliance for Democracy (PAD), a coalition of activist businesspeople and nongovernmental organizations, which organized street demonstrations, asked Thaksin to resign. He called for early elections in April 2006. His party won, but it did not have enough support to form a government. The PAD excoriated his liberal policies on loans and health care that benefited the poor. Thaksin was deposed on September 16, 2006, in a bloodless military coup supported by the palace; the military declared a state of emergency in several cities, including Bangkok, the nation's capital, and Chiang Mai, a Shinawatra power base. In October 2006, he resigned as TRT leader. In May 2007, the Constitutional Court found him guilty of election irregularities and banned TRT from engaging in political activities for five years.

A yearlong military rule, led by an appointed government headed by General Surayud Chulanont as prime minister, resulted in a new constitution and an electoral process that would ensure that the new government was inarguably anti-Thaksin. But in the December 2007 election, the electorate voted for pro-Thaksin parties, resulting in the election of Samak Sundaravej, an avowed admirer of Thaksin's, as prime minister. On February 28, 2008, Thaksin, who had been banned from politics, returned from exile in England to face fraud-related charges. Samak's People's Power Party had attempted to amend the constitution to allow for the forgiveness of Thaksin and had sought to placate the protesters through seeking a compromise in parliament. The PAD, which disbanded when Thaksin went into exile, was reinvigorated; it organized massive protests in August 2008 to oust his successor. PAD demonstrations escalated, as were investigations into and charges on a series of Thaksin's corruption cases, forcing the former prime minister into exile again, this time in Dubai. On October 21, 2008, he was sentenced in absentia to a two-year jail term for conflict of interest in a land transaction. And on February 26, 2010, the Supreme Court confiscated his family's assets worth $1.4 billion, arguing that they were ill-gotten.

Situation Analysis

Abhisit Vejjajiva of the Democrat Party and a military-supported candidate assumed office on December 15, 2008, based on the outcomes of a parliamentary vote. He became the nation's fifth prime minister in a year. His government, like those of two of his predecessors, did not have a strong power base and was not popularly elected. In April and May 2010, Thailand was thrust into the vortex of a political crisis that pitted two warring protest groups: the pro-Thaksin Red Shirts (Figure 2.22) supported by the Blue Shirts, and the anti-Thaksin Yellow Shirts (Figure 2.23). The Yellow Shirts, spearheaded by PAD, were conservatives and royalists who supported the monarchy (and King Bhumibol Adulyadej, who has been on the throne since 1946), and protested against the one-person, one-vote democracy of Thaksin's government. A familiar argument of the Yellow Shirts was that the populace was not sufficiently literate to reap the real benefits of such universal suffrage, even as the nation's adult literacy rate was at 94.1 percent.

In response to protesters' labeling his government as illegitimate and calling for it to resign, Abhisit said, "We assumed office under the same means, under the same rules, by the same vote of parliament as the two previous

Figure 2.22 Red Shirts gearing up for action in Bangkok against the Thai government.

Source: Courtesy of Voja Miladinovic, Bangkok. Reprinted by permission.

Figure 2.23 Yellow Shirts protesting in Bangkok on behalf of the Thai government.
Source: Courtesy of Voja Miladinovic, Bangkok. Reprinted by permission.

administrations" ("Thai PM," 2010). Yet, anti-government protesters stepped up their insistence that he dissolve parliament, call for new elections, and grant amnesty to Thaksin who had been accused by the government of funding the protests. On April 7, 2010, Abhisit declared a state of emergency for the Thai capital and for some other parts of the country; in July it was extended to more than one-third of the country. The protests still raged. And on Sunday,

September 18, 2010, to mark the four-year anniversary of the September 2006 coup that deposed Thaksin, several thousand anti-government protesters rallied against the Abhisit government.

Problem and Opportunity (PO) Statements

In this case study, we view problems not entirely as dysfunctional, problematic occurrences, but also as opportunities for engaging in communication excellence. The Chinese have offered the world an instructive, insightful expression for crisis, interpreting it as *"dangerous opportunity"* (Ulmer et al., 2011, p. 3), or *wei ji*, which means *both* a crisis and an opportunity. Therefore, protest movements in Thailand and elsewhere, in the Chinese dialectical view, also present opportunities for a national reflection on and an integration of disparate constituents' interests. Even though the statements below are prima facie problem-focused, they are at bottom presented here also as opportunities for promoting national reconciliation and for fostering unity.

Glassman (2011) identifies three generally discrete publics in Thailand's political crisis: (a) the royalist elites who comprise members of the palace, leaders of the military, and the Democrat Party (hereinafter referred to as the Royal Thai government); (b) Thaksin supporters who include Thai capitalists, the large rural population, and the industrial working class (hereinafter referred to as the pro-Thaksin protesters); and (c) class-privileged defenders of royalist hegemony and Bangkok professionals (hereinafter referred to as anti-Thaksin protesters). The remainder of this chapter will be presented in line with those three publics.

- *The Royal Thai government's PO statement*: Thailand's electorate, as a primary public, and the international community are unaware of the full range of political issues in the country's protest movements.
- *Pro-Thaksin protesters' PO statement*: TRT's rural programs and business orientation threaten Thailand's aristocratic class.
- *Anti-Thaksin protesters' PO statement*: Thailand's politics are dominated by TRT's business interests, rendering democratic institutions ineffectual and making governmental agencies broadly malfeasant.

Government's Initial Responses

The Thai government's immediate response was meeting fire with fire, using police and military forces to crack down on protesters. On April 7, 2010, under the "Emergency Decree on Government Administration in States of Emergency, B.E. 2548," it declared a state of emergency in six provinces: Ayutthaya, Bangkok, Nakon Pathom, Nonthaburi, Pathum Thani, and Samut Prakan. By May 19, that number was 24. That decree proscribed public gatherings and restricted public communications. The government also stifled communications by shutting down broadcast stations and social networks associated with the Red Shirts.

Communication Goals, Objectives, Strategies, and Tactics

The crisis-communication goals, objectives, strategies and tactics will be presented from a three-pronged perspective: those of the Thai government, of the pro-Thaksin protesters, and of the anti-Thaksin protesters. We must note that even though the Thaksin government was overthrown in a military coup on September 19, 2006, Thailand's politics, Hewison (2010) writes, have revolved around Thaksin and his government since the 1998 founding of the TRT, which has changed the operational landscape of Thailand's political parties. McCargo and Pathmanand (2005) argued that Thaksin dominated Thailand by (a) transforming his Shin Corporation to telecommunications leadership in the Thai market and in those of other Asian countries; (b) founding a political party that eclipsed all others; (c) securing military support for his party and government, thus protecting him from the volatility of Thai's electoral politics; (d) communicating consistently with stakeholders, particularly voters; and (e) creating an elaborate, innovative political economy network of his business, TRT, the military, the news media, and other constituencies. Little wonder, then, that all street protests during nearly a decade had references to the "Thaksinization" of Thailand and to its "Thaksinomics," by which government protected domestic firms from the competition of advanced economies.

1. Royal Thai Government

Goal 1: To manage protesters' demands and concerns.

Objective: To increase significantly and urgently government's actions in managing or resolving the nation's political turmoil.

Strategy (a): Demonstrated that democracy bereft of mammoth opportunities for *civil* disagreement and engagement and for expressing those actions hamstrung the political and social well-being of Thais.

Strategy (b): Demonstrated that the ongoing protests could be potentially transformative—politically, socially, economically.

Tactics:

- invited select leaders of the protest movements—that is, representatives of the Red Shirts and leaders of the Yellow Shirts—for more government-protest movement dialogue in an attempt to address head-on the concerns of angry, anxious protesters;

- organized counter-demonstrations of government supporters who carried banners and placards, some of which read "No Parliament dissolution for peace of the country" and "No more Thaksinomic"; and wore yellow T-shirts emblazoned with "WE LOVE THE KING";
- invited leaders of the Yellow Shirts of the PAD to discuss the latter's objection to Abhisit's proposed five-pronged road map for national reconciliation;
- met one-on-one occasionally with the leadership of the United Front for Democracy Against Dictatorship (UDD; the Red Shirts), in government officials' attempt to ensure a broad, robust understanding of that leadership, of other slivers of protest groups, and of government's efforts to resolve conflicts;
- announced on live television on May 3, 2010, government's response to the crisis (Abhisit's five-pronged road map for national reconciliation called for (a) "upholding the monarchy," (b) "resolving fundamental problems of social injustice," (c) "enabling media's constructive operation," (d) "establishing facts about violent incidents," and (e) "establishing mutually acceptable political rules") ("Prime Minister," 2010);
- appealed to the country in a televised broadcast on June 10, 2010, to join in efforts to mend the social, economic, and political divides in the country;
- closed some opposition news organizations, for example, the People's Channel TV, while using ASTV, a satellite channel, to broadcast government-favored information;
- limited public communication networks by invoking special powers under the Internal Security Act, by which it banned public gatherings of more than five people, prohibiting protests; and
- piggybacked on the neutral White Shirts' "I Love Thailand" campaign theme by organizing its own national anthem-singing campaign that iterated that theme.

Goal 2: To increase public awareness of the government's position on the protesters' claims and concerns.

Objective: To increase significantly and urgently the number of channels for disseminating public information on the protest movements, their demands and counter-demands.

Strategy (a): Provided the Thai electorate with streams of detailed information about the ongoing crisis and its aftermath.

Strategy (b): Kept some opposition news organizations on a "tight leash."

Tactics:

- developed partnerships for communicating with key nongovernmental organizations in Bangkok that helped spread the government's take on the crisis;
- made major nationally televised announcements in the presence of General Anupong Paojinda, head of the Thai army, in a show of unity between the Abhisit administration and the military;
- re-energized electorate's mindset through emphasizing government programs focused on national unity, not partisan, sectarian interests;
- mounted exhibits of caches of weapons, including assault rifles, grenades, improvised explosive devices, and homemade bombs it said had been seized from anti-government protesters, in an attempt to respond to and ameliorate public criticisms of Thai government's use of excessive force to contain the protests;
- held scores of public hearings such as discussion fora and town hall meetings on the nation's crisis;
- included more crisis-related information on government-managed blogs, microblogs, and websites in which the public participated in decision-making on the nation's crisis;
- recruited protest-management ambassadors to assuage public anxiety and to placate the opposition; and
- monitored and censored the information media, particularly those of the opposition.

Goal 3: To expand government's diplomatic exchange of information on the crisis.

Objective (a): To increase significantly and urgently diplomatic opportunities for face-to-face dialogue on the crisis internationally.

Objective (b): To cultivate significant and immediate international media interest in the government's position on the crisis, thereby strengthening and deepening its media relations.

Strategy: Kept the international community apprised of political and social developments.

Tactics:

- invited diplomats to exhibits of caches of weapons the government said it had seized from the protesters, in an attempt to respond to the barrage of international criticism of Thailand's abuse of human rights; and

- granted to the international media several interviews, some streamed live in Thailand (Abhisit used those interviews to explain to the world his government's perspectives on the crisis).

2. Pro-Thaksin Protesters (the Red Shirts)

Goal 1: To increase public awareness of pro-Thaksin protesters' demands.

Objective 1: To increase significantly and urgently the number of domestic channels for disseminating public information on pro-Thaksin protesters' demands.

Objective 2: To increase significantly and urgently networks for recruiting supporters and for disseminating information on protesters' demands.

Strategy (a): Demonstrated that the ongoing protests were an unequivocal message to the government that it had abused the democratic process and the rights of citizens.

Strategy (b): Reinforced demand for the government to step down and for a general election to be held.

Strategy (c): Demonstrated the dual nature of TRT's political base, that is, as a coalition of the rural poor and the corporate elite.

Tactics:

- used symbols (red shirts), protests, rallies, and demonstrations to communicate their case and to express group oneness during several weeks in April and May 2010;
- used additional communication vehicles such as banners and slogans, some of which read "Stop Killing People," "Stop double standard! Dissolve parliament", and "New thinking, new ways for all Thais";
- called for dissolving government agencies such as the NCCC and for the ousting of Thaksin's successor governments;
- delivered fiery, incendiary speeches immediately before and after each demonstration or rally;
- used multiple channels, (e.g., traditional news and information media, websites and social media, and banners) as communication channels of choice to call for new elections, particularly on the assumption of office after September 19, 2006, by prime ministers of the People's Power Party and of the Democrat Party;
- called for calm and understanding of the non-violent nature of the movement (while there were allegations of the protesters' using dangerous

weapons, the leadership of the protesters insisted on peaceful non-violent demonstrations and called for a peaceful transition of government);

- used firearms and explosives to set buildings on fire, a tactic not publicly accepted by the protesters' leadership;
- used satellite television, YouTube, Paltalk, Facebook, Twitter, text messages, and blogs to communicate and illustrate instances of victimhood of the protesters (for example, protesters' fatalities went viral on the Internet, were widely featured on YouTube and streamed live on video feeds, as occurred on May 13, 2010, when Major General Khattiya Sawatdiphol, a red-shirt endorser, was fatally shot); and
- re-energized the movement (and its message) by marking the four-year anniversary of the 2006 coup that toppled the Thaksin government with rallies and demonstrations, all as a reminder of a struggle yet to attain its goals.

Goal 2: To increase third-party endorsement and enhance the credibility of pro-Thaksin protesters' demands and messages.

Objective: To increase significantly and urgently the number of high-profile spokespersons for disseminating pro-Thaksin protesters' demands.

Strategy: Made movement appealing to hitherto inactive but admiring personalities in the struggle.

Tactic: Sought high-profile endorsements, from Major General Khattiya Sawatdiphol, as a marquee endorser; General Chavalit Yongchaiyudh, a former prime minister; General Pallop Pinmanee, a vocal Pheu Thai Party member; and Prime Minister Hun Sen of Cambodia.

3. Anti-Thaksin Protesters (the Yellow Shirts)

Goal 1: To increase public awareness of anti-Thaksin protesters' demands.

Objective: To increase significantly and urgently the number of channels for disseminating public information on anti-Thaksin protesters' demands.

Strategy (a): Defused and counteracted protesters' demands for the government to step down and for a general election to be held.

Tactics:

- used symbols (yellow shirts of the PAD) and counter-activities—protests, rallies, demonstrations—to communicate their case that the government, which was of the people and by the people, was a respecter of the democratic process and of the rule of law;

- used fiery speeches to enunciate their cause and to express group solidarity for it;
- held protest rallies and demonstrations, some of which resulted in skirmishes with government security forces, during several weeks in April and May 2010;
- used at least five languages (Arabic, French, Dutch, Spanish, and Chinese) on PAD's website to marshal its case against anti-government protesters and to endorse government's handling of the billionaire-turned-fugitive case of Thaksin; and
- used a mantra on its website to solidify its position in the crisis: "People's Alliance For Democracy Against Thaksin, the International Terrorist Criminal."

Strategy (b): Demonstrated that the ongoing protests were as myopic as they were misguided.

Tactics:

- expressed the notion that TRT's political activities and policies were inconsistent with the well-being of Thais and their democratic institutions; and
- insisted that due process and the rule of law can resolve the nation's challenges.

Goal 2: To increase third-party endorsement of anti-Thaksin protesters' demands.

Objective: To increase significantly and urgently the number of high-profile spokespersons who reinforce anti-Thaksin protesters' demands.

Strategy: Demonstrated that democracy and respect for the monarchy, as symbolized by the tutelage of King Bhumibol Adulyadej, were not exclusive of each other.

Tactic: Used the king's public rebuke of the Thaksin government as a platform to further their cause.

Outcomes Assessment

What has become of Thailand since the Thaksin government was overthrown in a military *coup d'état* in 2006? Abhisit's Democrat-led government has quelled the riots and rallies. The streets have been cleaned up and a normalcy of sorts has returned to Bangkok. Abhisit is on track to accomplishing his government's overarching goal of managing or resolving the nation's political crisis. But his earlier plan for a November 14, 2010, general election has been shelved because, as he put it, of the fragility of the nation's reconciliation and the depth of the divisions that occurred in the aftermath of the ouster of Thaksin.

Assessing the outcomes of the communication goals, objectives, strategies, and tactics presented in this case requires an analysis of the three key publics.

1. Royal Thai Government

From the government's standpoint, there is every reason to be optimistic about the future of Thailand: that it is again becoming well positioned to reclaim its glory days as a leading economy in Southeast Asia and as a widely known tourism haven of tranquil beaches, of safe urban centers, and of accessible rural areas. At the core of this case is the protest movement as a vehicle of national reflection and of political and social reform. Thailand is a constitutional monarchy and a parliamentary democracy. Even so, its monarchy expresses publicly its displeasure with governments, as occurred in December 2001, when the king said to then-Prime Minister Thaksin:

> At present everyone knows that the country faces a catastrophe . . . because now everything seems to be in decline. The prime minister is making a long face. He's not pleased I talked about catastrophe. But that's the truth, because whatever is done seems to be a problem.
>
> (in Baker, 2005, p. 135)

And its king was not reluctant to express his displeasure with the numerous political and business controversies that rocked Thaksin's government and to throw his weight behind the military's intervention in 2006 in government operations. Its parliament was not averse to a revolving door for premiership: in 2008 alone, Thailand had five prime ministers.

Thaksin's government had drawn fire from segments of the electorate for its dominance of and entanglement in most aspects of Thai life. Aside from his charismatic personality (he was the first Thai prime minister to serve two consecutive terms), his party won the 2005 general election by a landslide and had a significant parliamentary majority, and was largely unconstrained in passing legislation, unlike the weak coalitions of preceding governments. Such enormous powers stoked the ire of the conservative elements in the country, led to a coup and to the "2007 Constitution to weaken political parties, the executive, politicians and parliament. This means that the parliament has again become a place of shifting loyalties" (Hewison, 2010, p. 123). The Thaksin government had set the tone for governmental and bureaucratic reform, an element that continues to this day.

Abhisit's Democrat Party is guided by the principles of participation and justice. His road map for national reconciliation is a formidable attempt to mend fences, to bridge the social and political divisions, and to restore

Thailand to economic viability. It is plausible, then, that given the proposals laid out by the Abhisit administration, the Thaksin-style governance, one in which stakeholder interest in big business and in poor rural areas was explicitly catered to in his policies, is being overtaken by one focused on national reconciliation and attention to disparate national interests. The long-drawn riots, as well as government's response to them, are catalysts in ensuring that calm and progress return once again to modern Thailand.

2. Pro-Thaksin Protesters (the Red Shirts)

The Red Shirts focused their discontent on the Thai military, which they saw as an ardent supporter of Prime Minister Abhisit. A Red Shirts' demand was that the prime minister step down and that the government offer amnesty to Thaksin. Both were rejected and Abhisit ordered his security forces to crack down on the protesters, even as they were being invited for discussions with administration officials.

The Red Shirts have well-organized communication networks and can congregate promptly publicly, as necessary. Their use of social media (viral video, social networking sites, YouTube, blogs and microblogs) accounts for the speed with which they assemble to challenge the government. Their demands, from the government's perspective, have been inappropriate. And their occasional use of firearms and violence has been deemed excessive and illegal. Dialogue bereft of violence can ensure that discussion of the political and economic future of Thailand is a topic for a broad national debate.

3. Anti-Thaksin Protesters (the Yellow Shirts)

The continuing success of the PAD, a key anti-Thaksin stakeholder, is largely attributed to three factors: (a) its tacit support from the monarchy, (b) its support by the military, and (c) its support from the government. Whereas the Red Shirts are clearly at odds with the government and the Thai military, the PAD occasionally disagrees with government's policies, particularly with some aspects of Abhisit's five-pronged national reconciliation proposals. But the PAD is a bulwark of democratic governance—not subservient to the government and not antagonistic to it, either. It is able to enjoy co-governance of sorts with the Abhisit administration.

Lessons Learned

At the outset, we noted the ubiquity of protests, rallies, and other forms of social movements, all seemingly justified by the political currents that loom large in "the enduring logic of Thai elite politics: clientelism, cronyism, and patrimonial use of the state that the political reform movement sought to eliminate" (Connors, 2007, pp. 252–253). This case study demonstrates one of the strengths of those social causes: they are a vehicle of participatory democracy that requires a government to be transparent, fair, and accommodating. The Thai government, in its continuing search for social and political equity, on the one hand, passed the 1997 Constitution, which reduced the likelihood for the emergence of splinter political parties and for the instability of party coalitions and governments. On the other, the military's 2007 Constitution, for all intents and purposes, was designed to weaken elected governments, to make weak coalitions normative, to increase the likelihood of extra-parliamentary interventions in government, and to enhance the power of the judiciary to proscribe political parties. Those constitutional developments were the military's response to the growing need for public participation in a government that had a streak for dominating all aspects of civil society; it was the military's attempt to weaken parliament vis-à-vis external stakeholders.

The first lesson is that protest movements, particularly when the full panoply of communication networks is used, have the potential to facilitate shared governance, to destabilize a government, to get governments to listen to and seek buy-in from other stakeholders, and, if necessary, to adjust accordingly rather than further stoke stakeholder resistance and ire. One may conclude that because Prime Minister Abhisit encouraged consistent dialogue and discussions with the leadership of protest groups, and pleaded with them to support his reconciliation program, this made a difference between the collapse of his government and its survival. At the very least, his government did not turn its back on the protesters, but reached out to them in many strategic ways. And that his government allowed demonstrations to be held on September 19 and November 19 (the latter to mark the six-month anniversary of military crackdown on Red Shirts), even though Bangkok and several other provinces were under an emergency decree that prohibited large political gatherings, is a public acknowledgement of the importance of democratic governance to the government. As Smith (2008) argues, "Public deliberation is an essential element in democratic governance. And public deliberation can only take place where there is a public sphere where large numbers of well-informed citizens can discuss problems and the variety of possible solutions to them" (p. 156). And vibrant protest groups such as the Red Shirts (or the UDD) and the Yellow Shirts (or the PAD) are critical to cultivating and nurturing active public spheres within which discussions and social networking can take place for the benefit of the entire nation.

The second lesson is that government's rhetoric should be sensitive to the possibility of the emergence of new publics—the Blue Shirts and the White Shirts—and of notable defections (à la Major General Khattiya) from the government. Protest movements result in new stakeholders and loyalties and in shifting allegiances.

Finally, government's planning efforts should be explicitly cognizant of the growing importance of relationship management, dialogue, and argumentation, all of which are critical to accomplishing the nation's communication goals and objectives. Rather than squelch the opposition and exacerbate the conflict, the deep divisions between the Red Shirts and the Yellow Shirts could have been mitigated if the government, with its high resource capacity, had sought better ways to engage in—and sustain—an open dialogue, a reasoned argumentation, and a relationship-building program with the warring parties.

Discussion Questions

1. From a crisis-communication management standpoint, how would you argue that the Thai government, as represented by the Abhisit administration, lost a tremendous opportunity to place Thailand on the map as a model practitioner of a two-way symmetrical communication model in its original Grunig and Hunt (1984) formulation?
2. Did the Red Shirts really have to organize a protest movement after all? Assume that you had been invited to counsel that group on how it could better advocate and communicate its position publicly. What new perspectives would you have offered—and why?
3. Position yourself as King Bhumibol's chief public information counselor. Engage in a point–counterpoint discussion on the following topic: King Bhumibol was plainly out of place to have taken sides of sorts with the Yellow Shirts movement.
4. This case study provides key elements in the Abhisit government's public affairs response to an ongoing crisis. Assume that there is a continuing interest to consolidate—and extend—its initial successes in managing the anti-government protests. What *additional* communication elements will you use in a plan that you are about to launch to help accomplish Abhisit's objectives? Justify each element.
5. What broader role do you envisage for third-party endorsements in political conflicts?

References

Baker, C. (2005). Pluto-populism: Thaksin and popular politics. In P. Warr (Ed.), *Thailand beyond the crisis* (pp. 107–137). Abingdon, UK: Routledge Curzon.

Beyeler, M., and Kriesi, H. (2005). Transnational protest and the public sphere. *Mobilization: An International Journal, 10*, 95–109.

Chambers, P. (2010). Thailand on the brink: Resurgent military, eroded democracy. *Asian Survey, 50*, 835–858.

Connors, M. K. (2007). *Democracy and national identity in Thailand*. London, UK: Routledge/Curzon.

Crossley, N. (2002a). Global anti-corporate struggle: A preliminary analysis. *British Journal of Sociology, 53*, 667–691.

Crossley, N. (2002b). *Making sense of social movements*. Buckingham, UK: Open University Press.

Crossley, N. (2003). Even newer social movements? Anti-corporate protests, capitalist crises and the remoralization of society. *Organization, 10*, 287–305.

Dalton, R. (1996). *Citizen politics in western democracy: Public opinion and political parties in advanced western societies*. Chatham, NJ: Chatham House.

Fisher, D. R. (2010). On social networks and social protest: Understanding the role of organizational and personal ties in large-scale protest events. In P. G. Coy (Ed.), *Research in social movements, conflicts and change, Vol. 30* (pp. 115–140). Bingley, UK: Emerald Group Publishing.

Fuchs, C. (2006). The self-organization of social movements. *Systemic Practice and Action Research, 19*, 101–137.

Glassman, J. (2011). Cracking hegemony in Thailand: Gramsci, Bourdieu and the dialectics of rebellion. *Journal of Contemporary Asia, 41*, 25–46.

Grunig, J. E., and Hunt, T. (1984). *Managing public relations*. New York: Holt, Rinehart and Winston.

Hewison, K. (2010). Thaksin Shinawatra and the reshaping of Thai politics. *Contemporary Politics, 16*, 119–133.

Klandermans, B. (1984). Mobilization and participation: Social psychological expansions of resource mobilization theory. *American Sociological Review, 49*, 583–600.

Klandermans, B. (1997). *The social psychology of protest*. Oxford, UK: Blackwell Publishers.

Klandermans, B. (2004). The demand and supply of participation: Social-psychological correlates of participation in a social movement. In D. A. Snow, S. A. Soule, and H. Kriesi (Eds.), *Blackwell companion to social movements* (pp. 360–379). Oxford, UK: Blackwell Publishing.

Martin, A. W. (2010). Movement publications as data: An assessment of an underutilized resource. In P. G. Coy (Ed.), *Research in social movements, conflicts and change, Vol. 30* (pp. 271–299). Bingley, UK: Emerald Group Publishing.

McAdam, D., McCarthy, J. D., and Zald, M. N. (Eds.). (1996). *Comparative perspectives on social movements: Political opportunities, mobilizing structures, and cultural framings*. New York: Cambridge University Press.

McCargo, D. (2000). Thailand: Crisis or reform? *Asian Affairs, 31*, 131–137.

McCargo, D., and Pathmanand, U. (2005). *The Thaksinization of Thailand*. Copenhagen: Nordic Institute of Asian Studies Press.

Minkoff, D. C., and McCarthy, J. D. (2005). Reinvigorating the study of organizational processes in social movements. *Mobilization: An International Journal, 10*, 298–308.

Oommen, T. K. (2010). Introduction: On the analysis of social movements. In T. K. Oommen (Ed.), *Social movements I: Issues of identity* (pp. 1–46). New Delhi: Oxford University Press.

Peleggi, M. (2007). *Thailand: The worldly kingdom*. London, UK: Reaktion Books Ltd.

Phongpaichit, P., and Baker, C. (2004). *Thaksin: The business of politics in Thailand*. Chiang Mai, Thailand: Silkworm Press.

Phongpaichit, P., and Baker, C. (2008). Thaksin's populism. *Journal of Contemporary Asia, 38*, 62–83.

Porta, D. D., and Diani, M. (2006). *Social movements: An introduction* (2nd. ed.). Malden, MA: Blackwell Publishers.

Prime Minister Abhisit Vejjajiva declares five-point road map for national reconciliation leading to elections by November 14, 2010. (2010, May 3). Retrieved from www.thaiembdc.org/Ann_Doc/thailandupdate05_10.pdf

Rosen, D., Kim, J. H., and Nam, Y. (2010). Birds of a feather protest together: Theorizing self-organizing political protests with flock theory. *Systemic Practice and Action Research*, 23, 419–441.

Smith, J. (2001). Globalizing resistance. *Mobilization: An International Journal*, 6, 1–20.

Smith, J. (2008). *Social movements for global democracy*. Baltimore, MD: The Johns Hopkins University Press.

Stekelenburg, J. V., and Klandermans, B. (2009). Individuals in movements: A social psychology of contention. In B. Klandermans and C. Roggeband (Eds.), *Handbook of social movements across disciplines* (pp. 157–204). New York: Springer.

Thai PM says he is seeking political resolution to opposition standoff. (2010, April 27). Retrieved from http://amanpour.blogs.cnn.com/tag/abhisit-vejjajiva/

Ulmer, R. R., Sellnow, T. L., and Seeger, M. W. (2011). *Effective crisis communication: Moving from crisis to opportunity* (2nd ed.). Thousand Oaks, CA: Sage.

Valocchi, S. (2010). *Social movements and activism in the USA*. Abingdon, UK: Routledge.

Walgrave, S., and Klandermans, B. (2010). Open and close mobilization patterns: The role of channels and ties. In S. Walgrave and D. Rucht (Eds.), *The world says no to war: Demonstrations against the war on Iraq* (pp. 169–193). Minneapolis, MN: University of Minnesota Press.

Walgrave, S., and Rucht, D. (2010). Introduction. In S. Walgrave and D. Rucht (Eds.), *The world says no to war: Demonstrations against the war on Iraq* (pp. xiii–xxvi). Minneapolis, MN: University of Minnesota Press.

Ward, J. C., and Ostrom, A. L. (2006). Complaining to the masses: The role of protest framing in customer-created complaint web sites. *Journal of Consumer Research*, 33, 220–230.

VIEWS FROM AN EXPERT

BERTIL LINTNER

Bertil Lintner, a Swedish citizen who has been living in Thailand since 1979, is Asia correspondent for the Swedish daily Svenska Dagbladet, *and a contributor to* Jane's Information Group *in the United Kingdom, as well as to several regional publications in Asia. He is a former correspondent for the* Far Eastern Economic Review *and the author of 10 books on Asian politics. His work in English can be viewed at www.asiapacificms.com*

Soldiers attempting to keep the peace on the streets and protesters clamoring for democracy—the scenes are reminiscent of those of October 1973, when students and others took to the streets of Bangkok, forced the country's then-military rulers into exile, and ushered in a new, but brief, period of democracy in Thailand. Three years later, the dictators returned, resulting in a new wave of protests, which were brutally crushed. In May 1992, hundreds of thousands of people protested against the appointment of an unelected general, Suchinda Kraprayoon, as prime minister. Scores were killed, but Suchinda was forced to resign.

There are fundamental differences between those upheavals and events in 2010 and 2009. The 1973, 1976, and 1992 protests were genuine anti-authoritarian uprisings that enjoyed broad popular support. The military opened fire on unarmed demonstrators. In 2010, the Red Shirt movement—the popular name for the United Front for Democracy against Dictatorship (UDD)—had its own black-clad commandoes, and soldiers and policemen were killed as well. UDD activists threatened journalists and others; some were injured. The UDD also had, and still has, solid financial backing from former Prime Minister Thaksin Shinawatra and some of his business associates.

And it is not, as depicted by an almost unanimous chorus of the international media, a struggle between the "haves" and the "have nots." While the top three leaders of the UDD all come from southern Thailand, where there are also many poor people, the movement has no base there at all and its influence in Bangkok and the central provinces is limited. It is largely a regional phenomenon with its main stronghold in the northeast. The north, where Thaksin comes from, is bitterly divided between pro- and anti-Thaksin forces, probably equally strong, as reflected in recent by-elections.

The clash in Thailand should be described as a clash between two oligarchies. On one side is the traditional elite, consisting of the old Sino-Thai plutocracy that for years had enjoyed a symbiotic and mutually beneficial relationship with the military, bureaucracy and monarchy. On the other is the nouveau-riche elite that began to emerge during the Vietnam War era, when the economy took off and culminated in the boom of the 1980s. Lacking the political connections of the old elite, Thaksin and his business associates built up their own power base by forming the Thai Rak Thai Party in 1998. Hardly by coincidence, Thaksin, a telecommunications tycoon and a multi-billionaire, entered politics in the early 1990s after he lost some lucrative contracts to one of the politically better-connected old elite companies.

Thaksin launched a string of populist policies, which won him many admirers in certain parts of the country. His party won spectacular victories in the 2001 and 2005 elections, but once in power, he was anything but democratic. Thaksin tried to stifle the media, silence critics of his regime—and launched a vicious "war on drugs" that claimed more than 2,000 lives in extrajudicial executions. Provinces where his party had not won were threatened with fewer subsidies from the central government.

But it was the clash with the old elite that became his downfall. Ousted in a military coup in September 2006, he now spends most of his time in Dubai, Montenegro, and Russia, but still commands his forces back home in Thailand. Just before the most recent wave of unrest in March–May 2010, he told his followers over a video link that "I'm going to fill your pockets with money. I have plans for your children's education." In more recent "phone-ins" to meetings in the northeast, he promised to resolve the poverty in that part of the country "in no time at all." Rather than being a movement by the poor, Thaksin has successfully managed to capitalize on social injustices in the country, and on genuine grievances.

It is not only Thaksin's democratic credentials that are weak, to say the least. The main UDD leader, Jatuporn Promphan, served as a cabinet secretary in Thaksin's government, and, in 2003, he and other officials ordered 1,000 police to retake a large tract of land in the south, which had been taken over by poor farmers. They accused the government of leasing land to big oil palm producers instead of redistributing it to the farmers. Jatuporn defended the police action, saying the peasants were "armed" and "broke the law." When Thai Rak Thai's successor, the People's Power Party, won the December 2007 election, it chose as its prime minister Samak Sundaravej, a right-wing politician who had played a prominent role in suppressing the student movements in the 1970s. Thai Rak Thai's last incarnation, Pheu Thai, had announced that its candidate for the premiership was Chalerm Yubamrung, a traditional *chao pho* or "godfather," and one of Thailand's most controversial politicians with an extremely checkered past.

Whatever the outcome of the present crisis, the future for Thai democracy looks bleak. In fact, a country that only a few years ago was a pillar of economic and political stability risks becoming a failed state. This frightening scenario—rather than whether the UDD will succeed in bringing the government down—can only be thwarted if Thailand gets solid, independent state institutions that can handle a crisis like this one—and bridge the gap between various elites, different parts of the country, as well as society's rich and poor.

Section 3
Australia

Australia

Victoria Burning: Confronting the 2009 Catastrophic Bushfires in Australia

Christopher Galloway and Kwamena Kwansah-Aidoo

Introduction

In February, 2009, a series of devastating fires, the worst of which occurred on February 7—since known as "Black Saturday"—roared through vulnerable communities in Victoria, Australia. The eventual death toll was 173, with estimates of more than a million animals dead, and widespread property damage and destruction. The financial cost has been calculated at more than $4 billion. The fires were not only a crisis for the individuals and communities in harm's way, but also for the Victoria state government and its emergency services agencies. In the cauldron of the conflagrations, serious problems were revealed in these agencies' responses, producing not only a physical, emotional, and financial crisis but also significant reputation and legitimacy issues for the government. Because the fires created complex, multilayered issues in Victoria, this study concentrates on only one key area: communication strategy.

Background of the Crisis

Victoria, Australia's second most populous state, has "a long, sometimes devastating history of fire" (2009 Victorian Bushfires Royal Commission, 2010, p. 3). Regarded as one of the world's most bushfire-prone regions, in the world's driest inhabited continent, Victoria had experienced disastrous fires in 1983, in which 47 people died, and fires in 2003 and 2006–7, which burned 1.3 million and 1.1 million hectares of land respectively. In late January, 2009, the state sweltered through one of its most severe and prolonged heatwaves, which in itself resulted in the deaths of more than twice as many people as died in the subsequent fires (Maslen, 2010, para. 5). In the capital, Melbourne, temperatures topped 43°C (109.4°F) for three consecutive days for the first time since records began, reaching 46.4°C (115.52°F) on 7 February (2009 Victorian Bushfires Royal Commission, 2010, p.2). The Premier, Hon. John Brumby (MP), described the state as "tinder dry." On Saturday, 7 February, very dry fuels in forest and bushland and strong surface winds—reaching storm force during the day—produced particularly destructive fires. The Fire Danger Index (FDI), a measure of fire weather and the risk of a bushfire starting, has a scale of 0–100. On 7 February, it registered 328. Direct fire suppression is considered difficult above an FDI of 50 and impossible above 100. Together, the fires produced one of Australia's worst natural disasters, causing the deaths of 173 people and devastating entire rural and urban fringe communities.

On what quickly became known as "Black Saturday," emergency services attended or patrolled 316 fires of different types. In a number of cases, fires spread so rapidly they could not be contained by responding ground crews (2009 Victorian Bushfires Royal Commission, 2010, pp. 2–3). During the crisis, emergency controllers responded as best they could in conditions of rapid, uncontrollable fire progress, incomplete information and stretched resources, but later analysis also revealed deficiencies in responses that led to the resignations of four top officials and other organizational changes.

Black Saturday became a crisis of legitimacy for the state government as a whole and for the individual emergency agencies for which the state is responsible. In terms of how extensively their activities were covered in mass media reports, the most prominent of the agencies are the Department of Sustainability and Environment, which manages fire on Victoria's 7.6 million hectares of public land (roughly one-third of the state); the Country Fire Authority, one of the world's largest volunteer-based emergency services organizations, part-funded by the state government, reporting to the Minister of Police and Emergency Services; and Victoria Police. All three organizations have emergency-related responsibilities, while the premier, as the state's top politician, also had a leadership role.

In the aftermath of the devastation, the state government established a Royal Commission. Its mandate included reviewing the preparation and planning before the fires as well as all aspects of responses to the fires themselves (2009 Victorian Bushfires Royal Commission, 2010, p. 3). The government also set up a Bushfires Reconstruction Authority to oversee all aspects of recovery and rebuilding.

Situation Analysis

The key stakeholders for this crisis included:

- more than 78 communities directly affected (Country Fire Authority, n.d., para. 2);
- emergency responders dealing with the fires themselves and with the effects, such as arranging shelter for people whose homes had been burned;
- emergency organizations' leaders;
- the premier;
- mass media (local and international); and
- Victorians with family or friends in affected areas.

Although these were key stakeholders, in one sense it seemed that all Victorians were involved: everyone seemed to know someone who was affected in some way. Smoke from the bushfires drifted across unburnt and urban areas, bringing the scent of disaster to those removed from its immediate impact.

Initial Response

The Bushfires Royal Commission noted that

> The response to the fires on 7 February was characterised by many people trying to do their best in extraordinarily difficult circumstances ... Nevertheless, some poor decisions were made by people in positions of responsibility and by individuals seeking to protect their own safety.
> (2009 Victorian Bushfires Royal Commission, 2010, p. 4)

The initial response was to:

- deploy more than 4,000 firefighters to fire-affected areas;
- mobilize humanitarian responses, including an appeal for funds to aid affected people and wildlife;
- extend media news bulletins to cover the unfolding devastation;
- set up a message board at the Australian Broadcasting Corporation, to offer or request help (this was inundated with replies); and
- use Twitter to post updates.

Goals and Objectives

The Victorian State Government did not specify goals and objectives for its crisis communication. However, we infer that its overall goal was related to reputation:

- To present the government's response as timely, appropriate, and effective in the circumstances.

We infer that specific objectives were:

- to ensure that threatened communities received appropriate information about fire spread in time to act upon it;
- to ensure that affected communities were aware of the support and assistance available both during the fires and afterwards;
- to ensure that emergency services were communicating effectively both internally among themselves and to stakeholders;
- to position Premier Brumby and emergency services leaders as providing appropriate leadership in the face of fires whose severity and scale far exceeded worst case planning scenarios; and
- to assure the entire Victorian community that affected and threatened communities were being appropriately protected and supported.

As later analysis indicated, neither the goal nor the specific objectives were fully attained and in some cases, such as ensuring that threatened communities received timely warnings, performance fell well short of what residents expected—and needed.

Strategies and Tactics

Before Black Saturday

Strategy 1: Set expectations.

Tactic: The government sought to prepare Victorians for the worst by setting expectations in advance, through statements made by the premier, John Brumby. On February 6, 2009, he advised Victorians to cancel whatever plans they might have had for the following day, telling them to prepare for what was expected to be

> the worst day in the history of the state . . . It's just as bad a day as you can imagine and on top of that the state is just tinder-dry . . . If you don't need to go out, don't go out, it's a seriously bad day . . . Don't go on the roads. If you don't need to use the public transport system, don't use it. If you can stay at home, stay at home. If you've got relatives who are elderly, if you've got friends, if you've got neighbours, please call on them. Ring them . . . it's going to be a terrible day for anyone who is ill or who is old.
>
> (Moncrief, 2009)

After Black Saturday

Strategy 2: Present problems as systemic rather than owing to individual organizational failures.

Tactic: After the Bushfires Royal Commission criticized failures of leadership by the police minister and the chief commissioner of Police, and the head of the Country Fire Authority, Premier Brumby—for the first time—apologized. "There were system failures on that day and for that all of us who were involved from me [sic] we're obviously sorry those systems failed" (McMahon and Ross, 2010). However, this apology was delivered more than a year after the events to which it related. While Mr Brumby's own leadership and empathy attracted "deserved acclaim" (Austin, 2010, para. 9), the government he led was criticized for a history of ignoring recommendations about how to make Victoria safer from bushfires. For example, in 2006 the government had been advised to upgrade a bushfire information line, while in 2007 and 2008 it was advised to upgrade the 000 emergency line (the equivalent of 911 in the USA, or 999 in the UK). Neither upgrade occurred; and on Black Saturday, around 80 percent of calls to the bushfire information line went unanswered because of insufficient staff.

Because of this poor record, the Bushfire Royal Commissioners said there should be an independent monitor to report on the implementation of their recommendations (Austin, 2009). Further, this strategy may have been intended to deflect attention from individual failures. For example, the Victoria Police Chief Commissioner, Christine Nixon, left the emergency coordination center despite being told it was likely that Victorians had been killed. She went home and then had dinner with friends. Subsequently she tried to justify her decision by saying, "I had to eat," before later apologizing for her action ("Christine Nixon apologises," 2010, para. 12). Premier Brumby himself said that Ms. Nixon should have stayed at the incident control center ("Christine Nixon apologises," 2010).

Strategy 3: Position the disaster as so overwhelming as to exceed the limits of reasonable planning and preparation.

Tactic: The government used a dramatic metaphor to underscore the exceptional nature of the complex cauldron of risks and crises facing emergency services in order to minimize the perceived organizational failure. Speaking on February 9, Premier Brumby said:

> What broke over the state was like a tsunami. It didn't matter how good people's fire plans were. When the wind changed—particularly around Kinglake [one of the worst affected townships]—when it came back up the hill there was nothing that anybody could have done. It wouldn't have mattered if you had 1000 tankers there.
>
> (Austin, 2009, paras. 10–13)

This tactic was necessary, because commentators such as blogger Guy Rundle were claiming that "some or many [deaths] were caused by a fatal paralysis of action and initiative, a sheer lack of audacity and leadership, an inability to take control in a situation which has totally engulfed and undermined any notion of normality" (Rundle, 2010, para. 10).

Strategy 4: Direct attention to the future while aiming to be seen as making an effective response in the present.

Tactic: Speaking on February 10, Premier Brumby made it clear that the inflow of donations for relief and recovery from around the world meant that money would not be an issue when it came time to rebuild fire-ravaged communities (the appeal eventually raised more than $A379 million). Mr Brumby commented: "I've made it clear, and the [Federal] Prime Minister has made

it clear . . . that we will do whatever it takes to rebuild these communities."
He continued:

> And I've got to say I think that is the aspiration of Victorians as well. We've
> already seen . . . more than $30 million in donations to the bushfire relief
> fund and it's only been operating for less than 48 hours. So, money is not
> the issue for us, it's making sure that we get this right.
>
> ("Money no issue," 2009)

The Victorian Bushfire Reconstruction and Recovery Authority (VBRRA)
was established on the same day, February 10, by the Federal and Victorian
governments ("About the Victorian Bushfire Reconstruction and Recovery
Authority," n.d., para. 3).

Outcomes Assessment

The Brumby government's response may have contributed to its defeat at the
state election in November 2010, when a coalition government under Ted
Baillieu took power in a close election. Political commentator Paul Austin
noted that Baillieu had been "chipping away at Brumby's credibility on
bushfire safety" and that "The problem for the [then] Premier is that as the
evidence has come in, it has vindicated Baillieu's position" (Austin, 2010,
paras. 12 and 13).

A delay in apologizing for the failures of the state's emergency services
management on Black Saturday may have played a part in Mr Brumby's defeat:
It was not until August 1, 2010, that he personally apologized to Victorians.
He commented:

> There are many people who in hindsight should have done things
> differently on that day. There were system failures . . . and for that all of
> us who were involved from me [sic] we're very obviously sorry those
> systems failed. And I personally feel the weight of responsibility to get the
> arrangements and system right for the future so that we never again see
> a repeat of those circumstances on February 7.
>
> (McMahon and Ross, 2010, paras. 6–8)

As one might expect with a complex, multilevel crisis such as the Victorian
fires, the state government's strategies achieved mixed success. The strategy
of setting expectations may have helped many Victorians to be at least mentally
prepared for the devastation of Black Saturday—but in many cases, the
preparation did not seem to go far enough: analysis of research reports
presented to the Bushfires Royal Commission has shown a significant gap
between people's intentions and their actions. One study found that in three
districts where a Code Red day had been declared (the highest level of fire

danger) two-thirds of residents were at home on the day. Of the third that were not at home, only 1.5 percent left because it was a Code Red day (Whittaker and Handmer, 2010).

Presenting problems as systemic left the government open to calls for system change. Some change has occurred, such as the appointment of a fire services commissioner and state controller to assume overall command of fire management. This was a necessary development: one crisis management expert opined that the Victorian bushfires had shown how confusion in leadership could have disastrous effects (Atfield, 2010, para. 2). But focus on systemic issues not only resulted in personnel changes; it also highlighted the authorities' failure to adequately respond to the ramifications of previous fire disasters. One environmentalist, concerned about the way public land is managed to minimize fire risk, commented: "Apart from the terrible human and animal suffering from the continuing bushfire crisis in Victoria, the tragedy of this event is the failure of public land managers to heed lessons already learned from past holocausts" (Rheese, 2009, para. 1; see also www.firecrisis.com/royal-commission-into-victorian-bushfires-14-09-09/w1/i1061253/ para. 2). However, it was not just the authorities who failed to heed past experience: one academic commented that Victorians themselves had refused to learn the lessons from past bushfires (Buxton, 2010).

The government's approach of presenting the disaster as so overwhelming as to exceed the limits of reasonable planning and preparation was understandable in the cauldron of the immediate crisis. The total of fatalities put Victoria's bushfires in the top ten of bushfire crises ever recorded any-where (Cameron et al., 2009). However, the approach appeared less reasonable under the scrutiny of the Bushfires Royal Commission. Of the Commission's 67 recommendations, only five related directly to the Commonwealth Government ("Commonwealth response," 2010); the others addressed the Commission's views on what the state government should do. Equally, the strategy of directing attention to the future while aiming to be seen as making an effective response in the present fell short: the unprecedented toll of people, property, animals, and bushland resulted in intense scrutiny of what happened and why. While this scrutiny resulted in various plans and proposals for the future, it meant that the government could not avoid having to respond to criticism of its past performance.

That performance needed adjustment in certain areas, according to the Bushfires Royal Commission, which called for a change in fire and emergency services' priorities in dealing with especially fierce bushfires:

> The most fierce fires call for a different approach to community safety, for different advice, support and responses from fire agencies. On such days, if the initial attack fails to contain a fire, the operational focus and mindset of fire agencies should move to providing information and attending to community safety, rather than fire suppression.
> (2009 Victorian Bushfires Royal Commission, 2010, p. 5)

Lessons Learned

The 2009 bushfires crisis had many elements, ranging from communication issues to on-the-ground fire management practices to organizational structures and accountabilities, to community infrastructure problems and individual citizens' diverse interpretations of the dangers facing them and the nature and effectiveness of the warnings about these risks. Therefore, the lessons to be learned are too many for all to be dealt with here. However, focusing on communication, some points emerge:

- Communication is central to pre-crisis, crisis event, and post-crisis management.

Yet it is not communication as such that is important but rather, communication that motivates people to act. They need not only information sufficiency, that is, enough information about the risk to make them feel in control of it (Griffin et al., 2004), but also instructing information (Coombs, 2007) that tells them specifically what they should do. There were "prior warnings and 'estimative forecasts' that could have been heeded" (Burns and Eltham, 2010, p. 97), had the communication been succinct enough.

- For communication to be effective, it has to be timely and must reach its intended audience.

Examples abound of instances on Black Saturday where urgent information about the imminent fire danger did not reach residents on time. In one instance, Kissane (2010, pp. 86–89, 170–171) reports that the Urgent Threat Message for Kinglake issued at 4.10 p.m. was delayed by internal coordination problems and broadcast by ABC Radio at 4.43 p.m. and then published online at 5.55 p.m. A minimum of 33 precious minutes was lost which could have made the difference between life and death for some. As Kissane puts it: "Small decisions separated the survivors from bushfire victims, and that involved chance, hazard and luck" (p. 144). In another example, Burns and Eltham (2010, p. 97), recount the case of Kevin Tolhurst, the fire simulation expect who was at CFA headquarters on February 7, actively forecasting the spread and severity of the Kilmore East fire. "But his warnings never reached key fire controllers because of breakdowns in the CFA's communications and decision-making process" (Bushfires Royal Commission, 2009, p. 256). There is no substitute for clear communication, delivered to the target audience at the precise time of need during a crisis and the lack of it, as this case has shown, can have catastrophic effects.

- Authorities must understand what constitutes effective communication *from the point of view of the message recipients*.

As the Bushfires Royal Commission noted:

> Advice about bushfires must also be provided to the community in a way that engages them . . . It is essential that there be a continued focus on providing frank and meaningful advice about the risks and what is required to adequately prepare for and survive a bushfire. (2009 Victorian Bushfires Royal Commission, 2010, p. 6)

- If the crisis is sufficiently severe (affecting a high number of people with major property damage) it is not possible to deflect attention to the future until the immediate past has been analyzed.

In the case of crises with severe impact on people and the environment, individuals will not "move on" and refocus fully on the future until explanations have been offered and blame, where appropriate, has been assigned. In this sense, for the state government, the crisis was protracted considerably beyond the immediate crisis events by media coverage of Commission hearings and of recovery efforts. The media reports served to recapitulate central issues in the crisis, such as the government's bushfire safety policy, thereby underscoring difficulties and dilemmas as well as highlighting government initiatives to support recovery efforts.

- Publics expect authorities to keep them safe but differ as to how that should be done.

As Heath and O'Hair note, "society is organized on the rationale of collective risk management" (2009, p. 19). On this basis, many if not all citizens expect authorities to help keep them safe. While the Victorian state government did have plans, policies, and procedures in place to manage bushfire risk and response, they fell short in the face of the furious onslaught of the Black Saturday conflagrations. The resulting attributions of blame were not unique to this case: as Bushnell and Cottrell report, "The government . . . is often blamed in the event of a bushfire" (2007, p. 34). Citing a 2002 study by Odgers and Rhodes, Bushnell and Cottrell commented that, "there appears to be a general public opinion that governments are ineffective in their efforts to mitigate bushfire" (p. 34).

While traditionally bushfire risk reduction was the responsibility of government and government agencies, more recently there have been moves to place more responsibility on the public's shoulders (Winter and Fried, 2000, in Bushnell and Cottrell, 2007, p. 3). Studies have shown that people do perceive some level of personal responsibility, with only a minority seeing the government solely responsible for protection (Bushnell and Cottrell, 2007, p. 16). But "although there is the general expectation that governments need to take action, which actions and to what extent can vary considerably from person to person and area to area" (Bushnell and Cottrell, 2007, p. 29).

The Bushfires Royal Commission recognized that responsibility for preparing for fire and improving people's safety is a shared one, involving individuals, fire agencies and governments (2009 Victorian Bushfires Royal Commission, 2010, p. 2). But in the view of one researcher, some of its recommendations "reverse the trend to shift most of the responsibility onto the people at risk." Recommendations for refuges or shelters were "probably well aligned with community expectations" (J. Handmer, in "Rapid roundup," 2010, para. 2).

Communities, therefore, may adjust their expectations of governments in the light of a disaster experience, especially an unprecedented one such as the 2009 fires, as they recognize the limits to their own ability to prepare for and mitigate the risks of a major bushfire.

Discussion Questions

1. The Victorian state government was dealing with a disaster that was far worse than its regular bushfire planning envisaged. If you had been Premier Brumby's media adviser, what key messages would you have suggested he use?
2. Do you think that in order to reduce confusion, the state government and its agencies should have attempted to coordinate their messaging about the development of the fires and their impacts?
3. In a crisis with a natural disaster at its center, should the authorities use only one spokesperson, such as the premier?
4. In a crisis such as the Victorian bushfire case, should authorities take entire responsibility for what happened, or should they publicly state that their responsibility has limits—citizens need to play a part, too?

References

2009 Victorian Bushfires Royal Commission (2010). *Final report*. Melbourne: 2009 Victorian Bushfires Royal Commission.

About the Victorian Bushfire Reconstruction and Recovery Authority. (n.d.). Retrieved from www.wewillrebuild.vic.gov.au/about-us.html

Atfield, C. (2010). Flood warnings: "Learn the lessons of Victorian bushfires", 15 October. Retrieved from www.brisbanetimes.com.au/environment/weather/flood-warnings-learn-the-lessons-of-victorian-bushfires-20101015-16myg.html

Austin, P. (2009). Brumby announces Royal Commission into bushfires, 9 February. Retrieved from www.theage.com.au/national/brumby-announces-royal-commission-into-bushfires-20090209-81zx.html

Austin, P. (2010). Strength in Baillieu's stride as bushfire critique trips Brumby, 12 August. Retrieved from www.theage.com.au/opinion/politics/strength-in-baillieus-stride-as-bushfire-critique-trips-brumby-20100811-11zni.html

Burns, A., and Eltham, B (2010). "Catastrophic failure" theories: Evaluating media explanations of the Black Saturday bushfires. *Media International Australia*, *137*, 90–99.

Bushnell, S., and Cottrell, A. (2007). *Living with bushfires: What do people expect?* Townsville: Centre for Disaster Studies, James Cook University.

Buxton, M. (2010). Next generation needs action now. *The Age*, Melbourne, August 5. Retrieved from www.cfa.vic.gov.au/about/history/about_black_saturday.htm

Cameron, P. A., Mitra, B., Fitzgerald, M., Scheinkestel, C. D., Stripp, A., Batey, C., Niggemeyer, L., Truesdale, M., Holman, P., Mehra, R., Wasiak, J., and Cleland, H. (2009). Black Saturday: The immediate impact of the February 2009 bushfires in Victoria, Australia. *The Medical Journal of Australia, 191*(1), 11–16. Retrieved from www.mja.com.au/public/issues/191. . ./cam10194_fm.html

Christine Nixon apologises for dining out on evening of Black Saturday. (2010, 7 April). Retrieved from www.news.com.au/national/christine-nixon-apologises-for-dining-out-on-evening-of-black-saturday/story-e6frfkvr-1225851139175

Commonwealth response to the Final Report of the Victorian Bushfires Royal Commission. (2010, October 25). Retrieved from www.jennymacklin.fahcsia.gov.au/mediareleases/2010/Pages/cwlth_resp_vic_bushfires_25oct10.aspx

Coombs, W. T. (2007). Crisis management and communications. Retrieved from http://ucf.academia.edu/TimothyCoombs/Papers/302066/Crisis_Management_and_Communications

Country Fire Authority (n.d.). About Black Saturday 2009. Retrieved from www.cfa.vic.gov.au/about/history/about_black_saturday.htm

Griffin, R. J., Neuwirth, K., Dunwoody, S., and Giese, J. (2004). Information sufficiency and risk communication. *Media Psychology, 6*(1), 23–61.

Heath, R. L., and O'Hair, H. D. (2009). The significance of crisis and risk communication. In R. L. Heath, and H. D. O'Hair, (Eds.), *Handbook of risk and crisis communication* (pp. 5–30). New York and London: Routledge.

Kissane, K. (2010). *Worst of days*. Sydney: Hachette Australia.

Maslen, G. (2010). *Victoria vulnerable as heat rises*, 6 December. Retrieved from www.theage.com.au/victoria/victoria-vulnerable-as-heat-rises-20101205-18lc8.html

McMahon, S., and Ross, N. (2010). Premier John Brumby expresses sorrow over Black Saturday, 1 August. Retrieved from www.heraldsun.com.au/news/special-reports/black-saturday-royal-commission-releases-final-report/story-e6frf8zx-1225899489577

Moncrief, M. (2009). "Worst day in history": Brumby warns of fire danger, 6 February. Retrieved from www.theage.com.au/national/worst-day-in-history-brumby-warns-of-fire-danger-20090206–7zf1.html

"Money no issue" in bushfire rebuild: Brumby (2009, 11 February). Retrieved from www.abc.net.au/news/stories/2009/02/11/2487945.htm

Rapid roundup: Victorian bushfires Royal Commission experts respond (2010). Australian Science Media Centre, 31 July. Retrieved from www.aussmc.org/2010/07/rapid-roundup-victorian-bushfires-royal-commission-experts-respond/

Rheese, M. (2009). Lessons not yet learned: A bushfire tragedy. AEF Online. Retrieved from http://aefweb.info/articles68.html

Rundle, G. (2010). Nixon should resign—but so should Brumby, 8 April. Retrieved from http://blogs.crikey.com.au/thestump/2010/04/08/nixon-should-resign-but-so-should-brumby/

Whittaker, J., and Handmer, J. (2010). Community bushfire safety: A review of post-Black Saturday research. *The Australian Journal of Emergency Management, 25*(4), 7–13.

VIEWS FROM AN EXPERT

TONY JAQUES

Dr Tony Jaques is an internationally recognized authority on issue and crisis management who was living in Melbourne on Black Saturday. He has been widely published around the world and is a leading champion of the concept that prevention and crisis preparedness are critical elements of crisis management. He teaches in the Masters programme at RMIT University Melbourne, and is founding Director of the consultancy Issue Outcomes (www.issueoutcomes. com.au)

The bushfires of Black Saturday—7 February 2009—were a devastating event for the State of Victoria, and Australia's worst natural disaster in terms of lives lost.

But for communications professionals and students, the sad truth is that many of the lessons to be learned were the same old problems, repeated again and again. As Shrivastava (1988), has noted, the one thing more tragic than the crises that occur is the failure of organizations and organizational scholars to learn from them. And the same idea was later expressed by Stocker, who commented that when you look at the majority of crises that occur, what happened should have been on or near the top of the list of possible events. "Why," he asked, "wasn't anyone prepared?" (1997, p. 192).

It is often argued that a crisis—by definition—is a situation out of control, when managers and other leaders find that normal systems and processes are unable to cope with events. This was certainly true for communication on the day of the bushfire, when there was a failure of message content—providing information and advice quickly and effectively—and also a failure of the physical communication system itself, which simply did not work under the stress of the crisis.

There are some basic principles that apply to just about every crisis, and the Victorian Bushfires highlighted three of those important factors—that most crises are not unexpected, that most crises are followed by a hunt for scapegoats, and that iconic images often come to symbolize the event.

Research around the world shows that the majority of crises are not sudden, unexpected events at all, but are preceded by a string of "red flags" and other warning signs. After any crisis there are always people who will start to talk about how they saw the warning signs and—often—that no one would pay attention. This was certainly the case with the Victorian Bushfire, and communicators need to be ready for the fact that such revelations will almost inevitably surface and plans need to be put in place to respond.

There is an old saying that the hunt for someone to blame is always successful, and every crisis is very quickly followed by the hunt for scapegoats, sometimes while the crisis event is still under way. The bushfires highlighted that it is very easy for the media and the public to rush to judgment on who to blame. In this case one of the key leaders failed to understand that it is not just a question of who is in charge, but who is *seen* to be in charge. That mistake cost the former chief commissioner of police her career and her reputation. The role of communicators is certainly not to cover up wrongdoing or failure of leaders, but there is a very important role in providing sound advice to leaders, and in providing balanced information to help the public properly understand what happened and who was responsible.

In the same way that every crisis leads to a hunt for scapegoats, every crisis always throws up highly visible symbols that become iconic images of the event. These symbols may be negative, like oft-repeated footage of a leader stumbling over basic facts, or positive, like a rescued victim being carried to safety.

For the bushfires, one of the most memorable images was a firefighter pausing to share his water bottle with an orphaned koala. This iconic photograph spread around the world and came to symbolize humanity in the midst of disaster. Good communicators understand the difference between "photo ops" designed for the vanity of politicians and managers, and truly effective moments that progress the story. Every crisis will produce iconic images, and the communicator can help determine whether these images are positive or negative. The orphaned koala, and the high-profile priority on rebuilding community halls and schools destroyed in the fire rather than houses and shops, provide a reminder that communication is about a lot more than just words.

References

Shrivastava, P. (1988). Industrial crisis management: Learning from organizational failures. *Journal of Management Studies*, 25(4), 283–284.

Stocker, K. P. (1997). Strategic approach to crisis management. In C. L. Caywood (Ed.), *The handbook of strategic public relations and integrated communications*, (pp. 189–203). New York: McGraw-Hill.

Section 4

Europe

England

"Climategate": UK Climate Researchers' E-mails Cast Doubt on Scientific Support for Global Warming

Doug A. Newsom

The Climate Research Unit (CRU) at the University of East Anglia in Norwich, United Kingdom, is recognized as one of the world's leading institutions on climate change. CRU pioneered research using tree rings, anthropogenic climate change studies, and historical reports on natural environments around the world before thermometers and other scientific measurement tools were available to evaluate the patterns of climate change. Since the CRU has its own code for analysis, which it refuses to share, a scandal arose when the unauthorized publication of internal emails, just before the 2009 Intergovernmental Panel on Climate Change (IPCC) in Copenhagen was to meet, created doubt about the authenticity of its findings. External audits that failed to find CRU responsible for misleading researchers and the public, were rejected so that reverberations from "Climategate," as it was called in the UK, continued into 2010. Then in 2011, just before the international meeting in Durban, South Africa, thousands more messages, apparently from the same, original source, were made public, to little consequence. The crisis continues.

Introduction

Recognized as one of the world's leading institutions on climate change, the Climate Research Unit (CRU) at the University of East Anglia in Norwich, United Kingdom, incorporates research using tree rings, anthropogenic climate change studies, and historical reports on natural environments around the world before thermometers and other scientific measurement tools were available to evaluate the patterns of climate change. The CRU developed its own code for analysis and refused to share it. When computer hackers accessed the CRU computers, they got a treasure trove of e-mails and documents that revealed damaging communication between British and U.S. climate scientists involved with the Intergovernmental Panel on Climate Change (IPCC). The scandal, known as "Climategate," not only cast doubt on scientific support for global warming, it also highlighted the triumph of politics over science in policy decisions affecting global warming.

Background of the Crisis

Critics of scientific evidence for global warming found support for their accusations of false conclusions from "bad science," after documents and personal e-mails between scientists working in the CRU at the University of East Anglia in Norwich, United Kingdom, were posted online on November 20, 2009. Hackers were assumed to be involved. However, on December 10, 2009, Lord Christopher Monckton, adviser to CFACT, an organization that "defends the environment and human welfare through facts, news and analysis," said the e-mails were released by a "whistleblower" insider, not obtained by a hacker (CFACT NEWS: All pain no gain, 2009, December 7).

More than 1,000 private e-mail messages and other documents between CRU Director Phil Jones and other CRU staff were captured—leaked or hacked. Information drawn from the captured material resulted in allegations that the scientists had manipulated data to support global warming. The CRU responded to the e-mail situation on November 23 and issued a follow-up on November 24, 2009. Excerpts from the electronic break-in reinforced critics of human beings as major contributors to climate change at a critical time, 15 days before the December 7, 2009, conference in Copenhagen, Denmark, to reach an international accord on controlling carbon emissions. Extractions from the e-mails seemed to support critics' accusations of manipulation of data and exaggeration of findings being used to create a global alarmist agenda (University of East Anglia CRU Update 1, Update 2, 2010).

In Copenhagen, CFACT attended the conference to brief attendees on its perspectives. On December 7, a video filmed at Berlin's Melia Hotel on December 4 at a climate conference sponsored by CFACT and some European think tanks was released. The lead in the CFACT news release about the video said:

> Lord Christopher Monckton appears today in a powerful new video by CFACT in which he exposes the deception involved in Climategate, scientist by scientist. These scientists received more than $21 million in public funding, yet used deception to ensure that real world data did not interfere with the selling of global warming.
> (CFACT News: All pain no gain, 2009, December 10)

CFACT Executive Director Craig Rucker said:

> When you listen to Chris Monckton clearly, logically and succinctly take you through what transpired at the University of East Anglia, it's like having a bucket of cold water thrown in your face. ... These scientists whom Lord Monckton exposes using tricks in place of science are no bit players ... (t)hese scientists are founding fathers of global warming and their credibility now lies in tatters.
> (CFACT News: All pain no gain, 2009, December 7)

Why and How it Occurred

Political effort to discredit evidence of global warming obviously was the objective, but exactly how the e-mails were captured is not known with any certainty. In the November 20, 2009 release, the message was "... random selection of correspondence and documents too important to be kept under wraps" (Searle, 2010).

Situation Analysis: Consequences

The CRU was not aware that its electronic communication system had been compromised until the e-mails were released, which occurred shortly before the United Nations Climate Change Summit in Copenhagen on December 7, 2009. At this fifteenth summit, the goal was to replace the Kyoto Protocol, which the USA never signed, with a binding global agreement on greenhouse gas emissions. After two weeks, there was only a nonbinding agreement by 193 of the attending parties to keep the rise in global average temperatures under 2°C (3.6°F). There also was an agreement to provide $30 billion short-term aid to less developed countries until 2012 (Allaby, 2010, p. 237).

Because one of Director Jones's e-mails said he used a "trick" to "hide the decline" (in global warming) by splicing together proxy temperatures and instruments data, CRU scientists were criticized for providing a misleading figure for the front cover of the 1999 World Meteorological Organization's report. It wasn't the technique itself that was the problem, but not labeling it was, according to the investigating panel's report (Adam 2010). That is not likely to have helped CRU's cause, though, as Jones's choice of the word "trick" certainly suggests intent to mislead (University of East Anglia CRU Update 1: Comment from Jones, 2009).

Priority Publics/Stakeholders

Major:

- University of East Anglia (administration and scientists working with the CRU).
- Intergovernmental Panel on Climate Change (IPCC).
- UK government (the university is publicly funded).
- UN summit on climate change, country participants.
- News media in UK, especially *The Guardian*—founded 1821, owned by Foundation, The Scott Trust, second largest English language online newspaper (*New York Times* is first). Has a sister Sunday broadsheet, *The Observer*, both owned by the Guardian Media Group. Additionally: BBC News, Reuters, *The Times*, *Daily Telegraph*.
- UK bloggers.

Others:

- World Meteorological Organization.
- London-based International Institute for Environment and Development.
- Grantham Institute of the Imperial College of London.
- Editors of scientific journals in the field.
- U.S. climate researchers.
- UN World Economic and Social Survey.
- World Bank.
- U.S. Congress.
- Worldwide organizations involved in the green movement.
- Worldwide climate control research scientists.
- Critics of global warming, organizational and individual.
- High profile individuals such as:
  - Sir (Alistair) Muir Russell KCB DL, former chairman of the Judicial Appointment Board for Scotland and former principal and vice chancellor of the University of Glasgow, chair of the investigation of the e-mail situation.
  - Lord (Ernest) Ronald Oxburgh (Baron Oxburgh), member of the House of Lords, educated and taught at Oxford with a Ph.D. from Princeton. A geologist and geophysicist and known to be a supporter of the climate change study and initial investigator of some concerns about the CRU. He was appointed September 25, 2009, as Chairman of the House of Lords Select Committee on Science and Technology.
  - Lord Christopher Monckton, although the title is questioned since his background is in journalism and he is not in the House of Lords, but in the House of Commons, is an adviser to CFACT. His criticism of CRU that appeared in Anthony Watts's blog, "WattsUpWithThat", claimed he had been climate change adviser to former British prime minister, Lady Margaret Thatcher. That was not true, according to Bob Ward, policy and communications director at the Grantham Research Institute on Climate Change and the Environment at the London School of Economics and Political Science. Ward's comments initially appeared in *The Guardian* but were included in DeMelle's piece in the *Huffington Post* (DeMelle, 2010).
  - Al Gore, USA, joint recipient of Nobel Peace Prize 2000 with the Intergovernmental Panel on Climate Change and specifically for his book *An Inconvenient Truth*, is also founder and chair of the Alliance for Climate Protection, also past (forty-fifth) vice president of the United States under the Bill Clinton administration.
  - Sarah Palin, USA, past governor of the State of Alaska, where she set up a sub-cabinet level climate change committee to prepare the state for global warming, but denied the warming was caused by human action and became the USA's leading spokesperson against that concept.

Initial Response from CRU Director Phil Jones

Jones, in responding to the November 23, 2009, inquiry about the e-mail messages attempted to lay that aside with this explanation:

> The following e-mail, which I can confirm is genuine, has caused a great deal of ill-informed comment, but has been taken completely out of context and I want to put the record straight. Quoting from the e-mail:
> "I've just completed Mike's (Michael Mann) Nature trick of adding in the real temps to each series for the last 20 years (i.e., from 1981 onwards) and from 1961 for Keith's (Keith Briffa) to hide the decline. Mike's series got the annual land and marine values while the other two got April–Sept for NH land N of 20N. The latter two are real for 1999, while the estimate for 1999 for NH combined is +0.44C wrt 61–90. The Global estimate for 1999 with data through Oct+ is 0.35C cf. 0.57 for 1988."
> The first thing to point out is that this refers to one diagram—not a scientific paper—that was used in the World Meteorological Organisation's statement on the status of the global climate in 1999 (WMO no. 913). The diagram consisted of three curves showing 50-year average temperature variations for the last 1000 years. Each curve referred to a scientific paper and a key gives their details. Climate records consist of actual temperature records from the mid-19th century and proxy data (tree rings, coral, ice cores, etc.), which go back much further. The green curve on the diagram includes proxy data up to 1060 but only actual temperatures from 1961 onwards. This is what is being discussed in the e-mail. The word 'trick' was used here colloquially as in a clever thing to do. It is ludicrous to suggest that it refers to anything untoward.
> (University of East Anglia CRU Update 1)

Four Investigations, Three Outcomes

1. UK House of Commons Science and Technology Select Committee questioned Phil Jones and others in person.

Outcome: Concluded that the reputation of CRU was sound, but that University of East Anglia (UEA) needed to respond to accusations of no access to data. A problem, later brought out, was that Sir Russell never asked the other CRU scientists any questions and was not there when the final report was signed. Also, that meeting where the report was signed was attended by only four of the fourteen members of the Science and Technology Select Committee involved in the investigation. Submission was not made and put up on UEA's website until February 25, 2010, after pressure on the university to release its submission to the two independent reviews in memorandum submitted by the University of East Anglia (CRU Statements: university reaction, 2010) and the outcomes of all three reviews and response: Lord

Oxburgh Report April 14, 2010, Sir Muir Russell Report July 7, 2010 and March 31, 2010 (CRU Statements: Independent reviews, 2010).

2. A short report by Lord Ronald Oxburgh was an effort to determine the integrity of the research.

Outcome: Although the scientists were not accused of flawed research, the report did say that that public data should be made available by those collecting it, including national weather services around the world. The UEA "welcomed the findings that cleared them of any scientific impropriety and dishonesty and the suggestions made for improvements in some areas." Critics challenged the findings.

3. UEA asked for an independent review by Sir Muir Russell, who headed a panel of experts. The panel recreated its own study without access to the CRU code using information in public databanks. The panel, working independently, arrived at the same conclusions as the CRU had reported, which indicated global warming. This was the most comprehensive review.

Outcome: All scientists were cleared of adjusting data to falsely make the case for global warming. A charge of mishandling data from China resulted in the investigators saying they saw nothing to dispute the validity of the scientists' work to support global warming. The CRU was also cleared of the accusation that in the peer-review process the scientists had prevented publication of articles of dissent in scientific journals. They also were cleared of efforts to affect the IPCC's reports by silencing dissent. Because the IPCC was a team responsibility, there was "no improper exclusion of material," investigators ruled.

However, the CRU's refusal to turn over its code in freedom of information requests drew a reprimand about transparency. The panel reported:

> We note that much of the challenge to CRU's work has not always followed the conventional scientific method of checking and seeking to falsify conclusions or offering alternative hypotheses for peer review and publication. We believe this is necessary if science is to move on, and we hope that all those involved in all sides of the climate science debate will adopt this approach.
>
> (Adam, 2010)

Critics of the global warming prognosis called the investigation a whitewash.

4. Ongoing Norfolk Police inquiry to determine how the e-mails were made public.

Outcome: Although the police were on the scene investigating the day the e-mails were released, no developments were reported as of September 2010.

A summary of the three investigations appeared in a 54-page report, "The Climate Gate Enquiries" by the Global Warming Policy Foundation. The outcomes of each, discussed by Donna Laframboise, creator of Toronto-Canada-based NOconsensus.org, echoed the complaints of critics (Laframboise, 2010).

Climategate Crisis Process in Brief

Since nothing in the Climategate case mentions either goals or objectives, the mission statements of UEA and CRU were examined and assumptions drawn from these for both:

Goal 1: To preserve the reputation for both.

Strategy: To use a series of investigations with high-profile individuals as judges to clear the organizations of accusations of deliberate distortion of climate warming reports.

Tactic 1: Made results of investigations public by posting on website.

Tactic 2: Used outreach to other scientists who helped gather data and contributed to the research reports.

Tactic 3: Positioned the CRU as a "victim" of illegal hacking into private e-mail correspondence, although there is as yet no evidence to indicate whether it was an invasion or a leak.

Goal 2: To maintain government support, basically retaining public funding, especially for the research unit.

Strategy: To create an appearance of "openness" to discourage and overcome perceptions of disingenuousness if not actual dishonesty.

Tactic 1: Prompted responses to government and media inquiries.

Tactic 2: Encouraged media coverage of investigations.

Goals and Objectives

Since goals and objectives should be based on an organization's mission statement, the first effort is to look at both the University's and then its research division's mission statements.

University of East Anglia Mission Statement: Our mission is to understand, empower and act, to enhance the lives of individuals and the prospects of communities in a rapidly changing world (www.uea.ac.uk).

In addition to the overall university mission statement, it has mission statements for all units, such as on equal opportunities in which it defines itself as "a premier research and teaching university," on disabilities, and for each discipline. Most Western universities follow the same procedures (www.cru.uea.ac.uk).

Climate Research Unit: The aim of CRU is to improve scientific under-standing in:

- past climate history and its impact on humanity; and
- prospects for the future.

Although nothing specific appears in the UEA or CRU on particular goals or objectives for surviving the crisis, from these two statements, it seems obvious that preservation of reputation for both the university and its climate research unit are primary for attracting and retaining students, faculty, and outstanding researchers in all fields. The CRU in its responses clearly indicates that it understands that research findings almost always are controversial, particularly in the area of climate. Furthermore, since this is a government supported university and research unit, clearly survival is critical. A provable scandal in the research unit jeopardizes public funding.

Strategies and Tactics

As in many crisis situations, this event was not anticipated. The CRU did not even know that the e-mails had been intercepted until these were made public. There is no detectable evidence that the university or the research unit had a crisis plan in place. Thus both the strategies and tactics were reactive.

Strategies: In this case, the principal effort was to get cleared of accusations that the CRU's data was manipulated to support the position that global warming was occurring and that human actions were a major contribution to the acceleration of warming, primarily through excessive emissions from carbon-based fuels.

The effort to do this was through investigations looking at the work product and communication from the CRU. An incomplete investigation is tracking how the private communication among the scientists was captured and made public.

A second strategy was to respond to inquiries from government and news media to emphasize that there was no attempt to mislead, and to show that excerpts from e-mails that were made public were taken out of context in a way that distorted the reality of the situation.

The motive was to prevent government intervention, particularly in the funding for the research, and to take away critics' ability to focus on the "bad science" that supported global warming from carbon emissions. The flip side of that is to support organizations involved in reducing the human "carbon footprint" globally.

Tactics: News releases were posted on the university's website, and the CRU's director participated in a news conference when the crisis first broke.

Outreach to contributors to the research and to other scientists most likely through private correspondence, although there was no discoverable public evidence of other scientists coming to the CRU's defense.

Critical Response to Investigations

Detailed responses to three of the completed investigations appear in *The Hockey Stick Illusion: Climategate and the Corruption of Science*, a book by Andrew Montford. His findings were released in a 54-page report from Global Warming Policy Foundation as a PDF, September 14, 2010. The critique is based on documents of the investigations released to the public late in 2009. A summary of Montford's criticism of each investigation can be found in "Nofrakking Consensus" website at http://nofrakkingconsensus.wordpress. com/2010/09/14/the-shoddy-climategate-inquiries/.

Lessons Learned

CRU's director said his unit regretted not having shared its code for analysis and for not responding to questions that came under freedom of information requests. The CRU claimed confusion about handling such requests and a "lack of engagement" on the part of the scientists and senior university officials. Although deleting other e-mails not specifically requested before they were revealed is acceptable in responding to FOI requests, the panel said, "Nonetheless, the requirements of the legislation for release of information are clear and early action would likely have prevented much subsequent grief." Critics later claimed that the e-mails were deleted after FOI requests were sent. The deletions were not considered "acceptable policy." In any case, Jones' defense of "confusion" seems a bit disingenuous. The UK is one of the 85 countries in the world with some sort of FOI Act, although there are differences in some places about privacy and open meetings. The UK's Freedom of Information Act 2000 includes all but Scotland, which has its own FOI. Environmental information disclosure is covered in the Environmental Information Regulations 2004 (Campaign for Freedom of Information-UK, 1984).

CRU needs to consider more openness in publicly funded scientific research, the panel noted, especially in light of changes in the law and the new communication climate of Internet bloggers—citizen journalists (Carrington,

2010, July 7, 11). In terms of more immediate action, there is no evidence that the CRU was at the Copenhagen conference to present its position on the released e-mails. Nor does it appear that the CRU had a dark website ready to activate in case of a crisis. The releases seemed to be on the University of East Anglia's principal website.

Other Lessons from the Case CRU should have Learned

Credentials of examiners and the process followed are critical to credibility. Although both chairs of the two major investigations have impeccable reputations; nevertheless, their positions on global warming were known. Two of the most important investigations in this case, then, had some problems that any critic could use to taint the outcomes.

Although use of the Internet was initiated by scientists to exchange information, by 2009 they should have been aware that the Internet is a public global network and that messages can be made public no matter how personal or private the intention. Furthermore, in a country with more national newspapers than any other in the world and the world's best-known global broadcast network, it would seem that residents there would be aware that anything written or spoken is likely to be widely disseminated. Casual comments any time, anywhere can have global consequences. In this situation, the captured e-mails only gave more ammunition to opponents of the idea that human behavior is affecting, if not causing, global warming.

Since the U.S. government is accustomed to granting requests for information based on the Freedom of Information Act, there is some reason to suspect that the whole effort of discrediting the CRU's research, perhaps even capturing of the e-mails and making them public, might have its origins in the USA. However, it was not wise to say that the e-mail deletions that Jones admitted to occurred when there were no FOIs outstanding at the time. All computers can yield date and time.

With so many global misunderstandings of the meaning of the same words in a language by different users of the language, it seems remarkable for Jones to use what he admits is colloquialism in correspondence, in this case the word, "trick." Had he used only scientific terms that would have at least enabled other scientists familiar with the terms to come to CRU's defense. Furthermore, relative to word use, when *The Guardian* newspaper labeled its coverage "Climategate," the newspaper's word choice implies not just wrongdoing, but very bad wrongdoing.

Finally, the scientists had to be aware that their research had critics. Critics can become motivated to become active adversaries. Allowing unprotected e-mails to escape is nothing new, and even some data thought to be protected can be "shared." There is no evidence of internal sabotage, though, in this case, nor is it indicated that the messages were in an encrypted Intranet.

Best-case scenario is that CRU has a crisis plan in place. The argument over the cause of global warming is not nearly over.

Some Theories that Apply

Although it is not possible to list all of the theories that can be applied to Climategate, some are so obvious that it seems irresponsible not to mention them, at least by general points. Before doing that, it is important to point out that UEA has a communication staff made up of a head of communications, one communications officer, two communications assistants and two "press" officers. These have responsibility for the external and internal communications, which includes a monthly university newsletter (*Broadview*), postings in the Campus News Section of the Portal/Intranet, and the campus e-mail system at these two sites: (www.uea.ac.uk/mac/comm/media and www.uea.ac.uk/mac/comm/internal)

There are many elements of building and sustaining a reputation, but in this case five are particularly significant.

1. Trust

Persuasion relies on: personal identification; suggestion of action; familiarity and trust; clarity (Earl Newsom quoted in D. Newsom et al., 2010).

Although the scientists might say they are just trying to examine global warming, when they present their findings, surely they are hoping for, even expecting, acceptance. That depends upon how much the receivers are willing to believe the message and the source.

Of all the various message theories, two seem especially relevant here. Information is judged by consistency (Leon Festinger, 1957 and Milton Rokeach, 1989 in Littlejohn, 2002) and authority (legitimate). Consistency draws from Festinger's theory of cognitive dissonance that says that information is evaluated by its relevance or irrelevance and by whether it is consistent or inconsistent, which he calls dissonance. Consistency also finds a place in the theory of beliefs, attitudes, and values from Rokeach. The one that applies so strongly here is consistency. (Judging, Rokeach (1989) says, also includes: reciprocity, social validation, and scarcity.) Rokeach noted that core beliefs resist change. Values are central to these core beliefs, and both affect your self-concept. Only when inconsistencies impact your self-concept are beliefs likely to change (Littlejohn, 2002).

2. Strategic Relationships, Cooperative Communities

Cooperative communities developed around issues, mutual interest, proximity and function, strengthened by focused efforts over a long period of time and trust is the first and most important characteristic of cooperative relationships, according to Laurie J. Wilson (Culbertson and Chen, 1996).

3. Public Diplomacy

In a section titled "Public diplomacy: Government goes global," W. Timothy Coombs and Sherry J. Holladay note that public diplomacy, a sub-field of diplomacy, overlaps with public relations because the target is to influence public opinion in another country and particularly to impact its foreign policy. "Public diplomacy," the authors say, "provides a global arena for issues management and reputation management, two broad areas of public relations" (Coombs and Holladay, 2007, p. 105).

Climategate did impact global public policy and did no good for the reputation of CRU.

4. Beyond the Website—Participating in Global Conversations

In their preface to a book on international cases, Danny Moss and Barbara DeSanto write:

> [O]ne of the key tenets of effective public relations practice is that practitioners should operate as an organization's "antenna," constantly scanning the organization's environment and alerting management to new threats and opportunities, and helping frame responses to emerging issues. Here practitioners only function effectively if they are taken seriously by management and their advice listened to by key decision-makers.
>
> (Moss and DeSanto, 2002)

5. Planning for a Crisis: Anticipation

With so much international discussion about global warming, causes and consequences, it is difficult to imagine that CRU did not have a darksite prepared with basic information about its work and principal scientists involved in each segment as well as contact information for a principal spokesperson. But, it apparently did not. Some organizations resist planning for a crisis because they think there are too many types of crisis. There are only six. If an organization takes a careful look at what it is, what it does, how it does those things, it is easy to develop some scenarios for anticipation and response.

Crises fall into two broad categories: Violent: cataclysmic—immediate loss of life or property or Non-violent: sudden upheaval but damages, if any, are delayed. Intersecting both of these two broad categories are three others, resulting in six type of crises: act of nature, intentional, and unintentional (Newsom et al., 2010).

With information and images reaching global audiences in seconds every hour of every day, being prepared, generally, if not specifically, is essential. In this case, scientists have learned that strategic, skillfully planned and executed communication is as important as the science itself.

Reverberations from Climategate were still resonating in 2010. *The Enclyclopaedia Britannica 2011 Book of the Year* that covers 2010 had two references, one in the section in Earth Sciences on "Meteorology and Climate" and the other in the book's section on "The Environment" where the Climategate case (called Climategate Scandal in the subheadline) was the introductory piece.

The Meteorology section, written by Douglas Le Comte, observed that reviews had generally supported the integrity of the scientists involved and particularly mentioned the findings of the Muir Russell investigation as being the most thorough examination. In quoting from the final report of the event there was a "consistent pattern of failing to display the proper degree of openness" among the researchers and the UEA. Le Comte included the continuing criticism of the event:

> the deletion of emails to avoid complying with the Freedom of Information Act, the withholding of temperature and other climate data, and the interference with the peer-review process that prevented the publication of research disputing the notion that human-induced climate change was occurring.
>
> (*Encyclopaedia Britannica 2011 Book of the Year*, p. 227)

In the yearbook's section on "Environment," under "International Developments," "Climategate" is the next subheading. This report includes information about the CRU behavior pattern, over 13 years, of withholding information, showing contempt for those who disagreed with them, and by discrediting and attempting to boycott journals that published papers by their opponents. This article details the relationship between Jones and his Chinese-American colleague WeiChyung Wang of the State University of New York at Albany who reported information from 84 Chinese weather stations. These reports supporting the warmer weather argument depended on some stability in the location of the weather stations, when actually 51 of the reporting stations had moved, 25 had not, and there was no information on the other eight. Jones repeated Wang's statement that "few, if any" stations had moved, which was not true.

This report says that on September 14, 2010, the non-partisan think tank, Global Warming Policy Foundation (GWPF), concluded that the investigations of Climategate lacked sufficient consideration in choice of panel members resulting in imbalance, lack of independence, and objectivity. Finally, GWPF observed that the way investigations were conducted made it unlikely that these would restore confidence in CRU's work (*Encyclopaedia Britannica 2011 Book of the Year*, p. 231).

Discussion Questions

1. Do you think this crisis could have been anticipated or not? For either "Yes" or "No," explain why.
2. What do you suggest that CRU do now to recover its reputation?
3. How should the university and the research unit plan to present their findings going forward?
4. Are there some management issues that need to be addressed? Where and by whom?
5. For senior scholars, what other theories apply to Climategate? How?

References

Adam, D. (2010). "Climategate" report: The main points: From manipulating data to censoring articles, 150-page report clears scientists of main allegations against them. *The Guardian*, July 7. Retrieved from http://guardian.co.uk/environment/2010/jul/07/climategate-scientists-main-points

Allaby, M. (2010). Environmental issues: Climate change. In *Encyclopaedia Britannica 2010 Book of the Year*, (pp. 236–238). Chicago, IL: Encylopaedia Britannica, Inc.

Campaign for Freedom of Information-UK (1984). Retrieved from: www.cfoi.org.uk

Carrington, D. (2010). Q&A "Climategate." *The Guardian*, July 7. Retrieved from http://guardian.co.uk/environment/jul/07/climate-emails-question-answer

Carrington, D. (2010). "Climategate" shows the need for openness by scientists. *The Observer*, July 11. Retrieved from cache www.guardian.co.uk./environment/hacked-climate-science-emails.

CFACT News, All Pain No Gain (2009, December 7). (Global warming File). Retrieved from www.cfact.org/a/1652/Monckton-names-names-on-Climategate

CFACT News, All Pain No Gain (2009, December 10). (Video, Copenhagen, Climategate File). Retrieved from www.cfact.org/a/1652/Lord-Monckton-on-Climategate-Whistle-Blower-not-Hacker

Coombs, W.T., and Holladay, S.J. (2007). *It's not just PR: Public relations in society* (p.105). Malden, MA: Blackwell.

Culbertson, H.M., and Chen, N. (Eds.). (1996). *International publicrelations, A comparative analysis*, (p. 76). Mahwah, NJ: LEA Publishers.

DeMelle, B. (2010). Lord Christopher Monckton exposed again as fabulous fabricator. *Huffington Post*, June 22. Retrieved from www.huffingtonpost.com/brendan-demille/lord-christopher-monckton_b_621816.html

Encyclopedia Britannica 2011 Book of the Year (2011). (pp. 227, 231). Chicago, IL: Encyclopedia Britannica, Inc.

Festinger, L. (1957). In S. W. Littlejohn (2002). *Theories of mass communication* (pp. 125–8). Belmont, CA: Wadsworth Publishing.

Laframboise, D. (2010). The shoddy Climategate Inquiries, September 14. Retrieved from http://nofrakkingconsensus.wordpress.com/2010/09/14/the-shoddy-climategate-inquiries/

Littlejohn, S. W. (2002). *Theories of Mass Communication* (pp. 128–30). Belmont, CA: Wadsworth Publishing.

Moss, D., and DeSanto, B. (2002). *Public relations cases: International perspectives* (p. 8). London and New York: Routledge.

Newsom, D., Turk, J.VS., and Kruckeberg, D. (2010). *This Is PR: The Realities of Public Relations* (10th ed.). Boston, MA: Wadsworth division of Cengage Learning.

Rokeach, M. (1989). In S. W. Littlejohn (2002). *Theories of Mass Communication* (pp. 128–30). Belmont, CA: Wadsworth Publishing.

Searle, A. (2010). Timeline of events, hacked science emails. *The Guardian*, July 7. Retrieved from http://guardian.co.uk/environment/jul/07/hacked-climate-science-emails

University of East Anglia CRU Update 1 (2009, November 23) and Update 2 (2009, November 24). Retrieved from www/uea.ac.uk/mac/comm./media/press/2009/nov.CRUupdate

University of East Anglia. Three independent reviews. Reports available: Muir Russell Review, July 2010; Lord Oxburgh Scientific Assessment Panel, March 2010; Parliamentary Science and Technology Select Committee, March 2010. Related statements Independent Review: The Independent Climate Change E-mails Review—July 2010 sent 2010, September 2; University response to Sir Muir reports, sent 2010, July 7; Response by the University of East Anglia to the Report by Lord Oxburgh's Science Assessment Panel, sent 2010, April 14; Statement in response to the Science and Technology Committee Report, sent 2010, March 31; The University of East Anglia Website. Retrieved from www.uea.ac.uk/mac/comm/media/press/CRUstatements/independentreviews

VIEWS FROM AN EXPERT

BARBARA DESANTO

Barbara DeSanto Ed.D, APR, Fellow PRSA, Professor of Communication and Communication Program Director at Maryville University, Saint Louis, Missouri. Dr. DeSanto, lecturer at universities in Scotland, Sweden, Germany, the Netherlands, New Zealand, is currently Maryville University's Australia/New Zealand Study Abroad Summer Program Director. DeSanto's latest book, Public Relations Management, *(Sage: in press) with co-author, Dr. Danny Moss, University of Chester, England, is based on research with public relations managers in the UK and USA.*

According to several well-respected British communication professors and scholars, the far-reaching consequences of Climategate generated a bit of heat, but no fire. This case study, however, does provide important issues management lessons.

The British academic research process and the research itself pose two important considerations in this case. British research is important not only for adding knowledge to their disciplines, but for securing research funds for their universities. All public universities are awarded government research funds based on the government's Research Assessment Exercise (RAE). One of the main funding determinants is the status of the research outlets in which academics distribute and publish their research. This competitive funding process creates a rivalry among universities in the new British academic environment where there have been more polytechnic institutes becoming public universities and fewer research dollars to go around. It is not difficult to imagine researchers taking care to protect their discoveries to make sure they get all of the dollars they can for their efforts.

While funding is an important consideration, so is protecting individual and university research reputations. Questions about data handling and research "tricks" to make data say what the researchers want can have far-reaching consequences—yet another reason to guard against any public discussion until researchers are sure of their results and their ability to defend—and protect—them.

The issues management lesson here is that academics must not only be aware of the "new" public environment created by the "new" media, the demand for transparency by anyone who has the technology, but be prepared to respond to a media environment in which everyone has the potential to play a media role because he or she has a personal media device. Britain has long had a popular press that enjoys adding sensational touches to its stories. With so many more potential sources of leaks, researchers and universities working on projects need to plan strategies that build relationships with key stakeholders in media and the scientific community that can be used as credible resources when incidents such as the Climategate leak occur.

Britain also has a very public and strong environmental tradition along with a very strong public protest culture. In the scientific realm, Brits have long championed a myriad of green causes, including climate change. Environmental groups are among the most vocal public pressure groups. Protests about some facet of conservation or a green cause occur daily. Another real possibility is that one of these environmental pressure groups was responsible for hacking into the university's e-mail and feeding that information to the media. The lesson to be considered here is that universities, traditionally bastions of free expression, must be aware of their internal employees and stakeholders. The rather sensationalist popular press routinely goes "undercover" to find stories that make great reading, or cooperates with pressure groups to pursue stories. This again suggests having an issues management/crisis strategy in place to specifically deal with situations involving internal as well as external stakeholders.

In addition to having strategies to deal with building trust and credibility with internal and external stakeholders, such as the scientific community and the government RAE funding body, Climategate is a lesson that words do matter. Researchers and scholars often speak in academic language where words mean very different things when used in non-academic conversation. "Tricks" is such a word. Anyone not educated about working with statistical data in the British university research community would find many words that do not mean what they mean in colloquial speech. The very important lesson here is that highly technical or complex communication subjects must be thought about and addressed from other stakeholder perspectives. To not have a plan that carefully releases information in words designed to inform and build trust with important stakeholders is to risk not only having to explain "tricks," but, in this case, to suffer consequences ranging from increased public scrutiny to reduced research funding.

In this case, the consequences were mild compared to what they could have been. The hope is that the scientists have learned that strategic and skillfully planned and executed communication is just as important as the science itself.

Euro Zone

Eurovision 2010: A Security Breach Endangers Europe's Largest TV Show

Alfonso González-Herrero

The Eurovision Song Contest is Europe's largest television production and the biggest non-sport event in Europe. Organized each year by the European Broadcasting Union (EBU) and a leading national television broadcaster, the 2010 final was broadcast from Oslo (Norway) to 45 countries, with an estimated audience of 69 million viewers and more that 2,000 journalists from 70 countries accredited to cover the event. This chapter analyzes the crisis communications planning and response actions undertaken by the EBU and NKR (Norway's national broadcaster) after Jimmy Jump, a notorious pitch invader, intruded on the stage and took part in the choreography during the live performance of the Spanish singer. The security breach was widely criticized across Europe, affecting Norway's reputation as organizer of future events. The issue was labeled in Norway as a "national drama" and a "national embarrassment."

Background of the Crisis

The Eurovision Song Contest is Europe's largest television production and the biggest non-sport event in Europe. Organized each year by the European Broadcasting Union (EBU), Eurovision is the oldest and most popular song contest across the continent too. Stars such as Celine Dion, Cliff Richard, Julio Iglesias, and ABBA took part and are famous thanks to the Eurovision Song Contest.

An estimated 16,000 people attended the 2010 Eurovision Grand Final at the Telenor Arena in Oslo, Norway, which was broadcast to 45 countries, with an estimated audience of 69 million viewers. More than 2,000 journalists from 70 countries were accredited to cover the event.

One of the 25 countries represented in the 2010 final was Spain, one of the "Big Four" country delegations, along with the United Kingdom, France, and Germany. During the live performance of the Spanish singer, Daniel Diges, something unexpected happened before the stunned and bewildered eyes of the singer, dancers, and the audience. Jimmy Jump—a notorious pitch invader who had previously interfered in several major sporting events in Europe in search of publicity—invaded the stage and joined in the dance routine for 20 seconds (as shown in Figure 4.1), the time it took the organizer's security to chase him off the stage.

Because of the incident, the organizers allowed Spain to perform for a second time after the last regular performance. Nevertheless, the security breach was widely criticized across Europe—particularly in Norway and Spain. It was the first time that something like that had happened in the 54 years that the song festival has been running.

The Norwegian press catalogued the issue as a "national drama" and "national embarrassment" (EFE, 2010; Fondenes and Oksvold, 2010; Gonsholt, 2010) while the Swedish daily *Expressen* labeled it as a "scandal" (Julander, 2010). In mid-August, the BBC YouTube video alone had been watched by more than 1.4 million people (BBC, 2010), before it was blocked for allegedly infringing copyright.

Coincidentally, a few months after the 2010 edition, Eurovision's executive supervisor resigned after eight years on the job and the European Broadcasting Union had to undertake an important internal reorganization (Bakker, 2010b).

Figure 4.1 Jimmy Jump (wearing a red cap and a T-shirt with his name) appears on stage as Spain's Daniel Diges performs his song during the Eurovision Song Contest 2010 final.

Source: Photograph by Kim Erlandsen. Copyright 2010 by NRK. Reprinted with permission.

Situation Analysis

Eurovision

Eurovision is the oldest and most popular song contest across Europe. The Eurovision Song Contest has been broadcast every year since 1956 without interruption, making it one of the longest-running television programs in the world (Eurovision, 2010d). It is one of the few truly pan-European television programs transmitted live via the Eurovision satellite network, on prime time television.

The Eurovision Song Contest claims to be Europe's largest television production and the biggest non-sport event a European city can host. It consists of three live shows (two semi-finals and the grand final), which are currently seen by a steady and growing audience of more than 100 million people.

The competition is broadcast every year throughout Europe, but also in Australia, Canada, Egypt, Hong Kong, India, Jordan, Korea, New Zealand, and the United States, even though these countries do not participate.

The 2010 Edition

The 2010 Eurovision Song Contest took place May 25–29 in Oslo, Norway. The event was attended by some 16,000 people at the Telenor Arena, and 2,007 journalists from more than 70 countries were accredited (Bakker, 2010a).

NRK, the host broadcaster in the Eurovision 2010 edition, reportedly spent somewhere between €25 million and €30 million (US$32–39 million) on the production of the show (Schader, 2010).

The Final was watched by 69 million viewers from no less than 45 countries. An impressive figure if we take into account that, for example, the 2010 Oscar's ceremony was seen in the United States by a record 41 million people (*Telegraph*, 2010).

The average audience share for the Final across the nations where it was broadcast was 40 percent, compared to the usual Saturday night average of 18.4 percent recorded by public broadcasters. In some countries, such as Norway, it reached more than 88 percent of share (NRK, 2010).

Stakeholders Affected by the Crisis

The crisis provoked by Jimmy Jump had a negative impact—to a lesser or greater extent—on several of the organizations involved in the development of the Eurovision Song Contest.

The European Broadcasting Union

The European Broadcasting Union (EBU) is the largest association of national broadcasters in the world. Founded in 1950 and headquartered in Geneva,

Switzerland, it comprises 86 national media organizations in 56 countries in and around Europe. Some 75 percent of EU citizens regularly watch EBU members' main channels. The EBU employs 320 professionals in Geneva and 68 in its various offices around the world, representing about 50 nationalities (European Broadcasting Union, 2010a).

Much of the organization of the Eurovision Song Contest is in the hands of the host broadcaster of the event. However, the EBU—through a separate division and brand name called Eurovision—supports the host broadcaster and is the link with the participating EBU member broadcasters. As initiator of the Eurovision Song Contest, the EBU is also taking care of brand management, international marketing activities, general communications, and the official website.

The Reference Group

The Eurovision Song Contest Reference Group is the executive expert committee for all members, whose purpose is to control and guide the Eurovision Song Contest. It is in charge of approving the development and future format of the Eurovision Song Contest, securing the financing, modernizing the brand and raising awareness, and overseeing the yearly preparation by the host broadcaster (Eurovision, 2010c).

One of its members, the Eurovision Executive Supervisor, has a mandate to take decisions under any kind of challenging situations. (S. Bakker, personal communication, September 21, 2010).

The Host Broadcaster, NRK

Traditionally, the Eurovision Song Contest is produced by the national public broadcaster of the country that won the year before. In 2010, the Norwegian public broadcaster, NRK, took care of the production, in close cooperation with the EBU.

NRK (in Norwegian, Norsk rikskringkasting AS), is the Norwegian government-owned radio and television public broadcasting company, and the largest media organization in Norway. A founding member of the European Broadcasting Union, it is, however, a small broadcaster, compared with the major media houses of Europe.

G4S and Oslo Police Department

Security was the responsibility of the host broadcaster. NRK commissioned security of the event to G4S (S. Bakker, personal communication, September 21, 2010), one of the leading security companies worldwide. Security was also coordinated with the Oslo Police.

Among the discussion topics during security meetings before the event, NRK and the police discussed whether there should be a fence around the stage, a measure that was eventually rejected by the broadcaster. The police asserted then to organizers that they could not guarantee 100 percent security during the event (Pettersen et al., 2010).

National Delegations

Each public broadcaster taking part in the Eurovision Song Contest sends a national delegation to the host city; 1,014 delegates from the 39 participating countries were in Oslo, and 212 of them appeared on stage. The head of the delegation is the European Broadcasting Union's contact person.

Radio Televisión Española, RTVE

Radio Televisión Española (RTVE) is Spain's public TV broadcaster. RTVE is in charge of selecting the singer that represents the country each year at Eurovision.

Spain is one of the "Big Four" country delegations, together with the United Kingdom, France, and Germany, since it is one of the largest financial contributors to the show. As such, it enjoys certain privileges, qualifying directly for the Grand Final every year.

The Host City and Host Country

Since Eurovision is one of the most important events that a European country can organize, the logistical and security failures also affected the reputation of the host city and country: Oslo and Norway.

Eurovision 2010 Partners

TEAM (Television Event and Media Marketing AG) is Eurovision's worldwide exclusive marketing agency for the commercial rights of the Eurovision Song Contest.

For the 2010 edition, TEAM negotiated three sponsoring contracts on behalf of the EBU with three partners:

1. Telenor, one of the leading mobile operators in the world, became Presenting Partner of Eurovision. As part of the sponsorship agreement, the event took place at its own Telenor Arena in Oslo (Eurovision, 2010a).
2. Nivea Visage, a brand of the Beiersdorf Group was named Official Partner.
3. Norwegian Airlines also entered into a partnership agreement with the EBU to become the Official Airline of the Eurovision Song Contest 2010.

Fan Clubs

There are several Eurovision Song Contest fan clubs across Europe, all aiming at promoting the contest and its contestants. Although the contest does not have an official fan club, the Organisation Générale des Amateurs de l'Eurovision (OGAE) is the most popular fan organization. Active OGAE branches can be found in many of the participating and non-participating countries (Eurovision, 2010b).

Initial Response

Vigilant Monitoring

Organizations must monitor and scan their environment in search of public trends (or single issues) that may affect them in the near future (Gonzalez-Herrero and Pratt, 1995, 1996). This can be done by establishing an online alert system that includes monitoring of websites, blogs, newsgroups etc. (Gonzalez-Herrero and Smith, 2008).

Eurovision monitors the Web through Google News, Twitter, Facebook, and several other platforms to know what is being said about the brand. It also has a group of "ambassadors," or true fans of the event, who can let Eurovision know what is relevant in the fan community (S. Bakker, personal communication, September 21, 2010).

In the Jimmy Jump case, however, Eurovision and NRK failed to detect the announcement made by the invader three weeks before the grand final in an Internet interview to the Sport24.gr Greek website (Georgopoulos, 2010; Sport24, 2010). His announcement was subsequently echoed in several other Internet blogs and forums (Coroneri, 2010). Even friends of Jimmy Jump had announced in Jimmy's open wall on Facebook that he was in Oslo just a couple of days before the Eurovision show (Tobiassen, 2010).

Should the issue have been detected, Eurovision and NRK would have been able to prevent its occurrence or—at least—they would have been able to put in place a specific plan to address the issue in a coordinated manner.

A hard task, though, according to NRK's Head of Press, Peter Svaar, who believes that it is not realistic to think that a better monitoring system would have detected this issue among the thousands of posts the Eurovision generates, especially the days before the grand final (P. Svaar, personal communication, September 29, 2010).

However, today there is a diverse array of monitoring and information services provided by companies such as PR Newswire, Cymfony, Intelliseek and Biz360 that analyze hundreds of newsgroups and blogs, and filter millions of messages daily. Some of these services also track online media coverage in search of commentary about a specific organization. Monitoring allows companies to decide quickly how to react to adverse information, recognizing potential problems (Gonzalez-Herrero and Smith, 2008).

Planning

Both the EBU and NRK had developed for Eurovision a comprehensive crisis communications plan, which included contact details of stakeholders, procedures to follow, a kit with templates, examples of situations, action lists, etc. Although a stage invasion was not part of their plan as a specific case, a "disruption of the show during the live broadcast" (e.g., a bomb threat) was one of them (S. Bakker, personal communication, September 21, 2010; P. Svaar, personal communication, September 29, 2010).

Eurovision and NRK also had a crisis team (in charge of dealing with the operational aspects of a crisis) and a crisis communications team (to manage communication around the issue).

Eurovision's crisis plan determines that local authorities must be in charge of the crisis when it is related to safety and security. At the same time, Eurovision's Executive Supervisor has the responsibility over issues related to regulation of the song contest. A total of four public relations professionals (two of them from EBU's Eurovision division, and another two from NRK) made up the whole communications team for the event (P. Svaar, personal communication, September 29, 2010).

The invasion of Jimmy Jump posed EBU, NRK, and local authorities, however, with a real coordination challenge. They had to deal with a security breach (responsibility of NRK and local enforcement authorities), but the issue had also altered the proceedings of the contest (responsibility of the EBU), and the individual responsible for the incident was arrested by the police (who subsequently had to inform the press about his whereabouts). This implied that Eurovision and NRK struggled to coordinate the execution of their crisis plans.

Initial Response

The initial response from NRK security services was poor. It took them 20 seconds to appear on stage—even when there was no indication that the invader was harmless. The security assessment was that they waited a few seconds to arrest Jimmy Jump, according to NRK press officials. Had they stormed on stage before, they would have disrupted Spain's performance even more (Pettersen et al., 2010).

This delay led to additional criticism, since NRK and Eurovision not only had to give explanations later about the security breach, but also about the reason why the show had been a priority over personal safety of the Spanish team members.

Afterwards, following RTVE complaints, the reaction of EBU was swift (20 minutes), publicly announcing that Spain would be allowed to act a second time. "We consider it fair that the Spanish participant gets the chance to perform their song again without interference," said the EBU in a statement to the media (Fondenes and Oksvold, 2010).

NRK also distributed a press release to the commentators from the different countries who were broadcasting the show live and to all the accredited press at the Telenor Arena. In the release, NRK apologized for the incident, explained the reasons for the security failure, commented that the EBU had decided to let Spain sing again, and emphasized that new security measures had been taken (P. Svaar, personal communication, September 29, 2010).

Press officers from both EBU and NRK made themselves available for interviews backstage while the song contest continued, since numerous news media as well as blogs were broadcasting the show live over the Internet. Prompt backstage interviews allowed organizers to be part of those conversations and online media stories.

NRK and EBU did not consider it appropriate, however, to hold a more general press briefing or conference to address the issue, either during or after the event. The reason was to downplay the issue and to avoid attracting further attention. For the same reason, EBU decided not to make available any press release on Eurovision's online press center. Similarly, the following day's press releases (from EBU, Eurovision, and NRK press centers) completely ignored the issue and focused exclusively on the winner of the contest, Germany. Eurovision went even further and decided to delete from its website any reference to the incident, including those in its online forums (S. Bakker, personal communication, September 29, 2010).

These decisions meant that only the media accredited at the event received direct communications from Eurovision and NRK, while the rest of the European press reported the issue with the partial information obtained from news wires. As a consequence, particularly in Spain, Eurovision's image was affected in an important way.

Communication goals, Objectives, Strategies, and Tactics

Although the EBU and NKR shared the main goal and objective, we can also distinguish some specific ones, each with their own strategies and tactics.

Main goal and Objective of the European Broadcasting Union

Goal 1: To control the severity of the issue and to avoid magnifying it further.

Objective (a): To interpret rapidly Eurovision's contest rules in a way that would avoid further debate and criticism by the stakeholders, minimize the impact of the stage invasion on the live broadcast, and not interfere in the final voting process.

Objective (b): To achieve full and immediate public awareness of EBU's decision to let Spain sing again.

Strategy 1.1: Defined clear guidelines of action regarding responsibility: NKR agreed with the EBU that the regulatory implications of the issue—a participant being disturbed on stage and the decision that he would sing again—were an EBU responsibility and, therefore, Eurovision took the responsibility for those aspects of communications (S. Bakker, personal communications, September 21, 2010).

Strategy 1.2: Defined crisis management guidelines that facilitated swift decision-making: EBU assigned sole responsibility of taking a fast and fair decision to Eurovision's Executive Supervisor.

Strategy 2: Gave information about EBU's decision, primarily to the media and commentators present at the event (P. Svaar, personal communications, September 29, 2010).

Tactics:

- exchanged e-mails between Eurovision public relations officials and the Executive Supervisor's desk in the arena immediately after the incident with Jimmy Jump;
- established an on-site crisis communications team to coordinate responses;
- followed the guidelines that had been developed in the crisis communications plan in the scenario "disruption of the show during the live broadcast";
- Eurovision communicated the decision of allowing Spain to sing again through a press statement within 20 minutes, distributed to all accredited media via e-mail (Figure 4.2);
- decided not to upload the press statement to the Eurovision virtual press center and did not hold a press conference, to avoid magnification;
- wrote a press release the day after the event and held a press conference focusing, exclusively, on the artistic aspects of the show; and
- deleted any reference to the incident from its website and online forums in the subsequent days.

Goal, Objective, Strategies and Tactics of the EBU and NKR

Goal 2: To convey a sense of normality that allowed normal development of the song festival and a global positive evaluation of the event.

Objective: To minimize the negative impact of Jimmy Jump's stage invasion on live and next-day media coverage across Europe.

Strategy 1: Showed promptness and responsiveness in answering media need for information.

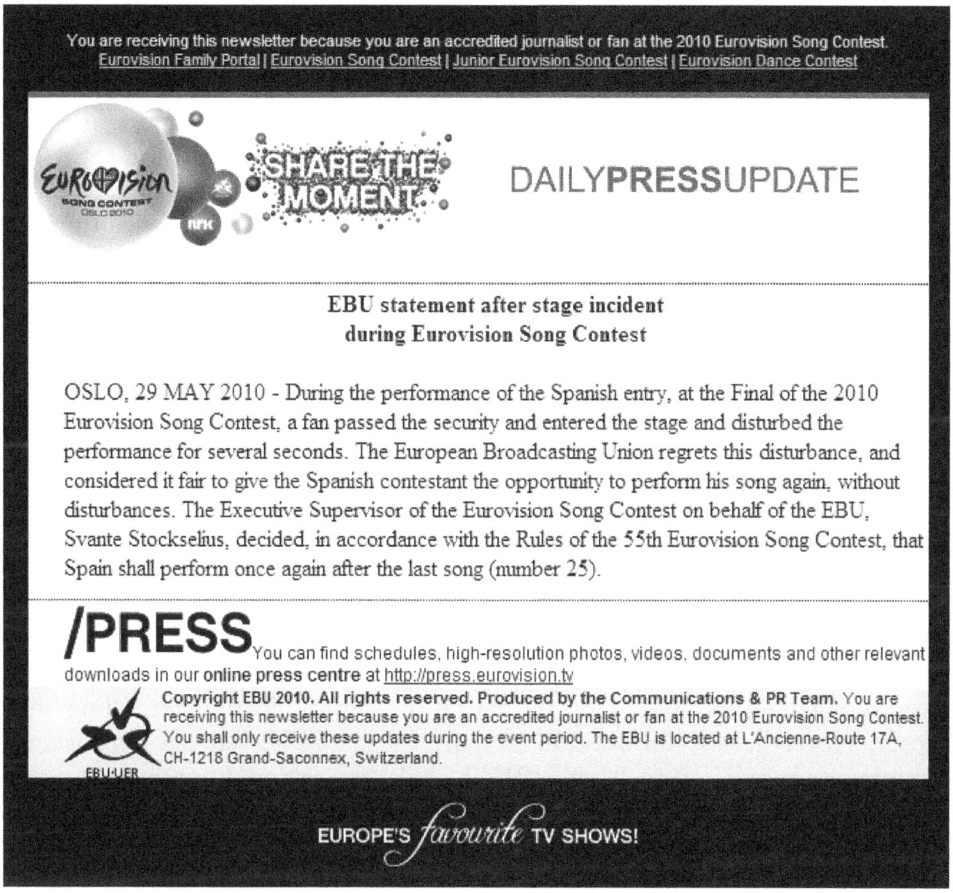

You are receiving this newsletter because you are an accredited journalist or fan at the 2010 Eurovision Song Contest.
Eurovision Family Portal | Eurovision Song Contest | Junior Eurovision Song Contest | Eurovision Dance Contest

SHARE THE MOMENT

DAILY**PRESS**UPDATE

EBU statement after stage incident during Eurovision Song Contest

OSLO, 29 MAY 2010 - During the performance of the Spanish entry, at the Final of the 2010 Eurovision Song Contest, a fan passed the security and entered the stage and disturbed the performance for several seconds. The European Broadcasting Union regrets this disturbance, and considered it fair to give the Spanish contestant the opportunity to perform his song again, without disturbances. The Executive Supervisor of the Eurovision Song Contest on behalf of the EBU, Svante Stockselius, decided, in accordance with the Rules of the 55th Eurovision Song Contest, that Spain shall perform once again after the last song (number 25).

/PRESS You can find schedules, high-resolution photos, videos, documents and other relevant downloads in our **online press centre** at http://press.eurovision.tv

Copyright EBU 2010. All rights reserved. Produced by the Communications & PR Team. You are receiving this newsletter because you are an accredited journalist or fan at the 2010 Eurovision Song Contest. You shall only receive these updates during the event period. The EBU is located at L'Ancienne-Route 17A, CH-1218 Grand-Saconnex, Switzerland.

EUROPE'S *favourite* TV SHOWS!

Figure 4.2 Twenty minutes after the incident, Eurovision communicated the decision to allow Spain to sing again through a press statement, distributed to all accredited media via e-mail.

Source: Copyright 2010 by EBU. Reprinted with permission.

Strategy 2: Communicated the correct information, clearly and completely, to all relevant stakeholders (S. Bakker, personal communication, September 21, 2010; P. Svaar, personal communication, September 29, 2010).

Strategy 3: Apologized to the public (and the Spanish delegation).

Tactics:

- relayed Spain's second chance live;
- wrote and distributed an EBU press release;
- hand-delivered a NRK press release to the accredited media on-site;

- wrote shorter website postings, Facebook messages, and Twitter tweets on Eurovision's website;
- offered interview slots to key media with Eurovision and NRK spokespeople;
- held one-on-one meetings with representatives of the Spanish delegation; and
- held meetings with police and authorities to reinforce security during the rest of the show and communicated it to the media.

Secondary Goal and Objective of NRK

Goal 3: To protect NRK's image as a trustful and competent international event organizer.

Objective: To show immediate responsiveness and transparency to all EBU's national delegations in Oslo and the accredited media.

Strategy: Defined guidelines of action regarding communication about the security breach: EBU and NRK agreed that the incident—someone on the stage who should not be there—was the responsibility of the host broadcaster and that, as such, NRK should be in charge of communicating regarding that aspect. Nevertheless, Eurovision, as part of the EBU, had to approve all outgoing communication from NRK (S. Bakker, personal communications, September 21, 2010).

Tactics:

- issued a press release by NRK to all accredited media apologizing for the incident, explaining the reasons for the failure, and emphasizing that new security measures had been taken;
- made a spokesperson available for media interviews backstage;
- coordinated a consistent answer with the authorities and the police for the media about Jimmy Jump's legal situation once he was arrested;
- included written news and video images in its website explaining NRK's position regarding the issue;
- remained transparent through the post-crisis stage, keeping news and photos of the incident visible on its website; and
- produced a one-hour documentary on the making of the song festival, showing the complexity and professionalism of the team involved.

Other Tactical Considerations

The EBU considered media relations the priority. Therefore, at the time of the show, it was not considered relevant to have specific communications with the different national delegations. According to Eurovision, only the Spanish delegation was affected, so it was the only one receiving information directly from the production staff (S. Bakker, personal communication, September 21, 2010).

The same consideration was made regarding communications with the host city and host country officials. From Eurovision's point of view, at the time of the incident that was not relevant. On the internal communications side, Eurovision normally uses an intranet to communicate EBU members and partners Eurovision-related issues. In this case, however, since this issue happened during the live show (when the intranet was not being used by most country members), Eurovision decided to inform them using that tool afterwards. If it had been crucial for them to be informed, Eurovision could have used its SMS platform and send out an SMS alert to them (S. Bakker, personal communication, September 21, 2010).

Outcomes Assessment

This case presents several challenges from a communications perspective. First, the fact that there were several actors involved in the organization of the song contest did not make it easy to establish clear responsibilities for communication. Second, the fact that 25 countries participated in the event, although the issue mainly affected two of them (the host country, Norway, and the affected country, Spain), posed great difficulties regarding the level of communication that should have been taken in the different countries involved. And third, the lack of resources assigned to communications both by NRK and by the EBU for the Eurovision song contest made it impossible to consider implementation of a variety of tactics, which may have affected Eurovision's brand image badly in some markets.

Responsibility Over Communications

Responsibilities for communications of EBU and NRK were defined in EBU's and NRK's crisis plans, so that—according to Eurovision—it was clear who was in charge at all times (S. Bakker, personal communication, September 21, 2010). NRK, however, admits that defining each other's communication responsibilities was not easy and presented certain areas of ambiguity, being an area for future improvement (P. Svaar, personal communication, September 29, 2010).

A clear indication of this is that none of the organizations took responsibility for Eurovision's brand image. That is, while NRK's main objective was to explain the reasons of the security breach and EBU's objective was to inform about the ruling of the event, none took care of the Eurovision brand itself, and evaluated what was needed to protect it—in the short and long term—in the different countries.

Level of Communication Required for each Market

It seems obvious that the impact of the crisis was more severe in Norway or Spain than in the rest of the European countries. Thus, while NRK's only market is Norway and, accordingly, its communications efforts did focus on its country almost exclusively, it seems reasonable to argue that the EBU should have followed a different strategy. It should have adjusted its crisis response and tactics to the severity of the issue in the different countries where it has presence. Thus, it should probably have had a higher and more proactive role in Norway and Spain and lower in the rest of the countries that broadcast the show.

Use of the Internet

On the Internet, which today reaches more than 475 million people in Europe (Internet World Stats, 2010), Eurovision downplayed the issue and avoided any relevant mention of it. For example, the day after the Grand Final, Eurovision's press release omitted any mention of the incident (and focused exclusively on the results of the contest), which was inappropriate for the Norwegian and Spanish markets, where Jimmy Jump's incident was the main subject of public conversation and was front cover of many newspapers. Days later, Eurovision even decided to delete most postings about the issue from its website.

In contrast, NRK, in a web page with anecdotes about the grand final, under the title "the uninvited guest", admitted that "[it] was so bad that the incident should probably have been passed over in silence." At the same time, it said that "this is what everyone was talking about during and after the final, and is an event that will be shown on the web in years to come" (Bakken and Saleem, 2010), and included video images of a NRK spokesperson explaining NRK's position about the issue. NRK also included statements from its broadcast manager in several Internet links that referred to the issue.

Lack of Resources

NRK spent more than €25 million (US$32 million) on the production of the event (Schader, 2010). However, its public relations team was composed of only two people, a similar figure of Eurovision's very limited public relations team, composed by two external public relations-consultants.

Since neither NRK nor Eurovision had any public relations agency support to manage this crisis (P. Svaar, personal communication, September 21, 2010), the resources assigned to communications were scarce and inadequate.

Lessons Learned

The Eurovision case has been a wake-up call for the entire show business and entertainment industry in Europe, since learning from others' mistakes is an effective principle of crisis communications.

An efficient monitoring system, proper planning, and good coordination in execution among the different organizations involved are keys to success. Without a well-defined crisis plan and clear guidelines and responsibilities to execute what has been planned, even a minor issue can get out of hand.

- Vigilant monitoring is necessary to prevent or minimize the impact of crises.

Vigilant monitoring in the age of the Internet is now a key part of crisis communications. An early analysis of web-based content might provide the early warning needed to develop appropriate corporate plans and responses, and enable companies to avoid the situation in which EBU and NRK found themselves.

- Crisis planning and execution readiness become critical.

Proper planning can allow organizations to respond effectively to crises, even if their surveillance was not adequate. "Good preparation is crucial," says Eurovision's manager of communications, Sietse Bakker (S. Bakker, personal communications, September 21, 2010).

Planning, however, is not enough. All parties involved in the response must be well coordinated, so previous simulations and tests should be part of the process of crisis preparedness.

- On-site media relations are not enough, especially at international events.

"Think globally, act locally" is a phrase being used in many different contexts. Applied to this case, it would mean that crisis response at international events—or when multiple countries are affected—requires a common substrate, but that it must be adjusted to the reality of each country involved.

Thus, while NRK's and EBU's top priority to inform the media and commentators on-site was correct, hundreds of other media outlets across Europe (and particularly in Norway and Spain) would have required greater, targeted attention, specially by the EBU, which has operations all across Europe.

- Organizations need to control issues, but ignoring them is not the answer.

Communications materials need to be easily accessible by the media, accredited or not. However, media statements were not available on neither Eurovision's nor NRK's online press centers. Eurovision deliberately chose not to offer that option, allegedly to avoid any further media attention on Jimmy Jump. The result was that many articles were written and TV news were broadcast without Eurovision's positioning about the subject.

Similarly, while accredited media received information both from EBU and NRK, other stakeholders (from national delegations, to sponsors of the event, or the general public) did not, however, receive any direct communication about the incident. Partly owing to lack of resources by the PR teams, which made it impossible to target specific communications to relevant stakeholders such as the host city and host country officials, but also owing to misuse of existing communication tools, such as the Internet.

• Communications structures need to be empowered and simplified.

For example, EBU is taking measures to increase the efficiency of its communication services and it will create in 2011 a new Department of Public Affairs and Member Relations. The objective is to bring together a centralized communications function, the Brussels office, the Strategic Information Service, and various related support services (European Broadcasting Union, 2010b).

Long-lasting Effects of Crises

Today, organizations should accept that it is almost impossible to eradicate negative publicity from the Internet, even when a crisis is over. The Web perpetuates bad news. It is no longer the one-day story it used to be in traditional mass media (Gonzalez-Herrero and Smith, 2008). Video-sharing websites such as YouTube mean that footage about the Eurovision crisis can be viewed repeatedly, so the organization response must also remain there.

The main lesson, though, is that the basics of crisis management remain the same, and that effective monitoring and planning give organizations the tools they need to protect their organization's corporate image. The tactics and tools to respond may need to be revised and adapted to today's digital environment, but yesterday's principles of monitoring issues, preventive and advance planning, and quick, credible crisis response are still valid.

Discussion Questions

1. If you were appointed manager of public relations of Eurovision, what would you do to prevent or minimize the consequences of further incidents like this one?
2. What's your opinion about EBU's and NRK's response to the crisis? Do you think it contributed to lowering the profile of the issue—and, therefore,

it was correct—or that it damaged Eurovision's public image by not being more proactive in some markets?

3. In an incident like this, the news media typically have questions for the host broadcaster (NRK), the EBU organization, but also for the host city officials, country representatives . . . How do you think communications should be coordinated to ensure consistent responses?

4. Would you censor negative comments posted by fans on Eurovision's website? How would you handle criticism?

Appendix 1. Jimmy Jump

Jimmy Jump—whose real name is Jaume Marquet—is a notorious and prolific pitch invader born in Sabadell (Spain), who has made a name for himself by disturbing several major sporting events in Europe.

Before the Eurovision incident, he had also invaded the pitch during several soccer matches of the Spanish soccer league, the UEFA Champions League, and the UEFA Euro. In other sports, Jimmy had run through the starting lane during the warm-up lap of the 2004 Spanish Formula 1 Grand Prix. He also entered the court during a game between Memphis Grizzlies and FC Barcelona basket team; and at the start of the second half of the 2007 Rugby World Cup final between England and South Africa (Jimmy Jump, n.d.).

During the 2009 Men's Singles Finals of the French Open, he accosted eventual winner Roger Federer, and in July 2010, moments before the 2010 FIFA World Cup Final between Spain and the Netherlands, Jimmy Jump managed to evade security teams and attempted to hold the World Cup trophy before being apprehended by security guards (Lelliot, 2010).

Jimmy Jump recently warned that he would like to jump at the Oscars award ceremony (Pousa, 2010). Hollywood, watch out!

References

Bakken, H., and Saleem, N. (2010). Her er øyeblikkene vi aldri glemmer [There are moments we never forget]. NRK, May 31. Retrieved from http://nrk.no/programmer/tv/melodi_grand_prix/1.7147044

Bakker, S. (2010a). Oslo 2010: Let's share the numbers! Eurovision, May 19. Retrieved from www.eurovision.tv/page/news?id=12043&_t=Oslo+2010%3A+Let's+share+the+numbers!

Bakker, S. (2010b). EBU officially starts search for new song contest manager. Eurovision, September 19. Retrieved from www.eurovision.tv/page/news?id=20103

BBC (2010). Stage invasion during Spain's performance. YouTube, May 29. Retrieved from www.youtube.com/watch?v=7uWCTeIv-Tc

Coroneri, A. (2010). Eurovision 2010: Jimmy Jump aims to sing a song in Eurovision. *Oikotimes*, May 11. Retrieved from www.oikotimes.com/v2/index.php?file=articles&id=8059

EFE (2010). Bochorno en Noruega por los fallos de seguridad en el Festival de Eurovisión [Embarrassment in Norway for security flaws in the Eurovision Song Contest]. *El Mundo*, May 30. Retrieved from www.elmundo.es/elmundo/2010/05/30/television/1275217422.html

European Broadcasting Union (2010a). About the EBU. Retrieved from www.ebu.ch/en/about/index.php

European Broadcasting Union (2010b). EBU Annual Report 2010. Retrieved from www.ebu.ch/CMSimages/en/Rapport_UER_2010_EN_FINAL_tcm6–68194.pdf

Eurovision (2010a). Facts and figures. Retrieved from www.eurovision.tv/page/history/facts-and-figures

Eurovision (2010b). Fan clubs. Retrieved from www.eurovision.tv/page/fan-zone/fanclubs

Eurovision (2010c). The reference group. Retrieved from www.eurovision.tv/page/moscow2009/organizers/referencegroup

Eurovision (2010d). The story. Retrieved from www.eurovision.tv/page/history/thestory

Fondenes, E., and Oksvold, R. (2010). Mann i lue stormet scenen under MGP-finalen [Man in hat stormed the stage during the MGP final]. Nyhetene, May 29. Retrieved from www.tv2nyhetene.no/innenriks/mann-i-lue-stormet-scenen-under-mgpfinalen-3218220.html

Georgopoulos, J. (2010). Ο εισβολέας Jimmy Jump στο Sport24.gr. [The 'attacker' Jimmy Jump in Sport24.gr]. *Sport24.gr*, May 11. Retrieved August 14, from http://sport24.gr/football/mundial/mundial2010/article369513.ece

Gonsholt, C. (2010). Mann brøt seg inn på MGP-scenen. Spania fikk synge om igjen! [Man broke into the MGP-stage. Spain got to sing again!]. *VG Nett*, May 29. Retrieved from www.vg.no/musikk/grandprix/artikkel.php?artid=10007853

Gonzalez-Herrero, A., and Pratt, C. (1995). How to manage a crisis before—or whenever—it hits. *Public Relations Quarterly*, 40(1), 25–29.

Gonzalez-Herrero, A., and Pratt, C. (1996). An integrated symmetrical model for crisis-communications management. *Journal of Public Relations Research*, 8, 79–105.

Gonzalez-Herrero, A., and Smith, S. (2008). Crisis communications management on the Web: How Internet-based technologies are changing the way public relations professionals handle business crises. *Journal of Contingencies and Crisis Management*, 16, 143–153.

Internet World Stats (2010). Internet usage in Europe. Retrieved from www.internetworldstats.com/stats4.htm

Jimmy Jump. (n.d.). In *Wikipedia, The Free Encyclopedia*. Retrieved from http://en.wikipedia.org/w/index.php?title=Jimmy_Jump&oldid=375555829

Julander, O. (2010). Pressansvarig om ESC-skandalen: "Han är gripen och bortförd". [Press officer of ESC-scandal: "He is arrested and carried away"]. *Expressen*, May 29. Retrieved from www.expressen.se/noje/melodifestivalen2010/1.2005503/pressansvarig-om-esc-skandalen-han-ar-gripen-och-bortford

Lelliott, J. (2010). All's fine as Jimmy Jump hops free. *The Times*, July 13. Retrieved from www.timeslive.co.za/local/article547017.ece/Alls-fine-as-Jimmy-Jump-hops-free

NRK (2010). Eurovision samlet folket. [Eurovision gathers people]. Press release, May 31. Retrieved from www.nrk.no/informasjon/pressetjenesten/pressemelding sarkiv/?p_pressemelding_id=46363

Pettersen, J., Kristensen, E., Lundervold, L. K., and Sverrisson, J. (2010). Spansk presse raser mot NRK etter skandalestunt. [Spanish press rages against NRK after scandal stunt]. *Dagbladet*, May 29. Retrieved from www.kjendis.no/2010/05/29/kjendis/melodi_grand_prix/jimmy_jump/11923350/

Pousa, L. (2010). Jimmy Jump: "Me encanta el Camino de Santiago, porque yo me siento un peregrino de la vida." [Jimmy Jump: "I love the Camino de Santiago, because I am a pilgrim of life.] *La Voz de Galicia*, June 9. Retrieved from www.lavozdegalicia.com/sociedad/2010/06/09/0003_8537035.htm

Schader, P. (2010). Public broadcasters shudder at price tag for 2011 Song Contest. *Der Spiegel*, June 1. Retrieved from www.spiegel.de/international/zeitgeist/0,1518,698061,00.html

Sport 24. (2010). Το είπε στο Sport24.gr και το'κανε ο Jimmy Jump! [He told to Sport24.gr and he did the Jimmy Jump!], May 30. Retrieved August 8, from http://sport24.gr/Paraxena/article371247.ece

The Telegraph (2010). Oscars 2010: Highest US audience figures for five years. Telegraph.co.uk, March 8. Retrieved from www.telegraph.co.uk/culture/film/oscars/7400901/Oscars-2010-Highest-US-audience-figures-for-five-years.html

Tobiassen, M. (2010). Jimmy Jump is in Oslo, Norway. Tell your friends!, May 28. Message posted on Facebook at www.facebook.com/event.php?eid=1111789 85592901

Sources for Videos of the Incident

Videos of the incident can be accessed at the following sites:

www.eurovision.tv/page/multimedia/videos?id=19083

www.youtube.com/watch?v=_Unb161ZI-s

www.youtube.com/eurovision

www.youtube.com/eurovision#p/search/8/_Unb161ZI-s

www.rtve.es/mediateca/videos/20100529/final-eurovision-2010—-espana-1-actuacion/785749.shtml

VIEWS FROM AN EXPERT

SUZANNE SMITH

Suzanne Smith, Independent Communications Consultant and Founder of Text 100 Madrid. Suzanne has over 15 years of international communications consultancy experience working with brands such as IBM, Nokia, Microsoft, Vodafone, Skype, Electronic Arts, and Xerox. She is the founder of Text 100's Madrid office, which she ran successfully for eight years, building the business into one of the most

respected agencies in Spain. In her current role, Suzanne develops communications training programs for a range of European companies.

Despite the very complex setup regarding responsibility for communications—as described in the main text—NRK and Eurovision did two important things well in their crisis communications.

First, responsiveness is highly desirable in any crisis situation, and EBU and NRK reacted to the incident quickly and had communicated to the press their decision to allow Spain to perform again just 20 minutes after their first performance was disrupted. Second, they were open, honest, and transparent at the beginning, using wide-ranging tactics to reach both traditional and social media. This is important as it creates trust, which in turn limits damage to an organization's reputation.

In terms of what could be improved, it is clear that Eurovision, as a global event, requires a properly resourced, international and empowered crisis communications team acting as one entity with a consistent approach rather than each organization having their own communications plans and using different tactics. The unified team would be responsible for the development of one crisis communications plan that carefully considers all stakeholders (including the internal audience) in all regions and is put to the test prior to the event by running through crisis simulations, something that is now common practice in the corporate world.

The online component of the crisis communications strategy deserves a special mention since the Internet played a major role in raising awareness of the stage invasion. Comprehensive social media monitoring combining automated software tools tracking key words in different languages with human analysis would have alerted the organizers to potential crises. Once the crisis was under way, a consistent approach via different online channels (such as Twitter, or Facebook) driving people to a Eurovision response site should have been adopted. At this point, it should be noted that the crisis communications team do not have to handle all online communications alone. A clear social media policy in place prior to the event would allow them to empower employees and Eurovision ambassadors who are already active on social media to drive people to the response site.

In addition to improving crisis communications planning and their online communications strategy, EBU and NRK still need to communicate properly how they are addressing the underlying issue, which is the lack of security at the event. They need to show stakeholders that they are taking the problem seriously by communicating the actions they are implementing to ensure the same thing does not happen in the 2011 Eurovision contest in Germany. A good crisis communications strategy here would be to bring in a third party who is an expert in security and re-establish the credibility of Eurovision, especially among the countries affected by the stage invasion.

France

An Exceptional Fraud at Société Générale

Thierry Libaert

In January 2008, an exceptional fraud was detected at Société Générale, one of the ten major banks in the world. The bank discovered that one of its traders had managed to avoid its internal control systems and run up exposure totaling 50 billion euros. This coincided with a significant downturn in the global markets. The risk was considerable as, if the bank had been declared bankrupt, it could have put the entire global financial system under a lot of pressure.

This chapter analyzes the actions taken by Société Générale, the outcome of the action, and lessons learned.

Crisis Background

Timeline

Friday January 18, 2008: An exceptionally high counterparty risk was discovered on a broker, Jérôme Kerviel; the explanation given by the trader behind this position led to additional checks.

Saturday 19: The counterparty in question denied any knowledge of the transaction, which was therefore assumed to be false.

Sunday 20: The situation became clearer with the calculation of the directional position of 50 billion euros that resulted in a 4.9 billion euro loss after the unwinding of the positions.

Thursday 24: Daniel Bouton, Société Générale's CEO, announced that an internal fraud had been committed by one of its own traders, without naming the individual. The fraud had caused a loss of 4.9 billion euros, making it the largest fraud in banking history at that time.

The fallout following this revelation was quick: the CEO's resignation appeared to be only a question of time, rumors of the bank's impending sale circulated quickly. All this added to the prevailing climate of suspicion against banks and their practices (Figure 4.3).

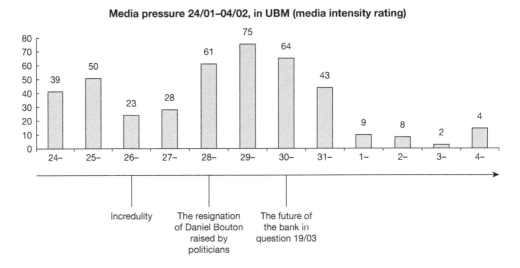

Figure 4.3 Traditional media pressure.

Situation Analysis

As explained in the diary of Société Générale's head of communication at the time (Hugues Le Bret, 2010), it was decided to focus on internal communication: the bank employs 160,000 people and so it was essential to keep them informed and prevent rumors or a decline in motivation. Letters to clients were sent (in French and in English) to the following groups: "individuals, professionals, craftsman, storekeepers, small and medium businesses, large organizations and investors." This was also based on the belief that employee confidence would work to reassure clients and shareholders.

The national authorities were the first to be informed and on Sunday January 20, the CEO notified the governor of the Bank of France and the secretary of the French Stock Exchange. However, the political authorities were told only three days later. The reason behind this was that Société Générale wanted to keep control of its communication and prevent potential scenes of panic with millions of people queuing in front of cash machines to withdraw their money. This seeming lack of confidence did not please the French government and on Monday, January 28, French President Nicolas Sarkozy declared that the crisis "could not be without consequences given the responsibilities involved." Overall, public opinion and the vast majority of politicians supported the trader, who they perceived as a scapegoat and was described as an ordinary young man by his friends and family.

The other stakeholder was the media. Media pressure was overwhelming and more than 2,000 journalists from different parts of the world covered the incident. On January 25, the day after the affair was revealed by Société

Générale, it was covered by 20,000 newspapers throughout the world. The bank's position was to be transparent but not proactive. Nothing would be done to sustain media coverage after the bank's initial press release on Thursday, January 24, the press conference and the interview with CEO Daniel Bouton, on French radio news station *France Info*. If there was an overwhelming coverage by the media, the online media and blog seem to have a relative minimal importance, especially just a few days after the starting point of the crisis (Figure 4.4).

Initial Response

The main point to highlight is the bank's decision to maintain secrecy during the most strategic period. This was a hard choice to make, as all the "guides" to crisis communication insist on immediate transparency. The strategy of secrecy involved alerting neither the Ministry of the Economy nor the head of state. The first alert on the rogue trader was triggered by internal controls on January 7, 2008, but it was only on January 19 that the full extent of the fraud became known internally. Société Générale found itself in a position where it had to get rid of a potential liability of 50 billion euros in the middle of a stock exchange debacle. The danger was that, if the fraud had been revealed internally, the bank would have been under immediate threat and would have been able to sell only under pressure because potential buyers would have been aware that it had to sell as quickly as possible. As a result, the total loss would have been much greater and the danger of a systemic crisis would have weakened the entire global financial system, in the aftermath of the bankruptcy of Lehman Brothers on September 15, 2008, which had a balance sheet that was half the size of Société Générale's (US$ 613 billion

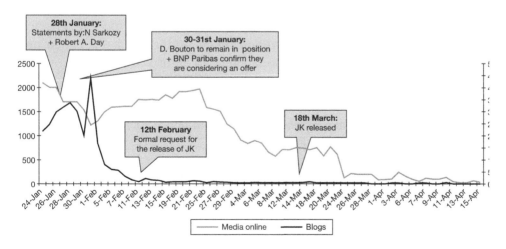

Figure 4.4 Online media pressure.

compared to US$1,100 billion). Between the discovery of the fraud, on Saturday, January 19, and the disclosure to the public, on January 24, there were only five days in which to unwind a position totaling 50 billion euros and to put in place an appropriate communication strategy. To illustrate this strategy of silence, only one trader was asked to unwind the 50 billion euros, which he did on his own in a separate room during the entire operation, which took three days. The trader was not informed of the reason for this massive sale; rather, he received selling instructions on a piecemeal basis, in successive fractions of the total sum.

Goals and Objectives

The only goal was to save the bank. Here, two main factors must be exposed. Immediately after the disclosure, the bank had to reassure its clients so that they did not run to cash machines to withdraw their money, which could have created a potentially deadly domino effect for Société Générale.

One week later, on January 31, BNP Paribas, the main French competitor of Société Générale, confirmed that it was considering making an offer to buy Société Générale. In addition, the fact that two days earlier, President Sarkozy had told the media that the crisis "could not be without consequences given the responsibilities involved" and asked for the resignation of Société Générale's CEO Daniel Bouton, meant that the bank's position was significantly weakened.

Strategies and Tactics

Goal 1: To reassure the stock exchange.

Strategy: Société Générale put in place a vast public relations campaign to reassure the stock exchange and investors.

Tactic: Top management met with members of the stock exchange and investors and ensured that they were adequately informed.

Goal 2: To use employees as a means of pressure and a symbol of legitimacy.

Strategy: Société Générale tapped into the confidence of its employees and worked to reassure clients and shareholders.

Tactic: The employees appear to have placed significant importance on the management of this crisis. Media coverage of the affair presented the fraudster as a modern-day Robin Hood working for a bank that seemed to shirk its responsibilities by making the trader a scapegoat in order to conceal the weakness of its control systems. All this profoundly exasperated employees, as they were from the outset regularly informed internally. They received e-mails, explanations on the Intranet (Sogenews), on the internal radio (Soge FM) and an e-mail chat was even organized with Daniel Bouton on January 29. This exchange allowed the 38,000 employees who logged in that day to address their questions directly to the CEO.

Consequently, when the rumors of a takeover bid were followed by the confirmation that BNP Paribas wanted to gain control of Société Générale, the employees did not hesitate to leave their offices and assemble outside the head office to demonstrate their loyalty to their bank and show the potential risk of internal crisis (Figure 4.5).

Goal 3: To keep the initiative and not be perceived as defensive.

Strategy: A major strategic element of this crisis management was that Société Générale understood that it had to provide a solution at the same time as it announced the problem.

Tactic 1: When Daniel Bouton revealed the 4.9 billion euro loss, he announced a capital increase that would provide the means to save the bank and preserve its potential expansion. This capital increase emphasized the perception that the company had a strategy. The operation was a success and was 1.8 times oversubscribed.

Figure 4.5 Demonstration of support by Société Générale employees.
Source: Photo taken January 30 by Philippe Zamora.

Tactic 2: To decrease the rumors of a possible collapse of the bank, Société Générale announced the acquisition of an important Russian bank, Rosbank. This operation was a success and the transaction was done on February 13. This contributes to the message of solidity: in spite of the crisis, we are continuing to do business.

Goal 4: To focus on the people involved with the company by means of communicating through osmosis.

Strategy: Do nothing ourselves to sustain media coverage.

Tactic 1: Put the focus on the most important type of public in a crisis. The head of communication chose to follow a strategy of silence, and to put the accent on the key stakeholders at the expense of the media and general public opinion.

• Clients: A letter was sent to them on February 2.
• Shareholders: A letter was sent to them January 26, and this letter was published in the national and regional daily press.
• A hotline to answer questions raised by shareholders and the clients was created.

Tactic 2: Cancel publicity campaigns. To avoid a crisis communication that might not be coherent with the publicity campaign, which was based on a message on the bank's leadership, all current publicity was instantly withdrawn.

Tactic 3: Cancel sponsorship activities. Société Générale is one of the main sponsors of rugby. Fearing that it could be perceived as inappropriate in the circumstances, the sponsorship was cancelled during the crisis period. This cancellation was explained by a press statement in support of the French rugby team, aimed at its enthusiasts and emphasized the values of team spirit and commitment.

Of course, the CEO could not escape a minimum media exposure. After the press conference on January 24, he gave interviews on French Television (*France 2*), to one of the main weekly news magazines (*Paris Match*), Reuters, and others. However, the goal was to limit media exposure to a minimum and to show that the bank was continuing with its business. One of the results was that media pressure decreased very rapidly, and, one week after the beginning of the crisis, media coverage was also considerably decreased.

Outcomes Assessment

The main result was that the bank still exists and keeps on growing. The clients remain confident, as shown in Figure 4.6:

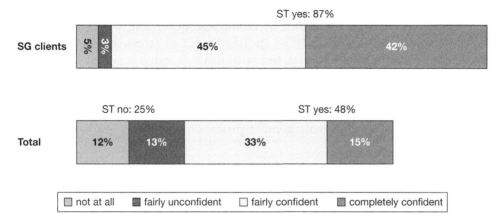

Figure 4.6 Société Générale Trust Barometer.

When clients were asked: "Do you think that the fraud perpetrated by Jérôme Kerviel on Société Générale could have taken place in other banks?", 95 percent of respondents answered "yes" to the question. Confidence was also very high among the employees and 92 percent said they were "proud to work for the SG group." It is possible that the strategy of discretion contributed to the fact that the media essentially focused on the personality of the rogue trader and that this story was called "the *Kerviel affair*" and not "the *Société Générale affair.*"

This affair came back in the news in October 2010 because of the trial of the trader Jérôme Kerviel. The courts ordered him to reimburse the sum of 4.9 billion euros to the bank and accept responsibility for his actions. The fact that the court of justice exonerated Société Générale from all responsibilities and the practical impossibility for Kerviel to pay the amount he defrauded led to a new current of sympathy for Kerviel, newly portrayed as the scapegoat for institutional dysfunctions.

Lessons Learned

- Focus on the dominant stakeholder and not necessarily on media and public opinion.
- Relating to your main stakeholder, traditional media can be of far more strategic importance than social networks.
- Make use of your employees as a shield and a means of relaying your messages.
- Be cautious with your competitors, they will probably try to take advantage of the situation and increase the intensity of the crisis.

- Another lesson could appear as anecdotal and was given to us by Denis Marquet, the former corporate communications director. When you are part of a crisis management team, you don't know when the crisis will stop and you will have to confront a lot of stress. It isn't generally explained in the crisis manual, but your health condition is very important. The fact that the members of the crisis team benefited from daily medical care, that fruit and fruit juices were freely and constantly available, that a psychologist was always close to the team, all of these facts contributed positively to the crisis management process.

Discussion Questions

1. Was it a mistake not to inform President Sarkozy of the crisis?
2. Organizations often forget employees in crisis communication and focus on relations with the media. Do you think this is a good idea? If so, why?
3. Is the fact that the banking sector in general has a bad reputation an inconvenience when it comes to handling crisis communication?

Reference

Hugues Le Bret (2010). *La semaine où Jérôme Kerviel a failli faire sauter le système financier mondial*, Les Arènes, p. 71.

VIEWS FROM AN EXPERT

CHRISTOPHE ROUX-DUFORT

Christophe Roux-Dufort is professor of strategic management at Laval University, Québec, Canada. He has written about 30 scientific and professional articles and five books. He also works as a consultant on crisis management for multinational companies in France, the United States, China and Thailand. His comments on corporate crises are regularly published in national newspapers. Christophe received his M.B.A. degree (1990) from the University Laval (Quebec, Canada) and his Ph. D. degree (1997) from University Paris Dauphine, France. His research interests lie in risk and crisis management.

Even though control is one of the absolute priorities in this type of business the system was vulnerable at least for three reasons. Knowing does not mean acting. Most of the time a crisis uncovers two complementary and cumulative processes: an accumulation of vulnerabilities and an accumulation of ignorance about these vulnerabilities that makes them more and more difficult to decipher up until the crisis erupts. Crisis is sometimes the only alternative to clean up the self-reinforcing process of vulnerability.

Second, repeated success leads to complacency. Up until the crisis, the communication of SG heavily insisted on the fact that SG was the second biggest bank in France, the best bank in the world in 2006 and that its shareholders had tripled their profits since 1999. It illustrates to what extent the size, the growth, and the prestige are sometimes major sources of inattention that could have kept the bank from being alert to warning signals about Kerviel's position.

Third, the best control system ever may reveal vulnerability because of the excessive trust it can generate. Before September 11, the security systems of airports covered a wide range of potential threats except . . . the use of cutters. The best architecture will never be able to counter the unanticipated nature of human behavior.

Germany

The Love Parade in Duisburg: Lessons from a Tragic Blame Game

Andreas Schwarz

During the Love Parade in Duisburg 2010, one of the largest techno music festivals in Europe, a panic in a tunnel at the festival site resulted in a stampede that killed 21 people and injured more than 500 revelers. Shortly after the incident, organizers of the festival as well as the police and the Duisburg authorities started publicly blaming each other for having caused the stampede. The detailed crisis response of the involved stakeholders is analyzed in this chapter. The objective is to better understand a complex crisis case and draw conclusions from the actors' strategic use of traditional media relations and web-based crisis communication. This case study shows that blame games in the context of tragedies such as the Love Parade do not pay off. Rather, they provoke stakeholders, fuel negative media coverage and amplify reputational damages.

Introduction

"I am 100 percent willing to take risks" (Arackal, 2009, p. 140) said Rainer Schaller, CEO of the German gym chain McFit Ltd., in an interview with a major German business newspaper in summer 2009. One year later he and his company Lopavent Ltd. were organizers of the largest techno music festival in Europe, the Love Parade in Duisburg. During the late afternoon of July 24, a stampede killed 21 people after mass panic broke out in a tunnel. More than 500 participants were injured. Quickly, the media remembered Schaller's statement and asked him whether cost savings regarding security at the festival were part of that business strategy. He denied it, and blamed the police for having caused the stampede. The police refused to take responsibility and blamed Duisburg authorities as well as Lopavent for security failures. Duisburg authorities and the mayor of Duisburg pointed to Lopavent and the police—the beginning of a tragic blame game.

The detailed crisis response of these actors will be analyzed in this chapter. The objective is to understand a complex crisis case and draw conclusions from the actors' strategic crisis communication. Methodologically, the case was analyzed by collecting all relevant press releases, speech transcripts, footage of press conferences and interviews, websites, and expert reports. In addition, a LexisNexis sample of the media coverage on the Love Parade between July 24 and November 1 was reviewed (major German news media).

Background of the Crisis

A Short History of the Love Parade

To understand the background of the Love Parade crisis in 2010 and the allegations against the organizers in Duisburg, some facts about the festival's history are essential. The parade was initiated by the techno DJ Matthias Roeingh, also known as Dr. Motte, in 1989. It started as a small party with 150 participants on the streets of Berlin that was officially declared a political demonstration that turned into an annual festival with steadily rising numbers of visitors from Germany and other countries. At its peak in 1999, 1.5 million people participated. In the next four years this number decreased from 1.3 million in 2000 to 500,000 in 2003. The festival organizers faced financial problems as the Love Parade had not been classified as a political demonstration since 2001. As a consequence, they had to cover most of the costs for security measures and cleanup. In 2004 and 2005 the festival did not take place due to lack of funding. One year later the largest German gym chain, McFit Ltd., became the main sponsor. Its CEO Rainer Schaller bought the Love Parade trademark and organized the festival as CEO of Lopavent Ltd. In 2006 the parade took place in Berlin for the last time with 1.2 million participants.[1] As the senate of Berlin refused to authorize the festival in 2007, the event moved to the city of Essen in the German Ruhr Valley. After the Love Parade in Dortmund in 2008, the music festival was cancelled in 2009 because the city of Bochum did not authorize the festival. The official reason was the lack of capacity of the city's central station.

The Love Parade in Duisburg 2010

In Duisburg the Love Parade took place outside Berlin for the third time. For the fourth time Rainer Schaller and his Lopavent Ltd. (formerly "Loveparade Berlin Ltd.") organized and promoted the event. The gym chain McFit Ltd. with CEO Schaller sponsored the festival. Instead of a procession through downtown as in the years before, the whole event was planned to happen on the grounds of a former railroad depot, a closed area that could be accessed solely through tunnels from the east and west side. Both tunnels met at a ramp, which was supposed to be the only entrance to the festival venue. At the same time, this ramp was the only point of exit (Figure 4.7). The following timeline, CET (Central European Time), describes the course of events and how the Love Parade evolved into a crisis on July 24 (Schwerdtfeger, 2010):

12:00 CET: The organizers opened the festival area with a one-hour delay. A big crowd of participants between Duisburg station and the old railroad depot was waiting to enter.

14:00 CET: The Love Parade with the slogan "the art of love" started. Fifteen floats from six countries circled the building of the old depot. According to the police 105,000 visitors had arrived by train in Duisburg. Rainer Schaller told Associated Press that the festival area had a capacity of 1.6 million people, but he would not expect more than 1.4 million to come.

16:20 CET: The police closed Duisburg central station as too many visitors were arriving and some began to cross the rail tracks. The first participants wanted to leave the festival through the ramp in the center and the tunnels while others pushed the crowd to access the festival area. The first panic reactions occurred.

16:44 CET: The organizers announced that the festival area had to be closed owing to overcrowding. Hundreds of thousands were still waiting to get access.

17:20 CET: More participants breached barriers to access the festival or to escape the overcrowded areas. Some tried to climb a stairway close to the intersection of the tunnels and the central ramp as the pressure in the crowd became intolerable. Several participants fell off the stairway on the crowd below while trying to escape.

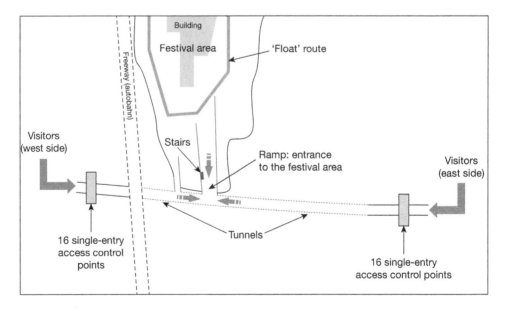

Figure 4.7 Outline of the festival venue and the flow of visitors leading to the stampede.

17:55 CET: The police announced that an accident occurred at the Love Parade. Ten people died, ten were revived, and 15 were injured. Later the number of deaths rose to 16 and the number of injured to 342.

After 18:00 CET: Most participants were not aware of the dramatic accidents. Many ambulances had problems in accessing the areas where they were needed. Mobile communications networks temporarily broke down.

19:00 CET: The crisis management team of the Duisburg authorities decided not to stop the festival to avoid further panic reactions or aggression among the participants. The police established a hotline for people looking for their friends or relatives.

19:45 CET: The first press conference of the crisis management team, the mayor of Duisburg and the Secretary of the Interior of the state of North Rhine–Westphalia (NRW) began.

23:00 CET: The Love Parade festival ended. The music was turned off.

After the festival had ended a further five participants died in hospital as a consequence of their injuries. Later autopsies revealed that all of the 21 deaths were to the result of crushed rib cages. Other participants, panicked by the pressure of the crowd, trampled them to death. Among the victims were 13 women and eight men, aged between 18 and 38 years, 13 from Germany, the remainder from Spain, Australia, Bosnia-Herzegovina, Italy, the Netherlands, and China.

Situation Analysis

The analysis of this case focuses on crisis communication strategies and activities of the organizations that were responsible for planning the Love Parade and the security measures at the festival venue. As these groups received most of the public attention and had to face accusations of wrongdoing, they were—from a public relations perspective—the main actors who had to respond to the crisis:

(1) *Lopavent Ltd.* and its *CEO Rainer Schaller* who, at the same time, was CEO of the festival's main sponsor McFit Ltd.: Lopavent was the organizer and responsible for financing and promoting the event. The company was in charge of setting up a security plan and putting all the necessary security facilities into place (e.g., security cameras, signs). Lopavent also had to contract private security firms to control the festival area and the access points.

(2) The *authorities of the city of Duisburg* with its highest official, the *mayor of Duisburg Adolf Sauerland*: Duisburg authorities were responsible for licensing the whole event to take place at the former railroad depot. They had

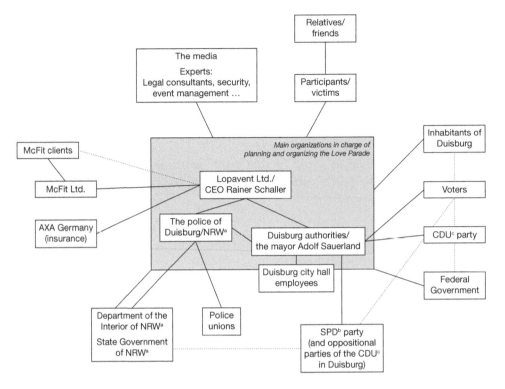

Figure 4.8 A stakeholder map of the Love Parade crisis.

a = the state of North Rhine–Westphalia; b = the Social Democratic Party of Germany; c = the Christian Democratic Union of Germany.

to review Lopavent's security plans, escape way concepts and fire prevention measures. After several meetings between Lopavent representatives, Duisburg authorities, and officials of the police, the fire departments and others, the permission was granted on July 21, three days before the Love Parade started.

(3) The *police* of Duisburg and the state of North Rhine–Westphalia were in charge of ensuring security at the festival area and the city of Duisburg. They were supposed to assist Lopavent's security staff in difficult situations. Before July 24, police officials from Duisburg participated in reviewing and discussing the security plans that Lopavent submitted to receive the permission for the festival.

In crisis situations it is essential for communication professionals to understand stakeholder relationships prior to the crisis and those that arise with the evolvement of the crisis. In the public relations literature stakeholders were described as "people who are linked to an organization because they and the organization have consequences on each other" (Grunig and Repper, 1992, p. 125). These individuals or organizations may vary according to the degree that they become active on a certain issue or a certain organization. Thus, stakeholders are of varying relevance for the crisis response of the respective organizations. This perspective will be used to identify the various stakeholders affected by the activities of Lopavent, the Duisburg authorities and the police of Duisburg in order of priority (Figure 4.8).

The people most affected in Duisburg were the *participants* of the festival, especially those who were part of the crowd in the tunnel and at the ramp where the fatalities occurred. In addition, their *relatives and close friends* belong to that group. Many of them were traumatized by hours of uncertainty and anxiety between the first media reports on the catastrophe and news on the whereabouts and the well-being of their relatives. In terms of crisis response, these stakeholders had substantial needs for information during and shortly after the catastrophe to cope with the consequences and the magnitude of the crisis.

Besides participants and their relatives, the *inhabitants of Duisburg* were substantially affected. Suddenly, their hometown was the subject of national and international news coverage. A tragic catastrophe had happened right on their doorsteps. In addition, the mayor they had voted for, the Duisburg authorities, and the local police seemed to be involved in the crisis. Thus, they had an interest in answers to the question of cause and responsibility as well as future prevention of such tragedies.

Further stakeholders were identified who had strategic interests in the consequences of the crisis for one of the three main crisis communicators. First of all, the *Department of the Interior* of the state of NRW, especially the *Secretary of the Interior Ralf Jäger*, had a stake in the crisis as his department is the superior authority of the police in Duisburg and NRW. Jäger, a member of the Social Democratic Party (SPD), was held accountable for the decisions and actions of the police authorities, although he was not directly involved in planning the police operation in Duisburg. In addition, the *government of the state of NRW* and its *governor Hannelore Kraft* (SPD Party) were affected by the situation for several reasons. First, this government had been in office for only ten days when the crisis erupted, having defeated the old government of the CDU Party (Conservative Party). Thus, the crisis was one of the first serious challenges for Kraft and Secretary Jäger. Second, the mayor of Duisburg was a member of the Conservative Party (CDU). Obviously, there was an interest of the state government and the *SPD party* to destabilize his position. Third, the crisis affected Hannelore Kraft personally as her son was among the participants of the Love Parade.

Besides the NRW government, two competing police unions were involved in publicly speaking for the police authorities: the German Police Union (DPolG) and the Union of the Police (GdP). These organizations primarily defended the police's position after the crisis and used it as an opportunity to gain support and members.

Regarding the organizers of the festival, the Love Parade's main sponsor McFit Ltd. was a relevant stakeholder. The economically successful gym chain had to fear substantial reputational losses, particularly because its CEO Rainer Schaller was one of the prime suspects allegedly responsible for the catastrophe in Duisburg. Instead of boosting the company's brand the sponsor engagement was potentially threatening its profitability as *McFit clients*—another stakeholder group of this crisis—might decide to boycott the company.

The festival's organizer Lopavent purchased insurance with liability limits of 7.5 million euros from the *German AXA Konzern A.G.*, a subsidiary of the AXA Group with headquarters in France. Therefore, the media observed AXA's reaction to the crisis and the handling of insurance payments. For both reasons the insurance company is part of the crisis's stakeholder network.

As for Duisburg's mayor, Adolf Sauerland, the Conservative Party (CDU) had an interest in the crisis as he and one-third of the city council were members of that party. Since 1948 all mayors of Duisburg had been SPD members. Sauerland was the first CDU candidate to win elections since that time. While local CDU members in Duisburg had an interest in keeping their candidate in office, the Federal Government of Germany and Chancellor Angela Merkel, also a CDU member, had to weigh their interests of staying in power in Duisburg or to minimize reputational losses among voters by refusing to support the mayor.

Finally *the media* played a pivotal role by covering the whole festival and the aftermath of the crisis. The regional public broadcaster, WDR (West German Broadcasting Station), with its numerous radio and television programs had reporters and cameras in place when the crisis started. However, WDR was not only covering the crisis, it had also substantially promoted the Love Parade in advance and organized one of the so-called "after parties." Even shortly before the first participants died, WDR reporters were inviting more people to join the festival, not knowing what was happening at the same time on the central ramp.

Initial Response

When a crisis hits it is crucial for organizations to respond within the first hours. Stakeholders, especially victims of a crisis, urgently need instructions on what to do or not to do in order to maximize their own safety. They also look for adjusting information to understand what exactly happened, why it happened and how it might affect them. This helps them to psychologically cope with the situation (Sturges, 1994).

On the other hand, organizations have the opportunity to show that they are in control of the situation and perform as well-prepared crisis managers. As the crisis evolves they can present their view of the situation and establish themselves as a valuable source of information. Practitioners and crisis communication scholars usually refer to form recommendations for the initial crisis response (Coombs, 2007a, p. 128). This includes the advice to respond quickly, to disseminate consistent messages, and to be open in terms of availability for the media, transparency, and honesty. In addition, the information should be accurate and easy to understand for stakeholders. Organizations should make safety their top priority and express concern or sympathy for victims (Coombs, 2007b). These recommendations are used to assess the initial crisis response of the organizers and the responsible authorities of the Love Parade. Part of the initial reactions comprised a number of statements, interviews, and a press conference between the occurrence of the first fatalities and the night of July 24.

The police made the first official announcements by releasing short notifications on its online news ticker. At 5:55 p.m. the police announced that an accident had occurred at the Love Parade with 10 deaths, 10 persons who had to be revived and 15 injured. Approximately one hour later a spokesperson of the Duisburg authorities explained that the crisis team of the Love Parade had decided not to cancel the festival to avoid further stampedes.

Around 7:45 p.m. a first press conference started where police officials, the Secretary of the Interior of NRW, Ralf Jäger, Duisburg's mayor, Adolf Sauerland, the chief of the crisis team, Wolfgang Rabe, as well as the spokesperson of Lopavent, Björn Köllen, informed the public about the incidents at the festival venue. Secretary Jäger started to express his compassion: "I am shocked and sad that people, who wanted to celebrate free of troubles, died. All my sympathy is with their relatives and friends." He also explained that his department ordered additional policemen, doctors, and staff for trauma counseling to help them.

The chief of the crisis management team, also high in rank among the Duisburg authorities, presented a mixture of instructing and adjusting information. According to his latest information, the death of 15 festival participants was probably related to falling off the staircase at the entrance ramp and the panic this might have caused. These persons removed a barrier that was supposed to block access to the staircase. He also repeated the crisis team's decision not to cancel the festival. In a later interview with the television news magazine *Spiegel TV*, he repeated that he wondered about how this could have happened right at this ramp, an open area with all the necessary security measures. During the interview he was walking on a parking lot with his hands in his pants pockets.

The mayor of Duisburg expressed his sympathy with the victims at the press conference as well: "The Love Parade evolved into one of the biggest tragedies in the history of Duisburg." But he also tried to speculate about the causes of the accidents and to downplay his own responsibility: "We did everything possible in advance to have a safe Love Parade." To the question of causality he said: "It was not due to the failed security plan but probably due to individual shortcomings."

The organizer, Lopavent, was represented by its spokesperson, Björn Köllen. He focused his response on expressing compassion with the victims followed by a promise to cooperate with Duisburg authorities to finish the festival peacefully. In an interview after the press conference he added that, in fact, there was still enough space on the festival terrain. Later Lopavent stopped live streaming of the event on its website (www.loveparade.com). Instead, a short text on a black background appeared saying: "Our intention to organize a happy gathering of people was overshadowed by tragic accidents today. We express our sincere condolences to all the families [who lost somebody] and our thoughts are with the ones who still need medical treatment." Since the media had become aware of the catastrophe Lopavent's CEO Schaller did not appear in public anymore on that day, while he had been quite active in promoting the event on television when the parade started in the early afternoon.

The same evening some of the speakers of the first press conference were giving interviews on major news programs and started speculating about causes and responsibility. Secretary Jäger emphasized that the accidents did not happen for lack of police control. Although he claimed that this would not be the day for quick speculations, Jäger also pointed out that Duisburg authorities and the organizer were responsible for security and that future analysis would have to show whether their security concept was appropriate. Right after this interview, Michael Schreckenberg, a professor from the University of Duisburg-Essen, commented on the case. Before the festival started he had been paid by Duisburg authorities to review the whole security concept. Now he insisted that the festival area as well as the tunnels were big enough for this number of participants. It was just not foreseeable that participants would remove the fences that blocked the access to the staircase at the ramp: "That people would fall down from above on the crowd was just not part of the security plan."

Finally, Hannelore Kraft, the governor of the state of NRW arrived in Duisburg to visit a hospital where some of the victims were being given treatment. She later gave interviews on television and radio in which she said that she hoped for all the families that their children would come back home safe: "Later we will have to analyze thoroughly what happened. Now, emotions are dominating." Kraft also mentioned her personal connection to the tragedy as her son attended the festival; although he had returned home safely. The governor's office disseminated a press release expressing her compassion: "The whole nation is mourning the death of these young women and men."

Strategies and Tactics

Duisburg Authorities and Mayor Adolf Sauerland

Goal 1: To keep the mayor in office and regain support for CDU politics in Duisburg.

Objective: There were two main objectives concerning crisis response that can hardly be separated from each other: (1) To regain popularity among Duisburg residents and (2) to prevent a no-confidence vote at Duisburg City Council or to prevent a majority of two-thirds of the council's representatives, once the no-confidence vote takes place.

Strategy 1: The mayor tried to demonstrate sincere compassion with the victims and residents of Duisburg. His crisis response was a mixture of excuses and victimage strategies.

Tactic 1.1: One day after the accidents the mayor brought flowers to the festival location in Duisburg to show his grief while being filmed by the media. As a result, people started to boo and threatened him physically. He fled the scene with the help of security staff.

Tactic 1.2: The mayor participated in a press conference that was held at 12:00 a.m., the day after the festival. Besides him, the CEO of Lopavent, the vice president of the police of Duisburg, and the chief of the crisis team (Duisburg authorities) spoke at this press conference. The mayor expressed his deepest sympathy for the victims and their relatives. He acknowledged that while the question of causes and blame was crucial, the public attorney's office in Duisburg would need time for investigation. For this reason and to protect his employees he would not say anything about the incident, but he would hand out all relevant documents to the investigators. He said it was very important for him to have time to take care of the victims and their relatives.

Rabe, the chief of the crisis team, explained that the whole security concept was reviewed by experts and agreed with all involved authorities and the organizer. He said the festival terrain was definitely big enough. A journalist asked about the rumors that officials of the fire department had criticized the concept prior to the festival. Rabe denied that he heard of such warnings.

Tactic 1.3: On July 26, the mayor published a personal statement on the website of the Duisburg authorities and his personal website. The statement was also sent out as a press release by his public relations office. Again, the mayor expressed his sympathy for the victims saying that he felt very sorry for what had happened. He would understand the public call for his resignation. But first, it would be necessary to have time to investigate the case and to look for answers. In case this investigation found evidence of wrongdoing by the city of Duisburg, he would take full responsibility.

A second personal statement followed on August 2. Besides his compassion, Sauerland emphasized that this incident deeply traumatized all his employees at city hall and himself (victimage). In addition, the message announced the establishment of an internal investigation group and a first report that would be submitted to the parliament of NRW. He also promised that he would hold a no-confidence vote at the city's council. Further, he encouraged the establishment of a parliamentary committee of inquiry to investigate the case in terms of political responsibility.

Tactic 1.4: Between July 26 and August 16, Mayor Sauerland gave interviews to some newspapers, news magazines, and television. He used them to underpin the statements he had published before. Meanwhile, Sauerland was physically attacked on the street and received death threats. He referred to these experiences during the interviews as a means to garner sympathy for his and his family's situation (victimage strategy). As to the calls for his resignation he argued that he needed to be in office to be able to play an active role in the investigation. Most of the interviews were rather short. A 20-minute long interview on WDR TV on August 15 was the exception.

Tactic 1.5: As the interviews mentioned above were published, at least two major newspapers quoted him as saying that he did not sign any authorization personally. This caused outrage among his city hall employees. In an internal letter to them, Mayor Sauerland apologized for his ambiguous wording, stating that he never meant to distance himself from his employees (excuse).

Strategy 2: Mayor Sauerland wanted to play an active role in the investigation of the case to underpin the necessity to stay in office. Part of the strategy was to diminish perceptions of responsibility.

Tactic 2.1: To demonstrate this intention an external law firm was contracted to review all the files related to the Love Parade that were available in city hall. A preliminary report was presented to the public on August 3, one day before the mayor was supposed to participate in a public hearing at the parliament of NRW. The report concluded that employees of the mayor's office did not violate any of their obligations. "External actors" were responsible. On the basis of this report the mayor read his statement at the public hearing on August 4.

A second "final report" was publicly presented on September 1. The mayor was not present. The conclusion was the same: The organizer, Lopavent, and the police were in charge of security at the venue, not the Duisburg authorities. Mayor Sauerland presented the conclusions at the second public hearing of the parliament on September 2, where he distanced himself from the blame game that was taking place. The results of both activities were published as press releases.

Strategy 3: The Duisburg authorities started some publicly visible activities to compensate victims and to help them to cope psychologically with the consequences of the crisis.

Tactic 3.1: A spokesperson announced that Mayor Sauerland would not participate in the official memorial service at the Salvatori Church in Duisburg. He did not want to provoke or hurt the victims' families. However, other representatives of his office were present.

Tactic 3.2: A press release on August 4 announced that the Duisburg authorities had established a hotline to offer trauma counseling.

Tactic 3.3: Duisburg authorities were part of a newly founded citizen's initiative that wanted to find ways to commemorate the tragedy. A press release on August 6 announced the group's first meeting in the city hall. Subsequent press releases discussed the progress of the group's work (such as, the installation of a glass cube with flowers, candles, and letters of condolence).

Tactic 3.4: After the insurance company AXA and Rainer Schaller announced that they would pay one million euros to help victims, on July 29, the city of Duisburg contributed an additional 500,000 euros to that amount (press release on August 12).

Lopavent Ltd., McFit Ltd., and CEO Rainer Schaller

Goal 1: To minimize reputational and financial losses of the main sponsor McFit Ltd. and CEO Rainer Schaller.

Objective 1: To minimize perceptions of the organizer's responsibility for the accidents.

Strategy 1: Lopavent used multiple channels of communication to express the organizer's compassion for the victims and to offer compensation.

Tactic 1.1: Rainer Schaller appeared personally at the press conference one day after the festival. He read a one-and-a-half minute long statement expressing his sympathy for the victims: "Words cannot express the grief we feel." He promised to do everything possible to clarify the causes of the incident. Out of respect for the victims he declared that this Love Parade was the last.

Tactic 1.2: A statement of grief was posted on the official website of the parade on a black background. Users were asked to express their condolences online. Some days later the digital book of condolences was removed (probably for too many critical postings).

Tactic 1.3: Schaller gave only a few newspaper and television interviews after the incident. On July 27, a video that showed Schaller in a castle reading a statement, was sent to major television networks and online news portals. In a later interview on August 31, he said, that as organizer he had a moral responsibility, but the investigation would have to find out who is to blame. He felt sorry for what had happened.

Tactics 1.4: The insurance company AXA and McFit Ltd. issued a press release to announce a payment of one million euros to victims of the Love Parade on July 29. The money came primarily from AXA and the private coffers of Schaller. It also said: "This aid package must not be understood as admission of guilt."

Strategy 2: Lopavent tried to demonstrate transparency and willingness to investigate the causes of the accidents.

Tactic 2.1: The interviews and statements mentioned above were all used to emphasize that Schaller would have an interest in clarifying the causes of the stampede. He also said that he never had the intention to earn money with the Love Parade. The festival was only sponsored and organized for marketing purposes (McFit Ltd.).

Tactic 2.2: On August 30, Lopavent published most of the footage of the security cameras of the festival on its website. Statements on this website and several interviews with Schaller on television, radio, and in news magazines emphasized that this decision was made to show the willingness to be transparent and help to throw light on the causes of the catastrophe.

Strategy 3: Lopavent tried shifting the blame onto the police (scapegoating).

Tactic 3.1: Schaller pointed to the police's role in his interviews several times. At the press conference on August 25, he mentioned that they never doubted the security concept as Duisburg authorities and the police had reviewed it. Subsequent questions by journalists on the festival's security measures were answered by his spokesperson. He tried to avoid saying anything about possible causes at the press conference: "We are not beating around the bush— we have to wait for the results of the attorney's investigation."

Tactic 3.2: Lopavent produced a six-and-a-half minute long documentary of the catastrophe. Animations, edited material of the security camera footage, and original documents were supposed to prove that the police caused the stampede. The movie was made available on Lopavent's website and circulated on Youtube (31,304 views on November 30).

Objective 2: To prevent McFit clients from canceling their contracts with local McFit gyms.

Strategy 1: McFit showed compassion to the victims.

Tactic 1.1: The company published a statement of grief on its website. Some McFit advertising posters in Duisburg were covered by black sheets with the statement: "We are mourning."

Strategy 2: The company kept silent in an attempt to avoid negative associations between Lopavent/the Love Parade and McFit. No press releases on the issue could be found at McFit's online press center. The only exception was AXA's and Rainer Schaller's announcement of the one million euros payment to the victims.

Strategy 3: To a certain extent McFit encouraged dialogue among its clients.

Tactic 3.1: McFit used some of its online platforms to stimulate dialogue and discussion among clients. On the discussion forum http://forum.mcfit.de users discussed questions such as "Still train at McFit gyms after Love Parade?" (82 replies and almost 10,000 hits) between August 2 and 28. Additionally, McFit's Facebook profile was used as a discussion forum where the company posted two statements from July 24 to 25. After that date the Facebook site was shut down for several weeks. "Respect for the victims and their relatives" was posted to explain this decision on August 16 when the profile went online again. No further postings on the topic followed.

Police of NRW, Police Unions, and the Department of the Interior of NRW

Goal 1: To maintain the government's support of the police and to prevent the Department of the Interior (DoI) from being held accountable for failures of the police.

Objective 1: To minimize perceptions of the police's responsibility for the accidents and to prevent the establishment of a parliamentary committee of inquiry from investigating the case in terms of political responsibility.

Strategy 1: The police, the DoI, and the police unions denied responsibility for the stampede and tried shifting the blame to Lopavent and Duisburg authorities (scapegoating).

Tactic 1.1: The vice president of the police of Duisburg spoke at the second press conference on July 25. He denied that the police was responsible and praised their good work. This position was also emphasized by interviews with Secretary Jäger on major television news shows, interviews with several presidents and vice-presidents of the police unions, as well as press releases of the DoI and the police unions. They emphasized that sufficient policemen were in place and did an excellent job in rescuing people. The organizers were formally in charge of security at the closed festival venue. They mentioned repeatedly that police officials had warned Duisburg authorities and Lopavent in advance.

Strategy 2: The DoI and the police wanted to appear as active investigators by demonstrating openness and transparency.

Tactic 2.1: Two days after the incident Secretary Jäger approached the parliament of NRW to inform members about all the available "facts," followed by a press release.

Tactic 2.2: Secretary Jäger and selected police officials attended two public hearings at the parliament of NRW on August 4 and September 2. Before these meetings on July 28 and August 17, additional press conferences were held. Most of the material including speeches, slides, figures, and expert reports were supposed to underpin their position that failures of the organizer and the Duisburg authorities led to the stampede. This material was made available on the website of the DoI.

Strategy 3: The DoI and the police unions started early to attack their accusers.

Tactic 3.1: Secretary Jäger and occasionally the Governor of NRW insisted publicly (in interviews) on the resignation of the mayor of Duisburg. Press releases and public statements of the police unions also reinforced this position.

Tactic 3.2: The police unions aggressively attacked Lopavent and its CEO in regular press releases and interviews. They also criticized Schaller for refusing to participate in the public hearings. Schaller instead sent his lawyers: "Schaller's refusal is cowardly and outrageous" (August 28).

Objective 2: To gain support and sympathy for the state government's crisis management among the population of the state of NRW.

Strategy 1: The DoI and the government of NRW showed compassion for the victims and their relatives.

Tactic 1.1: Together with Governor Kraft and a police official, Secretary Jäger was filmed bringing flowers to the place where most of the victims had died the day before.

Tactic 1.2: Secretary Jäger ordered all public institutions in the state to fly their flags at half-mast (press release). He and police officials expressed their sincere compassion at the beginning of most of the press conferences and public hearings. One police official almost started to cry while speaking at a press conference of the DoI on July 27.

Tactic 1.3: The government of NRW invited the media to film a "one-minute silence" in commemoration of the Love Parade victims on July 27. On July 29 a press release announced that the government's health institutions would offer trauma counseling for victims and those who were on duty on July 24.

Tactic 1.4: Kraft, Jäger, police officials, and others participated in a memorial service that was held at a church in Duisburg on July 31. This event was broadcast on major television channels in Germany. The governor's emotional speech received positive feedback from the media and the Internet community (Twitter, YouTube, Facebook). The government made the speech transcript and high quality pictures available on its website.

Strategy 2: The government of NRW and the DoI started corrective actions and offered compensation to the victims.

Tactic 2.1: On August 3, after governor Kraft had promised "quick and unbureaucratic help" during the memorial service, the government announced several forms of compensation and help, including a fund of one million euros, the appointment of an ombudsman to help victims, the establishment of a hotline and the encouragement of donations for the victims.

Tactic 2.2: Since August 4, the DoI publicly announced that it would change the laws and regulations concerning security measures at bigger festivals to avoid future catastrophes. Press releases, speeches at the two public hearings of the parliament and a press conference on August 17 were used for this purpose.

Strategy 3: The police and the DoI used strategies of ingratiation and victimage.

Tactic 3.1: Secretary Jäger used the press conferences and public hearings to praise the media for their active research on the causes of the incident.

Tactic 3.2: The police unions and the DoI used press releases and comments during press conferences to praise each other's crisis management and suggestions for corrective action.

Tactic 3.3: Since the second press conference on July 25, police officials and Jäger have mentioned the difficult and dangerous situation that threatened the policemen on July 24 in terms of both physical and psychological health.

Outcomes Assessment

100 days after the Love Parade a weblog journalist described the crisis as a "catastrophe without consequences" (Laurin, 2010). He referred primarily to the fact that none of the politicians involved in planning and authorizing the festival had to step down. Neither McFit, Lopavent nor CEO Rainer Schaller had to pay a lot of money. No high-ranking police officials lost their jobs. No one has been prosecuted at the time this chapter was completed.

However, media reports, Internet user comments, and reactions to public appearances of the actors in question indicated that they suffered substantial damages of reputation and trust. As a result of the case study, two major reasons led to this outcome. First of all, the mayor of Duisburg, the police, as well as Lopavent and its CEO were all perceived as being responsible for the crisis to a certain extent. A content analysis of 943 randomly selected guest book entries from the website of a major radio channel of the state of NRW (WDR 1Live) produced tentative evidence for that assumption. This guest book was set up by 1Live Radio on the evening of July 24, where users were asked to comment on the Love Parade catastrophe. Thirty-seven percent (or 345) of the entries until August 31 addressed the question of responsibility and blame; 41 percent of these 345 user comments blamed Mayor Sauerland and/or the Duisburg authorities, 66 percent blamed "the organizers" (including Lopavent) and 15 percent held the police responsible. Such attributions of responsibility have been proven to damage an organization's reputation (Coombs and Holladay, 2004).

Second, the public blame game that these organization started right after July 24 led to highly unfavorable media coverage and outrage among victims and other persons who felt they were affected by the crisis. The mayor of Duisburg, for instance, was booed and attacked by locals during most of his rare public appearances after the Love Parade. On November 11, he was even splattered with ketchup by a man wearing a T-shirt that said "21 who fell in silence accuse you." Whether Mayor Sauerland will be able to remain in office with such a lack of support among Duisburg residents is questionable. Rainer Schaller, who survived a car accident in his Lamborghini on August 6 without injuries, did not appear in public from August 30 to December 2, 2010. As for McFit Ltd., further research needs to be conducted to ascertain whether it suffered financial losses after the incident or not. According to an online news article from September 1, polls on McFit's image indicated substantial damages after the Love Parade crisis (Huth, 2010).

An investigation by the city attorney's office in Duisburg was still ongoing at the completion of this case analysis. Whether Love Parade 2010 remains a "catastrophe without consequences" remains questionable.

Lessons Learned

One lesson of this case is the selection of communication channels by the crisis communicators. Besides traditional media, the Internet was an important platform for information and dialogue on the crisis among stakeholders. Many participants uploaded private photos and videos showing the stampede and people falling off the staircase at the entrance ramp. The crisis was a major topic on weblogs, microblogs, and social networks where people, including festival participants and relatives of the victims, expressed their condolences and discussed what had happened or who had to be blamed. However, the police or the Duisburg authorities rarely used interactive online media (Web 2.0) to communicate with stakeholders. Only Lopavent was quite active in uploading statements and video footage on its website. Generally, strategies of interactive online communication were rarely used. Even McFit seemed to be afraid of negative postings. Most of the online crisis communication of the actors was limited to traditional media relations and one-way communication.

The case of the Love Parade showed that blame games in crisis communication do not pay off. Usually, these strategies are zero-sum games that nobody is able to win. Rather, shifting blame to others in the context of a severe crisis usually provokes stakeholders or the media and amplifies reputational damages. Most people perceived the catastrophe of the Love Parade as a human-error accident with high levels of attributed responsibility (Coombs, 2007b, p. 65). According to the situational crisis communication theory the gap between responsibility as perceived by stakeholders and responsibility as publicly accepted by an organization should be as small as possible (Coombs and Holladay, 2004). Hence, in the case of the Love Parade crisis, denial strategies were the wrong choice. The situation would have needed the involved actors to apologize, accept parts of the responsibility and offer compensation. Only the latter was applied in this case.

Showing compassion for victims and offering instructing as well as adjusting information as done by most of these organizations was fairly appropriate. However, the messages did not have much effect on their credibility as they were combined with denying responsibility and blaming others. It can be assumed that Governor Kraft's compassion was perceived as most authentic as she was personally affected, gave a very touching speech at the memorial service some days after the incident, and did not take part in the public blame game.

Discussion Questions

1. The initial response of the mayor of Duisburg, the police, and Lopavent, especially the two press conferences on July 24 and 25, were heavily criticized in public. What were the reasons and how could they have done better?
2. Four months after the Love Parade the mayor of Duisburg was still booed and attacked on the street. What tactics in crisis communication could have changed the outcome for him?
3. What kind of online communication strategy of either the police, the mayor of Duisburg, or Lopavent would have yielded better results in terms of reputation?
4. What are possible future outcomes for the police and secretary Jäger? Why was their approach the most risky regarding the strategic choices of the three main actors in this case?

Note

1   All participant numbers from 2006 to 2008 were officially announced by the organizers and may be "strategically" overestimated for marketing purposes (www.handelsblatt.com/politik/deutschland/loveparade-hohe-besucherzahl-angeblich-nur-marketingtrick;2636216).

References

Arackal, S. (2009). McFit-Chef Rainer Schaller: "Ich bin 100 Prozent risikobereit". Retrieved from www.handelsblatt.com/mcfit-chef-rainer-schaller-ich-bin-100-prozent-risikobereit-/3222188.html

Coombs, W. T. (2007a). *Ongoing crisis communication. Planning, managing, and responding* (2nd ed.). Los Angeles, CA: Sage.

Coombs, W. T. (2007b). Crisis management and communications. Retrieved from www.instituteforpr.org

Coombs, W. T., and Holladay, S. J. (2004). Reasoned action in crisis communication: An attribution theory-based approach to crisis management. In D. P. Millar and R. Heath (Eds.), *Responding to crisis. A Rhetorical approach to crisis communication* (pp. 95–115). Mahwah, NJ: Lawrence Erlbaum.

Grunig, J. E., and Repper, F. C. (1992). Strategic management, publics, and issues. In J. E. Grunig (Ed.), *Excellence in public relations and communication management* (pp. 117–157). Hillsdale, NJ: Lawrence Erlbaum.

Huth, D. (2010). Loveparade-Drama kratzt am Image von McFit. Retrieved from www.derwesten.de/staedte/duisburg/Loveparade-Drama-kratzt-am-Image-von-McFit-id3638080.html

Laurin, S. (2010). 100 Tage Loveparade. Retrieved from www.ruhrbarone.de/100-tage-loveparade/

Schwerdtfeger, C. (2010). Die Ereignisse des Tages zum Nachlesen: Tote und Chaos bei der Loveparade. Retrieved from www.rp-online.de/niederrheinnord/duisburg/loveparade/Toteund-Chaos-bei-der-Loveparade_aid_885642.html

Sturges, D. L. (1994). Communicating through crisis: A strategy for organizational survival. *Management Communication Quarterly*, 7, 297–316.

VIEWS FROM AN EXPERT

BRIGITTE KALTWASSER

Brigitte Kaltwasser, CEO of Kaltwasser Communications, Nuremberg, Munich and Berlin, started her career in 1982 as a journalist of major German newspapers. She has taught crisis communication at German universities for more than ten years and is a frequently booked speaker at international communication congresses. Ms. Kaltwasser has run her own PR firm since 1990 in Germany, consulting with international companies on crisis issues as well as corporate communication.

The first contact I had with the Love Parade crisis was on the evening of July 24 at 8 p.m. watching one of the major German television news shows. The Duisburg tragedy was the top story reporting that about 20 young persons had died, crushed on their way to or out of the music festival. The only interview that I was aware of at this time—the tragedy happened only 2 hours before—was given by the mayor of Duisburg, Adolf Sauerland. He stated that he was of course outraged and shocked. Right in the same sentence he claimed that it was not the fault of the Duisburg authorities. According to him, everything was perfectly organized by the municipal organizations. This was the start of the blame game. I immediately recognized, that—in addition to the tragedy itself—the reactions of the responsible actors would hurt the concerned people even more.

Overall it was one of the most tragic events that happened in Germany in 2010, amplified by a highly nonprofessional handling of this crisis.

Analyzing the case, I can clearly mention the following major problems regarding the crisis response of the three main actors as mentioned in this chapter:

- None of them took (adequate) responsibility.
- All of them blamed the others.
- They did not work together or communicate.
- They were totally overwhelmed by the situation.
- They were not familiar with crisis situations—at least this was not obvious.

The main sponsor of the Love Parade, Rainer Schaller, CEO of Lopavent and McFit, reacted inadequately. He hardly appeared in public in the first few days after the tragedy. It seemed that he tried to keep himself out of the game as much as possible. He hardly took part in most of the press conferences, held by the Duisburg authorities and the government of NRW. It was more than one week before Schaller offered financial and psychological support for the relatives of the victims. I do not have any reliable figures yet, but I expect this behavior to negatively impact his future business with McFit Ltd.

The police and the authorities of the state of North Rhine–Westphalia were the quickest to respond on television and radio—almost immediately after the tragedy happened. The police and Secretary Jaeger especially were the most active in fueling the blame game by completely shifting their own responsibility onto whomever.

The most tragic person in the aftermath was the mayor of Duisburg, Adolf Sauerland. From my perspective his crisis response was the worst among the main actors in this case. Sauerland used every "camera opportunity" to state that he and his office had made no mistakes. From a psychological angle it was clear that Sauerland was totally overwhelmed and only afraid of losing his job. He was not able to authentically express that he cared about the victims and their relatives or friends. He was just sticking to his story, obviously not using any consulting support on how to deal with this crisis in a professional way.

As a crisis communication expert, I am more than disappointed by the way these amateurish players handled such a severe tragedy. Their uncoordinated and selfish behavior even increased the pain for the victims' relatives and friends.

Even on an international scale, I consider the Duisburg tragedy to be an example of major failure and incapacity to manage crisis communication professionally. The involved actors failed not only regarding the content of their crisis response, but also the selection of communication channels was inappropriate. The use of dialog and social media was almost completely disregarded in this case—unbelievable in the twenty-first century!

Russia

Turnaround in Russia: Crisis Communication Campaign During the 2008 War in South Ossetia

Alexander G. Nikolaev

Government crisis communication skills are most visible during wartime campaigns. Since the collapse of the Soviet Union the field of public relations has experienced a tremendous growth in Russia. The new level of professional development in this area in the country became evident during the 2008 war in South Ossetia. The war communication campaign was handled quite successfully by Russian officials and public relations professionals. They were able to correctly identify key stakeholders and create effective strategies for working with them. Interestingly, they were able to catch the other side out on lies and fabrications and use that to their advantage.

Introduction

The evolution of the field of public relations and of the area of crisis communication in particular in Russia has been long and torturous (Nikolaev and Goregin, 1995; Goregin and Nikolaev, 1996). It developed from the old Soviet "administrative command" style (as the Russians call it) to the contemporary weird mixture of stoic toughness, cheap publicity, and traditional indifference toward public opinion. Until recently, it seemed as if Russians learned almost nothing in this area except for the art of spin. But some recent events showed something quite different.

Background of the Crisis

The Old Russian Crisis Communication Style

For the benchmark comparison reason it is important to see what the old Soviet/Russian style of government crisis communication looked like. If we look at some major past international disasters (such the Korean Air 007 incident of 1983 or the Chernobyl catastrophe of 1986) we shall see that the way the Soviet government tried to handle emergencies closely resembled (certainly, with some interpretational deviations) the Kübler-Ross model outlining the five stages of grief: denial, anger, bargaining, depression, acceptance.

Everything started with denial: "All this is not true and this is just capitalist propaganda." That was followed by the anger stage: "How dare you accuse us of something like that! Everything is good and perfect in our world." When concrete proof of the actual event became irrefutable—the bargaining stage followed: "Yes, maybe something like that really happened but there are certain conditions for us to admit it." (As, for example, the West would have to admit that the KAL-007 flight was in fact a spy plane.) After bargaining would certainly fail, a long-lasting stage of really depressed silence would follow. The Soviets hoped that the storm would just blow over and everything would simply be forgotten. But eventually (sometimes it would take decades) they would get to the acceptance stage and come clean, releasing related information and details about the crisis. That is, it was an emotional knee-jerk type of reaction rather than a planned and rational response to an unpleasant event.

It is also important to know that throughout all crises the Soviet population was completely blocked from any information coming from abroad. European and American media were not quoted; radio stations (such as the Voice of America) were electronically jammed all over the country. Information from the actual location of the crisis was also either severely limited or practically non-existent. The Russian population found out what was going on in Chernobyl only years after the catastrophe happened.

Taking into account that even after the collapse of the Soviet Union the country's communication culture did not change much and many Communist Party *apparatchiks* still remained in their places, any progress in the government crisis communication area was very unlikely and was actually almost invisible. But all that changed quite dramatically in August of 2008.

The Event—The 08/08/08 War

Some History Behind the Triple-Eight War

By 2008 the republic of South Ossetia had been a de facto independent state for almost 18 years. It seceded from the Republic of Georgia (one of the former Soviet republics). It is important to know that this conflict has a long and complex history. Throughout most of known history Georgians and Ossetians (the correct ethnic name is Alans or As-Alans) lived peacefully in harmony fighting together against common enemies. But the two nations became part of the Russian empire at different times and absolutely independently. Ossetia joined Russia in 1774. The process of Georgia's joining the big empire took

18 years (from the 1783 Georgia Treaty to the 1801 Manifesto by the Russian czar Alexander I).

It is interesting to highlight here that from that time Georgia and Ossetia both ceased to exist as independent states because in the Russian empire there were no national or ethnic formations. There were just districts directly ruled by Russian governors. So, each country was also broken into such smaller districts. At the same time, the czar government always especially safeguarded the national identity of Ossetians as a minor nation. For example, on September 12, 1852, the Russian government rejected all the attempts of Georgian princes to claim Ossetian peasants as their slaves (Dzugaeva, n.d.).

At the present time, some historians falsify history by claiming that Russians occupied Georgia by force. Indeed, Russians saved the Georgian nation from complete annihilation by Persian forces. In 1795 Agha Mohammad Khan conducted a campaign of genocide in Georgia, quickly killing more than 80,000 Georgians. So, they appealed to the Russians and on September 11, 1795, in a big Battle of Krtsanisi, the Russian–Georgian–Ossetian force defeated the army of the Persian ruler and, by so doing, ended the genocide. After that, Georgians (region-by-region) gladly and absolutely voluntarily joined the Russian empire (Dzugaeva, n.d.).

The big problem started after the Russian revolution of 1917. Georgia was one of the first republics to declare independence. Ossetia decided to stay with the newly-born Russian Soviet Socialist Republic. And the Georgians did not like that at all. They claimed the southern part of the Alania region (South Ossetia) as part of their homeland and in 1918 started the first ethnic cleansing campaign. In just one year, 1920, they killed or expelled one-half of the Ossetian population. Only the interference of the Red Army in 1921 stopped that genocide.

The early years of the Soviet era made the situation even more complex. Joseph Stalin became the Secretary General of the Russian Communist Party on April 3, 1922. His first order of business (on April 20, 1922) was to give South Ossetia to his native Georgia. He did it without asking anybody, using just his sheer power. There was a political reason behind that: at that time he conducted serious negotiations with different republics trying to convince them to join the future Soviet Union (which actually happened in December of 1922). He thought that such a gift would make Georgians more likely to join the future union. Maybe he was right, but, by so doing, he put South Ossetians for the first time under direct Georgian rule.

But the worst started happening around the time of the collapse of the Soviet Union. In 1989 the Georgian government deprived South Ossetia of its autonomous status. On September 20, 1990, South Ossetia proclaimed complete independence from Georgia. On September 1, 1991, the newly-born republic proclaimed itself a part of the Russian Federation. But on January 19, 1992, in a national referendum, 98 percent of the population voted for complete independence again. And that's when all hell broke loose.

The second twentieth-century ethnic cleansing campaign against Ossetians (after the 1918–1921 one) was led by Zviad Gamsakhurdia (who simply called Ossetians "human garbage"). Numerous horrendous crimes against humanity were committed. Entire Ossetian villages were wiped out along with their populations. For example, in 1991 in a village called Eredvi, Gamsakhurdia forces buried dozens of peaceful villagers *alive* and waited until they all died in the ground—when the soil stopped moving. A peace deal was brokered by the Russians and on July 14, 1992 a small United Nations peacekeeping force (just three battalions) was placed between the two sides in a small demilitarized zone, but not before between 2,000 and 4,000 South Ossetians were killed by the Georgians (Dzugaeva, n.d.).

The next Georgian leader, Mikheil Saakashvili, came to power as a result of a coup d'état in November of 2003. He failed to address the main problem in the country—the economy—and needed a small victorious war to hold on to power. As many times before, Ossetians were chosen as the scapegoats. So, the third anti-Ossetian ethnic cleansing campaign started in the summer of 2004. But Saakashvili forces were quickly and decisively defeated by the Ossetian militia. That humiliation was unbearable for the Georgian ruler but he could not do anything because of strong Russian warnings against any further military actions on his side. And from that time he started looking to the West for support for his genocidal ambitions and amazingly found it.

On August 15, 2006, the Republic of South Ossetia started issuing its own passports. At that time, Russian passports became available for those residents of South Ossetia who wanted to become Russian citizens. By August of 2008, more than 90 percent of South Ossetians had taken Russian citizenship.

At that point the August 2008 war became easily predictable. It is interesting that the author of this chapter warned about that war in his 2006 book. These words were written two full years before the war:

> The Americans installed and currently support the regime of Mikhail Saakashvili, a Georgian nationalist whose forces are poised to renew the campaign of genocide against the population of Southern Ossetia (an ethnic region in the republic of Georgia). The U.S. are directly financing and training the military forces of this dictator. Actually, the U.S. spent 64 million dollars to equip and train the Saakashvili forces. Some time earlier Russian forces stopped genocide in that region and signed a special agreement with the previous leader of Georgia—Shevardnadze. And now the only force that stands between the Saakashvili army—trained, equipped, and led by American instructors—and the population of Southern Ossetia is a small (about 500 soldiers) contingent of the Russian peacekeepers (stationed there according to that previous agreement). American administration many times expressed an explicit and official support for Saakashvili's actions.
>
> (Nikolaev, 2006, p. 214)

So, after having received such powerful support and after his personal meeting with Condoleezza Rice in Tbilisi almost exactly one month before the war (on July 10, 2008), Saakashvili decided to take his revenge. He honestly believed that the Russians would not dare interfere this time.

On the August 5, 2008, Tbilisi evacuated almost all the ethnic Georgians from South Ossetia (about 90 buses full of people crossed the border into Georgia). It became clear that a new war was coming. Saakashvili started the war on August 8 (quite cynically on the day of the opening of the Olympic Games), after promising not to start it just one day before that.

The Timeline

This timeline is a part of the official chronology of the war, which can be found on the website of the RIA Novosti news agency at this web address: http://rian.ru/osetia_spravki/20080811/150272529.html

August 8

00:06 a.m. Georgia starts shelling the capital of South Ossetia—a small township called Tskhinvali. They use a Multiple Launch Rocket System (MLRS) called Grad (Hail). This system is designed to destroy big tank formations on a mass scale. So, the use of this system against civilians officially constitutes a crime against humanity.

2:08 a.m. Georgia officially declares war on Ossetia.

3:46 a.m. A tank attack begins against the town.

4:20 a.m. A massive infantry assault starts. Infantry is followed by death squads. They mass murder Ossetian civilians, wiping out entire families, apartment buildings, and neighborhoods.

4:33 a.m. Russians call for an immediate UN Security Council meeting.

7:23 a.m. Georgian air force starts striking residential neighborhoods of Tskhinvali.

8:56 a.m. Saakashvili forces start an assault on the United Nations peace-keepers' positions.

12:37 p.m. The government and parliament of South Ossetia make a desperate and official plea to the Russian government to save the civilians.

1:34 p.m. Georgian army blows up all the utility pipelines, as well as the town hospital in Tskhinvali, and burns down the university.

4:14 p.m. First units of the Russian armored forces approach Tskhinvali.

6:23 p.m. Some units of the 58th Russian army take over the northern outskirts of the town.

7:32 p.m. Russians make their first airstrike against the Georgian airbase from which the town of Tskhinvali is being bombed.

August 9

2:14 a.m. Shelling of the parts of Tskhinvali that are still resisting the occupiers continues along with mass murder of civilians.

9:17 a.m. One of the tactical groups of the Russian 58th army brakes through the Georgian blockade to the UN peacekeepers and saves those who are still alive.

11:38 a.m. Some units of the Russian 76th and 98th paratrooper (airborne) divisions deploy in South Ossetia along with some other special forces. Russians start a full-scale campaign of liberation of Tskhinvali.

12:59 p.m. Saakashvili forces start surrendering or retreating from the town.

09:00 p.m. Some units of the 58th Russian army push the last Georgian forces from the southern outskirts of the town.

11:50 p.m. After a five-hour battle, Russians destroy 12 Georgian tanks stopping an armored counter-attack on Tskhinvali. They also destroy Georgian artillery positions, and by so doing, finally stop the shelling of the town.

August 10

10:25 a.m. The Ministry of Internal Affairs of Georgia declares the withdrawal of all forces from South Ossetia.

2:40 p.m. Russian air force bombs military installations around the Georgian city of Zugdidi.

6:39 p.m. The first convoy with wounded civilians leaves Tskhinvali for Russia. Before that Georgians did not allow injured to be evacuated and shot at every medical transport moving.

6:56 p.m. Tbilisi pleads for peace. The Russian ambassador receives a special note from Saakashvili.

8:20 p.m. Mass media report on new Russian airstrikes in Georgia, targeting military installations, fuel and ammunition dumps, command and communication centers. There are no reports of casualties or injuries. Russians are making a final push to leave Saakashvili without an opportunity to launch another war by destroying his military capabilities.

9:40 p.m. Tskhinvali is entirely cleared from the remains of Saakashvili death squads. Last Georgian military units hastily retreat to the administrative border between Georgia and South Ossetia.

10:16 p.m. Georgia agrees to let UN peacekeepers (manned exclusively by Russian soldiers and officers) back to their Zugdidi region (the former

UN-established demilitarized zone). The governor of the Zugdidi region officially gives his consent to the presence of the Russian military personnel on his territory.

August 11

00:23 a.m. Georgians start shelling Tskhinvali again but this time from the Georgian territory.

1:22 a.m. In response, Russian artillery starts shelling Georgian military installations and artillery positions around the Georgian town of Gori from which the shelling is conducted.

2:37 a.m. Russians destroy Georgian military installations—the shelling of Tskhinvali stops.

5:24–7:26 a.m. Georgians continue to shoot at the Russian peacekeepers from different locations. In response, Russians suppress military targets in Georgia continuing to degrade Saakashvili's military capabilities.

8:51 a.m. Georgian forces open river dams trying to drown South Ossetia's population and leave them without any opportunity to hide from continuing Georgian air and artillery strikes.

August 12

Throughout the day Georgian strikes and Russian counterstrikes involving air forces and heavy artillery continue.

Russian forces also enter into the Republic of Abkhazia (another independent state formed on the former territory of Georgia) trying to prevent genocide similar to that which had just happened in Ossetia. The jubilation in Abkhazia is overwhelming. People celebrate on the streets greeting their saviors.

1:00 p.m. The president of Russia, Dmitry Medvedev, officially declares that the operation to "pacify Georgia" is over.

The Outcomes of the War

As a result of this war Saakashvili forces murdered more than 2,000 Ossetians (mostly, women, children, and elderly people because all the men were fighting on the front line). About 1,700 of them were Russian citizens. Russian military casualties were: 74 killed, 19 missing in action, 171 wounded. It is especially important to note that among Russians killed were 66 United Nations peacekeepers. Georgia has carefully hidden the number of its military losses. The only thing that can be said here is that the number killed is somewhere between 228 and 3,000 soldiers and officers of all types (army, special, and security forces, ministry of internal affairs forces). Among civilians, Georgians officially reported 69 killed and 61 wounded.

We know what the Americans did after experiencing 2,974 casualties on September 11, 2001. Even more amazing was the fact that the Russians, after experiencing over 2,000 casualties as well, were fighting the war in white velvet gloves. They did not strike a single civilian target—any government buildings, etc. Probably for the first time in the history of warfare, they sent a warning to the personnel of every Georgian military installation before attacking or bombing it. It reduced the number of casualties dramatically. The only civilian casualties were those Georgians who either lived right next to ammunition dumps that were attacked by the Russians and, consequently, catastrophically exploded or those who worked at military installations and did not receive (or did not heed) the warnings. It is interesting that the Russians managed to deliver their warnings to Georgian people while Saakashvili did not find an opportunity to warn his own people living in danger zones. Probably, more civilian casualties were very profitable for his propaganda machine.

Finally, it is important to explain the unusual success of Saakashvili forces at the early stages of the campaign. They managed to take Tskhinvali in a matter of hours. Certainly, it is a fact that he sent his entire army of dozens of thousands of soldiers against a couple of thousand lightly armed militia men. But even in this situation his army had been defeated before. The difference this time was that his army was armed, equipped, and trained by the Americans and other Western countries. During the war several black (of African descent) bodies in uniforms were recovered by the Russian forces along with American documents and passports. There were also several video recordings found supporting this proposition. This fact put in doubt impartiality of the United States in this situation (RIA Novosti, 2008a).

Situation Analysis

Stakeholders Affected

As happens in case of any war there is usually a set of stakeholders involved but also there are some case-specific groups related to this particular situation:

1. As for any government during a war, the *country's citizens* is the most important group of stakeholders. The authorities have to assure significant public support for the war effort.
2. Also, it was important to make sure that the *international community*, especially the *European Union countries*, would be made aware of what was actually happening on the ground.

Under a different set of circumstances, the *people of Georgia* could have been an essential target audience because they were definitely stakeholders in that situation. But, as under any tyrannical regime, they were completely cut off from alternative sources of information and subjected to a powerful propaganda campaign. Therefore, the Russian government did not have any chance of communicating with them seriously, at length.

The Russian government identified a series of goals, objectives, strategies, and tactics for their wartime information campaign.

Goals

1. To mobilize public support for war in Russia.
2. To attain political support (or at least neutrality) of the governments of other countries, especially within the European Union (the geographical proximity factor).

Objectives

1. To have at least 80 percent support for the war effort among citizens and residents of the Russian Federation within the first 48 hours of the war.
2. To have at least two or three major European countries (such as Germany, France, and Italy) support Russian peace-enforcement efforts in the region within the first 96 hours (four days) of the war.

Strategies

To achieve these goals and objectives the Russian government:

- specifically highlighted the suffering of the people of South Ossetia and the horror of the ethnic cleansing campaign;
- exposed lies and fabrications spread by the Western propaganda machine in relation to the South Ossetia situation;
- rhetorically positioned Russian forces in the region as liberators (not occupiers) by explaining their motives and actions in the region; and
- emphasized its own complete openness and transparency during the crisis to increase public confidence in their communication campaign.

Tactics

With all this in mind the Russian government:

- Arranged for the Russian main figures of authority—the President and the Prime Minister—to deliver well-designed speeches during the first hours of the crisis, philosophically framing the situation in the context of liberation. All the speeches were broadcast live on all the Russian TV and radio channels as well as streamed live on the Internet.
- Organized and carried out a massive round-the-clock live-coverage electronic media (TV and radio) campaign. The coverage of the crisis was provided by all the state, public, and private media outlets. A substantial

number of journalists were working in the war zone. Most of them were closely cooperating with the Russian military forces but not embedded with them, which gave them much more freedom and credibility. They thoroughly documented all the events on the ground and immediately sent them to their editorial offices via satellite links. The stories were put on air immediately and practically unedited. Most stories were aired live.

- Ran daily press conferences with the highest-level Russian military officials participating. They were broadcast live by all the state, public and most private electronic media outlets (TV and radio) as well as streamed live on the Internet. The officials were instructed to be completely honest and open. They obviously had an appropriate level of media training. They provided good visuals as well as most up-to-date information (going sometimes overboard as will be shown below).

- Created a system of international media monitoring that helped them immediately detect and expose lies and fabrications spread in the West about the conflict. In each case they quickly issued a media release exposing the falsehood and also made sure that the Russian media was aware of each separate case and would cover it as fully as possible.

- Conducted a series of diplomatic meetings between top Russian officials and top European country leaders (of Italy, France, and Germany). During those meetings Russians explained their actions and political views in relation to the crisis situation. All such meetings were immediately covered by all the Russian state, public and most private electronic media outlets— TV and radio. Practically all Russian print media covered them in-depth a little bit later.

Outcomes Assessment

It is quite difficult to find a good set of recommendations as to how to conduct a government crisis communication campaign in wartime. Some military academies teach this but they keep their materials under wraps because this is where the border between propaganda and public relations becomes really blurred. There are some sets of guidelines for crisis situations. For example, Nikolaev (2009a) specified 30 common basic elements for crisis communication plans. But more appropriate here would be another article the same author wrote (Nikolaev, 2009b). In that work, he analyzed the U.S. communication campaign during the war in Kosovo. He conceptualized a media situation during wartime which he called the *agitation mode*. The agitation mode is a descriptive concept but it can also serve as a rough set of guidelines on how to conduct a government public relations campaign during international war crises.

The first thing that is important to highlight is that in August 2008 changes in Russian government crisis public relations were not evolutionary but revolutionary. Everything changed dramatically. Probably for the first time in

Russian government history the notion of "no PR is best PR" was completely rejected. Russian high-level political leaders stopped hiding behind public relations people and stepped into the light themselves. Even Russian military leaders were open and talked to journalists in a normal tone of voice (which had never occurred before). All this probably happened because Russians realized that if they did not do proper public relations, they would be simply overrun by the enormous Western propaganda machine. So, this time they were very smart.

They concentrated their main effort on their primary target audience—their own citizens. As Nikolaev (2009a) highlights, the internal public is the main one in any crisis situation because if these people defect—the organization (or country) is surely going to collapse. So, the government started talking to the Russians. But how easy was their job?

The first point in the agitation mode model states that in order for a wartime public relations campaign to succeed an important domestic political condition has to be present—"no significant political opposition should exist" in the country (Nikolaev, 2009b, p. 216). Within the first 48 hours the political support for the war within the Russian population went above 80 percent. Besides that, the author of this article was in the country at that time and was able to observe all the media interactions. And although some opposition was visible, it was mostly marginalized—approximately to the same extent as the opposition against the war in Kosovo was in the United States.

For the sake of fairness, it is necessary to say that it was difficult to be against the 2008 South Ossetia war for obvious humanitarian reasons. Therefore, there were just two groups opposing the war. The first one was political extremists. For example, die-hard communists called the war "imperialistic." The second group consisted of organizations and media directly managed and financed from the West. It is not really necessary to talk about them here because they do not reflect Russian public opinion (although, in the West they are mostly used as such for propaganda purposes). But in any case, the first condition was satisfied.

The second condition states that "low ego-involvement is required." This condition was only partly satisfied. On one hand it was a high-ego-involvement situation for most Russians. It was all happening right on the Russian state borders, Russian citizens were being killed, and many Russians had relatives and friends in that area. But what low ego-involvement mostly means is a low fear of losses. That was definitely the case. The Russians used in the operation only fast reaction professional military forces. Therefore, the fear that raw recruits would suffer was low. And certainly Russians did not fear any strikes by Georgians against their territory either.

The following several points were preconditioned by the very nature of the conflict. Definitely, the whole media debate was conducted in value-based (good versus evil) "good-guys/bad-guys" terms. The entire "drama" was shown to every Russian family on TV as it was unfolding. And the crimes committed by the Saakashvili regime indeed created "emotions of fear and anger against perpetrators" (Nikolaev, 2009b, pp. 126–127) without a huge effort on the Russian side.

The stage for a debate was indeed "preset and framed by a figure of authority" (Nikolaev, 2009b, p. 127). In this case, there were actually two figures—the President of Russia, Dmitry Medvedev, and the Prime Minister of the country, Vladimir Putin. They reacted to the event very quickly. A few hours after the attack on Tskhinvali started, both of them delivered very tough speeches and in unequivocal terms explained their stance on the issue. Since both leaders are still quite popular with the Russians (more than 70 percent support) their words were heeded and definitely made at least some impact on the public (Vesti, 2008a).

The last condition of the agitation mode was not satisfied. The last condition states that "a highly technologically developed society facilitates the media agitation mode because the war coverage is easily turned into a video game (for example, using camera shots from smart bomb warheads, etc.). No enemy's civilian casualties must be shown. This perception makes wars attractive and seemingly bloodless . . ." (Nikolaev, 2009b, p. 127). But in that article the author was talking about an aggressive war in which case civilian casualties are usually hidden. But the Russians were fighting a defensive war. So, it was in their interests to show civilian casualties as clearly as possible. And they were not shy about that; when one sees on live TV entire families executed in cold blood—the effect of this type of coverage is quite predictable. Therefore, instead of distancing the war, the Russian communication specialists actually placed it in every living room in the country.

But, certainly, not everything can be explained in "eight easy steps." Therefore, some other—more general—observations about the Russian communication campaign have to be made.

The first unusual thing was that the Russians went into a full 24-hour crisis communication mode that included daily full-scale press conferences (with long Q and A sessions) conducted by one of the highest Russian military officials—Colonel General Anatoliy Nogovitsyn, the Deputy Chief of General Staff of the Armed Forces of the Russian Federation. (That did not happen during previous conflicts—such as those in Afghanistan or Chechnya.) He had clearly received excellent media training. He was calm, well-informed, used appropriate visual aids, and communicated with journalists quite professionally. He was not hiding from the press—he was coming to them.

The next surprise was the complete honesty in Russian communications. Sometimes they even went overboard with it. For example, sometimes journalists complained that General Nogovitsyn was giving them contradictory information—such as about movements and current positions of the Russian troops. It turned out that the problem was that he was giving them overly detailed minute-by-minute information while troops were still fighting and moving around quite a lot. And as in any war, units were advancing and retreating depending on the situation, which confused many journalists who wanted to know specifically what parts of Tskhinvali were already finally and completely liberated.

The round-the-clock media coverage also surprised people with its openness and brutal sincerity. But that had its own purpose. Russians are usually deeply distrustful of the media. And what's the use in a media campaign if it is not credible? Consequently, they had to find a way to overcome that mistrust. And they chose to do it through the presence effect. It is difficult not to trust something you see unfolding with your own eyes. So, they decided to bring the war into every Russian living room and make the audience eyewitnesses to all the events.

Moreover, it is necessary to say that Russian journalists did a good job in this respect. They were actually on the front lines with the soldiers, even lending their cell phones to Russian commanders in difficult situations. They showed every dead child and woman in Tskhinvali, every destroyed house. Close-up shots produced the perfect presence effect. At the same time, they were not embedded with Russian military units which gave them much more freedom and credibility. Consequently, Russians saw the war as it was unfolding and were touched by it emotionally.

Finally, the most important and newest aspect of the communication campaign was the fact that this time the foreign coverage of the event was not blocked from the Russian audience but was completely open and even especially highlighted every day on Russian TV. But this fact had its own reason behind it and a special purpose.

Nikolaev (2009a) writes that in a crisis situation it is extremely important to monitor the media coverage of the event so that one can quickly react to any false, erroneous, or distorted information issued by the media. And any corrective action must be swift because damage is done immediately and any delayed correction is already too late. That is why Russians very carefully followed the foreign coverage of the event and found out that pretty much the entire coverage was falsified and distorted. But instead of blocking the lies—they decided to use them for their own public relations purposes.

Lying is one of the few sins that are recognized by all major world religions. It is so for two reasons. First of all, lies are dangerous socially. We rely on the honesty of others to run our lives and to maintain our civilizations. Second, lies are almost physiologically repulsive to people. People all over the world are appalled and repulsed when they hear a clear lie. Consequently, the best way to create the states of social indignation and emotional disgust is to expose a lie. And the Western media provided Russians with ample opportunities for doing this.

The Western media have been criticized for distorting the truth. Nikolaev wrote a detailed piece on this topic in 2004. Among others, Perlmutter (1998), in his book on international crises and journalism, wrote:

For example, in his recent memoir of experiences in former Yugoslavia, David Rieff admitted that he and his fellow journalists, very early in the war, "took the side" of the Bosnian government and subsequently consciously chose to maximize the production of evocative images of Serbian atrocities and horrors that they assumed would force the world to intervene. In other words, we have a member of the press claiming that many reports and pictures from Bosnia were (and presumably are) propaganda designed to affect foreign policy in Europe and America.

(Perlmutter, 1998, pp. 20–21)

The same happened in the Ossetia situation as well. And what the Russians did—they took the Western coverage of the event and exposed (almost with enjoyment) every bit of falsity in it. These are just two situations mentioned here as mere examples.

The Russian Information Agency RIA Novosti published a report by several journalists who worked in South Ossetia during the war. The journalists were outraged. They claimed that CNN used the video material they created inappropriately. CNN showed Tskhinvali razed to the ground by Saakashvili forces but reported that it was the Georgian town of Gori destroyed by the Russian air force. According to Arkhipov (2008), CNN refused to respond to any inquiries and never issued any correction. It is necessary to add that CNN had done this before—showing one thing and reporting the opposite. It happened, for example, during the Kosovo war and during the spring 2008 crisis in Tibet, China. All this creates a special pattern that, in turn, raises the issues of intentionality and professionalism.

The Russian TV channel Vesti (2008b) reported that Reuters distributed photos that had been allegedly taken in Georgia after so-called Russian air strikes. After a close analysis the channel described them as fake—they claimed the photos were staged. Experts pointed out that, for example, on some photos the same actor (in exactly the same clothing) was playing victims in different locations, just taking different poses (face-up, face-down). After that it became clear that the Russians were victims of a world-wide propaganda campaign, although conducted quite unprofessionally. Who did this?

PR Week UK (Cartmell, 2008) reported (although, no official confirmation has ever been released) that Saakashvili retained the services of a public relations firm called Aspect Consulting (with branches in Brussels, London, and Paris). This company became famous when it "defended some of the biggest companies during three of the biggest environmental and health scandals of recent times in the UK" (White, 2008). According to White, they

worked for Shell on the Brent Spar debacle in the mid-nineties, when Shell attempted to recklessly dump its redundant oil platform in the Atlantic. . . . [they] also worked for the global fast-food giant McDonalds over what was known as "mad cow disease" in the mid-nineties as well as working with biotechnology seed companies over their promotion of genetically-modified crops, despite known health and ecological risks that those crops entail. Aspect's current clients still include biotechnology companies such as Novartis and Exxon Mobil, the global oil company that has been at the forefront of action to deny climate change. Many would see his career as dancing with the devil, not flying with the angels.

(White, 2008)

Knowing all this, Russians made quite a controversial decision. They decided not to allow Western journalists into Tskhinvali during the actual battle phase of the war. They did this because they knew that the Westerners would distort and turn everything upside-down anyway. So, the Russians decided to deny them their presence and along with it an opportunity to create war footage and use it against them (as CNN did). In the long run it turned out to be the correct decision. This became clear when right after the liberation of Tskhinvali Western journalists were invited to come to the town. First they refused but then a small group of them did come, but obviously the images of ruins and dismembered bodies of little children did not make any impression on them—the trip produced no coverage in the Western media. It clearly shows that they were not interested in what was actually going on on the ground in the first place.

All this raises the question of intentionality on the part of the Western journalists. Certainly, it can be simply explained by century-long traditions of Russophobia in the Western media. But a better theoretical explanation was offered by Nikolaev (2009b). He suggested a theory of supply and demand of political news. And in this case the theory found its almost perfect empirical support.

We have to remember that in August 2008 the American presidential campaign was in full swing. Right before the war started, Senator McCain was losing to Barack Obama by about 5 percentage points (the ratio was somewhere in the region of 42 to 47 percent). Right after the war McCain was leading by 5 percent (the ratio was somewhere between 46 and 41 percent)—a complete turnaround within a few days because of a small war. That is, the Republicans clearly demonstrated a need for anti-Russian materials and journalists provided them, knowing that their work would be consumed by and for political campaigns. What's the use of telling the truth if the material is not in demand and would not be consumed (used by the media and politicians)? But if a journalist's materials are not used and published, and/or they are disliked by those whose opinions matter the most (the power holders)—he or she can lose everything (reputation, job, etc.). Therefore, any voice of truth in the West was effectively silenced (as it was in the Kosovo and Tibet cases as well). And, along with a well-orchestrated public relations campaign, all that produced an almost intoxicating effect on the Western public.

But an interesting question is: Who ultimately won this crisis communication war? And although there was no clear winner, it seems that the Russians fared better.

In relation to their primary audience—Russian citizens—they were extremely successful. Public opinion polls showed that over 80 percent of Russians supported the war effort. This is a very high percentage for such a critically thinking nation as the Russians—a nation that is practically invulnerable to what in the West is called the rally-around-the-flag effect (Mueller, 1970, 1973). The clear loser in Russia was the United States. In a few days the percentage of Russians who had a negative opinion of the United States jumped from 29 percent to 65 percent (RIA Novosti, 2008b). Certainly, Condoleezza Rice's trip to Tbilisi on August 15, 2008—where she again expressed America's complete support for the Georgian autocrat—did not help either. From the public relations point of view it was a disastrous step.

But the most amazing fact is that the Russians managed to do well even outside of their own borders. In a matter of months, the West restored absolutely normal relationship with the Russians. But the situation in Georgia was different. Most Western leaders rushed to distance themselves from Saakashvili. Violent and well-orchestrated anti-Saakashvili riots in Georgia clearly showed that Western governments and secret services were probing ground for a regime change in that country. And although the ruler managed to hold on to power (through brutal force) his international reputation was damaged beyond repair.

Lessons that Can be Learned

What lessons can be learned from this situation? And what recommendations can be made for the government crisis communication specialists all over the world?

The first (and probably the most important) lesson is that unethical behavior punishes its perpetrators first of all. Certainly, it is sad that not a single Western public relations practitioner or journalist has ever been officially punished or sanctioned for unethical professional acts committed by him or her at the international level (such as the video tape debacle before the 1991 Gulf war, Kosovo war fabrications, and many others). The only consolation here is that at least during the 2008 crisis the perpetrators punished themselves by getting caught.

The main recommendation is still the same good-old "never lie." You will get caught and it will be used against you in the court of public opinion. Consequently, the next advice—monitor your opponent and try to catch him on lies—will pay. Also, never hide, never shy away—do public relations aggressively and openly. Be honest—provide information round-the-clock by all possible means. Try to create a presence effect for your audience, by delivering images and sounds of the crisis right into their living rooms. Try to show how hard your own people work dealing with the crisis. Involve high-level people in your crisis communication efforts—presidents, prime ministers, generals, etc. If power-holders are not talking—people think that something is wrong. Although, this does not mean that if they do talk people will necessarily believe them. Try not to work with the "bad guys"—mafia leaders, genocidal dictators. Remember that the "questionable client" clause is still a part of most public relations codes of ethics. Consequently, do not associate yourself with a lost cause (as Condoleezza Rice did traveling to Tbilisi after the war).

The final advice is for non-Western professionals—concentrate on your own people. This is exactly what Nikolaev (2009a) means when he recommends against working with belligerent journalists. It will produce more problems than benefits.

Discussion Questions

1. What is always the primary public for any government public relations campaign during a military crisis?
2. What is always the primary goal for any government public relations campaign during a military crisis?
3. What would the main thrust of advice be for any public relations person in a military crisis?

References

Arkhipov, A. (2008). CNN presented footage from Tskhinvali as a report from destroyed Gori. *RIANOVOSTI* [Online], September 8 (Moscow, Russia). Retrieved from www.rian.ru/osetia_news/20080908/151078965.html

Cartmell, M. (2008). Georgia's PR agency lashes out at Russian "propaganda" [Electronic version]. *PR Week UK*, August 14 (London, UK). Retrieved from www.prweek.com/uk/news/839450/

Dzugaeva, K. (n.d.) The Republic of South Ossetia: History and the present time. Retrieved from www.spektr.info/articles/narodi/182

Goregin, A., and Nikolaev, A. G. (1996). Evolution of modern Russian communication. *Communication World*, *13*(6), 68–69.

Mueller, J. E. (1970). Presidential popularity from Truman to Johnson. *American Political Science Review*, 64 (May), 18–34.

Mueller, J. E. (1973). *War, presidents and public opinion*. New York: John Wiley & Sons.

Nikolaev, A. G. (2004). Can we trust what we see on TV about international politics and wars? Misrepresentation, bias, and ignorance. In A. Shostak (Ed.), *Defeating terrorism/developing dreams: Beyond 9/11 and the Iraq war: Vol. 1. Culture clash/media demons* (pp. 76–83). Philadelphia, PA: Chelsea House Publishers.

Nikolaev, A. G. (2006). Why the Russians did not support the 2003 Iraq war: A frame analysis of the Russian television coverage of the coming of the war in Iraq.

In A. G. Nikolaev and E. A. Hakanen (Eds.), *Leading to the 2003 Iraq war: The global media debate* (pp. 197–221). New York: Palgrave Macmillan.

Nikolaev, A. G. (2009a). Thirty common basic elements of crisis management plans: Guidelines for handling the acute stage of "hard" emergencies at the tactical level. In W. T. Coombs and S. J. Holladay (Eds.), *The Handbook of Crisis Communication* (pp. 261–281). London and New York: Wiley-Blackwell Publishing.

Nikolaev, A. G. (2009b). Images of war: Content analysis of the photo coverage of the war in Kosovo. *Critical Sociology*, *35*(1), 105–130.

Nikolaev, A. G., and Goregin, A. (1995). The value of a PR association to Russians. *Communication World*, *12*(10), 7–9.

Perlmutter, D. (1998). *Photojournalism and foreign policy: Icons of outrage in international crises*. Westport, CT: Praeger.

RIA Novosti (2008a). Interview of the prime minister of the Russian Federation Vladimir Putin on CNN network. Retrieved from www.ria.ru/politics/20080828/150771441.html

RIA Novosti. (2008b). After the war in South Ossetia Russians took offence at America. *RIANOVOSTI* [Online], September 10 (Moscow, Russia). Retrieved from www.rian.ru/society/20080910/151157631.html

Vesti (2008a). 77 per cent of Russians supported the actions of the president. Retrieved from www.vesti.ru/doc.html?id=205513

Vesti. (2008b). Photos from Georgian Gori—staged? *Vesti* [Online], August 10 (Moscow, Russia). Retrieved from www.vesti.ru/doc.html?id=199950

White, B. (2008). Georgia and the PR war. The Campaign for Press and Broadcasting Freedom [Online], September 10 (London, UK). Retrieved from www.cpbf.org.uk/body.php?subject=war&id=2071

VIEWS FROM AN EXPERT

ALEXANDER G. GOREGIN

Alexander G. Goregin holds an M.S. in communication from Oklahoma State University, United States, and a B.A. in journalism from Saint Petersburg State University, Russia. He is chief executive officer of Saint Petersburg Information Center, a full-service public relations firm in Saint Petersburg, Russia. From 1997 to 2003, he served as a public relations and international communication adviser to the vice governor of Saint Petersburg. From 1993 to 1994, he was a communication consultant to the Administration of the Plenipotentiary Representative of the President of the Russian Federation in the Saint Petersburg Region and in the Inter-Parliamentary Assembly of the Commonwealth of Independent States.

The triple-eight war was as much a media war as it was a military operation. It shows how powerful the media are. They can make up wars and they can make wars practically invisible. During that event both sides made some questionable and controversial public relations decisions. Saakashvili and the West put their stake on hiding and distorting the truth while the Russians, for example, did not allow Western journalists into the war zone.

One could even say that, if we look deep into the motivation of both sides, the 08–08–08 war was rather a media war than an actual military conflict. Saakashvili started the whole mess to show his ability to accomplish pretty much anything. And the Russians counteracted in order to show that they were still in charge in that part of the world and they were still capable of conducting effective military operations at least on their borders. And it is funny that probably as much money was spent on both sides' media campaigns as on their military operations.

At the end of the day, it seems as though, regardless of the fact that the darling of Europe and America—Mikheil Saakashvili—had initially held in the West a substantial advantage over the Russian government image-wise, he managed to lose a lot while the Russians came through the situation relatively unscathed (at least in the long run). It is not clear whether it was bad Georgian or good Russian public relations. But what is clear is the fact that PR people working for Saakashvili constantly twisted the truth, which did not help their situation. And it is also fairly obvious that improvements in Russian crisis communication strategies and tactics helped them quite a bit. The war showed the progress the Russians had made in relation to handling public relations crises. This time, they were much better trained and organized, demonstrated more openness and some ability to manage media messages. They were able to correctly identify key stakeholders and create effective strategies for working with practically all of them. The field of crisis communication in Russia is definitely improving.

At the same time, Saakashvili simply outsourced his public relations effort to a Western public relations firm that had little knowledge of the landscape on which its programs would be implemented. Saakashvili's war communications effort was primarily focused on speeches and his meetings with Western leaders, making it entirely *his* war—at the end, he owned both the war and the defeat. So, at least in this respect he definitely lost.

Section 5

The Middle East

Iran

"Iran's Twitter Revolution" from a Publics[1] Relations Standpoint

Chiara Valentini and Dean Kruckeberg

Iranian discontent that resulted in demonstrations in the streets over that country's 2009 disputed presidential election might well be regarded as the first "Twitter revolution." This chapter examines that recent political crisis, which demonstrated the power of social media to mobilize public opinion, perhaps to an extent not seen before. The authors present this case study from an independent perspective, not by identifying any of the actors in the case as having been the client of public relations, that is, as the focus of study, but rather by examining the crisis itself as a social phenomenon that swayed public opinion in multiple ways and with unpredictable results.

Introduction

> There is a long list of rebel students given to all universities, & security is to arrest them on sight.
>
> (Tweet from Tehran, 2009, June, 12:05 p.m.)

> We have to leave, it's not safe here anymore! wish us luck!
>
> (Tweet from Tehran, 12:15 p.m.)[2]

It is mid-June 2009, and Iran has just elected its new president. Groups of young people are demonstrating in the streets in several Iranian cities, protesting the outcome of the elections. Mass media were not free to report what was happening, and repression of dissidents was high. The only way to inform the world and to mobilize and coordinate actions within the country was through the use of social media. As the preceding quotations illustrate, social media, and particularly Twitter, became the means for the Iranian protests, which, today, are regarded as the first "Twitter Revolution." The use of social media during the Iranian elections is particularly interesting to investigate because these social media can be considered both the causes and the consequences of this political crisis.

In fact, in the global arena, it can be difficult to place a political crisis and any actor's attempts at crisis communication in the context of public relations and its literature; for example, who, in fact, is coordinating a campaign and for what organization or group's benefit and to what publics is a campaign directed? Widely disseminated communication, broadly defined, that may seem overwhelmingly pervasive and that may have evolved because of an unknown actor's public relations expertise may, in fact, have evolved chaotically and without unified strategies, with no one "managing" a campaign to any extent. Also, despite globalization, public relations as a set of knowledge, skills, and abilities nevertheless remains cultural, historical, and most certainly ideological. Nevertheless, public relations practitioners—particularly those who specialize in crisis communication—can learn much from studying political crises, which often directly and dramatically affect large numbers of heterogeneous groups within a nation. Public relations practitioners are society's students who must have a longitudinal, that is, an historical, under-standing of society, their clients' publics, and other stakeholders, as well as a latitudinal understanding, namely, a global perspective, particularly when examining political crises.

This chapter examines that recent political crisis that demonstrated the power of social media to mobilize public opinion, perhaps to an extent not seen before. The authors present this case study from an independent per-spective, not by identifying any of the actors in the case as having been the client of public relations, that is, as the focus of study, but rather by examining the crisis, itself, as a social phenomenon that swayed public opinion in multiple ways and with unpredictable results.

Background of the Crisis

A political crisis is defined as an unexpected and undesirable situation in the political sphere of a country that has the potential to become "a serious threat to the basic structures or the fundamental values or norms of a system," namely, the political system (Boin, 2005, p. 2). A political crisis may occur owing to religious disturbances, terrorist attacks, or even controversial comments by politicians in addition to a crisis that is caused by political developments (Dalei and Mishra, 2009, p. 4). Political crises can include the misconduct of a government and its leaders, such as a prime minister, president, or relevant political figure, as well as the instability of government formation and support. Political crises differ from organizational crises in the extent and magnitude of their consequences for a larger number of stake-holders. Political crises can damage the economic, financial, and social reputation of a country, with corresponding tangible costs for the whole society in terms of foreign investments, tourism, growth, and innovation as well as the life of indigenous populations. Media play a key role through the way in which they cover and frame political crises since one of their major roles is to be the "watchdogs" of governments' conduct (Dalei and Mishra, 2009). In the case of the 2009 Iranian election, the political crisis refers to a crisis of management misconduct, where the crisis is caused, not only by what must be regarded as deception and skewed values, but also by deliberate amorality and illegality. The Iranian government's major stakeholders questioned the transparency of the election process and accused those in charge of the elections of fraudulent behaviors in favor of one of the presidential candidates, who was, during that time, the president of the Islamic Republic of Iran. This political crisis, thus, directly threatened the person of President Mahmoud Ahmadinejad and his image domestically and internationally.

The tenth Iranian presidential election was held June 12, 2009. Over 46 million Iranians aged 18 and older were called to vote for the new leader of their country ("Iran's presidential candidates," 2009, June 12). Iran is a theocratic republic based on Islamic principles and rules. The current political system of the Islamic Republic of Iran is the result of the Islamic Revolution in 1979 (Iran Chamber Society, 2010). The most powerful political figure is the Supreme Leader, of whom there have been two since 1979: the founder of the Republic, Ayatollah Ruhollah Khomeini; and his successor, Ali Khamenei. The second most important position, as defined by the constitution, is the president, who is elected every four years by direct vote and who can serve a maximum of two consecutive terms. Members of other important offices in the Iranian government system who are also elected for four-year terms are members of the Parliament (the Majlis) and the Assembly of Experts, the latter being an all-clerical body having the primary task of selecting the Supreme Leader and the members of the Guardian Council (EIU, 2004).

The president, the Parliament, and the Assembly of Experts are subject to approval by the Guardian Council (Iran Chamber Society, 2010). The Guardian Council consists of six clerics who are appointed by the Supreme Leader and six jurists who are nominated by the judiciary and who must be approved by the Parliament. The Guardian Council has the right to vet all legislation passed by the Parliament and to veto any laws that this body judges do not comply with Islamic law or with Iran's constitution (EIU, 2004). The Guardian Council also vets the potential presidential candidates' Islamic credentials (Bazargan, 1997, August). The president is responsible for the implementation of the Constitution and for the exercise of executive powers, except for matters directly related to the Supreme Leader, who has the final say in all political matters. The president appoints and supervises the Council of Ministers, coordinates government decisions, and selects government policies to be placed before the legislature (EIU, 2004, 2008).

The 2009 presidential election saw 475 people registered to run in the election, including 42 women; none of the latter were authorized to stand (Jones and Steinfeld, 2009, June 4, p. 4). Following a vetting process by the Guardian Council, four candidates were judged to be eligible as candidates for the presidency. These were Mahmoud Ahmadinejad, Mir Hossein

Mousavi, Mohsen Rezai, and Mehdi Karroubi ("Iran's presidential candidates," 2009, June 10). Mahmoud Ahmadinejad, former mayor of the city of Tehran who was elected president of the Iranian Republic for 2005–2009, proposed himself for a second term. This ultra-conservative candidate had been domestically criticized for his fiery rhetoric and his verbal attacks on the United States and Israel, and for his failure to tackle the country's economic problems. Despite domestic criticism, Mr. Mahmoud Ahmadinejad had the support of the military, the Revolutionary Guards, and the state-owned media ("Iran's presidential candidates," 2009, June 12).

Mir Hossein Mousavi is a former Iranian prime minister and was widely regarded as the main challenger to incumbent President Mahmoud Ahmadinejad. He considered himself a reformist who intended to "combat Iran's 'extremist' image abroad" ("Iran's presidential candidates," 2009, June 12). Mr. Mousavi had called for greater personal freedoms in Iran and had criticized the ban on commercial television channels. But he had refused to back down from that country's disputed nuclear program, saying it was for peaceful purposes.

Mohsen Rezai is a former head of Iran's powerful Revolutionary Guards and, besides Ahmadinejad, was the alternative candidate who espoused conservative policies. Mr. Rezai had openly criticized Mr. Ahmadinejad for pushing the country to the edge of a "precipice" and had promised to reform Iran's struggling economy ("Iran's presidential candidates," 2009, June 12).

Mehdi Karroubi is a mid-level cleric and was speaker of the Parliament from 1989 to 1992, during a time when the Iranian parliament was dominated by Islamic radicals. Mr. Karroubi also had pledged to protect civil rights and to improve the status of women in Iran ("Iran's presidential candidates," 2009, June 10). He had openly opposed many of Mr. Ahmadinejad's policies and is one of the few politicians to have criticized the president's denial of the Holocaust. He told the AFP news agency he would "adopt the middle path" in Iran, to bring in social, economic, and political reforms without alienating hard liners ("Iran's presidential candidates," 2009, June 12).

Situation Analysis

During the first week of June 2009, the candidates participated in six live debates. The debate between incumbent President Mahmoud Ahmadinejad and reformist candidate Mir Hussein Mousavi was particularly heated, most notably because of Mr. Ahmadinejad's open criticism of Mr. Mousavi's wife, Zahra Rahnavard, who was involved in her husband's campaign and who had attracted a lot of support from the female electorate (Addis, 2009, June 6, p. 3). In general, opposition campaigns were being based on an attacking rhetoric. Opponent candidates accused Mr. Ahmadinejad of damaging Iran's national interests and of leading the country into diplomatic isolation in the way in which he had been handling foreign affairs. Opposition candidates also distanced themselves from Mr. Ahmadinejad's highly criticized speeches about the historical reality of the Holocaust, affirming thus that the president's oratory had provoked international hostility toward Iran. In general, each candidate had tried to present himself as a "change" for the country and as a more moderate alternative for Iran's leadership, for example, by promising to improve the conditions for women in the country as well as for greater freedom of speech (Jones and Steinfeld, 2009).

Addis (2009, June 6), quoting Iranian media reports, said between 40 and 50 million viewers had watched the political preelection debates and these offered for the first time to the public an opportunity to examine candidates' political platforms as well as their assessment of the president's political performance. What had emerged from the preelection debates was a stronger support for Mr. Mousavi, who was able to attract the support of the rural and urban poor populations of Iran who had previously backed Mr. Ahmadinejad. These populations, in fact, were now appearing dissatisfied with Mr. Ahmadinejad's past four years of government, particularly in relation to unemployment and inflation issues, international sanctions, and the global financial crisis (Erdbrink, 2009, June 7).

Censorship of news media coverage of the elections is officially forbidden under the Iranian constitution, but President Ahmadinejad was requiring all foreign journalists to obtain a special press card from the Ministry of Culture and Islamic Guidance to be allowed to work in Iran. Foreign journalists who needed translators would have to use those employed by official agencies, who were obliged to report where these journalists went, with whom they met, and whom they interviewed. Foreign journalists would also have to apply for permission to report from the streets or to go to the Parliament, with each activity requiring a different documentation (Batty and Dehghan, 2009, June 22). During the 2009 Iranian election campaigns, many foreign reporters were granted the opportunity to have access to the candidates and, above all, to report these candidates' views (Batty and Dehghan, 2009, June 22). This freedom was, however, only limited to the period of the election campaigns. The Tuesday after the election, foreign journalists were again banned from reporting from the streets, and media control and censorship began once again (Batty and Dehghan, 2009, June 22).

Problem and Opportunity (PO) Statements

To win the presidency of Iran, a candidate must receive more than 50 per cent of the total votes. Otherwise, the contest must go to a run-off vote, usually held the following week. The 2009 election saw as the winner the incumbent President, Mahmoud Ahmadinejad, with 63.3 percent of the 38,770,288 valid votes, whereas Mr. Mousavi officially received 34.2 percent, Mr. Rezai 1.7 percent, and Mr. Karroubi 0.9 percent of the valid votes (Mebane, 2010). The opposition candidates, however, refused to accept the results of the election, in particular the main opposing candidate, Mir Hussein Mousavi, who claimed that the election result was hindered by widespread fraud and vote-rigging. Besides these appeals by opposition candidates who were contesting the legality of the ballot, reservations were simultaneously being expressed by large elements of Iranian society concerning the results such as they had been proclaimed, as well as in their demands for transparency regarding the honesty of the ballot ("Iran blames U.S. for election chaos," 2009, June 18).

At the time of the election, proof had not been given of any deceitful manipulation of the voting process by the governing president, although a later analysis by Mebane (2010) supported the contention that the official results of the election that had been announced did not accurately reflect the intentions of the voters and that the vote counts for Mr. Ahmadinejad had been substantially augmented by inappropriate means.

Following Mr. Moussavi and other candidates' accusation of election fraud, Mr. Moussavi's supporters and others held public demonstrations in several major Iranian cities. Because of the fierce response by the president and by the ruling government, these street protests have been considered to be one of the most serious political crises for Iran's political system since the system emerged after the 1979 Islamic revolution ("Iranian opposition leader vows massive election protest," 2009, June 17).

Communication Goals, Objectives, Strategies, and Tactics

Violent clashes erupted after the election commission had announced Mr. Ahmadinejad had won in a landslide. Mr. Mousavi called for a mass demonstration from the population to show its disappointment in the way in which the elections had occurred. As Mr. Mousavi had said, "We want a peaceful rally to protest the unhealthy trend of the election and realize our goal of annulling the results" ("Iran blames U.S. for election chaos," 2009, June 18).

On Monday, June 15, 2009, hundreds of thousands of Iranians turned out in a huge procession, and seven demonstrators were shot by pro-regime militia ("Iranian opposition leader vows massive election protest," 2009, June 17). Despite this strong repression by the government, protesters continued their demonstrations, with thousands of people marching down a main street of the capital, Tehran, holding posters of Mr. Mousavi and flashing the V-for-victory sign in the air ("Iranian opposition leader vows massive election protest," 2009, June 17) or holding candle-light vigils in Tehran following Mr. Mousavi's call for a day of mourning for those killed in protests ("Iran blames U.S. for election chaos," 2009, June 18).

During a religious service on Friday, June 19, 2009, the Supreme Leader, Ayatollah Khamenei, confirmed that the election was legitimate and that the large voter turnout and resulting victory (for Mr. Ahmadinejad) was a "divine assessment." The opposition group did not accept this pronouncement and continued its mobilization of the population through the use of social media. Additional demonstrations in the streets followed, although on a minor scale. Violence occurred during several occasions, with people beaten and even shot by the militia. The case of a young Iranian woman, who was identified as Neda Agha-Soltan, became a symbol of freedom and of the young Iranian revolution. Her death, in fact, was recorded by cameras in Tehran and rapidly spread virally throughout the Internet after being posted on Facebook and YouTube.

Government oppression was backed by the Supreme Leader who, during the Friday prayers on live television on June 26, 2009, asserted that he who "fights against the Islamic system or the leader of Islamic society, fight him until complete destruction" and called for the execution of leading demonstrators because they were "people who wage war against God" (Fletcher, 2009, June 27). On Monday, June 29, 2009, the Guardian Council formally certified the re-election of President Mahmoud Ahmadinejad to a second four-year term and dismissed the charges of fraud (Slackman, 2009, June 30). This, however, did not put an end to the efforts of the dissidents. Throughout July 2009 and during the following months, protesters engaged in several actions against the government, such as boycotting goods that were being advertised on state-controlled television; attempting to deny power to state-run TV evening news broadcasts by turning on all electric appliances just before the news; setting up "blitz" street demonstrations; identifying paramilitary vigilantes linked to the crackdown and putting marks in the opposition color green; posting pictures of protest victims in front of their homes; and scribbling anti-regime slogans on money (Wright, 2009, July 27).

While citizens were protesting, the media were not allowed to cover the protests or to report on the situation. Following the government's decision to ban all foreign media outlets from covering the opposition's protests, non-Iranian media outlets were no longer allowed to cover postelection demonstrations ("Al-Jazeera TV report discusses role of media in postelections Iran," 2009, June 18). Censorship reached higher levels when several journalists, both Iranian as well as foreign, were persecuted, arrested, or deported from the country. But Iran's youthful and Web-savvy population had proven adept at using Twitter, blogs, mobile phones, and social networks to spread the word about the postelection discord.

Outcomes Assessment

Censorship, nonetheless, was not able to silence the protests. The spread and development of new communication technologies and, in particular, of social media in Iran have perhaps irrevocably changed the way in which the Iranian people interact, communicate, and engage in political, economic, and social issues. Political opposition groups had understood since the beginning of the election campaigns that a large part of the Iranian electorate had been born after 1979 and was very active in social media. Thus, these opposition groups employed social media and mobile phone-based organizing tactics, using Facebook, Twitter, websites, e-mail, mobile phones, and SMS, as well as the full suite of Web 2.0 tools, as mechanisms for political organizing (Faris and Heacock, 2009, June 15).

Although the government had tried to shut down SMS networks before the polls opened to avoid opposition supporters from collecting election results, controlling the flow of communication on the Internet was more difficult. Citizen journalism had become a reality. Videos, SMS, and Tweets were being used by Iranians to communicate to the outside world what was going on in the streets of the major Iranian cities.

Since the protests of the results of the presidential elections had broken out, social networking websites have turned into a principal podium for Iranian youths who are opposing President Ahmadinejad. YouTube, for instance, has turned into the world's window into Iran. Facebook and Twitter have given supporters of Mir Hoseyn Mousavi room to coordinate positions, organize demonstrations, and provide constant updates on the security situation. Many Iranians have set up blogs that have overflowed with messages defying the authorities and supporting Mousavi, and one of these websites had garnered more than 50,000 supporters. The Iranian authorities noted with concern this electronic activity, which drew the admiration of those abroad ("Al-Jazeera TV report discusses role of media in postelections Iran," 2009, June 18). The protests thus had moved from the street to cyberspace, which is the appellative of a "Twitter revolution." Cyberspace, of course, knows no national boundaries. As one U.S. newspaper had reported:

> With the foreign press corps expelled from the country or confined to their hotels and the Internet disrupted by the regime, the story of Iranian government oppression of citizen dissent has been courageously told through the messages delivered by Twitter users and the images of bloodied demonstrators transmitted by iPhone.
> ("This time the revolution will be tweeted," 2009, June 20)

The country was estimated to have had more than 100,000 blogs (Jaafar, 2009, June 16). In the United States, hundreds of protesters, echoing friends and relatives in Tehran, demanded new elections in Iran during a march on the United Nations. "We want the United Nations to hear us when we ask them to get rid of the dictators," said Sheva Khatami, 18, of Woodcliffe Lakes, N.J. "This is not an election. It was rigged" (Ransom and McShane, 2009, June 22).

Stakeholders in the Iranian Political Crisis

To identify the main stakeholders[3] of the Iranian political crisis, two frameworks are considered to be most appropriate: Grunig (1997) and Grunig and

Hunt's (1984) situational theory of publics, and Mitchell et al.'s (1997) stakeholder salience model. These two frameworks, one from the public relations literature and the other from the stakeholder management school, complement one another.

The situational theory of publics defines and classifies an organization's main publics according to their level of awareness of a problem and the extent to which these publics can do something about the problem. This theory considers three independent variables—problem recognition, constraint recognition, and level of involvement—and two dependent variables—seeking information and processing information—as factors to classify and prioritize an organization's attention to publics. Four types of publics are possible: *nonpublic*, *latent public*, *aware public*, and *active public*. Accordingly, in the case of the Iranian elections, we can see that all of the government's major stakeholders had moved toward more compelling roles, that is, there was no *nonpublic*, but all were either *latent*, *aware*, or *active publics*. The active group had high levels of all independent and dependent variables. This group of stakeholders consisted of opposition leaders (other presidential candidates) and dissident citizens. The aware group had high levels of problem recognition, but low constraint recognition, and a medium level of involvement, since this public either was not part of Iranian society or had limited connection to it. This group sought information primarily as a reaction to the media coverage of the controversy of the election process. This public tended to process information, but to a lesser extent than did the earlier-mentioned group of stakeholders. This second group consisted of Iranian expatriates, international news media, and international organizations, such as Reporters Without Borders, Open Society Foundations, Center for the Defenders of Human Rights, and others. A group that had high levels of all independent and dependent variables, but because of government control had limited possibilities to become active, was the national news media. They are thereby classified in the aware group. Finally, foreign governments/heads of states of other countries and international supporters of the protesters were latent publics, because they recognized there was a problem, but were not directly involved in or affected by the crisis, i.e., they had no particular constraint recognition (Table 5.1).

The situational theory of publics, however, shows some limitations in explaining the level of salience of these different stakeholders for the organization, namely, the government, during the crisis because it fails to consider the power and legitimacy dimensions of stakeholders' demands. Mitchell et al.'s (1997) stakeholder salience model identifies primary and secondary (for the organization) stakeholders and prioritizes activities toward the primary stakeholders on the basis of their power, legitimacy, and urgency. Those stakeholders who have high power to influence and affect an organization, who have high legitimacy to question the actions and behavior of an organization, and have the urgency to be listened to and to be taken into consideration can be classified as definitive stakeholders and should be the priority of an organization's communicative efforts (Table 5.2).

In this political crisis, two *definitive stakeholders*, two *dependent stakeholders*, and four *demanding stakeholders* are evident. Definitive stakeholders were those who had high power, legitimacy, and urgency to be heard and could influence the political system in Iran. These were the opposition candidates as well as the dissident Iranian citizens. Dependent stakeholders have high legitimacy and urgency, but have lower power. These were the national media and expatriates. The media had lower power because they were directly controlled by the government and thus could not perform freely their role as the watchdog of Iranian society. The expatriates also had limited power. Although they held voting rights and thus were entitled to express their political opinions in relation to their motherland, they were perceived to have been less relevant since they lived outside the immediate political context of Iran.

The demanding stakeholders were those who had some urgency, but limited power and legitimacy, in relation to the Iranian government. These stakeholders included the international media and international organizations. Since they operated and were embedded in an external (to the Iranian) society, their power in requesting the Iranian government to invalidate the elections was limited, and their legitimacy was limited to the sphere of human rights and freedom of expression. Such stakeholders, by their nature, have limited influence in decisions of a political nature. Foreign governments/heads of states and international supporters of protesters were also part of the demanding stakeholder group, but they had lesser urgency than did the earlier-mentioned ones. Foreign governments/heads of states and international supporters recognized that there was a problem with the way in which the election had taken place, but as "outsiders" of the Iranian political, economic, and social systems, they did not hold legitimacy or power attributes to question Iranian governance and the way in which the political elections had been held. Nonetheless, they had felt a medium level of urgency in this political crisis, because the stability of Iranian government was seen as an important element for future Middle-East relations. On the other hand, foreign supporters had some urgency because of the moral and ethical issues that were based on democratic principles. The reasons for cheering on the Iranian citizens were predicated upon their desire to express their sympathy toward the proponents of a more democratic Iran.

Each of these groups of stakeholders had different concerns toward the elected Iranian president and the government and demanded different answers. In the following section, we analyze how the government and, *in primis*, the re-elected president, Mr. Ahmadinejad, had responded to the crisis and to its main stakeholders' requests.

Table 5.1 The stakeholders of the Iranian crisis, according to the situational theory of publics

Publics	Levels of engagement							
	Prepresidential elections				*Postpresidential elections*			
	No public	*Latent*	*Aware*	*Active*	*No public*	*Latent*	*Aware*	*Active*
Political opponents				x				x
Iranian citizens								x
Iranian expatriates		x					x	
Iranian media		x					x	
International media	x						x	
International organizations		x					x	
Foreign governments/heads of states	x					x		
Foreign supporters	x					x		

Table 5.2 The stakeholders of the Iranian crisis, according to the stakeholder salience model.

Publics	Levels of salience					
	Prepresidential elections			*Postpresidential elections*		
	Power	*Legitimacy*	*Urgency*	*Power*	*Legitimacy*	*Urgency*
Political opponents	H	H	H	H	H	H
Iranian citizens	L	H	L	H	H	H
Iranian expatriates	L	M	—	L	H	H
Iranian media	L	H	M	L	H	H
International media	—	—	L	L	L	H
International organizations	L	L	L	L	L	H
Foreign governments/heads of states	L	—	—	L	L	M
Foreign supporters	—	—	—	L	L	M

H= high; M= medium; L= low; — = no salience

The President's Response to the Political Crisis

Past literature in relation to damaging organizations' or political figures' images has emphasized that responses by organizations or political personalities often aim at protecting or repairing their image (Allen and Caillouet, 1994; Benoit, 1995) and that the management of a crisis depends very much on the type of threat (Boin, 2005). As Huang (2006) had identified in her study of four different political crises, the crisis communication strategies adopted by the parties involved were *denial, excuse, justification,* and *concession.* Romenti and Valentini (2010) integrated crisis response strategies from Coombs (2001), Sturges (1994), and Bradford and Garrett (1995) to analyze a mismanagement type of crisis involving the Italian government and Alitalia's management by adding *attack the accuser, ingratiation, providing information, corrective action,* and *apology strategies* to those used by Huang (2006).

Furthermore, crisis response strategies should take into consideration the situational and contextual dimensions of the crisis to be effective (Coombs, 1998). Particularly in the case of the Iranian 2009 postelection crisis, contextual parameters in relation to the role of religion in politics, the type of political system, the type of media system, the level of development of human rights, as well as the economic and social factors of the country should be taken into consideration to understand the impact of the government's selected strategies in accordance with the configuration of elements in the crisis situation and the relevance of stakeholders' requests. In the following section, the government's response strategies and tactics are analyzed according to three major moments—precrisis phase, initial crisis phase, and crisis climax phase—of the unfolding Iranian political crisis.

Phase 1: Precrisis

Fearing the possibility of not being re-elected and acknowledging the power of social media in mobilizing the youth in the country, Mahmoud Ahmadinejad had decided to block access to Facebook three weeks before nationwide elections. This action drew strong criticism among the opposition groups, who had sought to use this channel to mobilize the youth and to unseat President Mahmoud Ahmadinejad. "Facebook is one of the only independent sources that the Iranian youth could use to communicate," said Mohammed Ali Abtahi, a former vice president who had become adviser to another pro-reform candidate, former Parliament speaker Mahdi Karroubi. More than half of Iran's population had been born after the 1979 Islamic Revolution, and young voters made up a huge bloc—which had helped former reformist President Mohammad Khatami to win back-to-back victories in 1997 and 2001, but which had failed to rally strongly behind Mr. Ahmadinejad's opponent, Akbar Hashemi Rafsanjani, four years previously (Dareini, 2009,

May 25). By blocking access to Facebook, Mr. Ahmadinejad had indirectly acknowledged that social media could become a powerful means for those who opposed the government's politics and policies to enhance public discussion as well as public participation in opposing the government. Rather than attempting to counter-argue opponents' discourses using the same tool, Mr. Ahmadinejad had decided *tout court* to block the flow of information in Facebook among the media, the other political candidates, and citizen stakeholders.

Phase 2: Initial Crisis—after the Election

To counter the accusation of having altered the results of the elections, Mahmoud Ahmadinejad at the same time used *denial* and *excuse* strategies to deny the accusation of mismanagement by attempting to move the responsibility of protests to external enemies.

First of all, not only did he deny the accusation of fraud, but he tried to build a new agenda and to attack the accusers, especially Mr. Mousavi, by delivering an uncompromising reply to questions about his political legitimacy by casting his re-election as a democratic triumph and by mocking his opponents for failing to provide evidence to support their claims of fraud. He claimed an 85 percent turnout from this election and stated that this was a sign of the "highest rate of democracy." Furthermore, he claimed the election had been "the most free of its kind" because it had allowed candidates open criticism, televised debates, and access to state media. The mandate supplied by his re-election would be used to tread his chosen path "more powerfully than before," he said (Tait and Black, 2009, July 8).

Second, Mr. Ahmadinejad played the role of a victim of a conspiracy against the Islamic Republic of Iran by blaming external enemies for the instability of the political system. In particular, he openly accused the United States of meddling in the deepening crisis ("Iranian opposition leader vows massive election protest, 2009," June 17), thus shifting the blame for the political crisis to other agents.

Phase 3: Crisis Climax—Following Weeks

When the protests had not stopped after the first week, the Guardian Council, which supervised the election, tried to pacify the opposition by offering to recount votes in a limited number of districts. This strategy that, upon first look, may have appeared to have been a shift toward a corrective action by the government, was, in fact, perceived as a cynical gesture because the authorities had made clear that the recount would not change the final result ("Iran's nonrepublic," 2009, June 18).

Protests continued to unfold for sixteen consecutive days from June 15 to June 30, 2009, making this political crisis one of the most serious since the

Islamic Revolution in 1979. Since denial and excuse strategies were not working to settle down the rampant unrest of significant numbers of Iran's citizens, Mr. Ahmadinejad's response to this political, institutional, and personal crisis was to adopt an *attack the accuser* strategy, whereas, in this particular context, the attack was not only verbal, but, above all, physical, against any perceived enemy of the government. The underlying tactic was thus increased oppression: first, by restricting the flow of information within and outside the country through censorship of news media, with the intent to mitigate Mr. Ahmadinejad's personal negative image in the news media as well as to limit public discussions on the topic; and, second, by oppressing dissidents through physical and psychological coercion. Media can play a crucial role in defusing tension during a crisis and in creating awareness among the people about the nature of the problem, its origin, and the way in which to resolve or face it (Dalei and Mishra, 2009, May 20, p. 5).

While control of national news media was increased, the foreign press corps was either expelled from the country or these foreign journalists were confined to their hotels to avoid their coverage of the street protests. Those who dared to report street protests were either arrested, such as were the cases of BBC journalist John Simpson and his camera operator, as well as another television camera operator, or even beaten with batons by riot police while filming a march and then briefly detained, such as was the case of Bill Neely, the international editor at ITN, and his camera operator (Batty and Dehghan, 2009, June 22). The news media, witnessing the Iranian political crisis and government's response to the crisis, were considered an inconvenient and bothersome means to be "disturbing" the government's intention of controlling the Iranian public opinion. Access to the news organization's popular Farsi-language website and the U.S. government-funded Voice of America was also partially blocked (Jaafar, 2009, June 16). Furthermore, foreign news correspondents were perceived to be the perpetuators of Iranian protests (Batty and Dehghan, 2009, June 22) to the extent that they came to be considered enemies of the country, and, as such, were persecuted and arrested while performing their jobs. Reporters Without Borders claimed that several Iranian journalists had been arrested, while the offices of Mr. Mousavi's newspaper had been ransacked and its computers destroyed by Mr. Ahmadinejad's supporters (Jaafar, 2009, June 16).

Iranian police said that, in the first month of protests after the elections, they had detained more than one thousand political activists, journalists, and protesters during the demonstrations (Tait and Black, 2009, July 8). The official death count was 37, but opposition groups reported approximately 70 individuals had died, and human rights organizations suggested as many as 200 may have died. In August 2009, the judiciary estimated that the authorities had detained approximately 4,000 persons. Authorities continued to arrest numerous political activists throughout the rest of the year 2009 (Human Rights Practices, 2010, March 11).

Lessons Learned

In 21st-century global society, political crises have changed in fundamental ways, and communication technology has become the most influential and powerful intervening variable that simultaneously permits and encourages a global discourse that is made possible through the compression of time and space while paradoxically exacerbating social conflicts. This compression of time and space, however, is no more relevant to today's global public opinion environment than is the minimal expense of sending and receiving messages; that is, communication has become inexpensive, with those wishing to communicate with others no longer needing printing presses or radio or television stations or, for that matter, physical proximity. A mobile phone and access to the Internet works just as well, and any other communication media dependency has ceased for "professional communicators" to communicate messages, although the outcome of such easy and inexpensive access by senders to receivers of messages has resulted in the erosion of professionalism (and its professional values) of mass communicators. Today, no one holds a monopoly of knowledge, and many media offer only the channels of communication with consumers providing their own content. Thus, citizens have great influence in setting news agendas. "Professional communicators," such as news reporters, have lost their monopoly of knowledge to this immense number of purveyors of user-provided content traveling on inexpensive and easily accessible electronic channels of communication. Messages can emanate from any user (known or unknown, credible or not) to any consumer irrespective of time and space. Further, much of the content of the social media has become ideological, with no attempt at fairness and objectivity according to traditional concepts of news and news values.

This case study illustrates that, today, we must question the continuing utility of the concept of segmented publics (plural) in an era of globalism, easy and immediate re-segmentation into multiple worldwide publics, and amid the dangers of what was once private becoming globally public. With incendiary immediacy, previously unidentified publics can form globally and can act unpredictably and seemingly chaotically—and with unseen power. This challenges public relations practitioners' historic contention that public relations programs seldom will be effective if they are directed to a mass audience and that the costs of a campaign will be much greater when messages are directed to "nonpublics" as well as to identified and targeted strategic publics. Indeed, one could argue that, in today's global milieu, the only truly "strategic" public that can be identified with any certainty is the "general public" (Kruckeberg and Vujnovic, 2010). Further, the "general public" has no pre-determined "rules of behaviors" or pre-determined concerns to address, but acts case-by-case upon different circumstances and situations.

Discussion Questions

1. In what ways could these elections have been contested before the advent of social media?
2. What implications can social media have in political elections in more democratic, less authoritarian governments?
3. What are the benefits and disadvantages of using social media for political leaders when signs of a crisis are visible?
4. What changes do you predict for future elections in democratic forms of government?
5. The authors assess this political crisis using the frameworks of Grunig (1997) and Grunig and Hunt's (1984) situational theory of publics, and Mitchell et al.'s (1997) stakeholder salience model. What other theoretical frameworks might be appropriate to examine this political crisis?

Notes

1   In this chapter, we use "publics" and "stakeholders" interchangeably when referring to groups of people who are affected by and can affect an organization's existence. In the *Encyclopedia of Public Relations*, Rawlins and Bowen (2005), when referring to Grunig and Hunt's work (1984), affirm that groups and individuals, when they recognize a certain problem and act upon it, can be described as a type of stakeholder (p. 719).
2   Tweets retrieved from www.timesonline.co.uk/tol/news/world/us_and_americas/article6531831.ece.
3   Mitchell et al. (1997) identify seven typologies of stakeholders depending on their level of power, legitimacy, and urgency. These are *latent-dormant, latent-discretionary, latent-demanding, expectant-dominant, expectant-dependent, expectant-dangerous*, and *definitive stakeholders*.

References

Al-Jazeera TV report discusses role of media in post-elections Iran. (2009). *BBC Monitoring: International Report*, June 18, News transcript of BBC Monitoring—International Report available in LexisNexis.

Addis, C. L. (2009). Iran's 2009 presidential elections. *Congressional Research Service*, June 6, R40653. Retrieved from www.fas.org/sgp/crs/mideast/R40653.pdf

Allen, W. M., and Caillouet, R. H. (1994). Legitimation endeavors: Impression management strategies used by an organization in crisis. *Communication Monographs*, *61*(1), 44–62.

Batty, D., and Dehghan, S. K. (2009). Media: Struggling to be heard in Iran: Tight restrictions have stifled media coverage and made it difficult to get to the root of the story. *The Guardian*, June 22, p. 7.

Bazargan, D. (1997). Iran: Politics, the military and Gulf security, *Middle East Review of International Affairs*, *1*(3), August. Retrieved from www.gloria-center.org/meria/1997/09/bazargan.html

Benoit, W. L. (1995). *Accounts, excuses and apologies: A theory of image restoration strategies*. Albany, NY: State University of New York Press.

Boin, A. (2005). *The politics of crisis management: Public leadership under pressure*. Cambridge, UK: Cambridge University Press.

Bradford, J. L., and Garrett, D. E. (1995). The effectiveness of corporate communication responses to accusations of unethical behaviors. *Journal of Business Ethics, 14*(11), 875–892.

Coombs, T. W. (1998). An analytic framework for crisis situations: Better responses from a better understanding of the situation. *Journal of Public Relations Research, 10*(3), 177–191.

Coombs, T. W. (2001). Designing post-crisis messages: Lessons for crisis response strategies. *Review of Business, 21*(3/4), 37–41.

Dalei, P., and Mishra, K. (2009). Role of media in a political crisis. *Proceedings and E-Journal of the 7th AMSAR Conference on Roles of Media during Political Crisis, Bangkok, Thailand*, May 20. Retrieved from http://utcc2.utcc.ac.th/localuser/amsar/PDF/Document52/Prabash_template%20_2_.pdf

Dareini, A. (2009). Facebook block ahead of Iran vote hampers youth. The Associated Press, May 25. Retrieved from *The Jakarta Post*, www.thejakartapost.com/news/2009/05/25/facebook-block-ahead-iran-vote-hampers-youth.html

EIU (2004). Country profile: Iran. *The Economist Intelligence Unit*, 1–67.

EIU (2008). Country profile: Iran. *The Economist Intelligence Unit*, 1–33.

Erdbrink, T. (2009). Rural Iran may shift its loyalty. *Washington Post*, June 7. Retrieved from www.washingtonpost.com/wp-dyn/content/article/2009/06/06/AR2009060602177.html

Faris, R., and Heacock, R. (2009). Cracking down on digital communication and political organizing in Iran. *OpenNet Initiative*, June 15. Retrieved from http://opennet.net/blog/2009/06/cracking-down-digital-communication-and-political-organizing-iran

Fletcher, M. (2009). Leading demonstrators must be executed Ayatollah Khatami demands. *The Times*, June 27, p. 28.

Grunig, J. E. (1997). A situational theory of publics: Conceptual history, recent challenges and new research. In D. Moss, T. MacManus, and D. Vercic (Eds.), *Public relations research: An international perspective*. London, UK: International Thomson Business Press.

Grunig, J. E., and Hunt, T. (1984). *Managing public relations*. New York: Holt, Rinehart and Winston.

Huang, Y. H. (2006). Crisis situations, communication strategies, and media coverage. A multicase study revisiting the communicative response model. *Communication Research, 33*(3), 180–205.

Human Rights Practices (2010). *2009 Human Rights Report: Iran*, Bureau of Democracy, Human Rights, and Labor, US Department of State, Diplomacy in Action, March 11. Retrieved from www.state.gov/g/drl/rls/hrrpt/2009/nea/136068.htm

Iran blames U.S. for election chaos. (2009). *Belfast Telegraph*, June 18, p. 24.

Iran Chamber Society (2010). *The Constitution of Islamic Republic of Iran*. Iranian Laws and Government, Iran Chamber Society, November 12. Retrieved from www.iranchamber.com/government/laws/constitution.php

Iran's nonrepublic. (2009), *The New York Times*, Editorial, June 18, p. 36.

Iranian opposition leader vows massive election protest, Associated Press. (2009). *Fox News*, June 17. Retrieved from www.foxnews.com/story/0,2933,526829,00.html

Iran's presidential candidates. Read our quick guide to the four candidates in Iran's 2009 presidential election. (2009). Al Jazeera, June 10. News article retrieved from http://english.aljazeera.net/focus/2009/06/200968114647880273.html

Iran's presidential candidates. (2009) *BBC News*, June 12. News article retrieved from http://news.bbc.co.uk/2/hi/middle_east/8060304.stm

Jaafar, A. (2009). Iran feels the Tweet. *Daily Variety*, News, June 16, p. 4.

Jones, S., and Steinfeld, R. (2009). *Iranian presidential elections 2009*. UK Parliament, International Affairs and Defense Section, document SN/IA/05084, June 4. Retrieved from www.parliament.uk/briefingpapers/commons/lib/research/briefings/snia-05084.pdf

Kruckeberg, D., and Vujnovic, M. (2010). The death of the concept of "publics" (plural) in 21st century public relations. *International Journal of Strategic Communication*, 4(2), 117–125.

Mebane, W., Jr. (2010). Fraud in the 2009 presidential election in Iran?, *Chance*, 23(1), 6–15.

Mitchell, R. K., Agle, B. B., and Wood, D. J. (1997). Towards a theory of stakeholder identification and salience. *Academy of Management Review*, 22(4), 853–886.

Ransom, J., and McShane, L. (2009). Crowd at UN demands action. *Daily News (New York)*, June 22, p. 7.

Rawlins, B. L., and Bowen, S. (2005). Publics. In R. L. Heath (Ed.), *Encyclopedia of Public Relations*, (pp. 718–721). Thousand Oaks, CA: Sage Publications.

Romenti, S., and Valentini, C. (2010). Alitalia's crisis in the media: A situational analysis. *Corporate Communications: An International Journal*, 15(4), 380–396.

Slackman, M. (2009). Iran Council Certifies Disputed Election Results. *New York Times*, June 30, p. A4.

Sturges, D. L. (1994). Communicating through crisis: A strategy for organizational survival. *Management Communication Quarterly*, 7(3), 297–316.

Tait, R., and Black, I. (2009). International: Ahmadinejad mocks rivals and trumpets "free" vote: Live television address all but ignores mass protests: Opponents vow to fight on using concerted action. *The Guardian*, July 8, p. 14.

This time the revolution will be tweeted. (2009). *St. Petersburg Times (Florida)*, June 20, p. 12A.

Wright, R. (2009). Iran's Protesters: Phase 2 of Their Feisty Campaign. *Time*, July 27. Retrieved from www.time.com/time/world/article/0,8599,1912941,00.html

VIEWS FROM AN EXPERT

JOHN PALUSZEK

John Paluszek APR, Fellow, Public Relations Society of America, is senior counsel at Ketchum Public Relations and 2009 to 2011 chair of The Global Alliance For Public Relations and Communication Management

To address the issues in this case study, let us first temporarily widen the aperture of our lens. "Temporarily" because, even as we venture to draw conclusions about "Iran's Twitter Revolution," the subject of social media in crisis management evolves virtually moment-by-moment—(not unlike the behavior of sub-atomic particles as presented in the Heisenberg Principle[1]). And the subject is not only elusive, but it may be only as achievable as trying to travel to the horizon. "Widen" because many related developments have occurred, and will continue to occur, worldwide since the 2009 Iranian national election. That said, public relations professionals and geopolitical analysts have been well-served by the research and analysis that have been presented in this case study, including:

Context

Ironically, Iran presents an interesting historic context for analyzing the impact of social media in a crisis, first with its 1979 revolution, which was transmitted globally in fascinating—albeit disturbing—detail using what we now call traditional ("mass" or "old" media). Events leading to the 1979 revolution centered on the about-to-be-deposed Reza Shah Pavlavi. Through the grim visage of the Ayatollah Mostafawi Khomeini (a master of the use of communications technology of the day, namely, the tape cassette), and especially in the hostage-taking at the American Embassy, the 1979 revolution suggests how the Iranian election of 2009 *might* have unfolded without the use of social media.

Such historic context introduces the critical aspect of media (both traditional and new) of "reliable sources," which is too complex for in-depth analysis in this limited space. Here, we perhaps must settle for the hoary-tale punchline: "Who do you believe, me, or your lying eyes?"

The Wide Angle

So much has happened in global communication—both technologically and sociologically—since the 2009 Iranian election that only a cursory summary of "Iran's Twitter revolution" can be framed by these contemporary questions:

- How will "WikiLeaks" affect the management of diplomacy and reporting of international relations by traditional media? Are the selected national media that are receiving the "leaks" complicit when they publish selected portions, even though many bloggers have done likewise?
- What is the long-range significance of "organized" hackers ("anarchists unite!"), who have confronted search engines that have "disconnected" WikiLeaks?
- Will the current issues of privacy and censorship on the Internet metastasize, both in democracies and authoritarian regimes alike, when consumers and governments increasingly object to content that they judge to be injurious?
- In election campaigns in democratic societies, will politicians learn to live-and-or-die "by the sword" of the immense and growing power of social media—media that generate not only recruitment and organization of supporters (à la Barack Obama in 2008), but also the instant transmission of faux pas (in too many cases to mention)?

A Pleasant Surprise

As a former journalist from a bygone era, I was happily surprised by a key conclusion of an earlier Kruckeberg and Vujnovic study cited in "Iran's Twitter revolution": "Indeed, one could argue that, in today's global milieu, the only true 'strategic' public that can be identified with any certainty is the 'general public.'"

Many recent studies have documented that, even with the critical and growing importance of social media—not only in crises, but in virtually every transmission of information and knowledge—the most efficient way to reach the "general public" is still through traditional "general media."

There is still hope for quasi-Luddites like me.

Note

1   The Heisenberg Principle—"It is impossible to specify completely the position and momentum of a particle, such as an electron, at the same time."

Lebanon

Risk Perception and Change Management: Strategic Efforts to Restore Lebanon's Tourism Sector

Ali M. Kanso, Joseph Ajami,
and Abdul Karim Sinno

For years, tourism was an integral component of the Lebanese national economy but the Lebanese civil war (1975–1991), two Israeli invasions (1982 and 2006), and internal clashes between pro-government and opposition forces (2008) hurt the reputation of a country that was often called the "Switzerland of the Middle East." While the Lebanese government has made some efforts in recent years to revive the tourism sector in the country, carefully planned and well-executed public relations activities are still needed to eliminate war-torn images. This case study reviews the conditions of tourism in Lebanon and assesses the public relations efforts of the Ministry of Tourism in Lebanon after the 2006 Israeli war.

Introduction

Since 2005 the world has witnessed countless developments, disasters, breakthroughs, crises, revolutions, and many other noteworthy events. In spite of the unrest in several parts of the world and all aviation disasters and natural catastrophes such as tsunamis, earthquakes, and more volcanic eruptions in Europe and other places, the world remains relatively a safe and beautiful place to explore and enjoy. Tourism and travel remain two vibrant activities throughout the globe.

Lebanon, a small yet beautiful spot in the Middle East region, continues to be a fairly popular destination for hundreds of thousands, if not millions, of people from the Middle East, Europe, and other parts of the world. The country, once dubbed the "Switzerland of the Middle East," has suffered tremendously in its recent history from political instability and at times this has been translated into wars such as the Israeli venture in 2006. Not only were human and military targets attacked but the country's infrastructure and economy were hit as well. Prior to the 2006 events, the 17-year civil war (1975–1991) and Israel's occupation of large chunks of South Lebanon (1978–2000) robbed Lebanon of its prized reputation as the region's quintessential vacation spot (Kanso et al., 1997; Kanso and Sinno, 1999).

However, the Lebanese government and the private sector have been able to recover after each major war or disaster. Resiliency remains a major trademark of both the Lebanese people and the country's economy. Government and private endeavors have helped put the country back on its feet but negative publicity has acted as a major reason behind a diminishing tourism industry in a country that largely depends on this productive, money-generating sector.

In this context and in light of the current stable political situation in Lebanon, this case study assesses efforts of the Ministry of Tourism to restore Lebanon's once prosperous tourism industry by attempting to attract large numbers of visitors, tourists, and Lebanese expatriates from all parts of the globe.

Owing to lack of a written crisis plan on the part of the Ministry of Tourism in Lebanon, this chapter infers what the Lebanese government has done in terms of establishing public relations objectives, articulating strategies, identifying tactics, and assessing outcome. The study draws heavily on literature and interviews of high-ranking officials in the Ministry of Tourism. But before delving into the role of the Ministry of Tourism in revitalizing tourism in the country, an updated brief summary of the characteristics of Lebanese society seems to be essential.

Characteristics of Lebanese Society

The Lebanese Republic is one of the smallest nations in the world. It borders Syria on the north and east, and Israel on the south. The country sits on the eastern shore of the Mediterranean Sea with an area of 4,019 square miles. Lebanon has witnessed many civilizations and conquests. One can easily find traces of the Egyptians, Phoenicians, Persians, Babylonians, Greeks, Romans, Byzantines, Arabs, Crusaders, Ottoman Turks, French, and others.

The country's essentials and fixtures remain intact: natural beauty, spring-like weather and temperatures for more than eight months of the year, rich history, remarkable experience in tourism and hospitality, private-enterprise economy, fairly democratic political system, and free economy. More significantly, however, remains the Lebanese people's expertise in "selling" the attractions of their small nation to potential seekers of beautiful and affordable sites.

Few countries enjoy the climate or scenic variety of Lebanon. Capsule descriptions of this country usually label its climate "temperate," with 200 days of sunshine, moderate rainfall, a warm "cold" season, and pleasant "hot" months. The country's weather satisfies residents and guests alike. If the coastal towns get too hot or humid for them a half-hour drive eastward gets them into the invigorating coolness of Mount Lebanon.

Throughout its long and rich history, Lebanon has been known as a jewel in the Middle East region, a miracle of nature, and an attractive destination for tourists from all parts of the world. The country has beautiful mountains, serene and golden beaches, and fertile plains. Its small size allows a prospective tourist to visit all attractions in a matter of days rather than weeks or months. In addition to its natural beauty, Lebanon offers limitless opportunities for fun, night entertainment, renovated downtown Beirut, and all sorts of indoor and outdoor activities. A January 2009 *New York Times* article listed the Lebanese capital, Beirut, as the first destination among 44 places to visit in 2009. The article mentioned that in the recent détente Beirut is poised to reclaim its title as the Paris of the Middle East. The *NYT* also reported the opening of new luxurious hotels and a clutch of high-profile restaurants. A more recent article in *USA Today* (Stoddart, 2010) made the same observation of the capital but further highlighted Beirut's sizzling nightlife. The writer pointed out that the exuberant atmosphere is drawing mainly Gulf Arabs for the liberal lifestyle and Mediterranean climate and beaches, and returning Lebanese expatriates and Westerners.

Also in 2009, and according to statistics released by the official website of Lebanon's Ministry of Tourism, and based on an article published in the leading French daily newspaper in Lebanon, *L'Orient Le Jour*, more than 1.85 million people visited Lebanon in 2009, a 38.9 percent increase from the previous year. Visitors from 21 Arab countries represented 42 percent of the total number of tourists while Europeans came in second at 25 percent. Saudis comprised the biggest bulk of tourists (17 percent) whereas French represented 14.5 percent of all tourists. In a country that is not bequeathed with minerals and natural resources and where various industries are fighting for their mere survival following bloody conflicts, it is rather amazing that the tourism sector is showing such vitality.

Situation Analysis

Following Hezbollah's kidnapping of two Israeli soldiers who infiltrated Lebanese territories on July 12, 2006, Israel launched a 34-day destructive war against Lebanon. The war, which resulted in the death of nearly 1,200 people on the Lebanese side and 200 on the Israeli side, was ended by United Nations Resolution 1701 after feverish diplomatic efforts. Only a day after the abduction of the two soldiers, Israel responded with airstrikes and artillery fire on targets in Lebanon and damaged Lebanese civilian infrastructures, including Beirut-Rafic Hariri International Airport (CNN, 2006).

Most of those killed in Lebanon (some say about 65 percent) were Lebanese citizens and the war displaced more than one million Lebanese and 300,000 to 500,000 Israelis (BBC News Online, 2006). UN Resolution 1701, which was adopted by the Security Council on 11 August 2006, and accepted by the Lebanese government and the Israeli government, called for a full and immediate cessation of hostilities. The Resolution also called for: (1) the withdrawal of Israel from Lebanon, (2) the deployment of Lebanese army, and (3) the enlargement of UN forces in South Lebanon (UN News Centre, 2006). While the United Nations-brokered ceasefire went into effect on August 14, 2006, the war actually ended on September 8 after Israel lifted its naval blockade of Lebanon.

The 2006 round of hostilities between Israel and Lebanon was the latest in a long and bloody history between the Jewish state and its neighboring Arab countries before and since the establishment of Israel in 1948. This time, however, Hezbollah was the main target of Israel's massive operations that engulfed large parts of Southern Lebanon and expanded all the way to the Lebanese capital, Beirut, and especially to the Dahia area, which is Hezbollah's main stronghold outside the South. Hezbollah's operations were also able to hit hard and deep inside Israel. The party is a heavily armed, paramilitary Shiite group whose main goal has been to liberate Lebanese territories from Israel's occupation of parts of South Lebanon.

News accounts of world news agencies (Long, 2006) reported that large parts of the Lebanese civilian infrastructures were destroyed, including 400 miles of roads, 73 bridges, and 31 other targets such as Beirut-Hariri International Airport, ports, water and sewage treatment plants, electrical facilities, 25 fuel stations, two hospitals and 15,000 homes. In addition, more than 130,000 homes were damaged.

As the fighting intensified, countries such as Australia, Canada, France, Italy, the United Kingdom and the United States sent either cruise ships or warships to evacuate their citizens from Lebanon. Two of the authors of this chapter were caught in war activities and one of them had to be evacuated to the U.S. by sea and air.

Owing to the widespread devastation that captivated vast worldwide media coverage that included live and shocking images of the war, it was a foregone conclusion that Lebanon's summer season, the backbone of its tourism industry, was essentially over. With its international airport closed, its land borders with Syria jammed with thousands of displaced Lebanese and many Arab and non-Arab visitors fleeing the country and seeking safety, and with Western and other nations pulling out their citizens from Lebanon by land and by sea, the country's tourism sector was among the early victims of this war. The conflict forced hundreds of thousands of Lebanese compatriots and potential Arab and non-Arab visitors to scrap their plans to visit this small and beautiful country.

The War's Impact on Tourism

Traffic for Lebanon's tourism industry had unfortunately become a one-way exit from this small nation, a direct result to the 34-day war between Israel and its foes in Lebanon. The country, which depended heavily on its natural beauty, cultural and historical attractions, and on its reputation as a destination for those seeking pleasure and great times, was now facing a very serious problem: lack of safety and tranquility.

The war left a detrimental impact on one of Lebanon's more productive industries, tourism. After all, tourism flourishes when safety and peace go hand in hand with the country's natural beauty and attractions. The industry continued to suffer for a period of time as sizable numbers of potential visitors and tourists stayed away, fearing a renewed conflict in Lebanon. Many reservations by non-Arab and Arab visitors, including Lebanese compatriots who are spread the world over, were canceled. The extensive media coverage of the war had a chilling effect on potential visitors. Scenes of destruction in Beirut suburbs, South Lebanon, and Bekaa Valley became familiar sights to media users throughout the world.

Added to the plight of the tourism industry was the fact that the conflict occurred in July and August, the most critical months for the industry in Lebanon. The obvious decline in the number of visitors had naturally affected those who constitute the tourism sector in the country, namely the Ministry of Tourism (MOT), the touristic resorts, hotels, sites, travel agencies, and others connected to tourism in one way or another.

Efforts to Restore Tourism After the War

Soon after the hostilities ceased, the Lebanese government along with the country's private sector had to confront a twofold challenge: (1) controlling the damage that resulted from the relatively short but destructive war, and (2) re-launching of Lebanon as an attractive touristic spot. As expected under similar circumstances, the Lebanese government got busy rebuilding roads and bridges and seeking financial aids from Arab and non-Arab countries. Several private initiatives helped in the process as well. Aside from handling damages in the country's infrastructure, the government attempted to persuade tourists that life was back to normal in Lebanon. The latter mission was assigned to the Ministry of Tourism and other touristic boards and organizations in the country.

There was no specific written plan that explains how the government dealt with the crisis, simply because the efforts were reactionary. However, one can draw some remarks and conclusions from monitoring the website of the Ministry of Tourism and from reading and watching news that followed the crisis. The authors noted that the short-term goal of Lebanon's Ministry of Tourism was to control damages that resulted from the recent conflict, a necessary step in any crisis management situation. The efforts focused on reassuring potential tourists, as well as the rest of the world, that the crisis had ended and the country was headed back to normalcy. News and images of tourists and visitors flooding Hariri International airport occupied the front pages of the Ministry's website as well as other media outlets in Lebanon. In addition, nightly newscasts included images of returnees to "Switzerland of the Middle East." In general, various types of media were used to communicate with potential visitors and tourists.

Objectives

To articulate the objectives that the Ministry of Tourism attempted to achieve in its endeavor to restore tourism, the authors counted heavily on: (1) conducting interviews with high-ranking officials in the Ministry of Tourism, (2) analyzing stories published or broadcast in media, and (3) monitoring the website of the Ministry of Tourism for four years. The authors were able to identify the following objectives:

1. To restore confidence in the country and hence in matters related to the safety of Lebanon's guests.
2. To stress Lebanon's beauty and charm especially during summer time.
3. To reaffirm Lebanon's efforts and commitment to list the Jeita Grotto, one of Lebanon's most beautiful and popular attractions, as one of nature's Seven Wonders of the World, the upcoming version.
4. To promote Lebanon's readiness to receive large numbers of tourists through its international airport and through the Syrian borders, a very vital crossing point for Arab visitors who come from various countries.
5. To communicate to potential visitors through local, regional, and international travel agencies and through various media venues, Lebanon's ability to accommodate large numbers of visitors in the country's hotel sector and at affordable prices.
6. To inform potential tourists that Lebanon's four regular seasons make their visit to the country an unforgettable one.

Strategies

As for the use of strategies, the Ministry of Tourism, in coordination with other tourism offices and bodies, embarked on the following activities:

1. Launching massive advertising campaigns in Arab and non-Arab media outlets.
2. Signing bilateral protocols and agreements with other nations to revive the tourism industry.

3. Keeping close and frequent contact with travel agents to update them on new incentives that entice world travelers to place Lebanon on their list of destinations.
4. Soliciting endorsements and testimonials from world celebrities and selected groups and individuals about the normal life in Lebanon and their pleasant experience.
5. Highlighting Lebanon as an attraction for people from different faiths and religions since the country is an amalgam of various religions and creeds.
6. Promoting Lebanon as a first-rate fashion capital in the Middle East to highlight beauty and elegance.
7. Establishing close and working relationships with the private sector to promote Lebanon as a safe and attractive place.

Tactics

1. Buying full-page advertisements in world-class newspapers and commercial time in regional and global television stations.
2. Holding meetings and public appearances (press conferences and visual presentations) to reconfirm Lebanon as a hotspot for world's tourists.
3. Conducting concerts by famous Lebanese, Arab, European, and American musicians and singers in downtown Beirut, the ground zero point of the past, to project an image of peace, tranquility, creativity, and fun.
4. Inviting world-renowned Lebanese designers Abed Mahfouz and Elie Saab to participate in fashion shows.
5. Organizing special events such as inviting representatives of various governmental and nongovernmental agencies/offices connected to the tourism industry in Lebanon on a well-orchestrated tour of the country's major touristic and cultural attractions.
6. Reactivating programs and accords with neighboring countries to exchange travel tours.
7. Participating in regional and international fairs and exhibits.

Outcome Assessment

As for the outcome assessment of the efforts to put Lebanon back on the world's points of attraction, it is impossible to draw concise and precise conclusions on the effectiveness of these efforts in the absence of measurable objectives. The large numbers of people who returned to Lebanon or visited the country for the first time in the last four years seem to suggest that these efforts have been successful to a certain extent. Official statistics publicized by the Ministry of Tourism and based on registered numbers of those who entered Lebanon by land or by air indicate that almost 1.9 million visitors entered Lebanon in summer 2009. These involved Arab nationals, Lebanese expatriates, Americans, Europeans, and others. Larger numbers visited the country in summer 2010, according to the MOT's official website.

As mentioned earlier, Beirut was recognized in 2009 as a top tourist destination among 44 cities. It remains to be seen, however, whether this distinction is clear, direct, and accurate evidence of the government's efforts or is a result of several other factors. One may argue that advertising campaigns, media coverage, foreign governments' directions and instructions, affordable packages, and other forces may have contributed to the tourist influx in Lebanon.

Lessons Learned

The Lebanese government's efforts to revamp tourism after the 2006 war have been adequately but not fully articulated and executed. Time will tell whether or not these activities have fulfilled their potential. One has to remember that the activities went into effect only in 2006. A drawback of long-term activities in a developing country such as Lebanon is that those activities change almost every time with the new Ministry of Tourism. Continuity, commitment to previous plans, persistent follow-ups and evaluative research during the campaign implementation are essential ingredients in the formula for success of any endeavor. Frequent interventions by task forces assigned to monitor any long-term plan is a must to determine whether the efforts have been faithfully and fruitfully carried out.

The Lebanese government's efforts have missed out on several tools that are now deemed vital to the success of any crisis management program. The post-2006 activities did not use the latest communication tools and gadgets, media such as Twitter, Facebook, and other social networks. These and other techniques have been credited for assisting in the overthrow of governments in places such as the Philippines, Tunisia, and Egypt, among others. Use of these new forms of media makes them indispensible in any political, economic, cultural, and other endeavors.

Crisis management plans should carefully and meticulously pinpoint the various groups that have a stake in the plan outcome. We live in an ever-changing world, especially in terms of technological advances, something that requires us to keep a very close eye on the latest innovations.

The government could not rebuild Lebanon's reputation and stature in the tourism industry without active and continuous involvement of the private sector. At times it appeared that the government and the private sector each had its own agenda in the general scheme of things. A successful tourism industry is the integration of numerous efforts by various stakeholders.

Other lessons learned is the need to seek new groups of potential tourists. These groups include lovers of outdoor activities and lovers of shopping. According to the official MOT site (www.Lebanon-tourism.gov.lb), Lebanon has six ski resorts catering to skiers and snowboarders of all skill levels. The country is still heavily dependent on its summer season and its summer attractions. Selling Lebanon as a year-round attraction should be a key strategy. In addition, Lebanon provides shoppers with the latest from the worlds of jewelry, fashion, gadgets, and other commodities. The country adopts a free enterprise system that allows for a healthy competition and may lead to better prices. Thus, the months of February and August which are considered by the government as "sales" months should be publicized and marketed appropriately.

Other potential money-generating venues include rural tourism, religious tourism, and medical tourism. In 2009, Lebanon was ranked on the top list of nations for performing plastic surgery. Countries such as India, Brazil, and Argentina have been very successful in attracting people interested in this area.

The Lebanese government and other agencies must appeal to the 12 million people of Lebanese origin who live in all countries of the world but most notably in Brazil, Australia, and North America. These people should be a highly significant target public, a true priority. Thus, serious attempts should be made to lure them back to their land of ancestry. Tourism in Lebanon has all the potential to attract tourists but the industry remains, sadly, a second-tier priority to all successive Lebanese governments.

We have noted that most of the Ministry of Tourism's actions are temporary remedies. More carefully planned actions are needed to generate long-lasting effects. War-torn images cannot be fixed solely by publicity efforts. Continuous public relations efforts are required to: (1) build strong relationships between the Lebanese government and various stakeholders and (2) rebuild tourists' confidence in Lebanon. The public relations industry around the world is evolving from publicity-oriented practices into varying degrees of professionalization and sophistication (Sriramesh and Verèiè, 2003). L'Etang et al. (2006) posit that tourism is a vulnerable industry heavily affected by global events and incidents, and public relations helps the industry engage with such issues and maintain relationships between tourists and hosts.

In order for an organization to practice public relations from a relational perspective, it must recognize that both the organization and key publics can affect each other (Broom et al., 1997; Bruning and Ledingham, 1999; Hon and Grunig, 1999; Grunig and Huang, 2000; J. Grunig and Hung, 2000). While a variety of environment developments have made all types of organizations susceptible to crisis, tourism is exceptionally vulnerable to all kinds of risks and crises. This is partly owing to its intangibility (L'Etang et al., 2006). Lebanon's Ministry of Tourism can consider various techniques that support proactive planning and strategy development for the prevention of crises and disasters (Gonzales-Herrero and Pratt, 1998). Among these techniques are: contingency planning, strategic forecasting, issues analysis, stakeholder considerations, and feedback and media relations.

Coombs (2000) argues that the organization and its stakeholders have a connection that binds them together through economic, political, or social concerns. To strengthen the relationships between the Ministry of Tourism and various stakeholders concerned with the revival of tourism, we propose a five-year public relations plan guided by the theoretical framework of Grunig and Hunt's (1984) two-way symmetric model. The literature has shown that a large number of studies applied Western public relations theories, models and concepts in non-Western countries (VanSlyke Turk and Scanlon, 1999; Parkinson and Ekachai, 2006; Gupta and Barlett, 2009).

Organizations practicing the two-way symmetric model use bargaining, negotiating, and strategies of conflict resolution to bring about symbiotic changes in the ideas, attitudes, and behaviors of both the organization and its publics (Grunig and Grunig, 1992; Grunig et al., 1995). The Lebanese government is not the only beneficiary of full recovery of tourism in Lebanon. Other beneficiaries should include groups such as workers, entertainers, airliners, cab drivers, touristic guides, shop owners, and supermarkets. Each group can contribute to the success of any recovery plan by making sure that visitors feel at home. Thus, the Ministry of Tourism must seek feedback from all these publics with regard to offering the best services to Lebanon's guests.

The list of target publics of future plans should include leisure travelers, business travelers, travel reporters, travel agencies and organizations, religious groups, historians, foreign consulates, hospitality industry professionals, sports and leisure professionals, web masters, celebrities of Lebanese descent, international students, Lebanese citizens, and others. The plan has to allow for development of appropriate messages and provide necessary information that helps modify perceptions.

Conclusions

In the wake of the 2006 Israeli war, the tourism industry in Lebanon has witnessed some recovery. Continuous progress in the finance and investment sectors has made tourism in this Middle Eastern country more resilient than in other parts of the world. Some writers attribute this recovery to new governmental policies, which have promoted Lebanon as an exotic destination (Jallat and Shultz, 2011). However, in reviewing the literature and conducting online research, we did not find tangible evidence of new policies. In fact, an interview of three high-ranking officials in the Ministry of Tourism reported a lack of genuine public relations efforts to promote tourism for the last ten years. We believe that most of the official efforts to restore tourism in the last three decades have been based on impressions and not sound research.

Regardless of the disagreement on the existence of new policies, empirical evidence (Kanso, 2005) clearly suggests that tourists' negative perceptions of tourism in Lebanon remain strong. Serious efforts are needed to alter tourists' negative perceptions of Lebanon. Crisis management often places heavy emphasis on public relations to recover associated damages. If done correctly, managing a crisis may represent opportunities for the firm to strengthen its relationships with the customers (Coombs and Holladay, 2001).

Lebanon is not the only tourist destination that has suffered from negative publicity as a result of wars and or political instability. Scholars have provided evidence from Austria, Cyprus, Greece, Ireland, Italy, and other destinations, exemplifying the negative impact of political violence on tourism (Enders et al., 1992; Mansfield and Kliot, 1996; Wall, 1996; and Wahab, 1996, all cited in Neumayer, 2003). The literature has not documented empirical evidence on the role of public relations in shifting tourists' perceptions since civil unrest was settled. Anecdotal evidence, however, suggests that tourism was restored in troubled countries such as Egypt, Ireland, and Turkey after their governments implemented plans to erase negative images from the tourists' minds. Ireland, in particular, successfully overcame a situation similar to that of Lebanon. The country suffered a big shock from negative publicity associated with political violence, but it did a major turnaround relative to repositioning it as a tourist destination.

The revitalization of tourism in Lebanon after crises is not an easy task. It requires carefully planned public activities along with the use of state-of-the-art technologies. Hit-and-miss policy is doomed to failure.

Discussion Questions

1. How would you describe the role of public relations in the tourism industry?
2. What would you advise the Lebanese government and the private sector to do in a five-year plan? Be specific in making your recommendations.
3. Do you think that the Ministry of Tourism has been successful in its attempts to restore tourism in the country following the 2006 events?
4. What other communication tools would you use in the ongoing program to regain Lebanon's stature in the world of tourism?
5. Name and discuss the variables that a potential tourist might and should consider before he/she makes his/her decision to visit another country or region.
6. What major impediments remain to expanding tourism in Lebanon?

References

BBC News Online (2006). Middle East crisis: Facts and figures, August 31. Retrieved from http://news.bbc.co.uk/1/hi/world/middle_east/5257128.stm

Broom, G. M., Casey, S., and Richey, J. (1997). Toward a concept and theory of organization—public relationships. *Journal of Public Relations Research*, 9(2), 83–89.

Bruning, S. D., and Ledingham, J. A. (1999). Relationships between organizations and publics: Development of a multi-dimensional organization–public relationship scale. *Public Relations Review*, 25(2), 157–170.

CNN (2006). Israeli warplanes hit Beirut suburbs, July 14. Retrieved from http://edition.cnn.com/2006/WORLD/meast/07/13/mideast/

Coombs, W. T. (2000). Crisis management: Advantages of a relational perspective. In J. A. Ledingham and S. D. Bruning (Eds.), *Public relations as relationship management: A relational approach to the study and practice of public relations* (pp. 73–94). Mahwah, NJ: Lawrence Erlbaum Associates.

Coombs, W., and Holladay, S. (2001). An extended examination of the crisis situation: A fusion of relational management and symbolic approaches. *Journal of Public Relations Research, 13*(4), 321–340.

Gonzales-Herero, A., and Pratt, B. (1998). Marketing crises in tourism: Communication strategies in the United States and Spain, *Public Relations Review, 24*(l), 83–97. Retrieved from Science Direct: www.sciencedirect.com/

Grunig, J. E., and Hunt, T. (1984). *Managing Public Relations.* New York: Holt, Rinehart and Winston.

Grunig, J., and Grunig, L. (1992). Models of public relations and communication. In J. Grunig (Ed.), *Excellence in public relations and communication management* (pp. 285–325). Hillsdale, NJ: Lawrence Erlbaum Associates.

Grunig, J. E., and Huang, Y. H. (2000). From organizational effectiveness to relationship indicators: Antecedents of relationships, public relations strategies, and relationship outcomes. In J. A. Ledingham and S. D. Bruning (Eds.), *Public relations as relationship management: A relational approach to the study and practice of public relations* (pp. 23–54). Mahwah, NJ: Lawrence Erlbaum Associates.

Grunig, J. E., and Hung, C. (2000). *Development of indices and an initial study of trust, control mutuality, commitment, satisfaction, and communal and exchange relationships as measures of organization–public relationships.* Paper presented at the Annual Conference of the International Communication Association, Acapulco, Mexico, June.

Grunig, J., Grunig, L., Sriramesh, K., Huang, Y-H., and Lyra, A. (1995). Models of public relations in international setting. *Public Relations Research, 7*(3), 163–186.

Gupta, C., and Barlett, J. (2009). Recruiting public relations professionals for global public relations, *Prism, 6*(2). Retrieved from http://praxis.massey.ac.nz/prism_online_Journ.html

Hon, L. C., and Grunig, J. E. (1999). *Measuring relationships in public relations.* Gainesville, FL: Institute for Public Relations.

Jallat, F., and Shultz, C. (2011). Lebanon: From cataclysm to opportunity—Crisis management lessons for MNCs in the tourism sector of the Middle East. *Journal of World Business, 46*(4), 476–486.

Kanso, A. (2005). Reinvigorating the "Switzerland of the Middle East": How the Lebanese government can use public relations to reposition the country as a premier tourism destination. *Journal of Hospitality & Leisure Marketing, 12*(1/2), 135–156.

Kanso, A., and Sinno, A. K. (1999). Attracting tourists to a new Lebanon: A two-phase plan. In J. VanSlyke Turk and L. Scanlon (Eds.), *Fifteen case studies International Public Relations. The evolution of public relations from countries in transition* (pp. 84–98). Gainesville, FL: The Institute for Public Relations, University of Florida.

Kanso, A., Sinno, A. K., and Nelson, R. A. (1997). Lebanon, tourism development, and the Internet: A plan of action for rebuilding from war. In A. F. Alkhafaji, and

Z. El-Sadek (Eds.), *International business strategies: Economic development issues* (pp. 96–106). Apollo, PA: Closson Press and the International Academy of Business Disciplines.

L'Etang, J., Falkheimer, J., and Lugo, J. (2006). Public relations and tourism: Critical reflections and a research agenda. *Public Relations Review, 33,* 68–76. Retrieved from Science Direct: www.sciencedirect.com/

Long, G. (2006). My beloved Lebanon: Crayons, glass, litter Lebanese school, August 30. Retrieved from www.mybelovedlebanon.com/2006_08_01_archive.html

Neumayer, E. (2003). The impact of political violence on tourism: Dynamic econometric estimation in a cross-national panel. Unpublished manuscript.

Parkinson, M., and Ekachai, D. (2006). *International and intercultural public relations: A campaign case study approach.* Boston, MA: Allyn and Bacon.

Shenwood, S., and Williams, G. (2009). The 44 places to go in 2009. *The New York Times,* January 11. Retrieved from www.nytimes.com/interactive/2009/01/11/travel/20090111_DESTINATION

Sriramesh, K., and Verèiè, D. (2003). *The global public relations handbook: Theory, research, and practice.* Mahwah, NJ: Lawrence Erlbaum, Inc.

Stoddart, V. G. (2010). Beirut is reborn as a glitzy playground for tourists. *USA Today,* January 22. Retrieved from www.usatoday.com/travel/destinations/2010-01-21-beirut-bounces-back_N.htm

UN News Centre. (2006). Lebanon: UN peacekeepers lay out rules of engagement, including use of force, October 3. Retrieved from www.un.org/apps/news/story.asp?NewsID=20106&Cr=Leban&Cr1

VanSlyke Turk, J., and Scanlon, L. (1999). *Fifteen case studies in international public relations. The evolution of public relations cases from countries in transition.* Gainesville, FL: The Institute for Public Relations, University of Florida.

VIEWS FROM AN EXPERT

RICHARD ALAN NELSON

Richard Alan Nelson (PhD, Florida State University) is professor of Mass Communication and Public Affairs at Louisiana State University where he teaches courses in public relations, advertising, ethics, and propaganda. He is editor of Journal of Promotion Management, *and past president of both the International Management Development Association and the International Academy of Business Disciplines.*

This case presents a good example of the challenge of applying public relations principles in an international context. More than ever before, public relations efforts are critical to the success of important travel, tourism, and hospitality market categories such as tourist destinations, attractions, hotels and lodging, restaurants, transportation, and other services.

A common denominator for each is to entice travelers and ensure their experience remains a positive one.

Perhaps most useful for readers will be a look at some of the issues raised in this case and some probing questions that result.

Since every tourism and travel sector has its own publics, messages, and public relations approaches, coordination between them can be especially difficult. As an example, travel agents and hotels tend to work closely with planners of large and small conventions, meetings, and events, but such contacts are of less importance to airlines and restaurants. What do the authors recommend in terms of building strong relationships between the government and various stakeholders to regain tourists' confidence in Lebanon? How could new social media be effectively harnessed as a method of reaching key audiences?

Having an educated workforce is always valuable. Therefore, close collaboration between universities and those engaged in the tourist trade is desirable. How prepared is the country in terms of its infrastructure? What is the status of public relations and tourism management in terms of Lebanese higher education?

Unfortunately, tourism is rather dependent on positive news reports and other media images, especially when the viewer or reader has no prior experience of a destination. As a result, individual and group travel and tourism decisions are especially vulnerable to threats of violence, crises, and other forms of risk. Fears of violence are an ongoing factor in the Middle East from which Lebanon is not exempt. It is a testament to the natural attractions of the country, that the tourism industry is vibrant once more.

Finally, can many of the lessons learned here be transferred to other nations? My own feeling is that while each country and culture is unique, there are indeed commonalities applicable in a variety of contexts and continents. All in all, this is a valuable contribution to the literature.

Section 6

North America

Mexico

Rosarito Beach: Mediated Reality and the Rebranding of a Mexican Border City

Robert Brown

The case study focuses on the damaging consequences of Mexico's ongoing violent drug cartel wars on the economic and perceptual health of Rosarito Beach, a once trendy and popular seaside resort city an hour south of the US–Mexican border in northern Baja. Rosarito's disastrous loss of tourism dollars and popularity was largely the result of mediated reality. The media-driven perception conflated the violence a thousand miles away from Rosarito in Ciudad Juarez and other distant Mexican locales with the reality of an essentially safe Rosarito Beach. To counter the damaging and misleading perception of Rosarito, a crisis communication and rebranding campaign was launched under the supervision of a coalition of students led by an Emerson College professor, a public relations consultant on the ground in Rosarito, and an active and courageous mayor of Rosarito. The mixed outcome of the campaign is analyzed.

Introduction

The problematic equation of perception and reality: That perception is reality has been the conventional wisdom of public relations, perhaps even before the rise of the modern public relations industry. To the extent that the strategies and tactics of public relations have been applied to communicating and managing in a crisis, the equation of perception and reality still holds.

But in the case at hand, a highly complex crisis indicates the limits of the public relations axiom that perception is reality—a conventional piece of wisdom that requires much closer critical inquiry.

For rhetorically oriented scholars of crisis management, the foundational perspective of organizational crisis theory is perceptual (Benoit, 1995; Coombs, 2007, p. 3).

Perception is reality. Except when it is not. Or, in the case of the crisis of Rosarito Beach, Mexico, when the boundary between perception and reality is as porous, troubling, and complex as the borderline that separates the U.S. and Mexico. That emotionally, culturally, and politically laden boundary has a metaphorical parallel in the gruesome, operatic drama, the bitter, high-profile contentiousness, and the mind-boggling ambiguities that frame the crisis of the pretty city of Rosarito Beach.

Crisis Background

The perception of Rosarito Beach as a city best avoided by travelers has emerged in the wake of Mexico's drug cartel wars. The U.S. State Department issues daily, cautionary travel warnings to American tourists. The media have reported on Mexico's president Felipe Calderón's counterinsurgency against the cartels. The tabloidish, body-count coverage of Mexico has created a poisonous perceptual frame for the nation of Mexico with political fallout north of the border: the bitterly contentious issue of illegal immigration.

The near-border city of Rosarito Beach has suffered as well from this relentless negativity. Hugo Torres, the former mayor of Rosarito Beach, attributed to these negative perceptions the devastating loss of 70 percent of the tourist revenue that is vital to this pretty, oceanside playground destination (Dibble, 2010b).

But even more devastating to Rosarito has been the degradation—although not the total loss—of its most important asset: its reputation. After the recent years of graphic media coverage of the violence in Juarez and several other locations elsewhere in Mexico, the perception and reputation of Rosarito Beach has been blurred and degraded with grisly imagery: decapitated bodies in the Sonoran desert; midnight machine-gun rampages in Juarez; and President Calderón's war against what is, in fact, not simply a Mexican crisis but a global crisis (Knight Center, 2010).

Until the drug cartel violence that was happening hundreds of miles from Rosarito Beach—most notably across the Gulf of California, in Juarez, the nation's third largest city—Rosarito had enjoyed a sunny reputation among Southern Californians. Tourists saw the city as a pretty, charming, seaside, romantic getaway, and expatriates saw it as a retirement community.

But the crisis of Rosarito Beach is ultimately inseparable from what Alma Guillermoprieto calls the "nightmare" of Mexico (Guillermoprieto, 2010, p. 48). Guillermoprieto resists what she calls the "easy conclusion" that Mexico, or even the nation's "drug war zone" of U.S./Mexican border cities and towns, constitutes a failed state. But she does note that the crisis in Mexico raises the question of whether "in the face of unstoppable activity by highly organized criminals, the Mexican government can adequately enforce the rule of law and guarantee the safety of its citizens *everywhere* in the country" (ibid., p. 48, italics hers).

It is on that italicized word *everywhere* that the crisis communication and rebranding strategy of Rosarito Beach has hinged—that is, on a public relations campaign that has attempted to distinguish the city from two critical dimensions of devastating, perceptual negativity: the localized crises of Juarez, Sinaloa, and Tamaulipas, the nuclei of drug cartel violence; and the negative perception of Mexico itself. The priority target of the public relations campaign (rebranding and crisis communication) has been the millions of Southern Californians who once constituted the thriving tourist trade of Rosarito Beach. The statistics are gaudy: 28,000 violent deaths have followed in the wake of Mexican President Calderón's declaration of a war on the nation's drug cartels in December 2006 (Beaubien, 2010; Bowden, 2003; Guillermoprieto, 2010, p. 48; Tuckman, 2010).

What makes the crisis of Rosarito especially interesting is the city's ongoing, daunting battle to restore its sunny image. Rosarito's crisis demonstrates that crisis is a perceptual–rhetorical phenomenon.

The city of Rosarito Beach, with approximately 130,000 souls and 15,000 expatriates, is situated about an hour south of, and across the border from, San Diego, California, and just south of Tijuana. Rosarito's neighboring proximity to the U.S. is one major driver of its crisis. Compared with remote Colombia—a nation that has suffered its own drug and violence crisis— Mexico in general and Rosarito in particular are too close to the U.S. border to be swept under the hemispheric rug.

The other driver of Rosarito's crisis is its perceptual identification with Mexico, itself—a nation embroiled in a brutal, complex, multifaceted crisis. Rosarito has watched its tourist-driven economy devastated by what Hillary Clinton, U.S. Secretary of State has called, quite controversially, "the Colombianization of Mexico" (Cardenas and Casas-Zamora, 2010).

Perceivers need not have considered Rosarito at all. The media and U.S. State Department narratives direct attention elsewhere, to other parts of the nation. Mexico is a land of more than 100 million, comprising 30 federal states, each with a number of cities with populations exceeding 20,000. (Brinkhoff, 2010). But in the degradation of Mexico's image, one city alone has dominated the perception of the nation the way Darth Vader dominates "Star Wars": Ciudad Juarez. Juarez is a metropolis of more than 1 million— a fraction of Mexico City, which ranks more than 20 million inhabitants. But *pathos* transcends *logos*: Mexico's homicide rate in 2009 was actually lower than it was in 1997, and its murder rate is less than one-third that of Washington, D.C. (Cardenas and Casas-Zamora, 2010).

Recognizing the grave economic, political, and cultural risk of a negative image, and to defend its reputation against misleading and incorrect information, President Felipe Calderón announced in June 2010 that Mexico would invest in a public relations campaign whose objectives would be to cleanse Mexico's image and promote the nation's appeal as a destination and haven for foreign investment ("Beyond beaches and pyramids: Mexico turns to PR to Repair Image," 2010) (Figure 6.1).

Enter: A college's crisis management team: The Emerson Coalition. Based in Boston, and led by J. G. Payne, Jr., a senior professor of political communication, Emerson College's crisis management team (CMT) based its strategy on one big idea: that the crisis of Rosarito Beach was an example of the theory of mediated reality (Gerbner, 1994; Jamieson and Waldman, 2003).

Murder By Media: What Misleading News Coverage Is Doing To Mexico

By Hugo Torres, Mayor
Rosarito Beach, Mexico

ROSARITO BEACH, BAJA CALIFORNIA, MEXICO---In Rosarito Beach, as in much of Mexico, we are fighting two battles these days.

One is against organized crime. The other is against misleading media coverage that wrongly implies that much of Mexico is unsafe for visitors and residents, and which is devastating our economy.

Some reporters, stories and outlets have been responsible and balanced, including some of those who know this area best. Many, perhaps most, have not.

The war that Mexico's President Felipe Calderon has launched against drug cartels (which are fed in part by a $38 billion yearly U.S. drug market) is indeed a serious one, one of vital concern for both our countries.

We welcome and invite serious and analytical coverage of this struggle. Such coverage can be of significant help to both countries, which have much at stake.

What we don't welcome is inaccurate, sensationalized, unbalanced and unfair coverage, which provides no insight but only promotes fear and misunderstanding. There has been far too much of this and it continues largely unabated.

Some media reports are simply biased and inaccurate. They are from individuals or media outlets that have an agenda against Mexico and will publish anything to promote it, whether or not it is true.

What is more troubling are reports from mainstream media that present an unbalanced, superficial and worrisome portrait of what life is like in Mexico, including Baja, California.

This is sometimes done because sensationalism sells; other times because of lack of understanding: many reporters never even visit. At other times, the situation in one city is presented as if it represents all of Mexico, a vast country.

Figure 6.1 Murder by media: what misleading news coverage is doing to Mexico.

Believing that Rosarito's crisis has been largely driven by relentlessly negative stories produced by distortions of mediated reality, Emerson's CMT focused a rebranding message on a priority public: revenue-generating Southern California tourists.

Mediated reality theory. Cultivation and mediated reality theorists have long made a compelling and epistemologically troubling case that in the late twentieth and twenty-first centuries we are faced with a great gulf between two very different and distinct pictures of reality: experiential and mediated (Gerbner, 1994; Jamieson and Waldman, 2003). This line of theory argues that the advent of television and other pervasive media has caused a distorting cleavage between perception and reality. For heavy consumers of media, particularly, mediated reality is not merely an alternate and equal reality, but it replaces personal, experientially-based reality. For Gerbner, the media "cultivated" the perception of reality (Gerbner, 1994).

This case study poses the following hypothesis: *That mediated reality (MR) contributed significantly to the crisis of Rosarito Beach.* (A quantitative study could be mounted to discover the amount of variance explained by MR.)

FOR IMMEDIATE RELEASE   JUNE 9, 2009

Baja Is Safe For Visitors,
Says Ranking U.S. Diplomat

ROSARITO BEACH, BAJA CALIFORNIA, MEXICO---Baja is safe for visitors and he hopes its tourism sector quickly rebounds, a leading U.S. diplomat told El Mexicano newspaper in a front-page story published Monday.

Ronald Kramer said that publicity about Mexico's war against drug cartels had falsely created the impression in the U.S. that the area is unsafe for visitors.

Kramer is head of the U.S. Consulate in Tijuana, which serves all of Baja.

While the bi-national effort against drug cartels is a serious one, visitors are not targeted, Kramer said. He also praised the Mexican army and authorities for their successes in the effort.

Kramer expects efforts by Mexican leaders, including Rosarito Beach Hugo Torres, to be successful in rebuilding Mexico's image, but said the country's economy and many of its people currently are suffering because of significant loss of tourism dollars.

Kramer also said concerns in past weeks about the H1N1 virus (also known as the swine flu) had hurt the area's economy.

He cited as an example some cruise lines canceling voyages to Ensenada and diverting them to San Diego, which actually had more confirmed cases of the flu.

Figure 6.2 Press release: Baja is safe for visitors, says ranking U.S. diplomat.

Experiential versus mediated. The leadership of the crisis management team relied on its salutary, positive, on-the-ground, direct, continuing, personal experience of Rosarito Beach, which was a far cry from the melodrama of the mediated Rosarito. J. G. Payne, a professor of political communication at Emerson College, who divides his time between his work in Boston and his family in Southern California, is a frequent visitor to Rosarito Beach and has close family ties there. Ron Raposa, a public relations practitioner, maintains residences in Rosarito Beach and San Diego, California. In interviews with both men, each expressed a highly favorable view of Rosarito Beach as a fundamentally safe and secure community under the leadership of Mayor Hugo Torres, an official they described in positive terms as a man of integrity, courage, and having the wisdom to embrace the concept and strategies of crisis communication. In a press release issued under the authority of Mayor Torres's office, Ronald Kramer, who was identified in the release as the head of the U.S. Consulate in Tijuana, which serves all of Baja, proclaimed the safety and security of Baja ("Baja is safe for visitors," 2009) (Figure 6.2).

Emerson Coalition Strategy. From the outset in 2007, the Emerson Coalition's strategy was to rebut the mediated reality of Rosarito Beach. The Coalition's message: the city remains a charming, convenient, and affordable destination. The Coalition emphasized the leadership of Rosarito's strong mayor who took action to fire corrupt police and open the lines of communication with partners on both sides of the border.

In 2008, the Coalition ramped up its efforts, focusing its messaging on the city's priority stakeholders: 30 million Southern Californians have avoided Rosarito Beach, depleting tourism by 70 percent (Torres, 2009).

Situation Analysis

In 2008, a crisis management team (CMT)—a coalition of Emerson College faculty, graduate students based in Boston, Massachusetts, and a public relations practitioner based in San Diego, California and Rosarito Beach, Mexico, was created to address the crisis of Rosarito Beach. The CMT developed a crisis management plan (CMP). (Baja, California: See for Yourself, 2009).

The CMP analyzed the situation as follows:

- Baja North, the region where Rosarito Beach is located, has seen a significant decline in tourism revenue.
- Intensely negative publicity has created the overall impression of Mexico in general as a dangerous and violent place, best avoided if possible.
- The romantic, tranquil, and glamorous image of Rosarito Beach, which held sway particularly during the 1990s and into the middle of the next decade, has been largely dismantled.

- The establishment of Juarez as "murder city," and the rhetorically driven conflation of Rosarito Beach with Juarez and certain other high-crime Mexican communities, has created doubt, anxiety, and fear.
- Rosarito's brand has suffered degradation.

Objectives

- To prevent the misperceptions of Baja from continuing to tarnish the brand of this beautiful region.
- To bring back tourism.
- To reposition Baja as a safe and secure place for expats to retire, for second vacation homes, and for seasonal tourists.
- To regain self-confidence and positive image.
- To increase economic development, including small and emerging businesses.

Strategies

The strategic plan developed for Rosarito Beach was an integrated one. It wove together proactive crisis management and communication with marketing strategies. The strategy called for the building of a "community" around Baja by means of the following tactics:

- targeting influential traditional and social media;
- reaching opinion leaders in government, education, religious communities and sports;
- targeting the U.S. State Department, which issues travel advisories; and
- building partnerships with key individuals in business and civil society on both sides of the Mexican/U.S. border.

Tactics

- *Grassroots projects*
  - Southern California college campus-targeted events and promotions
  - word of mouth marketing (WOM)
  - focus groups for stakeholders and targeted audiences
  - street interviews
  - expat liaisons
- *Mass media marketing*
  - advertisements (testimonials/outdoors)
  - media relations and publicity
  - media advocacy

- *Online marketing*
  - social media networking
  - social media marketing
  - search engine optimization (SEO)
  - distribution of monthly press releases via PR Newswire
- *Public affairs*
  - lobbying: a strong name for Baja
  - editorial tours
  - events marketing
  - hosting special events (conferences, conventions, advising and consulting)
- *Infrastructural improvements*
  - spokesperson training
  - developing a regional crisis communications team
  - developing a crisis management team (CMT)
  - tourist security forces (San Diego Police Department partnership with Baja)
  - other infrastructural improvements.

Timeline

The program was scheduled to begin immediately upon proposal and budget approval—ideally, December 2009. The thinking behind the timing was that it would take approximately three months to have all the elements and materials developed, plus time for the campaign to impact audiences. For this reason, fast approval was considered to be a critical part of the plan if it were to have a significant impact on the 2010 tourist season in Northern Baja.

Target Audiences

- U.S. families/tourists
- U.S. students/tourists
- American senior citizens (retirement communities; health care services)
- U.S. and Mexican media
- travel agents
- medical industry/medical bloggers
- travel bloggers
- stakeholders from both sides of the Mexican/U.S. border

  - local businesses (Baja, Mexico, and Southern California)
  - local governments (Baja, Mexico, and Southern California)
  - residents/citizens/expats
  - state governments of Mexico and California.

Budget: $840,000

Crisis Management Team: The Emerson Coalition

Emerson College, based in Boston, with a small outpost in Hollywood, California, brands itself as the only institution of higher education in the U.S. dedicated solely to communications.

To address the crisis of Rosarito Beach, a four-tiered coalition team was assembled. Its collective background and experience had a range of critical assets to address the complex, international, bilingual shape of the crisis facing Rosarito Beach. The membership is international, multicultural, multi-lingual and multigenerational. The CMT's skill set and background includes marketing public reations, media relations, political communication, public diplomacy, and crisis communication experience.

The team included a senior political communication professor at Emerson College, who has family ties and roots in Southern California; a cadre of Emerson College graduate students with diverse, international backgrounds including Spain, Greece, Turkey, and Saudi Arabia, as well the U.S.; a veteran public reations practitioner based in San Diego and Rosarito Beach who acted as media spokesperson and provided media training for the Mayor of Rosarito Beach; and two veteran, skilled communicators with U.S./Mexican trans-border experience.

Coalition's Outcomes Assessment Plan

Evaluation of objectives was planned to be implemented every six months beginning January 2010 through the following research methods:

- stakeholder and audience focus groups; and
- media audit.

Execution: A Selected Chronology

2007

Spring. Following negative media coverage of Rosarito, the Emerson Coalition leader, J. G. Payne, Jr., met with newly elected mayor Hugo Torres and Rosarito and San Diego-based public relations practitioner Ron Raposa. Coalition leaders surfaced risk management concerns related to President Calderón's plan to pursue a counterinsurgency "war."

Mayor Hugo Torres endorsed the need for crisis management.

Fall. Coalition leaders initiated media training of Mayor Torres.

Mayor Torres began identifying and dismissing corrupt police officers to demonstrate city management's credibility on safety and security.

2008

- Crisis team of Emerson College-led coalition created;
- Tijuana violence peaked at 844 homicides;
- Emerson Coalition began working with Rosarito businesses; and
- coalition developed website themed to *Rediscover Rosarito* in Spanish and English.

Summer. Grassroots campaign, including health communication. An Emerson College student from Saudi Arabia developed a juvenile diabetes program working with local Rosarito government and citizen groups.

Coalition launches Student Film Festival and produced rebranding short films that aired in Rosarito Beach's film studio.

Fall. Students worked with Rosarito local orphanage known as Cha Cha.

November. Coalition presented its campaign at National Communication Annual Convention (www.natcom.org), Chicago, Illinois.

2009

Spring. Presentation of creative and strategic work at annual convention of the International Academy of Business Disciplines (www.iabd.org).

June 9. Press release disseminated by Emerson Coalition partner Ron Raposa: "Baja Is Safe For Visitors, Says Ranking U.S. Diplomat" (2009).

Tijuana ran counter to national trends with 657 killings in 2009, a 20 percent drop from 2008.

Fall. Continued development of Rediscover Rosarito website to include advertisements from local businesses, tips for tourists, links to other sites; social media connections, such as Twitter and Facebook, featured appealing events in Northern Baja.

2010

January. Public relations practitioner Ron Raposa elaborates the crisis communication plan with additional rebranding strategies.

Summer. Third Annual Rosarito Student Film Festival.

- "Baja, Baseball and Burrito" project developed by an Emerson graduate student.
- Seminars in crisis communication management developed for and offered to Rosarito influencers.

Initial Outcome: Baja Government Selects Allison & Partners over Emerson Coalition

Despite its four-year investment in identifying, addressing, planning, and implementing its crisis communication management and rebranding campaign, the Emerson Coalition was not selected to be the consultant of record by the Mexican state of Baja, California. The Baja government believed that the campaign should emphasize safety first, then aesthetics.

In September 2010 the Baja government announced that it had selected Allison & Partners, a U.S. public relations firm headquartered in San Francisco, with offices in San Diego, Washington and elsewhere. The agency was awarded a $300,000 contract to provide communication services intended to repair Baja's battered image. A reporter for a San Diego newspaper interviewed Tim Wheatcroft, the general manager of Allison's San Diego office. Wheatcroft characterized the agency's strategy as what the reporter calls "a range of strategies," that, according to Wheatcroft, are intended "to make sure that the state has a more positive image" (Dibble, 2010a).

In a telephone interview with the author, Wheatcroft speculated that his firm was able to win the crisis management business of the Baja government because of Allison & Partners' "very deep experience" with tourism, including a campaign focused on Lake Powell, Utah, which had been experiencing low water levels that damaged tourism.

Wheatcroft indicated that the agency was just beginning to develop and implement its crisis management program to address the crisis affecting Rosarito and Northern Baja. The fundamental message of the Allison program would be to stress that Baja was a safe and secure region because in contemplating their travel plans to Baja, "people have felt unsafe." Wheatcroft added that the message would be that, "If you do travel down to Baja, you'll be safe," adding that once there, tourists will be able to experience the fishing, food, and other appealing features of the region. As far as the thesis about mediated reality was concerned, Wheatcroft believed that the media in San Diego actually "has been somewhat fair in its reporting" (Wheatcroft, 2010).

In contrast to the Emerson Coalition strategy, which tended to emphasize the appealing attributes of Rosarito Beach, Allison & Partners offered a two-phase strategy that would emphasize tourist security until the message was assessed to be credible, and then (and only then) to build a secondary message emphasizing the appealing attributes of the entire Baja region.

Theoretical Frame Analysis

Frame 1: The media narrative. Three narratives have competed to frame the perception of Rosarito. The first is the *media narrative*. Putatively objective, the media narrative of Rosarito is sometimes, if not always, difficult to distinguish from the sensationalistic, tabloid coverage of Mexico's drug cartel's localized violence. As a Knight Foundation study reports, journalists missed the real story: that drugs and violence are not a police story by an international one (Knight Center, 2010).

Lost in the body counts of Juarez, Monterrey, and other beleaguered Mexican localities is what the Knight report identifies as the real news story: that the Mexican crisis is in reality a localized spoke in an international web with hubs in locations including Cali, Colombia, Moscow, and the poppy fields of Afghanistan (Knight Center, 2010).

Frame 2: U.S. State Department narrative. The second narrative frame is visible on the website of the U.S. State Department:

> Millions of U.S. citizens safely visit Mexico each year. This includes tens of thousands who cross the border every day for study, tourism or business and at least one million U.S. citizens who live in Mexico. The Mexican government makes a considerable effort to protect U.S. citizens and other visitors to major tourist destinations. Resort areas and tourist destinations in Mexico do not see the levels of drug-related violence and crime reported in the border region and in areas along major drug trafficking routes. Nevertheless, crime and violence are serious problems. While most victims of violence are Mexican citizens associated with criminal activity, the security situation poses serious risks for U.S. citizens as well.
>
> (U.S. State Department Travel Warnings, 2010)

While attempting a balanced message, the thrust of the State Department's warning is clear: Travelers, beware!

Frame 3: Rebranding: The Emerson Coalition. The third marketing-driven narrative sought legitimacy over mediated reality.

Outcomes Assessment

Assessment 1: Mixed Results in the Short Term

Crime is down but tourism is not recovering. Three observations emerge from the Rosarito-based actors in the city's drama: Mayor Torres, whose term of office ends on the final day of November 2010; and Ron Raposa, the public relations practitioner who has worked closely with the mayor. In the fall of 2010, Raposa offered these observations:

1. Notwithstanding the multi-year rebranding efforts of the Emerson coalition, tourism is not recovering. It will be down slightly in 2010 compared with the previous year (Raposa, 2010).
2. While Rosarito's neighbor city, Tijuana, has seen its crime rate decline in 2009, its murder rate is expected to rise in 2010 (Raposa, 2010).

3. Rosarito continues to experience a reduction in crime, including violent crime, over the previous three years. Its crime rate is the lowest since it began keeping records in 2000. Baja's crime rate ranks lower than that of many U.S. cities, including Washington, D.C. and New Orleans (Raposa, 2010).

Assessment 2: Safety Message Trumped the Marketing of Aesthetics

After reviewing the Emerson Coalition Rebranding and Crisis Communication Plan, the Baja government selected Allison & Partners. The Coalition plan and execution sent a mixed message intended to reframe Rosarito. While public relations practitioner Raposa issued news releases in 2009 that reported Rosarito was experiencing reduced crime rates, the Emerson Coalition's emphasized rebranding Rosarito in terms of its legacy image of aesthetic and entertainment attributes. But amid the perception of danger and risk, the Coalition's strategy might have been more effective by focusing more heavily on a safety message. Safety and security was the message prioritized by Allison & Partners' successful pitch of its services to the Baja government.

Assessment 3: The Complexity of Political, Cultural, Geographical, and Organizational Systems Contributed Significantly to Creating and Extending the Crisis

The crisis of Rosarito Beach is ongoing. The nexus of geography, culture, and politics has played a major role in the crisis of Rosarito Beach. One of the hot-button issues in U.S. politics has been the bitterly debated issue of illegal immigration of Mexican citizens across the border into North America. U.S. elections have turned on just this issue, and a search and seizure law passed in 2010 by the state of Arizona faces U.S. federal and judicial challenges. The geographic locus of this controversy is the Mexican/U.S. border stretching about 3,000 miles from San Diego on the Pacific Ocean eastward past El Paso to Brownsville, Texas. Both Juarez and Rosarito are border cities. To be a border city is in itself a potential crisis. But the similarity ends there, if not in the perception of worried travelers.

Assessment 4: History Indicates Longer-Term Optimism for Rosarito

History offers hope. As of the Fall of 2010, while drug war violence continued to flare up in specific hotspots, a very different wind was blowing in from the opposite direction. Investment dollars were not only flowing into Mexico, they were flowing in at a faster rate than ever, suggesting that as far as foreign investor perception is concerned, Mexico has highly promising prospects for economic growth. Foreign investment in Mexico soared 28 percent in 2010 compared with the previous period of 2009. But even more surprising is the trend in tourism (United States—Mexico Business Network, n.d.). According to reliable sources, upwards of four million Americans flew to Mexico in one period during 2010, a surge of 15 percent compared with the same period of the previous year (Drake, 2010).

History—looking not only backward but forward—offers a possible explanation for this apparent paradoxical perceptual endorsement of Mexico, amid the reputationally damaging effects of mediated reality.

Investors have apparently discounted the drug war violence as a short-term phenomenon that a sovereign nation can manage. With its natural resources, including petroleum, and its long history of robust trading partnerships with the U.S. and other nations, Mexico offers the possibility that like other nations in Latin America—notably, Brazil—it is a good bet for economic growth. In essence, foreign investors have bet on Mexico's ability to manage its crisis and with its wealth of petroleum and other natural resources, grow profitably in the future.

In the fall of 2010, Hillary Clinton, U.S. Secretary of State, made the controversial observation that Mexico, amid its drug cartel wars, had been "Colombianized" (Booth, 2010). While that observation seemed to imply that Mexico had devolved into the nearly failed-state condition that characterized Colombia in the 1990s, a very different and far more hopeful conclusion can be drawn. Today, Colombia is in the midst of a political, economic, and reputational resurgence. Bogota, Medellin, and Cali—more than a decade ago as drug-ridden and murderous as Juarez and other localized areas of Mexico are today—have become magnets for U.S. and other tourists. Under the security-minded administration of former president Alvaro Uribe, Colombia has turned the corner from chaos to civility. Comparing Mexico to Colombia is only superficially negative, but historically speaking, a light at the end of the reputational tunnel.

The Lessons of Rosarito

1. Mediated Reality is a Crisis Generator

If, as rhetorically based crisis communication theory indicates, crises are perceptual; and if the epistemological problem implicit in mediated reality is that consumers of mass media cannot fully rely on their own perceptions of a reality they perceive through the distorting lens of the media—then Rosarito offers a vivid and troubling illustration of this principle.

2. The Perception of One Crisis can Color the Perception of Another Crisis

The rhetorical trope known as metonymy may have played a role in the crisis of Rosarito Beach. Metonymy is the rhetorical substitution of the part for the whole or the whole for the part. The apparent substitution of Mexico and Juarez for Rosarito Beach, generated by the mediated and State Department narratives, created a devastating image problem for Rosarito.

3. Crisis Management's Efficacy is Limited and Bounded by Complexity, Uncertainty, and Contingency

Ours is an era of astronomical speed that runs far ahead of human capability; intricate systems can malfunction. As Mitroff (2004) has argued, we have created highly complex systems and organizations that tend to generate unmanageable crises. In such an era as ours, management—whose normative attributes are planning, organization, and control—can be simply overwhelmed by contingency: what can neither be controlled nor predicted (Brown, 2010).

4. Crisis Communication and Public Relations Take Precedence Over Marketing, Advertising, and Rebranding

Where a crisis of safety and security exists, safety and security messaging should take priority over rebranding, marketing, and advertising messaging.

5. More Research is Needed to Expand Existing Crisis Theory

Coombs's elegant (2007) taxonomy of crisis works toward identifying discrete crisis types such as accident and human error that are associated with a hierarchy of stakeholder blame and rhetorically indicated rhetorical strategies. But even Coombs's sophisticated taxonomic approach warrants future research to account for the type of highly complex crisis exemplified by Rosarito Beach.

Discussion Questions

1. Despite the Emerson Coalition's continuing efforts to rebrand Rosarito Beach, the Baja government selected Allison & Partners, a public relations agency, to help restore the good image of Rosarito, Tijuana, and Baja. In your opinion, what could be the reasons for the Baja government's decision to offer the public relations firm a contract, rather than select the Emerson Coalition?
2. Can you identify a current organizational crisis that could be the result of the damaging effects of mediated reality?
3. How could the Emerson Coalition have emphasized more effectively the theme of safety and security?
4. Aside from rhetorical theory, what other theories or principles can you offer to explain the crisis facing Rosarito Beach?
5. Would you have created a different kind of crisis management team than the Emerson Coalition? Why? Why not?

References

Baja, California: See for yourself. (2009). Rebranding and crisis communication plan. Prepared by the Emerson Coalition. R. Raposa and J. G. Payne, Jr. (Eds.).

"Baja is safe for visitors," says ranking U.S. diplomat. (2009). News release issued by Rosarito Beach office of the Mayor, June 9.

Beaubien, J. (2010). Mexican election to proceed despite assassination. National Public Radio story online, June 30. Retrieved from www.npr.org/templates/story/story.php?storyId=128203784

Benoit, W.L. (1995). *Accounts, excuses, and apologies: A theory of image restoration.* Albany, NY: State University of New York.

Beyond beaches and pyramids: Mexico turns to PR to repair image. (2010). Retrieved from www.wharton.universia.net/index.cfm?fa=viewArticle&id=1942&language=english.

Booth, W. (2010). Secretary of State Clinton compares Mexico's drug violence to Colombia's, September 8. Retrieved from www.washingtonpost.com/wp-dyn/article/AR2010/09/08AR2010090806882.html

Bowden, C. (2010). *Murder city: Ciudad, Juarez and the global economy's news killing fields.* New York: Nation's Books.

Brinkhoff, T. (2010). City population: Mexico. Retrieved from www.citypopulation.de/Mexico.html

Brown, R. (2010). Seven ways of looking at a crisis. Speech. *Vital Speeches of the Day, LXXVI*(6), 250–254.

Cardenas, M. and Casas-Zamora, K. (2010). *Brookings Institution Report.* Retrieved from www.brookings.edu/opinions/. A Spanish-language version was published in *Reforma*, a Mexican newspaper, September 21, 2010.

Coombs, T. (2007). *Ongoing crisis communication.* Thousand Oaks, CA: Sage.

Dibble, S. (2010a). Baja launches drive to rehab image. *San Diego Tribune*, September 1. Retrieved from www.signonsandiego.com/news/2010/sep.01

Dibble, S. (2010b). Baja tourism seeks more government aid. *San Diego Tribune*, October 26. Retrieved from www.signonsandiego.com/2010/oct/26/baja-tourism-industry-seeks-more-government-aid

Drake, M. (2010). Despite news, Mexico grows as destination. *The New York Times*, Sunday Travel, October 24, p. 2.

Gerbner, G. (1994). *Growing up with television: The cultivation perspective.* Mahwah, NJ: Lawrence Erlbaum Publishers.

Guillermoprieto, A. (2010). The murderers of Mexico. *New York Review of Books, LVII*(16), 46–48.

Jamieson, K., and Waldman, P. (2003). *The press effect: Politicians, journalists, and the stories that shape the political world.* New York: Oxford University Press.

Knight Center for Journalism (2010). *Journalism in time of threat, censorship, and violence.* Report from the Seminar Cross-border coverage of U.S.–Mexico Drug Trafficking, conducted March 26–27. Austin, TX. Author: Medel, M.

Mitroff, I. I. (2004). *Crisis leadership: Planning for the unthinkable.* Danvers, MA: John Wiley & Sons.

Raposa, R. (2010). Email correspondence, November 3.

Torres, H. (2009). Murder by media: What misleading news coverage is doing to Mexico. Undated news release issued by Rosarito Beach, Mexico, mayor's office.

Tuckman, J. (2010). Mexico looks to legalization as murders hit 28,000, August 4, Retrieved from www.guardian.co.uk/world/2010/aug/04/mexico/legalisation-debate-drugwar.

United States—Mexico Business Network (n.d.). Mexico foreign direct investment rose 28% to $12.24B. Retrieved from www.usamexico.org/index.php?option+com_content&view=article&id=46:mexico-foreign-direct-investment-rose-28-to-1224b-in-1h-2010

U.S. State Department Travel Warnings (2010). Retrieved from http://travel.state.gov/travel/cis_pa_tw/tw/tw/4755.html

Wheatcroft, T. (2010). Telephone interview with Tim Wheatcroft, September 21, 2:35 p.m. EST.

VIEWS FROM AN EXPERT

J. E. HOLLINGWORTH

J. E. Hollingworth is an Associate Professor, Department of Communication Studies, Emerson College, Boston, MA. He is also a consultant, trainer, lecturer, author, and teacher specializing in communication and management for colleges, universities, government, private and nonprofit organizations throughout North America.

Rosarito and the Emerson Coalition

It appears that the community of Rosarito finds itself caught in "a perfect storm"—the Mexican drug wars and the U.S. financial downturn. The unfortunate result for Rosarito was a dramatic drop of 70 percent in its economically vital tourist trade. The management challenge was to reverse the downward trend, recover losses, regain the status quo, and even to keep the tourist industry growing in the future.

Conventional and oft-tested managerial objectives in such a case are as follows: In order to successfully meet the challenge, the manager(s) needs to (1) assess the moods and emotions surrounding the problem, (2) uncover every piece of related information available (or not), (3) build a project team, (4) carefully and accurately state the problem in clear, focused terms that everyone grasps and agrees upon, (5) trace the causes and effects leading from the problem back to the root cause or causes, (6) create and identify options, (7) pro/con those options, (8) build a plan that is viable and cost-effective, (9) then sell, implement, tweak, and evaluate the results of the entire process.

The following observations can be offered about the Emerson Coalition:

1. Had a clear idea that personal safety was a powerful concern of potential tourists. It is not clear that the team fully examined the economic downturn implications.

2. Was secondarily aware of many variables in the situation, but did not appear to be fully aware of many primary points such as reasons why 30 percent of tourists came to Rosarito in spite of the "fear factor" or specifically why 70 percent did not.
3. Was made up of what was essentially a well-intentioned, intelligent, dedicated, and creative but random group of volunteering students, rather than seasoned crisis management professional troops. Problems of this magnitude require full-time, totally committed professionals.
4. Appeared to have a clear idea of what the basic challenge is—get the tourists to come to Rosarito.
5. Was not convincingly persuasive regarding its full understanding of the multiple causes and effects relationships regarding the problem. There were many assumptions involving media, governments, and wide varieties and sources of statistical data.
6. Applied a "shotgun" approach to the many opportunistic solutions that seemed more geared to what and who is available (rather than what will really work) such as student involvement in an orphanage, a diabetes clinic, graduate student papers at conferences, exposure at academic meetings, and student-created documentary films. Each may have a purpose and be noble in itself, but the real question should be, "Is this the best use of resources to impact the achievement of the goal or is it simply an inexpensive, easy 'I can do this' thing?"
7. Did not (and perhaps logistically could not) thoroughly and objectively evaluate the pros and cons of each activity—especially from the point of real connections with the targeted past, present, and future tourist.
8. Developed and presented a plan that was rejected in lieu of a competing plan.

In summary, the Emerson Coalition mounted a noble and creative endeavor burdened by mixed agendas, randomly focused efforts, a less than optimal skill and experience mix, and a not soundly articulated concept of project management.

As with most "perfect storms," controlling or even impacting the causes and effects may be well beyond many or most of the victims. Sometimes we have to do whatever we can to survive, hope for the best, and ride it out.

USA

No Walruses in the Gulf: BP's Need for Effective Issues Management

Ashli Quesinberry Stokes

This chapter provides an initial explanation of how BP could have been spared some of its public lashing following its Gulf oil spill disaster through greater attention to careful issues management. In 2000, BP sought to rebrand itself after the acquisition of Amoco, Castrol, and Arco petroleum, and positioned itself as an environmentally friendly, forwarding thinking oil company that sought to look "Beyond Petroleum." Rebranding aside, however, its new campaign neglected to integrate its image efforts with its business plan through issues management. I first provide a situation analysis and explain how an issues management approach would have better met stakeholders' expectations. This case also describes how the company relied on three main strategies, each complemented with respective tactics, in order to meet its short-term objectives and long-term goals. Viewing BP's varied public relations efforts through an issue management perspective provides insight for other practitioners and scholars looking to help avoid crises of BP's magnitude.

Introduction

BP has the unfortunate distinction of being linked to the largest man-made environmental disaster in the history of the United States. In the six months following the April 20, 2010, explosion of the Deepwater Horizon oil rig and subsequent massive spill into the Gulf of Mexico, BP's corporate image and reputation became tattered. This chapter provides an initial explanation of how BP could have been spared some of its public lashing through greater attention to careful issues management. Following an earlier 1989 campaign promoting a greener, more socially responsible image, in 2000, BP sought to rebrand itself after the acquisition of Amoco, Castrol, and Arco petroleum (Beder, 2002). Seeking an aggressive identity change, BP positioned itself as an environmentally friendly, forward-thinking oil company that sought to look

"Beyond Petroleum" (A.L., 2005). Professing an interest in alternative energy sources such as solar power and a desire to move beyond its core business of hydrocarbons, BP chose a new logo. Based on the ancient Greek sun god Helios, the logo really looked like a green and yellow sunflower. BP released a series of ads positioning itself as a friend to the environment and promoted its $4 billion investment in alternative energy sources (though its investment in branding cost more than its investment in solar power). Nevertheless, as one practitioner noted, BP "nailed their colors very firmly to the environmental mast" and this branding "hit," becoming regularly featured in university classes (A.L., 2005, p. 1). Rebranding aside, however, BP has the worst safety record of all the major oil companies (*The Independent*, 2007), and its new campaign neglected to integrate its image efforts with its business plan through issues management. First, this chapter analyzes how an issues management approach would have better met stakeholders' expectations. Then, it examines BP's initial ineffective response to the crisis. It then describes how the company relied on three main strategies, each complemented with respective tactics, to meet its short-term objectives and long-term goals. Viewing BP's varied public relations efforts through an issue management perspective provides insight for other practitioners and scholars looking to help avoid crises of BP's magnitude.

Background of the Crisis

The disaster is well known, but it bears detailing how BP's disaster became the world's largest accidental release of oil into marine waters (*New York Times*, 2010). After the Deepwater Horizon rig caught fire and sank off the Louisiana coast, killing 11 crew members, BP spiraled into the worst environmental crisis the country has seen. Nearly five million barrels of oil flowed into the Gulf, topping the estimated 3.3 million barrels that spilled there in 1979, creating the worst spill in American waters since the Exxon Valdez (*New York Times*, 2010). As one plan after another failed, the company seemed clueless as to how to stop the gush. By June 15, 2010, President Obama used his first address from the Oval Office to order BP to set aside whatever resources were required to compensate workers and business owners harmed by the spill (Jensen and Snyder, 2010). On July 15, 2010, for the first time in 86 days, BP temporarily capped the Macondo well, followed by a more permanent plugging on August 5, and a full sealing on September 19. A cascade of public relations problems emerged for BP as the days of the disaster wore on. The public was outraged about the loss of life on the rig. Harsh questions about the state of the oil industry arose, concerning offshore drilling moratoriums, the regulatory regime overseeing offshore drillers, and the potential long-term environmental damage.

Further battering BP's reputation was the release of an Associated Press story detailing the 582 pages of its crisis plan. The Regional Oil Spill Response Plan for the Gulf of Mexico contained a host of errors and omissions and detailed no clear role for public relations during the event of a crisis. Approved by the Federal government in 2009, the plan included references to protecting walruses, sea lions, and seals, wildlife that does not live in the Gulf. In addition to appearing copied from a crisis plan better suited to an Alaskan spill, the document listed a wildlife expert who died in 2005, incorrectly listed the contact information for marine specialists at Texas A&M University, and cited a marine mammal rescue network that was no longer in business. In the plan, spokespersons were advised not to assure the public that an ecosystem would be back to normal after such a spill. Although the crisis plan is clearly egregious, the seeds for BP's disaster were planted even earlier.

Situation Analysis: Rebranding and the Need for Issues Management

As the company began its rebranding efforts in 2000, BP continued to invest more in fossil fuels than ever before. It spoke to consumers about environmental themes, but it faced a series of environmental, worker safety, and corporate conduct fines. An explosion at a Texas refinery in 2005 killed 15 workers and injured 170, with the company receiving a fine of $50.6 million. An oil pipeline leak in Alaska in 2006 led to a fine of $20 million. The company was fined $300 million in 2007 for manipulating the market price of propane. BP's decision to position itself as an environmentally concerned energy company as these infractions and continued investments in traditional energy sources continued was risky: "I remember hearing somebody talking about how Beyond Petroleum was going to be the poster child for this new environmental mind-set, and somebody else saying, 'Yeah, that'll work until they have their own plant explosion'" (Goodman, 2010, p. 2). Indeed, some have argued that the amount of public rage now centered on BP is a direct reflection of it having fallen victim to greenwashing, or cloaking itself in environmental messaging without the corresponding internal changes to become more sustainable (Garfield, 2010). The spill did reveal a disconnect between the global company and its stakeholders' myriad concerns. In addition to its shareholders, everyone from Gulf-area residents, BP-branded gas station owners, BP consumers, national and global media audiences, the Gulf-area tourism industry and tourists, Gulf-area seafood industry and consumers, environmental groups and activists, and State and Federal regulatory bodies were possibly affected by BP's actions; certainly, many publics had an interest in BP's handling of the spill.

Issues management helps us in understanding how the company squandered the opportunity to guide itself through the crisis more successfully. The practice helps organizations take a more proactive, rather than reactive, stance on important political issues, such as concerns over the environment or rising energy costs. Although Crable and Vibbert (1985) point out that the government possesses the actual authority to determine public policy, organizations can employ issues management to resolve an area of concern in their favor by responding to public interest, changing organizational policy, and/or shaping legislation. Should organizations not exercise public sensitivity on issues of concern, however, they can face regulation that forces them to adopt more socially responsible practices, the position in which BP now finds itself.

Issues management helps organizations integrate public relations, government and legal affairs, and strategic planning. Early on, issue management took the form of issue advocacy advertising, where organizations headed controversial issues through skillfully designed controlled media. Mobil Oil, for example, famously argued for openness in the heated 1970s energy debate in its aggressive op-ed campaign. While early discussions did not recognize that organizations might need to adapt their internal cultures to successfully manage an issue and forestall regulation, today savvy organizations recognize they may need to change to foster mutual interests in the public policy arena. Several issue management models detail this process. In 1979, Jones and Chase (1979) identified the "issue change strategy options" managers can select to deal with an issue. Organizations can adopt a reactive stance where they "stonewall" an issue, an adaptive stance where they indicate openness to change and willingness to participate in the public policy process, or a dynamic stance where organizations attempt to direct and shape the direction of public policy through strategic activities. Crable and Vibbert (1985) later offered another issue change strategy option, the catalytic stance, which tries to enter into the decision process even earlier, something difficult to do for an oil company. Here, organizations determine what public policy outcome they are trying to achieve and nurture their position through the issues management life cycle. A catalytic stance may have been difficult, but instead of engaging in a reactive position during the spill, attention to issues management years earlier might have helped BP avoid the crisis or at least given it a better position from which to operate.

BP's Initial Response

Initially, BP decided to downplay, indirectly address, and shift the blame for its role in the oil spill crisis. This reactive response was a particularly poor choice given the level of interest and scrutiny from so many different publics. When using a reactive stance, organizations attempt to "ride out" the developments occurring around them (Crable and Vibbert, 1987, p. 8). Over the years, BP had touted its concern over the environment, but its corporate policies did little to implement the message. In fact, by 2005, BP had spent $64 billion in fossil fuels, compared with $500 million in solar, representing a drop in the bucket for such a large company (A.L., 2005). BP's initial decision to focus on shareholders and minimize the crisis echoed its plan to remain committed to its fossil fuels business. A day after the Deepwater Horizon rig exploded, for example, it shared a news release stating it would offer its "full support to Transocean," noting only that it operates the license on which the rig was drilling (bp.com, April 21).[1] Later, it chose in an earnings statement to footnote that the crisis "might" impact shareholder dividends. This focus on shareholders continued when the company did address the crisis directly, with BP insisting that it was not solely at fault for the spill. During an appearance on the "Today Show," for example, Mr. Tony Hayward, BP's CEO, said "Well, it wasn't our accident, but we are absolutely responsible for the oil, cleaning it up" (Elliott, 2010, p. 2). Although the company stated in numerous media outlets that it would take full responsibility for cleaning up the spill, it pointed fingers at its contractors for the explosion of the rig and seemed to focus its efforts only on containment.

Overall, the company's initial public relations response could be categorized as sharing information about its containment resources. For example, as of April 22, BP posted news releases on its websites detailing the resources it was sending to the Gulf, including its vessels, boom, and storage capacity. Hayward echoed this focus noting:

> We have assembled and are now deploying world-class facilities, resources, and expertise, and can call on more if needed. There should be no doubt of our resolve to limit the escape of oil and protect the marine and coastal environments from its effects.
>
> (bp.com)

BP specified its efforts to contain the spill, providing numbers of vessels and the like to show the extent of its recovery efforts; for example, "supplies of more than 100,000 gallons of dispersants and four aircraft ready to spray dispersant to the spill, and the pre-approval of the US Coast Guard to use them" (bp.com). Although the company could have done a better job explaining how dispersant worked or why 100,000 gallons was a good volume to have on hand, it did try to quantify its efforts.

Nevertheless, BP's reactive stance, focusing on working to contain the spill, rather than reassuring or apologizing for the worsening environmental tragedy, made the crisis worse. Further, its decision to feature CEO Hayward as spokesperson poured salt on America's environmental wound and made for some very insensitive media remarks. Hayward continually tried to downplay the environmental magnitude of the leak, saying on one occasion, "The Gulf of Mexico is a very big ocean. The amount of volume of oil and dispersant we are putting into it is tiny in relation to the total water volume" (BBC, 2010). Four days later, Mr. Hayward echoed this sentiment, saying that "the environmental impact of this disaster is likely to have been very, very modest" (BBC, 2010). BP attempted to remain responsible only for the clean-up and continued its operations without suffering fundamental or marked change, highlights of a reactive position. This stance made Hayward's apologies for BP's role in the spill seemed insincere and self-interested: "We're sorry for the massive disruption it's caused to their lives. There's no one who wants this thing over more than I do. I'd like my life back" (Zarroli, 2010). As one reporter noted, this comment "opened the gates to Sound-Bite Hell, one that burned brighter as Hayward was then photographed a few days later spending time with his family in a yacht race" (Elliott, 2010, p. 2). As the days wore on, BP attempted to change its public relations approach, but its attempts were hampered because of its lack of issues management years before.

Implementing the Public Relations Response

As public rage deepened, with 76 percent of Americans disapproving of BP's crisis response, the company began a more planned approach to public relations. BP began a "Making it Right" public relations campaign designed to convey its commitment in remedying the harm the spill caused to the Gulf and thus achieve the (likely unattainable):

Goal 1: To save its reputation and rebuild stakeholder trust. This goal featured seven ill-defined objectives:

1. To communicate its efforts to seal the well.
2. To communicate its clean-up of the region.
3. To communicate its clean-up of the beaches.
4. To communicate its response to insurance claims.
5. To communicate its rehabilitation of wildlife.
6. To communicate its environmental restoration efforts.
7. To stimulate economic investment.

BP created a specific part of its website detailing these campaign objectives (www.BP.com/GulfofMexicoResponse) (Figure 6.3). To achieve them, BP loosely embraced three strategies: advocacy, transparency, and partnership. Ironically, though, each of these strategies designed to take a more planned approach to public relations still echoed a reactive issues management stance because they reacted to public sentiment and responded to the directives of officials. BP's stance caused it to become a victim, rather than a proponent, of change. After examining each of these strategies and their respective tactics, I argue that following a dynamic stance years earlier would likely have spared BP at least some of its many public relations problems.

To address objectives 2, 3, 6, and 7, BP employed an advocacy strategy.

Strategy 1: Used controlled media to convey its commitment, responsibility, and competence in responding to the crisis.

bp

Contact us | Reports and publications | BP worldwide | Home

Search [   ] Go

About BP   Products and services   Environment and society   Investors   Press   Careers   Gulf of Mexico response

You are here: BP Global   ▸ Gulf of Mexico response

Making it right - highlights
Response timeline
Response in pictures
Response in video
Response maps
Claims
Supporting materials
Contacts
BP internal investigation

Follow us on:
BP on Twitter
BP on Facebook
BP on YouTube
BP on Flickr
RSS Feed

Gulf of Mexico response

Gulf of Mexico response

The completion of the relief well operation in the Gulf of Mexico is an important milestone in our continued efforts to restore the Gulf Coast. However our work is not finished. BP remains committed to remedying the harm that the spill caused to the Gulf of Mexico, the Gulf Coast environment, and to the livelihoods of the people across the region

Latest reports:

Online Q&A, with Dave Rainey, VP of Science and Technology for BP's Gulf Coast Restoration Organization
More details here

BP Pledges Collateral for Gulf Of Mexico Oil Spill Trust
Read the press release

BP and the Gulf of Mexico Alliance Announce Implementation of BP's $500 Million Independent Research Initiative
Read the press release

BP has confirmed that well kill operations on the MC252 well in the Gulf of Mexico are now complete, with both the casing and annulus of the well sealed by cement.
Read the press release

BP has published its internal investigation team's report into the accident on the Deepwater Horizon rig in the Gulf of Mexico on 20 April 2010.
Visit the investigation report page

Official BP
BP_America

Dr. Sam Walker leads @usNOAAgov subsurface monitoring to '[meet] the needs of #Gulf citizens': http://bit.ly/b2Vr7j
4 minutes ago

(Video) 2k+ miles boom deployed during #oilspill What's #BP doing to minimize amt of waste material in landfills? http://bit.ly/cL9tpU
about 1 hour ago

Find a one-stop hub for #oilspill response activities and info on our Facebook page: http://on.fb.me/dznHaz
about 1 hour ago

Join the conversation

Latest video
Assessing the environmental impact of the spill
Watch the video

Share this article: Share on Twitter   Post on Facebook

Sealing the well
See how we're tackling the leak at its source

Cleanup
See how we're capturing oil from the ocean surface

Beaches
See how we're cleaning Gulf beaches 24/7

Claims
We're committed to paying all legitimate claims for losses

Wildlife
See how we're rehabilitating birds and other wildlife

Environmental restoration
Supporting ecological research and other projects

Economic investment
Helping to restore jobs and livelihoods

Response in video
Watch videos documenting our efforts to stop the leak, protect the shore and support the local community
▸ Video listings

State response websites
▸ Alabama
▸ Florida
▸ Louisiana
▸ Mississippi

Figure 6.3 Gulf of Mexico response overview webpage.

Tactic 1.1: Employed public relations advertising.
In its advocacy ads, BP attempted to demonstrate its concern for the public by vowing to clean up the spill and engage in "Making it Right." Tactically, the company first released ads featuring CEO Hayward. In one televised 60-second ad, Hayward tells viewers as they hear the sounds of seabirds and ship bells in the distance, "BP has taken full responsibility for cleaning up the spill in the Gulf. We'll get this done. We'll make this right" (bp.com). Similarly, BP bought ad space in major newspapers such as the *Washington Post* and in major magazines. In these ads, BP frequently employed rhetorical strategies that positioned the spill as a common enemy that it, as a consumer ally, was determined to fight (White, 2010). In one ad, for example, an employee in charge of capturing and cleaning up oil in the Gulf talks in aggressive language about "hunting down" remaining oil using satellite images, helicopters, strike teams, and the like. Viewers see planes flying above the Gulf and boats using skimming devices, which in concert with the text, gives the ad an almost military operation-like feel. These efforts at portraying the oil leak as the enemy, however, fell short. In light of BP's initial response, shifting the blame for its responsibility for the spill, *it* remains the enemy, not the spill it has helped create. Especially in light of Hayward's earlier rhetorical missteps, BP's later ads featuring New Orleans natives who work for BP were better at humanizing the company and supporting its clean-up efforts (Goodman, 2010).

Tactic 1.2: Used the Gulf Response website to communicate its advocacy efforts.
One webpage addressing BP's beaches objective, for example, uses an ongoing cleaning metaphor to convey its dedication in restoring the beaches. Website users can read about how rapid response teams "are scouring" the Gulf beaches for oil, "patrolling" the coast daily, employing "vacuum boat patrols" to reach the less accessible parts of the terrain, and using a "Sand Shark" cleaning vehicle to "wash" the sand. Combined with the continuing use of military-like language, users are encouraged to view BP as dedicated fully to the beaches and clean-up objectives, and therefore committed to "cleaning up" itself.

Tactic 1.3: Used news releases to convey commitment to protecting the Gulf shoreline from the oil.
One release, for example, noted that BP was "determined to fight this spill on all fronts," and "defend the shoreline." Again, though, these efforts to generate approval of BP's military-like handling of the spill's aftermath were hampered by the ongoing realities of the crisis; namely, that BP could not shut down the gushing well for months. Coupled with its insistence that it was helping fight the enemy rather than admitting it *was* the enemy in many publics' minds, these advocacy efforts were incomplete.

To bolster its advocacy strategy, BP employed a transparency strategy to address objective 1, but only did so in response to a letter from the EPA and DHS asking the company to be more open about its clean-up efforts.

Objective 1: To communicate its efforts in sealing the well.

Strategy 2: Appear transparent in releasing data and information to the public.

Tactic 2.1: Used website to upload and share information generated by itself and credible agencies.
BP first began working with the Coast Guard and EPA to upload materials to its website on an ongoing basis in order to "provide the American people with the information they need to understand the environmental impact from the spill and the response steps that have been taken."

Tactic 2.2: Used the web to provide regular updates on BP's subsea operations.
BP provided live feeds of remotely operated vehicles (ROVs), designed to help seal the well. The efforts largely backfired, however, as the days wore on and users could see underwater cameras documenting the pouring of oil into the ocean.

Tactic 2.3: Created state-specific response web sites, such as www.mississippigulfresponse.com, to provide residents with the most current information about the spill in the area.
Residents could sign up for e-mail updates, follow a RSS or Twitter feed, or connect with a Facebook page. As BP noted about the state-specific websites, "these community focused web sites are part of BP's effort to engage with the communities of affected areas, their residents, local leaders, and other stakeholders" (www.bp.com). BP began other types of data sharing designed to portray corporate transparency in dealing with the spill, but many of these efforts also fell short.

Tactic 2.4: Posted Gulf-based news dispatches and video reports to its website to humanize its image.
BP engaged a pair of reporters to travel the Gulf and upload first-person accounts to the Web. After one of these pieces, called "Ballet at Sea," "fetishized the beauty of shrimping boats weaving a web of oil containment booms during clean–up operations," the press criticized these efforts for again being tone-deaf (Houpt, 2010, p. 2).

Tactic 2.5: Used social media to communicate transparency.
BP hired Ogilvy Public Relations to advise the company on how to best use Facebook, YouTube, and Twitter to engage audiences. These efforts largely worked to magnify the disaster and poke fun at the company. For example,

a satirical Twitter feed was created, purporting to be from BP's communications department. It garnered 160,000 followers, dwarfing the company's legitimate feed followers of 11,500 (Houpt, 2010). BP was further damaged by social media when one blogger discovered that it was posting doctored images of its response efforts to its website. One blogger posted a doctored image of a BP command center to Flickr, a social media picture-sharing site, that drew much negative attention among social media users.

Tactic 2.6: Tried to direct the electronic media tide.
BP bought the rights to oil spill-related search terms online, so that consumers would see a sponsored link to BP's corporate messages whether they entered "I hate" or "I love" BP (NPR Staff, 2010). This tactic hampered its efforts at appearing transparent. Although consumers would then have had a greater chance at seeing the messages BP wanted to share with them, this practice sneakily directed consumers away from the volumes of criticism found online.

Some of the tactics BP used to achieve its partnership strategy fared a bit better, but the approach did not begin well.

Objectives 1–3: Communicate efforts in 1) sealing the well, 2) cleaning up the region, and 3) cleaning up the beaches.

Strategy 3: Partnered with various entities, community programs, and agencies to demonstrate commitment and credibility in responding to the crisis.

Tactic 3.1: Partnered with the Federal Government to clean up the spill.
BP partnered with the Federal government, but it only did so after being required. This "partnership" worked poorly for both parties: as the Government put more responsibility on BP, BP continued to have difficulty in stopping the flow, leading to criticism from both sides of the political spectrum. Further, because the Government was dependent on BP's equipment and expertise to stop the spill, it really did not have the power to take charge of the operation (Liasson, 2010).

Tactic 3.2: Began a compensation initiative, by which it appointed an independent mediator charged with overseeing the claims process for those who filed claims for loss or damage from the spill.
The company faced criticism here as there were several groups not entitled to compensation from the $20 billion fund. These limitations could exclude a large majority of spill victims from compensation, including fishermen operating on a cash basis and tourism and home owners "not directly affected" by the spill. Further, because BP stressed it would fund all "legitimate" claims, the burden of proof for meeting the definition of legitimate was placed on the spill victims.

Other tactics in positioning itself as a community partner were more successful.

Tactic 3.3: Used advocacy ads to demonstrate commitment to community partners.

One ad featured Iris Cross, director of BP Community Outreach, discussing BP's efforts in meeting its objectives (6) environmental restoration and (7) economic investment (Figure 6.4).

Ms. Cross's status as a lifelong Gulf-area resident, coupled with the ads' discussion of its varied initiatives to address the Gulf area residents' concerns, did convey a measure of compassion and responsibility. The ad's language that it would "help people get back on their feet" and reassurance that "We haven't always been perfect, but we will be here until the oil is gone and the people and businesses are back to normal" helps convey the right tone.

Tactic 3.4: Created Vessels of Opportunity program, where BP paid local commercial and charter fishing vessels to help in the clean-up and recovery efforts.

This tactic was wise. Website video of the fishermen using their own boats to tow boom and support skimming operations, all the while talking about their appreciation of the program, helps position BP as a community investment partner.

Tactic 3.5: Invested $500 million in the Gulf Research Institute (GRI), a research program staffed by independent experts. By involving distinguished academics from around the country in the areas of public and environmental health, this tactic helped bolster BP's credibility.

Tactic 3.6: Partnered with Tri-State Bird and Rescue to help recover and clean affected wildlife. BP featured this initiative on its website, where users could learn more about what to do if they spotted oiled wildlife. The use of another independent agency also helped bolster BP's claims that it was working with experts in handling the spill.

Initial Outcomes Assessment

Even in light of the more concerted public relations efforts of the Make it Right campaign, BP's reputation continued to suffer. It was further harmed once a hearing in late July found that the company had made several questionable decisions before the Deepwater Horizon rig exploded (White et al., 2010). These decisions included permitting the rig to operate in the face of a highly critical maintenance report, using a cheaper well design, and skipping tests that might have detected problems in the well (White et al., 2010). BP continued to face problems because its public relations efforts seemed to

I was born in New Orleans. My family still lives here. We have to restore the Gulf communities for the shrimpers, fishermen, hotel and restaurant owners who live and work here.
- Iris Cross, BP Community Outreach

Making This Right

Beaches
Claims
Cleanup
Economic Investment
Environmental Restoration
Health and Safety
Wildlife

No oil has flowed into the Gulf for weeks. But we know this is just the beginning of our work. BP has taken full responsibility for the cleanup in the Gulf and that includes keeping you informed.

Restoring Gulf Communities
We can't undo this tragedy. But we can help people get back on their feet. We have been working with impacted communities since day one.

Partnering with local governments and community organizations, my job is to listen to people's needs and frustrations and find ways to help. We have 19 community centers and teams in four states, listening and helping.

Restoring The Economy
BP is here in Gulf communities with shrimpers, fishermen, hotel and restaurant owners, helping to make them whole.

More than 120,000 claim payments totaling over $375 million have already gone to people affected by the spill. We have committed a $20 billion independent fund to pay all legitimate claims, including lost incomes until people impacted can go back to work. And none of this will be paid by taxpayers.

BP has also given grants of $87 million to the states to help tourism recover and bring people back to the Gulf beaches.

Restoring The Environment
We're going to keep looking for oil and cleaning it up if we find it. Teams will remain in place for as long as it takes to restore the Gulf Coast.

And we've dedicated $500 million to work with local and national scientific experts on the impact of the spill and to restore environmental damage.

Thousands of BP employees have their roots in the Gulf. We support over 10,000 jobs in the region and people here are our neighbors. We know we haven't always been perfect, but we will be here until the oil is gone and the people and businesses are back to normal. We will do everything we can to make this right.

For general information visit: bp.com
For help or information: (866) 448-5816

restorethegulf.gov
Facebook: BP America
Twitter: @BP_America
YouTube: BP

For claims information visit: bp.com/claims

Figure 6.4 Advocacy ad featuring Iris Cross.

contrast with its corporate activities. Rather than using issues management to guide its business as a whole, BP's reliance on public relations to staunch its wound after the crisis was not effective.

To evaluate the outcomes of BP's public relations efforts, it is useful to assess how a differing stance could have helped create perhaps different realities for the company. If BP had employed a dynamic position when rebranding its image back in 2000, it could have positioned itself as a new type of environmentally conscious energy company and influenced public policy in its favor. Instead of choosing to wed its image positioning to its strategic planning, BP now finds itself facing regulation and legislation rather than shaping it. Its decision to pursue a reactive stance, especially coupled with its rebranding campaign that celebrated environmentally conscious values without putting them fully into place, compounds each of the public relations outcomes discussed herein. Even granting that it would be difficult for an energy company of BP's magnitude to assume the position of an environmentally conscious company, recognition of the issue management process would have helped the company resist definition by others. Over time, BP became one of the big, bad energy companies. Through the dynamic strategy, BP could have taken an offensive, affirmative issue stance that considered the public's growing concern about environmental issues (Crable and Vibbert, 1987). Instead, ten years after its rebranding campaign, BP faced the following problems with its reactive response to the spill.

The biggest mistake BP made was that it created expectations it did not meet. It said it cared about the environment in its branding materials, and then did not live up to these claims. It not demonstrate environmental stewardship and tried to pass the blame when crisis erupted. By attempting to deflect blame for the spill by pinpointing its contractors as responsible, BP appeared more interested in avoiding legal liability than in being willing to accept responsibility (Goodman, 2010). The company maintained this stance into September, when a news release following its internal investigation of the crisis announced, "It is evident that a series of complex events, rather than a single mistake or failure, led to the tragedy. Multiple parties, including BP, Halliburton, and Transocean, were involved" (see Figure 6.5).

This position counters all three of BP's strategies, but particularly defeats its claim of being a trustworthy community partner. With contractors Transocean and Halliburton pointing fingers at each other, and BP pointing fingers back, the message was that no one was culpable. BP's inability to be forthright and instead pass the buck earned a failing grade from the public and experts alike:

> It was one of the worst PR approaches that I've seen in my 56 years of business. They tried to be opaque. They had every excuse in the book. Right away they should have accepted responsibility and recognized what a disaster they faced.
>
> (Goodman, 2010, p. 3)

bp

Contact us | Reports and publications | BP worldwide | Home

Search: Go

About BP | Products and services | Environment and society | Investors | Press | Careers | Gulf of Mexico response

You are here: BP Global ▸ Press ▸ Press releases

Press releases

Speeches

Features

Images and graphics

Press contacts

RSS

▸ What is RSS?

BP Releases Report on Causes of Gulf of Mexico Tragedy

Release date: 08 September 2010

No single factor caused the Macondo well tragedy. Rather, a sequence of failures involving a number of different parties led to the explosion and fire which killed 11 people and caused widespread pollution in the Gulf of Mexico earlier this year.

A report released by BP today concludes that decisions made by "multiple companies and work teams" contributed to the accident which it says arose from "a complex and interlinked series of mechanical failures, human judgments, engineering design, operational implementation and team interfaces."

The report – based on a four-month investigation led by Mark Bly, BP's Head of Safety and Operations and conducted independently by a team of over 50 technical and other specialists drawn from inside BP and externally – found that:

- The cement and shoe track barriers – and in particular the cement slurry that was used – at the bottom of the Macondo well failed to contain hydrocarbons within the reservoir, as they were designed to do, and allowed gas and liquids to flow up the production casing;
- The results of the negative pressure test were incorrectly accepted by BP and Transocean, although well integrity had not been established;
- Over a 40-minute period, the Transocean rig crew failed to recognise and act on the influx of hydrocarbons into the well until the hydrocarbons were in the riser and rapidly flowing to the surface;
- After the well-flow reached the rig it was routed to a mud-gas separator, causing gas to be vented directly on to the rig rather than being diverted overboard;
- The flow of gas into the engine rooms through the ventilation system created a potential for ignition which the rig's fire and gas system did not prevent;
- Even after explosion and fire had disabled its crew-operated controls, the rig's blow-out preventer on the sea-bed should have activated automatically to seal the well. But it failed to operate, probably because critical components were not working.

Commenting on the report, which he commissioned immediately after the Macondo explosion, BP's outgoing chief executive Tony Hayward said: "The investigation report provides critical new information on the causes of this terrible accident. It is evident that a series of complex events, rather than a single mistake or failure, led to the tragedy. Multiple parties, including BP, Halliburton and Transocean, were involved.

"To put it simply, there was a bad cement job and a failure of the shoe track barrier at the bottom of the well, which let hydrocarbons from the reservoir into the production casing. The negative pressure test was accepted when it should not have been, there were failures in well control procedures and in the blow-out preventer, and the rig's fire and gas system did not prevent ignition.

"Based on the report, it would appear unlikely that the well design contributed to the incident, as the investigation found that the hydrocarbons flowed up the production casing through the bottom of the well," Hayward said.

BP's incoming chief executive Bob Dudley said: "We have said from the beginning that the explosion on the Deepwater Horizon was a shared responsibility among many entities. This report makes that conclusion even clearer, presenting a detailed analysis of the facts and recommendations for improvement both for BP and the other parties involved. We have accepted all the recommendations and are examining how best to implement them across our drilling operations worldwide.

"This was a tragic accident that resulted in the loss of 11 lives and impacted the communities and the environment along the Gulf Coast region. We deeply regret this event. We have sought throughout to step up to our responsibilities. We are determined to learn the lessons for the future and we will be undertaking a broad-scale review to further improve the safety of our operations. We will invest whatever it takes to achieve that. It will be incumbent on everyone at BP to embrace and implement the changes necessary to ensure that a tragedy like this can never happen again."

Chairman of the Board Carl-Henric Svanberg commented: "I believe this report will be of significant value in helping the overall understanding of how this tragedy occurred. It is of the utmost importance to the Board to ensure that BP learns from this and further enhances the safety of its operations for the future."

Based on its key findings, the investigation team has proposed a total of 25 recommendations designed to prevent a recurrence of such an accident. The recommendations are directed at strengthening assurance on blow-out preventers, well control, pressure-testing for well integrity, emergency systems, cement testing, rig audit and verification, and personnel competence.

The company said it expected a number of the investigation report's findings to be considered relevant to the oil industry more generally and for some of the recommendations to be widely adopted.

BP said the report was based on information available to the investigating team. It noted that additional relevant information may be forthcoming, for example, when Halliburton's samples of the cement used in the well are released for testing and when the rig's blow-out preventer is fully examined now that it has been recovered from the sea-bed. There will also be additional information from the multiple ongoing US government investigations.

The investigation report is available online at www.bp.com, together with an accompanying video.

Further information:

BP press office, London: +44 (0)20 7496 4076, bppress@bp.com
BP press office, Houston: +1 281 366 0265, uspress@bp.com
www.bp.com

In this section

▸ Brendan Nelson and Frank L "Skip" Bowman to Join the BP Board

▸ October is Busiest Month Yet for Rumaila Operations

▸ BP Awarded Seven Exploration Licences in UK North Sea

▸ BP Returns to Profit in Third Quarter with Strong Operating Performance

▸ Third quarter 2010 results

▸ More

Related link

▸ BP internal investigation

Figure 6.5 Press release on causes of Gulf coast tragedy.

The company's inability to accurately assess or report the amount of oil leaking into the Gulf furthered the perception that it was trying to deny responsibility and hampered its transparency strategy. BP chose to focus its efforts on containing the spill, rather than measuring the outflow of oil spilling into the Gulf. To observers, this tactic gave the impression that the company was hiding information. People simply wanted to know how much oil was spilling into the Gulf: "You need to either give us an estimate, a number, or tell us why you can't" (Neary, 2010, p. 1). Its repeated underestimate and the 24-hour news cycle made this visually-oriented crisis worse. Continually cycling images of oil-drenched sea creatures, of oil gushing into water, and images of BP trying a parade of techniques to stem the flow, did much to worsen the image of the disaster.

BP's unwillingness to acknowledge its confusion as to how to fix the leak became lampooned in the media and the company's credibility sank along with its equipment. Some crisis observers noted that BP would have been better off just admitting that they did not know exactly what it would take to stop the leak: "What would have helped from the very beginning is for them to say, 'we're in uncharted waters.' Because they did not do that, they created the expectation they knew how to fix it" (Houpt, 2010, p. 2). Frequently, in crisis situations, problems need to be solved before apologies can be effective:

> BP could apologize every day. They could have a situation where the CEO goes on an environmental pilgrimage and falls on his knees going up a mountain, and it wouldn't do them any good. Until the oil stopped, there was nothing that could be done to make it better, but there was plenty that could be said to make it worse.
>
> (Goodman, 2010, p. 7)

Finally, the company's insensitive public tone did not meet contemporary crisis expectations and hampered its advocacy strategy. As crisis expert Eric Dezenhall pointed out:

> It's the height of arrogance to assume that in the middle of a crisis the public yearns for chestnuts of wisdom from people they want to kill. The goal is not to get people not to hate them. It's to get people to hate them less.
>
> (Goodman, 2010, p. 3)

BP's choice of Tony Hayward as spokesperson magnified the level of public hate. Mr. Hayward's aloof and tone-deaf public comments alienated the public, with Americans finding issue with everything from Mr. Hayward's British accent to his pin-striped suits. One reporter somewhat cheekily suggested that BP needed a "high-profile, plain-talking, media friendly, all-American tough guy to act as the company's official spokesman" (Reguly, 2010, p. 2). The missteps BP had in selecting the right tone indirectly points to the need to select the right public relations agency. Although Brunswick Public Relations is a well-known international public relations firm, its expertise lies more in financial, not crisis, public relations. The firm does not have a large U.S. presence, making managing the crisis on the ground perhaps more difficult.

Criticism about BP's public relations has been varied, frequent, and ongoing. Practitioners have offered suggestions to help BP fix its image, ranging from becoming the "ultra-green" industry leader to offering free gasoline to churches, schools, and charities (Horovitz, 2010). Some have suggested that BP change its name and image (again); for example, Philip Morris became Altria in 2003 after ongoing criticism. Following an increased dedication to issues management, BP may need to again participate in a rebranding exercise (Horovitz, 2010). Critically, however, rebranding should reflect, not merely rename, a change in corporate culture. Putting new lipstick on the proverbial pig would only worsen BP's situation, as it has learned from trying to present itself as an environmental leader without following through internally (Bush, 2010).

Lessons Learned

Ultimately, BP's efforts can be read as a clarion call for a renewed focus on issues management. The stakes in crisis have been raised:

> When we used to say you have the first 24 hours to respond to a crisis, you probably know you have the first 24 minutes. As a company, as an organization, when an unforeseen crisis smashes down on you, you need to have a protocol in place where you're ready to respond.
>
> (Houpt, 2010, p. 2)

The BP disaster has been called oil's Three Mile Island, meaning that the industry can expect more regulation, as the nuclear industry did following the 1979 accident at the Pennsylvania reactor (Vaida, 2010). Following the Three Mile Island incident, the nuclear industry was deeply affected, with no new plant license occurring since that time. For the oil industry, deepwater drilling could be similarly affected. A moratorium about new deepwater offshore drilling in the Gulf of Mexico is being debated. Congress is focusing on energy legislation as well as discussing raising the industry's legal liability, designed to hold oil companies more accountable (Vaida, 2010). From an issues management perspective, BP failed to manage the public's interest in environmental issues and is now paying the hefty price of increased business scrutiny and regulation. Indeed, in the final report released by the National Commission on the BP Deepwater Horizon Oil Spill and Offshore Drilling in early January, 2011, commissioners called for "significant reform" in both industry practices and government policies in order to prevent a similar disaster from occurring

(BBC, 2011). Calling the root causes of the tragedy "systemic" and a result of "bad management," the report concluded that the catastrophe could have been avoided (BBC, 2011). BP may have returned to profit, but its inability to follow through on its brand promise that it was moving "Beyond Petroleum," will cause it to occupy the role of "Big Polluter" in the minds of many stakeholders for a long time.

Discussion Questions

1. Can you think of other public relations cases where an issue management perspective would have been beneficial?
2. Does applying an issues management perspective help public relations practitioners become part of the management team? Why or why not?
3. Do you find BP's public relations decisions to be unethical, or just examples of bad public relations? Can you think of public relations cases where practitioners made bad public relations decisions that were also unethical? Is there a connection between the two?

Note

1   All statements and images analyzed on behalf of BP can be found on www.bp.com

References

A.L. (2005). BP. *Fortune*, October 31. Retrieved from the Ebscohost Database.

BBC (2010). BP boss Tony Hayward's gaffes. *BBC*, June 20. Retrieved from www.bbc.co.uk

BBC (2011). US oil spill: 'Bad management' led to BP disaster, January 6. Retrieved from www.bbc.co.uk

Beder, S. (2002). BP: Beyond petroleum? In E. Lubbers (Ed.), *Battling big business: Countering greenwash, infiltration, and other forms of corporate bullying*. Totnes, UK: Green Books.

Bush, M. (2010). Brunswick put to ultimate test as BP grows increasingly toxic. *Advertising Age*, June 7. Retrieved from the Ebscohost Database.

Crable, R. E., and Vibbert, S.L. (1985). Managing issues and influencing public policy. *Public Relations Review, 11*, 3–16.

Elliott, D. (2010). BP's PR doesn't make things right with locals. *NPR*, June 5. Retrieved from www.npr.org

Garfield, B. (2010). From greenwashing to godwashing, BP and Obama fail at image control. *Advertising Age*, June 21. Retrieved on September 5, 2010, from the Ebscohost Database.

Goodman, P. (2010). In case of emergency: What not to do. *The New York Times*. Retrieved from www.nytimes.com

Horovitz, B. (2010). BP's image won't be easy to clean. *USA Today*, June 14. Retrieved from Ebscohost Database.

Houpt, S. (2010). "Junk shot" PR? BP veers into uncharted territory. *The Globe and Mail*, July 7. Retrieved from the LexisNexis Database.

Independent (2007). British Petroleum, January 17. Retrieved on September 5, 2010, from the LexisNexis Database.

Jensen, K., and Snyder, J. (2010). Outrage grows, so does BP's beltway crew. *Bloomberg Businessweek*, June 6. Retrieved from the Ebscohost Database.

Jones, B.L., and Chase, W.H. (1979). Managing public policy issues. *Public Relations Review*, 5, 3–23.

Liasson, M. (2010). As spill gets bigger, so does White House PR problem. *NPR*, May 24. Retrieved on September 5, 2010, from www.npr.org

Neary, L. (2010). Crisis communication requires "common sense." *NPR*. Retrieved from www.npr.org

New York Times (2010). The Lede Blog. *New York Times*, August 6. Retrieved from www.nytimes.com

NPR Staff (2010). BP buys oil spill-related search terms. *NPR*, June 8. Retrieved from www.npr.org

Reguly, E. (2010). No accents please: BP's PR woes start at the top. *The Globe and Mail*, June 17. Retrieved from the LexisNexis Database.

Vaida, B. (2010). Oil's Three Mile Island? *National Journal*, June 15. Retrieved on September 5, 2010, from the Ebscohost Database.

White, R. (2010). For BP, oil spill is a public relations catastrophe. *Los Angeles Times*, April 30. Retrieved from www.latimes.com

White, R., Huffstutter, P., and Fausset, R. (2010). BP chief Tony Hayward might be out sooner than later. *Los Angeles Times*, July 26. Retrieved from the LexisNexis Database.

Zarroli, J. (2010). Before gulf spill, BP CEO Tony Hayward won praise. NPR.org. Retrieved from www.npr.org/templates/story/story.php?storyId=127884525

VIEWS FROM AN EXPERT

RAYMOND C. JONES

Raymond C. Jones is director of Public Relations at Carolinas HealthCare System in Charlotte, N.C. After college, he worked for 15 years as a newspaper reporter and editor. He later managed public relations at three colleges: Monmouth University, Winthrop University, William Jewell College. Before entering the healthcare field, he managed a consulting business in Kansas City, Media Ink Communications, which specialized in crisis communications.

Where Did British Petroleum Go Wrong?

My first big insight regarding crisis communications came two decades ago, when I attended a workshop and heard a retired news anchor say: "Nothing makes you look more foolish than denying there's a body bag, when the body bag is lying at your feet. As your denials are quoted in the voice-over, the camera will focus on the body bag."

Since hearing that advice I have weathered dozens of PR challenges, mostly in college and university settings where the number of things that can go wrong is practically limitless. I've learned a lot in the process, although I've never understood why corporate executives believe so uniformly that the laws of public relations don't apply to them.

Today I lead my own workshops, using tip sheets that reflect my own hard-won insights about the "laws of public relations." Let's score BP accordingly.

Tip 1—Come clean immediately.

Rationale—People can handle the truth, but they have no patience for a steady cascade of revelations.

BP Score—F. BP grossly minimized the consequences of their initial platform explosion. Government estimates immediately gained more credibility, as video images of gushing pipes made it clear BP's lowball numbers were unrealistic.

Tip 2—Apologize immediately. Assure the public there will be full account-ability, regardless of consequence.

Rationale—One of Richard Nixon's most enduring legacies is public suspicion that every big scandal will be followed by a cover-up.

BP Score—D. They did some positive things to convey a sense of concern, such as TV ads showing real employees pledging not to rest until the clean-up was complete. Unfortunately, such promises were quickly overcome by the sheer scope of the disaster. Too much oil; too many places that could not be protected.

There's no "spin" that can neutralize the image of a dying, oil-soaked cormorant. And how do you convince people crude oil isn't dangerous when everyone involved in the clean-up is wearing a haz mat suit?

Tip 3—People judge actions, not words.

Rationale—Before promising that nothing can go wrong, keep Murphy's Law in mind.

BP Score—F. When BP filed for permission to drill, they offered unequivocal assurances that blowout preventers were fail-safe. Consequently, when an explosion occurred, their executives joined the rogue's gallery of those who said Titanic wouldn't sink, Hindenburg wouldn't explode, and Three Mile Island wouldn't melt down.

BP's credibility had no place to go but down, particularly when it was revealed that the people approving drilling applications were in cahoots with the industry.

Tip 4—When the chips are down, put your strongest performer in front of the media, not your most senior executive. (Note: If your governing board has any brains, this will be one and the same person).

Rationale—People judge what they see on TV. They don't care about someone's résumé, tenure or technical expertise. If your CEO doesn't come across well, find someone else who does. Remember that when Congress gets involved, it's the CEO who will inevitably be required to testify—another reason why the senior executive and the person who best communicates under pressure should be the same person.

BP Score—F. BP's CEO, Tony Hayward, should never have been put in front of a camera. In his press appearances he came across as arrogant. In his Congressional testimony he came across as clueless.

Fairly or unfairly, his upper-class British accent was an inflammatory reminder that control of a vital American resource was in foreign hands. It was perhaps a fitting outcome that Hayward was ultimately sent to Siberia, literally. But it was too little, too late.

Section 7

South America

Chile

The 2010 Chilean Mining Accident: The Triumph of Transparency and Calm Leadership

Emmanuel C. Alozie

For more than a month, Chile and the world held their collective breath as they watched, listened, or read about the plight and fate of 33 Chileans miners trapped underground following the 2010 San José mine collapse on August 5, 2010. Reluctant to be engaged during the first few days after the collapse, the Chilean government took charge when the owners of the mine stated they did not have the resources to mount a rescue. Once engaged, the Chilean government exerted every effort to rescue the miners by inserting its resources and seeking assistance from foreign governments, institutions and mine experts. The rescue effort riveted the world. On October 13, 2010, when the last of the 33 miners emerged from the earth, the world took a collective sigh of relief. The rescue inspired Chileans and people worldwide. The successful rescue was viewed as a milestone in international cooperation. The Chilean government was praised for its handling of the crisis and rescue efforts. Considering the worldwide acclaim the Chilean government garnered from its handling of the mining collapse and search and rescue effort, this chapter is aimed at identifying the objectives, determining the strategies, and also tactics the administration employed to manage the crisis. The study found that the Chilean government did not employ an established crisis communication management procedure, but the willingness of the government to remain transparent and seek international assistance accounted for the success of the rescue effort.

Introduction

Out of the 33 trapped miners rescued from the 2010 San José mine accident, Carlos Mamani was the only non-Chilean. The 23-year-old Bolivian had worked for only five days as a mechanic at the mine when the accident occurred. The collapse of the small-sized mine owned by San Esteban Mining

Company, Copiapó, Chile, captured worldwide attention (Govan, 2010, October 14; Euronews, 2010, October 13). As for the whole world, Mamani's 69-day plight occupied the minds of people in his native land—men and women, young and old, rich and poor—owing to the fact he is one of the millions of their young and poor of working age who left to seek greener pastures in neighboring countries as a result of lack of economic opportunity in their homeland. The fourth to be rescued safely aboard the Phoenix capsule, his emergence from the deep and that of the other 32 miners was greeted with great jubilation in Bolivia, Chile, and worldwide (Govan, 2010, October 14; Richwebnews/Allvoices, 2010, October 13).

When Mamani surfaced from the deep, he received a visit from Bolivian President Evo Morales. His Chilean counterpart Sebastián Piñera and his wife were at the scene of the accident to greet the trapped miners as they emerged. During his visit, Morales offered the young compatriot a job and a house if he would return home. The Bolivian president offered to fly home with the young father of one (a daughter). Mamani had been married for just a year. As the eighth of eleven children, whose poor family eked out a living cultivating potatoes and herding sheep and cattle (Govan, 2010, October 14), the presidential offer was quite enticing, but Mamani, who had resided in Chile for four years as he searched for a job, thanked his president, but declined the offer. He said he would like to remain in Chile for a while to meet up and deliberate with his fellow miners.

To express his sentiments and gratitude toward the Chilean people and government for working hard to save his life and the lives of his miner brothers, Mamani pointed at the Chilean flag on his T-shirt and shouted "Gracias, Chile!" upon emerging from the capsule. On Independence Day, he joined other trapped miners to sing the Chilean national anthem while still trapped. His gestures won wide acclaim among Chileans (Govan, 2010, October 14). Mamani must have been stunned at the sight of Chile's president and the first lady waving the Bolivian flag. It should be noted that for years Chile and Bolivia had frosty relations stemming from philosophical differences, border disputes, and presumed poor treatment of Bolivian immigrants in class-conscious Chile. Morales's visit to Chile and the gesture of waving the Bolivian flag by the Chilean president and the first lady were regarded as milestones that might lead to the warming of relations between the two nations as well as the region.

Morales's visit to Bolivia, the Bolivian president's offers of a guaranteed job and a home to his compatriot, Mamani's refusal of the presidential offers, the young man joining the other 32 trapped miners to sing the Chilean national anthem, pointing at the Chilean flag upon his emergence and the waving of the Bolivian flag by the president and first lady of Chile received some degree of international coverage. However, these acts did not gain as much public salience as other events surrounding the mining accident and rescue. Despite the lack of public salience, domestic and international public opinion leaders regarded these acts as public relations successes for the Piñera administration stemming from its handling of the mine disaster derived from crisis communication and management.

Considering the worldwide acclaim the Chilean government has garnered from its handling of the mining collapse, search and rescue, this chapter is aimed at identifying the objectives, determining the strategies, and tactics the administration employed to manage the crisis. The chapter also attempts to discern what lessons could be derived from the management of the crisis for possible implementation in future crisis incidents. Other subjects explored in the chapter include: (a) historical evolution of Chile; (b) background of mining accidents in Chile and the world; (c) history and role of Chilean mass media; (d) conceptual exploration of crisis communication and management; (e) situation analysis; (f) communication goals, objectives, strategies, and tactics; (g) outcomes assessment, and (h) conclusions and lessons learned from the conduct of the government. The chapter includes "views from an expert" in international public relations.

Historical Evolution of Chile

Politics and economy: Regarded as the fastest-growing economy since the 1990s and having weathered the economic instability in the region during the 2000s, Chile is often described as the most stable country in Latin America economically, socially, and politically. For most of its history since independence from Spain in 1818, Chile has enjoyed political plurality anchored on constitutional provisions, as well as conservative and collectivistic orientations where relationships were tied to family and friends that promoted group solidarity. Religion—especially Catholicism—has occupied and continues to occupy a significant place (BBC News, 2010, August 12; Ferrari, 2003; History of Chile, 2011, January 4). However, there are some occasions when Chile constitutional plurality was abrogated following military takeover of power. These include General Luis Altamirano from 1924 to 1932, and General Augusto Pinochet from 1973 to 1990. In the 1973 coup, Pinochet overthrew the elected left-leaning administration of Salvador Allende (New World Encyclopedia, 2008, November 17).

Ferarri (2003) pointed out that the Pinochet administration is regarded as the most controversial in Chilean history. She stated that contemporary Chilean history could be split into three eras: before, during, and after Pinochet's reign. In his 17 years as head of state, in the guise of fighting communism at the peak of the Cold War, Pinochet instituted political repression, social and economic policies that promoted an uneven distribution and muzzled opponents (Ferrari, 2003). During his reign, it has been estimated that more than 3,000 political opponents were killed. These killings and his draconian measures divided the country into two camps—those in favor and those against the Pinochet regime. His reign produced a profound impact on the psyche of Chileans. With a weakened social cohesion, Chile shifted its values from a collectivistic to an individualistic orientation where personal socioeconomic survival became the dominant consideration in the lives of 17.1 million Chileans. That shift, Ferrari stated, produced an era where "group participation generally occurs when there is a threat to public safety or to personal and family integrity" (Ferrari, 2003, p. 391) rather than the collective yearning of the masses.

A copper-dependent economy, Chile's other main exports include fish, fruit, paper, pulp, and chemicals. Chile has a GNI per capita of $9,420 and life expectancy of 76 years (men) and 82 years (women). It is regarded as the most urbanized and industrialized society in Latin America with a 95 percent literacy rate. Chile is also one of the few Third World countries with a privatized and stable social security funded by individual capitalization mechanisms. From the late 1980s and early 1990s, when Chile started the transition from dictatorship to democratic rule, an era when capitalism had become the dominant force in an increasingly interconnected global economy, Chile encountered financial challenges that adversely affected socioeconomic growth. Like most Latin American and other developing countries, this period of transition from industrial- to information-based global economy created employment dislocations. As in most developing economies, worldwide economic dislocation has affected every facet of Chilean life—individual, environmental, sociocultural, political, and psychological (BBC News, 2010, August 12; Ferrari, 2003; History of Chile, 2011, January 4).

History of Mining Disasters: The World, Chile and the 2010 Mining Accident

Synopsis of Global Mining: About 12,000 people die in mine accidents every year worldwide (ABC News, 2010, November 20). The U.S. Mine Safety and Health Administration describes a mine disaster as an accident in which five or more people are killed. The cost of accidents is estimated to run in the hundreds of millions of dollars annually worldwide (*New York Times*, 2010, April 12; BBC News, 2010, October 7; BBC News, 2010, October 18b). Causes of mine accidents include poisonous gas leaks, collapsing of mine stopes, mining-induced seismicity, underground flooding, extraction method, general mechanical errors from improper use or malfunctioning mining equipment, and poor regulation and failure to enforce to safety rules (Mining Accidents, 2010, December 31; BBC News, 2010, October 18b). While everyone agrees with President Piñera, who said that some accidents are beyond human control (BBC, 2010, October 18a), experts contend that standardization of equipment, inspection, and adequate regulations and enforcement have contributed to the reduction of mine accidents, thus saving human lives (BBC News, 2010, October 18b; *Christian Science Monitor*, 2010, October 13).

At the height of industrialization—during the last decades of the nineteenth and the turn of the twentieth century—mine accidents were common. At the time, accurate records of accidents and casualities were not kept. It has been assumed injuries and death tolls from mine accidents were quite high and generally acceptable. This was in view of the mindset that mining was more hazardous than most occupations (*Christian Science Monitor*, 2010, October 13). However, following decades of research, technological innovations, preventive measures, and better regulations and enforcement, the number of accidents, injuries and loss of lives stemming from them had been on the decline. As stated earlier, injuries and deaths from mine accidents have become increasingly unacceptable, which may be true in most developed countries where regulations are strictly enforced, but not necessarily in developing nations.

In the less developed nations such as China, India, and South Africa, accidents occur more frequently. However, studies have found that whether in developed or less-developed countries, the degree of safety standards, observance of regulation, and emergency responses at mines tend to be dependent on the size of the mine, the size and policies of the company operating the mine, and enforcement of regulations (*Christian Science Monitor*, 2010, October 13; Scher, 2010; BBC News, 2010, October 7). Globally, it has been established that large companies and mines maintain high safety standards and deal with emergencies swiftly. On the other hand, small-to-medium-size mines, owned by small companies, are plagued with poor safety standards and are slow to respond to emergencies. The difference could be attributed to the fact that large company-owned mines tend to have better resources than small-company owned ones. Smaller mines are affected by economic pressures as was the case with the San José mine, a small to medium mine, owned by a small size company. Records indicated that the mine had inadequate infrastructures, coupled with safety practices and standards that are not up to par. On the other hand, the infrastructures and safety standards in larger Chilean mines, owned and operated by government entities and large companies are considered adequate (*Christian Science Monitor*, 2010, October 13).

Synopsis of Chilean Mining: For an economy such as Chile and those of other countries dependent on mining, any mine accident produces an adverse economic effect. Chile is the world's top producer of copper. Mining developed in Chile in the twentieth century. There are more than 4,000 mines employing hundreds of thousands of people. Though Chile is considered by some to have a strong safety record (Cambero, 2010), the National Geology and Mining Service (Sernageomin), the agency responsible for regulating the mining and supervising mining safety standards, reported that since 2000 an average of 34 people have died yearly in mining accidents, with a high of 43 in 2008 and 40 in 2007 (Long, 2010, October 5; 2010; "2010 Copiapó mining accident," 2011, January 10). Prior to 2010, Chile had experienced two major mine accidents that captured international attention. In June 1945, during a fire, 355 men died in El Teniente, by inhaling carbon monoxide, while in January 2006, an explosion occurred in a mine in Copiapó, leaving 70 miners trapped underground. The miners were rescued after a short period of time. Only two died ("Mining accident," 2010, December 31). Mining regulators stated that the number of incapacitating injuries per million work hours fell from 33 in 1989 to 4 in 2010 (*Christian Science Monitor*, 2010, October 13).

Although some insist that Chile represents one of the few countries with a decent record with regard to mining disasters, injuries, and deaths—especially in large-size mines, like their counterparts in other parts of the world, the small and medium-size mines in Chile are prone to accidents stemming from the aforementioned problems that small mines are plagued with (Bonnefoy, 2010, August 28; *Christian Science Monitor*, 2010, October 13). For years, mine workers, labor leaders, and unions at the San José mine and other small mines have complained about these issues. They voiced their concerns to the regulators, government officials, and mine owners. When concerns are presented to some Chilean mine owners and management such as the San Esteban Mining Company, the owners usually pay lip service with promises of improving mine infrastructures and safety standards, but end up doing nothing.

When irregularities and poor safety standards are brought to the attention of government officials and regulators, not much is done with regard to enforcing established regulations, or initiating new ones to address the concerns raised (BBC News, 2010, October 18b). For instance, after the August 5, 2010, collapse, the 33 trapped miners started climbing the emergency ladder in a ventilation shaft to take them to the surface 2,300 feet above after the dust from the collapse settled. But they were unable to get out because the escape ladder was unfinished (Bonnefoy, 2010, August 28). In 2007, Sernageomin had required the mine to install the ladder following a January accident in which a geologist's assistant died following a rock explosion. At the behest of the agency, the mine closed, but opened in less than one year without installing the escape ladder. Back in 2006, a truck driver in the mine was also killed in an accident. The family was paid $170,000 in compensation. Also in 2006, 182 workers at the mine were injured. Out of the 182, 56 were considered to be in a serious condition (Bonnefoy, 2010, August 28). The Chilean Safety Association (ACHS), a nonprofit group, reported eight workers have been killed at the San José mine in 12 years. Between 2004 and 2010, the 120-year-old mine received 42 fines for breaching safety regulations ("2010 Copiapó mining accident," 2011, January 11). Less than two months later before the August 2010 mine accident, a miner suffered the amputation of his leg in an accident that has been described as avoidable. Despite its failure to observe basic safety measures, the San José mine remained open. It continued to attract workers by offering higher than average salaries and benefits ("2010 Copiapó mining accident," 2011).

With the spotlight shed on the Chilean mining industry as a result of the 2010 San José ordeal, President Piñera vowed his administration would henceforth enforce mining regulations strictly and protect whistleblowers. The Piñera administration is recomposing the mining agencies. It has set up an inquiry to investigate accusations of flouting mining rules leveled against the San Esteban Mining Company, owners of the mine. However, union activists are pressing for the ratification of the International Labour Organization (ILO) Convention 176 by the Chilean government. The convention requires governments to enforce safety regulations and provide protection for any miner who raises safety concerns. It should be noted there is a culture of fear among Chilean mine workers. They shy away from expressing their true feelings and concerns owing to intimidation from management and fear of losing their jobs (BBC News, 2010, October 18b; BBC News, 2010, October 7; Bonnefoy, 2010, August 28). It has been reported that some activists and workers quit the mine as a result of intimidation.

The 2010 San José mining accident: The cave-in that occurred at the San José copper–gold mine on August 5, 2010, did not come as a surprise to labor activists, union leaders, workers at the mine, and their families. They knew of the hazardous conditions and lack of safety equipment that existed at the mine. They were aware of the need to install safety facilities and observe mining rules. They were aware that the management ignored those concerns. They were also aware safety regulations are weakly enforced by regulators. Throughout the crisis, mine experts pointed out that if the mine owners had installed the exit ladder as they were required to, the trapped miners would have escaped through the evacuation exit because it remained clear for 48 hours after the collapse (Bonnefoy, 2010, August 28). Reaching the ladder, finding it unfinished, thus making the escape impossible, the miners were stuck. They had to cope for 17 days without any contact, ultimately spending about 69 days before resurfacing following a painstaking rescue effort.

Seventeen days after the cave-in without a connection to the trapped miners, hope dimmed that any of the 33 remained alive. The gloomy outlook changed and hope returned and anticipation surged when a small borehole reached the miners' refuge, and rescuers received a message that the 33 had survived. Armed with the knowledge of their survival, a video camera was threaded deep underground, capturing the first image of the miners. When their images were broadcast, anticipation for their rescue rose globally. As the news of survival was transmitted instantaneously to a global audience, it spread like wildfire. It prompted nationwide jubilation. Finding them to be in good health, Chileans and the international community were energized to ensure a successful rescue. The miraculous survival of the miners after 17 days in the deep elicited a variety of assistance globally—human talent, material and moral support. Assistance came from every part of the world—rich and poor. The miners celebrated their survival and discovery by using a modified telephone to send the Chilean national anthem to the hundreds of teary-eyed relatives

(*New York Times*, 2010, October 25; BBC News, 2010, October 18b; BBC News, 2010, October 7).

It was reported that miners survived because the ventilation shafts had withstood the mine's cave-in, allowing enough fresh air to reach the chamber where the miners huddled. To survive, they used heavy equipment to provide light and charge the batteries of their head lamps. They drank water from storage tanks. They also stripped off their shirts to endure the stifling heat. Mine experts said the survival of the miners could be attributed to the fact they did not appear threatened by toxic gases such as methane that usually occur and poison trapped miners after cave-ins. As the rescue efforts continued, food was in short supply (*New York Times*, 2010, October 25; BBC News, 2010, October 14). With rescuers relying on a tiny borehole to send down tubes containing sugar, water, and liquid nutrients to nourish the 33 trapped miners, they were forced to consume an average of 8 kilograms (18 lb) each ("2010 Copiapó mining accident," 2011, January 11). The tube became a life source for the miners. In addition to being the source of food, the tube also served as the vehicle for exchanging information between the trapped miners, their rescuers, families, and officials (*New York Times*, 2010, October 25; BBC News, 2010, October 14).

On October 9, 2010, after two excruciating months of painstaking work drilling a tunnel with the potential of prompting another collapse, a sizable drill finally broke through to the miners, creating a space for a rescue shaft through which the miners were raised in a capsule. On October 12, 2010, Florencio Ávalos, 31, became the first miner to emerge to the surface to a worldwide audience. About 1,300 journalists were on hand to cover the search and rescue efforts and the emergence of the 33 miners. On October 13, 2010, Luis Urzúa, 54, a shift leader who organized the miners' lives while trapped became the last miner to ascend to a hero's welcome and warm embrace of family members, rescue workers, government officials and friends (*New York Times*, 2010, October 25; BBC News, 2010, October 14).

History and Role of Mass Media in Chile

To understand how the Chilean government used mass communication and why that influenced its conduct and handling of the 2010 San José crisis, it becomes necessary to trace the historical role of media in the country. Ferrari (2003) stated that the political plurality that existed in Chile prior to 1973 contributed to the emergence of a free media and public expression where the mass media served as a forum for the discussion of important political, socioeconomic and religious issues. Chile's mass media are also credited with assisting the various administrations in promoting economic development, political stability, and social order.

Print and broadcast: Since their introduction, the press has been regarded as the principal arm of mobilization of public opinion and the government watchdog, while television has been viewed as the primary source of entertainment. Radio offers both news and entertainment. The key roles of the press could be attributed to the fact that until 1973 it was highly politicized and tied to political parties and other principal components of power in Chile such as the state, business, and the church (BBC News, 2010, August 12; Ferrari, 2003; History of Chile, 2011, January 4). The print sector can be described as vibrant. The country has several newspapers and magazines that circulate locally, regionally, and nationally. The most popular six are: *La Nacion*, government-owned daily; *El Mercurio*, conservative daily; *La Segunda*, conservative evening daily; *Diario Financiero*, business daily; *La Tercera*, mainstream daily; and *Santiago Times*, the only English-language newspaper (BBC News, 2010, December 8 and August 12).

Radio serves as an important source of news and information. Chile has about 1,300 stations, of which about 220 are community radio stations. The major radio outlets are: Radio Cooperativa, a news-based, national, private network; Radio Horizonte, a music-based, private network; Pudahuel, Bio Bio La Radio, and El Conquistador FM, all private networks (BBC News, 2010, December 8 and August 1). Chile has six television stations, of which three have national reach. They are: National Television of Chile, state-owned but not under direct government control; TV Universidad Catolica de Chile (Canal 13), and Universidad Catolica de Valparaiso (UCV), both owned by Catholic universities; and Chilevision, Megavision, and Red TV, all privately owned. The local terrestrial TV channels operate alongside extensive cable TV networks that carry many US and international stations—a development some Chileans view as harming cultural values owing to a lack of broadcasting of domestic-produced programs.

Before the Pinochet administration, governments contributed and funded the media outlets—especially television. After Pinochet came to power, the administration stopped funding mass media. That change in policy forced the Chilean mass media to rely on market forces. Another legacy of Pinochet's 17-year-long military rule concerned the introduction of draconian rules that restricted press freedom, promoted media self-censorship and inhibited individual expression. With the lack of freedom, Chileans distrusted their media. They viewed the industry as kowtowing to the wishes of the Pinochet regime, saying what they wanted them to say to avoid offending the regime and doing what they had to do in order to survive.

With the return of democratic rule in the 1990s, constitutional reforms culminated with the passage of the 2001 Press Freedom Act. The act swept away the vestiges of Pinochet's draconian press rules, ushering in an era of press freedom and speech. With the passage of the act, the authorities generally respected the press. The mass media now strive to maintain their independence by objectively criticizing the government and covering sensitive issues. For a growing number of Chileans, the mass media are regarded as the fourth estate, having regained their reputation and now increasingly respected by the public who use them to air their grievances, seek action or redress, as the families of the 33 trapped miners did when the mine management seemed to be reluctant to embark on a long-term search and rescue effort. The attention given to their complaints by the Chilean mass media forced the government to take over the search and rescue effort (BBC News, 2010, August 12; Ferrari, 2003; History of Chile, 2011, January 4). Notwithstanding these manifestations, critics contend that "Chile had a good name for press freedom" but added that the police and military "have not lost repressive habits left over from the military dictatorship" (BBC News, 2010, August 12).

Public relations and strategic communications: Ferrari (2003, 2000) stated that foreign manufacturing companies introduced the practice and conduct of public relations and other forms of promotional communications into Chile in the 1950s. She pointed out that despite the existence of seven university-level programs, the public relations profession was not fully developed, nor understood, and was often confused with journalism. It was not until the 1990s with the return of democratic rule and the globalization of the world economies, which led to the expansion and internationalization of Chilean business, that professionalization and increased recognition of public relations and strategic communication came about (Ferrari, 2003).

In a study that examined the conduct of public relations and strategic communication in thirteen Chilean organizations, Ferrari (2000) found that the model adopted by an organization was usually based on organizational culture, and prevailing political, economic, and philosophical orientation. Of the thirteen, Ferrari found six that could be characterized as having authoritarian bent, four were making the transition from authoritarian to participatory, while three exhibited a full participative cultural model. Her study also found that six of the organizations engaged in a two-way asymmetric model anchored on a reactive program, but administratively operated within an authoritarian cultural framework. Six of the multinational organizations studied relied on a symmetrical model that made provisions for negotiation and mediation. The six, she argued, used that model because they existed in a highly dynamic industrial environment. These organizations, she pointed out, were in vulnerable economic sectors—such as mining—that compelled them to rely on the proactive stance with their various publics. Of the thirteen, only one company employed the public information model.

Crisis, Crisis Communication and Management: A Conceptual Exploration

The thrust of communication—the transference of information from a source to a destination in order to influence conduct—and its cousins—public relations, integrated marketing communications, risk communications, issues management, crisis communication and management—is to promote under-standing, and establish and maintain mutual relations and outcomes between an entity and the public or publics it serves. Thus, any persuasive communication effort must be carefully planned and managed. It must be adaptable to changes as needs arise if it is to achieve a stated objective (Newsom et al., 2000; Wilcox and Cameron, 2007; Seitel, 2011).

Although most forms of strategic communication are aimed at influencing the conduct of a target group and their perception of an organization—small or large—a number of factors influence the model, processing, production, and transmission of media artifacts an organization develops and adopts. These factors include economic, social, cultural, political, technological, and historical accounts of the organization and society where it operates. In an increasingly global world, where nations have become interconnected and economically interdependent, and the movement of information has become instant, strategic communication such as crisis communication and management has gained increased importance (Alozie, 2009); for example, when a crisis occurs in a remote part of the world such the Atacama Desert in the northern region of Chile, that event gains international salience whether the crisis has affected an individual, a small or large group, or one or more organizations. In the case of the 2010 San José mine accident, it could be argued that it had a direct and immediate impact on the trapped miners, and their families and mine owners, that might be considered small. However, the collapse of the mine gained quick public salience as a result of the evolution of information and communication technologies that make possible split second transmission of the accident to a global audience.

The instantaneous transfer of information in this era of globalization, coupled with the preceding factors usually influences the conduct of individuals, governments, and organizations when a crisis strikes—whether natural or man-made. Coombs (2007) defined crisis as "the perception of an unpredictable event that threatens important expectancies of stakeholders and can seriously impact an organization's performance and generate negative outcome" (pp. 2–3). Whether a crisis is natural or man-made, violent, or nonviolent, it is unpredictable, unexpected, and unanticipated, which could produce a negative perception and impact on an organization, if not handled with careful planning and execution. Considering the unexpected and unpredictable nature of crises, organizations had begun to develop policies and procedures to deal with crises when they occur (Newsom et al., 2000; Coombs, 2007; Wilcox and Cameron, 2007; Seitel, 2011).

When struck with a crisis, an organization relies on crisis communication and management to deal with and overcome the incident, which when unattended may harm the organization. It relies on the protocol to address specific constituencies, and society at large. Crisis communication is the reliance on mass media to relay transparent information on an event with concerned groups by adhering to a systematic strategy that outlines the rules and conducts that guide an organization (Newsom et al., 2000; Coombs, 2007; Coombs and Holladay, 2010). The process of developing and implementing a strategy for combating the escalation of a crisis so as to diminish the degree of harm to an organization wrought by a crisis is called crisis management. Crisis communication and management are not two separate things, but are interrelated and involve a set of measures that include the adoption of a plan, assembling of a team, and creation of strategic messages and tactics for dissemination and public consumption (Coombs, 2007; Coombs and Holladay, 2010). Coombs and Holladay identified three phases of a crisis: (a) precrisis (if possible steps are taken to avoid occurrence); (b) event-crisis (taking control to control the event and avoid doom), and (c) postcrisis (evaluating what happened and how it was handled in order to make alterations in case of a future unforeseen event). They stated that the phases are interrelated and the strategies adopted to overcome an ongoing crisis in its course must be adaptable if the objectives set are to be achieved.

Grunig and Hunt (1984) identified two dominant communication models that organizations have historically employed when dealing with and using mass media to direct and influence public opinion on issues. The models are: (a) one-way asymmetrical (press agentry/publicity and public information), and (b) two-way asymmetrical model. Press agency/publicity, described as the act of planning news in the mass media in an effort to attract favorable publicity for an organization, began in the late nineteenth century as the United States was industrializing. Aimed at mainly propagandizing, the model was criticized because it was unconcerned with the accuracy of the information being provided (Haque, 2004). By the beginning of the twentieth century, as the United Sates became increasingly industrialized, the conduct of industrialists, their treatment of workers and quality products came under severe attack by muck-raking journalists. The attacks produced a negative of perception of business practices and of industrialists among the American public.

To counter those attacks, and redirect the growing negative public opinion, industrialists hired journalists as public relations practitioners with the aim of developing and transmitting positive messages. A public information model delivers only desirable information about an organization. It should be noted that both press agency/publicity and public information are described as one-way asymmetrical communication because they are not aimed at eliciting feedback from the public; they are aimed at propagandizing. If feedback is received, it is not acted upon (Grunig and Hunt, 1984). Haque (2004, p. 354–355) noted that

> even though these resident public relations practitioners focused only on good things about their organizations, they disseminated factual information with some in-depth explanations of issues and problems. Both press agentry and public information models represent one-way public relations approaches, but the goal is for the practitioner to disseminate certain kinds of information about the organizations to the public through the media.

See also Grunig and Hunt (1984).

With time, studies found that organizations that acted on the feedback they received from the public found their decision to be beneficial. The need to transmit information to the public, receive feedback, and evaluate feedback in order to make adjustments that could shift public opinion and perception in the right direction transformed one-way asymmetrical communication into two-way asymmetrical communication. It should be noted that until the middle of the twentieth century, most studies in mass media were based on a rhetorical approach, not scientific. With the introduction of the scientific approach, studies on promotional communications have increasingly grown and are being relied upon by organizations when dealing with crisis and non-crisis events.

Haque (2004) and Ferarri (2000, 2003) pointed that whether one-way assymmetrical (press agentry/publicity and pubic information) or two-way symmetrical communication, the particular model adopted by an organization depends on the socioeconomic and cultural contexts prevailing in the society and/or organization. For example, Ferarri's (2000) study of practice of public relations in Chile reflected this assertion. The study established publicity and public information that dominated early public relations practice. In recent years, the study found that both models are currently being practiced. However, she noted that the model an organization adopts is dependent on its culture and management. It could be argued that these factors may have influenced owners of the San José mining company as well as the Chilean government, which managed the crisis.

Situation Analysis

The August 2010 San José mine collapse had been described as a "disaster waiting to happen" (Morgan, 2010). It had also been described as an "accident that should not have happened" (Bonnefoy, 2010, August 28). Some of the phrases used to describe the management and physical state of the mine after its collapse include constant rockbursts, uncontrollable rock explosion, violations of safety standards, poor infrastructure (inadequate ventilation, failure to install a ladder in the ventilation shaft, lack of gates and escape routes), coupled with management neglect. For years, miners and union officials have brought these concerns to the attention of the management and various governments. The management disregarded the requests to address these concerns; rather, whistleblowers were intimidated and some were forced to leave. Few workers, especially union officials, left voluntarily. Those who remained worked with fear, declining to speak out about their concerns (BBC News, 2010, October 18b).

When the government officials did act, they failed to hold the management fully accountable for the poor conditions that had existed and endangered mine workers. For example, Morgan (2010) stated that the mine was closed twice, partially in 2006, and, after a fatal accident in 2007, definitively, but it was given permission to re-open in May 2008. The permission to re-open followed a promise by the mine owners to repair and install safety equipment. Installing a ladder in the ventilation shaft was among the promises, a commitment that was never carried out. If government inspectors had conducted a proper inspection, they would have discovered the mine owners had not installed the ladder. If they had, the trapped miners would not have had to go through a 69-day ordeal. Morgan pointed out that Sernageomin was not primarily a safety inspectorate, but was given the responsibility for safety, displacing the labor inspectors who work in every other sector of the economy. He stated that the agency has 16 inspectors for 8,000 mines, and just two for the 2,000 in the Atacama Desert in the northern region of Chile. He reported about four deaths and several workers suffered debilitating injuries from hundreds of accidents that occurred at the San José mine from 2001 to 2010 (Morgan, 2010).

While agreeing that the mine accidents cannot be totally prevented, trade union leaders and experts point out that they can be managed when they occur if the safety rules and requirements are met and enforced. Considering these issues explored, it could be argued that a number of factors influenced how the San José mine management and the Chilean government reacted to and handled the accident. The dominant factors include the Chilean psyche, the prevailing political and socioeconomic circumstances in the country, the policies of the government in power, the conduct of the owners of the miners, enforcement, or lack of mining regulations and safety measures, and the reaction of the trapped miners' families. Dependence on information and communication technologies played an important role. These technologies have interconnected the world and made the world a much closer place where transmission of events that occurred in a remote place is instant, reaching a worldwide audience within minutes—everyone in the world is made a stakeholder in an event such as the San José mine disaster.

To understand how the psyche of Chilean people influenced the conduct of the Piñera administration, one has to look at its distant and contemporary history and socioeconomic development. During its almost two centuries of independence, Chile has enjoyed a stable constitutional plurality. Though a conservative nation and class-conscious society, Chileans have had the right to express themselves freely, except on occasions when the military encroached into power—under Altamirano, 1924 to 1932, and Pinochet, 1973 to 1990 (*New World Encyclopedia*, 2008, November 17). Pinochet came to power at the peak of the Cold War. In the guise of fighting communism and promoting neoliberal economic policies, his administration instituted repressive and draconian polices that adversely affected the political, sociocultural, and economic conduct of Chileans. During his reign, thousands of people disappeared, or were killed. Some accused him of mass murder. With the murders and freedom of expression curtailed, Chileans muzzled their political expression and personal opinions out of fear (Ferrari, 2000, 2003). Historically, Chileans

—especially those of European descent—have been known to freely express and protest government policies. It should be pointed out that indigenous Chileans have often accused the European-dominated governments of discrimination. Under the Pinochet regime, most Chilean segments of Chilean society kept silent and shied away from activism out of fear because the administration had a tendency to engage in witch hunts.

Under Pinochet, the country was divided between those in favor and those against his administration—a division that continues to date. Division exists between the haves and the have-nots as well as in ideological terms—politically and socioculturally. A highly stratified society economically, Chile's top 10 richest percentile possesses 47 percent of the country's wealth. Within Latin America, Chile has been characterized as having one of the most uneven distributions of wealth in the world, ahead only of Brazil and Guatemala. It lags behind even that of most of the nations in sub-Saharan Africa (*New World Encyclopedia*, 2008, November 17; *Encyclopedia of the Nations*, undated). Since the start of the Pinochet administration, the business community and bourgeois class supported him and other administrations in power because government policies favored businesses at the expense of the masses. Business owners have had a free hand to do what they want to promote free enterprise and commerce. As economic liberalism took hold and government subsidies and support grew increasingly less, economic well-being preoccupied the masses. Competition was high, while economic survival became the priority of the masses. Every Chilean fought to climb the economic ladder at the expense of cultural obligations and political expression.

A collectivistic culture turned individualistic. Government oppression and poor social policies were not contested by the government as individuals focused on their welfare and that of their families. Faced with these harsh conditions, the Catholic Church became the moral compass of the nation during the Pinochet regime and succeeding administrations. With the fall of communism in the late 1980s, political pluralism and democracy returned to Chile as reforms were introduced. Leftist and socialist influences staged a comeback with the election of a left and socialist-tilting government. Despite these facts, Chileans have not completely rid themselves of the repression and individualistic nature they acquired under Pinochet—individualistic economic tendencies among Chileans are growing in the face of pressures coming from the current global economic context. It should be noted that with the introduction of political plurality, social consciousness and activism are on the rise. Through elections, and sociopolitical activism, Chileans are able to express their concerns to elected governments. Notwithstanding social isolation and political repression of activism, some critics contend the fears Chileans nursed under Pinochet have not been completely wiped out.

It was the realization that the less privileged in Chile now had a stake in that society to address the government without fear of retaliation that might have influenced the families of the 33 trapped miners to call to express their fears that the management of the San José mine would not bring all forces to bear in the effort to rescue their loved ones. That lack of trust, which raised the need to bring to the attention of the government the straddling efforts of the mine owners to rescue their loved ones is well founded, considering the mine management had been known to ignore safety issues when concerns were raised. Their insistence that management must mount and continue the rescue efforts paid off. That insistence, coupled with the changing political landscape in Chile might have influenced the conduct of the mine management. Grudgingly, the management continued to search for miners a couple of days after they had not been heard from and were feared dead. To get the management to keep searching, the miners' families formed a camp at the site and openly spoke to the press. They made it known that the management of the mine disregarded safety rules and the poor infrastructure at the mine.

When the management of the mine started protesting that they did not have the resources to embark on a long-term search, the families made their concerns known to the government, insisting the government must take charge of the search and rescue efforts. While these families were protesting and calling for continued efforts to secure their loved ones, the management of the mine attempted to camouflage its failures. The management insisted that it adhered to safety rules, took care of its workers, and exhausted every effort to return the miners to their families. Nonetheless, it was alleged that the management was working to stop the rescue just days after the collapse without any contact having been made with the trapped miners. While the management made much of paying the workers, it indicated it was filing for bankruptcy as a result of the accident and costs stemming from the collapse and rescue efforts.

It could be argued that if the accident had occurred during the Pinochet administration, the management would have been able to hold its ground knowing it would enjoy the regime's backing. On the other hand, the miners' families would not have stood firm in their demands for action from the company and government. Chile's mass media might not have covered the protests of the miners' families which helped give the issue a public salience nationally and internationally. It could also be argued that if the administration in power was undemocratic, and its electoral fortunes and perceptions depended on how it handled the accident (the rescue of the trapped miners), it might not have taken over the rescue effort, which was estimated to have cost over $20 million (Lane, 2010). It is more likely a dictatorial regime would have acquiesced with the views of the management of the mine. Based on this exploration, it could be argued the government key target groups are:

- the families of the 33 trapped miners, other Chilean mine workers and their families;
- the 33 trapped miners;

- Chilean electorate and population, as well as press; and
- the international community (governments, investors, and world audience and to a lesser degree—the international media).

These direct (trapped miners, and their families), and indirect constituencies (other Chilean mine workers and their families, Chilean electorate and population as well as press, and the international community) influenced the objectives, strategies, and tactics used by the Chilean government during the crisis. The degree of influence that the changes in information and communication technologies had on the conduct of the government cannot be discounted even though it might be considered intangible.

Communication Goals, Objectives, Strategies, and Tactics

As stated earlier, it should be noted that the Chilean government did not have an established crisis communication management plan when it took over the management of the 2010 San José mine crisis. The government made one up and adapted it as the situation commanded during the crisis. Based on its conduct and a variety of reports and examinations, the following goals, objectives, strategies, and tactics were derived by the Piñera administration during the 69-day ordeal as it managed the 2010 San José mine crisis.

Goal 1: Assure the families of the 33 trapped miners and Chilean mine workers and their families that the Chilean government would not leave any stone unturned in the search and rescue of their loved ones.

Objective: To win and maintain the confidence and trust of Chileans and the international community by relying on their resources and foreign assistance to keep the search and rescue effort going.

Strategy: Mounted a round-the-clock search and rescue effort, assisted the families to maintain their vigil at the site of the accident, and kept the family members informed.

Tactics:

- The president, ministers and officials spoke to families often about the search and rescue effort.
- The president, ministers and officials paid constant visits to Camp Hope.
- The ministers and officials provided advice and counsel to the families.
- The government built and equipped Camp Hope (including media to be apprised of the search and rescue efforts).
- The government provided food and provisions for the families of the trapped miners.

- The president postponed a foreign trip to monitor the search and rescue efforts.
- When the trapped miners were found, efforts were made to exchange information between them and their families.

Goal 2: For the first 17 days before the 33 trapped miners were found, the goal was to determine their fate—whether they were dead or alive—after being found—the goal changed to ensuring the trapped miners the government, is doing and would do everything, in its power to rescue them.

Objective: When the fate of the 33 trapped miners was unknown, the government employed a variety of techniques (Plan A, B, and C) to find out their fate. When discovered alive, the government and rescuers relied on the plans to rescue them.

Strategy: Maintained a round-the-clock search and rescue effort, and when the 33 trapped miners were found, informed them of the plans and round-the-clock effort to bring them out, as well as provide them information about their families.

Tactics:

- Officials kept the trapped miners informed of the all-out effort being made to rescue them.
- A mechanism was developed to exchange letters and photos between the miners and their families.
- At the request of the miners, the government built a temporary school for the children of the miners.
- Provisions and food were provided to the miners using pipes.
- Officials provided counsel and encouragement for the miners.

Goal 3: To keep the public (Chilean electorate and population, as well as press) informed that an all-out search and rescue effort was being undertaken to find and rescue the trapped miners.

Objective (a): To keep the public aware of its effort to rescue the trapped miners; the government hoped it would gain support for its conduct and policies from the Chilean public.

Objective (b): To assure the public that the administration listens and is there for its citizens when they are faced with difficult issues and life threatening situations.

Strategy: Officials used mass media and new information and communication technologies to reinforce the government's search-and-rescue efforts.

Tactics:

- Chilean officials and the president granted interviews and participated in press conferences for the international media.
- The president cancelled a foreign trip to monitor the search and rescue effort.
- The president attended every occasion when a milestone was reached (discovery and emergence of the miners).
- Assistance and facilities were provided for the media covering the search and rescue.
- Social networking forums and new technologies were used to update the public and press about the search and rescue efforts.

Goal 4: To maintain contacts with the international community (governments, investors, world audience, and—to a lesser degree—the international media) regarding search and rescue efforts, as well as the activities and conduct of the administration.

Objective (a): To keep the interest of all segments of the international community, solicit and attract aid and assistance.

Objective (b): To demonstrate that Chile is politically stable so as to attract future investment.

Strategy: To inform and update the international community (governments, investors, world audience, and—to a lesser degree—the international media) regarding the search and rescue efforts, as well as the activities and conduct of the administration.

Tactics:

- Chilean president and officials held constant conversations about the search and rescue efforts with foreign heads of state, diplomats, and officials of foreign leaders.
- Chilean president and officials held constant conversations about the search and rescue efforts with foreign heads and officers of supra-national organizations.
- Chilean president and officials held constant conversations about the search and rescue efforts with heads and officials of multinational corporations with expertise and technologies on rescue.
- Chilean officials granted interviews and participated in press conferences for the international media.
- Assistance and facilities were provided to the media covering the search and rescue.

- Social networking forums and new technologies were used to update the global audience about the search and rescue efforts.

Outcomes Assessment

Any outcomes assessment of the Chilean government's handling of the 2010 San José mine accident should be conducted from two interwoven dimensions: communication, and socioeconomic and political. Studies on crisis communication management have found that the successful handling of a crisis hinges on a number of elements and considerations. These include establishing a plan beforehand, assembling a crisis crew, establishing a site presence, and appointing a spokesperson (Newsom et al., 2000; Wilcox and Cameron, 2007; Coombs and Hollady, 2010). Other considerations include initiating dialogue between an entity and the group affected, recognizing the public as partners, instituting two-way communication, and ensuring honest and truthful exchange of communication. Understanding and meeting the needs of news media are of great importance. It is also important to develop trust early with those that disagree, or mistrust the affected entity and address any extraneous direct and indirect concerns as they arise (Zoda in Wilcox and Cameron, 2007).

Despite the generally accepted view that the Chilean government did not possess an established crisis communication management program (Crean, 2010; Yaxley, 2010), its conduct during the crisis demonstrated it reacted well and followed some of the preceding principles. Relying on these principles, albeit unplanned, resulted in a successful outcome, although it took the government two or three days to get engaged after the collapse of the mine, when the owners indicated they could not handle the accident and were about to declare bankruptcy (Black, 2010; Gonzales, 2010). The Chilean government delegated Coldeco—the state-owned mining company and the largest copper producer in the world—to take over management of the crisis (Yang, 2010). After taking over, and without sparing any expense, Coldeco worked earnestly to ensure rescue of the miners (Bodzin, 2010, October 13). With Chilean Mining Minister Laurence Golborne and Health Minister Jaime Manalich as the key spokespersons (Bodzin, 2010, October 13; BBC News, 2010, October 14), Coldeco and government officials established an on-site presence. Equipment and experts were brought in to facilitate the rescue (Figure 7.1). The minister of mining served as the official spokesperson on the rescue efforts. After the miners were found alive, the health minister was added as a spokesperson, but addressed the health of the trapped miners only. The president occasionally served as a spokesperson when a milestone was reached. This process enabled the Chilean government to produce and deliver centralized messages to the target public and the global audience.

The messages offered were truthful and transparent and dealt with every aspect of the rescue efforts. The spokesperson offered explanations of what

Figure 7.1 Private companies pitched in with specialist equipment such as the Schramm T130 drill.

the government and rescuers were doing, what they could do, or could not do. Officials gave information on the rescue process and efforts (Plans A, B, and C) and updated the public as needed (Grinam-Nicholson, 2010; Bodzin, 2010, October 13). Without hesitation, government officials communicated their needs to the global audience and sought assistance from any sources, hence expressing their willingness to accept any offers. It should be noted that officials provided the media access to the miners' families and spoke to them often about the progress of the rescue effort. When the miners were found alive after 17 days—their discovery and the information relayed from miners were made available to the waiting media. With the mining minister as the lead spokesperson, the health minister and Coldeco officials were often present at Camp Hope to interact, welcome, and deliver information as new developments evolved. The president came whenever a milestone was reached—for example, when the miners began to emerge (BBC News, 2010, October 13; Bodzin, 2010, October 14; Geiger-Hemmer, 2010).

A key process in handling a crisis concerns the relationship between the organizations involved (the government and the San José mine owners) and those involved in the crisis (trapped miners and their families). Every Chilean mine worker, his or her family, the Chilean public, and the global audience could be added as the nimbus public since they were not directly affected, but had a great of interest in the outcome (Newsom et al., 2000). When the Chilean government took over the management of the crisis, it established a good rapport with the families of the trapped miners. The government improved the infrastructure of the camp site. With charities in the region and local government authorities, the administration offered the trapped miners' families provisions. Members of the Piñera administration provided them with information and assurance that the government would do everything within its power to rescue their loved ones. Government officials offered counsel and sympathy (Barrionuevo, 2010). By doing so, officials built and won the trust the trapped miners' families.

Prior to the accident, Chilean mining families were critical of the government for failing to establish firm mine regulations and strictly enforcing those on the books. They also accused the government of not holding Chilean mine owners responsible for their conduct and poor mine safety (Bonnefoy, 2010, August 12). The trapped miners' families threatened to sue the government and mine owners (Giovani et al., 2010). However, after the government started managing the crisis, rather than take issue with the government for its inaction on mine regulation and for getting involved in the rescue effort late, the trapped miners' families evolved from criticizing to praising the government's handling of the crisis. They interacted and greeted officials with cheers and expressed their gratitude. When the trapped miners were found alive, government officials ensured they communicated the efforts being made to rescue them by supplying them with vehicles that enabled them to exchange information. Messages were exchanged between the trapped miners and their families, their rescuers, government officials, and even the media. Provisions were also provided to the miners through these vehicles to keep them healthy. Government officials provided information the rescuers received from the trapped miners to the various publics through the global media. At the request of the trapped miners, the government set up a school for their children (BBC News, 2010, October 14). The positive relationship, feedback, and interaction that developed touched the Chileans as well as the global audience.

Polls taken during and shortly after the rescue showed that the Piñera administration's handling of the crisis received high approval from Chileans. Stemming from the handling of the crisis, the Piñera administration's overall policies received high marks from the people of Chile as well. A poll taken during the rescue showed the administration's approval rose from 46 percent in July to 56 percent (Nelson and Llana, 2010). Still basking in nationalism, pride, and patriotism, the administration's approval rating remained fairly high weeks later in spite of what critics view as its shortcomings. Critics contended that despite Piñera's promise to introduce a new way of governing, he remains a control freak who prefers centralized decision making. They alleged he intended to impose a private managerial style on government entities that might not necessarily benefit the masses—only a few elites (Bonnefoy, 2010, October 11; BBC, 2010, October 18a). Bonnefoy stated that his handling of two earthquakes that occurred shortly after he came to power was adequate, but that his management of the reconstruction efforts almost a year after had been inadequate. Despite these criticisms, she noted his proposal to raise mining royalties was considered center-left, instead of center-right as his supporters expected. He seemed to have deviated from his past conservative stance on policies. Some of the reforms the president advocated—such as the move to center—have remained just promises, as yet unimplemented. His association with the Pinochet dictatorship and a hostile political climate may hamper his ability to push through the reforms. His party does not enjoy a majority in congress (Business Monitor Online, 2011, January 17). The left distrust him and this remains a stumbling block. His base, the right-wing conservative bloc, may not necessarily put its weight behind his reforms on the grounds they are too liberal.

As stated earlier, the Chilean government provided access and facilities to the world mass media that gathered to cover the crisis (Guardian.co.uk, 2010, October 13). It has been reported that about 1,300 journalists representing 50 Chilean media outlets and another 200 foreign journalists from 33 countries offered continual coverage of the accident from the inception to rescue (Barrionuevo, 2010). Instead of distancing themselves from the media, Chilean government officials cultivated their friendship. Officials provided amenities, technical assistance for journalist to do their work, and access to the miners' families at the camp. Officials also provided information regarding rescue efforts and processes. For example, officials used new information and communication technologies to connect the media center to the rescue site where the rescuers worked. These provisions enabled the reporters to witness the rescue efforts firsthand, receive firsthand information from the rescuers and government officials as well as the reactions of trapped miners and their families. The spokespersons adjusted and corrected information as need arose.

The success of the Chilean government's management of the crisis could also be discerned from the degree of lavish and uncritical coverage given to its handling of the crisis, the rescue processes, and the positive public reactions of the Chilean people and world audience derived from the accounts they received from the media. By cooperating with the media, Chilean government officials influenced the coverage of the crisis during and after the crisis. During the crisis, few media outlets or journalists questioned the past conduct and policies of the current and former governments with regard to mine regulations and crisis management. Even though the Piñera administration was under six months old when the crisis occurred (Gallacher, 2010, March 11), the administration did express a strong orientation with regard to mine regulation during the election. However, on assuming power, the administration did not address the concerns that already existed and were known. These concerns included the harsh and unsafe conditions at San José and other mines in Chile as well as his decision to build the HidroAysen complex, which could impact the environment negatively (Woods, 2010, August 14). Pinera's seemingly unfair policies and harsh treatment toward Mapuche Indians were disregarded in the media (Sepúlveda, 2010), and largely unknown to the over one billion global audience members that witnessed the rescues, even though a number of the trapped miners were of indigenous descent (Carroll, 2010, October 17). It should be noted that the number of journalists present and the extent of coverage given to the accident in the face of other pressing issues in the world have come under attack (Littau, 2010).

In addition to the traditional mass media that provided instantaneous coverage as development warranted, the Chilean government employed a variety of non-traditional channels to transmit its messages worldwide, to gain and maintain global attention. These included social media, mobile phones, and websites (Hicks, 2010). By employing these non-traditional channels, the worldwide audience could access information whether at home, away, at work, or at leisure, thus keeping people highly engaged.

Following the crisis, the government announced that it would strengthen mine regulations and policies, strengthen agencies that regulate the mine industry and business, and prosecute businesses that do not adhere to labor rules and safety regulations (BBC News, 2010, October 18b). The legislature launched an investigation (Bonnefoy, 2010, August 28), and President Sebastián Piñera established a commission to look into safety standards at Chilean workplaces across the economy (BBC News, 2010, October 5). A few of the world media and journalists reminded their audience about the president's long-term support of neoliberal policies that benefited a narrow segment of the Chilean populace, considering he supported and executed Pinochet's policies as his minister of mines. As a member of the Pinochet cabinet, he strongly advocated the privatization of social welfare systems (Progressive Populism for the 21st Century, 2010; Guardian.co.uk 2010, October 13). It should be noted the president's older brother, José Piñera served as minister of labor under the Pinochet administration (Progressive Populism for the 21st Century, 2010). It was during his brother's reign as minister of labor that the mine industry was deregulated, thus weakening mining rules and general labor regulations, while strengthening management, not just in the mining industry, but in the private sector at large. He also relaxed labor rules, gutting the influential trade union. Prior to the Pinochet administration, Chile was regarded as one of the few Latin American countries with strong labor rules and strong trade unions (Workers Vanguard No. 970, 2010, December 3).

Just days after the 33 trapped miners were rescued at San José mine, two miners died in a mine accident at Los Reyes mine about 60 miles from the former. Describing their deaths as a "rule rather than the exception," in Chile, Gonzales (2010) stated that their deaths "were not deemed worthy of a presidential visit, nor were their families offered compensation or any of the other prizes given to the 33." Traditionally, the Chilean mining industry has generally been credited with possessing strong mining safety records (Cambero, 2010). However, a report, "How safe are Chile's copper mines?" seemed to dispute that perception (Long, 2010, October 5). Long reported that historically the price of copper in the world market tends to influence the number of accidents and deaths that occur in Chilean mines. He explained that when the price of copper rises, accidents and deaths rise as well, but fall when the price declines. He stated that Sernageomin reported that there was an average of 0.41 deaths in Chilean mines for every one million hours worked during the 1980s. By the 1990s that figure dropped to 0.28 and by the past decade to 0.13. In 2009, there were 2.2 accidents in Chile's mines for every 100 workers. The safest year was in 1999 when the price of copper fell steeply. Chile's Department of Social Security reported that mining is among the safest industries in Chile (Long, 2010, October 5).

Shortly after the rescue, Piñera traveled abroad—a trip he planned before the accident, but cancelled after the collapse. His visit to Europe attracted a great deal of attention. While in England, he reaffirmed his resolve to tighten regulation, enforce regulations, and ensure equity, not just for mine workers, but for all workers in Chile. His statement implied that Chile has a stable political environment and eschewing the image it developed under Pinochet. He was not addressing just the media, but indirectly world businesses to invest in Chile (Bodzin, 2010, October 14). Queen Elizabeth of England and other European leaders hosted and toasted him. That sent a message to investors that Chile is stable and open for the world to come in. Voigt (2010) described his trip to Europe as a form of branding in which it would "be difficult to put a price on how much the good news exposure will be a boost to Chilean business abroad, tourism at home."

The Piñera administration's management of the crisis also helped Chile to build better relations with its neighbors. The Bolivian president visited Chile during the rescue. Bolivians welcomed the camaraderie of the Chilean government, thus improving their relations after years of estranged relations stemming from border disputes. Some opinion leaders share the view that this cooperation will help boost relations between Chilean and other South American governments (Kurczy, 2010, October 13; Monitor's Editorial Board, 2010, October 13). The handling and coverage of the crisis generated cooperation from every part of the globe. When sought, at times without asking, assistance for rescue poured in from South Africa, New Zealand, Australia, the United States, the Caribbean and the Middle East (Grinam-Nicholson, 2010).

The cost of the rescue has been estimated to be about $20 million—a sum the government intends to recuperate from the mine owners (Bonnefoy, 2010, August 28). The government has already sued the mine owners to recover what it spent (*New York Times*, 2010, April 12; BBC News 2010, October 7, October 18b). However, most experts agree the rescue does not match the exposure the Chilean government obtained from the free publicity stemming from the 69-day coverage of the rescue. The free publicity the Chilean government derived from the coverage if computed in equivalent advertising time runs into hundreds of millions. It should be noted that advertising equivalency for the coverage has yet been determined, but the estimate of hundreds of millions could hold considering Oakley, which donated about 53 pairs of sunglasses—valued at $180 a pair—to each miner, received $41 million in equivalent advertising time, according to Front Row Analytics (Voigt, 2010; Bodzin, 2010, October 13).

Conclusion and Lessons Learned

Before discussing the conclusions derived from this exploration regarding the relative success, or lack of success, of the manner in which the Chilean government handled the 2010 San José crisis communication and management campaign, one has to recall the attitudes of Chileans and the contemporary political and socioeconomic conditions manifesting in the country, as Ferrari (2003) pointed out. She contended that

> the legacy of military has resulted in a striking lack of solidarity among Chileans, who appear to have become more individualistic and self-centered. Paradoxically, the social, economic and cultural legacy created by the military, which was subsequently adopted by the new democratic regime, attempted to sell Chile as a jaguar or as a winner. As a result of this change where self interest and fear of reprisal stifled public debate,

participation and creativity, the Chilean cultural and communication system has been based on a mystified concept of reality which is a mix of nationalism, leadership, competitiveness, success, and innovation.

(Ferrari, 2003, p. 378)

Recalling these prevailing circumstances offers a mirror to discerning the conduct of the trapped miners, the reactions of the Piñera administration and mine owners, and the expectations of the Chilean public, the global audience, as well as the 33 trapped miners. It should be noted that the conduct of these groups stemmed their perceptions of what obtains in the country and what is possible.

The author agrees with those that claim that the Chilean government did not have an established crisis communication management plan when it took over the crisis, but made one up and adapted it as the situation commanded. The success of the government efforts could be attributed to quick thinking and ability to follow long-established protocols of crisis communication management by weaving together short-term objectives, strategies, and tactics. Without an established plan, the Chilean government initiated one, but adjusted it as needs arose. These protocols included the initiation of a plan, establishing an on-site presence, appointment of a spokesperson, and transparent communication stakeholders (Newsom et al., 2000; Wilcox and Cameron, 2007; Coombs and Holladay, 2010). It should also be noted that as a Western-trained media mogul, the president is considered publicity-savvy and knew how to exploit the media for his personal benefit—this time the benefit of his administration. Whether the use of three spokespersons instead of one, as experts advise, is a shorting, it did not create a problem because the feedback about the spokesperson remained during and after the crisis.

Considering the lack of an established crisis communication management plan and failure to enact and enforce strict rules and regulations to raise mine safety and workers' conditions, the author describes the government's overall handling of the crisis and policies as "reactionary"—developing and implementing plans and policies as events warranted. Trade unionists have often accused past government administrations of being reactionary when dealing with issues of safety and regulations with mine companies. Past and present administrations have been accused of being reactionary because they tend to handle issues on an ad hoc basis, or when one issue or another is brought to their attention instead of setting long-term goals to deal with the mining industry, or following established rules to be followed consequently.

In March 2011, five months after the 69-day ordeal in which 33 Chilean miners were buried at a depth of more than 700m (2,300ft) after a rockfall, the Chilean congressional committee investigating the accident issued a report. The report accused the mine owners of negligence. The report agreed with the miners who accused the owners of disregarding safety, considering their failure to install basic safety standards and equipment. Also, the report stated that Sernageomin was "administratively responsible" for the accident. The report implied as the families of miners had contended that Sernageomin should have shut down the company, considering there had been three deaths at their mines over six years, and dozens of accidents. The report is expected to play a great role as the Chilean government takes steps to strengthen mine safety. In keeping with the president's promise to raise safety standards, Sernageomin's budget and safety inspectors have already been increased (BBC News, 2011, March 2). One hopes that when the government initiates a crisis communication management plan, it would adopt some of the recommendations found in this and future reports.

Several lessons can be deduced from the Chilean government's handling of the crisis and its aftermath. With regard to communication, the lessons learned are numerous. The result demonstrates that when a crisis occurs, handlers should consider doing the following: (a) be proactive, take responsibility and demonstrate good leadership and judgment; (b) manage expectations, but provide hope to those affected and the public; (c) have a plan, if not—develop one and adjust as the situation warrants; (c) be open, communicate needs, accept assistance, but keep control; (d) communicate and exchange truthful information; (d) be accessible, be social, and offer assistance to the media and others; (e) provide training and help to your employees during and after the crisis; (f) work hard to fix problems, do not openly take credit for dealing with a problem, but don't apportion blame; and (g) keep learning and adjust as the need arises (National Law Review, 2010; Murray, 2010; DeVol, 2010; Yaxley, 2010).

Discussion Questions

1. Chile has experienced political plurality and dictatorship. It is also a society with a socioeconomic gap and cultural differences exist. These factors have influenced the conduct of the people, the mass media, and governments. Considering this, in what ways did Chile's political evolution, socioeconomic and culture influence how the government managed the 2010 San José mine crisis?

2. This exploration implied that the Chilean government does not have a crisis communication management plan. Assuming you are hired by the Chilean government to serve as a consultant to develop a plan, what would be your key advice and what would be the components of the plan you would develop? Please offer rationale for your advice and components for the plan.

3. The Piñera administration has been praised for the manner in which it managed the 2010 San José mine crisis with regard to crisis communication. Assuming you agree with the conduct of administration and what it did well—what suggestions would you offer to improve the process considering most of the administration's actions were ad hoc?

4. Disasters can occur in any part of the world. They are often unexpected and could spell doom. Select a country in Africa, Asia, the Middle East, or Eastern Europe—most of these areas are regarded as developing—do research on the political and cultural taxonomies of two or more of these countries. Based on these taxonomies, suggest how they would influence the crisis management plan for the countries if you were asked to assist during a crisis.

5. The Chilean president has promised to protect whistleblowers, reform and enforce mine regulations. However, many of his critics, including union officials and activists are skeptical. They contend he is paying lip service to reforms and would not engage in meaningful reforms once the media glare is over. If you are a strategic communication executive for a union— what would you do public relations-wise to hold the president accountable and ensure he initiates the reforms he has promised?

References

2010 Copiapó Mining Accident (2011). 2010 Copiapó mining accident, January 11. Wikipedia. Retrieved from http://en.wikipedia.org

ABC News (2010). Factbox: Mining accidents, disasters and escapes, November 20. Retrieved from www.abc.net.au/news/stories/2010/11/20/3071992.htm

Alozie, E. C. (2009). *Marketing in developing nations: Nigerian advertising in a global and technological world*. New York: Routledge.

Barrionuevo, A. (2010). Carnival air fills Chilean camp as miners' rescue nears. *The New York Times*, October 10. Retrieved from www.nytimes.com/

BBC News (2010). Chile Country Profile, August 12. Retrieved from http://news.bbc.co.uk/go/pr/fr/-/2/hi/americas/country_profiles/1222764.stm

BBC News (2010). How safe are Chile's copper mines?, October 5. Retrieved from www.bbc.co.uk/news/world-latin-america-11467279

BBC News (2010). Why are China's mines so dangerous?, October 7. Retrieved from www.bbc.co.uk/news/business-11497070

BBC News (2010). Jubilation as Chile mine rescue ends, October 13. Retrieved from at www.bbc.co.uk/news/world-latin-america-11469025

BBC News (2010). Jubilation as Chile mine rescue ends, October 14. Retrieved from www.bbc.co.uk/news/world-latin-america-11539182

BBC News (2010). Chile President Sebastián Piñera praises UK friendship, October 18a. Retrieved from www.bbc.co.uk/news/world-latin-america

BBC News (2010). Chile's Piñera "to protect mine safety whistle-blowers," October 18b. Retrieved from www.bbc.co.uk/news/world-latin-america-11565850

BBC News (2011). Chile Congress blames San José mine owners for collapse, March 2. Retrieved from www.bbc.co.uk/news/world-latin-america-12629647

Black, W. (2010). Capitalism would have killed the Chilean miners: A reply to Mr. Henninger. *The Huffington Post*, October 15. Retrieved from www.huffingtonpost.com

Bodzin, S. (2010). 5 reasons Chile mine rescue is so successful. *Christian Science Monitor*, October 13. Retrieved from www.csmonitor.com

Bodzin, S. (2010). Chile mine rescue a PR coup for Chile—and President Piñera. *Christian Science Monitor*, October 14. Retrieved from www.csmonitor.com

Bonnefoy, P. (2010). 33 miners buried alive in Atacama Desert. *Global Post*, August 12. Retrieved from www.globalpost.com/

Bonnefoy, P. (2010). Poor safety standards led to Chilean mine disaster. *Global Post*, August 28. Retrieved from www.globalpost.com/dispatch/chile

Bonnefoy, P. (2010). All Chile miners freed: Rescue succeeds. *Global Post*, October 11. Retrieved from www.globalpost.com

Business Monitor Online (2011). Key political challenges for 2011, January 17. Retrieved from www.allbusiness.com/

Cambero, F. (2010). SCENARIOS—Chile mine accident casts spotlight on safety. *Reuters*, August 6. Retrieved from http://uk.reuters.com/

Carroll, R. (2010). When the miners' leader met the president, two sides of Chile embraced. guardian.co.uk/*The Observer*, October 17. Retrieved from www. guardian.co.uk/

Christian Science Monitor (2010). Chile mine rescue shows how far mine safety has come, October 13. Retrieved from www.csmonitor.com/

Coombs, W. (2007). *Ongoing crisis communication: Planning, managing and responding* (2nd ed.). Los Angeles, CA: Sage.

Coombs, W., and Holladay, J. (2010). *PR strategy and application: Managing influence*. Malden, MA: Wiley-Blackwell.

Crean, J. (2010). Branding Chile through crisis, October 19. Retrieved from www.national.ca/johncrean/en/

DeVol, P. (2010). What the Chilean mine saga can teach you about crisis communications, October 13. Retrieved from http://devolpr.wordpress.com

Encyclopedia of the Nations (n.d.). Chile—Poverty and wealth. Retrieved from www. nationsencyclopedia.com

Euronews. (2010). Rescue: Morales visits freed Bolivian miner, October 13. Retrieved from www.euronews.net

Ferrari, M. (2000). A influencia dos valores organizaciones na determinacao practica das relacoes publicas em organizacoes do Brasil e do Chile (The influence of organizational values in the practice of public relations in Brazilian and Chilean organizations). Unpublished doctoral dissertation, Universidad de São Paulo, São Paulo, Brazil.

Ferrari, M. (2003). Public Relations in Chile. Searching for identity amid imported models. In K. Sriramesh and D. Vercic (Eds.), *The Global Public Relations Handbook*, pp. 378–395. Mahwah, NJ: Lawrence Erlbaum Associates.

Gallacher, A. (2010). New Chile quake as Piñera sworn in as president. BBC News, March 11. Retrieved from http://news.bbc.co.uk/

Geiger-Hemmer, A. (2010). It's Hemmer time. Living in country, October 19. Retrieved from www.livinglakecountry.com/

Giovani, F., Laing, A and Allen, H. (2010). Chile mine firm ignored warnings on safety, say families. *Times Colonist*, August 26. Retrieved from www.timescolonist.com/

Gonzales, M. (2010). Back to business as usual in Chile's mines. Guardian.co.uk, November 14. Retrieved from www.guardian.co.uk/

Govan, F. (2010). Chile miners rescue: Bolivian miner emigrated in search of work. *The Telegraph*, October 14. Retrieved from www.telegraph.co.uk/news/worldnews

Grinam-Nicholson, Y. (2010). Leadership lessons from the mines. *Jamaica Observer*, October 20. Retrieved from www.jamaicaobserver.com/

Grunig, J., and Hunt, T. (1984). *Managing public relations*: New York: Holt, Rinehart and Winston.

Guardian.co.uk (2010). Chile miners: rescue joy must not derail focus on why mine collapse happened, October 13. Retrieved from www.guardian.co.uk/global-development/poverty-matters

Haque, M. (2004). Around Asia: Overview of public relations in Asia. In D. Tilson and E.C. Alozie (Eds.), *Toward the common good: Perspectives in international public relations*, pp. 346–362. Boston, MA: Pearson.

Hicks, D. (2010). Communicating through a crisis: Chile Miner rescue captures the world's attention, October 13. Retrieved from http://crisisexperts.blogspot.com

History of Chile (2011). History of Chile, January 4. Wikipedia. Retrieved from http://en.wikipedia.org/wiki

Kurczy, S. (2010). Chile mine rescue unites a fractured world. *The Christian Science Monitor*, October 13. Retrieved from www.csmonitor.com/

Lane, E. (2010). Chile mine rescue "to cost $20m". BBC News: Business, October 14. Retrieved from www.bbc.co.uk

Littau, J. (2010). Chile is a story about journalism's failure (updated), October 13. Retrieved from www.jlittau.net/

Long, G. (2010). How safe are Chile's copper mines?, October 5 Retrieved from www.bbc.co.uk

Mining accidents (2010). Mining accidents, December 31. Wikipedia. Retrieved from http://en.wikipedia.org

Monitor's Editorial Board (2010). Chile rescue of miners recalls "better angels". *The Christian Science Monitor*, October 13. Retrieved from www.csmonitor.com/

Morgan, D. (2010). Remembering why the Chilean mining disaster happened. Front-line of Revolutionary Struggle, October 10. Retrieved from http://revolutionary frontlines.wordpress.com

Murray, T. (2010). Chile mine rescue—Seven lessons on leadership. Ezine Articles, October 14. Retrieved from http://ezinearticles.com/

National Law Review (2010). Eight crisis management lessons from the Chilean mine rescue, December 27. Retrieved from www.natlawreview.com/

Nelson, A., and Llana, S. (2010). Chilean miners trapped, but citizens approve government response. *Christian Science Monitor*, September 7. Retrieved from www.csmonitor.com.

New World Encyclopedia (2008). Chile, November 17. Retrieved from www.new worldencyclopedia.org/

New York Times (2010). Mining disasters, April 12. Retrieved from http://topics. nytimes.com/topics/reference

New York Times (2010). Chile mining accident (2010), October 25. Retrieved from http://topics.nytimes.com/top/reference

Newsom, D., Turk, J., and Kruckeberg, D. (2000). *This is PR: The realities of public relations* (7th ed.). Belmont, CA: Wadsworth.

Progressive Populism for the 21st Century (2010). The hidden truth behind the Chilean miner rescue, October 13. Retrieved from http://open.salon.com/blog/

Richwebnews/Allvoices (2010). Carlos Mamani non- Chilean miner captivates Bolivians—even Pres. Evo Morales, October 13. Retrieved from www.allvoices. com/contributed-news/7010263

Scher, B. (2010). They never should have been trapped in the first place, October 13. Retrieved fromt www.huffingtonpost.com

Seitel, F. (2011). *The practice of public relations* (11th ed.). Boston, MA: Prentice Hall.

Sepúlveda, P. (2010). Chile: Discrimination directed against the Mapuche Indians. Mapuche set up Autonomous Legal Defence Unit. Center for Research on Globalization, February 12. Retrieved from www.globalresearch.caindex/

Voigt, K. (2010). Big day for Brand Chile. *CNN*, October 14. Retrieved from http://business.blogs.cnn.com

Wilcox, D., and Cameron, G. (2007). *Public relations today: Strategies and tactics* (8th ed.). Boston, MA: Pearson.

Woods, R. (2010). Piñera losing environmental credentials as Endesa Seeks power in Patagonia. Bloomberg, August 14. Retrieved from www.bloomberg.com

Workers Vanguard No. 970 (2010). The Chilean miners and Pinochet's murderous legacy, December 3. Retrieved from www.icl-fi.org/

Yang, J. (2010). From collapse to rescue: Inside the Chile mine disaster. Thestar.com, October 10. Retrieved from www.thestar.com/

Yaxley, H. (2010). An international view of crisis management of the Chile mine disaster. PR Conversations, October 14. Retrieved from www.prconversations.com/

Zoda, S. (2007). In D. Wilcox and G. Cameron (Eds.), *Public relations today: Strategies and tactics* (8th ed.). Boston, MA: Pearson.

VIEWS FROM AN EXPERT

CLARKE CAYWOOD

Professor Clarke Caywood is director of the Graduate Program in Public Relations and past chair of the Department of Integrated Marketing Communications at Medill School at Northwestern University, United States. He teaches graduate classes in crisis management, communications management, marketing and public relations. Professor Caywood is editor of the best selling Handbook of Strategic Public Relations & Integrated Communications *(McGraw Hill, 1997) and has published numerous articles and book chapters on advertising and marketing. He was named Educator of the Year by the Public Relations Society of America in 2002–2003.*

A key issue in crisis management is how the corporation, NGO, or government agency responds. It is imperative that a leader in the organization respond. It is important that the organization "be out front" with a message that represents its values and concern. In work reported at http://jimc.medill. northwestern.edu/JIMCWebsite/2003/caywood.pdf with my professional colleague Hud Englehart, we outlined the responses that leaders must consider for a crisis. It is also useful to know that the responses can often be planned ahead so that there are no delays when time is critical. Naturally each crisis demands careful planning and implementation, but the following seven steps may be helpful for the crisis team. Each step contains some language that might be used by leaders in various crisis situations. This process should not be so mechanistic that the public or the press see you following a script. The intent is to provide the crisis team with a beginning point of planning long before a crisis occurs.

Respond—Some communication, even limited, is necessary to be transparent and avoid the appearance of indifference: "Today, we were told that our company would be . . ." Most responses to most types of crisis can be anticipated and pre-checked within the company hierarchy and attorney for permission to release in advance of the emergency.

Regret—Some form of human concern must be communicated with or without accepting responsibility even if the facts are not fully known: "We regret the harm caused to our customers and their families by our product . . ."

Resolution—Some promise must be stated to insure that the specific or general event is being investigated and some action is being taken to solve a problem. "We are shutting down the plant."

Restitution—As the crisis unfolds and facts are known; the message must be conveyed that the organization is able and willing to "make good" to those harmed even if the promise is simply one that meets the normal warrantee and guarantees of the products or services. Again, planning ahead may help the process move quickly with regulatory agencies, lawyers and investors.

Reform—As the facts are gathered and known, some honest promise of action that will prevent any reoccurrence must be stated. "We have found that currently accepted industry and regulatory standards are not sufficient to protect our employees; we are improving our program . . ."

Responsibility—At some time in the midst of or after a crisis someone (a single leader in the company) and the company must accept responsibility for either the specific event or for a management process that failed to prevent the crisis. "As CEO of this firm I accept that it was my responsibility to ensure that the investors of this company were protected . . ." must be stated.

Reputation/Brand Rebuilding—To reestablish the reputation of the organization and its employees, the management must reaffirm its intention to be considered a premier company among leaders in the industry. "Our reputation in business and society will depend on our ability to promise and deliver the safest . . ."

Colombia

"Nothing Will Be The Same; Everything Will Be Better": Floods in Colombia's Atlántico State

Jaime S. Gómez and Soledad Leal

Natural disasters create special crises that have provided many of the frameworks for analyzing and evaluating the way in which organizations, especially governments at the local, state, and national levels, have managed (or mismanaged) crises and emergency communication strategies. This case study examines the framing of the crisis communication strategy and tactics of Atlántico State Governor's Office in its response to the Canal del Dique flooding that left thousands of people homeless, destroyed hundreds of acres of crop, killed hundreds of livestock, and caused considerable environmental damage. The scale of the disaster prompted the governor of the Atlántico State, Eduardo Verano, to quickly mobilize emergency resources and to design a plan to address issues of recovery and reconstruction. The data for this study were collected from semi-structured interviews with Sandra Devia, the governor's director of communications and protocol, and with journalists who covered the event for weeks. The study also used observational field trips at the affected sites and at temporary shelters and reviewed newspaper articles about the crisis. The chapter starts with a crisis background followed by the situation analysis. It then concludes by presenting an outcomes assessment and a summary of lessons learned from this experience.

Indeed, the best crisis is the one prevented!

(Barton, 2001, p. 14)

The atmospheric phenomenon known as "La Niña" has been blamed for the weather pattern that caused severe floods in Australia, Africa, Asia, and South America during 2010 and early 2011. Colombia, located at the northwest tip of South America, suffered an unusual rainy season during the last three months of 2010. The loss of lives—more than 300 people—and the enormous economic damage, estimated in the billions of dollars, forced the government to declare a national disaster in 28 of the 32 departments (states) and develop a crisis management strategy with three basic phases: first, to save lives; second, to provide humanitarian aid; and third, to reconstruct. One of the most affected areas was the Atlántico State, situated in northern Colombia in the Caribbean basin (see Figures 7.2 and 7.3) where a breach in the levees of the Dique Canal created a serious institutional crisis.

Figure 7.2 Map of South America, showing the location of Colombia and Atlántico State.

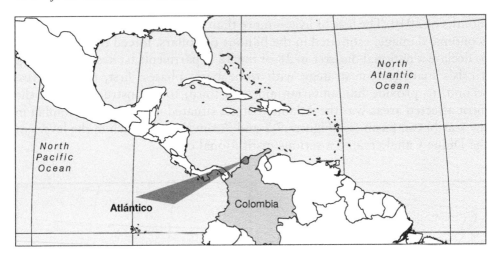

Figure 7.3 Atlántico State.

"Nothing will be the same; everything will be better" was the succinct phrase that a young girl, living in a shelter for the flood victims, wrote over a drawing she made when the children at the shelter were asked to make drawings about their experiences during the flood and their vision of the future. The phrase and drawing (see Figures 7.4 and 7.5), depicting a happier past, a sad present, but a hopeful future, came to the attention of the governor of the Atlántico State, Eduardo Verano, and his communication team. The crisis communication management team decided to use the phrase as a key message of hope, recovery anticipation, and also as an implicit reference to the fact that disasters offer the opportunity for rebuilding a damaged community into a buoyant one if adequate resources and investments are brought into the affected area. Ulmer et al. (2007) note that "focusing on renewal is a way of making sense of a crisis by revealing the crisis-induced opportunities"(p. 132).

Crises and Natural Disasters

A crisis is an event that presents a major threat to an organization and its stakeholders. Crises have the potential to disrupt organizational operations and inflict damage in three basic areas: public safety, financial, and reputation and image (Barton, 2001; Coombs 2007). Gonzalez-Herrero and Pratt (1996) assert that every crisis has a life cycle that can be influenced and that the best strategy to avoid negative media exposure is to "engage in symmetrical, reputation-enhancing, socially responsible activities" (p. 80). Farazmand (2007) states that "crises are borne out of short chains of events, often unpredicted and unexpected, but they develop with dynamic and unfolding events, over months, days, hours, or even minutes" (p. 150). Natural disasters, such as floods, fall within this category of often unpredicted and unexpected events. They usually produce crises that impact all aspects of the community's life, causing emotional and physical traumas among the victims. In an ideal scenario, crisis and disaster management prevention, planning, and preparation should be of high priority on institutional and policy agendas but because they are low-probability events—low incidence and high impact—planning and policy are given inadequate resources, although a response to the crisis may place a large demand on available resources (McDonnel and Drennan, 2006; Williams, 2008).

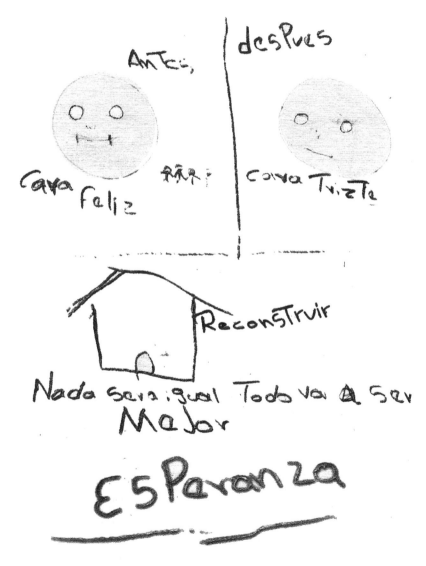

Figure 7.4 Young girl's drawing.

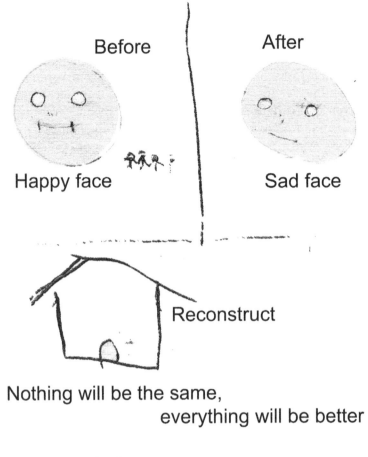

Before

After

Happy face

Sad face

Reconstruct

Nothing will be the same,
everything will be better

Hope

Figure 7.5 Young girl's drawing translation.

The breach in the Dique Canal was considered by the state government as a natural disaster and it was attributed to torrential rainfalls that affected the area in the preceding months. However, some residents of the affected communities attributed the incident to human error, mainly, the improper maintenance of the canal and irrigation procedures by one or more land tenants adjacent to the canal. Like hurricane Katrina, to which experts have compared the Atlántico flood, the Dique Canal event was most likely owing to a combination of both natural (excessive rains) and technological (improper maintenance and irrigation methods) factors (Buitrago, 2011). This is important for disaster researchers must be able to distinguish natural from technological disasters in terms of approaches to response, practices, policies, and ultimately to the assignment of blame. As Williams (2008) states:

Briefly, natural disasters have long been accepted as "acts of God" whilst technological ones are attributed to human error or a technical failure. More nuanced distinctions now suggest that natural disasters tend to include damage to the built environment and have legitimate victims, garnering government response . . . In contrast, technological disasters are usually less visible, contaminating the biophysical environment often without warning, and they fail to follow a clear path of specific stages while also delaying any recovery.

(Williams, 2008, p. 1120)

Natural disasters create special crises that have provided many of the frameworks for analyzing and evaluating the way in which organizations, especially governments at the local, state, and national levels, have managed (or mismanaged) crises and emergency communication strategies. Furthermore, research conducted in the wake of hurricanes Katrina and Rita found that most Public Relations professionals representing local, state, health, nonprofit, education, and corporate organizations, were unprepared to cope with these catastrophic events (Lundy and Broussard, 2007). Globally, there are various examples that illustrate how some governments are more prepared than others to manage calamities or crises.

United States

Hurricane Katrina hit a large region in the Gulf of Mexico on August 29, 2005, killing almost 2,000 people and causing damages in excess of 125 billion dollars. Louisiana was the hardest hit with about 1,500 people killed, most of them residents of New Orleans. Katrina, considered by many experts in the crisis communication field as a "grand failure" in emergency management (Farazmand, 2007, p. 150; Garnett and Kouzmin, 2009), has been, and continues to be, the subject of a vast array of studies that analyze the federal government's performance under many perspectives and theoretical frameworks. Gecowets and Marquis (2005) focused on response time frames and activities by the military; Spence et al. (2007) surveyed Katrina evacuees and findings indicated differences in crisis preparation and in information-seeking patterns on the basis of race. Boin et al. (2010) researched the Bush administration's response to analyzing crisis management, political leadership, and blame game. Liu (2007) used image repair theory discourse to examine President Bush's speeches and their effectiveness in trying to repair his image after Katrina.

Crisis communications during natural disasters have also been the subject of much research and criticism by scholars and public relations practitioners across the globe. Following is an overview of some cases in Asia and Latin America.

Japan

In Japan, the 1995 Kobe earthquake killed more than 6,000 people, caused an estimated US$100 billion in economic losses and enormous damage to buildings and infrastructure, and sent about 300,000 residents to shelters and relief centers. The Japanese government's response to the earthquake was widely criticized for being too slow, and its lack of preventive and preparation planning was also criticized. Tierney and Gotz (1997) attribute this unpreparedness to the fact that the earthquake occurred in a zone where seismic activity was not a major concern for the government or the general population. If anything, it was in the Tokai region, located 50 miles southwest of Tokyo, where a major earthquake was (and still is) anticipated. They also claim that the earthquake illustrated the need to establish effective ways during an emergency of communicating with the public to disseminate information relevant to transportation and other emergency services. Taguchi (1995) points out that, although the earthquake was a natural and unavoidable disaster, the absence of a public relations mentality in the government "caused a second, avoidable disaster for Japan's relationships with the international community and its citizenry" (p. 31). In the end, the lack of a crisis management strategy tarnished the government's image.

Hong Kong

In Hong Kong, SARS (severe acute respiratory syndrome) created a major health crisis in 2003. The epidemic infected about 1,800 residents and took the lives of 300 people. The handling of the emergency by the Hong Kong government was considered a major crisis mismanagement by media and citizens alike. Lee (2007) asserts that the government's handling of media was highly secretive, denying the widespread reach of the disease, and with most of its efforts geared toward minimizing media scrutiny. In addition, the secretary of health accused the media of exaggerating the situation and trying to create panic among the population. Furthermore, Lee claims that the inconsistent and anarchic messages coming from different government officials "reflected a lack of control center and the breakdown on the intra-bureaucratic communications among government units" (2007, p. 76). Zhang and Benoit (2009) focus on the issue of government's image restoration strategy. They claim that messages from the health minister, Zhang Wenkang, were not timely or accurate. They conclude that, even though the minister used several image repair approaches, such as denial, minimization, and corrective action, all of his efforts were unsuccessful and he was finally removed from office.

The cases described above have illustrated the failures of crisis communication mismanagement and lack of preventive and preparation planning by state and national governments. However, there have been cases in which governments' responses and strategies to crisis have been successful and have been praised by the public, the media, and public relations practitioners.

China

In 2008, the Sichuan province in China was struck by an earthquake of 8.0 on the Richter scale that killed over 70,000 people, left more than five million homeless and affected more that 45 million people overall. Contrary to the Hong Kong experience, the Chinese government was very open to media inquiry, allowing reporting from the onset of the disaster, and broadcasting live through national television images of the affected area (Fu et al., 2010). The government ordered a rapid deployment of several officials from the Ministry of Environmental Protection, the Ministry of Agriculture, and the China Seismological Bureau, among others, to the disaster zone to perform rescue and recovery operations. Wang (2009) states that "this time, the Chinese government disclosed the disaster and their corresponding reactions by implying the fastest and most proactive crisis communication" (p. 39). Zhao (2009) notes that the *New York Times* gave positive coverage to the military actions in Sichuan and the *Washington Post* praised the Chinese government for its rapid response. Chen (2009) asserts that the Chinese government handling of the Sichuan emergency illustrates how the government has institutionalized its public relations in the area of crisis communication and management with very visible results.

Chile

In Chile, on August 5, 2010, the San José copper mine located in the Atacama Desert, collapsed, trapping 33 miners 2,300 feet below the surface. The story of "Los 33" (the 33), as it became known, attracted global attention through live television broadcasts and the successful crisis communication strategy enacted by the Chilean government became an exemplary case in the public relations field. PR practitioners and scholars all over the world praised the Chilean government for the open communication approach and for its crisis management style that kept families and media informed of the event developments during the whole saga. President Sebastián Piñera showed remarkable leadership and communication skills by "being there," representing the solidarity of the Chilean people, and taking personal responsibility for the rescue operation. Crenshaw (2010) states that the Chilean government's communication strategy during the crisis provided eight lessons in crisis management; high among these were taking responsibility, being transparent, accepting help but maintaining control, and being there. On October 13, millions of viewers across the globe watched on live television how the miners, after 69 days underground, one by one, emerged to the surface to be hugged by the president and then be reunited with their families in a very emotional scene. The los 33 saga had captured the world's attention and, as the drama unfolded into its climax, the safe recovery of all the miners, millions of viewers experienced the happy ending of a "real" reality show.

The Method

This chapter examines the framing of the crisis communication strategy and tactics of Atlántico State Governor's Office in its response to the Canal del Dique flooding. We begin with the crisis background followed by the situation analysis. We then look into the way that tactics were used to implement the strategy and to accommodate the stakeholders, both those affected directly by the flooding and people on the periphery, such as the residents of nearby areas, media, and other agencies involved in relief or recovery operations. We conclude the chapter by presenting an outcomes assessment and a summary of lessons learned from this experience.

Methodologically, this case study has been informed by findings and theories in the preceding literature review and sample cases. The data were collected from semi-structured interviews with Sandra Devia, the governor's director of communications and protocol, and with journalists who covered the event for weeks. The study also used observational field trips at the affected sites and at temporary shelters and reviewed newspaper articles about the crisis. The newspaper articles studied were published between November 30, 2010, when the levees broke, and January 26, 2011, when the breach was sealed, 57 days after it wreaked havoc in the region. We particularly used articles published by *El Heraldo*, the most important local and regional newspaper. Finally, there was also a careful review of the information posted on the website of the Atlántico State government, which dedicated most of its content to the Dique Canal crisis.

As a framework for analysis we use Timothy Coombs's situational crisis communication theory (2007) because it provides a set of organizational best practices to be carried out during the three phases of a crisis communication management process: pre-crisis, crisis response, and post-crisis. We focus on the first two phases, pre-crisis and crisis response, because, at the time of this writing, plans for recovery, reconstruction, assistance, and residents' return to evacuated areas had just begun to be implemented. The pre-crisis phase is concerned with prevention and preparation processes. The crisis response phase presents the Atlántico State government's strategy and tactics used to face the emergency.

Background of the Crisis

On November 26, 2010, a breach in a levee of the Dique Canal, Atlántico State, in Northern Colombia, caused a major flood that covered five towns in water and forced the evacuation of thousands of people. Although there was no loss of lives, the event became a major crisis for the state government and the residents of a large area known as the South Cone of the Atlántico State (Figure 7.6). The towns with the most severe damage were Santa Lucia, Campo de la Cruz, El Suan, Manati, Candelaria, and Repelón (Figure 7.7).

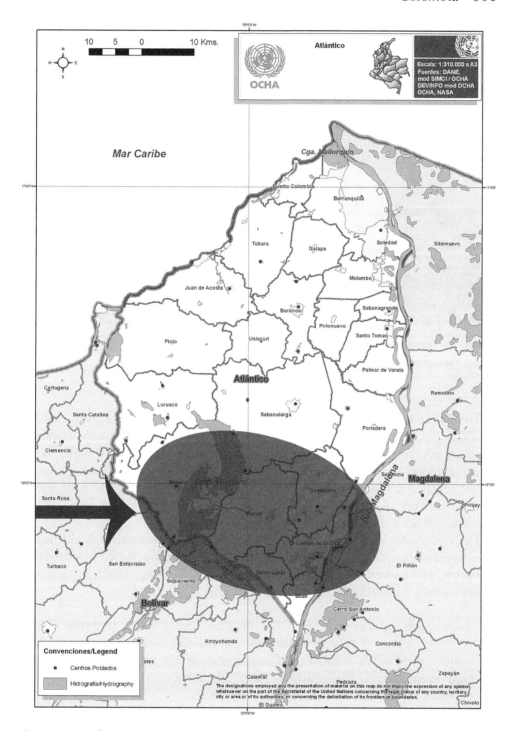

Figure 7.6 Atlántico State's South Cone.

Figure 7.7 Santa Lucia.

Source: Photograph by Halo Osio/Atlántico State Governor's Office of Communication. Reprinted by permission.

The Dique Canal is a cut-off canal from the Magdalena River, which runs north to the Caribbean city of Barranquilla. The breach in the cut-off canal, which flows to the Caribbean port of Cartagena, started as a 10-meter-wide opening; in less than one hour it was 50 meters wide; and in less than 24 hours it had reached a width of 250 meters. It spilled millions of gallons of water into a vast area of the region's coastal plains causing the worst flood of the past five decades (Figures 7.8 and 7.9).

The disastrous breach of the levee, worsened by heavy rainfall, displaced thousands of people, destroyed hundreds of acres of crop, killed hundreds of livestock, and caused considerable environmental damage. The news website "Hispanically Speaking News" (2010) posted:

> To understand the extent of the disaster, every week that the Canal remains ruptured is approximately equivalent to dumping the entire volume of St. Clair, one of the Great Lakes, on the region. It is estimated that even after the rupture is repaired, homes in the area will stay submerged for at least two to four months.

David Brauner, a former deputy director of U.S. Federal Emergency Management Agency (FEMA) who traveled to the area in mid-December as part of an American team of engineers sent to the area to provide support and

Figure 7.8 The breach.

Source: Photograph by Halo Osio/Atlántico State Governor's Office of Communication. Reprinted by permission.

Figure 7.9 The breach and the flood.

Source: Photograph by Halo Osio/Atlántico State Governor's Office of Communication. Reprinted by permission.

advise government officials, expressed the following upon seeing the scene "I'm an old FEMA guy, and I've never seen anything like this." Jeff Bedey, another member of the visiting team and former commander of the U.S. Army Corps of Engineers' Hurricane Protection Office, who was responsible for rebuilding storm-surge defenses around New Orleans after Hurricane Katrina, stated: "The breach is humongous. That isn't going to be an easy animal to close. It's riverine flooding—not a hurricane where the storm comes and goes, and you can deal with it" ("No quick fix in sight for Colombia flood," 2010).

Likewise, Guillermo Toro, the Disaster and Risk Reduction Manager for Oxfam, an international confederation of 14 nongovernmental organizations, based in Oxford, United Kingdom, said: "The image we faced on arrival in the Atlantic zone was one of just roofs above the waterline. Two days later, everything was below water—even the roofs" (Oxfam, 2010) (Figures 7.10 and 7.11).

Thousands of people were forced to live in makeshift camps built by the side of roads and others had to move to shelters established around the affected areas. Canoes, as the type of boats used in the region is called, became the main means of transportation as streets and roads were totally submerged (Figures 7.12 and 7.13).

Figure 7.10 Houses under water.

Source: Photograph by Halo Osio/Atlántico State Governor's Office of Communication. Reprinted by permission.

Figure 7.11 The flooded area.
Source: Photograph by Halo Osio/Atlántico State Governor's Office of Communication. Reprinted by permission.

Figure 7.12 Makeshift tent by the road.
Source: Photograph by Carlos Capella. Reprinted by permission.

Figure 7.13 Canoes on the street.

Source: Photograph by Halo Osio/Atlántico State Governor's Office of Communication. Reprinted by permission.

The scale of the disaster prompted the governor of Atlántico, Eduardo Verano, to quickly mobilize emergency resources and design a plan to address the crisis, which also involved other official agencies such as the Office of Disaster Prevention (CREPAD), Environmental Regional Corporation (CRA), the Dique Corporation (Cardique), and the Río Grande Regional Corporation of the Magdalena (Cormagdalena). These agencies were being harshly criticized and faced potential liabilities for the absence of preventive measures and maintenance of the Canal del Dique and Magdalena River itself.

Given the number of people affected, the economic losses, and the magnitude of the catastrophe, it became clear that the situation required a crisis communication strategy to handle all information needed to cope with the disaster, to organize both the victims and those who were assisting, and to guide and coordinate all rescue and recovery efforts.

Situation Analysis

Floods caused by heavy rains, which raise the Magdalena River water levels, have periodically inundated the Atlántico State. The latest of these floods occurred in 2008 and inundated, but to a much lesser level, the area of the current flooding. This event prompted the recently elected governor, at the time, Eduardo Verano, to design a plan to build an effective defensive infrastructure to protect the towns and agricultural lands adjacent to the river. The defense infrastructure was built during the next two years and was completed in 2010. After completion of the works, the office of the governor organized tours for media representatives and journalists to show the reinforced and new infrastructure. This led to journalists from RCN and Caracol, two national news networks, to point out, 87 days before the rupture of the Canal del Dique, and when other states in the region were registering severe flooding, that the Atlántico State was "shielded or flood-proof." (Sandra Devia, personal communication, January 10, 2011). Indeed, the works had been executed according to a well elaborated plan, designed through collaboration with national, regional, and local agencies, and met all the engineering requirements to prevent floods from rising water levels of the Magdalena river. It seems that all these works may have instilled false confidence within the state and municipal governments, environmental agencies, and the area residents. However, the Dique Canal was not part of the governor's flood protection plan for its maintenance fell under the responsibility of Cardique and Cormagdalena, two environmental agencies created specifically to monitor and maintain the canal and to execute flood preventive projects along the Magdalena River. The Dique Canal broke unexpectedly, at a place where governmental agencies did not see a critical rupture point. Nevertheless, the media indicated that days before the breaking of the levees, mayors of small municipalities such as El Suan and Campo de la Cruz warned that the works were insufficient and called for stronger measures. At the end, part of the blame fell upon Governor Verano, who had recently been rated with a 91 percent approval and then was forced to apply an image repair strategy (Benoit, 1997) based on denial, evasion of responsibility, and offensiveness of event reduction by taking corrective, solution actions, and a constant presence in the affected area.

The Stakeholders

One of the most important tasks in every crisis management scenario and one of the first to be performed is the identification of all stakeholders. All communication actions and messages must target specific groups and depending on the desired effect of the message it must be tailored to that specific audience. Not all people affected by the crisis have the same "stake" and as such the crisis team must consider all audiences in advance (Barton, 2001). In the case of the South Cone crisis, Sandra Devia (personal communication, January 10, 2011) notes that her office was prompt to identity the groups that were affected directly by the tragedy and those others that were likely to play important roles during the crisis response and the aftermath of recovery and reconstruction (Figure 7.14).

Victims. Although no lives were lost, approximately 300 thousand people lost their homes, household goods, livestock, crops, and a life of organized

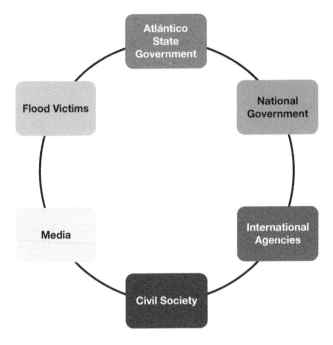

Figure 7.14 Stakeholders' diagram.
Source: Sandra Devia/Governor's Director of Communications.

labor in their communities. They were displaced into crowded, temporary shelters or had to stay with friends and relatives in neighboring villages. Some of them moved to higher ground or by the roads where they built makeshift tents. Victims and journalists interviewed expressed that there were insufficient preventive measures and mechanisms to mobilize and evacuate people despite warnings about possible floods announced by the National Institute of Hydrology, Meteorology, and Environmental Studies (IDEAM). Some journalists pointed out that in the initial stages of the incident neither the state government nor other state agencies were prepared to carry out a census or count of households and people affected because nobody knew who was responsible for that task. Emelina Martínez, a 73-year-old victim (personal communication, January 7, 2011) stated that

> I did not receive aid for several weeks because I was not registered in the census of victims generated by Civil Defense Office. But no one seemed able to fix my problem even though my house was under water and I had lost everything, my pots, food, clothing and household appliances.

Atlántico State Government. As previously stated, the breach in the Dique Canal was an unexpected event for the state government and therefore it was not prepared for such an emergency. Sandra Devia (personal communication, January 10, 2011), the governor's director of communications, explained that

Mr. Verano responded immediately by setting up a strategic committee and convened the so-called Crisis Situation Room, integrated by officials from three committees. Coombs (2007) notes that every organization should have a multifunctional crisis control center that can be used by the crisis management team to discuss the crisis, to collect information, and to brief the media. The crisis room acted as a communication center equipped with television monitors, computers, phones, and other equipment required to monitor information. The committee was kept permanently in session during the emergency. All communications with the media were conducted through a liaison—a one-person voice for the sake of message consistency—that was appointed three days into the emergency. To this effect, Coombs (2007) notes that consistency does simply consist of just one person speaking for the organization but that there should be a coordination of efforts from all official spokespersons and unofficial statements by other members of the organization should be avoided. It is important to note here, that the "being there" attitude of Governor Verano was very noteworthy and received ample recognition and praise by the press, the victims, and the general public.

National Government and the environmental public agencies. The national government was mainly involved through environmental agencies, such as the Office of Disaster Prevention (CREPAD), Environmental Regional Corporation (CRA), Cardique, and the Río Grande Regional Corporation of the Magdalena (Cormagdalena). This was the starting point for criticism after the tragedy when TV journalist Johnny Romero stated: "the Corporation of the Río Grande de la Magdalena, Cormagdalena, assigned in December 2009 the consortium of the Canal del Dique US$185 billion to work strengthening the Dique. Here was a liability." The results show that the plan of strengthening the Dique did not work, or it was done in non-critical points. With the passage of days it became clearer that the public environmental agencies had a lot of responsibility in the tragedy of the South Atlántico state to the point that the President of the Republic, Juan Manuel Santos, announced it would study the restructuring of these bodies to establish how they invest the budgets they manage.

The local and national media. Journalists and experts interviewed for this case agree that although the end result was positive communication management in the early stages of the Dique Canal crisis, the response showed that there was no training or previous contingency plan to handle these emergencies. As Rosario Borrero (personal communication, January 10, 2011), a journalist from *El Heraldo*, pointed out:

> There was much improvising in the beginning, to the point that when you needed to know specific information, the Communications Office referred to the journalist on his team, or to the secretary of the topic, and they did not respond to the phone. When they did, they were upset, saying they were very busy and that taking care of victims of the emergency had priority, without stopping to think about the crucial role that the media played in the tragedy.

Also, the consultant and image management expert German Hennessy (personal communication, January 14, 2011) said that: "Through the media information management I didn't perceive a different media management to what I usually see in normal times. That is, I saw a good job, but not characteristics of crisis communications."

He also noted that the crisis communication process was definitely affected by the following two factors: First, the situation could not be predictable and exceeded all previous experiences; and second, it was difficult to guide the management of information due to the complexity of the situation: number of persons affected, geographic extent, and the impact on various communities, among others.

International NGOs. The effectiveness of communications with NGOs became a controversial issue and a focus of criticism against the state government. Critics claimed that there were insufficient efforts to seek international aid and that most communications were directed toward local and national audiences. The director of regional TV news program "Televista," Humberto Mendieta (personal communication, January 10, 2011), expressed that the governor's communication team concentrated most of the attention on closing the Dique so people could return and reconstruction could begin. In this aspect, the communication goal was accomplished. However, Mendieta notes, most of the humanitarian aid came from domestic agencies while international aid was relatively low if we take into account the social dimension of the tragedy.

Civil society. You can divide the civil society between those directly affected and those indirectly involved by the calamity. The directly hit are the victims, now homeless (these are discussed in a separate section above). The indirectly affected are those who were impacted by the situation: donors who came at the height of Christmas, the inhabitants of the nearest capital city and surrounding municipalities, who were receiving in their streets hundreds of victims and felt threatened by the lack of public safety. In general, all the people in the country were affected at some point: roads, food supplies, public health, and other important social issues. For these people, information and press releases through media were crucial and the only source of information to learn about the enormous dimension of the tragedy.

Goals and Objectives of the Government Communication Plan

Goals

According to Sandra Devia, the governor's Communications Office drew a clear goal:

> To use a comprehensive communications process through the join efforts of all regional sectors in order to coordinate the necessary solidarity work

between the media, private sector and state government. This goal addresses the need to overcome the rainy season emergency, creating an atmosphere of transparency and trust to consolidate a process of recovery and reconstruction of the South of the Atlántico State. (personal communication, January 10, 2011).

To achieve this goal the following objectives were established.

Objectives

- To define information needs and provide logistical support for key media organizations and for the different levels of government agencies involved in emergency care.
- To survey communities affected in order to estimate the socioeconomics effects of the tragedy including a quantitative expression of the number of families and their characteristics.
- To maintain updated information on grants and other forms of aid received from NGOs, civil society, the national government and all stakeholders in this process.
- To instill messages of hope in the community, through the many communication tools and instances.

Strategy and Tactics

Strategy

Using a multiple media platform as the foundation for reaching all stakeholders, the governor's communication team designed a communication structure supported by two important columns as the central strategy:

- the Office of Planning responsible for providing technical data, financial, environmental and social conditions in general;
- the Information Technology Department charged with providing all the technological support to implement the various communication and informational channels with target audiences.

Tactical media

Governor Verano and his crisis communication team defined three basic areas as targets of tactical actions: emergency care, inventory of damages caused by the disaster, and regular operation of administrative and state government affairs. Each area had a subcommittee, which were integrated into a larger strategic committee. To implement the strategy, the communication team used a multimedia platform, including the Internet, intranet, radio, television, newspapers, etc. in order to reach all stakeholders. Coombs (2007) points out the special value of intranets and the Internet. The former provide members of the crisis team who have the proper clearance with access to sensitive information and it also allows for information to be stored or distributed. The Internet is very valuable for communicating with outside stakeholders and to reach media representatives, government officials, or simply to post updated information for all stakeholders including aid information for victims.

Direct communication: face to face, was essential. Almost daily Governor Verano met with various groups and leaders of affected populations to discuss the best ways to overcome the emergency. "Being there" became an important tactic for the governor's reputation management and believability. It also served as an effective vehicle for expressing sympathy and concern for the victims and to reassure them of his personal and institutional commitment to relief and renewal.

Group presentations: The communication team designed a series of Power Point presentations with basic news and information about emergency aid and other specific topics as needed.

Community radio: 18 local radio stations were networked and broadcast information about the emergency. It became an important resource because they broadcast information in each town about emergency aid and actions and also entertainment for children and adults.

The institutional newspaper, which was ordinarily issued bi-monthly, began to be distributed on a weekly basis. It was distributed among the victims to inform about the emergency situation, the procedures for receiving humanitarian aid, and the work being done to overcome the flooding. It also provided official information about efforts by the state government and other agencies to care for their needs and immediate concerns: the education of their children, sustenance for the coming months, and the recovery and reconstruction of the area and their homes.

The website of the state government was specially redesigned to address the emergency and to establish links with social networks Facebook and Twitter, to seek international aid. This is how they contacted Shakira's Pies Descalzos Foundation (Shakira was born in Barranquilla, the capital of Atlántico State), which donated 20 thousand pairs of shoes, six water treatment plants and food for children. In addition, this tool allowed contact with a Colombian host of CNN in Spanish, who in one of his programs interviewed and showed the tragedy of over 158 thousand people in the South of Atlántico State. CNN showed images daily, links to websites organizing humanitarian aid so people would be motivated to help the victims.

Through agreements with the Facebook pages of various media local citizens were encouraged to participate in the great Day of Solidarity with the victims. In the end they collected 15 tons of food, clothing, and cookware.

The communications strategy for delivering more aid for flood engineering works and humanitarian assistance to the victims did not neglect the international community. Through e-mails and personal selected contacts, information on different international institutions such as USAID, the diplomatic mission of South Korea, institutions of Israel, the United States and other countries, was obtained and aid requested.

Thirty-nine videos of the tragedy that were uploaded to YouTube in a month exceeded 121 thousand hits. Videos were also published on CityTV's website and on CNN's iReport, in its daily broadcasts of the U.S. news network. The videos, recorded over a period of time, showed different stages and development of the tragedy. The first videos were carrying the message of what was happening, later how people could help, and finally how the state administration was addressing the needs of all those affected. Internet was also used for mass mailings with links, and live streaming from the breach of the Dique during the days before closing the huge gap.

Besides text messaging through cellular phones, the state government established special agreements with telephone companies to install portable emergency stations so the victims could make long distance calls to relatives and call centers specially set up to handle the emergency.

Television: because all municipalities of the Atlántico state are connected via optical fiber, broadcast stations were installed in various locations and programming related to the event was broadcast live through the Telecaribe regional channel. The governor's communication team made extensive use of live television broadcasts to both provide information to all stakeholders and allow them to see the affected site, and to enhance the governor's image and protect his reputation. The latest generated some criticism by some journalists as most broadcasts focused on visits by the governor or the first lady to the affected area and not so much on the social, economic, and environmental devastation itself. However, some journalists did not recognize that the governor's team was doing its job and journalists had to do theirs. Carlos Toncel (personal communication, January 14, 2011), a television correspondent for RCN, one of the two private Colombian national networks, stated that "information was focused on the governor and his team and not on the tragedy itself. But we can say that it was also our fault." At the end, the governor's image came out stronger as stakeholder's perception of the handling of the crisis and response to it by the governor was very positive.

Outcomes Assessment

One of the special characteristics of natural disasters is the lengthy and complex recovery process that comes after the initial crisis response. The damage inflicted by the breach of the Dique on the communities and lands affected was devastating and for many of the victims life as they knew it will never be the same. Governor Verano's communication strategy and tactics, especially the act of being there, in the affected zone every day for long periods of time, turned out to be very effective and in tune with the victim's expectations of sympathy, compassion, and solidarity. Media messages coming from the governor's communication team were a mix of factual information and hope of an implicit opportunity for the future being better than what the past was because of the government plans for recovery and reconstruction. These messages of hope and permanent presence of the official agencies created a climate of credibility and trust, thus avoiding much feared violent reactions by victims or other stakeholders.

After a natural disaster, the road to recovery is always a bumpy one and requires a complex set of interactions by government, private, and in many cases nonprofit organizations. Although the breach was sealed after 57 days, the South Cone of the Atlántico State still has a long way to go in matters of recovery. The flooded land, three months after the incident, was still being drained and only one-third of the population had been able to return to their houses. The headlines of two stories from *El Heraldo* illustrate the frustration of, and loss of patience by victims with what they perceive as a very slow recovery and assistance process: "Flood victims block the oriental highway" (*El Heraldo*, 2011, February 22) and "Slowness in draining of waters worry flood victims" (*El Heraldo*, 2011, February 24). In the wake of the El Dique disaster, the government of the Atlántico State faces many challenges and in order to address them it must identify and tap traditional and new approaches that may help to speed the recovery and reconstruction process.

Lessons Learned

The training to deal with crises and emergencies should include all personnel involved directly with the Governor's Office and all officials involved in communications management, and not just the members of the technical area for disaster management. The communications office managing external publics should also be involved in this training.

The greatest success, even in the midst of the errors that occurred, was the coherence and consistency in discourse. We must focus and concentrate on one aspect and work on it consistently. In this case, the empathy and solidarity of the Governor Verano with the victims was the focal point and showed positive results, helping to protect his image and credibility.

The operating manual for the Office of Disaster Relief (technical area) should provide information for the management of communications and the links to be established with the Governor's Office communications team and the Office of the Governor (support area). This structure cannot work separately, it has to work synchronically. Also, manuals should be specifically elaborated to cover the needs of the local areas.

Use media in the Emergency Support Team. Through the media the government provided constant information on the availability of aid and the media also served as a bridge to collect information about needs and requested aid by the victims. This converted the media into a semi-official channel making the dissemination of information more efficient and tailored to meet state government needs.

Where necessary, provide the transportation and logistics support for the media. This was done in this case and it greatly contributed to enhancing the crisis management planning process of the state government from the stakeholders' perception. Media had ample coverage of the event and most of the time the news presented the Governor's Office in a very positive way.

Differentiate the operational management of local media from the nation-wide. The availability of the spokesmen and press links must adapt to the times required for live broadcasting of the national channels, while the locals may be scheduled at a different time.

Provide fast instructions through accessible channels to victims. It is important to note that the vulnerable population—low income and the very poor—may have no access to or do not know how to use certain technologies. For this group it becomes necessary to use traditional communication media, such as local radio, loudspeakers, and other face-to-face options such as focus groups and opinion leaders, which are more effective.

Discussion Questions

1. To what factors can be attributed the difference in perception about the management of crisis communications between journalists covering the emergency of South Atlántico and the Communications Team of the Government?
2. If the Government team got the news focused on the presence of Governor Verano instead of the social emergency and its effects, can we say that the strategy of the PR communication team was successful and the media perspective was wrong or incomplete?
3. How do you think the lack of prior training affected the governor's crisis communication team? They recovered from the initial lack of response but worked mostly to ensure the good image of the governor? Is it possible to relate these two processes?
4. How can an organization reach international organizations efficiently to seek humanitarian aid and other types of assistance?

References

Barton, L. (2001). *Crisis in organizations II*. Cincinnati, OH: South-Western College Publishing.

Benoit, W. L. (1997). Image repair discourse and crisis communication. *Public Relations Review*, 23(2), 177–186.

Boin, A., Hart, P., McConnel, A., and Preston, T. (2010). Leadership style, crisis response and blame management: The case of hurricane Katrina. *Public Administration*, 88(3), 706–723.

Buitrago, J. (2011). Controversia pot tuberias en la zona del boquete. *El Heraldo*, February 3. Retrieved from www.elheraldo.com.co/local/controversia-por-tuberías-en-la-zona-del-boquete

Chen, N. (2009). Institutionalizing public relations: A case study of Chinese government crisis communication on the 2008 Sichuan earthquake. *Public Relations Review, 35*(3), 187–198.

Coombs, T. W. (2007). *Ongoing crisis communication: Planning, managing, and responding* (2nd ed.). Thousand Oaks, CA: Sage Publications.

Crenshaw, D. (2010). 8 crisis management lessons from the Chilean mine rescue. *Risk Management, 57*, December. Retrieved from www.rmmag.com/Magazine/Printtemplate.cfm?AID=4220

El Heraldo. (2011). Damnificados bloquearon la Oriental durante 7 horas, February 22. Retrieved from www.elheraldo.co/damnificados-bloquearon-la-oriental-durante-7-horas-9029

El Heraldo. (2011). Lentitud para evacuar aguas preocupa a los damnificados, February 24. Retrieved from www.elheraldo.co/local/lentitud-para-evacuar-aguas-preocupa-los-damnificados

Farazmand, A. (2007). Learning from the Katrina crisis: A global and international perspective with implications for future crisis management. *Public Administration Review, 1*(67), 149–159.

Fu, K., White, J., Chan, Y., Zhou, L., Zhang, Q., and Lu, Q. (2010). Enabling the disabled: Media use and communication needs of people with disabilities during and after the Sichuan earthquake in China. *International Journal of Emergency Management, 7*(1), 75–87.

Garnett, J., and Kouzmin, A. (2009). Crisis communication post Katrina: What are we learning? *Public Organization Review, 9*(4), 385–398.

Gecowets, M., and Marquis, J. (2008). Applying lessons of hurricane Katrina. *Joint Force Quarterly* (48), 70–76.

González-Herrero, A., and Pratt, C. B. (1996). An integrated symmetrical model for crisis-communication management. *Journal of Public Relations Research, 8*(2), 79–105.

Lee, B. K. (2007). The HKSAR government's PR sense and sensibility: Analysis of its SARS crisis management. *Asian Journal of Communication, 17* (2), 201–214.

Liu, B. F. (2007). President's Bush's major post-Katrina speeches: Enhancing human repair discourse theory applied to the public sector. *Public Relations Review, 35*(1), 40–48.

Lundy, L., and Broussard, J. (2007). Public relations in the eye of the storm: Lesson from professional in the wake of hurricane Katrina and Rita. *Public Relations Review, 33*(2), 220–223.

McConnell, A., and Drennan, L. (2006). Mission impossible? Planning and preparing for crisis. *Journal of Contingencies and Crisis Management, 14*(2), 59–70.

No quick fix for Colombia flood (2010). *Contractor City Blog.* Retrieved from http://contractorcity.com/blog/general/no-quick-fix-in-sight-for-colombia-flood

Oxfam (2010). Oxfam gears up its flood aid in Colombia but is in desperate need of funds, October 31. Retrieved from www.oxfam.org/en/pressroom/reactions/oxfam-gears-its-flood-aid-colombia-desperate-need-funds

Spence, P., Lachlan, K., and Griffin, D. (2007). Crisis communication, race, and natural disasters. *Journal of Black Studies, 37*, 539–554.

Taguchi, J. (2005). Japanese officials and PR mentality: Will they learn this time? *Public Relations Quarterly, 40*(1), 31–36.

Tierney, K. J., and Gotz, J. D. (1997). Emergency response: Lessons learned from the Kobe earthquake. *Preliminary Paper no. 260.* Disaster Research Center. University of Delaware.

Ulmer, R., Seeger, M., and Sellnow, T. (2007). Post-crisis communication and renewal: Expanding the parameters of post-crisis discourse. *Public Relations Review*, 33(2), 130–134.

Wang, R. (2009). The relevance of Western crisis communication theories to authoritarian Chinese practices: A study on the SARS epidemic and the Wenchuan earthquake. Master thesis, Norwegian School of Economics and Business Administration, Bergen, Norway. Retrieved from http://docs.google.com/viewer?a=v&q=cache:2EB XrFJ4DTUJ:bora.nhh.no/bitstream/2330/2342/1/Wang%25202009.pdf+renna+ wang+and+The+relevance+of+western+crisis+communication+and+wang+2009 &hl=en&pid=bl&srcid=ADGEESi8UA5FB6WBy2WOGuD1wSe43n1xVAzprt MKLSXKKSmpljxLSngOkI1o8d-K3zDp6r55165pMyl-vsAzKADjSMzSFW DjYyrfiWTitkhdo2g5ePqPe9I3X1jckGV3Tga1aZrKMOf8&sig=AHIEtbTAHuBwI VT6fkhkcz-JxrVi-QqpUw

Williams, S. (2008). Rethinking the nature of disaster: From failed instruments of learning to post-social understanding. *Social Forces*, 87(2), 115–138.

Zhang, E., and Benoit, W. L. (2009). Former minister Zhang's discourse on SARS: Government's image restoration or destruction? *Public Relations Review*, 35, 240–246.

Zhao, H. (2009). Chinese government's role in crisis management-cases studies of three major crises in recent years. Unpublished doctoral dissertation, University of Southern California, Los Angeles.

VIEWS FROM AN EXPERT

FEDERICO SUBERVI-VELEZ

Dr. Federico Subervi-Velez, Ph.D. is professor and director of the Center for the Study of Latino Media and Markets at the School of Journalism and Mass Communication, Texas State University—San Marcos. Since the early 1980s, he has been conducting research, teaching and publishing dozens of works on a broad range of issues related to the mass media, especially Latinos in the U.S. In 2008 he authored and edited the book The Mass Media and Latino Politic. Studies of U.S. Media Content, Campaign Strategies and Survey Research: 1984–2004. *In 2010, he authored a report entitled "An Achilles Heel in emergency communications: The deplorable policies and practices pertaining to non-English speaking populations."*

Catastrophes attributed to nature such as floods and earthquakes are much too often in reality *social catastrophes*: the outcomes of human folly and neglect. Urbanizing a narrow river delta region at the foot of steep mountains known to be prone to massive and sudden downpours; erecting homes and buildings with low quality materials that cannot withstand strong tremors in an earthquake zone; and not inspecting and securing dams that could succumb to extraordinary rainstorms are among the patterns of human folly and neglect that contribute to innumerable *social catastrophes*—not "natural" catastrophes or disasters, and much less "acts of God."

The massive flooding and its consequences resulting from the breach in the Dique Canal in Colombia's Atlántico State was yet another *social catastrophe*. The "writing was on the wall" that the Dique Canal might not withstand massive rainstorms. Yet the signals were ignored or downplayed until the social catastrophe unfolded.

Having bypassed the *preventive* phase of a potential catastrophe, and then being faced with the actual crisis and calamity, the government of Atlántico State seems to have worked rapidly and relatively efficiently to deal with the *mitigation* of the unfolding social catastrophe. Multiple teams and committees were assembled and put into action, and the governor himself and other technical and civic leaders were present at the local level to handle to the best of their means the day-to-day recovery efforts and information flows. What could have been yet another type of crisis—such as that which emerges when all or most communication channels are blocked, censured, or totally centralized to curtail potentially negative information about the authorities, all of which then feeds the flames of fear of the unknown—was turned into a productive crisis management strategy.

The "branding" of the crisis was particularly laudable. "Nothing will be the same, everything will be better" is a white propaganda slogan that served its main purpose quite well: promoting a vision of hope in the midst of utter chaos. Those few words convey an acknowledgement that the flood had affected and would continue to affect the homes, land, social fabric, and culture of the victims. At the same time, the second part of the slogan carried an underlying promise—true or only wishful thinking that it may be—that with good leadership and collaboration the recovery could lead to an even better life. As Gómez and Leal state, the "messages of hope and permanent presence of the official agencies created a climate of credibility and trust thus avoiding much feared violent reactions by victims or other stakeholders." For people who had little or nothing to begin with, the rescuing governor and his team might have well been perceived as "redentores," that is, redeemers; like religious figures redeeming lost souls.

However, the *recovery* phase of any catastrophe is a long one. As the popular Spanish saying goes, "*de lo dicho al hecho hay un largo trecho.*" The road to recovery in the Atlántico State is very long and one for which judgment should be withheld about the government's public relations and communication strategies. That assessment should wait until the *hechos* (facts) show that the recovery is actually happening for the vast majority of the 300,000 victims, and that the economic, social, and cultural structures are again in place for their *sustained* livelihood. Most importantly, the judgment should await until the policies *and practices* are implemented to assure the structure of the Dique Canal, and *preventive communication strategies* that would inform and mobilize to safety populations that might be affected by crises caused by human oversights, or by truly unpredictable natural events.

Section 8

Tying it all Together:
Social Media and Revolution

Crisis and *Kairos*
Social Media Activists Exploit Timing to Support Anti-government Protests

Jacqueline Lambiase

Introduction

Moldova. Iran. Tunisia. Egypt. Saudi Arabia. Sudan. Libya. These nations and their citizens engaged in varying dialogues between 2009 and 2011, resulting in government accommodations of demands, regime change, hard-line responses, or civil war. Frequently, these dialogues occurred in computer-mediated spaces, especially blogs and social media. While all of these engagements existed in online spaces, some burst into protests in public squares and most resulted in violence, both small and large. This chapter primarily traces social media efforts to raise awareness of revolutionary ideas, garner support for these efforts and transform this spirit from digital expression to flesh-and-blood resistance. To a lesser extent, this chapter tracks government efforts to suppress online activism, in order to capture activities of both activists and their opponents. Except for a few recent studies, most crisis communication research has focused on responses by companies and governments, rather than activists who oppose them (for a review of activist-oriented studies, see Coombs and Holladay, 2010.)

Many political scientists, journalists, and their sources have commented on the ways that social media sparked or supported these revolutions and protests (Agence France Presse, 2011; Barry, 2009; Cohen, 2009; Eltahawy, 2011; Rich, 2011; Vick, 2011). One common objective of social media efforts was to ignite and unite the body politic. One widely recognized strategy was timing. Insiders and outsiders of these governments invoked "timing" as being right or wrong. On January 28, 2011, a minister in Israel's government was quoted as saying, "I'm not sure the time is right for the Arab region to go through the democratic process" (Vick, 2011, p. 3). One day later, an Egyptian writer in Great Britain praised "Generation Facebook," which has "kicked aside the burden of history, determined to show us just how easy it is to tell the dictator it's time to go" (Eltahawy, 2011, p. 2). However, Libya's citizens struggled to maintain opposition to their dictator's brutal crackdown, which turned into civil war; the press reported in March 2011 that the opportunity is slipping away, that "time (is) running out" (Reuters, 2011).

Much of crisis communication literature mentions time as an element for communication professionals to ignore at their peril (Baron, 2003; Dilenschneider, 1990; Levine, 2002). In the business culture of Westernized nations, "fast honesty" is a valued principle when compared to stonewalling (Lambiase and Dempsey, 2006), and "tell it all and tell it fast" advice is common among crisis communication experts (Dilenschneider, 1990, p. 169). The "golden hour" after a crisis begins is perceived as the most critical time for an organization's narrative to be established (Baron, 2003, p. 251). In social media and online news media, with constant deadlines and demand for new content, this short time frame for making statements is seen as more imperative than ever. Time, however, is reduced to the ticking of a stopwatch in this conceptual framework. Yet seasoned crisis communicators know that while *time* is of the essence, *timing* is everything. More important than the channel— whether radio, television, newsreel, telephone, voice, mail, newspaper, social media, or copy machine—may be choosing the correct message at the optimum time to communicate the most important information. Known more commonly as analyzing the rhetorical situation, this ancient conceptual framework is also known as *kairos*.

Kairos and Crisis

What is *kairos*? In ancient Greece, rhetoricians used the term *kairos* to describe the cultural circumstances that led to a "provisional truth" (Bizzell and Herzberg, 1990, p. 28). Other scholars (Kinneavy, 1986; Kinneavy and Eskin, 1994) use the work of Aristotle to explore *kairos* as situational context; Smith (1986) describes *kairos* as qualitative time "when something appropriately happens that cannot happen just at 'anytime' . . . an opportunity which may not recur" (p. 4). Lanham (1991) uses the work of sophist Gorgias to explain *kairos* as the means for decision-making, since only time, place, and circumstance matter when no absolute truth exists. When this timing and circumstance fell into place, then a rhetorician who understood *kairos* could use that opportunity to arrange words, images, and delivery for communicating messages.

Across these definitions, *kairos* also indicates understanding of the audience's frames of mind and reference at a particular moment in time. If competing speakers vie for the attention of the same audience, then one of those speakers could gain an advantage by grasping that cultural moment through use of the rhetorical situation, in which timing, message, channel, and style of delivery meet with an audience through *kairos*. Kinneavy and Eskin (1994) use Aristotle's *Rhetoric* to argue that *kairos* may include a crisis situation tinged with emotion. In this circumstance, "those . . . who have been wronged in the past should be feared because 'they are forever on the lookout for an opportunity'" (Kinneavy and Eskin, 1994, p. 138, quoting Aristotle).

Kairos, then, seems especially apt for describing the crisis communication feats used during citizen demonstrations of nations in northern Africa, the Arab world and Eastern Europe, starting in 2009 through 2011. In these disparate nations, citizens gained power through social media, and hierarchies shifted. Hierarchies between major news media and their audiences have been leveled, too. One early social media example in the U.S. occurred when a bystander's cell phone video and student-generated online discussions rivaled major news media for attention during the Virginia Tech shootings of 2007 (Palen et al., 2007).

In much the same way, a few activist groups in Moldova in 2009 crafted messages and scheduled protests, "making" content. A large number of others "moved" this content, sharing it with their networks. Thus, movers are as important, perhaps more important, than the makers of the original content. While some observers called the actions of these movers and makers "Twitter Revolutions," that moniker trivializes the risks, relationship-building, and hard work behind the messaging and planning made visible through social media (Gladwell, 2010, 2011; Rich, 2011; for more on this debate, see Agence France Presse, 2011). Even Twitter co-founder Biz Stone downplays his company's role in the real actions required for revolution (Gross, 2011). Yet there is no doubt that through social media, these political movements were nurtured and enlarged through blogs, Facebook pages, and Twitter messages. Alec Ross, senior innovation adviser for the U.S. Department of State, said social media helped to accelerate revolutions and merged protest efforts across tribal, class, and racial groups (Agence France Presse, 2011).

For this moment of revolutions and protests, *kairos* includes the many voices advocating freedom in social media, competing successfully with one-voice, state-controlled media. As a nation surrounded by revolutions and protests in early 2011, at least one Saudi Arabian official seemed to understand the moment. In an interview with Public Radio International's program *The World*, in early March 2011, Saudi Arabia's minister of information, Abdul Aziz Khoja, said "we have to talk with (young people) in Facebook, in Twitter, and on Youtube. We have to know how they think. They now represent 60 percent of our population and they are the future of our country" (Lynch, 2011).

Saudi Arabia's information minister most certainly did not mean his nation would engage in two-way symmetrical conversation with younger citizens. In fact, many nations responded not by embracing social media, but by blocking access to it. Yet Saudi Arabia's Khoja clearly recognized what that moment in history demanded, that communication with younger Saudis must involve communication within their channels, rather than through his state-owned traditional media. And he clearly recognized a moment that requires words, not weapons. Perhaps he came late to the conversation, but Khoja knew the implications of *kairos*. Like much of rhetorical theory, *kairos* first and foremost demands an understanding of audience needs and desires.

Overview of Social Media's Role During Protests and Revolutions

Social media's contours include the best and worst that computer-mediated communication can offer. Some organizations and people use social media as monologue, as a one-way channel, as a primitive mass media form. In this model, social media can be silencing and authoritative, not unlike traditional mass media; in fact, Twitter serves as a propaganda tool of dictators, such as Hugo Chavez of Venezuela (Rich, 2011). At its best, social media is richly interactive and multidimensional, serving as a network of relationships, voices, and resolve. Activists and revolutionaries of many nations used strategies and tactics from 2009 to 2011 with one *goal* in mind: freedom. The *objective* of some protesters was regime change, pure and simple, while for others, the *objective* was more accommodating government that allowed for free speech and open debate, transparent elections, economic assistance, more jobs, and other demands.

The reactions of these governments ranged from civil war in Libya, to crackdowns and censorship (Moldova, Iran, Sudan), to acquiescence to some demands by the ruling family in Saudi Arabia, to ousters of dictators (Tunisia, Egypt and Libya). The first two types of results—civil war, crackdowns, and censorship—are timeless tactics of totalitarian regimes. The last two results—acquiescence and regime change—illustrate the power of *kairos*. These governments understood some sort of temporal, provisional truth from the many voices calling for freedom, assisted in part through the multiplication of voices and amplification of demands carried in social media.

The following five short case studies of social media usage in Moldova and Iran during 2009, and in Tunisia, Egypt, and Sudan during 2010 and 2011, are based on keyword searches in Google and in LexisNexis Academic using the nations' names plus the words "social media," "Twitter," "Facebook," and "YouTube." In addition, the author collected articles on these revolutions during early 2011 and tweets containing these hashtags: #Tunisia, #Egypt, and #Jan25. To avoid redundant observations about activities used by citizens in all five nations, each short case study focuses primarily on strategies and tactics different from those discussed in the other cases. In this way, saturation occurred so that the variety of social media activities could be discussed, rather than trying to determine which were the most popular or most successful strategies and tactics.

Moldova, April 2009

When communists won a national election in Moldova in spring 2009, young activists organized protests against the long-standing Communist Party, in part using a blog on LiveJournal.com, Facebook postings, tweets, and phone text messaging (Barry, 2009). While Twitter was credited with helping to organize the protests, it was used mainly to keep people outside of Moldova informed of events in the nation's capital, Chisinau, even though Internet access had been curtailed by the government (Cohen, 2009). One of the organizers of ThinkMoldova, Natalia Morar, created a protest movement called "I am not a Communist," describing it on her blog as "six people, 10 minutes for brainstorming and decision-making, several hours of disseminating information through networks, Facebook, blogs, SMSs and e-mails" (Barry, 2009). In speculating about ThinkMoldova's efforts, which turned into a sometimes violent protest with thousands of people, an English-language Twitter user from Moldova attributed it to trust, saying "when you follow somebody, you usually know this person, so you trust this person. It is coming from a real person, not an institution" (Cohen, 2009).

Strategy 1: Involve disparate citizens in a common movement.

Tactic 1: Create a website or blog attached to a movement called "I am not a Communist." Ask for pledges of support, by adding names to a petition or voices within comment sections of websites.

Strategy 2: Keep the outside world informed of protests inside a nation.

Tactic 2(a): Use Twitter messages as testimony, providing eyewitness accounts, photos to outsiders, and links to video.

Tactic 2(b): Use Twitter hashtags (#Moldova) so that others may follow events within that nation.

Tactic 2(c): Use activists in Twitter who can tweet in multiple languages, including English.

Iran, June 2009

Just a few months after Moldovans protested their election results, so too did Iranians after their presidential election on Friday, June 12, 2009. Relying on text messaging and Twitter, supporters of opposition candidate Mir-Hossein Mousavi began to panic when Twitter announced that it would be shut down for maintenance during protests. Many users—including Iranian activists, their supporters worldwide, and the U.S. government—appealed to the U.S.-based company and one of its founders, Biz Stone, to delay maintenance (Gross, 2011). Twitter complied with these requests. In the meantime, Iranian newspapers ran blank spaces where government censorship had occurred (Grossman, 2009).

During the Iranian protests, journalists and pundits offered more testimonials to the power of Twitter over traditional media. *Time* magazine's lead technology writer called it "the medium of the moment" because "it's free, highly mobile, very personal and very quick. It's also built to spread, and fast" (Grossman, 2009). In his analysis, he describes Twitter as "promiscuous by nature: tweets go out over two networks, the Internet and SMS, the network that cell phones use for text messages, and they can be received and read on practically anything with a screen and a network connection" (Grossman, 2009). One of those tweeting and retweeting information about the Iranian protests, "jennyrae," asked Twitter users worldwide to "change ur location timezone to Iran/Tehran (GMT +3:30) make it harder to track Iranians #IranElection" (Latest tweets, 2009). In other ways, protesters stayed ahead of censors and government surveillance by accepting outside dissidents' help. According to *The Times*, "an ad hoc network of volunteer Internet users outside Iran has been creating proxy servers, or false IP (Internet protocol) addresses to reroute online traffic and fox censorship software" (Evans, 2009).

Strategy 3: Build redundancy into the system of communication.

Tactic 3: Use both Twitter and phone text messages for information about timing of protests and events.

Strategy 4: Acknowledge surveillance within social media and protect communicators.

Tactic 4(a): Ask outsiders to help insiders in social media, by establishing false IP addresses, false accounts, and other diversionary actions.

Tactic 4(b): Shut down government computing systems, through the anonymous "hacktivist" network, using denial of service strategies (Proudfoot, 2009).

Tunisia, December 2010 and January 2011

In late 2010, activist bloggers and online videos shared dramatic stories occurring in Tunisia, with little or no coverage in traditional Western print or broadcast media (Hopkins, 2011). One story seemed to capture the brutal essence of daily life in that nation, when on December 17, 2010, a street vendor named Mohamed Bouazizi set himself on fire. About an hour before this act, Bouazizi's fruit and vegetables had been confiscated, followed by a fine, and then he was humiliated or ignored by Tunisian authorities. Following Bouazizi's death in early January 2011 and after four weeks of protests against his government, Tunisian President Zine El Abidine Ben Ali left office, and the nation began the process of writing a new constitution and holding elections.

During those weeks surrounding Bouazizi's death, protesters used Facebook and Twitter to organize and to announce protest locations, but those online actions were not easy. The Committee to Protect Journalists reported that the Tunisian government blocked sites (including access to WikiLeaks), inserted script into Facebook pages to harvest user names and passwords, and arrested bloggers, journalists, and activists (Anderson, 2011). One activist blogger who was arrested was Slim Amamou, who used the geolocation service FourSquare to let his colleagues know that he was at the Ministry of the Interior after his arrest (Malek, 2011). However, despite these government tactics, those using social media "gave us a front seat in this uprising," said London-based Egyptian journalist Mona Eltahawy (Brown, 2011). Eltahawy noted Twitter helped those inside Tunisia, too, when "Tunisians were warning each other of where the regime snipers were, using Twitter" (Brown, 2011).

Strategy 5: Use emotional appeals and storytelling to garner support.

Tactic 5: Provide online stories, testimony, and videos focused on revolution martyrs such as Mohamed Bouazizi or on those arrested such as activist blogger Slim Amamou.

Strategy 6: Use geolocation and digital mapping to track arrests and to chart movement of government snipers, troops, and tanks.

Tactic 6: Publicize arrests and government activities related to snipers, police actions, barricades, and tanks.

Egypt, Summer 2010 and January–February 2011

Kairos seems most apt for explaining communication successes that supported the Egyptian revolution. In June and August 2010, a few thousand people protested the beating to death of Khaled Said, who had been dragged from an Internet café by police for posting videos online about police brutality. This incident was chronicled on a Facebook fan page called "We are all Khaled Said" and, later that fall, it was linked to more stories of police brutality ("Egypt police," 2010; see Figure 8.1). These publicity campaigns were then followed by Tunisia's successful use of nonviolent tactics in early 2011. At that moment, new and long-time activists seized on the "collective hope" that permeated Egyptian society after the Tunisian success in January 2011, and online organizers and activists each were asked to "bring ten non-connected people" to the protests (Graham-Felsen, 2011). "People who are on Twitter or Facebook in Egypt are often active in various other ways" and these influencers included Wael Ghonim, a Google employee, and Alaa Abd el Fattah, a long-time blogger who has been imprisoned for advocating for human rights (Connelly, 2011).

Using Facebook—plus Google Docs with guidelines and collateral for protests, e-mailing lists, and much offline planning—a massive demonstration

Figure 8.1 From YouTube, "Egypt police tortures Ahmed Saaban to death." Ahmed
Saaban's death was publicized by Mohamed Abdelfattah, an Egyptian
blogger from Alexandria who made and posted to YouTube a video
featuring interviews with Saaban's family.

against the government was set for January 25, 2011, led in part by Ghonim,
who had created the "We are all Khaled Said" fan page and who was later
arrested and released, just before Hosni Mubarak's resignation (Graham-
Felsen, 2011; see Figure 8.2). Because of the combination of robust offline
activists' networks and online organization starting in late January, protests
continued despite the government's shutdown of Internet and phone services
for several days, until Mubarak's resignation February 11.

Many other political, religious, and cultural efforts in Cairo's Tahrir Square
helped to bridge differences and were featured online, such as Egyptian Rami
Issam's "#Jan25 Tahrir," one of several protest anthems either performed in
the square or uploaded to YouTube, or both ("Protest singer," 2011; "Rami,"
2011). A popular retweet from January 27, 2011, also demonstrates this
solidarity: "Egyptian Christians said they will guard the Muslims from the
police while they are on Friday Pray. Amazing solidarity. #Egypt #Jan25."

Strategy 7: Gain momentum and support for risky internal protests by
connecting them to successful events in other nations.

Tactic 7: Use blogs, video, and tweets to share the stories from Tunisia and
to showcase the successes that are possible.

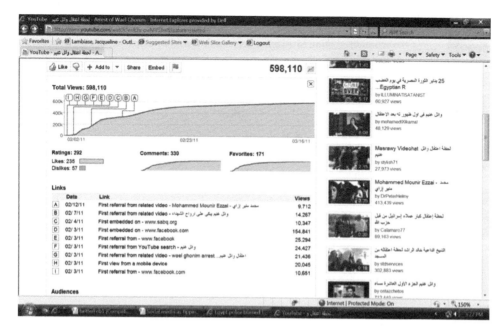

Figure 8.2 YouTube analytics for the "Arrest of Wael Ghonim." Web analytics
from YouTube show the numbers of views of the video growing from the
tens of thousands on February 3, 2011, to more than 150,000 later that
day after the video was embedded within Facebook. As of early March
2011, nearly 600,000 people had viewed the video.

Strategy 8: Publicize patterns of brutality and human-rights' abuses to national
and international audiences.

Tactic 8: Create videos and blog postings about stories of people's arrests,
killings by police, and experiences of torture, and seed them into social
networks and video-sharing sites, which may be viewed by citizens and
traditional media.

Strategy 9: Reach out to those not connected to online activism.

Tactic 9: Invite protesters who are not online to attend a protest or to provide
support in other ways, through monetary donations and support for activism.

Strategy 10: Bind protesters together in a common cause.

Tactic 10: Feature protest songs and other signs of solidarity, such as common
slogans, by offering online videos or downloadable collateral. Create stories,
tweets, and photographs that feature examples of solidarity.

andrewbonar Andrew Bonar
Everything __is_____ ____ ____fine ___ _ ____ love. ____ _____ the ___ Egypt ____
____ government __ #jan25 #Egypt #censorship 27 Jan Top Tweet

Khaledtron Khaled Akbik
This is #Epic, Fox News has no idea where Egypt is on a map:
http://plixi.com/p/73294801 #jan25 #egypt #USA (via @cheeseycelt)
30 Jan Top Tweet

ChristinaTwal Christina Twal
Retweeted *by Adi_Khair*
written on one banner: "،مبارك لقد جعلتنا نحب بعضنا ب " or "Mubarak, you made
us love each other" #Egyptians #Jan25

LOV3RENI Reni
Inspiring RT @jay2the9: "I dnt need Obama I dnt need Clinton,I will free Egypt
with my mom&dad" – Young Child at Tahrir Square #egypt #jan25

weddady weddady
Retweeted *by CineversityTV*
RT @acarvin 100's of thousands of protesters @ Tahrir "Freedom! Freedom!
Freedom! May God make it happen! May it be tonight!" #jan25

dougvought Doug Vought
ما اجمل الحرية #egypt #jan25

ramiar ramiar
Retweeted *by Jethro_Aryeh*
BBC says Mubarak will announce he will not run for sept elections, but he wants
to stay until then #jan25, #cairo, #egypt

Pharaonick Nick Rowlands
RT @arabian_babbler Ahmed Moor, Cairo: The people here determined & have
reached point of no return http://tinyurl.com/48er6yc #Egypt #Jan25

LaraABCNews Lara Setrakian
The crowd in Tahrir Square is going wild anticipating reported Mubarak speech
tonight #Jan25

ReemAbdellatif Reem Abdellatif
Egypt State TV: Mubarak to make statement shortly #Jan25 #Egypt

AfriNomad Amine
Retweeted *by usSup*
1st they say they won't run in next elections. Then they offer to organize early
elections. Then they flee to S. Arabia #Jan25

medeabenjamin Medea Benjamin
Retweeted *by joscottcoe*
The US gives $1.3 billion a year to #Egypt. Tell the US govt: Stop funding the
Mubarak regime now! http://bit.ly/fMEcC5 #Jan25

noornet Noor Al-Hajri
RT @HaninSh: Awww must be feeling left out now. its now Mu without Barack!
RT @JawazSafar: Obama is officially not supporting mubarak #Jan25

Figure 8.3 #Jan25 Twitter search on February 1, 2011, with top tweets from prior
days included.

Sudan, February 2011

Activists in northern Sudan arranged protests against the government in February 2011 through Facebook and text messaging by cell phone, according to Voice of America reporter Alsanosi Ahmed and Agence France Presse (Voice of America, 2011; Martelli, 2011). Ahmed also reported newspapers had been censored, with journalists and other media employees arrested, as well as protesters. Some activists were reported missing. In addition, security forces used social media to trick people about a protest location, so that "when people went there to protest they saw the security forces arresting them immediately when they arrived in the area" (Voice of America, 2011). "Future protests will probably be planned over different channels," Ahmed reported.

Strategy 11: Keep protesters' communication networks safe from disinformation of the ruling state.

Tactic 11: Protect planning by shifting channels of communication away from open social media.

Lessons Learned

The outcomes of these citizen protest movements differed by nation, but the stunning successes in Tunisia and Egypt demonstrate that social media efforts make a good partner for old-fashioned revolution when the circumstances and timing are right. Even lesser successes in nations such as Moldova and Iran show that social media offer a robust counterpoint to government suppression of dissent and communications technology. The lessons of other nations, such as Sudan or Libya, are less clear, since real-life protests were met with overwhelming shows of state power. Perhaps social media in those states can play a part in maintaining resistance until the right time, until *kairos*. In the case of Saudi Arabia and less brutal regimes, even the threat of prolonged demonstrations and social media campaigns can be an effective way to open dialogue and to gain concessions. In these latter examples, *kairos* may mean waiting, patience, and issues management for activists.

Another lesson may be the mental socialization that occurs in social media, where discourse is free. When people are able to operate under conditions when discourse is democratic, they are in effect practicing for their own projected futures. In Jürgen Habermas's reformulation of Robert Alexy's rules of reason, discourse is democratic when:

- every subject with the competence to speak and act is allowed to take part in a discourse;
- everyone is allowed to question any assertion whatever;
- everyone is allowed to introduce any assertion whatever into the discourse;

- everyone is allowed to express his [sic] attitudes, desires, and needs; and
- no speaker may be prevented, by internal or external coercion, from exercising his [sic] rights as laid down in the first guidelines (from "Discourse Ethics," in Herring 1993, p. 1).

In these free frontiers of computer-mediated communication, people may get used to speaking their minds. Indeed, Twitter, Facebook, and YouTube may be training grounds for the discourse required in developing democracies. Ong (1981) discusses this socialization of people in agonistic situations, who not only make themselves known to their adversaries, but who also "call their own attention to their own existence" (p. 203). Part of attending to their own existence may include attending to and getting used to their own democratic voices, and social media gave these activists space and time for this attention and nurturing.

In terms of *kairos*, it may be claimed as a more suitable explanation than Malcolm Gladwell's "tipping point," an explanation that even Gladwell himself has rejected. The tipping point for these events, using Gladwell's formulation, might be the combination of the right kinds and numbers of citizens plus their networks in social media (Gladwell, 2000). In this scheme, influential people collectively asserted their power when communicating within these networks, which were cobbled together before and during crises by activists, opinion leaders, and revolutionaries.

Yet, Gladwell had already disavowed social media's power to influence revolutions, just a few months before Egypt's 25 January Revolution. In a *New Yorker* article in October 2010, Gladwell discounted so-called "Twitter revolutions," writing that while social media make expression easier, it is "harder for that expression to have any impact. The instruments of social media are well suited to making the existing social order more efficient. They are not a natural enemy of the status quo" (Gladwell, 2010). After his article was published, Gladwell was criticized by columnists and bloggers, and his comments received more scrutiny during the December 2010–January 2011 demonstrations in Tunisia (Rich, 2011; for review, see Case, 2011). After the 25 January Revolution in Egypt, Gladwell responded to critics once again: "People with a grievance will always find ways to communicate with each other. How they choose to do it is less interesting, in the end, than why they were driven to do it in the first place"(Gladwell, 2011).

Yale genocide scholar Ben Kiernan disagrees with Gladwell's insistence that social media didn't matter much to these protests and revolutions:

> Whatever the grievances, a key political issue determining the outcome is the scale of mobilization. Other things being equal, additional or faster means of communication (social media offer both) will make mass actions easier and more likely, if not broader-based and more effective as well.
>
> (quoted in Case, 2011)

Certainly, social media provided crucial support for activists in Moldova, Iran, Tunisia, and Egypt. Yet, equating any one activity as the make-or-break happening in these revolutions shortchanges activists' hearts, minds, and spirits. A tipping point of any kind places too much emphasis on just one factor that makes a difference. *Kairos*, as a rhetorical strategy, simply recognizes that many situational and cultural elements must be aligned in time, and that all of these elements together work to enable the most proper and most effective persuasive communication.

In terms of modern issues management theory, *kairos* might be most akin to the catalytic model, through which activists gain power. This model "is rooted in legitimacy, the perception that something is appropriate," and in terms of the time element, this model also seeks to "build urgency by creating pressure to take action" (Coombs and Holladay, 2010, p. 93). In future research, scholars will certainly explore these revolutions in terms of catalytic theory, diffusion theory, or any number of other political, historical, economic, sociological, anthropological, or communication models. Certainly, studying the strategies and tactics used by activists, and sharing those activities, is important to the discipline of crisis communication and to an understanding of *kairos*. Yet unknowns will remain. "How a revolution comes to be is a mystery to me," says Twitter founder Biz Stone. "It's important to credit the brave people that take chances to stand up to regimes. They're the star" (Gross, 2011). Twitter, says one of its founders, is simply in a supporting role.

Discussion Questions

1. Why do you think so few scholars have studied crisis communication from the point of view of activists?
2. What is social media's role in revolutions and protests? Is it a neutral tool? Or does it demonstrate democratic or totalitarian qualities? If you choose one, explain why.
3. Explain your own understanding of *kairos*? Can you think of a crisis communication situation in which *kairos* played a part, when an organization decided to communicate at exactly the right time or cultural moment, or perhaps at the wrong time?

References

Agence France Presse. (2011). Social media, cellphone video fuel Arab protests. *France 24 International News*, February 22. Retrieved from www.france24.com

Anderson, N. (2011). Tweeting tyrants out of Tunisia: Global Internet at its best. *Wired*, January 14. Retrieved from www.wired.com

Baron, G. R. (2003). *Now is too late: Survival in an era of instant news.* Upper Saddle River, NJ: FT Prentice Hall.

Barry, E. (2009). Protests in Moldova explode, with help of Twitter. *The New York Times*, April 7. Retrieved from www.nytimes.com

Bizzell, P., and Herzberg, B. (1990). *The rhetorical tradition: Readings from classical times to the present.* Boston, MA: Bedford Books of St. Martin's Press.

Brown, J. (2011). Tunisia's upheaval resonates in Arab world. *PBS News Hour*, January 17. Retrieved from www.pbs.org/newshour

Case, D. (2011). Is Malcolm Gladwell wrong on Egypt and social media? *The Global Post*, February 19. Retrieved from www.globalpost.com

Cohen, N. (2009). Moldovans turn to Twitter to organize protests. *The Lede: A New York Times Blog*, April 7. Retrieved from http://thelede.blogs.nytimes.com/2009/04/07/moldovans-turn-to-twitter-to-organize-protests/

Connelly, P. (2011). Curating the revolution: Building a real-time news feed about Egypt. *The Atlantic*, February. Retrieved from www.atlanticmonthly.com

Coombs, W. T., and Holladay, S. J. (2010). *PR strategy and application: Managing influence.* Oxford, UK: Wiley-Blackwell.

Dilenschneider, R. L. (1990). *Power and influence: Mastering the art of persuasion.* New York: Prentice Hall.

Egypt police on trial for brutality. (2010). *Al Jazeera English*, July 27. Retrieved from http://english.aljazeera.net/news/

Eltahawy, M. (2011). We've waited for this revolution for years. Other despots should quail: Change is sweeping though the Middle East and it's the Facebook generation that has kickstarted it. *The Guardian*, January 29. Retrieved from www.guardian.co.uk

Evans, J. (2009). Iranian dissidents go online to defy government censors. *The Times*, June 16. Retrieved from www.timesonline.co.uk

Gladwell, M. (2000). *The tipping point: How little things can make a big difference.* New York: Little Brown.

Gladwell, M. (2010) Small change: Why the revolution will not be tweeted. *The New Yorker*, October 4. Retrieved from www.newyorker.com

Gladwell, M. (2011). Does Egypt need Twitter? *The New Yorker*, February 2. Retrieved from www.newyorker.com

Graham-Felsen, S. (2011). How cyber-pragmatism brought down Mubarak. *The Nation*, February 11. Retrieved from www.thenation.com

Gross, T. (2011). Twitter's Biz Stone on starting a revolution. *Fresh Air*, February 16. [Radio broadcast]. Philadelphia, PA: WHYY. Retrieved from www.npr.org

Grossman, L. (2009). Iran protests: Twitter, the medium of the movement. *Time*, June 17. Retrieved from www.time.com

Herring, S. (1993). Gender and democracy in computer-mediated communication. *Electronic Journal of Communication*, 3(2). Retrieved from http://ella.slis.indiana.edu/~herring/ejc.txt.

Hopkins, C. (2011). Traditional media abandon Tunisia to Twitter and YouTube. *ReadWriteWeb*, January 12. Retrieved from www.readwriteweb.com

Kinneavy, J. L. (1986). *Kairos*: A neglected concept in classical rhetoric. In J. D. Moss (Ed.), *Rhetoric and praxis: The contribution of classical rhetoric to practical reasoning* (pp. 79–105). Washington, DC: Catholic University Press.

Kinneavy, J. L. and Eskin, C. R. (1994). *Kairos* in Aristotle's *Rhetoric. Written Communication*, 11(1), 131–142.

Lambiase, J., and Dempsey, J. M. (2006). A scuffle, a stonewall, and a season: Football superstar fights off the field but his team isn't talking. In M. Land and W. Hornaday (Eds.), *Contemporary Media Ethics* (pp. 365–381). Spokane, WA: Marquette.

Lanham, R. (1991). *A handlist of rhetorical terms* (2nd ed.). Berkeley, CA: University of California.

Latest tweets on fallout from Iran's election. (2009). *Time*, June 15. Retrieved from www.time.com/

Levine, M. (2002). *Guerrilla PR wired: Waging a successful publicity campaign online, offline, and everywhere in between*. New York: McGraw-Hill.

Lynch, L. (2011). All quiet in Saudi Arabia? *The World* [Radio broadcast], March 2. Retrieved from www.theworld.org/2011/03/all-quiet-in-saudi-arabia/

Malek. (2011). Blogger, Global Voices contributor Slim Amamou arrested today. (Tran. Jillian C. York). *Global Voices Advocacy*, January 7. Retrieved from http://advocacy.globalvoicesonline.org/2011/01/07/tunisia-blogger-slim-amamou-arrested-today/

Martelli, S. (2011). 12 journalists held in Sudan crackdown: opposition. *Agence France Presse*, February 3. Retrieved from www.google.com/hostednews/afp

Ong, W. J. (1981). *Fighting for life: Contest, sexuality, and consciousness*. Ithaca, NY: Cornell University Press.

Palen, L., Vieweg, S., Sutton, J., Liu, S. B., and Hughes, A. (2007). Crisis informatics: Studying crisis in a networked world. Third International Conference on e-Social Science, Ann Arbor, Michigan, October 7–9. Retrieved from http://citeseerx.ist.psu.edu/viewdoc/download?doi=10.1.1.113.5750&rep=1&type=pdf.

Proudfoot, S. (2009). Social media breaks through Iran censorship. *National Post* (Canada), June 16. Retrieved from www.nationalpost.com/news/story.html?id=1702462

Protest singer brutally tortured. (2011). *Freemuse: Freedom of Musical Expression*, March 11. Retrieved from www.freemuse.org/sw40798.asp

Rami Issam's [revolution singer] testimony of his torture by Egyptian army. (2011). *Alive in Egypt* [Blog], March 10. Retrieved from http://egypt.alive.in/

Reuters (2011). As world talks, time running out for Libya opposition. *Al Arabiya News Channel*, March 13. Retrieved from www.alarabiya.net/articles/2011/03/13/141373.html

Rich, F. (2011). Wallflowers at the revolution. *The New York Times*, February 5. Retrieved from www.nytimes.com/2011/02/06/opinion/06rich.html

Smith, J. E. (1986). Time and qualitative time. *Review of Metaphysics*, 40, 3–16.

Vick, K. (2011). Israel has faith Mubarak will prevail. *Time*, January 28. Retrieved from www.time.com

Voice of America News (2011). Journalists arrested as crackdown continues in Khartoum, February 3. Retrieved from www.voanews.com/english/news/africa/Journalists-Arrested-as-Crackdown-Continues-in-Khartoum-115210639.html

VIEWS FROM AN EXPERT

RICHARD WELLS

Richard Wells, Ph.D. is professor emeritus at University of North Texas and visiting professor at the Naval Postgraduate School. His seminars/ workshops on strategic communications; public relations; leadership; interagency processes; and coping with crises, terrorism, and national security have been in Latin America, Asia, Eastern Europe, Africa, and the Middle East.

Jacqueline Lambiase's chapter on the use of social media as a method to garner support for anti-government protests clearly shows how this tool both mirrors communication techniques used for centuries as well as meeting modern cultural standards. It could be argued that the "social media" of the times—pamphlets, newspapers—met the standards of the late 1700s in the American Colonies and helped foment revolution. Certainly, timing is a key factor in successful use of such media.

Another important factor in helping fuel protests is whether there exists a legacy of distrust of the government as a whole or of government agencies. My recent experiences in several nations (democracies) reveal this legacy of distrust as a major obstacle when government agencies attempt to develop transparency, openness, and timeliness of communications. The Moldovan military's multi-year public relations campaign yielded a marked increase in the public's confidence level of the military after a legacy of Soviet-era distrust. However, the Moldovan Communist Party's lack of effective communications lent credence to the social media messages provoking protests.

The Moldovan example points to another important factor that social media can easily exploit in agitating protests: the lack of interagency coordination within governments. Most governments are notoriously inadequate in understanding the importance of coordinated communications. Chile, in contrast, enjoyed great success in the "one-message, many voices" communications campaign complementing the rescue of trapped miners. This success from a coordinated campaign is based on lessons learned from incidents such as the loss of soldiers who froze to death in 2005 and the government's response to the 2010 earthquake. Public confidence in government increased as the government responded better and when the communications were open and timely through all involved agencies. It's worth noting that in 2010 Chile's president and cabinet opened Twitter accounts. Here's what President Sebastián Piñera tweeted in October 2010 on the night before the rescue of the first miner: "Que emocion! Que felicidad! Que orgullo de ser Chileno! Y que gratitud con Dios!" ("What emotion! What joy! What pride of being Chilean! And what gratitude to God!"). This is *kairos* in action, considering audience, time, place, and circumstance—the "cultural moment" of a "crisis situation tinged with emotion."

What governments are learning is that social media provides a helpful tool that is a piece (albeit important in reaching specific publics) of an effective, honest public relations strategy. For instance, Sri Lanka's government wants to refute charges of brutality leveled largely by the diaspora of Tamil Sri Lankans via websites, e-mail, blogs, and other social media. The government plans to use a variety of social media in its strategic communications campaign. South Sudan, whose citizens have voted to become a separate nation, is using social media as part of its ongoing strategic communications campaign to help deal with meddling from the outside.

By its nature, social media can be used by all sides. Trying to censor it will be about as effective as the Stamp Act was in silencing American colonial separatists in the 1700s. The winner will be the side that most effectively employs social media in honest, two-way communications through a long-term trustworthy relationship as part of strategic communications.

Index

Please note that page references in *italics* refer to Figures or Tables.

For Product Safety Concerns and Information please contact our EU
representative GPSR@taylorandfrancis.com Taylor & Francis Verlag GmbH,
Kaufingerstraße 24, 80331 München, Germany

Printed and bound by CPI Group (UK) Ltd, Croydon, CR0 4YY
08/05/2025
01864366-0020